te shown below.

Fundamentals of Parallel Processing

Fundamentals of Parallel Processing

Harry Jordan
University of Colorado–Boulder
Gita Alaghband
University of Colorado–Denver

An Alan R. Apt Book

Pearson Education, Inc.
Upper Saddle River, NJ 07458

Library of Congress Cataloging-in-Publication Data

CIP data on file

Vice President and Editorial Director, ECS: *Marcia J.Horton*
Acquisitions Editor and Publisher: *Alan Apt*
Associate Editor: *Tony D. Holm*
Editorial Assistant: *Patrick Lindner*
Vice President and Director of Production and Manufacturing, ESM: *David W. Riccardi*
Executive Managing Editor: *Vince O'Brien*
Assistant Managing Editor: *Camille Trentacoste*
Production Editor: *Joan Wolk*
Director of Creative Services: *Paul Belfanti*
Creative Director: *Carole Anson*
Art Director: *Jayne Conte*
Art Editor: *Greg Dulles*
Cover Designer: *Bruce Kenselaar*
Manufacturing Manager: *Trudy Pisciotti*
Manufacturing Buyer: *Lynda Castillo*
Marketing Manager: *Pamela Shaffer*
Marketing Assistant: *Barrie Rheinhold*

© 2003 Pearson Education, Inc.
Pearson Education, Inc.
Upper Saddle River, NJ 07458

The author and publisher of this book have used their best efforts in preparing this book. These efforts include the development, research, and testing of the theories and programs to determine their effectiveness. The author and publisher shall not be liable in any event for incidental or consequential damages in connection with, or arising out of, the furnishing, performance, or use of these programs.

Printed in the United States of America.

10 9 8 7 6 5 4 3 2 1

ISBN 0-13-901158-7

Pearson Education Ltd., *London*
Pearson Education Australia Pty. Ltd., *Sydney*
Pearson Education Singapore, Pte. Ltd.
Pearson Education North Asia Ltd., *Hong Kong*
Pearson Education Canada, Inc., *Toronto*
Pearson Educación de Mexico, S.A. de C.V.
Pearson Education—Japan, *Tokyo*
Pearson Education Malaysia, Pte. Ltd.
Pearson Education, *Upper Saddle River, New Jersey*

Contents

Preface

To the Student

Computing is usually taught from a step-by-step or serial point of view. Algorithms are organized as a sequence of computational steps, programs are written one command after another, and machines are designed to execute a chain of machine instructions by performing a string of microsteps, one after another. While sequential formulation of a problem can lead to a solution, a tremendous performance advantage is available from doing many operations in parallel. The two principal approaches to speeding up a computation are a faster clock rate for the underlying hardware and doing more operations in parallel. Introducing parallel operations to speed up an application is a promising approach, because as tasks become larger, more operations can potentially be done in parallel. To realize this potential, three things must work together. Algorithms must involve many independent operations, programming languages must allow the specification of parallel operations or identify them automatically, and the architecture of the computer running the program must execute multiple operations simultaneously.

Parallel processing is the result of this combination of algorithm design, programming language structure, and computer architecture all directed toward faster completion of an application. The fundamentals of parallel processing emerge from an understanding of this combination of computing topics and their collaboration to achieve high performance. To gain this understanding, a basic knowledge of computer design and architecture, of programming languages and how they produce machine code, and of the elements of algorithm structure is required. Although some subsections focus exclusively on one of the three aspects of architecture, language, or algorithm, there are no such major divisions in the book. Treatments of all three are combined to expose the fundamental concepts that make up the discipline of parallel processing. We expect the reader to have a basic knowledge of algorithms and programming. To address the real goal of parallel processing—better performance—one must know how the program is executed by a computer at the machine language level. This requires an understanding of the specific organization of hardware elements constituting a machine architecture. Introductory experience in these areas constitutes the prerequisite material for reading this text.

To the Instructor

The goal of this textbook is to provide a comprehensive coverage of the principles of parallel processing. Integration of parallel architectures, algorithms, and languages is the key in gaining both the breadth and the depth of knowledge and expertise needed in designing and developing successful parallel applications. The book is organized and presented so that it continuously relates these subjects within the topic being studied. Discussions of algorithm designs are followed by the performance implications of each design on parallel architectures.

The rapid changes in technology and the continuous arrival of new architectures, languages, and systems demand a fundamental understanding of the field of parallel processing. The uniqueness of this book is that it treats fundamental concepts rather than a collection of the latest trends. The flow of information is carefully designed so that each section is a natural next step from the previous one. Detailed examples are used to clarify difficult concepts. The issues to be studied are posed early enough to motivate the reader to continue and to give a clear picture of what is to come next and why. The alternative approach of covering "recent" architectures, languages, and systems as a vehicle to teach the fundamental concepts is difficult and quickly dated. It is very hard to get to the heart of a subject without the readers feeling lost and confused about what is really being conveyed. Peeling off some layers of additional information and features is necessary before getting to the fundamentals in every case. For example, is it necessary for a language to provide numerous constructs? Or are some of them considered essential and some additionally provided for ease of use? Are they implemented with efficiency in mind for certain architectures or are they provided for portability? Are the constructs implementation dependent? Will their performance vary by much on different computer architectures? It is never possible to completely understand the trade-offs and the underlying concepts by going over example machines and languages alone. Once the fundamental concepts are understood, they can be applied to any architecture, system, or language.

Parallel processing is a relatively young academic discipline. The authors believe that it has developed to a point where fundamentals can be identified and discussed apart from individual systems. We have focused on presenting the fundamentals by architectural features, system properties, language constructs, algorithm design and implementation implications in a way that is as independent as possible of specific architectures, systems, and languages. In some cases, the original machine, language, or system introducing the concept being presented is covered. However, in a majority of cases we have intentionally refrained from expanding each topic to cover many specific machines or languages for the purpose of concentrating on fundamentals.

Although this is not intended as a parallel programming text, a real programming language is presented for each type of major parallelism concept introduced throughout the text. We selected Fortran as the base language whenever possible for several reasons. Much of the research literature in parallel processing is Fortran-based, and there are numerous parallel Fortran scientific programs and programmers. In addition, Fortran is a simple high-level language close to the machine level. It is easier to observe and explain the effects of executing Fortran statements on various machine architectures compared to high-level languages with many complex, user-friendly features. The Fortran program designer has much control over programming style, design, implementation, and execution. Fortran is a static language, so in comparison to dynamic languages or languages providing dynamic features, the programmer must be cautioned less regarding the use of high-level features and their parallel performance implications. The simplicity of the language helps keep the focus on parallel concepts and constructs. That multdimensional arrays are supported in Fortran is especially significant for vector processing. Maintaining the same base language throughout the book keeps the presentation consistent, and readers, not needing to switch between languages, will concentrate on parallel issues.

This textbook is designed and organized after many years of teaching and research experience in the field of parallel processing. It is intended for computer science or computer engineering seniors and graduate students. Students studying the book will be able to confidently design and implement new parallel applications, evaluate parallel program and architecture performance, and, most important be able to develop their skills by learning new parallel environments on their own. The major task of an educator is to nurture his or her students so that they can continue to grow and develop in their field of interest independently. This textbook is designed with this important goal in mind and will provide instructors with a comprehensive set of material to educate their students to be productive and successful.

Tailoring the Text to a Syllabus

The first seven chapters constitute an excellent first-semester course in parallel processing. They give an in-depth coverage of parallel algorithm design, vector, multiprocessor, and dataflow architectures, parallel languages for each machine type, synchronization and communication mechanisms, interconnection networks, data dependence, and compiler optimization techniques. The remaining four chapters are intended for advanced treatment of issues studied in the first part of the book. The focus is on various synchronization and communication implementations, influence of implementations on performance, interpretation of machine architecture and program performance, effects of program behavior on performance, and parallel I/O. This part of the book provides an excellent second semester for graduate students. They will gain insight into how to analyze machine architectures, parallel programs and systems, and understand how these components interact and influence overall performance. Many advanced research project ideas can be deduced from topics covered in Chapters 8 though 11.

The following chart shows the major dependencies among the chapters and suggests how they may be tailored to cover specific areas of emphasis.

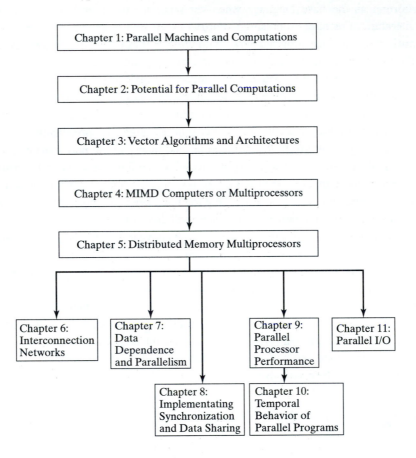

Chapter Contents

Chapter 1 briefly reviews the evolution of parallelism in computer architectures. It introduces the basic ideas of vector processing, multiprocessing, and parallel operations in algorithms. It establishes a framework for topics in the remaining chapters.

Chapter 2 introduces the key ideas of data dependence. The prefix computation is used to illustrate algorithm characteristics that make different ways of doing the same computation more or less parallel.

Chapter 3 examines the application of the same operation to multiple data items in parallel. It motivates the discussion with some simple algorithms from linear algebra and presents an architecture at the machine language level that incorporates vector operations. Fortran 90 is discussed as a language with high-level support for the unique features of machine level vector processing. Pipelined vector processing is discussed.

Chapter 4 briefly surveys multiprocessor architectural organizations and establishes the difference between shared and distributed memory multiprocessors. It proceeds to focus on shared memory by describing the extensions to sequential programming that are needed to coordinate multiple processes to perform a task. The OpenMP Fortran extension is used as an illustration of high-level constructs used to support shared memory multiprocessing. The chapter also establishes the basics of pipelined MIMD, or multithreaded, architectures.

Chapter 5 describes distributed memory multiprocessors using the message passing viewpoint to direct attention toward the dominant role of data communication in such architectures. Explicit send and receive programming is introduced, and the message passing interface (MPI) is used as an illustration of high-level language support for such programs. The basics of cache coherence and memory consistency are described in relation to shared memory and distributed memory multiprocessors.

Chapter 6 discusses interconnection networks in depth, including those for vector computers, and shared and distributed memory multiprocessors. Static and dynamic networks are compared and contrasted along with various topologies and their properties. Use of the network to combine messages, as in the NYU Ultracomputer, is discussed.

Chapter 7 is important in relating the ideas of data dependence that underlie the structure of parallel algorithms to the structure of a program. It covers code optimization techniques and topics of concern to a compiler writer having the task of generating code for a parallel computer. This chapter also introduces the ideas of dataflow languages and architectures that allow the elimination of nonessential dependences from programming languages and machines.

Chapter 8 expands the ideas of synchronization introduced in the shared memory discussion of Chapter 4 and integrates them with the data transmission point of view emphasized in Chapter 5. An in-depth understanding of key issues in synchronization is provided by a set of key topics, ranging from synchronization in cooperative communication, managing shared tasks, waiting mechanisms, to how to prove that a synchronization mechanism is implemented correctly.

Chapter 9 focuses specifically on the performance issues that have been continually referred to in previous chapters. It treats various performance models and illustrates their use through case studies of measurements on real systems. The impact of different scheduling and implementations of parallel constructs is discussed.

Chapter 10 relates performance of a parallel program execution to its temporal behavior. Experiments on real systems are used to illustrate performance characterization models. It examines temporal characterization from several viewpoints ranging from behavior in single cache systems, multiprocessor systems with distributed caches, to message passing systems.

Chapter 11 treats various aspects of parallelism in I/O operations. Parallel access disk arrays (RAID) are described as parallel I/O hardware. I/O dependence operations are introduced. Parallel input and output methods on files are discussed. Finally, parallelism in multiprocessors collective I/O operations is covered using MPI-IO.

Acknowledgments

Grateful acknowledgment is due to the Institute for Computer Applications in Science and Engineering, ICASE, which brought together a very stimulating group of computer scientists during the late 1970s and the 1980s. Considerable intellectual inspiration was derived from working with them. An important source of thoughts about the fundamentals of parallel processing came from the Conferences on High Speed Computing organized by Bill Buzbee and George Michael in 1980 and shepherded by them for 10 years. The effective mix of academics and application scientists they gathered at these meetings did much to establish the fundamentals of the field. Burton Smith has been a constant source of insight and perceptiveness. No technical conversation with him is ever very far from the fundamentals. Iain Duff at CERFACS, Centre European de Recherche et de Formation Avancee en Calcul Scientifique, provided a stimulating environment for collaboration with European scientists. We are grateful to Alan Apt, editor, and Prentice Hall for their invaluable support in completing this book.

The authors express their sincere appreciation to Chris Nevison, Wirg Wallentine, Pearl Wang, Tanya Zlateeva, Nan Schaller, David Kincaid, Norm Troullier, Steve Seidel, Hank Dietz, Richard Hughey, and Kathy Liszka for their diligent review of the book and constructive comments.

A very special thanks and deepest gratitude from Gita Alaghband to Harry Jordan to whom she is indebted for his years of generous guidance, mentorship, friendship, and support.

Finally, we express our appreciation to our families, Sue Jordan, Hamid, Sati, and Sara Fardi, for their loving support, patience, and encouragement throughout the years.

Fundamentals of Parallel Processing

Parallel Machines and Computations

In the quest for ever-faster computers, the technique of reducing execution time by doing several things at once is an obvious way to gain speed. The surprising thing is not that parallel computers and computation are attracting increased attention, but that so much of computing science and technology has revolved around a sequential, one-thing-at-a-time, style of algorithm specification, programming, and machine design. Parallel processing has evolved underneath an overall sequential world view, and only after considerable time has it emerged as a high-level principle to guide the design of algorithms, machines, and programming languages.

The subject of parallel processing is really a topic that integrates the needs of algorithms with the capabilities of architectures. The study of parallel architectures is sterile without the assurance that the parallel computation capabilities of the architecture can actually be used to speed up the execution of a sufficiently large set of real computations. In the same way, the study of algorithms to determine the operations that can potentially be executed in parallel is unexciting if no implementable architecture can be envisioned that can actually execute them in parallel. Parallel processing is thus a study that integrates parallel algorithms and architectures by way of parallel programming languages. Therefore, in what follows we do not attempt an overall organization that separates parallel processing into architectures, languages, and algorithms. Instead, we will move between these aspects of parallel computation in an attempt to underline the importance of their interrelationships.

It is useful to keep some general questions in mind while reading this chapter. What is the nature of the multiple computational units used to do operations in parallel? How can one write recipes that specify operations to be done in parallel and others to be done sequentially? What aspects of a particular algorithm for doing a computation influence what can and cannot be done in parallel?

1.1 The Evolution of Parallel Architectures

Several different forms of parallelism have been pursued to solve problems faster by doing several things at once. The main classes can be described by relating them to the standard sequential computational model. In this model, one operation: add, subtract, multiply, divide, or conditional branch, can be performed at a time. The first major division of kinds of parallelism is based on parallelism over multiple data items versus parallelism over multiple operations. There is probably a better understanding of the numerical analysis topic of transformation of data through a fixed set of operations than there is of flow of control transformations, which has a shorter history in the computer science field. Thus, the simplest step from sequential programs into the field of parallelism is probably to leave the control flow of the program alone and to do multiple operations on disjoint data items simultaneously. Flynn [110] characterized the concurrency of data operations with respect to instruction streams by dividing architectures into four categories based on the number of instruction streams and the number of data streams. Single (SI) or multiple instruction (MI) streams may be combined with single (SD) or multiple data (MD) streams to form an architectural category. Thus, the original von Neumann architecture is classified as SISD (single instruction stream, single data stream), vector computers are SIMD, because a single instruction stream directs operations on multiple data, and a multiprocessor is an MIMD computer. The MISD combination is not very useful, although there are a few research machines that it might fit.

Let us briefly describe the progress toward gaining computational speed from the computer architecture and system perspective.

1.1.1 Parallelism in Sequential Computers

The original von Neumann architecture, classified as SISD, performed computation by breaking them into a one-at-a-time sequence of machine operation. Figure 1-1 shows the major components of this early architecture, namely, the control unit (CU) and the arithmetic logic unit (ALU) together forming the central processing unit (CPU) and the main memory (M). The intent here is not to show detailed implementation but the high-level description of the operations as they lead to the discussion of parallelism. Upon start, the computer enters the fetch/execute cycle of Figure 1-2 until it is halted.

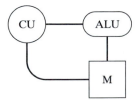

Figure 1-1   A typical von Neumann architecture.

1. Instruction fetch
2. Instruction decode and increment the program counter
3. Effective operand address calculation
4. Operand fetch
5. Execute
6. Store result

Figure 1-2 A simple fetch/execute cycle for a von Neumann machine.

Much improvement has been done to this early architecture to speed up the operations of the SISD computers. Interrupts have provided overlap between CPU operations and slow peripheral devices, input/output (I/O) processors provide concurrency between fast I/O devices and CPU while enabling the CPU and I/O processors to access the main memory directly, as shown in Figure 1-3. Multiplexing the CPU between programs in a multiprogrammed system has reduced the CPU idle time and maximized the system throughput and CPU utilization. Interleaving execution of several programs in this way led operating systems to have to manage concurrent processes, each at a different stage of its execution. High-speed block transfer between main and secondary memory made possible by I/O processors and the principle of locality have led to virtual memory management, where applications much larger than the size of the system's main memory can execute to completion. Combination of virtual memory and multiprogramming has resulted in the ubiquitous multiuser, time-sharing computing environments.

Pipelining is a powerful technique to overlap operations and introduce parallelism into a computer architecture. Through some additional hardware, the steps in the fetch/execute cycle of Figure 1-2 can be overlapped. Figure 1-4 shows a possible pipelined fetch/execute cycle. While instructions are still being executed sequentially by going through the different stages of the pipeline in the order they are fetched, several of them are being processed at different stages of the pipeline simultaneously. In this example, it takes four time units to complete the first instruction (pipeline start-up time). However, after this initial time, one instruction completes at every pipeline step. Figure 1-5 compares the non-pipelined fetch/execute cycle with the pipelined one to show the effectiveness of pipelining. There are, however, complexities associated with pipelining. For example, when a conditional jump instruction is encountered, the address of the next instruction is not usually known until after the execution phase of the jump instruction. In this case, the pipeline must be emptied and restarted with the next instruction when its address is known.

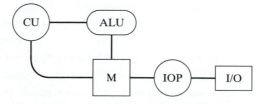

Figure 1-3 Adding an I/O processor to overlap I/O with CPU operations.

Instruction fetch	I1	I2	I3	Jump	–	–	–
Operand fetch	–	I1	I2	I3	Jump	–	–
Execute	–	–	I1	I2	I3	Jump	–
Result store	–	–	–	I1	I2	I3	Jump
Time	1	2	3	4	5	6	7

Figure 1-4   Overlapped fetch/execute cycle for an SISD computer.

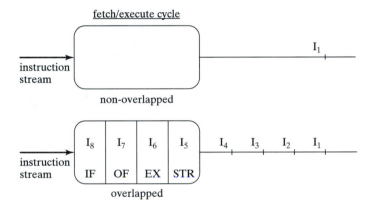

Figure 1-5   Comparison of SISD pipelined vs. non-pipelined fetch/execute cycle.

Several techniques to alleviate this problem and speed up the pipeline operation have been introduced, starting with an auxiliary instruction buffer introduced in the IBM system/370 model 165 [34,152,153]. The idea is to use two instruction buffers. Instructions are fetched into an instruction buffer sequentially addressed by the program counter. When a conditional jump is encountered, instructions will be fetched from the address of the target of the branch into the auxiliary instruction buffer. When the result is known, the buffers are switched if necessary.

The next major step of parallelism in sequential computers is the introduction of multiple arithmetic units in the CPU of the CDC 6600 [274]. In this situation, the CPU consists of several arithmetic units simultaneously capable of performing one operation each. To take advantage of this architecture, a local analysis of the instruction stream must be performed to determine which instructions in the stream can be processed simultaneously by the multiple arithmetic units. This *lookahead* analysis and its corresponding completion interlock, *scoreboarding*, was perhaps illustrated best in the CDC 6600 and its successors. The lookahead is used to prefetch instructions into an instruction buffer. The lookahead buffer is usually large enough to hold most scientific loops to optimize memory access. Scoreboarding is used to determine which instructions can be issued concurrently without a conflict. Conflicts may arise if two potentially concurrent instructions need to use the same arithmetic unit, *resource conflict*, or if they must store their results in the same output register, *output dependence*. Conflicts also arise if an input register of one instruction is used as output of the other, *flow* and *antidependences*. An interlock and reservation logic guarantees correct execution of the instruction stream as was intended by the original program. Therefore, even though some instructions are executed out of the original sequence, the result is the same as if they had been executed in the given order. Thanks to technological advances, most of these architectural techniques are featured in desktop computers of today.

Compilers play a significant role in generating code that can take advantage of the parallelism embedded in these complex computer architectures. Consider evaluating the expression

$$EXP = A + B + C + (D \times E \times F) + G + H.$$

Using a left-to-right evaluation of the arithmetic expression, the corresponding tree and code that are generated by a compiler are shown in Figure 1-6. The tree represents the order in which the operations are performed. It represents the data dependence relationship among the operations that are needed to evaluate the expression. For example, according to the tree of Figure 1-6, operations $A + B$ must be completed before the execution of $T_1 + C$ at the next level can start. Operation $D \times E$ must be completed before $T_2 \times F$ but can be done at the same time as $A + B$. The height of this tree, the longest chain from the root to any leaf node, indicates that it will take a minimum of five steps to evaluate the expression assuming addition and multiplication take one time unit. The five steps is only possible if the computer system has the arithmetic units to perform one addition and one multiplication simultaneously. A smart compiler may generate a more parallel code using associativity and commutativity laws of add and multiply operations to reorder the evaluation of the expression. The resulting tree evaluation of height four is shown in Figure 1-7. The expression can now be evaluated in four steps if the computer system can simultaneously perform two adds and one multiply. Arithmetic expression evaluation is further discussed in the next chapter.

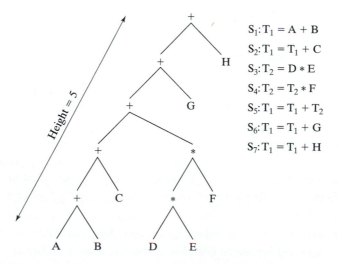

$S_1: T_1 = A + B$
$S_2: T_1 = T_1 + C$
$S_3: T_2 = D * E$
$S_4: T_2 = T_2 * F$
$S_5: T_1 = T_1 + T_2$
$S_6: T_1 = T_1 + G$
$S_7: T_1 = T_1 + H$

Figure 1-6   In-order tree traversal for evaluation of $A + B + C + (D \times E \times F) + G + H$.

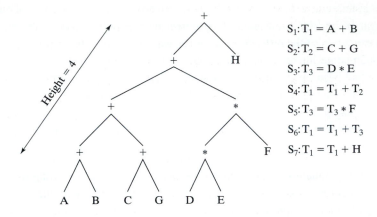

Figure 1-7   Commutativity and associativity applied to $A + B + C + (D \times E \times F) + G + H$.

These SISD parallelism techniques start with sequential code and do local reordering of operations using a combination of hardware and architecture specific code generation. This book does not specifically discuss instruction level parallelism (ILP), the parallelism that can be automatically extracted from sequential code and exploited by multiple arithmetic units in a very long instruction word (VLIW) or a superscalar machine. Our treatment is limited to explicitly parallel languages and machines. Of course, many of the fundamentals of parallel processing also apply to ILP, especially some of parallel algorithm characteristics discussed in Chapter 2 and some of the data dependence analysis framework established in Chapter 7, but we leave the direct treatment of ILP to other books.

1.1.2   Vector or SIMD Computers

The simplest step from sequential programs into the field of parallelism is to recognize that many inner loops are only used to specify that the same operations are to be performed repeatedly on a set of disjoint data items. These can be formulated as vector operations where the same operation is performed on each element of a vector. For example, a single vector add operation is used to produce a new vector, $C = A + B$, whose elements are component wise addition of two vectors, A and B. This single vector operation is equivalent to writing a sequential loop that adds corresponding elements of arrays A and B and assigns results to C one at a time.

The same operation can be carried out on multiple data items, that is, a vector operation, by a single control unit and replicated complete arithmetic units as in Figure 1-8(a). It can also be done by organizing the parallel hardware into a pipeline and processing the multiple data items in an assembly line fashion as shown in Figure 1-8(b). We will refer to the replicated, non-pipelined architectures of Figure 1-8(a) as "true" SIMD to distinguish them from the pipe-lined SIMD architectures. True SIMD architectures can be configured so that each arithmetic unit has access to its own private memory. In this configuration, the arithmetic units are connected to each other through an interconnection network so that they can exchange data with each other. Another possible configuration in true SIMD machines is to let the arithmetic units share the memory. In this model, an interconnection (alignment network) is needed between the memory modules and the arithmetic units so that any arithmetic unit can access data in any memory module.

In this discussion, the categories SISD, SIMD, and MIMD are used from the instruction set point of view without regard to whether multiple operations are carried out on separate complete processors or whether the "parallel" operations are processed by a pipeline. Pipelining is another method for introducing parallelism into the operation of a computer and, as we have seen, is an important topic in von Neumann computer architecture. We take the view that, independent of pipelining, a machine in which a single instruction specifies operations on several data items is an SIMD machine. The advantage of this point of view is that pipelining then becomes an independent architectural variable that may be combined with Flynn's categories in an orthogonal manner. Data operations in the SISD case do not become parallel until pipelining is applied; the simple technique of fetch/execute overlap is one application of pipelining to SISD computers. One of the earliest non-pipelined SIMD computers, which was designed for vector and matrix processing, was the Illiac IV computer [38]. A machine with a very similar instruction set architecture, but which uses pipelined arithmetic units to support vector operations, is the Cray-1 [76], which we call a pipelined SIMD computer.

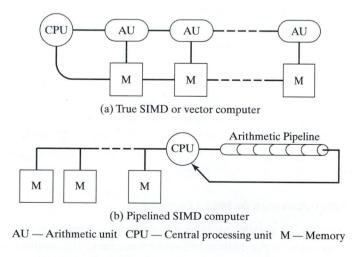

(a) True SIMD or vector computer

(b) Pipelined SIMD computer

AU — Arithmetic unit   CPU — Central processing unit   M — Memory

Figure 1-8   True and pipelined SIMD architectures.

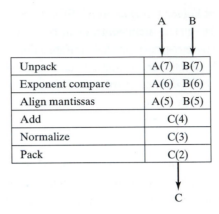

Figure 1-9   Example of an SIMD floating point addition pipeline.

In the true SIMD model, arithmetic units, also called PE for processing elements, perform the same operation, say floating point add, on a pair of vector elements that they are holding at the same time. Therefore, in the time it takes to do one addition, as many additions as there are arithmetic units are performed. Pipelining of arithmetic operations divides one operation, such as floating point addition, into several smaller functions and executes these subfunctions in parallel on different data. A snapshot of a floating point addition pipeline at a single pipeline minor cycle is shown in Figure 1-9. Pipelining can keep the amount of parallel activity high while significantly reducing the hardware requirement. Because the number of items inserted into the front end of the pipeline is not constrained by its length, pipelining also avoids the disadvantage of having vectors whose lengths are not even multiples of the number of arithmetic units in the true SIMD case. The vector pipeline usually empties after each vector operation and fills when a new vector operation begins; therefore, every new vector operation has a start-up cost associated with it.

True SIMD architectures have been used in numerous machines of a more special-purpose nature. General SIMD computers that have seen widespread commercial use have tended to be of the pipelined variety. Of course, no commercial machine uses a single form of parallelism. Multiple pipelines are used to enhance speed, and scalar arithmetic units are overlapped. The move from true to pipelined SIMD machines is dictated by an improved cost/performance ratio along with added flexibility in vector length. The numerous arithmetic units of the true SIMD computer are only partially used at any instant for short vectors. Chapter 3 provides a detailed treatment of SIMD computers.

1.1.3   Multiprocessors or MIMD Computers

Another way of introducing parallelism is to allow multiple instruction streams to be active simultaneously. This leads to the multiprocessor architectures. The analogy with organizing many people, each doing a small task to cooperatively perform a much larger task gives us some intuition about how to write programs for multiprocessors.

There are two prototypical forms of multiprocessor, distinguished by the way data are shared among processors. The shared memory form has a general interconnection network between multiple processors and multiple memories so that any processor can access any memory location. The distributed memory form associates a distinct memory with each processor with data being transmitted directly between processors. These two forms of MIMD computers or multiprocessors are shown in Figure 1-10(a).

The parallelism supported by multiprocessors may be used in two general ways. As each processor of the MIMD system is a complete CPU, each processor can execute a sequential program independently of the others; therefore, MIMD machines can execute multiple sequential programs in parallel for increased throughput. More interesting is to cause multiple processors to execute different parts of a single program to complete a single task faster. In this case, multiple processors will cooperatively and concurrently execute a parallel program. The cooperation and exchange of information among processors in shared memory MIMD is done through the read/write of shared memory locations by processors of a given task and through the use of synchronizations to control their access to shared data and the rate of progress of processes. In the distributed MIMD model, this is done by communication among processors through sending and receiving messages.

Successful systems of both the shared memory form and the distributed memory form have been built. Shared memory machines with tens of processors and distributed memory machines with hundreds of processors are commercially available. Figure 1-10(b) shows the configuration of an MIMD machine in which multiple instruction streams are supported by pipelining rather than by separate complete processors. The application of pipelining to multiple instruction stream execution can have the advantages of reduced hardware and increased flexibility in the number of instruction streams—the same advantages as were seen in the SIMD case. Because multiple, independent memory requests are generated by the parallel instruction streams, pipelining can also be applied effectively to the memory access path. Current terminology calls pipelined MIMD computers *multithreaded* machines.

In the SISD pipelined fetch/execute cycle of Figure 1-4, instructions that are in the pipeline come from a single instruction stream belonging to the process currently running. Dependences between instructions may introduce bubbles (null operations) into the execution pipeline. For example, if an instruction, I, needs the result of another instruction, J, ahead of it in the pipeline, then I cannot be issued until the result it needs is produced by J completing its execution. Figure 1-11 shows a snapshot of the operation of a multiprocessor pipeline. The instructions that are in the pipeline simultaneously come from different processes (instruction streams) and, therefore, do not (usually) need to wait on each other's completion. An explicit synchronization between instruction streams (because of communication between concurrent processes) may cause one process to be unable to proceed, in which case a null operation might proceed through the pipeline in the slot for that process until the delay condition is removed. Shared memory and distributed memory computers are presented in detail in Chapter 4 and Chapter 5, respectively.

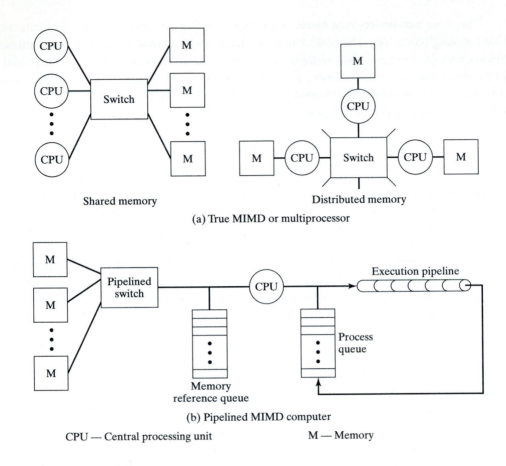

Shared memory   Distributed memory

(a) True MIMD or multiprocessor

(b) Pipelined MIMD computer

CPU — Central processing unit   M — Memory

Figure 1-10   True and pipelined MIMD architectures.

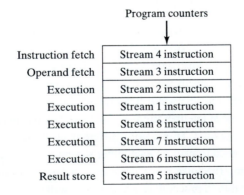

Figure 1-11   Pipelined fetch/execute cycle in shared-memory MIMD.

It is possible to discard the notion of flow of control entirely and take the attitude that it is only present as a vehicle for specifying how new data items depend on previous ones. This leads to a time-independent specification of data dependences and the complete elimination of the idea of control flow. The only remaining flow concept is the idea of data passing through, and being transformed by, operations that are successive in the sense that the input of one depends on the output of a "previous" operation. This idea is often denoted "data flow" and can be applied at the algorithmic, language design, or architectural level. The four categories of computer architectures defined by Flynn do not seem suitable for data flow machines, and we postpone their discussion until Chapter 7.

The increase in speed as a result of enhanced parallelism has been the province of computer architecture beginning with the move from serial by bit to parallel by word operation, moving through processor and I/O overlap and now focusing on the area of concurrent data operations. With the exception of the data flow idea mentioned above, one can almost trace a straight line evolution of the original von Neumann architecture into the parallel processors of today.

1.2 Interconnection Networks

An implication in all types of parallel architectures presented here is some form of connectivity between their components to facilitate the routing of data for the purpose of communication and cooperation between the parallel entities. This connectivity is provided through what is known as an interconnection network in the system.

In true SIMD computers, arithmetic units use the interconnection network to route data among themselves to get the right data to the processing elements needing them. In pipelined SIMD, an interconnection network enables parallel access to vector components stored in different memory modules. In shared memory MIMD, the interconnection network provides the processors access to the shared memory. Interconnection networks furnish the connectivity and the means for communication between processors of a distributed MIMD system. The implied interconnection networks in MIMD architectures are identified as "switch" in Figure 1-10.

An interconnection network is an important part of the parallel computer architecture. Its topology and structure directly influence the overall capability and performance of the system. A network structure can range from a simple bus structure connecting parallel processors to a complex, highly concurrent multistage network capable of performing all possible permutations of its inputs. Parallel machine performance is directly coupled with the degree of concurrency supplied by the interconnection network. To obtain high performance in a parallel system, the parallel entities must be able to communicate with each other concurrently. The higher the degree of concurrency in the interconnection network, the more concurrency is achieved by parallel units in a given system. In fact, concurrency in other units is wasted without a high concurrency network connecting them. With high concurrency come, however, design and cost complexities. While a fully interconnected network connects every processor to every other processor in an N-processor system, a bus interconnection allows all processors to connect to a single bus (Figure 1-12). The simple, low-cost bus allows only one communication at a time, while the fully connected network requires $N(N-1)/2$ bidirectional links and provides maximum concurrency at a cost that may be impractically high.

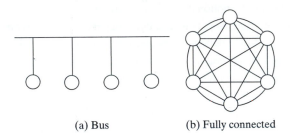

(a) Bus   (b) Fully connected

Figure 1-12 Two possible interconnection networks.

As some form of an interconnection network is needed by all parallel architectures that we will study, for the next four chapters we will assume its existence and will refer to it without too many details. We will study networks in detail in Chapter 6 once we have a clear understanding of the SIMD and MIMD computers and the need and importance of the role of interconnection networks in each.

1.3 Application of Architectural Parallelism

Applications programs for machines falling into different architectural categories require different structuring of solution algorithms for efficient operation. Put differently, given a program with a particular structure, the ways in which architectural parallelism can be applied are different. For example, programs written in a sequential programming language for a sequential machine take full advantage of a pipelined SISD machine. Programs for a SIMD machine can be written in one of a number of "vector processing" languages. On the other hand, it is possible to apply an SIMD machine to an already written, sequential program using an automatic vectorizing compiler that takes as input a sequential program written in a specific language and produces vector parallel code for the given SIMD machine. The degree of success of an automatic vectorizing compiler depends on program structure. MIMD machines can execute multiple sequential programs in parallel for increased throughput or language extensions can be used to cause multiple processors to execute different parts of a program written in a sequential language. Work on automatic parallelizing compilers to speed up the execution of a sequential program using an MIMD architecture is more recent than work on vectorizing compilers.

All forms of architectural parallelism are applicable to the many large problems arising out of numerical linear algebra, but SIMD machines are tailored to them and can achieve extremely high performance in operations on long enough vectors. It is easy to partition the components of a vector over different instruction streams, but the flexibility afforded by multiple streams is not needed, and synchronization overhead may be excessive if parallelism is restricted to the level of single vector operations. Vector processing may be performed quite efficiently with respect to other work on an SISD computer as a result of predictable lookahead characteristics, but again the architecture is not specialized to it. The number of linear algebraic applications, the often large size of these problems, and the considerable algorithm research that has taken place in this field, make this type of application an important standard against which to measure performance of any parallel architecture.

In numerous applications, the opportunity for parallel data operations is evident, but the operations differ from datum to datum, or there is enough irregularity in the structure of the data to make SIMD processing difficult or impossible. In these applications, one must either be content with pipelined SISD processing or move into the MIMD environment. Where multiple data items have irregular or conditional access patterns, MIMD processing may be preferred even when vectors are involved, as in the case of sparse matrix operations. At a higher level of algorithm structure is functional parallelism, in which large modules of the program operate in parallel and share data only in specific, easily synchronized ways.

1.4 Getting Started in SIMD and MIMD Programming

To start discussing the issues involved in parallel processing we need a way to show how a parallel algorithm might be executed by a given parallel processor; therefore, we need a parallel programming language. We really want a form of pseudocode that is not very machine-specific but reflects the features of the parallel computer architecture that are important for an understanding of the way operations are to be done simultaneously. We will start by characterizing, at the pseudocode level, the two types of parallel architecture that are closest to the traditional von Neumann computer, the SIMD and the MIMD.

We start with pseudocode for a traditional (SISD) computer that is similar to Pascal or C. We need assignment statements and a few control structures, as well as comments, to write readable pseudocode programs. Our initial constructs and the notation for them are specified by example in Table 1-1. Note that counted loops are more important to us than while loops, for example, because of the importance of an index in selecting from multiple data. We use the conventional mathematical relational operators, $>$, $<$, $=$, etc., for relational operations. To distinguish the relational "equal to," $=$, from an assignment statement we use ":=" for assignment. Because no modern language uses two key strokes for the ubiquitous assignment operator, this has the added advantage that the reader can easily distinguish pseudocode from actual programming language examples in later chapters.

As already mentioned, the SIMD mode of operation implies that the same operation is to be carried out simultaneously on multiple data items. The two ways of accomplishing this, with multiple arithmetic units or by means of pipelining, differ very little at the instruction set level. A single instruction must specify an operation and a collection of data items on which it is to be performed. (Two collections must be specified in the case of a two operand operation.) The simplest way of specifying a collection of data items of the same type, with the ability to select items using an index, is through the use of a vector. Hence, SIMD machines are often called vector computers. Either a multiple arithmetic unit or a pipelined SIMD machine can, therefore, be characterized by some way of specifying arithmetic operations applying to full vectors of data.

Table 1-1   Some pseudocode conventions.

Assignment	`:=`
End of statement	`;`
Statement grouping	**`begin`** ... **`end`** or `{` ... `}`
Statement label	`LABEL:`
Counted loops	**`for`** `i :=` `0` **`step`** `s` **`until`** `m` ⟨statement⟩`;`
While loops	**`while`** `(`⟨condition⟩`)` ⟨statement⟩`;`
Conditional	**`if`** `(`⟨condition⟩`)` **`then`** ⟨statement⟩ **`else`** ⟨statement⟩`;`
Comments	`/* Comments. */`
Exit a structured block	**`break`**
Procedure	**`procedure`** ⟨name⟩ `(`⟨parameter list⟩`)`
	⟨variable declaration⟩`;`
	⟨statement⟩`;`
	`return``;`
	`end procedure`
Procedure invocation	**`call`** ⟨procedure name⟩ `(`⟨parameter list⟩`)` `;`

To extend the serial processor pseudocode so that it can be used to describe programs for vector processors, we want a generalized method of specifying vector arithmetic. We do it by introducing a vector assignment statement of the form

$$\langle\text{indexed variable}\rangle := \langle\text{indexed expression}\rangle, \ (\langle\text{index range}\rangle);$$

The indexed variable on the left side of the assignment must depend on the index appearing in the parenthesized index range expression in such a way that the individual assignments that are made in parallel are all to different storage locations. An example might be

$$C[i,j] := C[i,j] + A[i,k]*B[k,j], \ (0 \le j \le N\text{-}1);$$

where assignments are made in parallel for different values of j, and, hence, to elements in different columns of the matrix C. With this simple extension, we can describe a matrix multiply as it would be performed on a SIMD computer as shown in Program 1-1.

In reading the pseudocode, it can be seen that there are two statements that specify parallel activity: one to initialize inner product sums to zero and the other to add the next inner product term. The second parallel statement would involve several machine instructions to do the two floating-point operations and to evaluate subscript expressions for the two dimensional arrays. If sufficient hardware units are available, either arithmetic units or pipeline stages, up to N operations may be performed in parallel. If only $M < N$ operations can be specified by a single machine instruction, the compiler will also have to generate code to sequence through the N vector elements, M at a time. Thus, the pseudocode is really at a higher level than the machine instruction set even though our SIMD parallel extension seems fairly low level. The fact is that, because SIMD parallelism occurs at the level of a single operation, it is necessarily reflected at a low level of program structure.

/* Matrix multiply, $C := A \cdot B$. Compute elements of C by

$$c_{ij} = \sum_{k=0}^{N-1} a_{ik} b_{kj} \qquad */$$

```
for i := 0 step 1 until N-1
    begin /* Compute one row of C. */
        /* Initialize the sums for each element of a row of C. */
        C[i, j] := 0, (0 ≤ j ≤ N-1);
        /* Loop over the terms of the inner product. */
        for k := 0 step 1 until N-1
            /* Add the kth inner product term across columns in parallel. */
            C[i, j] := C[i, j] + A[i, k]*B[k, j], (0 ≤ j ≤ N-1);
        /* End of product term loop. */
    end /* of all rows. */
```

Program 1-1   Matrix multiply pseudocode for an SIMD computer.

To characterize the operation of MIMD computers at a fairly machine-independent level, we need to extend the SISD pseudocode in a different way. Again, there is no difference between multiple processor and pipelined implementations. In either case, there are multiple processes that are capable of executing different code simultaneously. We will think of the code for a multiprocessor as constituting one program that is executed by all processes. Of course, each processor may be executing at a different place in the code, or even in a different procedure.

A note on careful use of terminology is important to keep the discussion from becoming confusing. The component of a computer that can run a program is called a *processor*. Because many processors can be running the same program simultaneously, we need to name the dynamic sequence of operations being performed by a specific processor so as to distinguish it from the static body of text that constitutes the *program*. We call this dynamic execution sequence a *process*. This is a fairly general use of the term *process*. Many authors use it to designate something more specific. Other terms that are sometimes used to describe what we call a process are an *instruction stream*, a *task*, or a *thread of execution*. In summary, our notation is

- processor—a physical unit capable of executing a program;
- process—the dynamic sequence of operations executed by a processor;
- program—a static body of code specifying a sequence of operations.

When multiple processes are used to solve a single problem, there must be a way for data computed by one process to be made available for use by a different process. Initially, the simplest way to provide such a capability is to think of all processes as sharing access to the same memory. It also must be possible for one process to exercise some control over the progress of another. It should at least be possible to start a new process executing at a specific place in the program and to determine whether it has completed a specified sequence of operations. A simple pair of operations to accomplish this control consists of `fork` and `join`. The fork operation takes a single argument that specifies a label in the program at which the newly started process will begin execution while the original process continues with the statement following the fork. The join operation takes an integer argument that specifies how many processes are to participate in the join. All processes but one that execute the join will be terminated, and that one "original" process will proceed only after the specified number have all executed `join`.

Another necessary pseudocode statement is declarative in nature. There should be a way to specify temporary variables that refer to a different storage location for each process. The corresponding feature in SIMD is handled by the index that appears in the index range expression. This index serves to separate different items of the multiple data. In MIMD it is natural to specify that a single variable name represents a different memory cell for each process. This can be handled by declaring the parallelism type of a variable, or more accurately its parallel storage class, as `private`. This means that each process has its own private copy of the variable referred to by that name. Although it is possible to have variables that are shared by some processes but not others, we start with the simple distinction between variables that are uniformly shared by all processes and those that are strictly private to a single process. A `shared` declaration means that the declared variables are shared by all processes.

A summary of our pseudocode extensions for describing multiprocessor algorithms is

`fork` ⟨label⟩	Start a process executing at ⟨label⟩;
`join` ⟨integer⟩	Join ⟨integer⟩ processes into one;
`shared` ⟨variable list⟩	Make the storage class of the variables shared.
`private` ⟨variable list⟩	Make the storage class of the variables private.

With these extensions it is possible to write pseudocode that gives a general understanding of the structure of a multiprocessor program without being specific to one machine or a limited class of machines. The matrix multiply program is written for a shared memory MIMD machine in Program 1-2.

In the multiprocessor pseudocode, it is somewhat difficult to see all the parallelism that exists in the program. The only explicit parallel extensions that appear are one occurrence each of `fork`, `join`, `shared`, and `private`. In reading the section of code between the label DOCOL and the `join` statement, it must be kept implicitly in mind that N processes, each with a different value of j, are executing the code simultaneously, although they are not necessarily executing the same statement at exactly the same time. MIMD parallelism can, thus, be thought of as asynchronous parallelism, whereas SIMD parallelism is synchronous at the statement level, with all the arithmetic for a parallel statement being complete before the next statement is executed.

1.5 Parallelism in Algorithms

One way to detect parallelism in a sequential algorithm is to look for operations that can be carried out independently of each other. The question then is how to identify the independence of operations.

/* Matrix multiply, $C := A \cdot B$. Compute elements of C by

$$c_{ij} = \sum_0^{N-1} a_{ik} b_{kj} \quad */$$

```
private i, j, k;
shared A[N,N], B[N,N], C[N,N], N;
/* Start N-1 new processes, each for a different column of C. */
for j := 0 step 1 until N-2 fork DOCOL;
/* The original process reaches this point and does column N-1. */
j := N-1;
DOCOL: /* Executed by N processes, each doing one column of C. */
for i := 0 step 1 until N-1
    begin /* Compute a row element of C. */
            /* Initialize the sum for the inner product. */
            C[i, j] := 0;
            /* Loop over the terms of the inner product. */
            for k := 0 step 1 until N-1
                /* Add the kth inner product term. */
                C[i, j] := C[i, j] + A[i, k]*B[k, j];
            /* End of product term loop. */
    end /* of all rows. */
join N;
```

Program 1-2 Matrix multiply pseudocode for a multiprocessor.

In general, we define three types of dependences between operations, namely, output, flow, and antidependences. Consider the sequence of statements in a sequential algorithm. For each statement, S_i, define the set of all variables read by S_i as its input set, $I(S_i)$, and the set of all variables written by execution of S_i as its output set, $O(S_i)$. Then two statements S_i and S_j are independent of each other if all three conditions of Eq. (1.1) hold.

$$1. \ O(S_i) \cap O(S_j) = \Phi \quad \text{output independence}$$

$$2. \ I(S_j) \cap O(S_i) = \Phi \quad \text{flow independence} \tag{1.1}$$

$$3. \ I(S_i) \cap O(S_j) = \Phi \quad \text{anti independence}$$

In other words, no two statements write to the same variables, and no input variable of a statement is an output variable of another. The conditions stated in Eq. (1.1) are known as Bernstein's conditions [47].

The statements in Eq. (1.1) may be considered at various levels of granularity. For example, at the level of multiple arithmetic units of an SISD processor as in the CDC 6600 example, the lookahead buffer and scoreboard essentially detect parallelism in the machine level instruction sequences using these conditions. At a higher level, one might consider the statements S_i and S_j as large-code segments or even entire procedures and detect dependence among pairs of procedures. It is important to note that parallelism is commutative but not transitive. In other words, if S_i is independent of S_j, and S_j is independent of S_k, S_i and S_k are not necessarily independent. Therefore, all pairs of statements that are being considered for concurrent execution must be tested for independence.

Compilers can use the conditions of Eq. (1.1) to generate parallel code from sequential programs. This approach of detecting parallelism in a sequential algorithm often does not result in the best parallel program and implementation. Most often, restructuring of operations must be done to reveal the hidden parallelism in the computation. In general, the type of parallelism we look for depends on the type of parallel architecture that implements the task at hand, and except in very simple cases, new parallel algorithms must be designed. For example, in the SIMD pseudocode for matrix multiply of Program 1-1, we have chosen the ordering of the three nested loops over i, k, and j indices that is different from the usual sequential algorithm order of i, j, k, respectively. In the typical sequential implementation order, the computation to produce the result matrix C is carried out by completing the calculation for $C[1, 1]$ before proceeding to calculate $C[1, 2]$ and so on. This sequential order performs the dot product of row i of matrix A and column j of matrix B to produce element $C[i, j]$. The component wise multiplication of row i of matrix A and column j of matrix B is an efficient vector operation for an SIMD type architecture. However, the dot product of the two vectors requires the summation of the product vector into a single element, known as a *reduction* operation. This reduction operation is not performed efficiently in most SIMD architectures. In the true SIMD case, for example, the arithmetic units must communicate via the interconnection network to do a pairwise summation of the product vector. Sequentially, the summation of N numbers can be computed in a loop by adding one number to the sum in each iteration. The summation can be done in its most parallel form if disjoint pairs of operands are added together first. Then disjoint pairs of partial sums are added next and so on until the single final sum is produced. The evaluation tree for this parallel summation will be a full binary tree if N is a power of 2. The pairwise summation of N numbers takes $\lceil \log_2 N \rceil$ steps even at the computer hardware level. Recall that the notation, $\lceil x \rceil$ denotes x if x is an integer and the next integer greater than x if x has a fractional part. In the SIMD version of the matrix multiply, we have reordered the operations to produce the elements of the C matrix one row at a time. This way the underlying architecture efficiently performs a scalar times vector operation and adds two vectors without the need for a reduction operation.

In the SIMD case, the attempt has been to identify efficient parallelism at the lowest machine instruction level. For the MIMD architecture, we applied parallelism at the highest possible level by partitioning the work so that each processor is assigned the largest amount of work to be done. All three algorithms for the matrix multiply do the same number of operations but in different orders. We will study parallel algorithms for various architectures and their properties in more depth in subsequent chapters.

1.6 Conclusion

A review of the evolution of sequential computers has revealed the many ways parallelism has been introduced into sequential computers over time. While the application of parallelism in sequential machines has been hidden from user programs, it has essentially been the key mechanism of delivering speed in computers from the architecture and system design perspective as opposed to advances in solid-state electronic technology. Parallel applications and architectures are, thus, the next natural step in our quest toward computational speed that can accompany and further the progress in the technology.

In this introductory chapter, we have seen two important architectures for parallel computation, the SIMD architecture that applies the same operation to multiple data items simultaneously and the MIMD architecture that executes multiple instruction streams simultaneously, applying multiple independent instructions to multiple data values in parallel. A brief sketch of programming for these two architectures showed that the foremost issue in SIMD programming is that of specifying operations on vectors at the statement level, while the paramount concern in MIMD programming is creating and coordinating multiple sequential instruction streams that share data.

Parallel algorithms are designed to take advantage of specific architectures. A sequential algorithm may have to be restructured to detect parallel operations. On the other hand, as we will see in the next chapter, completely new algorithms may have to be designed to perform the same task with various levels of parallelism.

The fundamentals of parallel processing, therefore, involve architectures, programming languages, and algorithms. The next four chapters consider major architectural styles and the languages and program types that go with them. Chapter 3 treats SIMD architectures and the vector-oriented algorithms and languages suited to them. Chapter 4 and Chapter 5 treat MIMD architectures in which processors do and do not share memory, respectively. Chapter 6 treats the interconnection networks that enable communication among processing elements and memories in both SIMD and MIMD machines. Chapter 7 examines the fundamental impact of data dependence on parallel execution, both in the context of extracting parallelism from sequential programs and in using data flow representations to avoid introducing artificial parallelism into programs when they are written.

1.7 Bibliographic Notes

The foundations of overlap processing in sequential machines are discussed in Baer's text [34] incorporating original parallel instruction scheduling work from the CDC 6600 scoreboard [274] and Tomasulo's algorithm [276]. A good survey of parallel architectures can be found in [150]. It covers architectures that are important from the architectural point of view, even if many are no longer available. An early survey [243] covers pipelined architectures, while a slightly later book by Kogge [178] is a classic work on pipelined architectures with a good discussion of pipelined SIMD. A survey of interconnection networks can be found in [106]. A broad survey of parallel algorithms across distinct architecture classes can be found in [74]. It includes algorithms for vector computers as well as for shared and distributed memory multiprocessors. The programming and design of vector computers is well treated in [144]. An integrated treatment of parallel architectures, algorithms, and languages is given in [15]. Trew and Wilson's book [278] is a nice survey of commercially available parallel computers in 1990. It demonstrates how quickly a list of current architectures becomes dated. It even has a section on machines from companies that had recently failed.

Problems

1.1 Write SIMD and MIMD pseudocode for the tree summation of n elements of a one-dimensional array for n a power of two. Do not use recursive code, but organize the computations as iterations. The key issue is to determine which elements are to be added by a single arithmetic unit or a single processor at any level of the tree. You may overwrite elements of the array to be summed.

1.2 What mathematical property do sum, product, maximum, and minimum have in common that allows them to be done in parallel using a tree-structured algorithm?

1.3 The SIMD matrix multiply pseudocode of Program 1-1 is written to avoid doing an explicit reduction operation that is needed for the dot product of two vectors. Write another version of SIMD matrix multiply pseudocode that avoids the reduction operation. Describe the order of operations and compare it with both the sequential version and the SIMD version of Program 1-1.

1.4 Apply Bernstein's conditions to the compiler codes generated for evaluation of expressions in Figure 1-6 and Figure 1-7. In each case, determine which statements are independent of each other and can be executed in parallel. Detect and identify the type of dependences for statements that are not independent. Explain what might happen if two dependent statements are executed concurrently.

1.5 To apply Bernstein's conditions to the statements of Figure 1-6 to determine the independence of operations between the statements, how many pairs of statements must be examined? How many conditions must be tested in general for a code consisting of N statements?

1.6 Assume each stage of the floating addition pipeline of Figure 1-9 takes one time unit. Compare the performance of this pipelined floating point add with a true SIMD machine with six arithmetic units in which a floating point addition takes six time units. Show how long it takes to add two vectors of size 20 for both true and pipelined SIMD.

1.7 Consider the execution of the sequential code segment

```
S1:      X = (B - A)(A + C)
S2:      Y = 2D(D + C)
S3:      Z = Z(X + Y)
S4:      C = E(F - E)
S5:      Y = Z + 2F - B
S6:      A = C + B/(X + 1)
```

(a) Write the shortest assembly language code using *add*, *sub*, *mul*, and *div* for addition, subtraction, multiplication, and divide, respectively. Assume an instruction format with register address field so that $R1 = R2 + R3$ is equivalent to *add R1, R2, R3*. Assume there are as many registers as needed, and further assume that all operands have already been loaded into registers, therefore, ignoring memory reference operations such as load and store.

(b) Identify all the data dependences in part (a).

(c) Assume that add/sub takes one, multiply three, and divide 18 time units on this multiple arithmetic CPU, respectively, and that there are two adders, one multiplier, and one divide unit. If all instructions have been prefetched into a lookahead buffer and you can ignore the instruction issue time, what is the minimum execution time of this assembly code on this SISD computer?

Potential for Parallel Computations

Having seen some generalized computer architectures capable of doing many operations in parallel, let us consider what kind of work is available to be done in parallel in common computing jobs, or algorithms. First, there is a very large amount of computing that is trivially parallel. Managing inventories of many different items or doing bookkeeping for many independent accounts involves separate, noninteracting operations that may be carried out in any order, including simultaneously. It is not because such work is unimportant or because there is only a small amount of it that it is largely ignored in our study of parallel algorithms. It is merely that there is little to study with respect to such work. Algorithms in which there is a rich dependence among operations are the ones that require the most study and reward new methods. There is one exception to the triviality of noninteracting operations, and that occurs when these operations are buried in a program written in a language that does not make the independence of the operations obvious. We then speak of analyzing a program for the purposes of parallelism detection.

It is helpful to try to answer some questions while studying this chapter. What does it mean for two parallel algorithms that compute the same result to be different algorithms? What quantitative measures can be used to distinguish different parallel algorithms? Must computations be very complex for there to be several different parallel algorithms for doing them? Can automatic parallelizing compilers replace the task of designing and implementing good parallel algorithms?

2.1 Parameters Characterizing Algorithm Parallelism

Consider a computation in which the result depends on all of the input data. If the result is a single number, the computation can be viewed as the evaluation of an arithmetic expression. As a concrete example, let us consider the problem of summing a set of N numbers again. If the numbers are organized as a vector V, the sequential pseudocode for this job is:

```
s := V[1];
for i := 2 step 1 until N
    s := s + V[i];
```

To analyze operation parallelism, it is useful to describe the computation by a graph that shows how operations depend on each other and on the input data. A *data dependence graph* for the sequential summation is shown in Figure 2-1.

The graph is a directed graph, although the arrowheads are not shown in the figure for simplicity; all lines are directed downward. Some simple characterizations of a computation can be defined on the basis of the data dependence graph. The total number of operations in the graph is called the *size* of the computation, and the number of operations encountered in the longest path leading from any input to any output is its *depth*. The sequential summation graph has both depth $N - 1$ and size $N - 1$. The ratio of size to depth gives a measure of the parallelism inherent in the computation. It is easy to see that the summation can be made more parallel by reorganizing the computation so that inputs, and then intermediate sums, are combined pairwise. That gives the computation with the dependence graph shown for $N = 8$ in Figure 2-2.

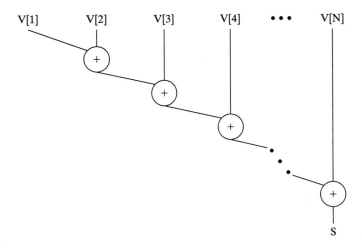

Figure 2-1   Data dependence graph for sequential summation.

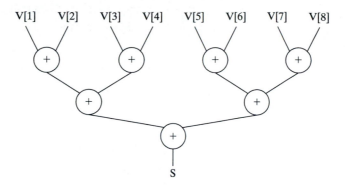

Figure 2-2   Data dependence graph for parallel summation.

From the graph, the size of the computation is still $N-1$, but the depth is reduced to $\lceil \log_2 N \rceil$. Thus, the computation still involves just as much work, in the sense of number of operations, but is more parallel in that it can be completed faster if there is the possibility of doing many operations simultaneously. Note that a simplification is being made in discussing the amount of work to be done. Only the operations that contribute to the numerical value of the answer are considered. If the input values are organized as a vector, the indexing operations on this vector are not counted. Also, we do not take into account any work that might be done to allocate operations to different processing units in a particular architecture. It is in this sense that we can say that we are considering the parallelism inherent in an algorithm rather than that of a particular parallel program for a particular architecture. Using an intermediate level pseudocode form of an algorithm, it is possible to estimate bookkeeping and overhead for algorithms implemented on a large class of machines, and we will have occasion to do this later. For the time being, however, the size and depth of the data dependence graph give a sufficient characterization of the parallelism inherent in a particular algorithm.

2.2 Prefix Problem

The previous computation is overly simple in that it represents a single arithmetic expression yielding one number as its result. A simple modification of the algorithm that now yields N results is

```
for i := 2 step 1 until N
    V[i] := V[i-1] + V[i];
```

An example where all sums are needed might be determining the starting page number for each chapter of a book given the number of pages in each chapter.

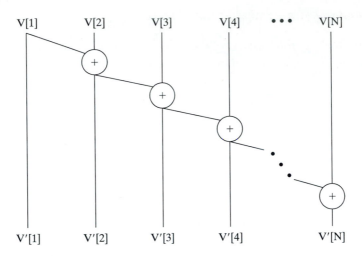

Figure 2-3   Data dependence graph for sequential summation.

This computation is called a *sum prefix computation* because, if the elements of V are written left to right with + signs inserted between them, all of the prefixes of this expression ending with each $V[i]$ are computed. Prefix computations with other dyadic operators such as multiply, logical *and* and *or* also find application. Several examples of applications of prefix computation can be found in the problems at the end of this chapter. The reader is especially encouraged to do Problem 2.9. The data dependence graph for this sequential version of the computation is shown in Figure 2-3. Its size and depth are the same as those of the sequential summation, but it is not as easy to parallelize because we also need all of the intermediate results that are computed by the sequential summation but not by the binary tree on which the parallel summation is based. In fact, it is possible to reduce the depth of this computation so as to make it more parallel, but only at the expense of increasing the total number of operations. We, thus, have an interesting middle ground between computations that are trivially parallel and those that can only be done sequentially, namely, computations that cost more operations to do in parallel. The following section presents an in-depth analysis of parallel prefix algorithms to show how parallelism and operation count can be traded off against each other in a nontrivial case.

2.3 Parallel Prefix Algorithms

A common way to produce parallel algorithms is the so-called *divide and conquer* approach, which involves separating a problem into two equivalent problems of half the size that can be done in parallel and their results combined to solve the original problem. In the sum prefix computation, the method would imply dividing an N element prefix problem into two prefix computations of $N/2$ elements each. There are several choices in how we divide an N element vector in half, each resulting in a different algorithm.

2.3.1   Upper/Lower Parallel Prefix Algorithm

We start with the simple idea of separating the lower numbered half of the elements from the higher numbered half. We call this the *upper/lower prefix*, P^{ul} for short, to distinguish it from a different partitioning of the indices to be considered later. If we can somehow compute the sum prefix on both the lower and upper halves of the input vector, then the final result can be obtained by adding the highest numbered result of the lower half computation to all $N/2$ results of the upper half computation, as shown in Figure 2-4. This division of the algorithm clearly introduces more operations because, even if the two half-size prefix computations are done with the minimum of $N/2 - 1$ operations each, we have added $N/2$ more operations, and $N - 2 + N/2 > N - 1$ for all but $N = 2$.

The key to the divide and conquer approach, of course, is to construct the two prefix computations appearing in the boxes by the same method, using two prefix calculations each of half their size. This would give a total of four prefix calculations of size $N/4$ each plus N extra add operations outside the boxes. We have been casual about assuming that $N/2$ and $N/4$ are integers. If they are not, we must introduce the *ceiling* and *floor* functions ($\lceil\ \rceil$ and $\lfloor\ \rfloor$) when dividing the computation into two parts as indicated in the figure. If we continue this division of the algorithm into two parts recursively, the computations in the prefix boxes eventually become trivial, consisting of only one or two inputs and outputs. At this point we simply introduce the direct implementations of the prefix computations in the boxes and obtain a parallel prefix computation for an N element vector that contains only add operations. The result of doing this recursive construction for $N = 8$ is shown in Figure 2-5. Even for only eight elements, we can see a fairly regular iterative pattern emerging, in addition to the recursive pattern used to generate the algorithm.

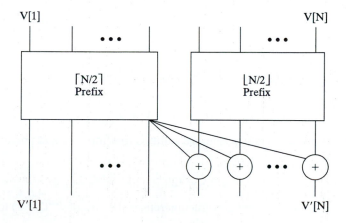

Figure 2-4   Upper/lower division of prefix computation.

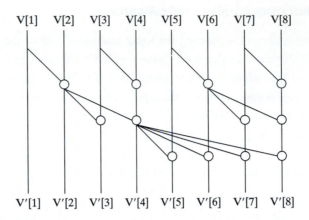

Figure 2-5   *Recursive upper/lower division for N = 8, $P^{ul}(8)$.*

It is interesting to consider the size and depth of this algorithm. The depth is easily seen to be $\lceil \log_2 N \rceil$, because each time the computation is split into two smaller ones, one more operation is added to the longest chain, and to reduce N to 1 it must be split this many times. The size is somewhat more difficult, but it seems simple for $N = 8$. At least for N a power of two, there are $N/2$ operations at each level of the computation. To illustrate how to obtain results for such recursive algorithms, consider a careful proof of the formula for the size of $P^{ul}(2^k)$. The technique of proof by induction is the appropriate method for dealing with recursive constructions.

THEOREM

Let $\sigma(N) = \text{Size}(P^{ul}(N))$. Then for N a power of two

$$\sigma(2^k) = k2^{k-1} = (N/2)\log_2 N, \tag{2.1}$$

where $N = 2^k$.

PROOF

As the initial condition for the finite induction, take $k = 1$. Then

$$\sigma(2^1) = \text{Size}(P^{ul}(2)) = 1 = 2^{1-1}, \tag{2.2}$$

so the result is true for $k = 1$. Now assume the result is true for $k = i$ and prove it for $k = i + 1$. Thus, we assume

$$\sigma(2^i) = i2^{i-1} \tag{2.3}$$

and calculate $\sigma(2^{i+1})$. The recursive construction relates the size of $P^{ul}(2^{i+1})$ to that of $P^{ul}(2^i)$ through

$$\sigma(2^{i+1}) = 2\sigma(2^i) + 2^i. \tag{2.4}$$

Thus, using our inductive hypothesis for $\sigma(2^i)$, we have

$$\sigma(2^{i+1}) = 2(i2^{i-1}) + 2^i,$$

$$= (i+1)2^{(i+1)-1}. \qquad (2.5)$$

Thus, if the result is true for $k = i$, it is also true for $k = i + 1$, and finite induction completes the proof for any finite k. ∎

The algorithm obtained from recursive upper/lower construction, thus, has depth $\log_2 N$ and size $N/2 \log_2 N$. If as many as $N/2$ operations can be done in parallel, the computation can be completed in $\log_2 N$ steps. The total amount of work done is $N/2 \log_2 N$ operations compared to $N - 1$ operations for the sequential algorithm. For a sum prefix on 1024 elements, the sequential algorithm does 1023 additions in 1023 time units, while the upper/lower parallel algorithm with at least 512 processors completes in 10 time units but does 5120 additions.

2.3.2   Odd/Even Parallel Prefix Algorithm

If we do not have unlimited processors, we may be interested in an algorithm with some parallelism but fewer operations. Such an algorithm can be obtained by a different divide and conquer approach. Divide the N inputs into groups whose indices are odd and even, respectively. A construction that makes use of only one prefix computation of half the size is shown in Figure 2-6. At the input we add the odd indexed values to those with the next higher even index. The prefix computation is then performed on the $N/2$ sums, yielding the correct result for all of the even numbered outputs. The odd numbered outputs are then obtained by adding each even numbered result to the next higher odd numbered input. Figure 2-7 shows the data dependence graph of odd/even algorithm for a vector of eight elements.

When this odd/even construction is applied recursively, two operations are added to the depth for each division of the size by two. This is not true for the special case of four inputs, see Figure 2-7. A simple diagram shows that the construction of $P^{oe}(4)$ from $P^{oe}(2)$ yields a depth of two instead of three. Doing the construction for $P^{oe}(N)$ where $N = 2^k$ down to $P^{oe}(4)$, the depth of which is 2, yields

$$\text{Depth}(P^{oe}(2^k)) = \sum_{i=k}^{3} 2 + \text{Depth}(P^{oe}(2^2)),$$

$$= 2k - 2 = 2\log_2 N - 2, k \geq 2. \qquad (2.6)$$

A similar repetition of the equation

$$\text{Size}(P^{oe}(2^k)) = \text{Size}(P^{oe}(2^{k-1})) + 2^k - 1, \qquad (2.7)$$

down to $\text{Size}(P^{oe}(2)) = 1$ yields

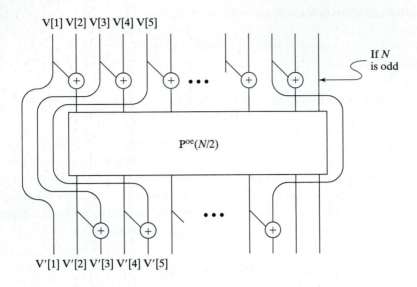

Figure 2-6   Odd/even construction for parallel prefix.

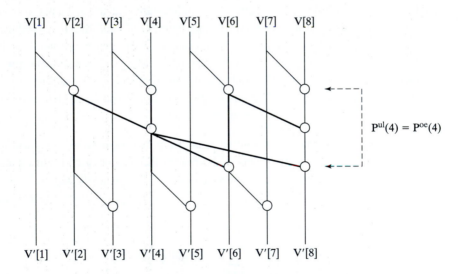

Figure 2-7   Recursive odd/even division for $N = 8$, $P^{oe}(8)$.

$$\text{Size}(P^{oe}(2^k)) = \sum_{i=k}^{1}(2^i - 1) = 2^{k+1} - k - 2,$$

$$= 2N - \log_2 N - 2, \, k \geq 0. \tag{2.8}$$

Thus, for large N, P^{ul} requires $1/4 \log_2 N$ times as many operations as P^{oe}, but P^{oe} has depth about twice that of P^{ul}. Thus, if the number of processes is very large, P^{ul} completes faster than P^{oe}. But if the number of processors is small enough that some work must be done sequentially merely from a lack of processors to do it in parallel, then P^{oe} may well complete faster than P^{ul}.

2.3.3   Ladner and Fischer's Parallel Prefix

The recursive upper/lower and odd/even parallel prefix algorithms are fairly straightforward applications of the divide and conquer method. The analysis of their size and depth involves only simple counting arguments. This section treats a better algorithm that requires more mathematics to compute its size. The flow of the chapter will not be disrupted for readers who wish to skip this section and take on faith the size of the algorithm $P_0(2^k)$ given in Table 2-1.

A parallel prefix algorithm, actually a class of algorithms, having some of the advantages of both P^{ul} and P^{oe} was developed by R. E. Ladner and M. J. Fischer [190]. The algorithms are called $P_j(N)$, where the integer subscript $j \geq 0$ distinguishes the different algorithms of the class. In some sense the algorithm $P_0(N)$, that has depth $\log_2 N$, is the most interesting, but the algorithm P_1 must also be used to define P_0, and the P_j for $j > 1$ allow very detailed trade-off of size versus depth. The odd/even construction is used to construct $P_1(N)$ from $P_0(N/2)$, and the upper/lower construction is used to define $P_0(N)$ in terms of both $P_1(N/2)$ and $P_0(N/2)$.

Table 2-1   Characteristics of parallel prefix algorithms.

Algorithm	Depth	Size
$P^{ul}(N = 2^k)$	k	$kN/2$
$P^{oe}(N = 2^k)$	$2k - 2$	$2N - k - 2$
$P_0(N = 2^k)$	k	$4N - 4.96N^{0.69} + 1$

Specifically, the general definition of Ladner and Fischer's class of algorithms defines $P_j(N)$ for $j \geq 1$ using the odd/even construction of Figure 2-6 with $P_{j-1}(\lceil N/2 \rceil)$ inside the box that does a prefix on the even numbered inputs. Thus, for $j = 1$, P_1 is defined in terms of P_0. To define P_0, which is the only algorithm of the class not defined by the odd/even construction, the upper/lower construction is used. However, the procedure is somewhat more complicated than simple recursive application of the construction to the same algorithm for different N. Instead, $P_0(N)$ is built by using the algorithm $P_1(\lceil N/2 \rceil)$ on the lower half of the inputs, but the algorithm $P_0(\lfloor N/2 \rfloor)$ on the upper half, and then combining them as shown in Figure 2-8. The key to maintaining a depth of $\lceil \log_2 N \rceil$ for P_0 is that, although $P_1(N)$ has depth $\lceil \log_2 N \rceil + 1$, which is one more than the minimum depth for N inputs, its use for the prefix of the lower half inputs does not lead to an increased depth for P_0. This is because the right most output has at most $\lceil \log_2 \lceil N/2 \rceil \rceil$ operators on any path to an input, and it is only this output that is combined with the upper half P_0 computation using one more level of operators. This construction, thus, maintains a depth of $\lceil \log_2 N \rceil$ for $P_0(N)$. Use of the odd/even construction along with the upper/lower construction tends to hold down the number of operators. In fact, the size of $P_0(N)$ is on the order of $4N$ instead of the $N/2 \log_2 N$ size of $P^{ul}(N)$.

To see how the size behaves, let $S_j(N) = \text{Size}(P_j(N))$. Then the basic size relationships obtained directly from the constructions are

$$S_j(N) = S_1(\lceil N/2 \rceil) + S_0(\lfloor N/2 \rfloor) + \lfloor N/2 \rfloor, \text{ and} \tag{2.9}$$

$$S_j(N) = S_{j-1}(\lceil N/2 \rceil) + N - 1, \text{ for } j \geq 1, \text{ even } N \geq 2,$$

$$S_j(N) = S_{j-1}(\lceil N/2 \rceil) + N - 2, \text{ for } j \geq 1, \text{ odd } N \geq 3. \tag{2.10}$$

From these relations we can get a closed form solution for the size when N is a power of two.

THEOREM

If $N = 2^k$ is a power of two, then

$$S_0(N) = 4N - F(2 + k) - 2F(3 + k) + 1, \text{ and}$$

$$S_1(N) = 3N - F(1 + k) - 2F(2 + k), \tag{2.11}$$

where $F(m)$ is the mth Fibonacci number.

Note: Recall that $F(0) = 0$, $F(1) = 1$, and the Fibonacci numbers satisfy the recurrence $F(m) = F(m - 1) + F(m - 2)$, for $m \geq 2$.

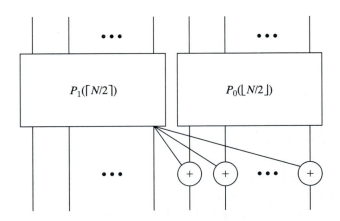

Figure 2-8   Definition of Ladner and Fischer's $P_0(N)$.

PROOF

We again use finite induction with the initial conditions

$$S_0(2^1) = 1 = 4 \cdot 2 - F(3) - 2F(4) + 1, \text{ and}$$

$$S_1(2^2) = 4 = 3 \cdot 4 - F(3) - 2F(4). \tag{2.12}$$

Now assume the result for $k = m$,

$$S_0(N) = 4N - F(2 + m) - 2F(3 + m) + 1, \text{ and}$$

$$S_1(N) = 3N - F(1 + m) - 2F(2 + m). \tag{2.13}$$

Using equations (2.9) and (2.10), obtained from the constructions,

$$S_0(2^{m+1}) = 4 \cdot 2^m - F(2 + m) - 2F(3 + m) + 1$$

$$+ 3 \cdot 2^m - F(1 + m) - 2F(2 + m) + 2^m$$

$$= 4 \cdot 2^{m+1} - F(3 + m) - 2F(4 + m) + 1, \tag{2.14}$$

$$S_1(2^{m+1}) = 4 \cdot 2^m - F(2 + m) - 2F(3 + m) + 1 + 2^{m+1} - 1$$

$$= 3 \cdot 2^{m+1} - F(1 + (m + 1)) - 2F(2 + (m + 1)). \tag{2.15}$$

Thus, under the assumption that the formulae of the theorem hold for $k = m$, we find they also hold for $k = m + 1$, and finite induction completes the proof of the theorem for any finite k. ∎

There are two things wrong with the result of the previous theorem. First, it does not say what happens if N is not a power of two, though we expect from the constructions that the size will increase more or less smoothly with N. Secondly, most people have little intuition about how Fibonacci numbers increase. The solution to the first problem is to find, not an exact formula, but an upper bound on the size of $S_j(N)$ for N not a power of 2. It can be shown that

$$S_j(N) < 2\left(1 + \frac{1}{2^j}\right)N - 2 \text{ for } N \geq 1. \tag{2.16}$$

Thus, in particular, $S_0(N) < 4N$ so the size of Ladner and Fischer's P_0 algorithm is no larger than four times the size of the sequential algorithm for any N.

The solution to the second problem is to use an asymptotic formula for the Fibonacci numbers to see how the size for $N = 2^k$ varies for large values of k. Using the method of generating functions (see, for example, [174]), it can be shown that

$$F(m) = \frac{\phi^m - \hat{\phi}^m}{\sqrt{5}}, \text{ where } \phi = \frac{1 + \sqrt{5}}{2} \text{ and } \hat{\phi} = \frac{1 - \sqrt{5}}{2}. \tag{2.17}$$

Because $\hat{\phi} < 1$ we have for large m, $F(m) \approx \frac{\phi^m}{\sqrt{5}}$. This allows us to write a size approximation

$$S_0(N) \approx 4N - \frac{\phi^{k+2}}{\sqrt{5}} - 2\frac{\phi^{k+3}}{\sqrt{5}} + 1,$$

$$= 4N - \frac{(1+2\phi)}{\sqrt{5}}\phi^2\phi^k + 1,$$

$$= 4N - \frac{(1+2\phi)\phi^2}{\sqrt{5}}2^{k\log_2\phi} + 1, \tag{2.18}$$

$$= 4N - 4.9597N^{\log_2\phi} + 1,$$

$$= 4N - 4.9597N^{0.69424} + 1.$$

In summary, we have the results of Table 2-1 for three different parallel prefix algorithms, P^{ul} obtained from repeated upper/lower construction, P^{oe} obtained from repeated odd/even construction and P_0 obtained from Ladner and Fischer's mixture of the two constructions. Thus, we do not need to use an algorithm whose size increases proportional to $N\log_2 N$ to achieve the minimum depth $\lceil \log_2 N \rceil$, but we can use one whose size is strictly less than $4N$.

2.4 Characterizing Algorithm Behavior for Large Problem Size

It is useful to be able to calculate the way the computational cost of solving a problem grows as the size of the problem grows. This information about an algorithm is usually most useful for large problem sizes, so the issue is that of characterizing the asymptotic behavior. This type of characterization is independent of the form of computational cost versus size for small problems. A example of an asymptotic statement would be that, if N measures the size of the problem data, then the computational cost increases by about a factor of eight when N is doubled.

Some notation and formal definitions are available to make such ideas precise and allow mathematical analysis to yield such information. Perhaps the most often used definition is that of the "big O" notation.

Definition: Let $f(n)$ and $g(n)$ be functions of an integer n. The notation $f(n) = O(g(n))$ means that there exists a constant c and an integer N such that for all $n \geq N$, $|f(n)| < c \cdot |g(n)|$.

In words, one could say that $f(n) = O(g(n))$ means that for large enough n, the magnitude of $f(n)$ grows no faster than that of $g(n)$ as n increases.

To get at the idea that a function grows at least as fast as another we have the following definition.

Definition: Let $f(n)$ and $g(n)$ be functions of an integer n. The notation $f(n) = \Omega(g(n))$ means that there exists a constant c and an integer N such that for all $n \geq N$, $|f(n)| > c \cdot |g(n)|$.

The prose form of $f(n) = \Omega(g(n))$ is that, for large enough n, $f(n)$ grows no slower than $g(n)$ as n increases. Combining this with the previous idea we get a definition that $f(n)$ is of the same order as $g(n)$, written $f(n) = \Theta(g(n))$.

Definition: If both $f(n) = O(g(n))$ and $f(n) = \Omega(g(n))$ then $f(n) = \Theta(g(n))$. Alternatively, let $f(n)$ and $g(n)$ be functions of an integer n. Then the notation $f(n) = \Theta(g(n))$ means that there exist an integer N and constants c_1 and c_2 such that for all $n \geq N$, $0 < c_1 \cdot |g(n)| < |f(n)| < c_2 \cdot |g(n)|$.

In addition to the ideas of a function growing no faster or no slower than another there are also precise definitions for the ideas of a function growing strictly slower and strictly faster than another. The formal definitions are as follows.

Definition: Let $f(n)$ and $g(n)$ be functions of an integer n. The notation $f(n) = o(g(n))$ means that for any $\varepsilon > 0$ there exists an integer N such that for all $n \geq N$, $|f(n)| < \varepsilon \cdot |g(n)|$.

This amounts to saying that the ratio $f(n)/g(n)$ tends to zero as n increases.

Definition: Let $f(n)$ and $g(n)$ be functions of an integer n. The notation $f(n) = \omega(g(n))$ means that for all C, arbitrarily large, there exists an integer N such that for all $n \geq N$, $|f(n)| > C \cdot |g(n)|$.

This says that the ratio $f(n)/g(n)$ diverges as n increases.

Note that $f(n)$ being on the order of $g(n)$, $f(n) = \Theta(g(n))$, does not mean that the graphs of $f(n)$ and $g(n)$ versus n resemble each other very much. For example,

$$f(n) = \frac{n^3}{M^3} + \sin\frac{2\pi n}{M} = \Theta(n^3), \tag{2.19}$$

but, especially for $n < M$, the graph of $f(n)$ looks very little like that of n^3. Also note that the statement "X is of the order 1,000," is a completely different use of the word "order." In fact, because of the constants in the definitions, if $f(n) = \Theta(g(n))$ then also $c \cdot f(n) = \Theta(g(n))$, and it is useless to write $f(n) = \Theta(c \cdot g(n))$ for any constant c other than one. The appearance of an expression like $\Theta(6n^3)$ (or O, o, Ω, or ω) in an order analysis is a sure sign that the writer is not using the above definitions or has not understood them.

Asymptotic statements are useful in some comparisons, and especially when the only information available is in the form of bounds. They are not a substitute for more precise information about the size and depth of an algorithm when it is known. From Table 2-1 we see that the depths of $P_0(N)$ and $P^{oe}(N)$ are both $O(\log N)$ and their sizes are both $O(N)$. Comparing them in this way neglects any distinction between these two, very different, algorithms.

2.5 Programming Parallel Prefix

So far we have discussed the parallel prefix algorithms without discussing any programs that might implement them. The data dependence diagrams show what operands are combined to produce each intermediate result, but they do not show how the operations are mapped onto a processor or processors that might perform them. As an example of programming parallel prefix, we consider the algorithm obtained by recursive odd/even partitioning.

Consider the odd/even parallel prefix algorithm $P_k(2^k)$, $N = 2^k$, which results from successive application of the odd/even construction. The pseudocode of Program 2-1 describes this algorithm for a sequential computer. Note that, although the algorithm was derived recursively, the code is not recursive at all. In general, iterations execute much more efficiently than recursions, and algorithms should be cast in iterative form if possible.

```
level := 2;
while level ≤ N
    begin
      for i := level step level until N
            V[i] := V[i] + V[i - level/2];
      level := 2*level;
    end;
level := level/2;
if level := N then level := level/2;
while level > 1
    begin
      for i := level + level/2 step level until N
            V[i] := V[i] + V[i - level/2];
      level := level/2;
    end;
```

Program 2-1   Sequential pseudocode for odd/even parallel prefix algorithm.

In Program 2-2 is the code for the same algorithm written for a multiprocessor with NP processors. The **fork** and **join** code to start up the processes and wait for their completion is not shown. Only the code executed by process j is shown. The relation between the number of processors, NP, and the number N of elements in the prefix vector is loose. Maximum speedup will be obtained if NP = N/2, and there is no benefit to having NP > N/2. Any NP < N/2 will work, including NP = 1.

The **barrier** function used in the MIMD pseudocode is a simple synchronization that operates as follows. When a processor executes a **barrier** statement, it waits until all other processors have entered their **barrier** statements and then continues. Thus, any work done by any processor before it executes its **barrier** is completed before any statement following the **barrier** is executed by any processor. Synchronizations will be treated in detail in connection with shared memory multiprocessors.

2.6 Speedup and Efficiency of Parallel Algorithms

For a given algorithm or computation, let T_p be the time to perform the computation using p processors or arithmetic units. Note that this makes T_∞ the depth of the algorithm. We define the *speedup* with p processors as

$$S_p = \frac{T_1}{T_p},$$ (2.20)

and the *efficiency* with p processors as

```
private level, j, i;
shared N, NP, V[1:N];
level := 2;
while level ≤ N
   begin
      for i := level + (j-1)*level step level*NP until N
         V[i] := V[i] + V[i - level/2];
      barrier;
      level := 2*level;
   end;
level := level/2;
if level := N then level := level/2;
while level > 1
   begin
      for i := level + level/2 + (j-1)*level step level*NP until N
         V[i] := V[i] + V[i - level/2];
      barrier;
      level := level/2;
end;
```

Program 2-2   MIMD odd/even parallel prefix code for process j of NP processes.

$$E_p = \frac{S_p}{p}. \tag{2.21}$$

Because p processors can do no more than p times as much work per unit time as one processor, the efficiency is theoretically bounded above by one.

Let π be the minimum number of processors required to achieve the maximum speedup according to some algorithm, so

$$\pi = \min\{p \mid T_p = T_\infty\}. \tag{2.22}$$

Then T_π, S_π, and E_π are the time, speedup, and efficiency for π, where π is the number of processors for the shortest known time.

Let $P^{ul}(N)$ be the parallel prefix algorithm obtained by recursive application of the upper/lower divide and conquer construction. Then

$$\pi(P^{ul}(N)) = \lfloor N/2 \rfloor \tag{2.23}$$

is the minimum number of processors for which the maximum possible speedup is obtained with this algorithm. The fastest time is given by the depth

$$T_\infty(P^{ul}(N)) = \lceil \log_2 N \rceil \tag{2.24}$$

while the time to execute $P^{ul}(N)$ with a smaller number of processors p where $p < \pi(P^{ul}(N))$ is denoted $T_p(P^{ul}(N))$. For the algorithm $P^{oe}(N)$ obtained by recursive application of the odd/even construction, we have a different characterization with

$$\pi(P^{oe}(N)) = \lfloor N/2 \rfloor, \; T_\pi(P^{oe}(N)) = 2\lceil \log_2 N \rceil - 2. \tag{2.25}$$

We must be careful how we use speedup figures. Because $P^{ul}(N)$ has $\lfloor N/2 \rfloor \lceil \log_2 N \rceil$ operations and one processor can do only a single operation at a time, we might be tempted to write the speedup as

$$S_\pi(P^{ul}(N)) = \frac{T_1}{T_\pi} = \frac{\lfloor N/2 \rfloor \lceil \log_2 N \rceil}{\lceil \log_2 N \rceil} = \lfloor N/2 \rfloor. \tag{2.26}$$

But this is a very misleading measure of what one can get in terms of improved execution by parallelizing the prefix calculation using the upper/lower construction. No one would compute the prefix on a vector by executing P^{ul} with only one processor. The correct value of T_1 to use is $N - 1$, which is obtained using the sequential algorithm, so the correct speedup and efficiency to cite are

$$S_\pi(P^{ul}(N)) = \frac{T_1(\text{sequential})}{T_\pi(P^{ul}(N))} = \frac{N-1}{\lceil \log_2 N \rceil}, \tag{2.27}$$

$$E_\pi(P^{ul}(N)) = \frac{N-1}{\lceil \log_2 N \rceil} \cdot \frac{1}{\lfloor N/2 \rfloor} \approx \frac{2}{\log_2 N}, \; N \geq 4. \tag{2.28}$$

Thus, we can talk about an algorithm-oriented speedup (2.26), which tells us only how a given algorithm will speed up with an increased number of processors applied to it, and a problem-oriented speedup (2.27), which tells us how much better we can really do by using parallel processing. We must also be careful about how we use the problem-oriented speedup. It is technically the ratio of the time obtained with the best sequential algorithm to the fastest parallel time. But we do not always know the best sequential algorithm in more complex cases, and we certainly are not always comparing it with the best parallel algorithm. It is always a good idea to specify carefully the comparison that is being made when quoting speedup results.

The previous discussion makes it clear that it is hard to talk about the parallelism and speedup achievable in a mathematical computation independently of the algorithm used to solve the problem. There are, however, a few areas where this is possible. Consider the evaluation of arithmetic expressions in the operations $+$, $-$, $\times$, and $\div$. The variables or constants appearing in an expression are known as *atoms*. Denote an arithmetic expression with N atoms by $E\langle N \rangle$. The minimum time to evaluate such an expression by any sequential algorithm is $N - 1$ steps, because each operation combines only two items. For the same reason we can obtain the following result.

Lemma 1

For any number p of processors,

$$T_p(E\langle N \rangle) \geq \lceil \log_2 N \rceil. \tag{2.29}$$

PROOF

Because there is a single result and all the operators are dyadic, that is, they combine two operands into a single result, there can be no more than two intermediate results at the next to the last step of the computation, no more than four at the step prior to that, and so on. In general, if there are k steps, there are no more than 2^{k-1} intermediate values at step 1. Because there must be N atoms at step 0, $2^k \geq N$, and the result follows. ■

One of the results that we can read from this lemma is that the depth of the parallel prefix algorithms $P^{ul}(N)$ and $P_0(N)$, which are both $\lceil \log_2 N \rceil$, are the minimum possible. This is true because the value of the last element of the prefix vector is given by an N element arithmetic expression, and the time for the prefix calculation must, thus, be at least as large as $T_p(E\langle N \rangle)$. That the lower bound can actually be achieved in this case is related to the fact that all the operators in the expression are the same and that the operator is associative.

Although the previous lemma gives a lower bound on the minimum evaluation time of an arithmetic expression, any specific expression may take longer as a result of evaluation order imposed by operator precedence or parentheses. For example, the expression $E\langle 8 \rangle = A + B(CDE + F + G) + H$, when evaluated from left to right, yields the expression tree of Figure 2-9. This does not mean, however, that the time required to evaluate this expression is equal to seven, which is the depth of the tree. If we are willing to make use of algebraic properties of $+$ and $\times$, namely, the associative and commutative laws, we can obtain the depth five tree of Figure 2-10(a), and if we are willing to increase the number of operations, we can use the distributive law as well to obtain the depth four tree of Figure 2-10(b). (The size of Figure 2-10(b) can be reduced slightly without changing its depth.)

Essential parentheses in an arithmetic expression are important to execution time of a parallel evaluation if we use only associativity and commutativity to transform the expression. The subexpression enclosed in a set of essential parentheses can only be changed by using distributivity. Nested parentheses increase the amount of time required to evaluate an arithmetic expression in parallel if these parentheses are essential. Therefore, it is not surprising that the time to evaluate an arithmetic expression in parallel, allowing only for associativity and commutativity, depends on d, the depth of nesting of parentheses. The main result in this case is embodied in the following theorem.

THEOREM

If $E\langle N|d \rangle$ is any arithmetic expression with N atoms and depth d of parenthesis nesting, then using associativity and commutativity only, $E\langle N|d \rangle$ can be transformed so that

$$T_\pi(E\langle N|d \rangle) \leq \lceil \log_2 N \rceil + 2d + 1, \text{ with } \pi \leq \lceil N/2 - d \rceil. \tag{2.30}$$

PROOF

A proof of this result can be found in [33].

The distributive law can be used to remove even essential parentheses by restructuring the expression. In general, this will introduce more operations into the transformed expression. An algorithm for evaluating an arithmetic expression that is obtained by using associativity, commutativity, and distributivity to reduce the evaluation time of some original form of expression evaluation is, in some sense, the best possible parallel algorithm for solving that problem. It, therefore, gives us the ability, in this special case, to talk about the best possible parallel execution time for the problem. The main result is

THEOREM

An expression $E\langle N\rangle$ with N atoms can be transformed using associativity, commutativity, and distributivity so that

$$T_\pi(E\langle N\rangle) \le \lceil 4\log_2 N \rceil, \text{ with } \pi \le 3N. \tag{2.31}$$

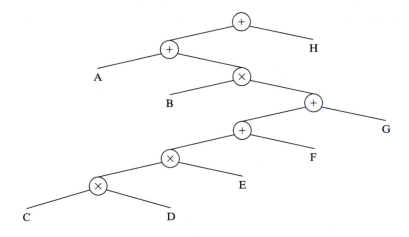

Figure 2-9 Expression tree for $A + B(CDE + F + G) + H$.

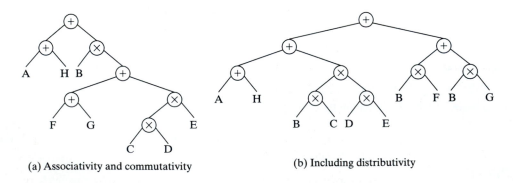

(a) Associativity and commutativity   (b) Including distributivity

Figure 2-10 Transforming the expression to minimize depth.

PROOF

Proof: See reference [33].

Note that if we are given an expression in some arbitrary form, it will require some time to transform it into the form required to obtain the parallel execution time given in the theorems. If the expression is to be compiled once and evaluated many times, the time required by the transformation is probably unimportant. If, however, the expression is transformed into the best parallel form and then evaluated only once, this time becomes very important. The transformation including distributivity is the most complex and requires $O(N\log_2 N)$ steps to perform. The time to do the translation, thus, grows proportionally to $N\log_2 N$, while the time to evaluate the resulting expression only grows proportionally to $\log_2 N$. Thus, for large N, the translation of the expression will take longer than its evaluation.

2.7 The Performance Perspective

At the outset we indicated that the whole purpose of parallel processing is to gain execution speed over a more serial approach. The last section discussed speedup from a very limited algorithmic viewpoint that considers only arithmetic operations and takes them all to be equal in time. While it is true that a machine with many arithmetic units is useless for an algorithm with small π, it is also true that general parallel expression tree evaluation cannot be performed on an SIMD computer, whose instruction set limits it to parallel instances of the same operation applied to regularly stored values. The programming language must also make a machine's parallel capability available to the program implementing an algorithm. For example, Fortran 90 has vector operations that can be implemented on an MIMD machine so that they execute efficiently in parallel, but it does not allow general parallel expression evaluation to be expressed effectively, even when running on the most general MIMD system.

Many studies of parallel processor performance have been stimulated by scientific computing tasks that are compute bound. For such tasks, the utilization of processors is most important, and use of other resources, such as I/O facilities, can be safely neglected. For these tasks, the best performance implies the smallest execution time. In parallel programs it is not the total number of processor cycles that is to be minimized but the time to completion of the job. Minimum processor cycles would probably imply sequential execution on a single processor, making parallelism unnecessary. Thus, execution time can be taken as the direct indicator of performance for compute bound parallel programs, and it remains to determine what factors determine the minimum execution time for a particular program run on a particular parallel computer system.

2.7.1   Factors That Influence Performance

Execution time is influenced by a wide variety of things. At the bottom is the hardware technology, which has a uniform scaling influence on all processors in the system. Processor architecture and system architecture come next, followed by the operating system, which is often characterized as an extension of the architecture. The language used to write the program, its compiler and run-time support libraries separate the program from the operating system extended architecture. The program structure, based on language and programming style can have a strong impact on performance and has the advantage of being accessible to the user. Finally, the algorithm selected can impact the available parallelism, and, thus, the execution time, in a significant way. Execution time is potentially influenced by all these levels, and experience shows that it is seldom attributable to only one of them. Table 2-2 lists six different levels of the computation that may impact performance. The user can influence these levels to varying degrees. He has total control over the program and algorithm but none at all over the hardware implementation. Limited control over the architecture might involve using fewer than the maximum number of processors in a multiprocessor system.

At the root of the hardware implementation is the digital logic technology, but other factors, such as the degree of integration, circuit interconnections and cooling, play a role in determining speed. The hardware influences can usually be summed up by stating the clock period of the machine. This is not entirely divorced from the architecture, because a single chip microprocessor with a 10 ns clock period is not the same as a supercomputer with the same clock rate.

Systems use parallel architecture to achieve a higher performance than would result from a sequential machine with the same clock rate. Architecture is often the target for performance studies, either for selecting a system or optimizing a design. The arithmetic unit, control unit, and memory impact the performance of each processor in the system. Total system performance is also influenced by synchronization and data movement among processors. Any of these architectural features can set an upper limit on the performance of a particular program. Perhaps a litmus test for a well-balanced architecture is the ability to find different programs whose performance is limited by each of these factors in turn.

Table 2-2   Levels that impact performance

Level	Notes
Hardware	Establishes fundamental speed scale
Architecture	Both individual unit and system level
Operating system	As an extension to the hardware
Language	Includes compiler and run-time support
Program	Control structure and synchronization
Algorithm	Data dependence structure

As well as being an extension of the hardware, the operating system also shares resources among multiple users of the system. As an extension of the role of sharing resources among users, it may also be involved in sharing resources among multiple processes belonging to one user's parallel program. Thus, process control, synchronization and interprocess data movement may involve the operating system. Input/output is managed by the operating system in more or less traditional ways, with some special techniques used with I/O devices that support parallel access.

The programming language influences performance through the operations made available to the programmer and through the efficiency of their implementation. Though based on the machine instruction set, the language influence on performance is strongly determined by the compiler and the run-time system. The important compiler features include not only the basic implementation of the language primitives but also global optimization and automatic parallelization, if used. A sizable run-time system often supports the language. Frequency and cost of linkages to the run-time package are often important performance influences. The degree to which the run-time relies on the operating system for support is also important. For example, it is possible that no low-cost synchronization whatever is available in a multiprocessor because all synchronizations use a two-level linkage through the run-time and operating systems, and may have a context switch for one or more processors.

The organization and style of the program have an important impact on performance, and almost all programmers make some degree of effort to structure their program to run fast on what they perceive to be the abstract model of the computer system. The choice of data structures, the program control structure, type of synchronizations used, and the management of I/O can all have a strong influence on performance. The result of many performance studies is to suggest modifications of program structure that will lead to better performance. Also, the ability to change parameters of the program can be used to advantage in studying the performance implications of lower levels of the computation.

While programming style can be considered the tactics of the computation plan, the algorithm constitutes the strategy. Aspects of the algorithm that relate directly to performance include the depth of the dependence graph, its size or number of operations, the maximum, minimum and average parallelism, and the fraction of the operations forming a strictly sequential chain. Different algorithms may be more vectorizable or parallelizable, and this may or may not trade off against the size of the computation. Although the choice of algorithm may be determined by an understanding of the system performance, algorithm variation often does not play a direct role in performance studies.

2.7.2   A Simple Performance Model—Amdahl's Law

As an introduction to mathematical characterization of parallel performance we introduce Amdahl's law, which we will refer to and extend several times in studying parallel processing. Amdahl's law is a very simple, general model of parallel processor performance. Not all of a program can be executed in parallel. Let f be the fraction of operations in the program that must be executed sequentially. Make the simplifying assumption that the remaining fraction $(1-f)$ of the program can be executed in parallel with 100% efficiency on the parallel hardware available. Let P be the degree of parallelism in the hardware. This degree of parallelism, P, varies depending on the type of the architecture.

- P is the number of processors in MIMD.
- P is the number of processing elements in SIMD.
- P is the ratio of vector speed to scalar speed in pipelined SIMD.
- P is the number of pipeline stages in pipelined MIMD.

Let $T(P)$ be the execution time with hardware parallelism P. If the time doing the sequential part of the work is S and the time to do the parallel part of the work sequentially is Q, that is, S and Q are the sequential and parallel amounts of work measured by time on one processor, the total time is

$$T(P) = S + Q/P. \tag{2.32}$$

Expressing this in terms of the fraction $f = S/(S+Q)$ of serial work, Amdahl's law becomes

$$T(P) = f \cdot T(1) + (1-f)T(1)/P. \tag{2.33}$$

The speedup is

$$S(P) = \frac{T(1)}{T(P)} = \frac{1}{f + (1-f)/P}, \tag{2.34}$$

and the efficiency is

$$E(P) = \frac{S(P)}{P} = \frac{1}{1 + f(P-1)}. \tag{2.35}$$

There are several consequences of this simple performance model. To achieve at least 50% efficiency on the program with hardware parallelism P, f can be no larger than $1/(P-1)$. This becomes harder and harder to achieve as P becomes large. Amdahl [18] used this result to argue that sequential processing was best, but it has several useful interpretations in different parallel environments:

- A very small amount of unparallelized code can have a very large effect on efficiency if the parallelism is large;
- A fast vector processor must also have a fast scalar processor to achieve a sizeable fraction of its peak performance;
- Effort in parallelizing a small fraction of code that is currently executed sequentially may pay off in large performance gains;
- Hardware that allows even a small fraction of new things to be done in parallel may be considerably more efficient.

Although Amdahl's law is a simple performance model, it need not be taken simplistically. The behavior of the sequential fraction, f, for example, can be quite important. System sizes, especially the number, P, of processors are often increased for the purpose of running larger problems. Increasing the problem size often does not increase the absolute amount of sequential work significantly. In this case, f is a decreasing function of problem size, and if problem size is increased with P, the somewhat pessimistic implications of equations (2.34) and (2.35) look much more favorable. See Problem 2.17 for a specific example. The behavior of performance as both problem and system size increase is called *scalability*.

2.7.3 Average Execution Rate

Many parallel processor studies use execution rate instead of execution time to measure performance. Popular units are millions of floating point operations per second (MFLOPS) and millions of instructions per second (MIPS). Because rate is the inverse of execution time, many architectural features that directly affect an execution time graph are harder to see in a rate graph. Citing the maximum rate achievable on any program has often been used to show a machine in the best light, but it is well understood that this is a bad measure of performance. A fair measure must consist of an average execution rate over different programs and/or parts of the same program.

The reciprocal relationship between execution time and execution rate means that rates are not simply averaged over the code. If the sequential execution rate is R_s operations per second and we take the execution rate for fully parallelizable code as $R_p = P \cdot R_s$, then the time to execute an amount of work W, of which a fraction f is not parallelizable and a fraction $(1-f)$ is fully parallelizable is

$$T_W = \frac{f \cdot W}{R_s} + \frac{(1-f) \cdot W}{R_p}. \tag{2.36}$$

This means that the average execution rate in operations per second for the work is

$$R_a = \frac{W}{T_W} = \left(\frac{f}{R_s} + \frac{(1-f)}{R_p} \right)^{-1}. \tag{2.37}$$

Thus, R_a is the *weighted harmonic mean* of R_s and R_p because the slower rate accounts for a proportionally larger fraction of the time, just as occurs in time, velocity, and distance traveled problems. The harmonic mean relationship is often written as

$$\frac{1}{R_a} = \frac{f}{R_s} + \frac{(1-f)}{R_p}. \tag{2.38}$$

If g is the fraction of time spent running at rate R_s instead of the fraction of work done at that rate, then the average rate is given by the arithmetic mean rather than the harmonic mean.

$$R_a = gR_s + (1-g)R_p. \tag{2.39}$$

The eventual dominance of serial execution in Amdahl's law can be seen to be closely related to the behavior of the harmonic mean as one of the two rates increases.

2.8 Conclusion

Recognizing that the ability to perform operations in parallel is both made possible by and limited by the underlying computation or algorithm, we looked at the degree of parallelism in different algorithms for performing the same task. We saw how to characterize algorithms in terms of properties including size, depth, speedup, and efficiency and discovered that, even for the simple prefix calculation, different parallel algorithms could be developed that traded off one characteristic for another. The operation dependence graph was seen to be an important tool for understanding algorithm characteristics. Arithmetic expression evaluation was treated as one of the few problems simple enough that the optimal parallel algorithm for it could be determined. We also introduced asymptotic analysis for cases where closed form expressions for algorithm characteristics are simply not available.

Enhanced performance is the ultimate goal of parallel processing. Performance depends on the interaction of algorithms, programming languages, and architectures and not on any one of these in isolation. After surveying some system features that impact performance, we introduced the characterization of parallel performance in terms of Amdahl's law and related the ideas to the harmonic mean of execution rates. We expand the Amdahl's law discussed here in Chapter 9 to develop surprisingly accurate models of performance for parallel programs and architectures, and in Chapter 10 we study the effects on performance of program execution demands resulting from a specific implementation of an algorithm.

2.9 Bibliographic Notes

Characterizations of algorithm parallelism can be found in [9] and [191]. A discussion of parallel prefix algorithms can be found in [157]. The Fibonacci numbers are well treated in [174]. An early discussion of asymptotic analysis is given in [175], and an engaging discussion of the topic appears in [15]. For details on transforming arithmetic expressions into parallel form see [33]. Almost all parallel processing books cover Amdahl's law. Gustafson [131] points out the pitfalls in a simplistic interpretation of the law.

Problems

2.1   Consider the program fragment consisting of the two lines:
```
x := (((((a*b)*c)*d)*e)*f)*g;
y := (a*b)*c;
```
   (a) Taking the parentheses as indicating the order of evaluation, what is the size of the computation for x? What is its depth?
   (b) Ignoring the specified evaluation order, find the minimum depth of a computation for x. What is the size of a minimum depth computation?
   (c) Taking advantage of the common sub expression, show a computation graph for both x and y using the evaluation order specified by parentheses. Reorder the evaluation to obtain a minimum depth computation for x and y. What is its size?

(d) If all the intermediate results obtained by evaluating x in the order specified were needed in subsequent statements, what could be said about the minimum depth computation and its size? That is, we need to store every subexpression enclosed in a pair of parentheses, as well as the final result x.

2.2 The sequential pseudocode below defines the bubble sort algorithm.

```
for j := N-1 step -1 until 1
    for i:=0 step 1 until j-1
    begin s := x[i];
        t := x[i+1];
        x[i] := min(s, t);
        x[i+1] := max(s, t);
    end;
```

In the analysis below consider only min and max as operations in the algorithm.

(a) Draw a data dependence diagram for the algorithm for $N = 4$.

(b) What are the size and depth of the algorithm for $N = 4$?

(c) Compute the size of the algorithm for arbitrary N.

(d) Compute the depth of the algorithm for arbitrary N.

2.3 The sequential pseudocode below is an idealized form of an iterative solution to a one dimensional Poisson's equation.

```
for k := 1 step 1 until M
    for i := 1 step 1 until N - 1
    a[i] := (a[i - 1] + a[i + 1])/2 + b[i];
```

a[0], a[N], and the b vector are constants.

(a) Diagram the data dependences for $N = 4$ and $M = 3$ taking the whole assignment statement as one operation. Give the size and depth.

(b) Calculate the size and depth of the algorithm for arbitrary N and M.

(c) Calculate the size and depth of the alternative algorithm below for arbitrary N and M. Show your work.

```
for k := 1 step 1 until M
begin
        for i := 1 step 2 until N - 2
            a[i] := (a[i - 1] + a[i + 1])/2 + b[i];
        for i := 2 step 2 until N - 1
            a[i] := (a[i - 1] + a[i + 1])/2 + b[i];
end;
```

2.4 We have two n bit numbers of the form $a = a_{n-1} \ldots a_1 a_0$ and $b = b_{n-1} \ldots b_1 b_0$. We want a small, fast circuit to compute the number $c = c_{n-1} \ldots c_1 c_0$ containing the left most string of bits for which a and b match, with the right hand portion padded with zeros. For example, if $a = 1101101$ and $b = 1101001$ then $c = 1101000$.

(a) Show how to do this with two input *AND*, *OR* and *XOR* gates and inverters. Hint: generate the prefix vector (1111000 in the example) that has a one in a given bit position only if a and b match in that position and in all positions to the left.

(b) What is the number of gates (not counting inverters) in the smallest circuit for generating c? How long, in gate delays, does it take to compute c? Count *AND* and *OR* as one delay, *XOR* as two delays and ignore inverters.

(c) How fast can c be computed if we are willing to increase the number of gates and about how many gates are needed? Answer the same question if we are willing to increase the number of gates by no more than 50%.

2.5   A priority circuit takes as input an n bit number $a = a_{n-1} \ldots a_1 a_0$ and outputs an n bit number $b = b_{n-1} \ldots b_1 b_0$ such that $b \equiv 0$ if and only if $a \equiv 0$. For $a \neq 0$ exactly one bit of b, b_i, is one and the rest are zero, where a_i is the left most bit of a that is one.

(a)   If the basic operations are two input *AND* and *OR* gates, give the design of the circuit with the fewest gates to perform this function. Assume inversion can be attached to any input or output at no cost so inverters are not counted. How many gate delays does it take to compute b?

(b)   What is the minimum possible delay for computing b? Design a circuit with minimal delay and determine the number of gates.

2.6   Write SIMD and MIMD pseudocode for the sum prefix algorithm obtained by repeated upper/lower construction for n a power of two.

HINT: Though the algorithm is defined recursively, that is not a good way to write the code. For the MIMD code, arrange to assign a processor number to each processor needed at one of the $\log_2 n$ levels of the dependence diagram and have the processor compute what adds to perform at that level. For the SIMD code, calculate index vectors giving the right things to add in terms of the level and the index of the arithmetic unit doing the add.

2.7   Consider Ladner and Fischer's sum prefix circuit $P_0(2^l)$ for $n = 2^l$. Show data dependence diagrams for $P_0(8)$, $P_0(16)$, and $P_0(32)$. Consider writing pseudocode for $P_0(2^l)$. Is the algorithm suitable for an SIMD architecture? An MIMD architecture?

2.8   Prove by induction the upper bound on Ladner and Fischer's parallel prefix calculation, i.e.,

$$S_k < 2\left(1 + \frac{1}{2^k}\right)n - 2 \text{ for all } n \geq 1. \text{ HINT: First show that } S_0 < 4n - 2 \text{ for all } n > 1.$$

2.9   Assume that we have $N = 2^l$ data structures, and that the amount of memory required by each is given by len[i], $i = 0, 1, \ldots, N-1$. It is desired to determine for all k whether data structures $0, 1, \ldots, k-1, k$ will all fit in a memory area of size M. The result of the computation is a logical vector fit[i], i $= 0, 1, \ldots, N-1$ such that fit[k] = **true** if and only if data structures $0, 1, \ldots, k-1, k$ will all fit together in a memory area of size M.

(a)   What is the size of a sequential algorithm to perform this computation? Note: Comparison of two numbers is counted the same as any other arithmetic operation.

(b)   What is the minimum depth for a parallel algorithm to perform this computation?

(c)   For $N = 8$ show the dependence graph of an algorithm of size no more than 19 operations and depth no more than 5 that does the computation.

2.10 Assuming an arbitrary number of processors, show a fast way to evaluate the expression:

$$\sum_{i=1}^{8} v_i(1-p)p^{i-1}.$$ (Hint: Consider doing a dot product of the vector v with a vector of values you produce in parallel from p and the constant 1.)

(a)   Show the data dependence diagram for your parallel algorithm.

(b)   If the upper limit on the summation is N instead of 8, what would the depth and size of your algorithm be?

2.11 N blocks of data of different sizes S_i, $0 \leq i \leq N-1$, are to be packed into a single area of memory, with block i starting immediately after block $i-1$. N processors can move the blocks in parallel once their starting addresses are known. Describe a parallel algorithm to compute the starting addresses in minimum time. Determine the number of processors required to execute the algorithm in minimum time, the time required, and the number of operations performed.

2.12 An arithmetic expression with N atoms can be transformed using commutativity and associativity so that its execution time using an optimal number of processors is bounded above by $\lceil \log_2 N \rceil + 2d + 1$. It can be transformed using commutativity, associativity, and distributivity so that its execution time with a (perhaps different) optimal number of processors is bounded above by $\lceil 4\log_2 N \rceil$.

What is d? Why does it appear in the expression for one upper bound but not the other?

2.13 Consider the arithmetic expression: $x = \dfrac{(a + bcd)e + f}{g} + pq$.

   (a) With the normal mathematical evaluation order, what is the size and depth of the expression tree?

   (b) Using only associativity and commutativity, transform the expression so that the tree has reduced depth. What are the new depth and size?

   (c) Using distributivity as well as associativity and commutativity, reduce the depth further. What are the size and depth of this expression tree?

2.14 Use associativity, commutativity, and distributivity to transform the expression
$a + b/c − d + e((f + g/h)/x + y)$ so that it can be evaluated in minimum time. Show the evaluation tree and find the minimum number π of processors needed for the minimum time evaluation, along with the time T_π, speedup S_π, and efficiency E_π.

2.15 Which of the following statements about Gaussian elimination can be concluded just from knowing that the size of Gaussian elimination on an $n \times n$ matrix is $\Theta(n^3)$?

   1. The size of Gaussian elimination for $n = 3$ is about 27.

   2. For large n, doubling n increases the size by 8 times.

   3. The size of Gaussian elimination increases monotonically as n increases.

   4. Tripling n increases the size by 27 times.

   5. The size increases monotonically as n increases for large n.

2.16 Suppose that a program obeys Amdahl's law with a sequential fraction $f = 5\%$ and that the execution time with one processor is 10 seconds. Graph $T(P)$, $S(P)$, and $E(P)$ for $1 \le P \le 100$.

2.17 Assume that the size of a problem obeying Amdahl's law is increased as the number, P, of processors increases. The absolute amount of sequential work is a constant, S (in seconds), but the amount of Parallel work, Q, increases with problem size, N, as $Q = qN$. The problem size scales with the number of processes as $N = cP$.

For $P = 10$ processors, an appropriate size problem has $N = 1{,}000$ and a sequential fraction of 5%. Graph the speedup and efficiency from $P = 10$ to $P = 100$ in steps of 10 processes.

2.18 In a certain computation, 90% of the work is vectorizable. Of the remaining 10%, half is parallelizable for an MIMD machine. What are the speedups over sequential execution for a 10 PE SIMD machine and a 10 processor MIMD machine on this computation?

2.19 Consider a parallel computer that can execute at three different degrees of parallelism at rates $R_1 < R_2 < R_3$. These correspond to using 1, 2, and 3 processors in an MIMD computer or 1, 2, and 3 arithmetic units in an SIMD computer. Suppose the fraction of total work W that can be executed at rate R_i in a particular program is f_i, where $f_1 + f_2 + f_3 = 1$. Work can be measured in terms of execution time on a single processor.

   (a) Give an expression for the harmonic mean execution rate R of the parallel computer in terms of f_i and R_i. How is the execution time of the parallel computer related to R?

   (b) What is the execution time T of the parallel computer on the given program if $f_1 = 0.5$, $f_2 = 0.3$, $f_3 = 0.2$, and $R_1 = 6$ MIPS, $R_2 = 11$ MIPS, $R_3 = 16$ MIPS. Why might we not have $R_2 = 2R_1$ and $R_3 = 3R_1$?

   (c) Suppose the program is rewritten to be more parallel, so that $f_1 = 0.1$, $f_2 = 0.3$, and $f_3 = 0.6$, with the same R_i as in part (b). What would the harmonic mean rate and corresponding execution time be in this case?

CHAPTER 3

Vector Algorithms and Architectures

An obvious place to extract parallelism from a computation is where multiple data items are operated on by the same operation. This so-called data parallelism is closely tied to the formulation of problem solutions in terms of vector, matrix, or multidimensional array operations. The vector is the simplest array structure and is next above the scalar as an elementary structure into which array operations may be decomposed.

Computers with special capabilities for operating on vectors were some of the first digital computers in which parallelism appeared at the level of the instruction set as well as in the hardware implementing individual instructions. The evolution of vector processors in the form of both true and pipelined SIMD machines has had a major impact on parallel processing and on high-speed scientific computation in general. In this chapter, we discuss algorithms for vector and matrix computation, the instruction set architecture of a vector processor, and some of the data movement and layout problems that must be addressed to supply the multiple operands needed for a vector operation. Emphasis on the instruction set of an SIMD machine is important because it is quite different from that of a uniprocessor. An SIMD instruction set contains a complete class of instructions that operate on vectors. The capabilities of the vector instructions set the ground rules for obtaining high performance on an SIMD computer.

Many language extensions for explicitly supporting vector and array operations have been made over the years, but Fortran 90 is the major language with matrix capabilities in wide use today. From the fundamentals point of view, the vector-oriented language extensions in Fortran 90 are representative of those in other vector languages. Fortran was originally designed with good capabilities for expressing serial access to multidimensional arrays and extends well to parallel array manipulation. Fortran is also the language used in many of the seminal research papers on vector and array processing, and familiarity with it is essential to an appreciation of this important body of literature. The fact that Fortran 90 is the only widely used vector language and our desire to compare and contrast algorithms for SIMD, shared memory MIMD, and distributed memory MIMD architectures is an important reason for our use of Fortran as a base language in subsequent chapters as well as this one.

Because even rudimentary computers are universal in their ability to perform computation, a specific architectural type will exhibit its characteristics not in what it can accomplish but in the performance level with which it accomplishes it. Thus, the questions to keep in mind while reading this chapter primarily have to do with performance. For example, a loop with independent body instances is vectorized and speeds up by a factor of P on a P processing element SIMD machine, while another loop, whose independent loop instances contain a data dependent conditional only speeds up by a factor of $P/2$. Why should this be so? In another case, a computation on columns of a two-dimensional matrix vectorizes well and speeds up proportional to the number of PEs while the same computation on rows of the matrix does not. Why might this happen? Why does the efficiency of processing vectors on an SIMD machine vary with vector length? At what vector lengths is the highest efficiency expected?

3.1 Vector and Matrix Algorithms

Vector and matrix algorithms not only are of fundamental importance in scientific and engineering linear algebra computations but also have a special property for parallel evaluation; the same operation is applied to all components of vectors simultaneously. For example, the addition of two vectors $x + y$ means component wise addition

$$x_1 + y_1, x_2 + y_2, \ldots, x_N + y_N. \tag{3.1}$$

Another important vector operation is the *dot product* (or *inner product*). It is component wise multiplication, followed by sum reduction over the products. Reduction is another concept of general use in vector computing. It is somewhat more complex than simple component wise operations of the same type. We have already discussed sum reduction, but it can be done with any dyadic operator. Especially useful ones are $+$, $\times$, *max*, and *min*. Reduction means writing the operator between all adjacent components of a vector and evaluating the arithmetic expression that results. The language APL has a reduction operator, written

$$\text{op}/V = v_1 \text{ op } v_2 \text{ op } \ldots \text{ op } v_N, \tag{3.2}$$

where op represents any dyadic operator. If the operator is associative and commutative, then left to right, right to left, and tree evaluation orders all give the same mathematical result. With finite precision arithmetic, round off or truncation may cause different evaluation orders to give different results. The inner product, $x \bullet y$, can be written as $+/x \cdot y$.

The *outer product* operation, $A = x \times y$, is also useful in linear algebra algorithms. This operation forms a two-dimensional matrix A with each element being a product of one element of x by one element of y, $a_{ij} = x_i y_j$.

Even the simple multiplication of a vector, x, by a matrix, A, illustrates some vector algorithm features. The simple mathematical expression

$$y = Ax \tag{3.3}$$

can be done by a sequential algorithm with the pseudocode of Program 3-1.

```
for i := 1 step 1 until N
        begin
            y[i] := 0;
            for j := 1 step 1 until N
                    y[i] := y[i] + a[i, j]×x[j];
        end;
```

Program 3-1   Matrix-vector multiply with dot product inner loop.

In this form, the outer loop is over the rows of A, and the inner loop represents the dot product of a row of A with the vector x. Because the dot product involves a sum reduction, it is not as efficient as a vector operation on independent pairs of vector elements. However, the dot product is not an inescapable feature of this algorithm. Another form of matrix-vector multiply arises from exchanging inner and outer loops, as shown in Program 3-2.

```
for i := 1 step 1 until N
        y[i] := 0;
for j := 1 step 1 until N
        for i := 1 step 1 until N
                y[i] := y[i] + a[i, j]×x[j];
```

Program 3-2   Matrix-vector multiply with SAXPY.

In this form, the outer loop is over columns of A, and the inner loop multiplies all components of a column of A by one element of x and adds this vector of products to the partial result, y. The initialization of the dot products to zero before summing is now a separate, single loop at the beginning. The basic vector operations in this form of the algorithm are multiplication of a vector by a scalar and vector addition. This operation is called SAXPY after the mathematical operation aX plus Y, where X and Y are vectors.

The simple loop interchange illustrated is an example of code restructuring, which can have a strong influence on the degree of parallelism apparent in a computation. Restructuring can also be done to the three nested loops of matrix-matrix multiply. The *kij* form of the algorithm shown in Program 3-3 can be described as:

1. Initialize the result matrix elements to zero.
2. Form the $N \times N$ outer product matrix of column k of A with row k of B.
3. Add the $N \times N$ matrix of product terms to C.
4. Repeat steps 2 and 3 for all N values of k.

```
for i := 1 step 1 until N
        for j := 1 step 1 until N
                c[i, j] := 0;
for k := 1 step 1 until N
        for i := 1 step 1 until N
                for j := 1 step 1 until N
                        c[i, j] := c[i, j] + a[i, k]×b[k, j];
```

Program 3-3   Matrix-matrix multiply in the *kij* form.

This form of the algorithm makes explicit the addition of $N \times N$ matrices. It is an alternative to the so called *ikj* form, which was used in Program 1-1 as an example of pseudocode for an SIMD computer. In the *ikj* form, the inner loop is over *j* and adds the *k*-th terms of inner products across a row of *C*.

Gaussian elimination is a more complex matrix algorithm that illustrates the basic pattern for the solution of a system of linear equations. The algorithm performs order N^3 operations on an $N \times N$ matrix, and it is usually complicated by the need to select an operation order on the basis of the data. This reordering of operations is called *pivoting* and is used to prevent round off error from destroying the accuracy of the result. The simplified version with no pivoting shown in Program 3-4 illustrates the triply nested loop structure. This form of the algorithm works in a row wise manner. The inner loop processes elements of a single row and can be looked at as adding a multiple of the portion of the *k*-th row to the right of the diagonal to the same portion of the *i*-th row. As in matrix multiply, various forms of Gauss elimination can be obtained by reordering loops. Care must be taken to handle initializations and index ranges correctly. If the loops over *i* and *j* in the row wise form are exchanged, one obtains the column-wise form shown in Program 3-5. This algorithm has an inner loop that can be seen as adding a multiple of the *k*-th column of *A* to the *j*-th column of *A*.

```
for k := 1 step 1 until N
        begin p := 1/a[k, k];
              a[k, k] := p;
              for i := k+1 step 1 until N
                      begin q := -a[i, k]×p;
                            a[i, k] := q;
                            for j := k+1 step 1 until N
                                    a[i, j] := a[i, j] + q×a[k, j];
                      end;
        end;
```

Program 3-4   Row wise form of Gaussian elimination without pivoting.

```
for k := 1 step 1 until N
        begin p := 1/a[k, k];
            a[k, k] := p;
            for i := k+1 step 1 until N
                    a[i, k] := -a[i, k]×p;
            for j := k+1 step 1 until N
                    begin q := a[k, j];
                            for i := k+1 step 1 until N
                                    a[i, j] := a[i, j] + q×a[i, k];
                    end;
        end;
```

Program 3-5   Column-wise form of Gaussian elimination without pivoting.

Including partial pivoting does not significantly alter the basic structure of Gaussian elimination. A search for the element with maximum absolute value in a column, followed by an interchange of rows, becomes the first step in the outer loop over the k index. The modifications are shown in Program 3-6. The pivoting modifications are also operations on vectors. The function idamax(a, k, N) finds the index of the element in the last $N - k + 1$ components of column k of A that has maximum absolute value. It is a maximum reduction over a vector with the feature that it returns the index of the maximum, or one of them if there are several, instead of its value. It can be defined with the sequential pseudocode of Program 3-7. The row swapping procedure swap(a, k, m, N) swaps the k-th through the N-th elements of row k with the same elements of row m. The sequential version shown in Program 3-8 can be vectorized easily by replacing the single temporary storage element tmp with a temporary vector of length N.

```
for k := 1 step 1 until N
        begin
            /*Index of maximum absolute value in column k.*/
            m := idamax(a, k, N);
            piv[k] := m;
            swap(a, k, m, N);  /*Exchange row k with row m.*/
            /*Program is identical from here on.*/
            p := 1/a[k, k];
            ...
        end;
```

Program 3-6   Modifications to Gaussian elimination to handle pivoting.

As an example of a vector-oriented algorithm that is not trivially vectorizable for a SIMD type of architecture we look at the solution of linear recurrences. A linear recurrence is distinguished by having dependencies between elements of the solution vector.

```
integer function idamax(a, k, N);
      m := k;
      s := abs( a[k, k] );
      for i := k+1 step 1 until N
          if abs( a[i, k] ) > s then
                begin m := i;
                      s := abs( a[i, k] );
                end;
      return m;
end function;
```

Program 3-7 Search for the maximum absolute value element.

```
procedure swap(a, k, m, N);
      for j := k step 1 until N
          begin tmp := a[k, j];
                a[k, j] := a[m, j];
                a[m, j] := tmp;
          end;
      end procedure;
```

Program 3-8 Procedure to swap portions of rows to the right of the diagonal.

Definition: An m-th order *linear recurrence* system of n equations, $R(n, m)$, is

$$x_i = 0, i \le 0,$$

$$x_i = c_i + \sum_{j=i-m}^{i-1} a_{ij}x_j, \ 1 \le i \le n, \text{ where } m \le n - 1. \tag{3.4}$$

The case $m = n - 1$ is called a general linear recurrence.

The recurrence can be written as an implicit matrix-vector equation $x = c + A \cdot x$, where the elements of the matrix A satisfy the restriction $a_{ij} = 0$ if either $i \le j$ or $i > j + m$. This means that the matrix A has the lower triangular form

$$A = \begin{bmatrix} 0 & 0 & 0 & \dots & 0 & 0 \\ a_{21} & 0 & 0 & \dots & 0 & 0 \\ a_{31} & a_{32} & 0 & \dots & 0 & 0 \\ a_{41} & a_{42} & a_{43} & \dots & 0 & 0 \\ \dots & \dots & \dots & \dots & \dots & \dots \\ 0 & 0 & 0 & \dots & 0 & 0 \\ 0 & 0 & 0 & \dots & a_{nn-1} & 0 \end{bmatrix}. \tag{3.5}$$

One way to express an algorithm for obtaining the solution to the recurrence is by writing separate equations for the components of x:

$$x_1 = c_1,$$
$$x_2 = c_2 + a_{21}x_1,$$
$$x_3 = c_3 + a_{31}x_1 + a_{32}x_2,$$
$$\ldots$$

(3.6)

This form seems to imply that all x components through x_{i-1} must be known before x_i can be computed. This is not the case. The x values can be evaluated with SIMD style vector operations, as shown by the SIMD pseudocode in Program 3-9 that implements what is called the column sweep algorithm. The algorithm does a series of vector multiply-adds, completing the computation of one more component of x at each step.

```
x[i]  := c[i],  (1 ≤ i ≤ n); /* Initialize the x vector making x[1] correct. */
for j := 1 step 1 until n-1
        x[i]  := x[i] + a[i, j]*x[j],  (j+1 ≤ i ≤ min(j+m, n));
/* Do all column i multiplies and add to x vector, completing x[j+1]. */
```

Program 3-9   Column sweep form of a linear recurrence solver.

Several characteristics of the column sweep algorithm for linear recurrence systems should be noted. All of the vectors in the multiply-add are of length m or shorter. The length starts at m and decreases as $n - j$ becomes less than m. For a general recurrence, the vector length starts at $m = n - 1$ and decreases by one at each step. The number of multiplies and adds at each vector step is $\min(n - j, m)$. For $m = 1$, the problem degenerates to sum prefix and the column sweep algorithm shown above becomes sequential. In this case, a vector algorithm would have to be derived from one of the parallel prefix algorithms.

The interesting situations are thus those in which the size of m is on the order of the number of operations that can be done in parallel. There are two interesting cases to analyze

1. a general recurrence—$m = n - 1$, and
2. a small bandwidth recurrence—$m \ll n$.

We compare column sweep to the simplest sequential algorithm by considering its speedup and efficiency with respect to that algorithm.

We start with the speedup of a general recurrence ($m = n - 1$) using column sweep. The minimum number of processors with which maximum speed can be obtained is $\pi = n - 1$. Because there are $n - 1$ steps in the **for** loop and each has a vector multiply and vector add, counting one unit of time for each vector arithmetic operation gives

$$T_\pi = 2(n - 1).$$

(3.7)

If the work were performed by a doubly nested loop on one processor, it would take

$$T_1 = 2[(n-1) + (n-2) + \cdots + 2 + 1] = 2\sum_{i=1}^{n-1} i = n(n-1) \tag{3.8}$$

scalar floating point operations. The speedup and efficiency available from the algorithm are, thus,

$$S_\pi = \frac{n(n-1)}{2(n-1)} = \frac{n}{2} \text{ and } E_\pi = \frac{n/2}{n-1} = \frac{1}{2}\left(1 - \frac{1}{n}\right)^{-1}. \tag{3.9}$$

The best speedup is about half the number of processors required to obtain it, and the efficiency of column sweep for a general recurrence is about 50% for large n.

For the case of a band limited recurrence, $m < n - 1$. In this regime, the minimum number of processors for maximum speed is $\pi = m$, and the time with m processors is still $T_\pi = 2(n-1)$. While the number of SIMD processing steps required to solve the recurrence is the same, the number of processing elements needed may be much smaller if $m \ll n$. The number of operations in the sequential algorithm for a band limited recurrence has the form

$$T_1 = 2[m + m + \cdots + m + (m-1) + (m-2) + \cdots + 2 + 1], \tag{3.10}$$

where the number of vector multiply-adds of length m is $n - m$. Thus, a closed form expression would be

$$T_1 = 2\left[m(n-m) + \sum_{i=1}^{m-1} i\right] = 2nm - m^2 - m. \tag{3.11}$$

An interesting and useful case arises when very large recurrence systems are solved with a limited number of processing elements, so that n is very large and m is such that $n \gg m$. In this case, the speedup and efficiency compared to the simple sequential algorithm are

$$S_\pi = \frac{(2n-1)m - m^2}{2(n-1)} \approx m \text{ and } E_\pi = \frac{(2n-1) - m}{2(n-1)} \approx 1. \tag{3.12}$$

Thus, even though only m processing elements can be used, the speedup nearly equals this number and the efficiency is nearly 100%.

3.2 A Vector Architecture—Single Instruction Multiple Data

Single instruction stream, multiple data stream computers first introduced parallelism in instructions for operations other than I/O. Because SIMD computers operate on multiple data items with one instruction and vector algorithms are dominated by component wise application of the same operation, SIMD machines are well suited to vector algorithms. Figure 1-8 shows that there are two versions of this type of architecture, the true SIMD and pipelined SIMD architectures. Both versions of SIMD have very similar instruction set architectures. The differences are primarily at the machine structure level and have their greatest impact on program performance rather than program structure. We consider first true SIMD architectures, in which different complete arithmetic units handle different components of the vectors.

We will use the PMS notation of Bell and Newell [44] to describe computer structure. It is essentially a version of the familiar block diagram notation but replaces blocks with single letters. The one letter codes are listed in Table 3-1. The letters may be augmented by following them with parenthesized lists of attribute:value pairs. The attribute name is often omitted when it can be inferred from the name of its value. Important one letter codes are M for memory, S for switch, P for processor (Pc for central processor), D for data processing unit (arithmetic unit), K for controller, T for transducer (an I/O device), and C for complete computer when the internal structure is not required. L is an explicit representation of a link between units, which is usually just represented by a connecting line. The L is used when it is important to introduce some attributes. Simple switches are also often hidden in junctions of several links on the diagram and may not have an explicit S shown. Figure 3-1 shows several variations on the internal structure of a computer, C, where := defines the left side symbol as the right side construct.

Switches are very important in parallel processing. Significant attributes of a switch are the bandwidth for transmitting data through the switch, the latency, or length of time it takes data to traverse the switch, the delay required to change the switch setting, and the concurrency, or how many transmissions between distinct source and destination pairs can be handled simultaneously. Building complex switching structures from simple switch components is the subject of interconnection network design.

Table 3-1   Summary of PMS notation.

P	Processor: including instruction interpretation and execution
M	Memory: registers, cache, main memory, or secondary storage
S	Switch: simple or complex; may be address decode; may be implicit in line junction
L	Link: often just a line, but shown explicitly when parameters are important
T	Transducer: input/output device changing the representation of information
K	Controller: generates microsteps for single operations applied externally
D	Data processing: usually arithmetic, but generally any transformation of data inputs
C	Computer: consists of P, M, and other components to form a complete system

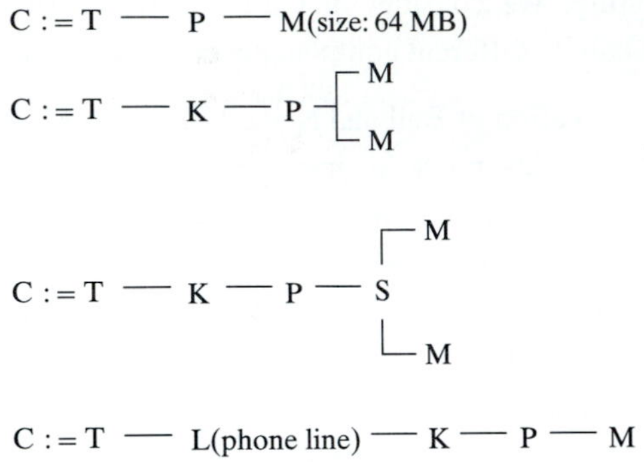

C := T ── P ── M(size: 64 MB)

C := T ── K ── P ──⌈ M
                                       ⌊ M

C := T ── K ── P ── S ──⌈ M
                                               ⌊ M

C := T ── L(phone line) ── K ── P ── M

Figure 3-1 Example PMS diagrams.

Two types of SIMD organization differ in the connection of memory modules, M, to arithmetic units, D. The architecture of the first type at the PMS (processor, memory, switch) level is shown in Figure 3-2. In this style of architecture, each memory module is uniquely associated with a particular arithmetic unit. Communication between units is done by way of explicit instructions, which permute data among specific registers in different arithmetic units.

SIMD machines are also designed with a configurable association between Ds and Ms. Communication of a data item produced as a result in one arithmetic unit to another for use as an operand is by way of memory. Such a shared memory SIMD machine has the configuration shown in Figure 3-3. The S(alignment network) in Figure 3-3 and the S(interconnection network) in the distributed memory architecture of Figure 3-2 have similar functions. They make the results produced by one processing element, D, available as operands to other D units. For an N PE vector machine, an index range $(0 \leq i \leq N-1)$ modifying a vector assignment maps directly to machine hardware, with i being the PE number.

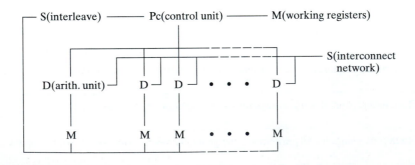

Figure 3-2 Distributed memory SIMD computer.

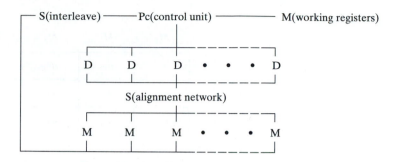

Figure 3-3 Shared memory SIMD computer.

In an SIMD architecture, the D units are usually called processing elements, or PEs. This designation can be somewhat misleading because of its close similarity to the term *processor*, which in Bell and Newell's notation and in most other literature implies a unit that includes instruction fetch and interpretation. In the vector processing literature, a PE contains only an arithmetic unit, associated arithmetic and address modification registers, and perhaps a portion of an interconnection network. The processor of a machine whose D units are called PEs is usually called a control unit, or CU.

At the structural level, there are two key issues that need to be addressed in the study of SIMD computers. Both have to do with supplying operands simultaneously to the arithmetic units so that all operations can, in fact, be done in parallel and are not sequentialized by delay in obtaining data.

1. How to partition data across memory modules so it can be accessed in parallel?
2. Once data is stored in different modules for parallel access, how does the interconnection or alignment network route it to the right D units simultaneously?

As an example of the requirements for accessibility of operands, consider the statement at the heart of the recurrence solver, Program 3-9,

$$x[i] := x[i] + a[i,j] \times x[j], \ (j + 1 \leq i \leq j + m); \tag{3.13}$$

The same D unit that has access to $x[i]$ must also access $a[i,j]$ for all j. Furthermore, all D units need access to $x[j]$. We say that $x[j]$ is broadcast to all the Ds. Because the control unit accesses the memory modules one at a time, it treats them as one memory instead of separate memories as the PEs use them.

If data is to be supplied to PEs in parallel, it must also be accessed from memories in parallel. A memory module is a unit of memory with the property that it can do only one fetch or store at a time. It is assumed that each M unit in Figure 3-2 and Figure 3-3 consists of one module. As an example of how data can be partitioned among memory modules, Figure 3-4 shows three versions of a 4×4 matrix stored in 4 memory modules. The *by row* and *by column* designations refer to the structure stored in a single module. Storage by row implies that parallel access is by column. With the skewed storage pattern, a permutation of the data must be performed in delivering it to the arithmetic units. The permutation is different for different columns.

By row

M_1	M_2	M_3	M_4
a_{11}	a_{21}	a_{31}	a_{41}
a_{12}	a_{22}	a_{32}	a_{42}
a_{13}	a_{23}	a_{33}	a_{43}
a_{14}	a_{24}	a_{34}	a_{44}

By column

M_1	M_2	M_3	M_4
a_{11}	a_{12}	a_{13}	a_{14}
a_{21}	a_{22}	a_{23}	a_{24}
a_{31}	a_{32}	a_{33}	a_{34}
a_{41}	a_{42}	a_{43}	a_{44}

Skewed storage

M_1	M_2	M_3	M_4
a_{11}	a_{12}	a_{13}	a_{14}
a_{24}	a_{21}	a_{22}	a_{23}
a_{33}	a_{34}	a_{31}	a_{32}
a_{42}	a_{43}	a_{44}	a_{41}

Routing to access

Column 1	Column 2
M_1 to P_1	M_2 to P_1
M_2 to P_2	M_3 to P_2
M_3 to P_3	M_4 to P_3
M_4 to P_4	M_1 to P_4

Figure 3-4 Matrix storage schemes in four modules.

Data layout in memory is the responsibility of the machine language programmer. If machine language is generated by a compiler, the compiler code generator must determine the layout. In some cases, the high-level source code may supply enough information for the compiler to determine an efficient layout. Many high-level languages, however, have constructs such as pointers that make it difficult or impossible to determine data access patterns at compile time. It is also possible that the same data structures are used by different parts of the program in ways that require a different memory layout. In such cases, a programmer may be required to supply layout information to the compiler and will surely need to control layout to optimize the performance of such a program.

As will be seen in Section 3.7, pipelined vector machines also have storage layout problems. In a pipelined SIMD machine, vector component accesses are not simultaneous, but the full bandwidth of a memory consisting of multiple modules cannot be attained unless some minimum number of successive references are to different memory modules. This leads to restrictions in some pipelined SIMD machines such as requiring successive vector components to be located in successive memory modules. These machines interleave memory modules on the low order address bits, so successive words are guaranteed to be in different modules. Thus, the requirement is usually that vectors accessed in an arithmetic operation must be "stride one" vectors, which have successive components separated by one address unit. The alternative to restricting vector stride is to allow multiple accesses to the same memory module, but at a reduced speed. We discuss pipelined memory access further in Section 3.7.

3.3 An SIMD Instruction Set

We present an example instruction set for a true SIMD computer that is simplified but contains all the elements of a vector computer. We study the SIMD instruction set to gain insight into the detailed workings of this type of computer. The way in which an algorithm implemented in a high-level vector language is translated into machine language has a significant impact on its execution performance. To obtain good vector performance, it is not enough to know a high-level vector language well, but it is also necessary to understand the underlying execution model realized by the architecture. Knowing what happens at the machine level as the result of executing high-level code gives one the tools to write better performing code and understand the reasons behind the resulting performance.

There are two major classes of instructions for this type of machine: single stream instructions and vector instructions. Single-stream instructions are further classified as control and scalar instructions. Vector instructions are processed by multiple arithmetic units, called processing elements (PEs). A control unit (CU) processes the single stream instructions. This control unit is also responsible for address calculations for the vector instructions and for sending detailed control signals to the PEs to accomplish the arithmetic operations. Some instructions involve cooperation between the CU and the PEs. They either replicate a single number and send it to all PEs or summarize information about all PEs into a single value. The type of instruction set we will discuss is very similar to one for a pipelined SIMD machine. This example machine assumes different numbers of bits for addresses, n_a, data, n_d, and registers having one bit for each of N PEs. Many machines make these numbers all the same. This machine also uses separate registers for address and data calculations, whereas the more popular architectures today use general registers for both address and data. The use of separate registers is a conscious choice to try to emphasize the function of different types of instructions.

To describe a computer at the instruction set level, a register transfer notation is needed. We will use the ISP notation of Bell and Newell [44]. Such a notation can describe not only static hardware structures, registers, and memories but also dynamic actions, register transfers, and operations. The ISP notation uses [ ] for word subscripts and ⟨ ⟩ for bit subscripts. A subscript range is denoted *left:right*. The primary dynamic operation in ISP is the register transfer, ←, that places the value of a right hand side expression into the register or memory cell on the left. There is also an infix *if-then* operation, →, that makes its right hand side, either a value or a register transfer, conditional on a logical left hand side. There is no *else*; a second *if-then* with complemented condition is required. The ISP notation is summarized in Table 3-2.

Table 3-2   Summary of the ISP register transfer language.

←	Register transfer: register on LHS stores value from RHS
[ ]	Word index: selects word or range from a named memory
⟨ ⟩	Bit index: selects bit or bit range from named register
n:m	Index range: from left index n to right index m; can be decreasing
→	If-then: true condition on left yields value and/or action on right
:=	Definition: text substitution with dummy variables
#	Concatenation: bits on right appended to bits on left
;	Parallel separator: actions or evaluations carried out simultaneously
;next	Sequential separator: RHS evaluated and/or performed after LHS
{ }	Operation modifier: describes preceding operation, e.g., arithmetic type
( )	Operation or value grouping: may be nested; used with operators or separators
$= \neq < \leq > \geq$	Comparison operators: produce 0 or 1 (true or false) logical value
$+ - \times \div$	Arithmetic operators: also $\lceil\ \rceil, \lfloor\ \rfloor$, and mod
$\wedge \vee \neg \oplus \equiv$	Logical operators: and, or, not, exclusive or, equivalence

Notes: LHS and RHS mean left and right hand sides, respectively. Expressions can be values and/or actions. Actions can be considered side effects if a value is present. A list of conditional expressions need not have disjoint conditions. Right hand sides of conditionals are evaluated for all conditions which are true. No sequencing is implied unless there are sequential separators between conditional expressions. There is no *else* equivalent.

Control Unit State

$PC\langle n_a{:}1\rangle$	Single program counter of n_a bits.
$X[1{:}2^j - 1]\,\langle n_a{:}1\rangle$	Address sized index registers.
$AC\langle n_d{:}1\rangle$	Arithmetic register of n_d bits; usually $n_d > n_a$.
$mask\langle N{:}1\rangle$	One bit for each PE, organized as a logical vector.
$len\langle m{:}1\rangle$	A length register may be present.
	Assume $m = \log_2 N$ is an integer.

Processing Element k State

$A_k\langle n_d{:}1\rangle$	Arithmetic register in each PE.
$R_k\langle n_d{:}1\rangle$	Routing register to communicate with other PEs.
$I_k\langle n_a - m{:}1\rangle$	Separate index for each PE. Addresses one module.
S_k	A single enable bit for each PE.

Figure 3-5   Processor state for an SIMD machine.

3.3.1   Registers and Memories of an SIMD Computer

The first thing to specify is the structures in the machine that store information. Most characteristic of these structures are the registers and flags constituting the processor state. In the true SIMD architecture, we have a control unit and N processing elements. The register declarations for the control unit and one of the identical PEs are given in Figure 3-5. In addition to the single program counter for the machine, the CU contains a set of index registers for address computation and some limited numeric data capability, represented by the single accumulator register. A mask register is a key concept in connection with data dependent conditional operations. There may also be a vector length register, but its function can also be incorporated into the mask. Registers in a PE are mainly devoted to numeric data, although there is an address index register. A special register in each PE serves as the interface to the interconnection network that routes data among PEs. A single enable bit controls the participation of each PE in a vector instruction, and, along with the mask, supports conditional operations.

The next thing to describe is the main memory. While there is only one set of memory modules, they are accessed by the control unit and the processing elements in different ways. We assume an architecture having a separate memory module for each PE and distinguish them by subscripting the name of the memory. The ISP declaration,

$$M_k[0:2^{n_a - m} - 1]\langle nd:1\rangle; \quad 0 \le k \le N - 1,$$

defines N memory modules with a total of 2^{n_a} words. The control unit sees the memory as a single n_a bit address space. The low-order m bits select the module. The memory seen by the control unit can be expressed using the ISP renaming operation (:=) as

$$M[adr \langle n_a:1\rangle]\langle n_d:1\rangle := M_{adr\langle m:1\rangle}[adr\langle n_a:m + 1\rangle]\langle n_d:1\rangle.$$

The PEs address only their own memory module with an address $n_a - m$ bits long. An address $pea_k\langle n_a - m:1\rangle$, developed in the k-th PE, addresses the word

$$M_k[pea_k]\langle n_d:1\rangle.$$

There are two forms of address calculation. For a CU address, no registers of the PEs may be used. Only CU registers and instruction address field bits are allowed. For PE addresses, the PE index register can also be used. Assume the instruction format is:

opcode	i	index	adr
	1	j	n_a

where adr is an address field, $index$ is a CU index field, and i specifies whether the PE index is to be used or not. An n_a bit CU address could be defined by

$$ca\langle n_a:1\rangle := (index = 0 \rightarrow adr\langle n_a:1\rangle);$$
$$index \ne 0 \rightarrow adr\langle n_a:1\rangle + X[index]\langle n_a:1\rangle);$$

An alternative to the special definition for the $index = 0$ case is to define a dummy index register, $X[0] := 0$, which is always zero. An $n_a - m$ bit address for PE number k that allows PE indexing can be defined by

$$pea_k\langle n_a - m:1\rangle := (i = 0 \rightarrow ca\langle n_a:m + 1\rangle);$$
$$i \ne 0 \rightarrow ca\langle n_a:m + 1\rangle + I_k\langle n_a - m:1\rangle);$$

A PE address can, thus, include indexing by a CU register (in ca) and possible indexing by the PE index, I_k, if $i = 1$. PEs could have multiple index registers, or arithmetic and index registers could be combined into a set of general registers for each PE. We treat separate arithmetic and index registers here to emphasize the distinct purposes for which they are used.

Typical SIMD instructions give insight into the operation of a vector computer. The insight can be used to understand capabilities, storage layout, and performance. We assume an assembly code line for our example machine of the form:

$$\langle\text{mnemonic}\rangle \quad \langle\text{address}\rangle[,\langle\text{CU index}\rangle][,i]$$

where the optional $\langle$CU index$\rangle$ is assumed zero if missing and the optional $,i$ specifies using the index in each PE. Vector instructions (PE instructions) manipulate multiple data items in parallel. They reference individual memory modules with PE addresses and/or PE registers. Whether any one PE takes part in a PE instruction is controlled by the enable bit S_k. CU instructions compute one result at a time. A CU address specifies one word from the set of all memory modules, and CU instructions can access control unit registers. Some instructions involve processor state registers from both the CU and PEs. These are information broadcast or collection instructions.

3.3.2   Vector, Control Unit, and Cooperative Instructions

The vector instructions are the most characteristic class for an SIMD computer. They include instructions to move vectors of data and to perform arithmetic on vectors. Figure 3-6 shows an example set of vector instructions for a machine with the processor state of Figure 3-5. In this architecture, one of the vector operands is in the set of accumulators, one in each PE, while the other can be in the memory modules or in the set of R registers. The complete set of $A(R)$ registers is often called the $A(R)$ vector register. An important characteristic of all of these instructions is that an operation only takes place in a specific PE_k if the enable bit S_k is set. The instruction format used in this example machine is a restricted form of the

```
register ← register + memory
```

format, with only two named vector registers. Introduction of a set of numbered vector registers would allow a load/store vector instruction set with arithmetic instructions of the form

```
register ← register + register.
```

Control unit instructions are mainly used for addresses and indexing. Many have a second index register specified in the opcode. Thus, for our example architecture,

opcode

becomes

cu op	*ix2*

for these instructions. Figure 3-7 shows an example set of control instructions. A real machine would probably have multiple data registers in the control unit, which are here represented by the single control unit accumulator. The multiple index registers for address modification would probably be combined with the data registers into general registers. They are kept separate here for the pedagogical purpose of underlining the distinction between the data manipulation and addressing functions of the control unit.

One-to-many and many-to-one data transmissions are done cooperatively by CU and PEs. Many cooperative instructions involve a *mask* register, which will be discussed later. One cooperative instruction that is independent of the mask is a second type of broadcast, where the source of the datum is the CU accumulator instead of a PE routing register. Figure 3-8 gives its description.

Instruction	Assembly code		Action
Vector load	lod	a, index, i	$S_k \rightarrow A_k \leftarrow M_k[pea_k], (0 \le k \le N-1)$
Vector store	sto	a, index, i	$S_k \rightarrow M_k[pea_k] \leftarrow A_k, (0 \le k \le N-1)$
Vector add	add	a, index, i	$S_k \rightarrow A_k \leftarrow A_k + M_k[pea_k], (0 \le k \le N-1)$
Vector subtract	sub	a, index, i	$S_k \rightarrow A_k \leftarrow A_k - M_k[pea_k], (0 \le k \le N-1)$
Vector multiply	mul	a, index, i	$S_k \rightarrow A_k \leftarrow A_k \times M_k[pea_k], (0 \le k \le N-1)$
Vector divide	div	a, index, i	$S_k \rightarrow A_k \leftarrow A_k / M_k[pea_k], (0 \le k \le N-1)$
Broadcast	bcast	index	$S_k \rightarrow R_k \leftarrow R_{X[index]}, (0 \le k \le N-1)$
Move PE register	mov $\begin{Bmatrix} A \\ R \\ I \end{Bmatrix}$ to $\begin{Bmatrix} A \\ R \\ I \end{Bmatrix}$		$S_k \rightarrow \begin{Bmatrix} A_k \\ R_k \\ I_k \end{Bmatrix} \leftarrow \begin{Bmatrix} A_k \\ R_k \\ I_k \end{Bmatrix}, (0 \le k \le N-1)$
Register add	radd		$S_k \rightarrow A_k \leftarrow A_k + R_k, (0 \le k \le N-1)$
Register subtract	rsub		$S_k \rightarrow A_k \leftarrow A_k - R_k, (0 \le k \le N-1)$
Register multiply	rmul		$S_k \rightarrow A_k \leftarrow A_k \times R_k, (0 \le k \le N-1)$
Register divide	rdiv		$S_k \rightarrow A_k \leftarrow A_k / R_k, (0 \le k \le N-1)$

Figure 3-6 Set of vector instructions for an SIMD machine.

Instruction	Assembly code		Action
Load index	ldx	ix2, a.index	$X[ix2] \leftarrow M[ca];$
Store index	stx	ix2, a.index	$M[ca] \leftarrow X[ix2];$
Load index immediate	ldxi	ix2, a.index	$X[ix2] \leftarrow ca;$
Increment index	incx	ix2, a.index	$X[ix2] \leftarrow X[ix2] + ca;$
Decrement index	decx	ix2, a.index	$X[ix2] \leftarrow X[ix2] - ca;$
Multiply index	mulx	ix2, a.index	$X[ix2] \leftarrow X[ix2] \times ca;$
Load data	cload	a, index	$A \leftarrow M[ca];$
Store data	cstore	a, index	$M[ca] \leftarrow AC;$
Compare and branch	cmpx	index.ix2, a	$(X[index] \le X[ix2]) \rightarrow PC \leftarrow ca;$

Figure 3-7 SIMD control unit instruction set.

Instruction	Assembly code	Action
Broadcast *AC*	cbcast	$S_k \rightarrow R_k \leftarrow AC, (0 \le k \le N - 1);$

Figure 3-8   A simple cooperative instruction.

N	DATA	64	Number of PEs and matrix size.
ZERO	DATA	0.0	Constant value.
I	EQUIV	2	Index 2 contains I.
J	EQUIV	3	Index 3 contains J.
LIM	EQUIV	1	Index 1 contains the loop limit.
A	BSS	64×64	Storage space for the arrays A,
B	BSS	64×64	B,
C	BSS	64×64	and C.

Program 3-10   Assembler pseudooperations to set up the matrix multiply.

	cload	ZERO	Initialize all
	cbcast		PE accumulators
	movR	toA	to zero.
	sto	C,I	Zero the I-th row of C.
	ldxi	J,0	Initialize the column index.
	ldx	LIM,N	Loop limit is the matrix size.
LOOP:	lod	A,I	Fetch row I of A,
	movA	toR	and set up for routing.
	bcast	J	Broadcast A[I, J] to all PEs.
	lod	B,J	Get row J of B and perform
	rmul		A[I, J]×B[J, k], for all k.
	add	C,I	C[I, k] ← C[I, k] + A[I, J]×B[J, k],
	sto	C,I	for all k.
	incx	J,1	Increment column of A.
	cmpx	J,LIM,LOOP	Loop if row of C not complete.

Program 3-11   Matrix multiply SIMD assembly code for one row of the product matrix.

As a simple example of SIMD assembly code we use matrix multiply. To set up the matrix multiply environment, we set constants in memory with the DATA pseudooperation, give names to registers with the EQUIV pseudooperation, and reserve blocks of memory with the BSS pseudooperation. Assuming 64 PEs and that 64×64 matrices are to be multiplied, Program 3-10 shows the assembler pseudooperations needed to set up the matrix multiply. Using this structure, Program 3-11 shows the section of code to compute one row of the product matrix C. Assume that all $S_k = 1$ and that register I indexes the row of C to compute. The function of routing registers is illustrated by the two broadcast operations, one from the control unit to all R registers and the other from a selected R to all others.

The form of the code has implications for data storage. For the above code to work correctly, memory module k must be organized as shown in Figure 3-9. A, B, and C are $n_a - 6$ bit addresses when used by the PE instructions. When used by the control unit the same symbols represent addresses extended to n_a bits by appending 6 zeros.

3.3.3 Data-Dependent Conditional Operations

Operations conditional on values of vector components are an important and unique feature of SIMD computers. Because there is only one program counter, this cannot be done by branching. A test instruction has N outcomes, one for each PE. A simple example of how data dependent conditionals might be used is to take the absolute value of all components of a vector.

$$(v[k] \geq 0) \rightarrow v[k] \leftarrow v[k];$$
$$(v[k] < 0) \rightarrow v[k] \leftarrow -v[k];$$

The PE enable bits, S_k, provide a way to restrict the performance of operations to a specified set of PEs. The mask register, with one bit per PE, provides a place to record N outcomes of a test on PE data. Transferring the N bit outcome of a vector test from the mask register to the PE enable bits provides a way to perform operations only for vector components corresponding to true values of a test.

Address	Contents
A:	$A[0, k]$
	$A[1, k]$
	...
	$A[N - 1, k]$
B:	$B[0, k]$
	$B[1, k]$
	...
	$B[N - 1, k]$
C:	$C[0, k]$
	$C[1, k]$
	...
	$C[N - 1, k]$

Figure 3-9 SIMD storage layout for matrix multiply.

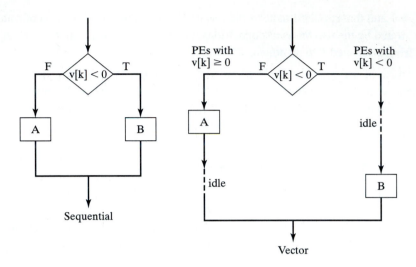

Figure 3-10   Data-dependent conditional operations on vectors.

A general procedure for data dependent conditionals uses the mask and the PE enable bits.

1. Save the PE enable bits S_k.
2. Record the results of a test in the mask bits.
3. Mask the PEs, i.e., set each S_k to the k-th mask bit.
4. Do code for the true case.
5. Complement the mask bit values and mask the PEs.
6. Do code for the false case.
7. Restore the original PE enable bits.

A pictorial representation of the situation is shown in Figure 3-10. An important performance aspect of this method of handling conditional execution is that the control unit executes both the operations for the true outcome and those for the false outcome sequentially. False enable bits prevent some PEs from performing operations but save no execution time. If t_A is the time for code block A in Figure 3-10 and t_B is the time for code block B, then excluding the test, sequential execution time is bounded above by $\max(t_A, t_B)$ while vector execution time is $t_A + t_B$. Of course, N executions of the sequential conditional are needed to do the same amount of work as the vector conditional.

Typical mask instructions for data dependent conditionals will now be described. We need instructions to perform tests, mask the PEs, save enable bits, and to communicate between the mask register and memory. Figure 3-11 shows a representative set.

The compare instructions enable us to obtain the results of vector tests, but the use of vectors of test results can be better supported. To build complex test expressions, it helps to have logical operations, selection operations, and summary branches which can be applied to vectors of test results. In Figure 3-12 are some useful logic operations, where $X[0]$ is used to refer to the mask register so that it can be combined with other test vectors. Selection operations on the mask vector are also important to select one out of a set of true responses to a test in cases where they must be handled one at a time. Figure 3-13 shows the two most important ones.

Branches based on a summary of test results can be used to skip code sections when a condition is nearly certain to be true or nearly certain to be false. These instructions only help if there is a sizeable probability that a test produces the same result for all N PEs, because both conditional code sections must be executed by the single control unit, even if only one PE produces a test result different from the others. Useful summary branch instructions are shown in Figure 3-14.

Instruction	Assembly code	Action
Compare $<$	clt a, index, i	$S_k \rightarrow (M_k[\text{pea}_k] < A_k) \rightarrow \text{mask}\langle k \rangle \leftarrow 1, (0 \le k \le N - 1);$
Compare $=$	ceq a, index, i	$S_k \rightarrow (M_k[\text{pea}_k] = A_k) \rightarrow \text{mask}\langle k \rangle \leftarrow 1, (0 \le k \le N - 1);$
Compare $>$	cgt a, index, i	$S_k \rightarrow (M_k[\text{pea}_k] > A_k) \rightarrow \text{mask}\langle k \rangle \leftarrow 1, (0 \le k \le N - 1);$
...	...	...
Mask PEs	mask	$S_k \leftarrow \text{mask}\langle k \rangle, (0 \le k \le N - 1);$
Save enables	stmask	$\text{mask}\langle k \rangle \leftarrow S_k, (0 \le k \le N - 1);$
CU move	$\text{move} \begin{Bmatrix} i \\ m \\ AC \end{Bmatrix} \text{ to } \begin{Bmatrix} i \\ m \\ AC \end{Bmatrix}$	$\begin{Bmatrix} X[j] \\ \text{mask} \\ AC \end{Bmatrix} \leftarrow \begin{Bmatrix} X[j] \\ \text{mask} \\ AC \end{Bmatrix};$

Figure 3-11   Cooperative SIMD instructions involving the mask.

Instruction	Assembly code	Action
Bitwise AND	and ix1, ix2, ix3	$X[ix1] \leftarrow X[ix2] \text{ and } X[ix3];$
Bitwise OR	or ix1, ix2, ix3	$X[ix1] \leftarrow X[ix2] \text{ or } X[ix3];$
Bitwise NOT	not ix1, ix2	$X[ix1] \leftarrow \text{not } X[ix2];$
...	... ...	...

Figure 3-12   Vector logic instructions useful for complex conditionals.

Instruction	Assembly code	Action
Select first	first	Reset all but leftmost one in *mask*.
Index of first	xfirst ix	$X[ix] \leftarrow$ index of leftmost one in *mask*, $X[ix] \leftarrow -1$ if *mask* $\equiv 0$.

Figure 3-13   Selection operations on the mask.

Instruction	Assembly code	Action
Branch if all	brall a,index	$(mask\langle k \rangle = 1, (0 \le k \le N - 1)) \rightarrow PC \leftarrow ca$:
Branch if any	brany a,index	$(not\ mask \equiv 0) \rightarrow PC \leftarrow ca$:
Branch if none	brnon a,index	$(mask \equiv 0) \rightarrow PC \leftarrow ca$:

Figure 3-14   Branches on test result summaries.

SIMD pseudocode can be extended by the mask idea. A mask is computed as a logical vector operation and then used to control a vector assignment. Evaluation and use of a mask can be expressed in pseudocode as shown in the patterns and example of Figure 3-15. The example shows vector absolute value written using this notation.

A larger example using the mask is scaling the columns of a matrix by their first element, unless that element is zero. The pseudocode for this operation and the SIMD assembly code to implement it are shown in Figure 3-16. Both this example and the vector absolute value are special cases in which no operations are executed for a false test outcome. They correspond to a sequential **if-then** construct with no **else** clause.

3.3.4   Vector Length and Strip Mining

So far, examples have assumed that the length L of vectors is the same as the number N of PEs. We now consider the control of the vector length in an SIMD computer. We must be able to process arbitrary length vectors. There are two cases.

1. $L \le N$: If the machine has a length register, *len*, set it to L. The mask can also control length by making it a vector of L ones followed by $N - L$ zeros, disabling unneeded PEs. Such a vector, of the form mask = [1 1 1 ... 1 1 0 0 0 ... 0 0] is called a prefix vector. We denote it $Pr(L)$.

2. $L > N$: This case is done by $\lfloor L/N \rfloor$ operations of length N followed by one operation of length L mod N.

Patterns

$$\text{mask}\langle k \rangle := \text{logical expression}(k), (0 \le k \le N - 1);$$
$$\text{vector assignment}(k), (\text{mask}\langle k \rangle \,|\, 0 \le k \le N - 1);$$

Example

$$\text{LT}\langle k \rangle := \text{v}[k] < 0.0, (0 \le k \le N - 1);$$
$$\text{v}\langle k \rangle := -\text{v}[k], (\text{LT}\langle k \rangle \,|\, 0 \le k \le N - 1);$$

Figure 3-15   Vector absolute value pseudocode using the mask.

Pseudocode

$NZ\langle k \rangle := B[0, k] \neq 0, (0 \leq k \leq N - 1);$
for $i := 1$ *step* 1 *until* $N - 1$
$\quad B[i, k] := B[i, k]/B[0, k], (NZ\langle k \rangle \mid 0 \leq k \leq N - 1);$

Assembly Language

N	DATA	64	Number of PEs and matrix size.
ZRO	DATA	0.0	Constant.
I	EQUIV	2	Row number is in index 2,
LIM	EQUIV	1	and the limit is in index 1.
B	BSS	64×64	Storage for the matrix.
	ldxi	I,0	Set I to start of columns.
	cload	ZRO	Set all
	cbcast		PE accumulators
	movR	toA	to zero.
	ceq	B	Test first row for zeros.
	not	mask, mask	Enable processors
	mask		corresponding to nonzeros.
	ldx	LIM,N	Set up loop limit.
ILP	lod	B,I	Fetch row I and
	div	B	scale it, and
	sto	B,I	store it, if scale factor ≠ 0.
	incx	I,1	Increment index and
	cmpx	I,LIM,ILP	loop if not complete.

Figure 3-16 Column scaling using the mask register.

For vector computers with a length register, setting the register to a value $L < N$ has the effect of automatically masking subsequent operations with a length L prefix vector.

Processing a long vector in *strips* of N or fewer elements at a time is an important idea in vector processing and is often referred to as *strip mining*. Vector computers with relatively complex instruction sets may support strip mining with special instructions. To do operations on several length N vectors followed by a wrap-up at the end, a special instruction to support looping when $L > N$ is useful. A vector looping instruction could have the form

```
vecloop     ix1,ix2,adr
```

where ix1 indexes a block of N components, ix2 is a loop limit, and adr is a loop start address. The instruction would perform the actions described by the pseudocode shown in Figure 3-17. The instruction counts, tests for completion, maintains an index to the next block of components, and adjusts the mask for the length of the last block. Its formal description is shown in Figure 3-18.

```
if X[ix1] < X[ix2] then
       begin
             X[ix1] ← X[ix1] + N;
             if X[ix2] < X[ix1] then
                          mask ← mask and Pr(X[ix2] mod N);
             go to adr;
       end
```

Figure 3-17   Pseudocode description of the vector looping instruction.

Instruction	Assembly code	Action
Vector loop	vecloop ix1, ix2, adr	$(X[ix1] < X[ix2]) \rightarrow$ $(X[ix1] \leftarrow X[ix1] + N); next$ $(X[ix2] < X[ix1]) \rightarrow$ $mask \leftarrow mask \wedge Pr(X[ix2] \bmod N); next$ $PC \leftarrow adr);$

Figure 3-18   A vector looping instruction.

Vector-length control is somewhat different in a pipelined SIMD computer, as will be discussed in more detail in Section 3.7. Because there is not a fixed number of arithmetic units, the vector length has different constraints. If the pipelined vector machine has vector registers, the length of the registers limits the vector length for a single instruction. If vector operands are fetched directly from memory and results returned there, then the limit on vector length may be very large. It is limited only by the size of the number that can be specified for the length in a single vector instruction. In machines with vector registers, long vectors must be broken into strips, as for the true SIMD case. Thus, a pipelined SIMD computer might also have a special instruction in its repertoire to support strip mining.

3.3.5   Routing Data Among the PEs

We now address the problem of how data computed by one PE can be made available to another PE for use in further computations. This is referred to as the problem of data routing among the PEs. We treat the problem in the context of an architecture with processor-memory pairs communicating by way of an interconnection network. The discussion applies to an alignment network between a set of processors and a set of memories if some software steps are shifted into hardware.

If there is no broadcast, that is, only one copy of a value is transmitted, then any exchange of data among PEs is a permutation of the set of data items associated with different PEs. We will consider permutations in some detail in relation to interconnection networks in Chapter 6, but to complete the SIMD instruction set description, we include the shift routing instruction of Figure 3-19. The permutation performed by this routing instruction is a circular right shift of data items in the routing registers of different PEs. It is right circular in PE index order, with PE0 at the left. The CU address ca is taken to be an integer shift distance modulo N and may either be a constant in the instruction address field or may be a variable specified in a CU index register.

As an example of an algorithm using shift routing, there is a form of parallel prefix computation using only these permutations. We assume an 8 PE machine and a vector length of 8. The data dependence diagram for this prefix algorithm is shown in Figure 3-20. Assembly code for parallel prefix on an 8 PE vector computer might appear as in Program 3-12. Assume all PEs are enabled at the start. Note that because the sender's mask bit determines whether a transmission occurs, the mask must be reset to all ones between vector additions. The extra wrap-around transmissions are not used by their receivers so it does not matter whether those transmissions are masked or not.

Figures 3-6, 3-7, 3-8, 3-11, 3-12, 3-13, 3-14, 3-18, and 3-19 present a fairly complete instruction set for an SIMD computer. We now have a detailed enough understanding of the architecture to return to the questions of storage layout and operand access identified at the outset as key issues in the study of SIMD computers.

Instruction	Assembly code		Action
Shift routing	route	a,index	$(S_k \rightarrow (R_{(k + ca)\bmod N} \leftarrow R_k), 0 \le k \le N - 1);$

Figure 3-19   A minimal set of routing instructions.

```
lod      V                           Get the input vector
movA     toR                            and ready it for routing.
route    +1                          All PEs send their data right,
ldxi     mask,  = (01111111)            but only the last 7
mask                                     perform the add
radd                                        of the received data.
movA     toR                         Results of
ldxi     mask,  = (11111111)            the add are
mask                                     sent two steps
route    +2                                 to right by all.
ldxi     mask,  = (00111111)         Received values are
mask                                     used only by
radd                                        the last 6 PEs.
movA     toR                         Results of
ldxi     mask,  = (11111111)            the add are
mask                                     sent four steps
route    +4                                 to right by all.
ldxi     mask,  = (00001111)         Only 4 additions
mask                                     are done in
radd                                        the last step.
```

Program 3-12   SIMD assembly code for parallel prefix using shift routing.

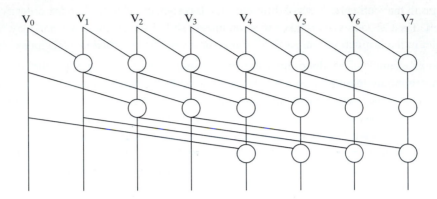

Figure 3-20 Data dependence graph for prefix using shift routing.

3.4 The Prime Memory System

Now consider a shared memory SIMD computer of the form shown in Figure 3-3. In principle, data in any memory module is available to any PE, but parallel access by multiple PEs can lead to conflict. When two operands needed by the same vector instruction are stored in the same memory module, there is said to be an access collision on that module. There are ways of avoiding memory module collision when "regular" access patterns are used. One way to avoid multiple references to the same memory module in vector access is to use what Lawrie and Vora [194] called the prime memory system. It is based on storing arrays to be accessed by P processors in M memory modules, where $M > P$. Most often $M = P + 1$. The scheme in its simplest form uses only P out of every M memory cells. For efficiency, M should be large and nearly equal to P. The scheme is illustrated by the 4-in-5 storage of an 8×8 matrix shown in Figure 3-21.

A formal definition of the prime memory storage scheme is as follows. Consider a two-dimensional array a_{ij} stored in column major order, beginning at memory location *base*, having I rows and J columns, and using zero origin indices i and j to specify elements. Define the module number:

$$f(i, j) = (j \times I + i + base) \bmod M \tag{3.14}$$

and define the row number:

$$g(i, j) = \lfloor (j \times I + i + base)/P \rfloor. \tag{3.15}$$

Note that the remainder is modulo M, but the integer quotient is modulo P. We assume that $P = 2^k$ is a power of two. The number of unused memory cells, or holes, is $M - P$ out of every M, so that a fraction $(M - P)/M$ of memory is wasted. Hardware tricks to avoid this wasted space can be found in the original article describing the scheme.

To see whether the scheme supports the parallel access requirements in matrix algorithms, one needs a characterization of important patterns of simultaneous access. Let P processes access a vector of P elements of the matrix A. The elements are ordered by an index k, $0 \le k < P$.

Many important vectors in a two-dimensional matrix can be specified by subscripts that are linear functions of k. If c_1 and c_2 are constants, some useful access patterns are:

$a_{c_1, k + c_2}$ P successive elements of a row.

$a_{k + c_1, c_2}$ P elements of a column.

$a_{c_1, 2k + c_2}$ P even elements of a row.

$a_{k + c_1, k + c_2}$ P elements of a forward diagonal.

$a_{k, I - k}$ P elements of the main reverse diagonal.

These access patterns are formalized by the concept of a linear P-vector.

Definition: A linear P-vector of a matrix A is the set of P elements:

$$V(a, b, c, e) = (a_{ij} | i = ax + b, j = cx + e, 0 \le x < P < M). \tag{3.16}$$

For linear P-vectors, the memory module accessed for a given value of x is

$$\mu(x) = f(ax + b, cx + e)$$
$$= ((cx + e)I + (ax + b) + base) \bmod M, \tag{3.17}$$

Memory Module

Address	0	1	2	3	4
0	a_{00}	a_{10}	a_{20}	a_{30}	-
1	a_{50}	a_{60}	a_{70}	-	a_{40}
2	a_{21}	a_{31}	-	a_{01}	a_{11}
3	a_{71}	-	a_{41}	a_{51}	a_{61}
4	-	a_{02}	a_{12}	a_{22}	a_{32}
5	a_{42}	a_{52}	a_{62}	a_{72}	-
6	a_{13}	a_{23}	a_{33}	-	a_{03}
7	a_{63}	a_{73}	-	a_{43}	a_{53}
8	a_{34}	-	a_{04}	a_{14}	a_{24}
9	-	a_{44}	a_{54}	a_{64}	a_{74}
10	a_{05}	a_{15}	a_{25}	a_{35}	-
11	a_{55}	a_{65}	a_{75}	-	a_{45}
12	a_{26}	a_{36}	-	a_{06}	a_{16}
13	a_{76}	-	a_{46}	a_{56}	a_{66}
14	-	a_{07}	a_{17}	a_{27}	a_{37}
15	a_{47}	a_{57}	a_{67}	a_{77}	-

Figure 3-21   Prime memory storage of an 8×8 matrix for $P = 4$, $M = 5$.

and the address specified within that module is

$$\alpha(x) = g(ax + b, cx + e)$$
$$= \lfloor ((cx + e)I + (ax + b) + base)/P \rfloor . \tag{3.18}$$

If we define $d = a + cI$ and $B = b + eI + base$ then the module number is $\mu(x) = (dx + B) \bmod M$, and the address in the module is $\alpha(x) = \lfloor (dx + B)/P \rfloor$. The goal is to have all the module numbers distinct so that the vector of P elements can be accessed in parallel.

The important question is, when are the components of a linear P-vector in different memory modules? The answer is contained in the following theorem, the proof of which is omitted.

THEOREM

The values of the memory module number $\mu(x)$, $0 \le x < P$, for a linear P-vector $V(a, b, c, e)$ are distinct provided that the parameter $d = a + cI$ is relatively prime to the number M of modules.

This is a more general form of the ancient Chinese Remainder Theorem, which tells us that a vector of stride d will reference M different modules if d is relatively prime to M. If M is a prime number, then only strides d that are divisible by M will fail to access different memory modules for all x. For example, $P = 16$ is a power of two, and $M = P + 1 = 17$ is prime. In a 16 PE vector computer with a 17 module prime memory system, an access to a row or a column of a 50×50 matrix references distinct modules. If the matrix is stored in column major order, column accesses have stride one and row accesses have stride 50, both relatively prime to 17. Unfortunately, access to the forward diagonal, represented by the linear P-vector $V(1, 0, 1, 0)$, has a stride of $51 = 3 \times 17$, so all forward diagonal elements are stored in the same memory module. A compiler that knows the P and M configuration could potentially detect array dimensions leading to module collisions when the array was declared and adjust the array dimensions up to numbers giving strides relatively prime to M for commonly used P-vectors.

The computation of module numbers, μ, and addresses, α, must be fast to take advantage of the prime memory scheme. Fortunately, the computation of the addresses can be distributed over the modules, with each module computing its own address on the basis of the parameters of the linear P-vector being accessed. A request for a P-vector can be sent to all memory modules, and the modules themselves can calculate their address on the basis of a, b, c, e, and μ. Solving for x in terms of μ:

$$x(\mu) = (\mu - B)d' \bmod M, \text{ where } (dd' \bmod M) = 1. \tag{3.19}$$

That is, d' is the reciprocal of d in the field of integers modulo M. d is guaranteed to have such a reciprocal because d is relatively prime to M. Then the address in module μ is:

$$\alpha(\mu) = \lfloor (d((\mu - B)d' \bmod M) + B)/P \rfloor . \tag{3.20}$$

In both the distributed memory architecture of SIMD Figure 3-2 and the shared memory architecture of Figure 3-3, a large switching network is shown connected to multiple PEs. In either case, the switch must be capable of simultaneously routing data from P sources to P destinations. In the situation we have just been describing, d relatively prime to M, the alignment network must be able to connect module $\mu(x)$ to PE x simultaneously for all x. We will discuss the structure and capabilities of such networks in Chapter 6.

3.5 Use of the PE Index to Solve Storage Layout Problems

The prime memory system is a hardware mechanism for supporting simultaneous data access, but skewed storage is not the only way to solve simultaneous access problems. Sometimes algorithm restructuring can accomplish the same goal. Returning to the distributed memory SIMD architecture of Figure 3-2, consider the straight storage of $A[i, j]$ with column k stored in PE memory k. If we want to form all the column sums, the storage layout allows us to write the highly parallel code of Program 3-13. For row sums, however, the storage layout does not allow us to write the key statement of the correspondingly simple code:

```
sum[k]  := sum[k] + A[k, j], (0 ≤ k ≤ N-1);
```

because it is not possible to access $A[k, j]$ for different k in parallel.

```
sum[k]  := 0, (0 ≤ k ≤ N-1);
for i := 0 step 1 until N-1
    sum[k]  := sum[k] + A[i, k], (0 ≤ k ≤ N-1);
```

Program 3-13   SIMD pseudocode for column sums.

We could attack this problem using the interconnection network. Assume a machine that includes shift routing of distance 2^k, $0 \le k < \log_2 N$. The recursive doubling technique could be used on such a machine to obtain row sums. Pseudocode for this algorithm might appear as in Program 3-14. The inner loop of this algorithm uses the trick of stepping by the current value of the loop index so that j goes through the values 1, 2, 4, ... up to the last power of two that is less than or equal to $N - 1$. Because the inner loop is executed $N\log_2 N$ times, the efficiency of the algorithm is:

$$E = \frac{1}{N}\frac{N(N-1)}{N\log_2 N} \approx \frac{1}{\log_2 N}. \tag{3.21}$$

By rearranging the algorithm and using the PE index, however, the more efficient algorithm of Program 3-15 is obtainable. This algorithm works by adding forward diagonals of the matrix. Unlike the elements of the columns themselves, the elements of forward diagonals are stored in different memory modules and can be accessed simultaneously without conflict. The diagonals are shifted so that elements of the same row are combined. The order of addition differs for elements of different rows, but the associativity and commutativity of addition make this irrelevant. A pictorial representation of the behavior of the algorithm on a 4×4 matrix is shown in Figure 3-22. Use of the PE index is inherent in the vector assignment

```
sum[k]  := sum[k] + A[loc[k], k], (0 ≤ k ≤ N-1);
```

where loc[k] has a distinct value for each PE k.

```
for i := 0 step 1 until N-1
    begin
            tmp[k]  := A[i, k],  (0 ≤ k ≤ N-1);
            for j := 1 step j until N-1
                tmp[k]:=tmp[k]+shift(tmp[(k-j) mod N],j), (0 ≤ k ≤ N-1);
                /* Sum pairs of groups of tmp. */
            sum[i]  := tmp[N-1];  /* scalar operation */
    end
```

Program 3-14 Row sums using recursive doubling.

```
loc[k]  := k,  (0 ≤ k ≤  N-1);  /* Initialize PE indices. */
sum[k]  := 0,  (0 ≤ k ≤ N-1);  /* Zero sums. */
for i := 0 step 1 until N-1
            begin  /* Add a diagonal. */
                sum[k]  := sum[k] + A[loc[k], k],  (0 ≤ k ≤ N-1);
                /* Now shift both index vector and row sums. */
                loc[k]  := shift(loc[(k-1) mod N], 1),  (0 ≤ k ≤ N-1);
                sum[k]  := shift(sum[(k-1) mod N], 1),  (0 ≤ k ≤ N-1);
            end
```

Program 3-15 Row sums using the PE index.

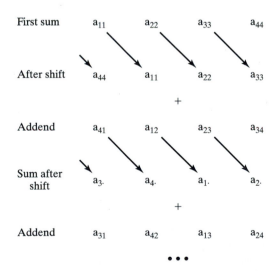

Figure 3-22 Routing and addition pattern for row sums.

The floating point vector add is executed N times in this row sum algorithm. If routing operations cost α units each, then the time with N processing elements is:

$$T_N = N(1 + 2\alpha),$$ (3.22)

and the efficiency becomes:

$$E = \frac{1}{N}\frac{T_1}{T_N} = \frac{1}{N}\frac{N^2}{N(1 + 2\alpha)} = \frac{1}{1 + 2\alpha}.$$ (3.23)

Thus, the efficiency is near one if routing is fast.

3.6 SIMD Language Constructs—Fortran 90

Numerous high-level languages with support for SIMD operations have been proposed and used in the scientific community. The most widespread one at this time is Fortran 90, as a result of its adoption as a standard by the American National Standards Institute. One feature that distinguishes Fortran 90 from previous versions of Fortran is the inclusion of the array as a first-class data type that can be manipulated and assigned within the language. Previous versions of Fortran allowed the declaration of arrays, but only individual elements of arrays could be elements of expressions or targets of assignments. The inclusion of array values and assignments in Fortran 90 was in direct response to the needs of users of SIMD processors and an attempt to standardize the various machine specific Fortran dialects supported by different manufacturers. Some early proposals for vector extensions to high-level languages limited parallel operations to one-dimensional vectors, but advances in compiler technology made it simple to build support for multidimensional array sections on the vector operations supplied directly by most SIMD machines. We will not present the Fortran 90 language in its entirety but only discuss those extensions that directly relate to SIMD operation.

3.6.1   Arrays and Array Sections

An *array* in Fortran 90 is a one or more dimensional collection of scalar *array elements*. All array elements must be of the same type. Each *dimension* has an *extent* representing the number of index values in that dimension. The number of dimensions of an array is its *rank*, and Fortran 90 arrays may have a rank up to seven. The *shape* of an array is a one-dimensional array, or vector, of integers, whose extent is the rank of the array and whose i-th element is the extent of the array in its i-th dimension. The *size* of an array is the product of its extents in all dimensions or the times reduction of its shape vector. A lower bound j_i and an upper bound k_i are also associated with each dimension i and are related to the extent, e_i, by $e_i = k_i - j_i + 1$. There is an inherent mapping between an array of any shape and a rank-one array of the same size. This mapping is called *array element order* and assigns the element $s_1, s_2, \ldots, s_m$ of a rank-m array to position,

$$1 + (s_1 - j_1) + (s_2 - j_2)d_1 + \cdots + (s_m - j_m)d_{m-1}\ldots d_1,$$

in the linear array, where $d_i = \max(k_i - j_i + 1, 0)$ and $j_i \le s_i \le k_i, 1 \le i \le m$. Because the first index varies most rapidly in mapping from an array of rank two to the rank-one array, the ordering is referred to as column major order. An intrinsic function allows a rank-one array to be reshaped into an array with any legal shape vector, discarding elements or adding padding elements if the size of the rank-one array does not match that of the target array.

An *array constructor* can be used to build a rank-one array from a sequence of scalar values. Arbitrary shape arrays are built by using the RESHAPE intrinsic function to restructure the rank-one result of an array constructor into an array of any specified shape. An array constructor has the form

(/ *ac_value*, *ac_value*, ... /)

where *ac_value* is a simple scalar value, an array whose elements are taken in array element order or an implied DO list. An implied DO list has the form

(*ac_value*, ..., *var* = *expr1*, *expr2*[, *expr3*])

where expressions in the list of *ac_value*s may include *var*. Thus, if A is $\begin{bmatrix} 1 & 7 \\ 3 & 9 \end{bmatrix}$, the array constructor,

(/ A, (I, I = 2, 8, 2) /)

produces the vector $\begin{bmatrix} 1 & 3 & 7 & 9 & 2 & 4 & 6 & 8 \end{bmatrix}$. Because the array constructor operates on scalars, the array A in the example is taken as its elements in array element order. Implied DO lists can be nested, making it easy to specify the elements of a multidimensional array in array element order using an array constructor. For example

(/ ((I**J, I = 2, 3), J = 2, 4) /)

constructs the rank-one array $\begin{bmatrix} 4 & 9 & 8 & 27 & 16 & 81 \end{bmatrix}$, which is the array element order vector for the rank-two array $\begin{bmatrix} 4 & 8 & 16 \\ 9 & 27 & 81 \end{bmatrix}$.

To flexibly specify array sections for building array values or as targets of array assignments, a way of specifying multiple index values along each dimension must be available. Fortran 90 uses subscript triplets and vector subscripts for this purpose. A *subscript triplet* has the form

lower_bound : *upper_bound* : *stride*

which specifies a vector of integers beginning with *lower_bound* and proceeding by successive additions of *stride* to the last value before *upper_bound*. If *stride* is positive and *lower_bound* < *upper_bound*, the last value is the last integer ≤ *upper_bound*, while if *stride* is negative and *lower_bound* > *upper_bound*, it is the last integer ≥ *upper_bound*. If *lower_bound* or *upper_bound* is omitted, its default value is the declared lower or upper bound for the corresponding dimension of the array. If stride and its preceding colon are omitted, the default stride is one. A subscript triplet consisting of a single : specifies the full set of indices declared for the corresponding dimension of the array. A *vector subscript* explicitly specifies a vector of integer subscripts as a rank one integer expression listing the subscript values rather than building the vector from bounds and stride. This form allows a subscript value to appear more than once in the list. An array section having a vector subscript with two or more equal values is called a *many-one* array section. If the array A is declared with dimension A(0:51, 0:51) then the array section A(0:50:2, :) is a 26×52 matrix consisting of even numbered rows of A. If V is the vector V = (/ (2*(I/2), I = 0, 51) /), then A(:, V) is a 52×52 many-one array section consisting of two copies of each even numbered column of A.

3.6.2   Array Assignment and Array Expressions

Array values may be assigned to arrays or array sections of the same shape. It is in assignment that the semantics of SIMD operation are clearly reflected in the high level language. The rule for array assignment is that the right-hand-side array expression is fully evaluated before any left-hand-side element is changed, and elements of the left-hand-side array or section are assigned in parallel, that is, no ordering is specified for assignment to individual scalar elements. This rule has the immediate consequence that a many-one array section is not allowed as the target of an array assignment because parallel assignments to the same array element would conflict. It also has consequences for compiled code when the array section on the left side overlaps an array section used in the right-hand-side expression. It is clear that the array assignment

```
A(7:36) = A(1:30)
```

cannot simply be executed element by element in order of increasing index values and achieve the semantics specified for array assignment. Perhaps more interesting is that a compiler for an SIMD machine with vector length ten could not strip mine the assignment into the form

```
A(7:16)  = A(1:10)
A(17:26) = A(11:20)      ! A(11:16)  have been altered by the first assignment
A(27:36) = A(21:30)      ! Similarly for A(21:26)
```

Vector registers or other temporary storage and/or careful reordering of operations must be used by the compiler to achieve the semantics of parallel array assignment. Some SIMD language proposals considered sequential semantics for array assignment, but this prevents the use of SIMD hardware in many cases and can always be achieved by element assignments enclosed in nested loops.

In expressions, scalar operators extend component by component to arrays. This is also true of scalar intrinsic functions, so if arrays A, B, and C have the same shape

```
C = sin(A + B)
```

assigns to each element of C the sine of the sum of the corresponding elements of A and B. This high-level expression evaluation mechanism is a direct reflection of the vector instructions in an SIMD processor. The broadcast operation is also reflected at the high level by allowing either operand of a binary operator in an array expression to be a scalar. In this case, a copy of the scalar is combined with each element of the array operand. An operator in an array expression, thus, either combines arrays of the same shape or combines an array with a scalar. If the right hand side of an array assignment is a scalar, the scalar is broadcast and assigned to each element of the array section on the left hand side.

We have seen the importance of the mask in evaluating data dependent conditionals on an SIMD machine. The function of the mask is accomplished in Fortran 90 by the WHERE statement. There are two forms of the WHERE statement, both of which use a logical valued array expression to control element assignment. The first form is a single statement with the syntax

WHERE (*mask_expression*) *array_section* = *expression*

The shapes of the *array_section* and both expressions must conform, and the elements of the *mask_expression* must be logical. An element of the *array_section* is assigned only if the corresponding element of the *mask_expression* is true and is unchanged if the mask element is false. The second form of the WHERE statement is block structured and has the form

```
WHERE  (mask_expression)
       array_assignment
       ...
ELSEWHERE
       array_assignment
       ...
END  WHERE
```

Each *array_assignment* between WHERE and ELSEWHERE is executed under control of the *mask_expression*, while each *array_assignment* between ELSEWHERE and END WHERE is executed under control of the logical complement of the *mask_expression*. ELSEWHERE and its corresponding assignments are optional. This form of a data dependent conditional assignment directly corresponds to the machine level mechanism diagrammed in Figure 3-10. The example given in Figure 3-16 of scaling columns of a rank two array by dividing each column by its first element, provided the latter is nonzero, could be written in Fortran 90 using the WHERE construct as shown in Program 3-16.

```
DO I = 1, N-1
        WHERE (B(0, :) .NE. 0.0) B(I, :) = B(I, :)/B(0, :)
END DO
```

Program 3-16   Column scaling using WHERE.

3.6.3   Fortran 90 Array Intrinsic Functions

In addition to extending scalar operators and intrinsic functions to take array sections as operands, Fortran 90 also includes intrinsic functions that take arrays as arguments and/or produce array results. Some of these intrinsic functions allow access to properties of an array, such as its shape, while others perform operations like reduction, which we saw to be important in vector algorithms. Other Fortran 90 intrinsics leave element values the same but rearrange them between source and destination arrays of the same or different shapes. Table 3-3 lists the intrinsic functions that give access to properties of an array. Square brackets surround optional arguments. Fortran 90 allows arguments to be specified by keywords, but we do not include this feature in our discussion. The SHAPE intrinsic returns a vector of integers that give the extents along each dimension of the array. This vector completely defines the structure of the array with the exception of the lower and upper index bounds along the different dimensions. The SIZE intrinsic, without the *dim* argument, returns the number of elements in *array* and in this case is equal to the product of the elements of the shape vector. With the optional *dim* argument, it returns the extent in that dimension. LBOUND or UBOUND, without the *dim* argument, returns a vector of lower or upper bounds, respectively, for each dimension. With the *dim* argument the scalar lower or upper bound in that dimension is returned.

The intrinsic functions that reorder array elements are listed in Table 3-4. RESHAPE treats a source array as a vector in array element order and forms it into an array with the specified shape vector. As mentioned earlier, it can be used with an array constructor to build an array of any shape. The two-dimensional array of squares and cubes discussed in connection with the array constructor can be built and shaped by the statement

```
RESHAPE((/ (( I**J, I = 2, 3), J = 2, 4) /), (/2, 3/))
```

PACK, UNPACK, and MERGE allow elements of an array to be placed in various ways under the control of a mask, which is an array of logical values. SPREAD provides a flexible broadcast mechanism that makes multiple copies of an array section. CSHIFT and EOSHIFT provide ways of shifting elements among array positions and generalize the machine language shift routing function of Figure 3-19. TRANSPOSE simply interchanges rows and columns of its rank two argument, *matrix*.

Table 3-3   Intrinsic functions that access array properties.

SHAPE (*array*)	Return vector of extents in each dimension.
SIZE (*array* [, *dim*])	Return size of array or extent in a given dimension.
LBOUND (*array* [, *dim*])	Vector of lower bounds or the lower bound in a given dimension.
UBOUND (*array* [, *dim*])	Vector of upper bounds or the upper bound in a given dimension.

Intrinsic functions that perform cooperative computations, that is other than element by element computations, on arrays are listed in Table 3-5. Emphasizing the importance of the reduction operation, there are eight different intrinsic functions that perform some kind of reduction. The reduction may be over the whole array, yielding a scalar result, or only over one specified dimension, yielding an array of rank one less than that of the source array. Plus, times, maximum, and minimum reduction can all be applied to arrays of numeric type. In addition, reduction with the logical functions OR and AND can be performed on arrays with logical valued elements. As an extension to the maximum and minimum reduction intrinsics, MAXLOC and MINLOC locate the position of the first maximum, respectively minimum, valued element in array element order and return its list of indices as a vector of integers of extent equal to the rank of the original array. Program 3-17 shows an example of finding the position of the minimum in an array and its value. The COUNT intrinsic can be viewed as a sum reduction over a logical array, where true values are mapped into ones and false values into zeros. Finally, the important functions of computing the inner product of two vectors, a matrix and a vector, or two matrices are supplied by the intrinsic functions DOT_PRODUCT and MATMUL. Restricting the ranks of their arguments allows them to be optimized for the most common cases.

Table 3-4 Intrinsic functions that reorder array elements.

RESHAPE (*array*, *shape*[, *pad*][, *order*])	Form the elements of *array*, in element order, into an array with shape vector *shape*, taking additional elements from the *pad* array and treating dimensions according to the permutation *order*.
PACK (*array*, *mask*[, *pad*])	Form a vector of values of *array* selected by true elements of the logical array *mask*, taking additional elements from *pad* if present and longer.
UNPACK (*vector*, *mask*, *field*)	Replace elements of array *field* corresponding to true elements of the conformable array *mask* with elements of *vector* in array element order.
MERGE (*Tsource*, *Fsource*, *mask*)	Return an array conformable with *Tsource*, *Fsource*, and *mask* having elements from *Tsource* where *mask* is true and from *Fsource* where *mask* is false.
SPREAD (*source*, *dim*, *ncopies*)	Replicate array *source*, *ncopies* times, along dimension *dim* to form an array of rank one more than source.
CSHIFT (*array*, *shift*[, *dim*])	Circular shift elements of all vectors of *array* along dimension *dim* (default one) by *shift*. Positive shift is toward beginning and negative toward end of vector.
EOSHIFT (*array*, *shift*[, *boundary*][, *dim*])	*array* is shifted end-off along dimension *dim* with end values filled from *boundary*, which is either a scalar or an array of rank one less than *array*.
TRANSPOSE (*matrix*)	Transpose the rank two array *matrix*.

3.6.4   Examples of SIMD Operations in Fortran 90

Some examples of the use of Fortran 90 can be drawn from the vector algorithms discussed in Section 3.1. Although there is an intrinsic function to compute the inner product of two vectors X and Y, it can also be written in Fortran 90 as SUM(X*Y), while the outer product of the vectors X and Y is the matrix.

```
A = SPREAD(X,1,SIZE(Y))*SPREAD(Y,2,SIZE(X))
```

Table 3-5   Intrinsic functions that perform cooperative computations on arrays.

SUM (*array*[, *dim*][, *mask*]) PRODUCT (*array*[, *dim*][, *mask*]) MAXVAL (*array*[, *dim*][, *mask*]) MINVAL (*array*[, *dim*][, *mask*])	Perform plus, times, maximum, or minimum reduction over the whole of *array* or along a single dimension if *dim* is specified. If *mask* is specified, reduce only over *array* elements corresponding to true values in *mask*.
ANY (*mask*[, *dim*]) ALL (*mask*[, *dim*])	Perform OR or AND reduction over the logical array *mask*, or only over dimension *dim* if specified.
MAXLOC (*array*[, *mask*]) MINLOC (*array*[, *mask*])	Return an integer vector of length rank(*array*) giving the position of the maximum or minimum element in *array* or the first one in element order. If *mask* is specified, consider only elements corresponding to true values in *mask*.
COUNT (*mask*[, *dim*])	Return integer count of true elements in *mask* or an array of counts of true elements along dimension *dim*.
DOT_PRODUCT (*vector_A*, *vector_B*) MATMUL (*matrix_A*, *matrix_B*)	Form the inner product of *vector_A* and *vector_B* or *matrix_A* and *matrix_B*. One of *matrix_A* or *matrix_B* must be rank two. The other may be either rank one or two.

```
INTEGER MN(3)
REAL A(4, 5, 10), VALMIN
MN = MINLOC(A)
VALMAX = A(MN(1), MN(2), MN(3))
```

Program 3-17   Fortran 90 code to find the location of the minimum and its value.

```
REAL A(10,10), B(10,10), C(10,10)
INTEGER K
C = 0
DO K = 1, 10
        C = C + SPREAD(A(:,K),2,10)*SPREAD(B(K,:),1,10)
END DO
```

Program 3-18   Fortran 90 matrix multiply corresponding to *kij* or *kji* form.

Without using the matrix multiply intrinsic function, the *kij* form of the matrix product of arrays A and B to get C corresponding to Program 3-3 can be written in Fortran 90 as Program 3-18. The first array assignment clears the whole matrix C, and the loop accumulates inner product terms for all elements of C simultaneously. Because two inner loops are accomplished by the array assignment body of the DO K loop, there is no distinction between the *kij* and *kji* forms of the algorithm.

The column sweep algorithm for the general linear recurrence that solves $AX = B$, where A is an upper triangular matrix is shown in Program 3-19. It is the same basic algorithm as that written in a sequential language in Program 3-9 except that here the A matrix is upper triangular and has non-zero diagonal elements. The sequential loop works backward, computing X(N) first and X(1) last. The only functional part of the DO loop for the first iteration, I = N, is the scalar assignment, but because Fortran 90 allows (null) computations with empty arrays, the code does not need to be specially modified to accommodate the last iteration.

```
PARAMETER N = 100
REAL A(N, N), B(N), X(N)
INTEGER I
DO I = N, 1
        X(I) = B(I)/A(I, I)
        B(1:I-1) = B(1:I-1) - A(1:I-1, I)*X(I)
END DO
```

Program 3-19   Fortran 90 version of column sweep.

As a final example of Fortran 90 usage, we can write a Gaussian elimination with partial pivoting to correspond to the sequential pseudocode of Program 3-6. The result is shown in Program 3-20. The intrinsic MAXLOC returns a rank-one vector of indices locating the maximum in a possibly multidimensional array. In this case, the rank-one array only has one element, but it must be declared as an array to satisfy Fortran 90 syntax requirements. The row swap required by pivoting is done with the help of the temporary vector, TMP. Efficiency could be improved by enclosing the row swap in an IF (MX(1) .NE. K) conditional block. Using the outer product, the inner DO I loop could be replaced by

```
PARAMETER N = 100
REAL A(N, N), TMP(N), PIV
INTEGER MX(1), IPIV(N), K, I
DO K = 1, N
    MX = MAXLOC(ABS(A(K:N, K)))
    TMP(K:N) = A(K, K:N)
    A(K, K:N) = A(MX(1), K:N)
    A(MX(1), K:N) = TMP(K:N)
    IPIV(K) = MX(1)
    PIV = 1/A(K, K)
    A(K+1:N, K) = A(K+1:N, K)*PIV
    DO I = K+1, N
        A(I, K+1:N) = A(I, K+1:N) - A(I, K)*A(K, K+1:N)
    END DO
END DO
```

Program 3-20   Row-wise Gaussian elimination with partial pivoting in Fortran 90.

```
A(K+1:N,K+1:N)  =  A(K+1:N,K+1:N)  - &
&          SPREAD(A(K+1:N,K),2,N-K)*SPREAD(A(K,K+1:N),1,N-K)
```

where the & is the line continuation character supported by Fortran 90 free form source.

3.7 Pipelined SIMD Vector Computers

A major advance in the cost effectiveness of vector computers comes from recognizing that an arithmetic operation like floating-point add carried out in parallel by all PEs is not done in a single-clock tick. Floating-point add might consist of the six steps:

1. Unpack operand exponents and significands.
2. Compare exponents.
3. Align significands.
4. Add significands.
5. Normalize result significand.
6. Pack result exponent and significand.

With multiple arithmetic logic units (ALUs), a pair of vector components would move through these steps in sequence in each PE, but a factor of six in hardware could be saved if each of six pairs of vector components were in a different stage of the addition pipeline at the same time. By staggering the starting times by one clock tick, a single pipelined addition unit can handle six additions nearly simultaneously. Figure 3-23 schematically shows the relationship between true and pipelined SIMD computers. Part (a) shows the overview that suggests that all PEs are busy, each adding a different pair of elements, $x_i + y_i$, while (b) shows that, in reality, five out of six hardware sections are idle in each PE. All sections of the pipeline are busy in part (c), where each operates on a different vector component addition.

For a vector length of six, a true SIMD machine with six complete ALUs would complete six adds in six cycles. A pipelined SIMD machine with a six-stage addition pipeline would complete the six adds using five cycles to fill the pipeline plus six more cycles to deliver the results, for a total of 11 cycles. The five-cycle start-up is a function of the pipeline length and is independent of the vector length. Longer vectors can be processed either by using one more pipeline cycle for each result or by having multiple pipelines, thus, mixing the true and pipelined SIMD architectures.

There is little difference between the instruction sets of true and pipelined SIMD computers. The characteristic division of the instruction set into scalar and vector operations still characterizes SIMD operation. Single vector instructions still implicitly include the arithmetic, indexed address modification, and iteration counting that would be required to do vector operations using scalar instructions. Data dependent conditionals on vectors must still be handled by a mask register instead of conditional branch. The memory interface can now be pipelined, but because the cycle time of a single memory module is longer than a pipeline cycle, successive vector elements must still be located in different memory modules for access to a vector in memory to proceed at full speed.

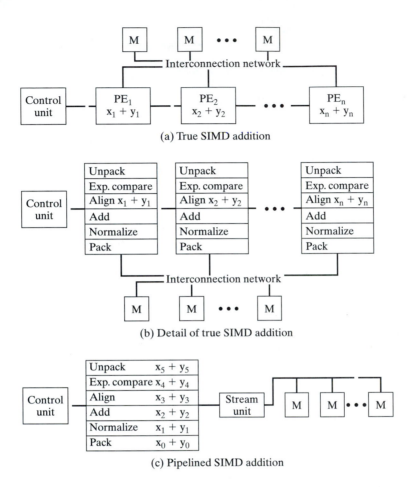

(a) True SIMD addition

(b) Detail of true SIMD addition

(c) Pipelined SIMD addition

Figure 3-23   Relation between true and pipelined SIMD operation.

3.7.1   Pipelined SIMD Processor Structure

The principal organizational distinctions between different pipelined SIMD computers can be classified under the headings of processor/memory interaction, number and types of pipelines, and implementation of arithmetic. The most pervasive architectural influence probably comes from the way in which operands and results move between memory and the processor pipelines. The overview sketch in Figure 3-23 suggests that vector operands come into the pipeline directly from memory and that results are returned to memory. The alternative to a memory-to-memory architecture, the load/store architecture, can be used with pipelined SIMD machines by supplying a set of vector registers in the CPU.

3.7.1.1   Processor/Memory Interaction

A vector register has a number, N, of full word cells to store a length N vector. A set of vector registers supplies all operands and receives all results from the arithmetic pipeline. Only load and store operations access memory, transferring vector data between memory and the vector registers. An ISP declaration of a set of eight vector registers of 64 elements, where elements are 64 bit words, would be

$$V[0:7][0:63]\langle 63:0\rangle .$$

The fixed length, N, of a vector register makes a pipelined load/store SIMD machine behave even more like a true SIMD computer with N PEs. In particular, the length N limit on vectors means that strip mining is important in both true and pipelined machines. In a true SIMD machine, adding a vector register means adding one register to each PE. Adding a length 64 vector register to a pipelined SIMD computer with, say, a ten-stage pipeline represents a larger percentage increase in hardware, and vector registers introduce an important new level into the storage hierarchy.

Figure 3-24 compares the load/store, or vector register, style of architecture of part (a) to the memory-to-memory architecture of part (b). The figure shows that either style can include multiple pipelines so that more than one vector operation may be in progress at a time. However, multiple pipelines make an even greater demand on the already high bandwidth needed in the stream unit, so multiple pipelines are more common in load/store style architectures. In the load/store architecture, the bandwidth to the vector registers must be high, but the memory interface can be simplified to the extent of loading or storing only one vector register at a time if desired. A load/store machine may use a vector length register capable of holding an integer $L \le N$, an N bit mask register, or both, to accommodate vector lengths less than N. A memory-to-memory style machine needs a length specification whose integer capacity could be comparable to the size of the memory.

Vector instructions must specify the locations of the first components of two operands and a result, a length, a mask, and the operation to be performed. The specification of three vector registers requires many fewer bits than the specification of three memory locations. Either memory-to-memory or load/store type architectures could specify the length in a vector instruction, but more bits would be needed by the memory-to-memory architecture. Bit vector masks are of variable lengths in the memory-to-memory architecture and must be stored in memory as are other vectors. Pipelined vector machines of the load/store type usually have special registers for the length and the mask and specify only three vector register numbers for a vector arithmetic instruction or one vector register and one memory address (and perhaps a stride) for a load or store. A vector arithmetic instruction for a memory-to-memory style machine may minimize instruction length by pointing to a parameter block that specifies starting addresses for two operands, a result, and a mask as well as a length. The stride in a memory-to-memory pipelined SIMD computer is usually restricted to one by the stream unit, as described in Section 3.7.2.

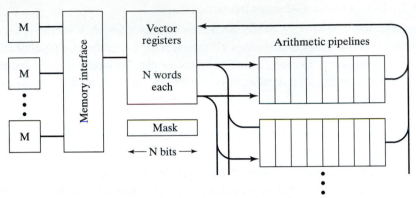

(a) Vector register pipelined SIMD architecture

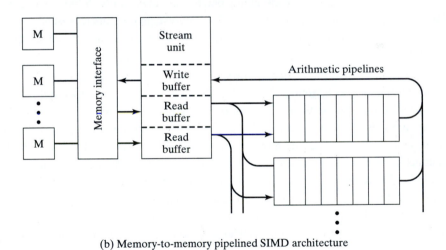

(b) Memory-to-memory pipelined SIMD architecture

Figure 3-24   Vector register and memory-to-memory pipelined SIMD architectures.

3.7.1.2   Number and Types of Pipelines

Multiple pipelines can be designed and used in different ways. A single pipeline may be designed to handle only a limited set of similar functions, such as add, subtract, and compare, or it may be more general purpose to handle any of the pipelined vector operations. Common restricted pipelines do addition, multiplication, or shift/logical operations. Division is not easily pipelined. There are two characteristic ways to use multiple pipelines: by starting an independent vector operation before another is finished using its pipeline or by *chaining*, which feeds the output of one pipeline into another as an operand. As an example of chaining, consider the so-called *linked triad* operation $W = X + Y*Z$, where all variables are vectors. A multiply pipeline can be started on operands Y and Z, and if issued soon enough, an instruction to add the result to X can take its second operand directly from the output of the multiply pipeline without waiting for the entire vector to fill a vector register. This situation is diagrammed in Figure 3-25, where the output of the multiply pipeline is sent both to its destination register V3 and to the first input to the add pipeline. To operate as shown, the add instruction must be issued before the first product exits the multiply pipeline. In the description of some Cray Research Corporation machines, this has been called *catching the chain slot.*

Any simultaneous use of multiple pipelines places increased bandwidth requirements on the sources and sinks of operands and results. In a vector register machine, two independent vector operations running simultaneously require four read ports and two write ports to the vector registers. The chain-linked triad operation of Figure 3-25 requires three read ports and two write ports. Additional ports to a register file are easier to supply than additional main memory ports, so simultaneous pipeline activity is harder to support in the memory-to-memory style of architecture. Chaining a vector register load with a vector operation that uses the register or chaining a vector operation with the store of its vector register result are also possible, and either of these makes the load/store architecture behave more like the memory-to-memory style, where memory read, arithmetic, and memory write are all included in the pipeline.

3.7.1.3   Implementation of Arithmetic

Because the same operation is applied to many vector elements, pipelines for one or a few related operations can often be more efficient than a general purpose pipeline. Addition/subtraction pipelines may use multiple pipeline stages to break the long carry propagation operation into shorter parts. In multiply pipelines, partial products can be generated in parallel early in the pipeline and summed in successive stages. Partial product summation usually uses carry-save techniques, propagating carries only in the last step. Because a pipelined multiplier must add a set of partial products, it is natural to think of adding independent vector elements to implement a pipelined sum reduction operation. Pipelined vector machines have included various forms of reduction, including sum reduction, inner product, and maximum reduction. Floating point vector operations are often handled by different pipelines than those for integers, with separate floating add and floating multiply pipelines being common. Other functional classes for pipelines may include shift and logical operations or population and lead zero counting.

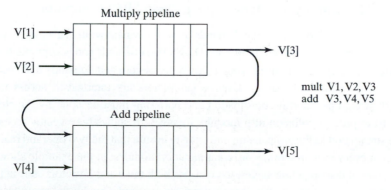

Figure 3-25   Chained vector multiply and add.

The fact that division is hard to pipeline efficiently can be addressed in different ways. A brute force approach is to supply multiple dividers that are started one by one as operands arrive from the vector registers and are reused when they become free. A more popular solution is based on reciprocal approximation and Newton iteration. If x_0 is an approximation to $1/b$, then $x_1 = (2 - bx_0)x_0$ is a better approximation with twice as many correct leading digits as x_0. Repeating this iteration doubles the number of correct digits each time, so if x_0 starts with, say, eight bits of accuracy, three iterations will produce a reciprocal with 64 correct bits. This technique reduces division to multiplication, subtraction, and reciprocal approximation. Reciprocal approximation can be done by simple exponent manipulation and table lookup for the significand and is easily pipelined. Thus, division, which is not easily pipelined, is replaced by reciprocal approximation, multiplication, and subtraction, which are. Because division of one vector by another is not a frequent operation, changing a vector division into one reciprocal approximation, seven vector multiplies, and three vector subtractions is an acceptable alternative to doing division one vector element at a time.

As with true SIMD computers, pipelined SIMD machines have scalar instructions that operate on single word operands. The degree of integration of the scalar and vector parts of a computer varies significantly. Many pipelined vector processors were built to be used as attachments to general purpose machines. An attached vector processor might execute commands prepared for it by a host machine in the same way an I/O processor executes input and output commands, competing for memory cycles for vector operands and results as a direct memory access I/O device would for input and output data. Even in integrated scalar and vector processors, functional units can be completely integrated between scalar and vector operations, or different functional units can be used for each type of operation. Separate functional units allow overlapping the execution of scalar and vector operations, provided there is no dependence between them, just as multiple vector pipelines allow the overlap of different vector operations. The Cray-1 processor, for example, had vector function pipelines for add, shift, and logical operations that were separate from the scalar function units but shared the floating point functional units for add, multiply, and reciprocal approximation between vector and scalar operations.

3.7.2   The Memory Interface of a Pipelined SIMD Computer

SIMD operation of any kind places high demands on memory bandwidth. In a memory-to-memory pipelined SIMD architecture, the memory must supply two operands and accept one result in every pipeline cycle. This requires a multiple module memory system and demands that successive vector elements be in different modules. Even when vectors are interleaved across modules and accessed with stride one, careful coordination and buffering must be done by the stream unit of Figure 3-24(b) to prevent collision at a module. Figure 3-26 shows how vector access is coordinated by the stream unit in this case, using buffering to ensure that the two operand reads and result write that occur every cycle reference different memory modules. In the example shown, with five memory modules and six pipeline stages, the fact that both the a and b vectors start in module zero and c starts in module two means that three buffers are required. One buffer separates the reads of a_i and b_i while two are needed to prevent the write of c from colliding with the read of either a or b.

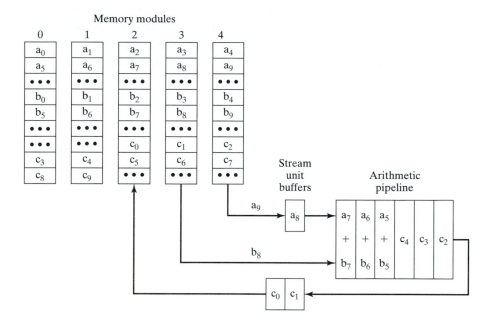

Figure 3-26   Stream unit coordination of vector element access in pipelined SIMD.

Problems with the three memory accesses per pipeline step can also arise if there are sources of memory requests other than the stream unit. Direct memory access I/O, for example, could steal a memory cycle and cause a disruption of the pipeline flow. Memory-to-memory pipelined SIMD machines usually have instructions to build stride-one vectors from elements stored in memory in other formats. A *gather* or *compress* operation corresponds to the Fortran 90 intrinsic, PACK, and could be used, say, to build a stride-one row vector from a matrix stored in memory by columns. The reverse operation that distributes a stride-one result vector over separated memory cells is called *scatter* or *expand* and corresponds to the UNPACK intrinsic of Fortran 90. Restrictions on the stride are also necessary for scatter and gather operations. In general, a stride-d vector has successive components stored in memory cells whose addresses are separated by d. If there are k memory modules interleaved on the low-order address bits, then a stride-one vector references the same module once every k components. A stride-k vector accesses the same memory module for all components. As with true SIMD machines, a stride d that is relatively prime to the number k of memory modules guarantees that successive accesses will be to distinct modules.

In the vector register style of architecture, the instantaneous requirements on memory bandwidth are not as strict. The vector registers serve as buffers between the memory and the arithmetic pipelines. Gather is performed in loading a vector register and scatter in storing it. A memory conflict stall in loading or storing a vector register does not affect flow in the arithmetic pipeline. The average memory bandwidth requirements, however, are still high in the vector register architecture. If the arithmetic pipelines are to be kept busy, memory must supply operands and absorb results at an average rate equal to the pipeline requirements minus the amount of reuse of the vector registers. Let p_{nr} be the probability that a vector operand is already in a register and need not be read from memory, and let p_{nw} be the probability that a result put into a vector register need not be stored in memory. Assume the probability of vector register reuse is $p_R = p_{nr} = p_{nw}$. Then if $\hat{k}$ is the average number of two operand pipelines active at any time, the memory bandwidth they require is

$$(3(1 - p_R)\hat{k})/t_p \qquad \text{words/second} \qquad (3.24)$$

where t_p is the pipeline cycle time. More detailed formulations that distinguish read and write bandwidth and take into account pipeline start-up and single operand vector operations are possible, but the principle is the same.

Another aspect of the pipelined SIMD memory interface is that it cannot use cache memory effectively. In the memory-to-memory style architecture, a cache miss would disrupt arithmetic pipeline flow. In the vector register style architecture, long-stride vectors have little spatial locality, and for direct mapped or low associativity caches, strides that are a multiple of the distance between addresses in the same index set cause very high miss rates. Thus, when SIMD operations are included in a uniprocessor based on cache, memory accesses for vectors usually bypass the cache. This requires extra address monitoring to prevent memory and cache from becoming inconsistent.

It might appear that the pipelined SIMD architecture is a good match to the pipelined designs currently popular for reduced instruction set (RISC) workstations, but there are several dissimilarities. Long vectors can be processed with no data dependence between pipeline stages and no pipeline interruption by branching. The balance between instruction and data access is also shifted significantly between SISD and SIMD operation. For these and other reasons, SIMD and SISD pipelines are usually separate hardware structures in machines that include both.

3.7.3   Performance of Pipelined SIMD Computers

Many overall performance issues are common to both true and pipelined SIMD computers, such as the need to execute code under complement masks for both the true and false cases of a data dependent conditional. Unique to the pipelined SIMD architecture is the detailed behavior of the vector pipelines. If N is the limit on vector length, such as might be imposed by vector register length, then the time to do a length $L \leq N$ vector operation in a K stage pipeline with cycle time t_p is

$$T(L) = T_{start} + Lt_p, \text{where } T_{start} = T_i + (K - 1)t_p. \qquad (3.25)$$

The start-up time, T_{start}, consists of instruction issue time T_i plus the $K - 1$ cycles to fill the pipeline before any result appears. The efficiency of pipeline usage is the number of element operations performed divided by the number of cycles required.

$$E(L) = \frac{L}{(T_i/t_p) + (K-1) + L} \tag{3.26}$$

For fixed pipeline length and instruction issue time, the efficiency approaches 100% as L becomes large. Because the bound N on L limits the efficiency, memory-to-memory pipelined machines that allow operations on very long vectors achieve a higher efficiency than vector register machines that must strip mine long vector operations into length N or smaller strips. For example, if vector registers are length $N = 64$, the pipeline length is $K = 8$, and there is an issue time $T_i = t_p$ of one cycle, the efficiency limit on a single vector instruction is 89%.

A way to characterize a pipeline, introduced by Hockney and Jesshope [144], uses two parameters called r_∞ and $n_{1/2}$. The parameter r_∞ is the asymptotic operation rate, $1/t_p$, of the pipeline while $n_{1/2}$ characterizes the start-up time by measuring the vector length that achieves 50% efficiency,

$$\frac{n_{1/2}}{(T_i/t_p) + (K-1) + n_{1/2}} = 50\%, \text{ or } n_{1/2} = (K-1) + T_i/t_p. \tag{3.27}$$

With chained operations, the pipeline length effectively doubles (assuming both pipelines have length K). The second instruction issue can be overlapped with the start-up of the first pipeline, so $n_{1/2}$ increases to

$$n_{1/2} = 2K - 1 + T_i/t_p. \tag{3.28}$$

The lower efficiency of the longer pipeline is compensated by the fact that the asymptotic operation rate doubles, $r_\infty = 2/t_p$, because two operations are performed on every result exiting the chained pipelines. In terms of the two parameters, the pipeline rate in operations per second for length L vectors is

$$r_L = (Lr_\infty)/(n_{1/2} + L). \tag{3.29}$$

In comparing pipelines used for vector operations to those used in RISC uniprocessors, we have already mentioned that the lack of dependence between pipeline stages and the absence of branches during long vector operations favors SIMD pipelines. Even more important is that vector instructions do not require the overhead instructions to increment operand and result addresses, count operations, and branch to the beginning of a loop that would be used to operate on vectors in a uniprocessor. Such overhead instructions need not be fetched, issued, or executed in a pipelined SIMD processor, and a useful, probably floating-point, operation is performed on each pipeline step.

Example   A comparison of two early representatives of the load/store and memory-to-memory pipelined vector architectures serves to illustrate some of the trade-offs in a simplified environment. The Cray Research Corporation Cray-1 and the Control Data Corporation Cyber 205 were comparable machines in terms of the date they became available and the technology used in their construction. Table 3-6 gives some of the parameters of the two machines. The multiply pipeline on the Cyber 205 is longer than on the Cray-1 because it includes the memory load and store functions, which are separate pipelines on the Cray-1.

We can compare the raw pipeline speeds of the two machines operating on vectors of their respective maximum lengths. We consider vector multiply and ignore instruction issue time.

$$\text{Efficiency(Cray)} = \frac{64}{64 + 7 - 1} = 91.4\% \tag{3.30}$$

$$\text{Efficiency(Cyber)} = \frac{4096}{4096 + 20 - 1} = 99.5\% \tag{3.31}$$

The pipeline efficiency of the Cyber is higher than that of the Cray, but when the r_∞ rates are taken into account, the Cray-1 achieves 73.1 MFLOPS while the Cyber 205 achieves only 49.8 MFLOPS.

This simple comparison of pipeline speeds is far from the whole story. Consider the multiplication of two length 1024 vectors stored in memory to produce a result in memory. Taking liberties with Cray-1 assembly language and representing looping with pseudocode, the Cray-1 would do this job with a code fragment resembling Program 3-21. The mask register is assumed to be set to all ones and the length register to 64. The Cyber 205 would do the same job with a single memory-to-memory instruction

Table 3-6   Hardware parameters of the Cray-1 and Cyber 205.

Cray-1	The machine has a load/store vector architecture.
	The vector register length is 64.
	A single pipeline can run at 80 MFLOPS.
	The pipeline length is 2–14 clocks, depending on the operation.
	The floating point multiply pipeline is 7 clocks.
Cyber 205	The machine has a memory-to-memory vector architecture.
	The limit on vector length is 4096.
	A single pipeline can run at 50 MFLOPS.
	The pipeline length is 18–70 clocks.
	The floating point multiply pipeline is 20 clocks.

```
for i := 1 step 64 until 1024
      begin
           vload        V1, A(I)
           vload        V2, B(I)
           vmul         V3, V1, V2
           vstore       V3, C(I)
      end;
```

Program 3-21   Strip mined Cray code to multiply length 1024 vectors.

```
vmul   (A, 1024, 0), (B, 1024, 0), (C, ones, 1024, 0)
```

where the format is

```
vmul        operand1: (base, length, offset)
            operand2: (base, length, offset)
            result: (result base, mask base, length, offset)
```

The offset is used for stepping through very long vectors, and separate lengths are specified for each vector. The address, ones, is the starting address of a mask vector of 1024 one bits occupying 16 words.

It is clear that only one out of four vector instructions in the Cray-1 code does floating point work while the rest are overhead not required in the Cyber 205, but there are several other factors that influence overall speed. Among them are:

- In larger program fragments some operands may remain in vector registers, so two loads and a store are not always needed.
- If elements are not in sequential memory locations in the Cyber another vector instruction is needed to gather them that way.
- The scalar instructions needed for the loop in the Cray and for the parameter set up in the Cyber must be considered.

Experience with the two machines indicated that the Cray-1 was faster on most codes, but that the Cyber 205 ran faster on programs that contained very many long vector operations. This probably reflected the importance of scalar operations, for which the Cray-1 was faster, as well as the predominance of short vectors in most programs.

3.8 Vector Architecture Summary

Vector or SIMD architectures are characterized by elementary instructions that operate on all elements of vectors of some length. By using parallel hardware, organized either as multiple arithmetic units or as multiple stages in one or more pipelines, length L vectors are processed in a time less than that required for L separate element by element operations in a sequential computer. This allows SIMD architectures to exploit the SIMD parallelism available in prevalent vector operations, where the same operation is applied repeatedly to independent vector elements.

Vendors of vector computers often quote an execution rate based on vector operations on maximal length vectors, no data dependent conditionals, and as many overlapped vector executions (e.g., chaining) as the hardware will allow. It is clear that such a rate cannot be achieved in practice. The highest level characterization of the advantage of SIMD over sequential computers comes from interpreting Amdahl's law, (Equation 2.33) from Chapter 2, in the vector environment. The speedup can be rewritten as

$$S = \frac{1}{f + (1-f)/V}. \tag{3.32}$$

Here V is the speedup that can be achieved by using vector rather than scalar operations on vectorizable code, that is, that part of the computation for which vector operations can be used. The fraction of the code that is vectorizable is $(1-f)$, so f is the fraction of the computation that is scalar, or not vectorizable. V is an average value that takes into account things like average vector length and the effect of data dependent conditionals. The insight this formula gives is as in Chapter 2. A speedup of V can only be achieved if $f = 0$, meaning that all code is vectorizable. Of course, even the most vector-oriented scientific programs have an appreciable fraction of scalar code. As in characterizing pipeline overhead by $n_{1/2}$, we can calculate a fraction $f_{1/2}$ of scalar code that reduces the speedup to half its maximum value, V,

$$f_{1/2} = 1/(V-1). \tag{3.33}$$

Viewed another way, when executing a computation with a fixed fraction f of scalar work, any machine with a vector speedup greater than $V_{1/2} = 1 + 1/f$ achieves less than 50% of that speedup.

In spite of the importance of SIMD operations in many data processing applications, not all computations can be cast into a vectorizable format. Of the scalar code that is left after vectorization, some is executable in parallel, but does not involve applying the same operation to multiple data items. As we move to a discussion of MIMD machines in Chapter 4, we can think of trying to reduce the fraction f of nonvectorizable code to a smaller fraction that is not parallelizable in any way.

3.9 Bibliographic Notes

Illiac IV [147] was one of the first true SIMD computers and much of our understanding of this architectural style rests on research done at the University of Illinois in connection with this machine. The ICL DAP [56, 144] in England and the Goodyear MPP [39] in America were true SIMD machines with bit-serial PEs. The Connection Machine [139], built by Thinking Machines, Inc., also employed bit-serial PEs and sparked much debate about whether many weak PEs were superior to fewer, more powerful, PEs. Thinking Machines partially resolved this debate, at least with respect to scientific applications, with the introduction of the CM-2 [279], which could be viewed as a Connection Machine with 32 times fewer PEs, each one of which had 32-bit parallel floating point capability. A good survey appears in [144], written at a time when "parallel computers" was viewed by some as synonymous with vector and array processors.

Pipelined SIMD computers appeared early at IBM as attached processors [151] and evolved into vector instruction set additions for their high-end processors [59]. Control Data Corp. and Texas Instruments both manufactured memory-to-memory pipelined SIMD machines, the CDC STAR-100 [140] and the TI-ASC [284], respectively. CDC's follow-ons to the STAR-100 were the Cyber 203 and Cyber 205 [200]. The Cray vector supercomputers, starting with the

Cray-1 [76] are register-to-register pipelined machines with more recent systems, for example, the Cray X-MP [70], being MIMD collections of pipelined SIMD processors. A detailed, cycle level description of the Cray X-MP can be found in [245]. Register-to-register pipelined SIMD machines were also produced in Japan, with a notable example being the NEC vector computers [283]. A comparison of the performance of two Japanese machines and the Cray X-MP can be found in [207]. An excellent treatment of the fundamentals of arithmetic pipelining and pipelined SIMD computers can be found in Kogge's book [178].

Vector languages and vector language extensions have a long history. An early one was VECTRAN [234] from IBM. Virtually all of the companies producing vector computers have produced their own, machine specific, vector languages or extensions. The abilities to manipulate full arrays or sections in a single assignment statement and mask with data dependent conditionals are common to many of these languages. Automatic vectorization of sequential code, especially code written in a language like Fortran that disallows many features that would complicate compiler analysis, has become quite mature. The Parafrase compiler [184] is an early good example of this technology. Automatic vectorization allows many vector machines to be programmed sequentially, at the cost of larger program size and reduced readability of code.

Problems

3.1 Write pseudocode for the *ikj* form of matrix multiplication and describe the algorithm in words.

3.2 Counting floating point operations is a way of estimating execution time. Use it to analyze the following code fragment written in SIMD pseudocode for a true SIMD computer with N processing elements. The scalars x, y, and s and the vectors a, b, and v are all floating point. Scalar operations are done using only one of the PEs.

$$s := (x - y)/(x*x + y*y);$$
$$v[i] := s*a[i] + b[i], (0 \le i < N);$$

(a) Give the speedup obtained by executing the above code on the SIMD (vector) machine versus doing the same computation on a SISD (scalar) computer.

(b) What is the largest integer value of N for which the processing element efficiency is still at least 50%?

3.3 An SIMD computer's vector unit executes at an average rate of 100 MFLOPS and its scalar unit averages 20 MFLOPS. What is the average execution rate of this machine on an algorithm in which 90% of the work is vectorized and 10% is scalar work?

3.4 An SIMD computer has a scalar execution rate of $R_1 = 10$ MFLOPS and a vector execution rate of $R_2 = 100$ MFLOPS.

(a) What is the average execution rate for a program in which 50% of the work is scalar and 50% vector?

(b) What is the average execution rate for a program that spends half its time executing in scalar mode and the other half the time in vector mode?

3.5 Write efficient vector pseudocode for a SIMD machine with N processing elements to do the following array computation.

```
for i := 2 step 1 until N
    for j := 2 step 1 until N
        X[i, j] := (X[i, j-1] + X[i, j+1])/2;
```

3.6   The following sequential pseudocode specifies a matrix-vector multiply:

```
for i := 1 step 1 until n
    begin
        y[i] := 0;
        for j := 1 step 1 until n
            y[i] := y[i] + a[i,j]*x[j];
    end;
```

(a)   Using SIMD pseudocode, write the matrix-vector multiply for a vector processor in which memory access is unrestricted.

(b)   If the pseudocode of part (a) is executed by a true SIMD machine in which each of n PEs has direct access only to its own memory module, how should the arrays x, y, and a be stored?

3.7   In one form of scaling a set of linear equations, each row of a matrix A is multiplied by the reciprocal of the maximum absolute value of any element in that row. A sequential algorithm for this would appear as follows.

```
for i:= 1 step 1 until n
begin
    max:= 0;
    for j:= 1 step 1 until n
        if abs(A(i,j)) > max then max:= abs(A(i,j));
    r:= 1/max;
    for j:= 1 step 1 until n
        A(i,j):= r×A(i,j);
end;
```

(a)   Using high-level pseudocode for an SIMD computer, write a vector version of this algorithm.

(b)   If the SIMD machine of part (a) has separate memories for each processing element, show the storage layout required by your solution in part (a).

3.8   Back substitution in Gaussian elimination is the solution of $y = Ux$, where $y = (y_1, y_2, ..., y_n)$ is given, $x = (x_1, x_2, ..., x_n)$ is to be found and U is an upper triangular matrix of the form:

$$\begin{bmatrix} u_{11} & u_{12} & u_{13} & \cdots & u_{1n} \\ 0 & u_{22} & u_{23} & \cdots & u_{2n} \\ 0 & 0 & u_{33} & \cdots & u_{3n} \\ \cdot & \cdot & \cdot & \cdot & \cdot \\ \cdot & \cdot & \cdot & \cdot & \cdot \\ \cdot & \cdot & \cdot & \cdot \cdot \\ 0 & 0 & 0 & \cdots & u_{nn} \end{bmatrix}.$$

Working backwards from x_n this is an $R\langle n, n-1 \rangle$ recurrence system:

$$x_i = \frac{1}{u_{ii}}\left(y_i - \sum_{j=i+1}^{n} u_{ij}x_j\right), i = n, n-1, \ldots, 2, 1,$$

which can be solved in parallel by the column sweep method.

Write vector pseudocode for the column sweep and indicate the memory layout required to achieve parallelism on an SIMD machine with separate memory-arithmetic unit pairs. You may assume n arithmetic units.

3.9 The sequential pseudocode below is to be parallelized for an SIMD computer with 32 PEs.

```
for i := k step 1 until n
        x[i] := (x[i] - y[i])/y[i];
```

(a) Ignoring questions of data layout, strip mine the above loop for execution on 32 PEs. $n - k$ may be much larger than 32 but does not have to be. Express your result using the SIMD pseudocode extensions.

(b) Suppose there are 32 memory modules with module i connected to PE number i. Suppose also that x[j] and y[j] are stored in memory module (j mod 32). Modify the strip mined code of part (a) for this case.

3.10 In a "true" SIMD computer with N processing elements and N memories, it is sometimes necessary to access rows of a matrix as parallel vectors, while at other times it is necessary to access all elements of a column in parallel. Show a storage pattern for the elements of an N by N matrix that will support both these needs.

What addition to the PE hardware will allow such different accesses to be done on matrices using a "straight" storage scheme, either by rows or by columns?

3.11 Consider an SIMD or vector processor with multiple arithmetic units and a single control unit.

(a) Use vector processor pseudocode to write a program to compute the square of an $n \times n$ matrix X. Call the result Y and assume that any arithmetic unit can access any memory cell.

(b) Show how to store data (and modify the program if necessary) to do the matrix squaring in Illiac IV type machine where n arithmetic units are attached to n private memories.

3.12 Consider an SIMD computer with N PEs, each having a private memory and capable of routing by a shift of one, either to the left or right. Find a storage layout for an N by N matrix such that column sums can be done optimally, in parallel, without routing, while row sums can be done in parallel using routing but not requiring PE indexing. Show pseudocode to accomplish row and column sums with this layout.

3.13 On a machine having no maximum operation, the computation of an N element vector C whose elements are the maxima of corresponding elements of vectors A and B can be done by comparisons.

```
for i := 0 step 1 until N-1
        if A[i] > B[i] then C[i] := A[i]
            else C[i] := B[i];
```

Using vector pseudocode, show how to do this operation on an SIMD machine with N PEs. What is the efficiency?

3.14 The following calculation, expressed in sequential pseudocode is to be vectorized for a true SIMD machine of the type considered in class having N PEs.

```
for i := 1 step 1 until N
    if (a[i] ≥ 0) then
        v[i] := (w + b[i])/(b[i] + a[i])
    else
        v[i] := (w + b[i])/(b[i] - a[i] + z);
```

Assume that we can estimate the execution time accurately by counting only floating point operations. On the SIMD machine, floating point operations are done by the PEs, and we assume that a vector floating point operation takes the same unit amount of time as a scalar floating point operation on a uniprocessor. All floating point operations take the same time.

(a) Suppose that the elements of the vector a[i] have a 50% probability of being negative. Give an execution time estimate for the calculation executed sequentially on a uniprocessor.

(b) Parallelize the computation for *efficient* execution on an N PE SIMD computer of the type discussed in Section 2.3. Express the parallelized algorithm in a restricted vector pseudocode that has a direct correspondence to the machine code that would be executed so that the execution time can be estimated.

(c) Under the same assumptions on the signs of a[i] as in part (a), give an execution time estimate for your SIMD computation of part (b).

3.15 Vectorize the following computation for a vector computer with length 64 vector registers. Express the result as SIMD pseudocode using vector statements with stride one index ranges starting at 0 and having restricted length. Hint: vectorize the index calculations.

```
k := 0;
m := 0;
for i := 0 step 1 until N-1
    begin
        a[i] := b[i] + b[m];
        k := k + 1;
        if (k = 4) then {k := 0; m := m + 1};
    end;
```

3.16 In a program that solves for the roots of N quadratic equations, part of the computation is described by the following sequential pseudocode:

```
/* a[i], b[i], and c[i] are input vectors and x[i] and y[i] are output
vectors, 0 ≤ i < N. */
for i := 0 step 1 until N-1
begin
    if a[i]=0 and b[i]=0 then
        begin x[i] := 0;
        y[i] := 0;
        end;
    else if a[i]× b[i] ≥ 0 then
        begin x[i] := (a[i] + b[i])/2;
        y[i] := c[i]/x[i];
        end;
    else if a[i]×b[i] < 0 then
        begin y[i] := (a[i] - b[i])/2;
        x[i] := c[i]/y[i];
        end;
end;
```

(a) Show how this calculation would be done on a "true" SIMD machine with N processing elements. You may use pseudocode, but be sure it is written at a low enough level to describe what happens at the assembly language level. In particular, it should be low-level enough to help answer part (b).

(b) Compute the speedup and efficiency of the SIMD parallel version compared to the sequential version. Assume that a comparison takes the same amount of time as any other floating point operation. Make, state, and justify reasonable assumptions about the distribution of outcomes of the three tests.

3.17 The sequential code below is to be vectorized for an SIMD computer with N PEs.

```
for i:=1 step 1 until N
    if a[i] < L
        then b[i] := f(i)
        else b[i] := g(i);
```

The computations $f(i)$ and $g(i)$ are both vectorizable but require different numbers of floating point operations. $f(i)$ uses W_f and $g(i)$ uses W_g operations.

(a) Write vector pseudocode using a mask to vectorize the above code.

(b) If the probability of a[i] < L is p, give an expression for the efficiency of the vectorized computation, counting only work involved in the floating point operations f and g.

(c) If $p = .5$, what is the efficiency?

(d) If $W_g = 2W_f$, over what range does the efficiency vary as p goes from zero to one?

3.18 In a "true" SIMD computer with one control unit and multiple PEs some **if** statements will compile into conditional branch instructions and some will not.

(a) How does the compiler determine which **if** statements will be implemented with conditional branches?

(b) List conditions that machine language branch instructions might test in a "true" SIMD computer.

3.19 Below is a fragment of vector pseudocode for a "true" SIMD machine with P processing elements.

```
        clt     zero        ; Set mask to result of testing PE accumulators <0
        brnon   L1          ; Branch if no mask bits set
        mask                ; Set PE enables according to mask
        add     b           ; Floating add vector b to accumulators
L1:     not     mask,mask   ; Complement test vector
        brnon   L2          ; Branch if no mask bits set
        mask                ; Set PE enables
        sub     c           ; Floating subtract vector c
L2:
```

Assume the floating point operations are the only instructions that take any time, and each executes in one unit of time. (They really represent larger code bodies.) If the signs of the PE accumulators are uniformly distributed on entry to the code fragment, write an expression for the execution time with P processors. Compared to sequential execution for a length P vector, how much do the branch instructions contribute to the efficiency with P processing elements?

3.20 An SIMD computer with $N = 2^n$ PEs has an architecture and assembly language like that of the machine described in the text. It uses a PE to PE routing network with a routing register in each PE that can be used in arithmetic or moved to or from the PE accumulator. Instead of shift routing, this machine has n exchange routing operations that exchange the contents of routing registers in PE_i and PE_j, $j = i \oplus 2^k$, $0 \leq k \leq n - 1$, $0 \leq j \leq N - 1$.

(a) Describe how these routing operations can be used to sum the values in the accumulators of all N PEs.

(b) Prove that the contents of a routing register in any one source PE can be moved to an arbitrary destination PE in n or fewer routing steps.

3.21 Consider the "column sweep" algorithm for solving a linear recurrence system R(n,m).

(a) Using pseudocode extended for SIMD machines write a vector version of the algorithm. Consider PE disabling and data layout in memory.

(b) Use the MIMD extensions to the pseudocode to write a multiprocessor version of column sweep.

(c) Discuss the effect of the order, m, of the system on efficiency in relation to the maximum vector length in the SIMD case and to the number of processors in the MIMD case.

3.22 Given an $n \times n$ matrix $A = (a_{ij})$, we want to find the n column sums:

$$S_j = \sum_{i=0}^{n-1} a_{ij} \quad \text{for } j = 0, 1, \ldots, n-1,$$

using an SIMD machine with n PEs. The matrix is stored in a skewed format, as shown below. The j-th column sum S_j is stored in location β in PEM$_j$ at the end of the computation. Using the type of SIMD machine described in class, write an SIMD assembly language program for the algorithm and indicate the successive memory contents in the execution of the algorithm.

Addr.	PEM$_0$	PEM$_1$	...	PEM$_{n-1}$
	.	.		.
	.	.		.
	.	.		.
α	$a_{0,0}$	$a_{0,1}$		$a_{0,n-1}$
$\alpha + 1$	$a_{1,n-1}$	$a_{1,0}$		$a_{1,n-2}$
	.	.		.
	.	.	...	.
	.	.		.
	$a_{n-1,1}$	$a_{n-1,2}$		$a_{n-1,0}$
	.	.		.
	.	.		.
	.	.		.
β	S_0	S_1		S_{n-1}
	.	.		.
	.	.		.
	.	.		.

3.23 For an SIMD machine with N arithmetic units, write a program in vector pseudocode to multiply the absolute value of an N by N matrix, A, times an N element vector, x. The pseudocode should correspond directly to the vector assembly language level so that you can answer the performance question that follows. Assume that there are no memory access conflicts. Absolute value is not an elementary operation but must be done with data dependent conditionals.

With a random, uniform distribution of signs, what are the expected values of the speedup and efficiency with respect to an efficient single processor program?

3.24 The following sequential pseudocode is to be vectorized for an SIMD computer with N PEs.

```
for i := 1 step 1 until N
    if (v[i] < a) then x[i] := exp(v[i] - a)
        else if (v[i] > b) then x[i] := exp(b - v[i])
            else x[i] := sin(v[i] - a);
```

   (a) Write vector pseudocode with masking to do the SIMD computation. The level of the pseudocode should be low enough to use in answering part (b).

   (b) Assume sin() and exp() each take 20 floating point operations while compare and subtract are each one floating point operation. Counting only floating point operations, what are the speedup and efficiency of the SIMD code if 50% of the v[i] are between a and b and the rest are equally divided between v[i] < a and v[i] > b?

3.25 Refer to the diagram in Figure 3-21 of the notes for the 4 in 5 skewed storage of an 8×8 matrix.

   (a) List all useful patterns that can be accessed in one memory cycle. Part of the problem is characterizing a "useful pattern" for matrix access.

   (b) Given a linear P-vector $V(1, 1, 1, 1)$. Calculate word addresses in memory modules.

3.26 Turn the SIMD pseudocode in the solution to Problem 2.6 into a Fortran 90 program for upper/lower parallel prefix. Notes: If two variables declared INTEGER, say I and N, are divided in Fortran, the integer result I/N is mathematically $\lfloor I/N \rfloor$ if they are both positive. Fortran has a modulo function, MODULO(J, M) = J mod M, for integer J and M.

3.27

   (a) Assume V is a 31 element vector declared in Fortran 90 as V(0:30). Strip mine the Fortran 90 assignment

       V(1:30) = 0.5*(V(1:30) + V(0:29))

       for a vector computer of 10 PEs. That is, write three Fortran 90 assignments with length 10 vectors that accomplish the same operation.

   (b) If V is a 32 element vector declared as V(0:31), strip mine the Fortran 90 assignment

       V(1:30) = 0.5*(V(0:29) + V(2:31))

   for a vector computer of 10 PEs. The bulk of the work should be done by vector assignments of length no more than 10.

3.28 The Fortran 90 code below is to be executed on a true SIMD architecture. It is known that the values of b(i) are equally distributed between zero and one. Comparison of real numbers takes one floating point (fp) operation, and sin() and exp() each take 20 fp operations.

```
real a(1:N), b(1:N), x(1:N)
where ( b(1:N) > 0.75 )
          x(1:N) = exp( b(1:N) )
    elsewhere
          x(1:N) = sin( b(1:N) ) + exp( a(1:N) )
end where
```

   (a) If the SIMD machine has N PEs, compute the speedup and efficiency of vector execution over scalar execution of the same computation, counting only fp operations.

   (b) If the machine has only 64 PEs, add Fortran 90 code to represent strip mining the computation when N is not necessarily a multiple of 64. Compute speedup and efficiency of the strip mined code.

3.29 Assume a, b, c, r, and s are vector registers in a pipelined vector computer. The computer has separate floating point add and multiply pipelines, each of length k. Vector registers have length n. The independent pipelines can be used simultaneously by chaining, as shown below.

Chained operations

```
r          :=          a + b
s          :=          c*r
```

It takes i clock cycles to issue a vector instruction, where $i < k$. Assume both pipelines are empty when the first instruction is issued. In these chained operations, what is the average number of floating point operations per clock cycle from the start of issuing the first instruction until the completion of the second? What is the efficiency of use of the hardware in the two pipelines?

3.30 Consider the following loop for adding two vectors:

```
      DO 10 I = 1, N
          C(I)  =  A(I)  +  B(I)
   10 CONTINUE
```

What would be the differences in the machine code generated by this loop for a register-to-register pipelined vector computer and for a memory-to-memory pipelined machine? Write example machine code for both cases; point out the differences; state any assumptions about the architectures needed to interpret your answer.

3.31 Consider a pipelined vector processor with a statically scheduled multifunctional pipeline (all vector operations use the same pipeline). The pipeline has k stages, each having a delay of $1/k$ time units. The pipeline must be drained between different functions, such as addition and multiplication or additions on different pairs of vectors. Memory-access time, control-unit time, etc., can be ignored. There are sufficient numbers of temporary registers to use.

(a) Determine the number of unit time steps T_1 required to compute the product of two $n \times n$ matrices on a non pipeline scalar processor. Assume one unit time per each addition or each multiplication operation on the scalar processor.

(b) Determine the number of time steps T_k required to compute the matrix product, using the multifunction pipeline processor with a total pipeline delay of one time unit (step time is $1/k$ time units).

(c) Determine the speedup ratios T_1/T_k, when $n = 1$, $n = k$, and $n = m \cdot k$ for some large m.

3.32

(a) A pipelined vector computer has a floating point add pipeline of 6 stages and a stage cycle time of 20 ns. Characterize this vector pipeline in terms of its asymptotic rate r_∞ (in MFLOPS) and the vector length $n_{1/2}$ required for 50% efficiency. Characterize only the pipeline behavior, i.e. ignore instruction issue time.

(b) Suppose the vector computer also has a floating point multiply pipeline of 9 stages and a 20 ns cycle time. The computer allows chaining the output of the multiply pipeline to the input of the add pipeline to do a SAXPY operation. Characterize the chained pipelines in terms of $n_{1/2}$ and r_∞ (MFLOPS).

MIMD Computers or Multiprocessors

Multiple instruction stream, multiple data stream (MIMD) computers are distinguished from SIMD or vector computers by having multiple control streams as well as multiple data streams. Thus, not only may multiple data items be operated on in parallel, but also the operations applied in parallel may all be different. The most trivial example is of multiple separate computers running independently, side by side on a tabletop. Computationally challenging problems can probably not benefit from such parallelism because of the need for results produced by one computer to be rapidly available to another for use in its part of the problem. A *multiprocessor* is a single integrated system that contains multiple processors, each capable of executing an independent stream of instructions, but one integrated system for moving data among the processors, to memory, and to I/O devices.

There are several degrees of cooperation among multiple processors. They may be used to run separate jobs and share only resources of the system, such as I/O devices and storage space. In this case, data movement among processors can be confined to the operating system that manages these shared resources. This mode of operation is called *multiprogramming* and can be done with a single processor also. It is not treated in this book. We are interested in the use of multiple processors to execute one application and contribute to the solution of a unified problem. This is the realm of parallel processing, whereas multiprogramming may simply be used to run several sequential programs simultaneously. Thus, not only system resources but also problem data must be shared among processors, with some processors computing intermediate results that are used as input operands by others. If data are transferred among processors infrequently, possibly in large chunks, with long periods of independent computation in between, the multiprocessing is called *coarse-grained*, or loosely coupled. In *fine-grained*, or tightly coupled, multiprocessing, data are communicated frequently in amounts of one or a few memory words. The *granularity* of multiprocessing may be at the program level, the level of subroutines and basic blocks, loop nest, statement, or machine operation level. There is no precise line between fine- and coarse-grained multiprocessing, and even a sequential program that reads a file written by another sequential program running on another processor might be viewed as very coarse-grained multiprocessing. Our focus will be on multiprocessing at a finer grain than use of the file system or long-distance communication network would imply, although some of the design and analysis techniques we discuss apply to very coarse-grained multiprocessing also.

A question for the reader to keep in mind in the course of this chapter is the difference between many independent computers running simultaneously and a multiprocessor. This difference leads to a focus on the interactions among processors. Interactions in shared memory multiprocessors are tied to synchronization operations, so special attention should be paid to such operations. Indeed, the presence of synchronization operations is the only major difference between the instruction set of a uniprocessor and the instruction set of one processor of a multiprocessor. We will use OpenMP as a high-level shared memory multiprocessing language in this chapter. The base language is taken as Fortran 77 so that the Fortran 90 extensions of Chapter 3 can be easily contrasted with the OpenMP facilities. The wide use of Fortran in the parallel processing literature and the lack of direct support for multidimensional matrices in C are also arguments for using Fortran as the base language in this chapter, although they are not as strong as in the vector processing discussion, where Fortran has an overwhelming dominance.

4.1 Shared Memory and Message-Passing Architectures

There may be very little difference between the programmer's view of one processor of a multiprocessor and that of the single processor of an SISD or uniprocessor computer. There is no separate class of parallel instructions as is the case in vector computers. The key issue is the way in which results produced by one processor are made available to others for use as operands. Just as in SIMD, there are two basic types of MIMD or multiprocessor architectures that differ with respect to whether data are communicated explicitly from processor to processor or implicitly by way of memory storage and retrieval. The two types have architectures that differ as in Figure 4-1. These diagrams are just those of Figure 1-10(a) using the PMS notation introduced in Chapter 3. In the organization of Figure 4-1(a), the memory is shared in the sense that any of the processors can read and write it using their normal memory reference instructions, that is, the memory is shared by the processors. In the *message-passing* configuration of Figure 4-1(b), processor instruction sets have commands, say, *send* and *receive*, to communicate data to other processors and can only read and write their own private memories. To see the correspondence to SIMD memory structures, compare Figure 4-1 to Figure 3-2 and Figure 3-3.

Interprocessor *send* and *receive* instructions are characteristic of a message-passing multiprocessor, but they may be adapted from I/O instructions and not stand out in the machine instruction set. Machines of the multicomputer style of Figure 4-1(b) are also called distributed memory multiprocessors, which makes the naming somewhat more symmetric. The important point, however, is not the physical distribution of memory over multiple modules packaged with different processors but the capability, or lack thereof, for multiple processors to reference the same set of memory cells.

The two switches in Figure 4-1 (a) and (b) have similar functions. Each must connect a number of transmitters and receivers with high efficiency. An interconnecting switch is usually implemented in a distributed manner, so it is commonly called an *interconnection network*. The key characteristics of an interconnection network are bandwidth, latency, and concurrency. The bandwidth is usually specified as the *bisection bandwidth*. This is defined as the number of bytes per second of information the network can transport across an interface that partitions the processors, or processors and memories, connected to the network into two equal groups. *Latency* is the total time from transmission of data into the network to its reception at its destination. If data messages are long, one can distinguish *start-up latency*, the time from the start of transmission to reception of the first byte, from *total latency*, the time from start of transmission to receipt of the entire message. *Concurrency* is the number of independent connections the network can make simultaneously. A bus, for instance, can interconnect many processors but has a concurrency of only one.

4.1.1   Mixed-Type Multiprocessor Architectures

Many variations of multiprocessor architecture are possible. Shared and private memories are not incompatible and may be mixed in a system. Each processor in a shared memory multiprocessor may also have some private memory that other processors cannot read and write, as shown in Figure 4-2. The diagram also shows the sharing of I/O device transducers, T, and their associated controllers, K, by all the processors. If information is moved in and out of the private memories under hardware control, the memories are local or private cache. Otherwise, the program determines the use of shared or private memory for data or instructions. Some uses for private memory in a shared memory multiprocessor are for program code, read-only data, and program stack frames.

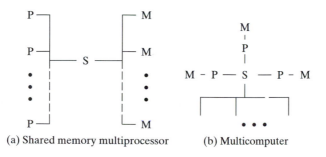

(a) Shared memory multiprocessor   (b) Multicomputer

Figure 4-1   Shared memory and message-passing multiprocessors.

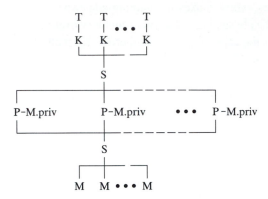

Figure 4-2   Shared memory multiprocessor with private memories.

There is also an important impact on performance if some locations in shared memory take longer to access than others. Such a computer is called a *nonuniform memory access* (NUMA) machine, as opposed to a *uniform memory access* (UMA) multiprocessor. This distinction is discussed further in connection with multiprocessor performance. It is also possible to connect few processor shared memory multiprocessors, often called *clusters*, using a communication network accessed by send and receive instructions, as shown in Figure 4-3. The shared memory of a cluster is then private with respect to other clusters.

Terminology for shared and private memories differs both historically and somewhat by the hardware or software point of view of a writer. Local, global, and distributed memory emphasize an architecture viewpoint from which memory is identified by its physical location in a system. Shared and private identify memory on the basis of the processors whose programs may reference it. Large shared memories, like large uniprocessor memories, are routinely implemented using several hierarchical types of memory and several memory modules of the same type distributed in different ways over the system. For this reason, we prefer to distinguish multiprocessor memory as shared or private rather than local, global, or distributed. It is true that shared memory is probably remote from at least some of the processors sharing it and that an advantage of private memory is that it can be integrated locally with its processor for fast access, but identifying memory by the processors that can reference it seems more general given the variability of implementations.

4.1.2   Characteristics of Shared Memory and Message Passing

Understanding that there are many variations and that the operating system and run-time software can purposely mask architectural features, we can give an initial differentiation of pure shared memory and message passing multiprocessors by listing some associated characteristics.

Shared memory multiprocessors

- Interprocessor communication is done in the memory interface by read and write instructions.

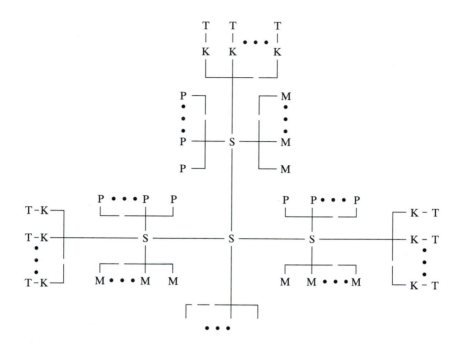

Figure 4-3 Interconnected shared memory clusters.

- Memory may be physically distributed and reads and writes from different processors, may take different amounts of time, and may collide in the interconnection network.
- Memory latency (time to complete a read or write) may be long and variable.
- Messages through the interconnecting switch are the size of single memory words (or perhaps cache lines).
- Randomization of requests (as by interleaving words across memory modules) may be used to reduce the probability of collision.

Message-passing multiprocessors

- Interprocessor communication is done by software using data transmission instructions (send and receive).
- Read and write refer only to memory private to the processor issuing them.
- Data may be aggregated into long messages before being sent into the interconnecting switch.
- Large data transmissions may mask long and variable latency in the communications network.
- Global scheduling of communications can help avoid collisions between long messages.

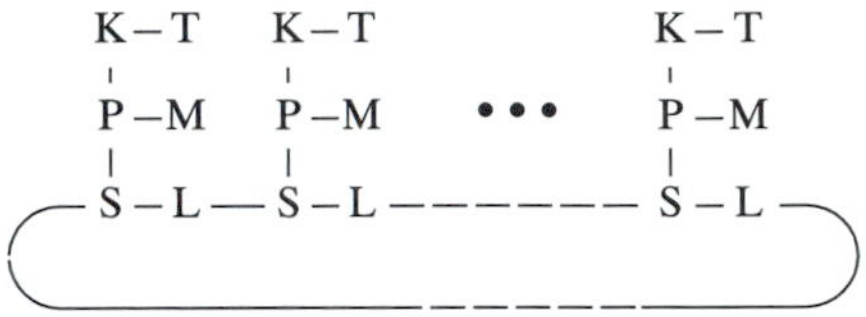

```
      K−T    K−T                 K−T
       |      |                    |
      P−M    P−M      • • •       P−M
       |      |                    |
      S−L — S−L  — — — — — —  S−L
```

Figure 4-4 Ring-connected message passing multiprocessor.

For any particular system, any of these characteristics may not hold, and at the software level, a language or runtime system may purposely make a system of one type appear to be of the opposite type. The underlying architecture, however, will usually reveal itself through performance.

As an example of the manifestation of some of the above characteristics, message passing architectures may favor coarse-grained multiprocessing. This is because send and receive operations can be designed to amortize latency over the long messages that are sent infrequently in coarse-grained programs. Shared memory multiprocessors communicate data using single word read and write, so they do not distinguish between fine- and coarse-grained computation. As a cautionary example of why things may not be so simple, a shared memory multiprocessor with hardware managed memory caches may transfer data between local cache and shared memory in units of cache lines. Such a machine might also benefit from coarse-grained operation.

4.1.3   Switching Topologies for Message Passing Architectures

Message passing multiprocessors are often distinguished from one another by the topology of their interconnection networks. For example, Figure 4-4 shows a ring network interconnecting processor-memory pairs. The links, L, shown in the PMS diagram are often suppressed but should be made explicit when they are major performance determiners as they are here. The links can be either unidirectional or bidirectional. Each has a bandwidth, B, in bytes per second in a given direction and a latency, R, from starting a send into the link to the delivery of the first byte at the other end. The network may be used for a single processor-to-processor transmission at a time or pipelined, so that different messages can occupy all links simultaneously. The behavior of the ring is a function of the number, n, of processors it connects.

Example   The ring interconnection of Figure 4-4 is just one way of building the interconnecting switch of Figure 4-1(b). Considered as a single (composite) switch, what are the bisection bandwidth, latency, and concurrency of the ring? Assume bidirectional links and that the ring is used in a pipelined manner.

Any bisection of the ring cuts two bidirectional links, for a bisection bandwidth of $4B$. At the maximum, a message may be travelling in each direction on each link, for a total of $2P$ messages simultaneously. Because this is larger than the number of processors, it assumes a processor can send a second message before receiving a reply to the first.

Given the start-up latency R of each link and assuming no overhead in passing a message through an individual switch on the ring, both maximum and average start-up latency for the ring can be computed. The maximum latency is just $\lfloor n/2 \rfloor R$. The average is obtained by summing the products of latency to a processor and the number of processors with that latency and dividing by the number of destinations, $n - 1$. There are two processors for each distinct latency, except for the maximum, where there are two processors if n is odd and one if n is even. Thus, the average latency, L_a, is

$$L_a = \left(2R \sum_{i=1}^{\lfloor n/2 \rfloor - 1} i + (1 + n \bmod 2)R\lfloor n/2 \rfloor \right)/(n-1),$$

$$= R\lfloor n/2 \rfloor(\lfloor n/2 \rfloor + n \bmod 2)/(n-1), \tag{4.1}$$

$$= \frac{R}{n-1}\left\lfloor \frac{n}{2} \right\rfloor\left\lceil \frac{n}{2} \right\rceil.$$

For large n, the overall start-up latency is about $n/4$ times the link start-up latency.

The example is simplified and blurs the distinction between long and short messages. We will take up the details of message passing, including the difference between message start up and link start up and the influence of cut-through versus store and forward routing, in the discussion of distributed memory architectures.

Other important topologies for message passing multiprocessors include the rectangular mesh and the hypercube. In a two-dimensional rectangular mesh, a processor has links to the two adjacent processors in its row and the two adjacent processors in its column. Processors at the ends of rows or columns either have fewer connections or link to the processors at the opposite ends by *wrap around* connections. This makes the topology of each individual row or column that of a ring. Figure 4-5 shows a 3×4 rectangular mesh with wrap around. Processor, memory, and I/O groups are abbreviated by C. Meshes can also be of three or more dimensions.

The hypercube topology of dimension d connects $N = 2^d$ processors numbered 0 through $2^d - 1$. Processor i connects to d other processors so that processors whose numbers differ by 2^j, $0 \leq j \leq d - 1$, are connected by a link. Figure 4-6 shows the form of a four-dimensional hypercube. It also makes it clear that a d-dimensional hypercube can be recursively constructed from two $d - 1$ dimensional hypercubes by connecting correspondingly numbered processors of the first and second $d - 1$ cubes and adding 2^{d-1} to the numbers of all processors in the second cube. A message may have to traverse up to d links to go from one of the 2^d processors to another. This makes latency proportional to the logarithm of the number of processors and is a major advantage of the hypercube for connecting many processors. A disadvantage is that the number of links to each processor grows with N, so processors already in the system may need to be changed if more are added. Hypercube concurrency and total bandwidth depend on whether links are bidirectional and on how many simultaneous messages a processor may transmit.

4.1.4   Direct and Indirect Networks

The distinctions among interconnection networks for shared memory and message passing multiprocessors are often in the details of the low-level switching protocol rather than in high-level switch topology. For example, the ring topology shown in Figure 4-4 connecting message passing processors could be packaged as shown in Figure 4-7 to connect processors to shared memories in the style of Figure 4-1(a). Nevertheless, a useful distinction in switch topologies is between the indirect networks often used in shared memory architectures and the direct networks more common to message passing architectures. In an *indirect* network, resources such as processors, memories, and I/O devices are attached externally to a switch that may have a complex internal structure of interconnected switching nodes, as in Figure 4-7. A *direct* network associates resources with the individual nodes of a switching topology, as in Figure 4-4.

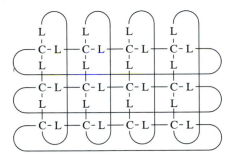

Figure 4-5   Two-dimensional mesh multiprocessor.

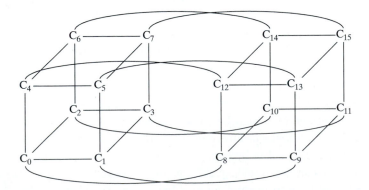

Figure 4-6   Hypercube multiprocessor connection.

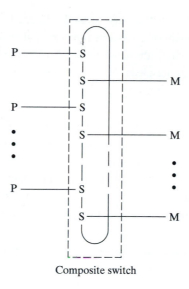

Composite switch

Figure 4-7 An indirect ring topology network for a shared memory architecture.

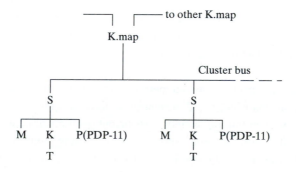

Figure 4-8 Architecture of the Cm*.

4.1.5 Classification of Real Systems

We sometimes think that the first machines of a given type are of a more pure type than those developed after the field has progressed, but this is not true in general. An important early research multiprocessor called Cm*, which was built at Carnegie Mellon University, is a good illustration of the unclear division between the various types of multiprocessor. The PMS diagram of the system, which consisted of clusters of PDP-11 computers, is sketched in Figure 4-8. Processors with memory and I/O devices form computer modules (Cm), which are grouped into a cluster by being linked by a cluster bus. Processors in different clusters can communicate through a set of interconnected communication controllers, called K.maps. The PDP-11 machines were small computers with a very limited address length. The Cm* used memory mapping to both extend the amount of accessible memory and as the mechanism for interprocessor data transfer. The way in which the Cm* system transmitted data illustrates a mixture of shared memory and message passing ideas. There are at least three different answers to the question, "Is Cm* a shared memory multiprocessor?"

- At the level of the microcode in the K.map, there were explicit send and receive instructions and message passing software. This is one of the characteristics associated with message passing and would indicate that Cm* was not a shared memory multiprocessor.
- At the level of the PDP-11 instruction set, the machine had shared memory. There were no send and receive instructions. Any memory address could be accessed by any processor in the system using read and write instructions, a clear indication that Cm* was a shared memory machine.
- Two operating systems were built for the machine. User processes under these operating systems could not share any memory. They communicated by making operating system calls to pass messages between processes. Thus, the applications programmer, as opposed to the systems programmer, wrote programs for a message passing multiprocessor.

Access to memory using a processor's read and write instructions took different amounts of time depending on whether the memory was attached to the processor, its cluster, or another cluster. The relative inefficiency of accessing the memory of another processor was one reason for supporting a process model that required operating system calls to communicate data among processors.

The artificial division between shared memory and message passing multiprocessors does allow us to organize our knowledge and present an orderly progression of ideas. The primary issue in shared memory programming is finding sufficient parallelism in an algorithm and dividing the work among the multiple processors. Message passing multiprocessor programming brings the additional problem of placing data in memories associated with the processors that will use it or that will produce it as intermediate results. We will start by discussing the topic of programming shared memory architectures and take up the added complexity of data placement afterwards in Chapter 5.

4.2 Overview of Shared Memory Multiprocessor Programming

Multiprocessors can certainly exploit vector parallelism and can, thus, execute versions of the algorithms suitable to SIMD, but the appearance of the algorithm may change, so it is instructive to look at a multiprocessor version of the recurrence solver whose SIMD pseudocode is Program 3-9. We consider a general recurrence system $R(n, n - 1)$. Preliminary pseudocode for a shared memory multiprocessor might appear as in Program 4-1.

To understand this code, we must imagine several things about its operation. First, processes must receive a private copy of i at the time they are forked from the initial process, and second, all processes must proceed together through the loop on j, so that the final value of an element, say x[k], is available just before it is accessed by processes having values of $i > k$. Additionally, the **join** operation should wait for the forked processes to complete and allow one of them to proceed. The argument n tells the **join** how many processes to wait for without explicitly identifying them. These ideas must be made more precise to have a coherent semantics for shared memory multiprocessor programming. Although the purpose of a multiprocessor is to execute processes on distinct physical processors, we use the term *processes* instead of *processors* when discussing programs because the general concepts are applicable to more than just the one process per processor case that we assume initially.

```
shared n, a[n, n], x[n], c[n];
private i, j;
for i := 1 step 1 until n-1 fork DOROW;
i := n; /* Initial process handles i = n. */
DOROW:   x[i] := c[i];
         for j := 1 step 1 until i-1
             x[i] := x[i] + a[i, j]*x[j];
         join n;
```

Program 4-1   Preliminary multiprocessor recurrence solver.

The appearance of column sweep differs from SIMD to MIMD. In MIMD, the loop over rows, i, creates a process to do each row. In SIMD, the loop over i is implicit in the vector operations. The loop over columns, j, is the outer loop in SIMD with an implicit inner loop over i internal to the vector instructions. In MIMD, the loop over i appears to be the outer loop creating processes with inner loops over j. In spite of appearance, the two programs are identical with respect to the order of execution of the multiply-adds. Multiply-adds for different values of i are executed simultaneously, either by separate PEs of the SIMD machine or by separate processors of the multiprocessor.

4.2.1   Data Sharing and Process Management

Even the simple introduction to MIMD operation in Chapter 1 showed the need to distinguish between private variables, with one copy per process, and shared variables. Another aspect of the data sharing problem arises in its interaction with *process management*, the creation and termination of processes. The **fork** operation is a simplified way for one process to initiate another, but we see from the need for each process to have a separate value of i in Program 4-1 that parameter passing is also a concern in instantiating processes. The mechanisms of parameter passing for function call in sequential languages can also be used for process instantiation in parallel languages. The variable i should be passed by value to the new process so that its private copy of i is set to the current value of i private to the process doing the fork. The shared arrays $a[,]$, $x[ ]$, and $c[ ]$ should be passed by reference, both to avoid copying of the shared variables and to allow x to be written. We can sharpen up the parameter passing specification by replacing **fork** with a **create** operation that is followed by a procedure name and parameters in the same way as a procedure call. The difference is that **create** starts a new instruction stream executing the procedure in parallel with the process doing the create, while the latter process continues without waiting for a return.

If we use **create** to instantiate processes, a reasonable way to handle process termination is to have created processes quit at the end of the procedure. A process that invokes the procedure with a **call** returns to the caller at the end of the procedure in the usual way. Thus, a **return** in a procedure that can be invoked by either a **call** or **create** is interpreted as **quit** if the procedure instance resulted from a **create** and as a sequential **return** if it was called. This form of process termination makes it necessary to use an explicit counter to determine when all processes have completed, as opposed to the implicit counter needed to implement **join** n. A **quit** statement can be used to terminate a created process regardless of its position in the procedure hierarchy. Replacing **fork** and **join** and their associated parameter passing ambiguities by create, the recurrence solver would appear as in Program 4-2.

```
procedure dorow(value i, done, n, a, x, c)
        shared n, a[n, n], x[n], c[n], done;
        private i, j;
        x[i] := c[i];
        for j := 1 step 1 until i-1
            x[i] := x[i] + a[i, j]*x[j];
        done := done - 1;
        return;
end procedure

shared n, a[n, n], x[n], c[n], done;
private i;
done := n;
for i := 1 step 1 until n-1
        create dorow(i, done, n, a, x, c);  /* Create n–1 procedures. */
i:= n;
call dorow(i, done, n, a, x, c);            /* Call the nth one. */
while (done ≠ 0)  ;      /*Loop until all procedure instances finished. */
        ⟨ code to use  x[]  ⟩
```

Program 4-2   Multiprocessor recurrence solver with parameter passing by **create**.

There is a possible confusion about name scope that can arise. The distinction between shared and private variables has no conceptual connection with the textual scope of variable names within the procedure hierarchy or file structure of a program. The confusion arises from a tendency to think of variables global to the procedure and its invoker as shared and those local to the procedure as private. This is an incorrect association of ideas. It would be perfectly sensible to have a variable local to the procedure `dorow` shared by all processes executing the procedure but not needed by the caller, and a private variable might appear that is globally referenced by several procedures invoked by a chain of calls in a single process. We will take care to use *local* and *global* to distinguish textual name scope and *shared* and *private* to refer to parallel scope describing access by multiple processes. Such care has not always been taken in the literature, and some multiprocessor languages have constructs that artificially connect the two concepts.

4.2.2   Synchronization

The major problem with Program 4-1 and its revised version, Program 4-2, is that there is no guarantee that processes proceed together through the loop over j. The program is only correct if a process i executes the j-th iteration of the loop over columns, and, thus, reads the value of $x[j]$, after process j has completed the $j-1$st iteration, and, thus, finished the computation of $x[j]$. As they stand, there is nothing in the programs to guarantee this. The guarantee must come from explicit synchronization operations. A *synchronization* operation delays the progress of one or more processes until some condition is satisfied. The condition can involve the progress of some other process(es), in which case it is a *control-based* synchronization, or the status of some variable, making the synchronization *data based*.

The natural way to synchronize Program 4-2 is based on the availability of the final value of $x[j]$ and uses a data-based synchronization known as producer/consumer. *Producer/consumer* synchronization associates a one bit full/empty state with each variable and uses synchronized read and write operations to access the value of the variable only when it has a specified state. The most important synchronized access operations are **produce**, which waits for the variable to be empty, writes its value, and sets it full, and **consume**, which waits for the variable to be full, reads its value, and sets it empty. Other operations on producer/consumer variables are **void**, which initializes the state to empty, **copy**, which waits for full and reads, but does not set empty, and passive tests of the full/empty state.

The MIMD recurrence solver program can be synchronized with respect to access to $x[j]$ as shown in Program 4-3. The pseudocode syntax assumed for producer/consumer variables is

```
produce ⟨shared var.⟩ := ⟨expression⟩
consume ⟨shared var.⟩ into ⟨private var.⟩
copy ⟨shared var.⟩ into ⟨private var.⟩
void ⟨shared var.⟩
```

Program 4-3 is almost in a form that would run correctly on a shared memory multiprocessor that supports the primitive operations introduced. There is one remaining problem that exposes an issue that is fundamental to the operation of all synchronizations.

4.2.3   Atomicity and Synchronization

The remaining problem involves the completion counter, `done`. The statement

```
done := done - 1;
```

may be executed simultaneously by several processes, but this statement is not a single operation. Almost all machines will read the value of done into a register, subtract one from it, and store the result back into memory. An incorrect result would be obtained if two processes read the value of done in some order, subtracted one from their respective registers, and wrote the results back in some order. In this case, done would end up decremented by one instead of two. A similar, but more subtle aspect of the same problem is that a simple read or write of a variable may take more than one operation. Numerous parallel programmers have been surprised by the failure of a program that ran correctly on a 64-bit computer when moved to a machine that supports 64-bit operations with 32-bit instructions.

```
procedure dorow(value i, done, n, a, x, c)
        shared n, a[n,n], x[n], c[n], done;
        private i, j, sum, priv;
        sum = c[i];
        for j := 1 step 1 until i-1
            {copy x[j] into priv;/*Get x[j] when available. */
            sum := sum + a[i, j]*priv;}
        produce x[i] := sum;/* Make x[i] available to others. */
        done := done - 1;
        return;
end procedure

shared n, a[n, n], x[n], c[n], done;
private i;
done := n;
for i:= 1 step 1 until n-1
        { void x[i];
            create dorow(i, done, n, a, x, c); }
i:= n;
void x[i];
call dorow(i, done, n, a, x, c);
while (done ≠ 0) ;
            ⟨ code to use x[] ⟩
```

Program 4-3   Recurrence solver producer/consumer synchronized on x[j].

The synchronization concept underlying the problems described is that of atomicity. Informally, an *atomic* operation is one that takes place indivisibly with respect to other parallel operations. All synchronizations rely on atomicity in some form. A **produce** operation must write a new value and set full atomically with the discovery that the variable is empty. Another process must not simultaneously discover the variable is empty and attempt to write it. Atomic operations are important in operating systems for uniprocessors, where parallel processing is achieved by time multiplexing a single processor using interrupts. In that environment, it is possible to make a sequence of operations atomic by disabling interrupts to prevent time multiplexing during the operations. Those who have been introduced to atomicity in the single processor setting must be careful to remember that multiprocessor atomic operation has nothing whatever to do with interrupts. Even with interrupts disabled on all processors, there are many running processors whose activity must be controlled to make a composite operation atomic.

One way, but not the only way, to implement atomic operations on shared variables in a multiprocessor is by *mutual exclusion*. In this method, atomic operations on shared variables are made into sections of code that mutually exclude each other's execution. Only one process may be executing within a mutually exclusive code region at a time. A mutual exclusion region is called a *critical section*. A multiprocessor may use a pair of statements `critical` and `end critical` to bracket mutually exclusive code in a control-based synchronization. If an operation on one set of shared variables must be made atomic with respect to parallel operations on the same set, but not with respect to operations on other disjoint sets, a name may be associated with each critical section. Critical sections of the same name exclude each other but may execute concurrently with critical sections of different names.

The final, synchronized, multiprocessor recurrence solver is shown in Program 4-4. Note that the use of different synchronizations, a data-based synchronization for x[j] and a control-based synchronization for done, is pedagogical. The critical section could be replaced by

> `consume` done `into` pdone;
> `produce` done := pdone - 1;

where pdone is declared private and done is initialized to full with value n. The ability to replace one synchronization with another is quite general, and synchronization methods are chosen on the basis of efficiency and ease of use rather than on the basis of intrinsic capability.

4.2.4 Work Distribution

Up to this point we have imagined that there are n processors executing the recurrence solver, one for the original and one for each of the created processes. If this is the case, the work load is poorly balanced. The process with $i = 1$ terminates without executing the loop over j, while that with $i = n$ executes it $n - 1$ times. An efficiency calculation similar to that for the SIMD recurrence solver gives an efficiency of about 50%. In general, the number, P, of processors is much less than n, for otherwise the amount of work per process would be far too small to justify the use of a multiprocessor to solve the problem. In this case, a decision must be made about which values of i are handled by each process. The discussion assumes one process per processor. More processes could be created than there are processors, and the run-time or operating system could manage the assignment of processes to processors. The work assignment decision must still be made, so we will discuss it as if it were explicit in the MIMD code.

The values of i can be divided into groups of n/P and each group assigned to a processor. If the groups consist of consecutive values of i, called *block mapping*, the load imbalance remains. Load balancing can be improved in the recurrence solver by *cyclic mapping*, where processor p, $0 \le p < P$, is assigned the values of i such that $p = i \pmod{P}$. See Problem 4.7. Both block and cyclic mapping are examples of *prescheduled* work distribution, where the pattern of assignment

```
procedure dorow(value i, done, n, a, x, c)
        shared n, a[n,n], x[n], c[n], done;
        private i, j, sum, priv;
        sum := c[i];
        for j := 1 step 1 until i-1
            {copy x[j] into priv;
              sum := sum + a[i, j]*priv;}
        produce x[i] := sum;
        critical/* Lock out other processes. */
            done := done - 1;/* Decrement shared done. */
        end critical/* Allow other processes. */
        return;
end procedure

shared n, a[n, n], x[n], c[n], done;
private i;
done := n;
for i:= 1 step 1 until n-1
        { void x[i];
          create dorow(i, done, n, a, x, c); }
i:= n;
void x[i];
call dorow(i, done, n, a, x, c);
while (done ≠ 0) ;
        ⟨ code to use x[] ⟩
```

Program 4-4   Final, synchronized, multiprocessor recurrence solver.

of *i* values to processes is determined by the programmer or compiler when the program is constructed. The alternative to prescheduling is *self-scheduling*. In this method, a shared value of *i* is
maintained, and each process atomically reads and increments it whenever it completes work for
a previous value of *i*. This method dynamically balances load, because processors doing more
computation for their *i* values will get fewer values before the supply runs out.

4.2.5   Many Processes Executing One Program

The ability to have a number of processes, $P \neq n$ allows us to decouple process creation from the
parallel loop over *i* in the recurrence solver. Processes can be created at the beginning of the program, execute a common set of code that distributes work in the parallel loop by either prescheduling or self-scheduling, and terminate at the end of the program. This style of shared memory
multiprocessor programming is known as *single program, multiple data*, or SPMD, in similarity
to the SIMD and MIMD notations. In this style, multiple processes, each distinguished by a
unique process identifier, $0 \leq id \leq P - 1$, execute a single program simultaneously but not necessarily synchronously. Private data may cause processes to execute if-then-else statements differently or to execute a loop a different number of times. The SPMD style of programming is

almost the only choice for managing many processes in a so-called *massively parallel processor* (MPP) with hundreds or thousands of processors. Distinct programs for each processor are simply intractable in this case.

Process creation for a SPMD program is shown in Program 4-5. The shared number, P, of processors and a unique private process identifier, id, are made available to all the processes executing the parallel main program, parmain, whose declaration must specify that the private variable id is passed by value. Depending on the implementation details, processes may be required to synchronize before ending parmain, or exit may be able to automatically wait for processes that have not finished. The variables P and id make up a rudimentary parallel environment in which the MIMD processes execute. Other items involved with process management and synchronization operations are natural additions to the parallel environment, as we will see when we discuss the implementation of such operations.

```
shared P;
private id;
for id := 0 step 1 until P-2
        create parmain(id, P);
id := P-1;
call parmain(id, P);
call exit();
```

Program 4-5   SPMD process creation and termination.

The parallel main program, now relieved of process management, can concentrate on data sharing, work distribution, and synchronization. A parallel main program for the recurrence solver is shown in Program 4-6. It uses the barrier synchronization mentioned in Chapter 1 to ensure that all processes reach a common point in the program, the barrier, before any of them proceed past it. The purpose of the first barrier is to see that all of x[] is initialized before computation begins on any of it, and the second barrier prevents use of x[] before it is all computed. The **forall** statement specifies a parallel loop whose work is distributed over the *P* processes. The user could be required to modify the forall by a work distribution strategy such as block, cyclic, or self-scheduled, or a clever compiler might analyze the body of the parallel loop to make the choice automatically.

Use of a **forall** usually implies that the loop body instances for different values of the loop variable are independent and can be executed in any order or in parallel. In cases like Program 4-6, where there is synchronized communication of values among loop instances, some restrictions apply to scheduling. In the **forall** i loop of Program 4-6, no value of i should be assigned to a process before all preceding values have been assigned. This prevents infinite waits at the copy operation. Some authors distinguish parallel loops with communication among body instances by calling them **doacross** while calling parallel loops with completely independent body instances **doall**.

```
procedure parmain(value id, P)
      shared P, n, a[n, n], x[n], c[n];
      private id, i, j, sum, priv;

      forall i := 1 step 1 until n
          void x[i];
      barrier;
      forall i := 1 step 1 until n
          begin
              sum := c[i];
              for j := 1 step 1 until i-1
                  {copy x[j] into priv;
                   sum := sum + a[i, j]*priv;}
              produce x[i] := sum;
          end
      barrier;
      〈 code to use x[] 〉
end procedure
```

Program 4-6   SPMD program for the recurrence solver.

The recurrence solver example is too simple an algorithm to make a good multiprocessor programming case study, but it has allowed us to introduce the major issues in shared memory MIMD programming with an example that can be understood at the lowest level. The mechanisms to address the various parallel programming issues that arose in the example were cast in the form of parallel programming language primitives. This is convenient but by no means necessary. The mechanisms can be built directly in terms of low-level primitives, embodied in macros, or called as run-time system library routines. We will continue to use the convenience of expressing mechanisms as programming language primitives as we discuss the basic issues of process management, data sharing, work distribution, and synchronization in a broader context.

4.3 Shared Memory Programming Alternatives and Scope

So far, we have not discussed the implementation of the mechanisms used to support parallel programming. Some can be supported fairly directly by hardware, while others are software level constructs consisting of nontrivial chunks of low-level code. An example is producer/consumer synchronization. Because it requires a variable to have a state as well as a value and needs a way for processes to wait for the correct state, it is a composite operation on many multiprocessors. However, there are architectures that have an efficient hardware waiting mechanism and support producer/consumer synchronization at the hardware level of memory read and write. There is a lack of agreement on which parallel programming primitives are fundamental, and, thus, a wide variation in what different machines support efficiently. The following sections discuss the variation and demonstrate implementations of mechanisms that may fit the programming problem in terms of others that may be available on a particular system.

Many parallel programming concepts arose in the operating systems environment, where concurrent operation is obtained by using interrupts to share one processor among many processes. The existence of many processors, so that many processes run simultaneously without need for context switching, and the decoupling of interrupts from concurrent operation combine to make some concepts that seem similar behave very differently in the multiprocessor and operating system environments. Some of these differences will be pointed out as new mechanisms are introduced.

4.3.1   Process Management—Starting, Stopping, and Hierarchy

The concept of a fork appears in the Unix operating system. A Unix fork replicates a Unix process, which has a large amount of associated structure. Not only is the memory state replicated to make the new process, but things such as process priority and open I/O channels are also associated with the new process. Processes with considerable associated structure are often called heavy weight processes. In a shared memory multiprocessor, it is possible to start a new stream of instructions executing by simply supplying a program counter value to an idle processor. The new process is very light weight and is often called a *thread* to distinguish it from the type of heavy weight process encountered in Unix and other operating systems. The words *task*, *chore*, and *stream* have been used to denote various forms of parallel process by different authors, with little consistency. We will use the historically earliest term, *process*, to denote a parallel activity when a weight-independent generic term is needed.

An important property that may or may not be associated with a process is its relation to other processes. Operating systems processes most often implement a parent/child relationship among processes with the parent able to exercise some degree of control over child processes, most often the ability to terminate a child. Other mechanisms can be used to allow operating system control over process termination, and correct user programs can cause processes to terminate themselves at the right point, so a flat process hierarchy with no relationship structure is also possible.

Message passing machines must establish a new address space when a process is started on another processor. Shared memory machines may or may not do so. We have seen that private variables are important to multiprocessor programming. These may either be handled by the compiler incorporating a process identifier into the access to a private variable or by having a different memory map associated with each process. Processes usually do not share registers or primary cache but might share second-level cache among a few processors if the hardware can implement this cost effectively.

Both *fork* and *create* are statement oriented operations, but parallel languages also have block structured process management constructs. Figure 4-9 shows nested use of the *cobegin/coend* mechanism for defining *parallel regions*. The diagram arranges statement sections vertically under the label *Pi* of the process that executes them. Compound statements (sections) enclosed by {} are executed in parallel. A separator, such as *par*, may be required by a language to distinguish parallel from sequential execution of the sections. The block structured nature of cobegin/coend demands that they appear in nested pairs, a requirement not imposed on fork/join or create/quit. In its simple form, the cobegin/coend construct ties process management to work distribution, because the statement sections to be executed by each process are specified explicitly.

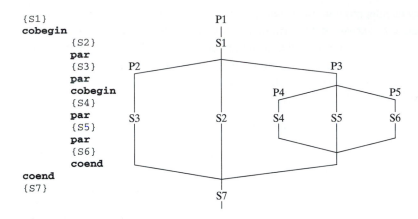

Figure 4-9 Nested serial-parallel execution using cobegin/coend.

The problem of process management is closely tied to that of processor management, but processors, being physical resources, are managed by the operating system rather than by parallel programming constructs. To yield good parallel performance, and even to avoid deadlock, the operating system must provide an execution model very close to that of a dedicated processor for every process. If many processes are time multiplexed on fewer processors, a given process must run often enough that other processes are not blocked waiting for a result it may produce. Time multiplexing may make individual processes execute slower than physical processors, but the environment should be that of all processes of a program making simultaneous progress at some rate of speed. In this method of allocating processors to processes the processes of a parallel program are said to be *coscheduled*. Operating system guarantees like coscheduling make it possible for a programmer to write good parallel code without accommodating the detailed scheduling policies of a specific system.

4.3.2   Data Access by Parallel Processes

Efficiency may be gained if the private variables of a process are placed in a memory that is private to the processor on which the process runs. Multiple copies of a private variable in the same memory may still be needed if several processes share a processor. Program stack, temporary variables, and code are types of data that are natural candidates for private storage. Program code is shared among all processes in a SPMD program, but because the code is read-only, no inconsistency will arise from making a private copy in each processor. Such data is called *cacheable* because it can be moved to a processor's cache without any overhead to keep the cache consistent with other caches or with shared memory. Note that loading a variable into a register makes that copy private, and inconsistent values may then exist in different processors. This can present special problems for optimizing compilers that attempt to maximize register reuse and thus the dwell times of variables in registers.

We use the term *parallel scope* of a variable to specify whether it is private or how it is shared among processes. With a block structured process management method such as cobegin/coend, the specification of shared and private variables is done on entry to the block and is thus closely tied to the lexical structure of the program. If procedures are called from within a *cobegin/coend* block, the specification of whether the local and global variables of the procedure are shared or private must be done explicitly. Such variables are outside the lexical scope of the cobegin/coend block but in its dynamic scope. All four possible combinations are useful. Beginning parallel programmers take the usefulness of global-shared and local-private variables for granted. Local-shared variables are used for interprocess communication among processes executing one procedure in an SPMD mode. It is an artificial work-around to declare such variables global when they are accessed only within a single procedure. Global-private variables are used when a group of procedures cooperate to do independent, data parallel computations. A package of linear equation solving routines that communicate through global private variables, for example, could be called by different individual processes within a *cobegin/coend* block to solve independent sets of linear equations in parallel.

If the parallel scope of a previously declared variable can be specified anew on entry to a nested *cobegin* block, then a hierarchical structure of parallel scopes arises. Figure 4-10 shows the possibilities for a depth two nesting of parallel regions. If all variables are actually located in a shared memory, then a private declaration only requires allocating a replicated copy of the variable for each process in the new parallel region. The initial values on entry and final values on exit need to be specified. Some parallel languages have *copyin* and *copyout* directives for this purpose, as does OpenMP, described in Section 4.4. If storage is to be partitioned between physically private and shared memories, the situation is more complex. A variable X may be placed in processor private memory inside the first parallel region but must be represented by n copies in shared memory inside the second region. The placement decision can be especially troublesome if the second *cobegin* is in another procedure, outside the static scope of the first *cobegin* but inside its dynamic scope. The language implementer, and perhaps the programmer, benefit from measurable simplification if the parallel scope of a variable may only be declared once. New variables can supply the different parallel scopes desired on entry to a new parallel region.

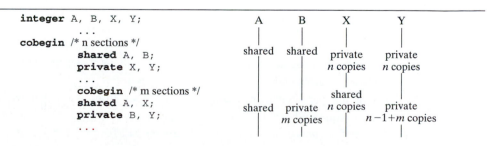

Figure 4-10   Nested parallel scopes of variables.

We briefly introduced the idea of passing parameters to a new process in connection with the *create* operation. If both shared and private variables are stored in physically shared memory, there is little intrinsic restriction on parameter passing. A private variable stored in a physically private memory cannot be passed by reference to a new process that may run on another processor. Call-by-value or call-by-value/result are the only ways to pass such private parameters, and call-by-reference can only be used for variables of shared scope. Even in shared address space systems, where it is feasible to pass a private variable to a created process by reference, doing so may be undesirable because the private variable becomes shared by the created and creating processes without an explicit declaration. When a shared variable is passed by reference, it must be remembered that during the shorter of the two lifetimes of the creating and created processes such a variable may be modified and/or read by either one. Thus, even a variable that is read-only in a created procedure can cause a synchronization problem unless it is passed by value, as we saw for the parameter *i* in Program 4-2.

The sharing of I/O devices by parallel processes has some similarities to sharing variables but also some differences. Like memory, an I/O device may be accessible to all processors in a system or physically connected to only one of them. I/O devices, however, are sequential and are usually accessed with a smallest unit of transaction, the byte, which is much smaller than the unit that must be kept coherent. Randomly interleaved output lines from different processes might be meaningful in some cases but interleaved characters would not. Because the operating system is usually involved in I/O, it can solve the accessibility and synchronization problems. Truly cooperative, parallel I/O requires random (or direct) access I/O devices so that each process may deal with a disjoint region of data.

4.3.3   Work Distribution

Work distribution is often closely tied to process management under the principle that a process is not needed unless there is work for it. Because it is hard to get much parallel activity by writing each section of parallel code in a *cobegin/coend* block explicitly, parallel regions are more often tied to a *forall* construct, designating that all instances of a loop body for different index values can be executed in parallel. The potential parallelism is equal to the number of values of the loop index and is usually much larger than the number of processors (or processes if there is time multiplexing) that are used to execute the parallel region. Large parallelism is less likely with explicitly written parallel code sections. The problem becomes one of allocating a number of discrete parallel tasks to a different number of parallel processes. Allocation can be done at program generation time by the programmer, or the compiler, or both, or at execution time by the run-time system or in-line program code.

Because much of the parallelism in a computation comes from work that would be expressed by loops in a sequential program, it is important to have work distribution mechanisms for parallel forms of sequential loops. Figure 4-11 shows SPMD code for one of np processes having identifier me executing its portion of a prescheduled loop

```
forall i := lwr step stp until upr
```

```
shared lwr, stp, upr, np;              shared lwr, upr, np;
private i, lb, ub, me;                 private i, me;
/* Compute private lower and upper bounds   for i := lwr + me*stp step np*stp
from lwr, upr, stp, process number me                        until upr
and number np of processes. */              ⟨loop body(i)⟩;
for i := lb step stp until ub
        ⟨loop body(i)⟩;
```

(a) Block mapping   (b) Cyclic mapping

Figure 4-11 Prescheduled loop code for an individual process.

```
shared lwr, stp, upr, np, isync;
private i;
barrier
        void isync;
        produce isync := lwr;
end barrier
while (true)
begin
        consume isync into i;
        if (i > upr) then                        mutual
            {produce isync := i;                 exclusion
             break;}   /* End while loop */   or
        else
            {produce isync := i + stp;
                ⟨loop body(i)⟩;}
end
```

Figure 4-12 Self-scheduling code for each process.

under both block and cyclic mapping. Block mapping requires computing lower and upper bounds for each process. See Problem 4.13. Figure 4-12 shows self-scheduling code for one process executing the same *forall*. Various forms of synchronization could be used for self-scheduling. The *produce/consume* used to update isync could be replaced by a critical section surrounding accesses to isync. The shared isync index is initialized using a variation on the barrier synchronization. Because parallel execution is the norm in SPMD programs, a way to introduce serial execution is needed. Choosing a particular process to execute the serial code is not very useful if np is not known, although the process with $id = 0$ is a reasonable choice. Another way is to associate a code body with a barrier, say by placing it between **barrier** and **end barrier** statements. The semantics require all processes to arrive at **barrier**, one process to execute the serial code body, and then all processes continue from **end barrier**. Another way to initialize isync would be to do it before processes are forked.

Because the consume of isync prevents any other process from consuming it, there is a mutually exclusive section of code from the consume to one of the two produces of isync, either that associated with the next loop body execution or that associated with the loop termination by **break**.

The mutually exclusive sections are executed serially by all np processes. If the amount of work in ⟨loop body(i)⟩ is small, processes may spend most of their time waiting for exclusive access to isync. This is a price paid for the dynamic load balancing ability of self-scheduling. Prescheduling has no mutual exclusion but cannot balance load if the amount of work in the loop body varies dynamically with i. Combinations of prescheduling and self-scheduling are also possible. Synchronized access to shared data may be used at execution time to allocate a range of index values to a process, which then computes individual index values independently. The size of the range may be fixed to simply aggregate small tasks into larger chunks or variable to provide dynamic load balancing.

Nested loops can be treated in several ways. Assuming the bodies of all loops in the nest are independent, it may be appropriate to parallelize only the inner or only the outer loop of the nest. It is also possible to parallelize over two or more loop indices simultaneously. In the case of two nested loops with indices i and j, loop bodies for different (i, j) pairs are treated as parallel tasks. The simplest case is that of *perfectly nested* loops. All loop body code in a perfect loop nest is contained in the single innermost loop of the nest. Imperfect loop nests can often be transformed into perfect loop nests for parallelization. The imperfect two loop nest of Figure 4-13(a) is transformed into the foralls of Figure 4-13(b), and index pairs (i, j) are generated in parallel from a one-dimensional index k, introduced by the transformation. Loop transformations will be treated in more detail in Chapter 7 on data dependence. The fixed upper and lower limits on i and j make the iteration space of Figure 4-13 rectangular. Other iteration spaces can also be handled when the inner loop limit depends on the outer loop index in a simple way. See Problem 4-9.

The dynamic scheduling concept extends from the simple idea of self-scheduled **foralls** to a situation where the amount of work to be done depends on the outcome of the ongoing computation. Adaptive quadrature, a method of integrating a function over an interval, will be used to illustrate the ideas. Adaptive quadrature is probably too simple to need the full power of the divide and conquer method we use it to illustrate, but its numeric simplicity focuses attention on the parallel processing techniques. Adaptive quadrature finds the integral of some function, $f(x)$, over an interval, $a \le x \le b$. To find the integral on any interval, an approximation and an error estimate are applied. If the error estimate is small enough, the approximation is taken as the answer. Otherwise, the interval is split in two and the answers for the two subintervals are summed. Applying the same method, recursively, to each subinterval results in adaptive quadrature. The example function, interval, and subdivisions shown in Figure 4-14 illustrate how the method "adapts" to the function, using larger intervals where it is smooth and smaller ones where it is not.

```
for i := 0 step 1 until n−1              forall i := 0 step 1 until n−1
   begin                                     s[i]:= f(i);
   s := f(i);                             forall k := 0 step 1 until m*n−1
   for j := 0 step 1 until m−1            i := ⌊k/m⌋;
      ⟨loop body(i, j, s)⟩;               j := k mod m;
   end                                                ⟨loop body(i, j, s[i])⟩;
```

(a) Serial imperfect two loop nest   (b) Split into parallel perfect nests

Figure 4-13   Parallelizing a simple imperfect loop nest.

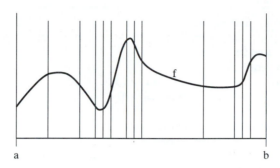

Figure 4-14 Adaptive quadrature behavior for a simple function.

Because computing on one subinterval may produce two more to be handled independently, this is a natural problem for multiple processes, but there are some pitfalls to be avoided. Forking or creating a new process to handle one of the subintervals every time a split occurs is not a viable solution. All of the processors in the system will rapidly be used up, and forking will either fail or produce processes that are time multiplexed on fewer processors. In the latter case, even a simple integral produces more processes than can be effectively time multiplexed and probably exhausts the system resources. The right approach is to decouple the number of pieces of work to be done, call them tasks, from the number of processes doing them. We will use a shared work list, from which tasks can be obtained and to which tasks can be added, with a fixed set of processes performing the work until it is exhausted.

The numerical analysis of the problem is embodied in two procedures. approx(a, b, f) returns an approximation to the integral of f over the interval (a, b), and accurate(a, b, f) returns true if the approximation is accurate enough and false otherwise. These routines could be as simple as an application of the trapezoidal or Simpson's rule, but we suppress the details to concentrate on the parallel processing. Of more interest here are three procedures that deal with the shared work list. workready() returns true if the work list is not empty and false otherwise, getwork(task) returns the same true/false indication along with a task from the work list in the true case, and putwork(task) puts a new task on the work list, returning false if the list was full and true otherwise. In our adaptive quadrature example, task is a structure consisting of the interval endpoints, task.a and task.b, and the function task.f. Program 4-7 shows the structure of an SPMD program for adaptive quadrature executed by P processes.

The program starts with one task, (a, b, f), on the work list and idle = P. The inner while loop terminates when there is no more work in the list, but there is a chance more work will be added if any processes are still executing tasks, so the outer while does not terminate until all processes have failed to find more work to do. The explicit synchronizations use named critical sections, but synchronization is also implicit in the procedures that access the shared work list. In this section we focus on the work distribution rather than the synchronization.

```
shared P, idle, integral;
private more, t, ok, cent, task, task1, task2;
while (true) begin
    critical work;
          more := workready() or (idle ≠ P);
          if (more) then idle := idle - 1;
    end critical;
    if (not more) then break;
    while (getwork(task)) begin
          t := approx(a, b, f); ok := accurate(a, b, f);
          if (ok) then
              critical int;
                    integral := integral + t;
              end critical;
          else begin
              cent := (task.a + task.b)/2.0;
              task1.a := task.a; task1.b := cent;
              task2.a := cent; task2.b := task.b;
              task1.f := task2.f := task.f;
              if (not putwork(task1) or not putwork(task2)) then
                  ⟨Report no room in task set.⟩;
          end;
    end; /* of while loop over available tasks */
    critical work;
          idle := idle + 1;
    end critical;
end; /* of while loop over available tasks or active processes. */
```

Program 4-7   SPMD adaptive quadrature program executed by P processes.

The order in which work is put onto, and taken from, the list is very important. The adaptive quadrature computation can be viewed as traversing a binary tree that is constructed as intervals are split in two. Binary trees can be traversed in a depth-first or breadth-first manner. Managing the work list in a last-in, first-out order gives a depth-first traversal, while using a first-in, first-out order gives a breadth-first traversal. It is important to use a depth-first traversal because a breadth-first order adds more and more tasks to the work list, generating new work much faster than work is completed until the end of the computation nears. The breadth-first traversal is the cause of the previously mentioned problem with forking processes recursively. Properly managed, the framework of a set of processes cooperatively accessing a shared work list can be a very effective form of dynamic scheduling.

Work distribution for parallel loops is particularly important because loops are the source of most of the parallel work in a program. The concepts used for loops extend to many situations where parallel tasks are generated in a different way. Parallel sections in a cobegin/coend block, for example, can also be prescheduled or self-scheduled, and in the shared memory environment, the ability to dynamically balance load is traded off against the overhead of synchronization needed to communicate among processes at run-time. In our discussion of message passing multiprocessors, we see that the placement of data in private memories presents another penalty for dynamic scheduling in the overhead of moving data from one processor's memory to another. This data layout concern is in addition to the load balancing and synchronization issues, which are also present in message passing systems.

4.3.4 Multiprocessor Synchronization

In the shared memory multiprocessor environment, the problem of one processor producing a value that another processor uses reduces to informing the consumer about when the new value is available to be fetched from the shared memory. This exchange of timing information is the function of synchronization. There is no need to move data, other than between processor registers and memory. A write to memory destroys the old value in the addressed location, replacing it with a new one. Not only must no process try to use the new value before it is written, but also the producer should not overwrite the old value before its value has been read by the consumer(s) that may need it. The *producer/consumer* synchronization already described captures the essence of this interprocessor communication of timing information. The information comes in the form of a restriction on the progress of a process. The consumer is delayed until the new value is present, and the producer is delayed until the old value has been used. This is a good form for the timing information if only a few cycles of delay are expected.

The problem of atomicity of synchronization is easy to understand from the *producer/consumer* perspective. If writing a value in memory and signaling its availability are two operations, in what order should they be done by a sequential process? If the signal occurs first, a consumer may see it and read the old value before the new one is available. If the write occurs first, a process reading the old value may get the new one without being informed that the state of the memory cell has changed. The solution is to have the two operations, writing and informing other processes of the new state, occur atomically (indivisibly) as far as their effect on other processes is concerned.

4.3.4.1   Atomicity

The fundamental nature of atomicity and its importance to correct and efficient operation of parallel programs makes it important to give a precise definition of the idea.

Definition: Let S be a set of processes and q be an operation (perhaps composite). q is *atomic* with respect to S if and only if for any process $p \in S$ that shares variables with q, the state of these variables seen by p is either that before the start of q or that resulting from completion of q.

The definition is careful to focus on the behavior of an atomic operation rather than on the way in which that behavior is achieved. This will be particularly important when we consider the performance implications of synchronizations.

There are two important concepts involved in atomicity—the set of processes with respect to which an operation is atomic and the shared variables through which a process might observe that the operation is not atomic. An operation q might have a complex internal structure, but if this structure is not observable by processes in the set S, q is atomic for the purposes of synchronizing processes in S. The processes of S can only observe the progress of q through variables they share with q. If q shares no variables with any process of S, its progress is not observable, and it is thus trivially atomic with respect to S. Limiting the set of processes with respect to which a complex q is atomic is essential because there is always some process, in the operating system or machine test hardware, that can observe the internal structure of q.

A common way of ensuring atomicity is by the use of mutual exclusion. Two processes are not both allowed to execute code inside a critical section simultaneously. Thus, if the compound operation q is enclosed in a critical section and all other processes sharing variables with q only access those variables inside corresponding critical sections, then those variables will necessarily have values from prior to the start of q or after its completion. Of course, if other processes access variables shared with q outside of a critical section, they can observe states internal to the compound operation q and mutual exclusion may be violated. Mutual exclusion is such a common way of implementing atomicity in synchronization that it has been claimed that all synchronizations are based on mutual exclusion at some level. The definition, however, makes no such demand.

The difference between indivisibility of operations and the appearance of indivisibility has important performance consequences for synchronization. We will illustrate the difference with a concrete example at the software level. The idea can equally well be applied to hardware design. Consider the problem of processes obtaining unique values of the shared index `isync` in the self-scheduling code of Figure 4-12. Assume that all operations on `isync` by any process appear inside of critical sections. Then a private index `i` may be obtained and the shared index `isync` updated by

```
critical
        i := isync;
        isync := isync + 1;
end critical
```

The performance problem is that if a large number P of processes attempt to execute the critical section simultaneously, one of them will have to wait for $P - 1$ others to execute it one at a time. Thus, the waiting time grows linearly with the number of processes.

To see that a solution with better performance for large P is possible, consider the recursive index update algorithm diagrammed in Figure 4-15. Eight processes obtain the old value of `isync` and increment it by one in the following way. Pairs of processes combine their operations at the first level of the tree by having one of them obtain the old value of `isync` and increment it by two. The old value is then returned to one of the processes and the old value plus one to the other. At the next level of the tree, processes incrementing `isync` by two are combined to increment it by four with one receiving the old value and the other receiving the old value plus two. At the root of the tree, `isync` is incremented by eight, and one of the two processes reaching the root returns the original value of isync, say one, and the other receives isync + 4, or five. Thus, each process receives a value of the shared index as if each fetch and increment had been done one at a time.

If the recursive operation is accessed at the leaves of the tree by the function call

```
i := incr(isync);
```

then it is correct to say that incr() atomically returns the old value of isync and adds one to it. This is also the behavior of the operations on isync inside the critical section. From the performance perspective, however, the behavior of incr() is very different from that of reading and incrementing isync in a critical section. At each level of the tree, a process synchronizes with only one other, and there are $\log_2 P$ levels for P processes. Thus, the time from processes entering incr() until the result is returned is $\log_2 P$ times the time at one level of the tree. The logic at a tree level is more complex than that in the critical section so if t is the execution time for the critical section and T is the time spent at a node of the tree, the incr() function performs better when $tP > T \log_2 P$. This is inevitably the case for large enough P.

There are numerous other considerations for the relative performance of the two methods for updating isync. The critical section only performs poorly and the tree algorithm well if all processes access isync simultaneously. Little delay may occur if processes reach the critical section at variable times, but the isync() function forces all processes to call it before any of them receives a result. Changes to the algorithm can address some of these issues, and we will see hardware support for the tree structured solution in Chapter 6. The point being made here is that the definition of atomicity in terms of results observable to other processes instead of in terms of mutual exclusion of operations opens up important possibilities for high performance implementations of synchronization.

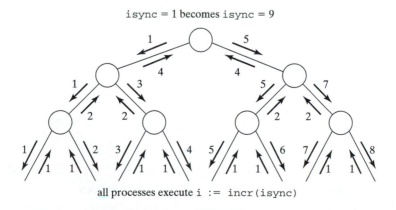

Figure 4-15 Cooperative simultaneous update of shared index.

4.3.4.2   Hardware and Software Synchronization Mechanisms

The fact that a complex synchronization operation like "get the next value of an index and incre-ment it" can be built upon a simpler mechanism like the critical section suggests looking for a basic set of synchronization building blocks. One could envision implementing the basic syn-chronizations in hardware and building more complex synchronizations on top of them using software. This idea is overly simplistic because there is no clear indication of the basic set of synchronizations. For example, a barrier might seem to be a complex operation because it involves communication of timing information among all processes, but architectures have been proposed and built with direct hardware support for barriers. Some things can be said, however, about the differences between hardware and software synchronization mechanisms.

Control-based synchronizations are primarily software mechanisms, while data based syn-chronizations can be implemented either in software or in hardware. The reason is that control flow is represented in hardware by a data item, the program counter. Mutual exclusion, which we illustrated using the critical section, must focus in hardware on entry to and exit from the range of program counter values associated with the critical section body. A shared-status flag indicates whether the critical section is available for execution or occupied by another process. The control-based critical section, thus, becomes one based on the status flag data item. The well-known *lock/unlock* operations are data-based synchronizations that directly embody this mechanism. The **lock** L operation waits until a Boolean data item L is clear, then sets it, and proceeds. An **unlock** L clears the lock. Named critical section entry and exit map directly into matched *lock/unlock* pairs, as shown in Figure 4-16. The name of the critical section can just be the name of the lock variable. The atomic part of **lock** L is discovering L clear, setting it, and proceeding. The atomic part of **unlock** L is just clearing L.

Another limitation on hardware synchronizations that is not as universal as the limitation to data-based synchronization is the common lack of a hardware waiting mechanism. Waiting can be done in software by retrying an operation in a loop or by using an operating system call to give up the processor. Calling the operating system often involves high overhead and is not appropriate for waits that are expected to be short. Hardware waiting mechanisms can disable instruction fetch until some condition is satisfied, but this is rarely seen. Multithreaded multipro-cessors can automatically transfer execution to another instruction stream that shares the proces-sor hardware and can thus implement a very low cost form of hardware waiting. In the absence of any hardware waiting mechanism, **lock** L and **unlock** L can be built on top of the opera-tions **test&set** L and **clear** L, as shown in Figure 4-17. A **test&set** L returns the old value of L and atomically sets it if it was clear. A **clear** L simply changes the state of L to clear.

Figure 4-16   Control-based and data-based mutual exclusion.

```
     lock L                              Loc: test&set L
                        ...                      branch_if_set Loc
     unlock L                                    ...
                                                 clear L
```

Figure 4-17 `lock/unlock` in terms of `test&set/clear`.

A possible scenario for implementing synchronization would be to support test&set and clear in hardware, do mutual exclusion by looping in software, called *busy waiting*, and implement all other synchronizations using mutual exclusion. This is probably a poor idea from the performance perspective because a small amount of additional hardware support can often significantly reduce the overhead of complex synchronizations. This approach also has no claim to being fundamental because mutual exclusion can be implemented using only atomic read and write of single bit quantities. The high complexity of such mutual exclusion algorithms translates into a very large performance penalty for their use. For this practical rather than fundamental reason, virtually all multiprocessors have supplied hardware support for a synchronization operation at least as powerful as **test&set**.

Some care must be taken in using mutual exclusion to make composite synchronization operations atomic. Consider implementing produce/consume using only critical sections for synchronization. We model a producer/consumer variable as a variable var and a full flag f. The implementation of **produce** is shown in Program 4-8. The **consume** operation is implemented similarly using a critical section to prevent incorrect interaction with **produce** and other **consume**s.

```
procedure produce(x, expr);
        shared struct {real var; boolean f} x;
        private ok;
        ok := false;
        repeat
           critical
           if (not x.f) then
              {ok := true;
               x.f := true;
               x.var := expr;};
           end critical;
        until ok;
end procedure;
```

Program 4-8 Produce implemented with mutual exclusion.

The most important thing to note about the implementation is that the repeat loop that waits for x to be full encloses the critical section. If the loop were inside the critical section, consume would be unable to enter its critical section to make x.f false, resulting in an infinite loop for produce. The second important note is that ok is a private variable that reflects what was observed about x.f inside the critical section and is not affected by a possible change to x.f after produce exits the critical section. Finally, note that using unnamed critical sections to implement produce/consume gives correct synchronization but may be inefficient because only produces and consumes on the same variable need to synchronize with each other, whereas the unnamed critical sections cause all produces and consumes to be mutually exclusive. A better implementation would use named critical sections with a distinct name for each producer/consumer variable or use a different lock for each variable.

4.3.4.3   Fairness and Mutual Exclusion

In operating systems texts, two topics are important to a discussion of mutual exclusion—exclusive access and fairness. The primary purpose of operating system synchronization is to control shared resource access by processes that are otherwise independent. It is not only important that a process gets exclusive access to the resource, but also that no one process waits indefinitely for access while others make progress. Preventing such a *livelock* or *starvation* situation can be done by including a *fairness* guarantee in the selection of the next process to enter a critical section. Such a mechanism is costly in terms of performance overhead because information on all waiting processes must be combined.

Fairness is not of the same importance to parallel processing as it is to operating systems. Parallel processes cooperate to solve a single problem, and lack of progress by one process due to competition by others often eventually stops the competing processes and allows the waiting one to proceed. In the self-scheduling example of mutually exclusive access to a shared index, repeated waiting by one process implies that other processes are successfully obtaining index values and completing the loop computations. Because at least two processes must be competing at all times for one to repeatedly lose, there must be more processes available than needed to complete the loop in minimum time. In either case, it is not cost effective to increase the overhead of critical section entry for all processes to ensure fairness. Low overhead monitoring of lack of progress by a process to reassign it might be beneficial, but only if the cost of monitoring and reassignment is less than the average loss of computing power to idle processes.

The concept of fairness is missing, for example, in the busy wait implementation of critical section entry using test&set shown in Figure 4-17. Operating systems often implement fairness by entering processes on a FIFO queue as they arrive at a critical section entry. Sequential access to a shared queue is not a problem in a uniprocessor operating system, where all processing is sequential in any case. On the other hand, coordinated access to a shared queue by a large number of processes can lead to significant synchronization overhead. Furthermore, the use of a queue is not simple because fairness in gaining access to the critical section can simply appear as the problem of fair access to the shared queue. Because fairness is generally unimportant in parallel processing, we will not pursue it further. Of course, deadlock, the mutual blockage of all processes in a synchronization, is just as important to parallel processing as to operating systems, and classic, deadlock detection and avoidance techniques can be important to some parallel programming techniques.

4.4   A Shared Memory Multiprocessor Programming Language

A high-level language for programming shared memory multiprocessors includes a selected set of constructs for process management, parallel scope declaration, work distribution, and synchronization. The language also embodies a model of parallel execution that may range from completely static to very dynamic. In a static model, a fixed number of instruction streams, or processes, usually associated with physical processors of the system, execute the program from start to finish. In a dynamic model, new processes may join those executing the program or processes may be taken away, under control of the operating system. Changes in the number of processes may be in response to the program's inherent parallelism at a given point in its execution or in response to the requirements of other jobs running on a multiprogrammed multiprocessor. Many compromises between static and dynamic execution are possible by restricting the allowable changes in the number of processes. Changes may be restricted to points such as specific user calls to the system, specific types of fork/join points, or synchronizations such as barriers, and there may be upper and lower bounds on the number of processes.

4.4.1   The OpenMP Language Extension

OpenMP is not a full parallel language but a language extension—a framework built on top of an existing sequential language. By limiting OpenMP constructs to compiler directives and library subroutine calls, and making the form of the directives such that they are treated as comments by a sequential compiler, it is guaranteed that an OpenMP program also corresponds to a legal program in the base language. Whether the base language program performs the same computation as the OpenMP version, or indeed any meaningful computation, is the responsibility of the programmer. OpenMP extensions exist for both C/C++ and Fortran. The extension is designated an Applications Program Interface, or API, and Version 1.0 of the OpenMP Fortran API specification appeared in October of 1997. We will keep the initial discussion as general as possible, but where language specifics are needed they will refer to the Fortran version.

The rationale for an extension rather than a separate parallel language is to allow existing compilers to be easily modified to support OpenMP and to allow a minimal addition of directives and subroutine calls to introduce some parallelism into an existing sequential program. Disadvantages of an extension arise from a mismatch between the underlying execution models for the parallel and sequential language interpretations. The fundamental dichotomy between a single and a multiple program counter interpretation of a base language construct can lead to obscure or ambiguous interpretations. If the standard for the extension does not anticipate and specify behavior in all such cases, a program may compute different results under different implementations of the extension. The problem differs from that of building a language around a single coherent execution model from the start.

4.4.1.1   Execution Model

The execution model supported by OpenMP is a form of fork/join semantics. Execution begins with a single sequential process that forks a fixed number of *threads* when it reaches the beginning of a so-called *parallel region*. The *team* of threads then executes to the end of the parallel region where they are joined back to the original process. On encountering a new parallel region a different number of threads may be forked, but the number remains fixed until the end of the region. If nested parallelism is allowed by the setting of an environment variable, a thread executing within a parallel region may fork a new team of threads on encountering the beginning of a nested parallel region. A thread entering a parallel region and forking others is called the *master thread* of the team. Three user-controllable environment variables manage parallel execution. An integer, `num_threads`, specifies the number of threads, a Boolean, `dynamic`, controls whether or not the number of threads may change from one parallel region to the next, and a second Boolean, `nested`, specifies whether nested parallelism is allowed or whether nested parallel regions enclosed by another are executed sequentially.

4.4.1.2   Process Control

Parallel regions are bracketed by *parallel* and *end parallel* directives. Other directives allow combining parallel regions with work distribution constructs using *parallel do* and *parallel sections*. We use the term *parallel construct* to denote a parallel region or a block structured work distribution construct contained in a parallel region. The *static scope* of a parallel construct consists of all the statements lexically between the start and end statements of that construct. The *dynamic scope* of a parallel construct consists of all statements executed by a team member between entry to and exit from the construct. This may include statements outside the construct's static scope reached by subroutine calls. Parallel directives that lie outside the static scope of a parallel construct but inside its dynamic scope are called *orphan directives* by the OpenMP standard. Such directives present special compiler problems when dynamic scope information is either not retained due to separate subroutine compilation or not available at compile time due to data dependent control transfer. Orphan directives are needed when fork/join constructs appear above the leaves of the call tree. Procedures executed independently on behalf of each thread range from functions of the mathematical library to complex user code subroutine packages. An SPMD-style program could be written in OpenMP by entering a parallel region at the beginning of the main program and exiting it just before the end, thus, including the entire program in the dynamic scope of the parallel region.

4.4.1.3   Parallel Scope of Variables

The parallel scope of data may be either *shared*, *private*, or *threadprivate*. Shared and private declarations may refer to variables or Fortran common blocks, while threadprivate only applies to common blocks. When the environment variable, `dynamic`, is false, thus, keeping the number of threads constant from one parallel region to the next, a copy of threadprivate common for each thread persists between parallel regions. Private variables have a separate copy for each thread executing the parallel construct in which the private declaration occurs, but only the master thread's copy survives on exit from the parallel construct. In general, the values of the master thread's private variables are undefined on exit from a parallel construct. Directives are available to initialize private or threadprivate variables to the value of the master thread's corresponding variable on entry to a parallel construct and to set the master's variable to a specific thread's private value on exit.

The parallel scope of variables in subroutines called from within a parallel construct is tied to their lexical scope. Local variables of the subroutine are private, except for those with the SAVE attribute, which are shared. Common blocks in the called subroutine are shared unless they are declared threadprivate. Actual parameters passed to the subroutine retain the parallel scope given them in the caller. Because parallel scope declarations only appear as clauses in a directive that begins a parallel construct, subroutines called in parallel do not declare parallel scope, other than threadprivate, unless they include a work distribution construct or a nested parallel region.

4.4.1.4   Work Distribution

Work distribution constructs consist of parallel loops, parallel code sections, single thread execution, and master thread execution. Parallel code sections represent the same concept as cobegin/coend except that the emphasis is on distributing code sections to parallel processes that may be already running rather than on forking processes. The directives, *sections* and *end sections*, begin and end the block structured construct, with each separate block of parallel code introduced by a *section* directive. The code between *single* and *end single* directives is executed by any thread, but only one, while code between *master* and *end master* directives is executed exclusively by the master thread. Allocating work specifically to the master thread is often done in support of synchronization, and the OpenMP Fortran API lists the master directive as a synchronization operation. The parallel loop construct, bracketed by *do* and *end do* directives, has the largest number of clauses that may be associated with it. In addition to parallel scope declarations, private variable initializations, and specification of reduction variables, the method of scheduling iterations over threads can also be specified. Prescheduling and self-scheduling are available under the names *static* and *dynamic*, respectively, and a generalization of block and cyclic mapping is available with a *chunk* of consecutive iterations assigned to each thread. The chunk size may be one for cyclic mapping, greater than one for general block mapping, or variable for a method known as *guided self-scheduling*.

4.4.1.5   Synchronization and Memory Consistency

OpenMP supports some control-based synchronizations by compiler directives and one data-based synchronization, locks, through subroutine calls. Locks can be initialized, destroyed, acquired, released, and passively tested. The control-based synchronizations are critical sections, single-point barriers, atomic updates, ordered sections of parallel loops, and memory consistency control. Critical sections are bracketed by *critical* and *end critical* directives and may be named. The single *barrier* directive behaves like the barrier/end barrier pair of Figure 4-12 with an empty code body. A barrier may also be implicitly associated with an *end do*, *end sections*, or *end single* directive. The *atomic* directive appears immediately before a statement of the form

    x = x op expression

where op is a two operand operation or intrinsic function. No modifications to x are allowed to occur between its read and subsequent write by the update statement. The effect of exclusive update could be obtained by critical sections or locks, but the atomic directive ties exclusive access to the specific variable x rather than an unrelated lock or critical section name. The *ordered* and *end ordered* directives are used in the body of a parallel loop to enclose a section of code whose instances must be executed in loop index order, even though the rest of the loop may be executed in parallel.

The *flush* directive forces a consistent view of memory by all processors at the point it appears in the program. Assignments to variables may become visible to different processors at different times as a result of a hierarchically structured memory. Multiprocessor memory structures will be discussed in more detail in Chapter 5, but the need for flush can be understood just by considering that each processor has a separate set of registers, which is true of virtually all multiprocessors. Modern uniprocessor compilers use fast registers extensively to minimize the number of slower memory accesses, but a new shared variable value in a register is not visible to other processors. Because correct parallel program behavior depends on mutual accessibility of shared variables, a program could fail without it. Two types of solutions to the problem are possible—never allocate shared variables to registers, or identify program points and/or variables for which mutual visibility affects program correctness. The first solution is seriously detrimental to performance and is impossible on modern processors that require operands and results in registers and maintain copies in an execution pipeline over several instruction executions. Fortunately, mutual accessibility of shared variables is only required at specific synchronization points for correct operation. A compiler can recognize the need to update shared memory at specific synchronization directives or subroutine calls. The *flush* directive is provided for the programmer to explicitly identify points where a consistent view of shared memory is required. By default, flush specifies that all variables visible to other threads must be made consistent, or a specific set of variables to be made consistent may be listed.

As in any shared memory multiprocessor language, OpenMP selects a subset of the possible constructs for process management, variable scope, work distribution, and synchronization. Selecting a few constructs makes the language easier to implement and learn, while supporting many constructs gives a parallel programmer more flexibility, allows some complex parallel algorithms to be written more compactly, and may improve performance over transcribing an unimplemented construct into a collection of those from a smaller set. OpenMP has one process management construct—the parallel region, three parallel variable scopes—shared, private, and threadprivate, four work distribution constructs—loops, sections, single execution, and master execution, and six synchronization methods—locks, critical sections, barriers, atomic update, ordered sections, and flush. This moderate sized set of constructs is sufficient for simple parallelization of sequential programs but may present challenges for more complex parallel programs.

4.4.2   The OpenMP Fortran Applications Program Interface (API)

OpenMP extends Fortran by adding OpenMP directives and the OpenMP Fortran API run-time library. Library routines are accessed by the standard call syntax for subroutines or functions in

Fortran. OpenMP directives are distinguished from ordinary Fortran statements by a sentinel beginning the line. The sentinel may differ depending on whether fixed form or free form is used for the Fortran source. In free form, the sentinel consists of the five characters `!$OMP` as the first characters of the line that are not white space. In fixed form, the sentinel must appear in columns 1–5, and in addition to `!$OMP`, the forms `C*OMP` and `*$OMP` are also allowed. Continuation lines of a directive must also have the sentinel and are identified in fixed form by a nonblank in column six. In free form, the directive to be continued must end in `&`, and continuation lines may have an optional `&` following the sentinel. As in ordinary Fortran, alphabetic characters may be upper or lower case. OpenMP also supports conditional compilation. Lines with `!$` in the first two columns will be treated in an OpenMP compilation as ordinary Fortran with the `!$` replaced by two blanks. Such a line is treated as a comment in a sequential compilation.

We will briefly describe the constructs of the OpenMP Fortran API and give some examples of its use. For complete details of the language extension, refer to the formal specification, [229]. An OpenMP directive consists of the sentinel, followed by the directive keyword(s), followed by zero or more clauses on the same line (or on continuation lines). While some clauses are specific to a single directive, many can appear with any one of several directives. In the description of OpenMP syntax, the characters |, {, }, [, and] and words in italics are metasymbols. Alternatives are separated by |, {} are used for grouping, and things in [ ] are optional. The meaning of an italicized name is usually evident from the name.

Parallelism is introduced into an OpenMP program by the parallel region construct

`!$OMP PARALLEL` [*clause*[[*,*] *clause* ...]]
block
`!$OMP END PARALLEL`

The *block* is a single entry, single exit group of statements that are executed by all threads of the team created on entry to the parallel region in SPMD fashion. Branching into or out of the block is illegal, except for subroutine or function calls, but different threads may follow different paths through the block. The number of threads executing the parallel region may be accessed using calls to the run-time library. The number of threads, `num_threads`, is set by calling

`SUBROUTINE OMP_SET_NUM_THREADS`(*integer*)

where the integer argument may be an expression. The number of running threads is returned by

`INTEGER FUNCTION OMP_GET_NUM_THREADS`()

and each thread gets its own unique integer between 0 and `num_threads` − 1 by calling

`INTEGER FUNCTION OMP_GET_THREAD_NUM`()

The integer 0 is always assigned to the master thread.

The parallel scope of variables inside a parallel region is specified by clauses attached to the `!$OMP PARALLEL` directive, except that threadprivate common blocks are specified by a directive. A list of variables or labeled common blocks can be specified as private by the clause

PRIVATE (*list*)

or shared by the clause

SHARED (*list*)

All copies of private variables disappear at the end of the parallel region except for the master thread's copy. A more complex parallel scope specification is that for reduction variables

REDUCTION ({*operator* | *intrinsic*} : *list*)

A variable X in *list* appears inside the parallel region only in reduction statements of the form

X = X *operator expression*

or

X = *intrinsic* (X, *expression*)

where *operator* may be +, *, -, .AND., .OR., .EQV., or .NEQV. and *intrinsic* may be MAX, MIN, IAND, IOR, or IEOR. The variable has shared scope, although the implementation keeps separate copies for each thread that are combined at the end of the parallel region using the specified reduction operation.

To show the structure of an OpenMP Fortran program, we use the directives, clauses, and run-time calls already described to build a trivial, but complete, main program to sum a ten-element array, as shown in Program 4-9. Because OpenMP programs must be portable among systems, there is no guarantee that an implementation will use ten processors to run the ten threads. There is a run-time system call to determine the number of processors available, but only the program's performance will reveal how much parallelism is actually exploited.

```
            PROGRAM MAIN
            INTEGER K
            REAL A(10), X
            CALL INPUT(A)
            CALL OMP_SET_NUM_THREADS(10)
!$OMP       PARALLEL SHARED(A, X) PRIVATE(K) REDUCTION(+:X)
            K = OMP_GET_THREAD_NUM()
            X = X + A(K+1)
!$OMP       END PARALLEL
            PRINT *, 'Sum of As: ', X
            STOP
            END
```

Program 4-9   Simple OpenMP Fortran example program.

4.4.2.1   Constructs of the OpenMP Fortran API

The directives, environment variables, and run-time library routines associated with creation, management, and termination of threads are shown in Table 4-1. The parallel region is the basic construct that introduces parallel execution. The structure and behavior of the team of threads that executes the parallel region is determined by parameters that can be read by the program using run-time library functions and can be set initially from environment variables with those settings possibly overridden by run-time library subroutine calls. The distinction between the functions that get the number of threads and its maximum is that the number of threads returned is the number currently executing, which is one outside any parallel region and may be less than the maximum inside a parallel region if the implementation is allowed to dynamically adjust the number of threads for efficiency. The maximum number of threads is determined by the environment variable or OMP_SET_NUM_THREADS call. If the nested parameter is false, nested parallel regions are executed sequentially.

Constructs that specify parallel data scope are summarized in Table 4-2. Except for THREADPRIVATE directives, scope is always specified by clauses attached to parallel region or work distribution directives. Many of the clauses are allowed in several directives. Note that the SHARED clause may not appear on a work distribution directive inside a parallel region, so variables that already have a copy for each thread cannot revert to being shared when parallel work is distributed. Values of private variables may be initialized on entry to a parallel construct using FIRSTPRIVATE, or COPYIN for threadprivate variables. A "last" value of a private variable may be passed out of a work distribution construct only when there is a distinguished last value, set by the last iteration of a loop construct or by the lexically last section of a sections construct.

Table 4-1   Thread management constructs in OpenMP Fortran.

Directives	
!$OMP PARALLEL [clause [[, clause]...]	Create a team of threads to execute
block	block in parallel; join to master
!$OMP END PARALLEL	thread at end.
Allowed clauses: PRIVATE, SHARED, DEFAULT, FIRSTPRIVATE, REDUCTION, IF, COPYIN	
Clause	
IF (logical_expression)	Parallel only if expression true, serial if false.
Environment variables	
OMP_NUM_THREADS	Number of threads to use, or maximum if dynamic adjustment allowed.
OMP_DYNAMIC	Change in number of threads allowed between parallel regions if true.
OMP_NESTED	May nested parallel region fork more threads?
Run-time library routines	
SUBROUTINE OMP_SET_NUM_THREADS (integer)	Set number or max number of threads.
INTEGER FUNCTION OMP_GET_NUM_THREADS ( )	Return number of threads in use.
INTEGER FUNCTION OMP_GET_MAX_THREADS ( )	Return max number of threads.
INTEGER FUNCTION OMP_GET_THREAD_NUM ( )	Return number of the calling thread.
INTEGER FUNCTION OMP_GET_NUM_PROCS ( )	Return number of processors available.

Table 4-1   Thread management constructs in OpenMP Fortran. (Continued)

`LOGICAL FUNCTION OMP_IN_PARALLEL()`	True if called from dynamic extent of a parallel region.
`SUBROUTINE OMP_SET_DYNAMIC (`*logical*`)`	Allow (true) or disallow (false) dynamic change in number of threads.
`LOGICAL FUNCTION OMP_GET_DYNAMIC()`	Return true or false setting of `dynamic`.
`SUBROUTINE OMP_SET_NESTED (`*logical*`)`	Allow nested parallelism or not.
`LOGICAL FUNCTION OMP_GET_NESTED()`	Return true if nested parallelism allowed.

Table 4-2   Parallel data scope specification in OpenMP Fortran.

Directive	
`!$OMP THREADPRIVATE  (/ `*cb*` / [, / `*cb*` /] ...)`	
Specifies that previously declared common blocks *cb* are private and persist across parallel regions.	
Clauses	
`PRIVATE (`*list*`)`	Variables or common blocks in *list* are private in block introduced by the directive.
`SHARED (`*list*`)`	Variables or common blocks in *list* are shared.
`DEFAULT(PRIVATE │ SHARED │ NONE)`	Default scope for all variables in block.
`FIRSTPRIVATE (`*list*`)`	Private variables in *list* are initialized to values on entry to block.
`LASTPRIVATE (`*list*`)`	The values of variables on *list* are set to values written by last iteration or section.
`REDUCTION ({`*operator* │ *intrinsic*`}: `*list*`)`	Reduce across threads by specified operation.
`COPYIN (`*list*`)`	Initialize threadprivate variables or common blocks on *list* to master's value on entry.

The work distribution constructs given in Table 4-3 include parallel loops, parallel independent code sections, and single-thread execution. Because loops are the most important way of exploiting parallelism, the most variation is included in their specification to maximize performance in different types of loops. Successive iterations of a Fortran loop are aggregated into chunks, and these chunks are distributed over threads statically by the compiler or dynamically at run-time. Dynamic scheduling may have a fixed chunk size or may exponentially reduce the chunk size in successive requests by threads for new work in the guided self-scheduling method. If scheduling is specified as `RUNTIME`, the value of the environment variable `OMP_SCHEDULE` determines the scheduling method. For example, in a Unix environment

```
setenv OMP_SCHEDULE "STATIC, 10"
```

specifies prescheduling with a chunk size of ten iterations. The `ORDERED` clause on a parallel loop directive indicates that one, and only one, `ORDERED` directive appears in the parallel loop. The `ORDERED` directive specifies that a block of statements must be executed in iteration order, even though the rest of the loop is parallel. In a `SECTIONS` construct, each separate section is executed by some one thread. A sequential block of code may be allocated to any available thread using the `SINGLE` directive or specifically to the master thread using `MASTER`.

As summarized in Table 4-4, all synchronizations are done by directives in OpenMP Fortran except for operations on locks, which are done by run-time library calls. Critical sections may be named or unnamed. All unnamed critical sections exclude each other. Both the CRITICAL and END CRITICAL directives must have the same, or no, name. In addition to the explicit BARRIER directive, a barrier is implied at an END DO, END SECTIONS, or END SINGLE directive unless the NOWAIT clause is attached. The ATOMIC directive modifies the following Fortran statement, which must be an update to a variable using one of the formats and an operator or intrinsic function allowed for the update of a reduction variable, as described previously. The expression value used for the update is evaluated in parallel, but the read, modify, and write of the left hand side variable is atomic. A FLUSH directive ensures that all threads see a consistent view of either all variables or just those on the attached list at this point in the program. Compiler movement of code affecting these variables past a FLUSH directive is not allowed. The ORDERED directive makes it possible to force iteration order execution of one or more statements in a loop while executing the rest of the loop body in parallel. The run-time library provides a standard set of operations on named locks. A lock name must be an integer variable large enough to hold an address. The SET_LOCK call waits for the lock to be available, sets it, and returns, while the TEST_LOCK call returns immediately with a .FALSE. value if the lock was unavailable and a .TRUE. value if setting it was successful. A lock should be unset only by the thread that succeeded in setting it.

The last two directives in OpenMP Fortran combine process management with work distribution as shown in Table 4-5. Either a DO or a SECTIONS work distribution construct is combined with the PARALLEL directive. These constructs allow a minimal modification of a sequential Fortran program to introduce parallelism into a computationally intensive part without restructuring the rest of the program.

Table 4-3   OpenMP Fortran work distribution constructs.

Directives	
!$OMP DO [clause [[, clause]...]	Distribute iterations of Fortran_do_loop
Fortran_do_loop	over threads of the team, and do a
[!$OMP END DO [NOWAIT]]	barrier at end unless NOWAIT is present.
Allowed clauses: PRIVATE, FIRSTPRIVATE, LASTPRIVATE, REDUCTION, SCHEDULE, ORDERED	
!$OMP SECTIONS [clause [[, clause]...]	Distribute execution of the blocks
[!$OMP SECTION]	for different sections over threads
block	of the team.
[!$OMP SECTION	
block]	
...	
!$OMP END SECTIONS [NOWAIT]	Do a barrier at end unless NOWAIT present.
Allowed clauses: PRIVATE, FIRSTPRIVATE, LASTPRIVATE, REDUCTION	
!$OMP SINGLE	One (arbitrarily chosen) thread executes
block	the block, and others wait at implicit
!$OMP END SINGLE [NOWAIT]	barrier at end unless NOWAIT is present.

Table 4-3   OpenMP Fortran work distribution constructs. (Continued)

Allowed clauses: PRIVATE, FIRSTPRIVATE	
!$OMP MASTER	Only the master thread executes the
block	*block* while other threads skip it with no
!$OMP END MASTER	synchronization at beginning or end.
Allowed clauses: None	
Clauses	
SCHEDULE (*type* [, *chunk*])	Distribute *chunk* consecutive loop iterations
type is STATIC|DYNAMIC|GUIDED|RUNTIME	by prescheduling (STATIC), self scheduling
ORDERED	(DYNAMIC), guided self scheduling, or as given by value of environment variable.
	Loop contains block that must be executed in iteration order.
Environment variable	
OMP_SCHEDULE	String value specifying *type*, *chunk*.

Table 4-4   OpenMP Fortran synchronization constructs.

Directives	
!$OMP CRITICAL [(*name*)]	Each thread executes *block*, but no other
block	thread may simultaneously be in this or
!$OMP END CRITICAL [(*name*)]	another critical section of the same name.
!$OMP BARRIER	No thread proceeds until all arrive.
!$OMP ATOMIC	Atomically do *update_statement*, having
update_statement	same allowed forms as reduction update.
!$OMP FLUSH [(*list*)]	Force consistent view by all processors of all variables, or only those in *list*.
Implicit in: BARRIER, CRITICAL, END CRITICAL, END DO, END SECTIONS, END PARALLEL, END SINGLE, ORDERED, END ORDERED (unless NOWAIT)	
!$OMP ORDERED	Execute *block* in a parallel loop in iteration
block	order. One and only one such block appears
!$OMP END ORDERED	in each loop with an ORDERED clause.
Run-time library routines	
SUBROUTINE OMP_INIT_LOCK (*var*)	Create and initialize lock with name *var*.
SUBROUTINE OMP_DESTROY_LOCK (*var*)	Destroy lock *var*, where *var* is type integer.
SUBROUTINE OMP_SET_LOCK (*var*)	Wait until lock *var* is unset, then set it.
SUBROUTINE OMP_UNSET_LOCK (*var*)	Release lock *var* owned by this thread.
LOGICAL FUNCTION OMP_TEST_LOCK (*var*)	Attempt to set lock var; return .TRUE. on success and .FALSE. on failure.

Table 4-5   OpenMP Fortran combined process management and work
distribution.

Directives	
`!$OMP PARALLEL DO` [*clause* [[,] *clause*…]]	Fork threads, and execute *do_loop* in
do_loop	parallel, joining back to a single thread
[`!$OMP END PARALLEL DO`]	at the end.
Allowed clauses: `PRIVATE, SHARED, DEFAULT, FIRSTPRIVATE, LASTPRIVATE,` `REDUCTION, SCHEDULE, ORDERED, IF, COPYIN`	
`!$OMP PARALLEL SECTIONS` [*clause* [[,] *clause*…]]	Fork threads, and execute each
[`!$OMP SECTION`]	independent section with one thread.
block	
[`!$OMP SECTION`	
block]	
…	
`!$OMP END PARALLEL SECTIONS`	Join back to single master thread at end.
Allowed clauses: `PRIVATE, SHARED, DEFAULT, FIRSTPRIVATE, LASTPRIVATE,` `REDUCTION, IF, COPYIN`	

Most of the restrictions on the way OpenMP Fortran constructs are allowed to interact can be derived from an understanding of the execution environment in which a construct makes sense. For example, a barrier assumes that all threads reach it and, therefore, makes no sense inside a sections construct, where only one thread executes each section. The same principle applies, somewhat less obviously, to exclude a barrier from a parallel loop. Depending on the number of threads and extent of the loop, a thread might reach a barrier zero, one, or several times. In general, the interior of certain parallel constructs is a sequential execution environment. This includes DO, SECTIONS, SINGLE, MASTER, and CRITICAL constructs. Constructs that assume a parallel execution environment, such as BARRIER, DO, SECTIONS, MASTER, and SINGLE, do not make sense in a sequential environment and, thus, must not be dynamically nested inside the previous constructs. Operations on locks and critical sections make sense in either a sequential or a parallel environment. Nested parallel regions can be viewed as having the enclosed parallel region act within the sequential execution environment of each separate thread. One OpenMP interaction restriction not easily interpreted on the basis of the logic described is that an ORDERED section is not allowed in the dynamic extent of a critical section.

4.4.3   OpenMP Fortran Examples and Discussion

There are two extreme philosophies that can be used to parallelize a program. In the minimal approach, parallel constructs are placed only where large amounts of independent data is processed, typically by nested loops, with the rest of the program left sequential. Two problems with this approach are that it may not exploit all the parallelism available in the program and that process creation and termination overhead may be invoked many times. Depending on the underlying hardware and implementation, this overhead may be large. The other extreme is the SPMD approach, which treats the whole program as parallel code, serializing steps only where required by the program logic. We give examples of each of these extremes, recognizing that many applications use a mixture of them. Although Fortran is case insensitive, upper case has been used consistently for OpenMP constructs to enhance readability of the examples.

Example   Our first example starts with a sequential program, locates large parallel loops, and places OpenMP PARALLEL DO directives around them. The program simulates the dynamics of n particles interacting in three-dimensional space by way of a pair potential between particle centers. The details of the physics are unimportant to the parallelization of the program except when they suggest where to look for independent computations. Parallelization is based on the control structure and data dependences of the program code.

The simulation represents n particles by four $3 \times n$ arrays, where the first index ranges over the x, y, and z space dimensions and the second index ranges over particles. The arrays are position, p, velocity, v, acceleration, a, and force, f. The potential energy, pot, and kinetic energy, kin, of the whole system are also computed. Like many simulations, this one evolves in discrete time steps that cannot be parallelized because virtually all of the information at a step depends on the previous step. The core of the main program is, thus, a sequential time stepping loop, as shown in Program 4-10. The loop calls a compute subroutine to calculate forces on the particles and total potential and kinetic energies and then calls the update subroutine to calculate new positions, velocities, and accelerations for all particles after a time step of length dt.

The body of the compute subroutine is shown in Program 4-11. It consists of three nested loops, with the innermost running over the three space dimensions and each of the outer two ranging over the number of particles. The simplest application of OpenMP applies a PARALLEL DO directive to only one of the loops. This should be the outermost loop so each thread does as much work as possible to amortize the time spent in thread creation and termination. Although it would be possible to coalesce the two loops over particles into one parallel loop (see Problem 4.20), if fewer than n processors are available, it would have little benefit. The subroutine dist calculates the vector distance between two particles and its magnitude, and the subroutine dot computes the scalar product of two 3-vectors.

The loop indices i, j, and k must be declared private because they differ among threads, and because rij and d depend on the pair of particles being considered, they must also be private. System potential and kinetic energies are summed over particles, so they are obvious candidates for reduction variables.

```
do i = 1, nsteps
   call compute(n, pos, vel, mass, f, pot, kin)
   call update(n, pos, vel, f, a, mass, dt)
enddo
```

Program 4-10   Time stepping loop central to the main particle dynamics program.

```
                    pot = 0.0
                    kin = 0.0
  !$OMP            PARALLEL DO&
  !$OMP&           DEFAULT(SHARED)&
  !$OMP&           PRIVATE(i, j, k, rij, d)&
  !$OMP&           REDUCTION(+: pot, kin)
                    do i = 1, n
                       do k = 1, 3
                          f(k, i) = 0.0
                       enddo
                       do j = 1, n
                          if (i .ne. j) then
                             call dist(pos(1, i), pos(1, j), rij, d)
                             pot = pot + 0.5*v(d)
                             do k = 1, 3
                                f(k, i) = f(k, i) - rij(k)*dv(d)/d
                             enddo
                          endif
                       enddo
                       kin = kin + dot(vel(1, i), vel(1, i))
                    enddo
  !$OMP            END PARALLEL DO
                    kin = kin*0.5*mass
```

Program 4-11   Body of the `compute` subroutine.

The body of the update routine, shown in Program 4-12, is a doubly nested loop with the outer loop over particles and the inner over space dimensions. Again, the simple approach parallelizes the outer loop of size n. Only the loop indices i and k need to be made private to ensure that different threads operate on disjoint portions of the p, v, and a arrays.

The sequential particle dynamics program of about four pages, including all subroutines, has been parallelized by the addition of only two PARALLEL DO constructs and their associated clauses. This is a minimal change to the program, but threads are created and terminated twice for each time step. If process management overhead is large, this can slow the program significantly. It should also be remembered that the time stepping loop and subroutine calls are executed sequentially. This is a small fraction of code if n is large, but Amdahl's law shows that even a small amount of sequential code can reduce efficiency if the number of processors is large.

Our second example illustrates the idea of writing a parallel program as a single body of program text executed by many instruction streams simultaneously, the so-called SPMD approach. The parallelization effort shifts from finding places to put parallel constructs to using synchronizations and sequential code sections to enforce the required data dependences of the program.

```
!$OMP       PARALLEL DO&
!$OMP&      DEFAULT(SHARED)&
!$OMP&      PRIVATE(i, k)
            do i = 1, n
              do k = 1, 3
                pos(k,i) = pos(k,i) + vel(k,i)*dt + 0.5*dt*dt*a(k,i)
                vel(k,i) = vel(k,i) + 0.5*dt*(f(k,i)/mass + a(k,i))
                a(k,i) = f(k,i)/mass
              enddo
            enddo
!$OMP       END PARALLEL DO
```

Program 4-12   Body of the `update` subroutine.

Example   Program 4-13 shows a complete OpenMP Fortran program for Gaussian elimination with partial pivoting. The program generates a test matrix rather than reading one,
does LU decomposition by Gaussian elimination, leaving L and U factors stored in place
of the original matrix, and prints the time for performing the elimination and, optionally,
the L and U factors. The execution time is calculated from calls to `timer()`, assumed to
return microseconds from start of job. Forward and back substitution for solving equation sets with specific right-hand sides using the L and U factors are not included in this
program.

The parallelism structure of the program is close to the SPMD model, with only input and
output being outside the single parallel region that encloses the rest of the program. The
generation of the test matrix is parallelized over rows, with different threads calculating
different rows and the inner loop over columns done sequentially. The `do 2000` loop over
diagonal elements is a sequential one that is executed independently by each thread. Barriers within the sequential loop ensure that threads will complete iterations of the loop in
close synchrony. For each diagonal element, a parallel search for the element with maximum absolute value in the pivot column below the diagonal is done. The small amount of
work for each iteration makes static scheduling appropriate to avoid the synchronization
overhead of dynamic scheduling, and some knowledge of the number of processors might
make a chunk size greater than the default of one appropriate. Swapping rows to bring the
pivot into the diagonal position is also statically scheduled because there is little work per
iteration. In the row reduction loop, each iteration involves a full row to the right of the
diagonal, so overhead may be small enough to make the better load balance resulting from
dynamic scheduling beneficial. This is not likely to help much here with processors of the
same speed because the work per parallel iteration is the same for all threads.

Synchronization in the program is partially explicit and partially implicit in the work distribution constructs. For example, the implicit barrier at the end of the matrix generation
loop ensures that all matrix elements are computed before anything else is done. At the

```
c               OpenMP Gaussian elimination program
c------------------------------------------------------
                program gauselim
                integer n,prflg,itim1,itim2,msing,pivind,nprocs
                real a(500,500),pivot,gmax,getim
                integer  i,j,k,indmax
                real pmax,temp
c
c               Read in matrix dimension and output flag
  5             write(*,*) ' Input the Following:'
                write(*,*) ' n = matrix dimension <= 500'
                write(*,*) ' prflg=1->print results;0->don"t'
                read(*,10) n,prflg
 10             format(2i4)
                if (n .gt. 500) goto 5
c
c               Use as many threads as there are available processors
                call OMP_SET_DYNAMIC(.false.)
                nprocs = OMP_GET_NUM_PROCS()
                call OMP_SET_NUM_THREADS(nprocs)
!$OMP           PARALLEL PRIVATE(i,j,k,indmax,pmax,temp) &
!$OMP&             SHARED(a,pivot,gmax,n,itim1,itim2,msing,pivind)
c
c               Generate the matrix
!$OMP           DO SCHEDULE(STATIC)
                do  i = 1,n
                   do  110  j = 1,n
                      if (i .eq. j) then
                         a(i,j) = i*i/2.0
                      else
                         a(i,j) = (i+j)/2.0
                      endif
 110               continue
                enddo
!$OMP           END DO
c               Implicit barrier at end of OMP DO
c
c               Initialize shared variables
!$OMP           SINGLE
                   itim1 = timer()
                   msing = 0
!$OMP           END SINGLE
c               Implicit barrier at end of OMP SINGLE
```

Program 4-13   OpenMP Fortran program for Gaussian elimination.

```
c                  Perform rowwise elimination
                   do 2000  k = 1, n-1
c
c                  Reset private and shared maxima
                   pmax = 0.0
!$OMP              SINGLE
                       gmax = 0.0
!$OMP              END SINGLE
c
c                  Find the pivot row
!$OMP              DO SCHEDULE(STATIC)
                   do  i = k, n
                       temp = abs(a(i,k))
                       if (temp .gt. pmax) then
                           pmax = temp
                           indmax = i
                       endif
                   enddo
!$OMP              END DO NOWAIT
!$OMP              CRITICAL(PIVLCK)
                       if (gmax .lt. pmax) then
                           gmax = pmax
                           pivind = indmax
                       endif
!$OMP              END CRITICAL(PIVLCK)
c
c                  If matrix is singular set the flag and quit
!$OMP              BARRIER
!$OMP              SINGLE
                       if (gmax .eq. 0) msing = 1
!$OMP              END SINGLE
                   if (msing .eq. 1) goto 9000
c
c                  Swap rows if necessary
                   indmax = pivind
                   if (indmax .ne. k) then
!$OMP                  DO SCHEDULE(STATIC)
                       do j = k, n
                           temp = a(indmax,j)
                           a(indmax,j) = a(k,j)
                           a(k,j) = temp
                       enddo
!$OMP                  END DO
                   endif
```

Program 4-13   OpenMP Fortran program for Gaussian elimination. (Continued)

```
c                      Compute the pivot
!$OMP                  SINGLE
                           pivot = -1.0/a(k,k)
!$OMP                  END SINGLE
c
c                      Perform row reductions
!$OMP                  DO SCHEDULE(DYNAMIC)
                       do  i = k+1, n
                           temp = pivot*a(i,k)
                           a(i,k) = -temp
                           do 410 j = k+1, n
                               a(i,j) = a(i,j) + temp*a(k,j)
 410                       continue
                       enddo
!$OMP                  END DO NOWAIT
c
 2000          continue           ! End of sequential loop
c
 9000          continue           ! Exit the parallel region
!$OMP          END PARALLEL
c
c                      Output section
                       itim2 = timer()
                       if (msing .eq. 1) then
                           write(*,*) ' The matrix is singular'
                       else
                           if (prflg .eq. 1) then
                               write(*,*) ' The eliminated matrix is as below:'
                               do 500 i = 1,n
                                   write(*,20) i
                                   do 510 j = 1,n,10
                                       write(*,30) (a(i,k),k=j,j+9)
 510                               continue
 500                           continue
 20                            format(//,2x,'Row  :',i4)
 30                            format(2x,10f6.2)
                           endif
                           getim = float(itim2 - itim1)/10**6
                           write(*,*) ' Time for performing the elimination with'
                           write(*,*) nprocs,' threads is ', getim, 'secs'
                       endif
                       end
```

Program 4-13   OpenMP Fortran program for Gaussian elimination. (Continued)

end of the parallel pivot search loop, NOWAIT is specified to allow a thread to request the critical section to make its contribution to the global maximum as soon as it has finished its share of the search. Using the REDUCTION clause to find the maximum here would be appropriate if the index of the maximum were not needed also. When all threads finish the do 2000 loop, the parallel region is completed, and the master thread does the output.

Minimal parallelization of an MIMD program follows a style that is almost SIMD in nature. A single stream of control characterizes the overall program structure, with parallel operations applied to large data structures with independent elements. In contrast, the SPMD style is cooperative, with the idea of a team doing work over the entire flow of control rather than at specific points in the computation. If sequential operation is required by the program logic, it is limited to specific program points where it can coordinate team activity. The SPMD style may exhibit replication of work over threads. For example, the do 2000 loop over pivots in Program 4-13 is executed independently by all threads, while the time stepping loop in Program 4-10 is executed by only one thread. However, other threads contribute nothing to program completion during execution of the sequential loop of Program 4-10 while no thread does any fork/join work in the do 2000 loop of Program 4-13. While the SPMD style may seem foreign to sequential programmers, it is quite familiar to managers, who commonly organize tasks to be done by teams of independent entities who coordinate their parallel activities by specific synchronizing meetings and memos.

4.5 Pipelined MIMD—Multithreading

Just as with SIMD operation, pipelining can be applied to MIMD computers to reduce the amount of hardware associated with multiple processors. The hardware savings comes because instruction execution is a multistep process, and different instructions from different instruction streams can use independent parts of the execution hardware simultaneously instead of having separate complete execution units for each stream. Pipelined MIMD is one way to achieve multithreading, and it is often identified by that name. *Multithreading* is a more general term for any fine-grained form of multiprogramming, where there is hardware for multiple instruction stream states, consisting of program counter, register set, and other process status for each stream. A fast context switch allows control to pass from one thread to another with minimum overhead, for example on a cache miss. The term *thread* is used for process or instruction stream in this context to indicate the "light weight" nature of a process, that is, the small amount of private state that distinguishes it. A thread shares its memory map, I/O bindings, and other system resources that might be associated with a heavier process with other threads in the system. Pipelined MIMD multithreading switches threads at every clock tick, inserting an instruction from a different stream into the pipeline on every cycle. Ideally, a new instruction from the same stream is not inserted into the pipeline until the previous instruction from that stream is complete. This ensures that instructions in the pipeline simultaneously are independent and eliminates many of the pipeline interlocks required in pipelined uniprocessors. Threads may interact through the shared memory, and appropriate synchronization operations must control this interaction.

An MIMD pipeline not only breaks down arithmetic operations into a series of pipeline stages, but also the instruction fetch, operand access, result store, and next program counter calculations are incorporated into pipeline stages. After being fetched, the instruction accompanies its data through the pipeline, determining the activity performed at each stage. Each process supported by the hardware can be represented by an ID number that points to the register set, program counter, and other items of its process state. Process IDs are then queued to enter the pipeline on the next available clock cycle, as shown on the right side of Figure 4-18. An implementation may use different pipeline hardware for different instructions, dividing into several special purpose pipelines after the decode stage, but our discussion takes a high-level view of a unified pipeline with instructions passing through the same stages, whose activity is modified by the specific instruction.

Memory access must be handled differently than other instruction activity for several reasons. First, an instruction access occurs on behalf of some process every clock cycle. Any data access by an executing instruction then represents a second memory reference in a single cycle. Instruction memory should, thus, be separate from data memory to support concurrent accesses. This can be done either by having a separate instruction memory, the so-called Harvard architecture, or by having an instruction-only cache service instruction fetches, as shown in Figure 4-18. The second unique feature of memory access is that, with current technology, it can take considerably longer than arithmetic instruction execution. It then becomes performance effective to separate load and store operations from register-to-register arithmetic as in a RISC architecture and handle them in a pipelined memory interface. When a memory reference instruction is decoded, it is sent to the memory access queue of Figure 4-18, and its process ID is removed from the execution queue and pipeline. Memory references may then propagate through pipelined connection network and memory modules without occupying execution pipeline resources. A memory reference that is blocked by synchronization or virtual memory activity can wait to retry in the memory access queue.

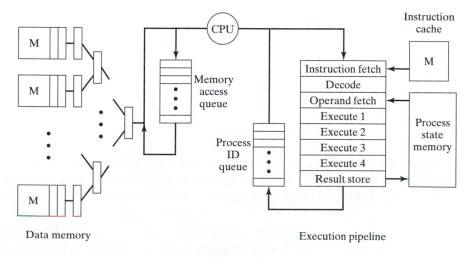

Figure 4-18 Pipelined MIMD computer architecture.

Because the number of process IDs in the execution unit varies with the number of outstanding memory requests, maximum pipeline utilization requires more active processes than there are execution pipeline stages. The goal is to have some process ID ready to enter the execution pipeline on each cycle. Each process ID requires a fair amount of storage for process state, probably on-chip in an integrated design. The need for on-chip register memory is offset by a reduced demand for on-chip data cache, because the pipelined memory interface tolerates longer data access latency.

A single hardware unit of a pipelined MIMD computer executes multiple processes sharing memory. We will call such a hardware unit a process execution module (PEM) to distinguish it from a uniprocessor. If multiple PEMs are connected to a common pipelined memory system, the total system simply supports more processes sharing memory. Thus, the programmer's model of the computer does not change in going from one to many PEMs in a system. That model is identical to that of shared memory MIMD with separate processors, except for some aspects of process control. Once created, processes act as if they were running on separate processors sharing memory and are programmed using the methods already described in this chapter. New processes are created, not by communication with a separate processor, but by assigning a set of instruction stream resources, including program counter and registers, to a new thread and starting it at some instruction location in the program memory. As long as process state sets are available, thread creation is simple, and may not even involve the operating system. Only if the PEM runs out of process states does the operating system need to be invoked to do resource management. In a multithreaded computer in which multiple PEMs share memory, the operating system probably is involved in the communication necessary to start threads on other PEMs.

In multithreading, part of the parallelism in a program is being used to mask pipeline and memory latency, and this is reflected in the evaluation of performance. An effective number of cycles per instruction can be computed as a weighted average of the number of pipeline stages in the execution unit and the memory access path. This effective number of cycles per instruction sets a target for the number of process IDs that should be supported by the hardware. Even a single PEM is a multiprocessor, and resources are surely under utilized if it runs only one process. If CPI is the effective number of cycles for an instruction, a multiple PEM system is well utilized on the average when

$$\text{number of processes} = \text{number of PEMs} \times \text{CPI}. \tag{4.2}$$

Having multiple memory requests outstanding simultaneously is the principle way to mask, or *tolerate*, memory access latency. The use of caches *reduces* memory latency when accesses conform to the principle of locality. Locality is harder to achieve with many processes cooperating in a computation, and *latency tolerance* becomes an important alternative to *latency reduction* in this case. Current uniprocessors expend considerable effort in compilers or dynamic instruction issue hardware to exploit instruction level parallelism (ILP) in sequential programs, partly to yield multiple outstanding memory references that help tolerate memory latency. The degree of independence enjoyed by multiple instruction streams makes this much easier to do in a pipe-lined multiprocessor. ILP extraction techniques can also be applied to individual threads in a pipelined MIMD system to allow more than one instruction per thread in execution at a time. If ILP techniques are used to allow multiple active instructions per process, the average number of processes required to use a multiple PEM system effectively are

$$\text{number of processes} = \text{number of PEMs} \times \frac{\text{CPI}}{\text{degree of ILP}}. \tag{4.3}$$

Thus, fewer processes are needed for effective hardware utilization when ILP is used in addition to multiprocess pipelining to get parallel activity running on the hardware.

We, thus, see that pipelined MIMD is related to "true" MIMD in the same way that pipelined vector machines are related to "true" SIMD computers. In both cases, multiple replicated hardware units of the "true" parallel architecture are replaced by a pipeline. The requirement for parallel operations with no interdependencies holds in both "true" and pipelined versions of the architectures, and except for performance, the programmer sees the same computational model in both architecture styles. Fortran 90 is, thus, well matched to both "true" SIMD and pipelined vector computers, while OpenMP is suitable for programming both "true" and pipelined MIMD architectures. Pipelined versions of either SIMD or MIMD architectures yield greater tolerance of memory latency by allowing multiple memory requests from a single execution unit to be outstanding simultaneously. One difference between SIMD and MIMD pipelining is in combining multiple pipelined processing units sharing memory in a single computer system. In the MIMD case, there is little change in the user's view of the system as multiple processes with a shared memory. In the SIMD case, the overall system appears as a multiprocessor, each of whose processors has vector instructions.

4.6 Summary and Conclusions

A multiprocessor or MIMD computer system supports the concurrent execution of multiple instruction streams that cooperate to solve a single problem. Intermediate result sharing to enable process cooperation is either by way of mutual accesses to a shared memory or by explicit communication operations. The underlying hardware organization predisposes a system toward either the shared memory or distributed memory interpretation, but the operating system layer may alter the user's view of the architecture. In shared memory multiprocessors, the pri-mary problem is work distribution, that is, which processes perform which operations. In distrib-uted memory machines, there is the added problem of distributing data among processor specific memory units. The treatment of MIMD programming in this chapter is limited to the shared memory system model.

In contrast to SIMD programming, where an entire new class of parallel operations and supporting hardware, comprising the vector unit, is added to the programmer's model of a com-puter, MIMD programming is based on the addition of a few process interaction operations to an otherwise sequential instruction set. The added instructions help to address the issues of process management, data sharing, synchronization, and work distribution. There are two main shared memory MIMD programming paradigms, that of a single master process that occasionally uses slave processes to accomplish sections of parallel work and that of single program, multiple data, or SPMD, where all processes are active from the beginning to the end of a program and cooperate to perform all required operations.

Although successful MIMD programming can be done using one or two extra constructs supporting each of the concerns of process management, data sharing, synchronization, and work distribution, many different mechanisms have been developed for these purposes. A particularly rich area is that of synchronization, where many ideas developed for operating systems also appear in the context of parallel processing. Distinct conceptual differences appear between synchronizing the tightly coupled processes of a parallel program and the relatively independent processes coordinated by an operating system. Fairness is less of a concern in parallel processing, and mutual exclusion cannot be assured by simply preventing the reallocation of a single processor, as it can in a uniprocessor operating system. A principle that underlies synchronization is the concept of atomicity, carefully formulated to both support correct synchronization and to allow for efficient, distributed implementations of synchronization operations.

OpenMP is an extension to a sequential programming language to support shared memory MIMD computation. It is presented here as an extension to Fortran 77, partly because that was its first defined version and partly to allow it to be easily compared and contrasted with the SIMD operations supported in Fortran 90 and described in the previous chapter. The OpenMP extensions are again grouped under the headings of process management, data sharing, synchronization, and work distribution within an execution model that begins with a single process and forks into multiple processes for the duration of specific parallel regions. The use of multiple parallel regions, each confined to one highly parallel portion of the computation corresponds to the master/slave style of programming, while starting a parallel region near the beginning of a program and maintaining it until the end corresponds to SPMD programming.

Finally, to show that the shared memory MIMD model of computation can be supported by different implementations, we discuss multithreading, in the form of pipelined MIMD. Operations from different instruction streams occupy a processing unit pipeline simultaneously with few pipeline interlocks being needed because instructions from different streams are quite independent. The ability of pipelined MIMD to have multiple memory requests occurring simultaneously can be used to mask memory latency, just as pipelined SIMD masks the latency of access to successive vector components. More efficient utilization of processor hardware and better tolerance of memory latency are the major drivers behind pipelined MIMD multithreading.

The idea of coordinating multiple independent entities to accomplish a single task is the unique feature of MIMD computation, though it is certainly not unique for managing large human endeavors. The ways in which independent workers share information, coordinate activity and partition the work to be done are the concerns of MIMD parallel programming. The degree to which processes share resources has an important influence on the character of an MIMD program, and the programming issues are simplest when shared access is allowed to variables in the computer's main memory.

4.7 Bibliographic Notes

For a historical review of early multiprocessors with only a few processors, as well as the larger scale Cm* and C.mmp systems at Carnegie Mellon University, see [253]. Another, more modern, treatment of MIMD programming and machines can be found in [270]. A broad discussion of all types of parallel processors with a good sampling of MIMD machines appears in [150].

Several shared memory programming languages were developed in research environments in the early 1980s. Some early ones were, the Force [10, 166], P4 [209], and EPEX/Fortran [86]. Commercial systems adopted many of the ideas of this work in their machine-specific languages. A good treatment of parallel programming for a specific commercial machine, the Sequent system, using the vendor supplied extensions to C, Fortran, and Pascal can be found in [230]. The programming extensions are quite typical of many commercial multiprocessors and are closely related to the facilities of OpenMP. The Parallel Computing Forum [233] discussed a Fortran extension that, while never adopted as a standard, laid the groundwork for OpenMP [229].

Surveys of multithreaded architectures have been presented in [226] and in [250]. Many of the machines using multithreading employ only a few threads and combine multithreading with other techniques for latency reduction and/or tolerance. The two commercial multithreaded MIMD machines, the Denelcor HEP [179] and the Tera Computer (now Cray, Inc.) MTA (multithreaded architecture) [16], have used multithreading as their primary latency tolerance method and employ hundreds of threads.

Problems

4.1   Rewrite the recurrence solver of Program 4-4 replacing the use of producer/consumer synchronization by critical section synchronization.

4.2   Why should the parameter i in Program 4-4 not be passed by reference because it is only read and not modified by the created processes? When are call-by-value and call-by-reference interchangeable in created processes of a parallel program?

4.3   In a shared memory multiprocessor in which all memory is shared and has the same access time, why might a parallel language supply a **private** declaration for variables?

4.4   Consider a shared memory multiprocessor in which a new process is started with a `create` statement and terminates with a `quit`. The `create` statement takes a subroutine name and a list of call-by-reference parameters. For synchronization, this machine has only the operations `lock` and `unlock`. Show code fragments needed in creating and created routines to make the statement `create sub(x)` act as if x were a call-by-value parameter. Your code should work even if the `create` statement is contained in a loop.

4.5   Calculate the efficiency $E(n)$ of Program 4-4 as a function of n assuming one processor per process.

4.6   Sequential pseudocode for Gaussian elimination without pivoting is shown below.

```
for k := 1 step 1 until N
    begin p := 1/a[k, k];
          a[k, k] := p;
          for i := k+1 step 1 until N
              begin q := -a[i, k]×p;
                    a[i, k] := q;
                    for j := k+1 step 1 until N
                        a[i, j] := a[i, j] + q×a[k, j];
          end;
    end;
```

Write shared memory multiprocessor pseudocode for Gaussian elimination on a system with NP processors. Assume NP << N. Use a minimum number of **fork** and **join** operations. Assume that **fork** assigns to the forked process a unique private variable, me, that contains the number, starting at one, of that process. The initial process will have me = 0. For synchronization use a **barrier** operation with a sequential body having the following format:

```
barrier
        ⟨Code body executed by one (any one) process⟩
end barrier
```

The behavior of the barrier is that all processes arrive at the **barrier** statement, one process executes the body of the barrier (process number is not specified), and then all processes exit the **end barrier**.

4.7   Consider both block and cyclic prescheduling of the **forall** over i in Program 4-6. Count the number of multiply-adds done by process k, $0 \leq k \leq P - 1$, in each case. How does the load imbalance between the process with the most work and that with the least work vary with P and n? Assume that P divides n evenly.

4.8   A job for a multiprocessor with P processors consists of N independent tasks of two types, long and short. Long tasks take T_L units of processor time, and short tasks take T_S. There are N_L long tasks and the rest are short. P divides N evenly and $m = N/P > N_L$. The N_L long tasks are randomly placed among the N tasks.

(a) If the tasks are executed by a prescheduled parallel loop, give an expression for the execution time in the worst case. Evaluate the worst-case execution time for $N = 100$, $P = 10$, $N_L = 5$, $T_S = 1$ ms, and $T_L = 10$ ms.

(b) If the tasks are executed by a self-scheduled parallel loop, find the worst case execution time and calculate it for the same parameter values.

Hint: Consider the worst case for processors being idle because there is no work left to do.

4.9   Write prescheduling code to enable a process with identifier $0 \leq id \leq P - 1$ to generate the set of index pairs (k, i) it will handle in executing a parallel two dimensional triangular loop corresponding to the sequential nested loops

```
for k := 1 step 1 until n
    for i := 1 step 1 until k
        ⟨ parallelizable loop body ⟩
```

Each process must compute its next index pair independently of other processes.

Hint: Linearize the index by numbering the pairs consecutively. For a given linearized index value handled by process *id*, find *k* by solving a quadratic and chopping to an integer.

4.10 Complete the implementation of producer/consumer variables using critical sections by writing critical section-based pseudocode procedures for **consume, copy,** and **void** to go with the **produce** implementation of Program 4-8.

4.11 A multiprocessor supports synchronization with lock/unlock hardware. The primitives are represented at the compiler language level by two subroutine calls, **lock**(q) and **unlock**(q). The **lock**(q) operation waits for the lock to be clear, sets it and returns, while **unlock**(q) clears the lock unconditionally. It is desired to implement produce and consume on full/empty variables where **produce**(x,v) waits for x empty, writes it with value v and sets full while **consume**(x,v) waits for x full, copies its value to v, and sets x to empty.

Using sequential pseudocode extended by the two operators **lock** (q) and **unlock** (q), write code sections that implement **produce** (x, v) and **consume** (x, v) on an asynchronous variable x and normal variable v. Carefully describe your representation for an asynchronous variable. No synchronization operations other than **lock** and **unlock** may be used.

4.12 What can happen if a processor is taken away from a process while it is in a critical section? Parallel programs may use many short critical sections to update shared variables. Must the operating system be notified on every entry to and exit from a critical section? What are the reasons for reallocating a processor in a shared memory multiprocessor? How do they differ from the reasons for reallocating a uniprocessor?

4.13 Write code to compute the lower and upper bounds, lwr and upr, for process me executing its portion of

    forall i := lwr **step** stp **until** upr

under block prescheduling. Balance the load so that each process handles at most one more value of the index i than any other.

4.14 A shared memory multiprocessor has the basic synchronization instructions **lock** and **unlock**. Some users have implemented the **barrier** synchronization using the pseudocode form:

```
procedure barrier(n);
private last;
shared n, count, b, c;
begin
    lock(c);
        count := count + 1;
        last := (count = n);
    unlock(c);
    if last then unlock(b)
        else begin lock(b); unlock(b); end
    lock(c);
        count := count - 1;
        if count = 0 then lock(b);
    unlock(c);
end barrier;
```

The parameter n is the number of processes to cooperate in the barrier, and initial conditions are: c-unlocked, b-locked, and count = 0.

The barrier behaves incorrectly when five processes execute the code:

```
phase1();
barrier(5);
phase2();
barrier(5);
phase3();
```

Tell what is wrong and show how to correct it.

4.15 The procedure below is called by all 2^k processors of a shared memory multiprocessor. The unique identifier of each processor is $0 \le me \le 2^k - 1$, V is a real valued variable, and k is an integer constant parameter. The function xor() returns the bit wise exclusive OR of its two integer arguments. All A[i, j] are initially empty.

```
procedure lep(me, V)
begin
      private me, V;
      shared A[0:k-1, 0:2^k-1];
      private i, j, T;
      for i:=0 step 1 until k-1
      begin
            j := xor(me, 2^i);
            produce A[i, j] := V;
            consume A[i, me] into T;
            V := max(V, T);
      end
end
```

   (a) What is the value of V returned in processor *me*?
   (b) Name the synchronization performed when all processors call the procedure.

4.16 Write efficient multiprocessor pseudocode for the computation:

```
for i := 1 step 1 until N
   for j := 1 step 1 until N
         a[j] := a[j] × (b[i, j]/c[i]);
```

Assume a **forall** construct (like the OpenMP PARALLEL DO), and assume that all processors are running and executing the same code. There are order N, and not order N^2, processors.

4.17 The following sequential pseudocode computes the histogram of a data array. x0 and x1 are the minimum and maximum values, respectively, in the data array x[1:N], and the histogram vector is h[0:M-1].

```
scale := M/(x1 - x0);
for i := 1 step 1 until N
      begin
            j := int(scale*(x[i] - x0));
            h[j] := h[j] + 1;
      end;
```

   (a) Write SIMD (vector) pseudocode for the histogram calculation. On the basis of the code, discuss what part of the calculation is vectorizable and not vectorizable, and why.

(b) Write MIMD pseudocode for the histogram calculation, extending sequential pseudocode with **fork/join**, shared and private variables, and using only unnamed critical sections for synchronization. Discuss the amount of parallelism achieved in your program.

(c) Would other hardware level synchronizations improve the parallelism in the MIMD calculation? Which ones and how?

4.18 Write two OpenMP subroutines that multiply $N \times N$ matrices. The subroutine parameters should be two operand matrices, the result matrix, and the dimension N. Do not use nested parallelism, but specify a fixed number of processes for the whole computation.

(a) Write the most straightforward OpenMP implementation in which the amount of work in each parallel task is $O(N^2)$ with $O(N)$ processes.

(b) Write a finer granularity program where each parallel task has only $O(N)$ operations with $O(N^2)$ processes. Suggest a new OpenMP construct that would better support this implementation.

4.19 A program with too many barriers can be safe because it is guaranteed to execute correctly in parallel, but unnecessary barriers have some performance penalty, if only because processes wait for the slowest at each one. For each OpenMP directive in Program 4-13 that allows a NOWAIT clause, tell whether such a clause is correct if present or may be inserted if absent to improve performance without damaging the program logic.

4.20 If the particle dynamics simulation is run on a system with more than n processors, it would be beneficial to combine the i and j loops in Program 4-11 to obtain $O(n^2)$ parallel work. Show how to do this by restructuring the code and introducing the appropriate OpenMP directives. It will be necessary to get perfectly nested i and j loops to combine them.

4.21 This problem considers two parallel organizations of code having the same serial time.

(a) The following OpenMP code is executed by P threads on P processors, where $N \gg P$. Write an expression for the execution time of the program. What is the speedup over a single processor execution if $N = 1{,}000$, $P = 50$, $t_0 = 1$ sec., $t_1 = 4$ sec., and $t_2 = 495$ sec.? Assume the single processor must execute the critical section body code, and assume that the time for all the OpenMP statements is negligible compared to the $\langle \text{code} \rangle$ sections.

```
!$OMP BARRIER
!$OMP SINGLE
          ⟨code: time t₀⟩
!$OMP END SINGLE
!$OMP CRITICAL
          ⟨code: time t₁⟩
!$OMP END CRITICAL
!$OMP DO SCHEDULE(STATIC, 1)
      DO 10    I = 1, N
          ⟨code: time t₂/N⟩
10    CONTINUE
!$OMP END DO
```

(b) Under the same assumptions as in (a), give an execution time expression for the code below, and estimate speedup over one processor using the numbers of part (a).

```
!$OMP BARRIER
!$OMP SINGLE
          ⟨code: time t₀⟩
!$OMP END SINGLE
!$OMP DO SCHEDULE(STATIC, 1)
        DO 10    I = 1, N
             ⟨code: time t₂/N⟩
!$OMP CRITICAL
             ⟨code: time t₁/N⟩
!$OMP END CRITICAL
10   CONTINUE
!$OMP END DO
```

4.22 Write an OpenMP program that eliminates the repeated barrier synchronizations in Program 4-13 for Gaussian elimination by implementing the algorithm described below.

Consider LU decomposition by Gaussian elimination organized as operations on columns. Column j is reduced j times, with the last reduction making it into a pivot column. A column j to the right of the pivot column $k < j$ is reduced the k-th time by exchanging two elements according to the number of the k-th pivot row and adding a multiple of the pivot column.

p_1	u_{12}	u_{13}	u_{14}	u_{15}	u_{16}	u_{17}	u_{18}
l_{21}	p_2	u_{23}	u_{24}	u_{25}	u_{26}	u_{27}	u_{28}
l_{31}	l_{32}	p_3	u_{34}	u_{35}	u_{36}	u_{37}	u_{38}
l_{41}	l_{42}	l_{43}	a_{44}	a_{45}	a_{46}	a_{47}	a_{48}
l_{51}	l_{52}	l_{53}	a_{54}	a_{55}	a_{56}	a_{57}	a_{58}
l_{61}	l_{62}	l_{63}	a_{64}	a_{65}	a_{66}	a_{67}	a_{68}
l_{71}	l_{72}	l_{73}	a_{74}	a_{75}	a_{76}	a_{77}	a_{78}
l_{81}	l_{82}	l_{83}	a_{84}	a_{85}	a_{86}	a_{87}	a_{88}

Column	1	2	3	4	5	6	7	8
Pivot row	3	7	5	—	—	—	—	—
Reduction	1	2	3	3	3	3	3	3

To make a column into a pivot column, a search for the maximum absolute value in the column locates the pivot row. The element in the pivot row is then swapped with the element in the pivot position, and the column is scaled to obtain the corresponding values of the L matrix.

The L and U values are computed once, as are the pivots, but there are several versions of most a_{ij}. Let the original matrix A consist of elements $a_{ij}^{(1)}$, $i = 1, 2, ..., n$; $j = 1, 2, ..., n$, where the superscript keeps track of the number of updates. Then the updates can be described by the formulas,

$$p_k = a_{kk}^{(k)}, k = 1, 2, ..., n;$$

$$u_{kj} = a_{kj}^{(k)}, k = 1, 2, ..., n; j = k + 1, k + 2, ..., n;$$

$$l_{ik} = \frac{a_{ik}^{(k)}}{a_{kk}^{(k)}}, k = 1, 2, \ldots, n; i = k+1, k+2, \ldots, n;$$

$$a_{ij}^{(k)} = a_{ij}^{(k-1)} - l_{ik} u_{kj}, k = 1, 2, \ldots, n; i = k+1, k+2, \ldots, n; j = k+1, k+2, \ldots, n.$$

Consider the problem of synchronizing updates on columns in this formulation of Gaussian elimination. The example Gaussian elimination program of Program 4-13 used a barrier to ensure that the $k - 1$st update was complete before the k-th update started. This is not necessary. Column j can be made a pivot column as soon as it has been updated $j - 1$ times. The j-th nonpivot column can be updated the k-th time as soon as it has been updated $(k - 1)$ times and the k-th pivot column has been produced. If column update tasks are represented by a pair (update level, column) and scheduled in the order,

$(1, 1), (1, 2), \ldots, (1, n), (2, 2), (2, 3), \ldots, (2, n), \ldots, (n-1, n-1), (n-1, n), (n, n),$

then a task will be assured that the tasks on which it depends have been previously scheduled.

This program is meant to give you experience in the SPMD style of programming. You may find it useful to think in terms of some of the pseudocode synchronizations we have discussed that are not available in OpenMP. In that case, design the program with those constructs, and then implement them with constructs that are available in OpenMP.

4.23 A pipelined MIMD or multithreaded computer inserts an instruction from a queued instruction stream into a 10-stage execution pipeline every cycle, as long as the queue is not empty. Memory reference instructions do not occupy the queue or execution pipeline while waiting for pipelined memory response. If the average memory request time is 50 cycles, and there is a 20% chance that a given instruction is a memory reference, how many instruction streams, N, must be active to ensure an instruction is issued every cycle?

Distributed Memory Multiprocessors

In distributed memory multiprocessors, every memory module is associated with some individual processor. For data to be available to a processor, it must be stored in a memory associated with, or *local* to, that processor. An intermediate result produced by a different processor must move to the memories of any processors that will use that result as an operand. This data movement may take place as a result of explicit send and receive commands executed by the processors producing and using the result, respectively, or it may be supported by hardware, where the local memory of each processor is treated as a cache, and data movement into the cache is managed by hardware invoked on a cache miss. In multiprocessor caching, considerable effort is required to maintain consistent values for data that appears in more than one cache. With either software or hardware management, data transmission between processors can have a large impact on the performance of a distributed memory multiprocessor.

As we saw in Section 4.1, it can be difficult to make a clear division between shared and distributed memory multiprocessors. One way to distinguish is based on the existence of a shared address space. If any processor can issue a memory read or write instruction referencing a memory cell in any other processor, the machine has a shared address space, and some authors declare that any such multiprocessor is a shared memory MIMD computer. Our presentation is organized somewhat differently. In our discussion of shared memory multiprocessor programming in Chapter 4, no consideration was given to where data was placed in the shared memory of the overall system, under the assumption that the programming and behavior of the system did not depend on data placement. We take this as the defining characteristic of shared memory multiprocessors, rather than the existence of a shared address space. Under the heading of distributed memory multiprocessors, we treat systems where the programming or performance of the computer, or both, depend strongly on how the data is placed in the aggregate memory distributed among the processors. Distributed caching techniques can make it possible to run shared memory style code on a distributed memory machine, but by our definition, its performance depends strongly on the placement of data in memory. Because user coded sends and receives make data movement among processors explicit, we begin the discussion of distributed memory systems from the *message passing* point of view, in which data moves between processors' local memories as messages sent by one processor and received by another. We return to the consideration of multiprocessor caching later in the chapter.

Questions for the reader to keep in mind through this chapter include the different amounts and types of overhead associated with data sharing by message passing compared to overhead in shared memory reads and writes. Do all reads and writes suffer the same latency overhead? What is the relationship of the time to transmit a one-byte message and the time to transmit a very long message? Can a program be reorganized to send and receive only long messages? Does data ever have to be completely redistributed in the course of a computation?

5.1 Distributing Data and Operations Among Processor/Memory Pairs

An important part of distributed memory multiprocessing is the placement of data in separate memories associated with individual processors and possibly moving it around as the computation progresses. There is a great deal of work in both software and hardware to isolate the users of distributed memory multiprocessors from the details of data placement, but the separate memory nature of such machines always has a performance impact, and much good science is embodied in the compilers, communications packages, and distributed cache management strategies that take on the memory placement problem on behalf of the user.

Memories store programs as well as data, and fast access to instructions is essential to good performance in any processor. A program must, therefore, be stored in the local memory of the processor executing it, and if, as is usually the case, many processors execute the same program, a replicated copy of that program must be present in the local memory of each processor executing it. Because programs are read-only, there need be no concern about the consistency of the multiple copies. As in shared memory multiprocessors, it is not feasible to write a unique program for each of a hundred or thousand processors so most distributed memory multiprocessor programs are of the SPMD type, where one program is executed by all processors. An exception is caused by the fact that many distributed memory multiprocessors have a processor that is physically distinct from all the others, with different interprocessor communications or I/O facilities and perhaps with the capability of starting and stopping other processors. This so-called *host* processor often executes a program that is different from that executed by the other, *worker*, processors. The distinction between host and worker processors may impose a master/slave character on the organization of a multiprocessor program.

A major concern in distributed memory multiprocessing is that message passing does not consume so much time as to slow computation, possibly even negating the speed benefits of parallel computation. This is not the case if the computation task obeys a form of principle of locality. Spatial and temporal locality are well known from virtual memory and cache design.

The locality of interest here is of a somewhat different sort. Spatial locality characterizes the fact that a program is more likely to access an address that is numerically close to that of a recently accessed location, while temporal locality gives a higher probability of access to one of the addresses accessed in the recent past as opposed to a related address. Both characterize the observed behavior of sequential programs with the layout of information in memory specified by the programmer, the compiler, or a combination of the two. Instruction access exhibits a great deal of spatial locality while data locality is primarily temporal, although stride one array accesses exhibit spatial locality also.

The type of locality required for good performance in distributed memory multiprocessors can be called *partitionable locality*. The principle states that there is a way of partitioning the total data of the program among the memories local to the processors and of partitioning the operations on the data among the processors, so that data accesses by a particular processor are more likely to be to data stored in its local memory than to data stored in other memories. Only data accesses are of interest because the program executed by each processor must surely be stored in its local memory, possibly having multiple copies of the same program. The large number of ways of partitioning data and operations over processor/memory pairs makes this principle of partitionable locality hard to verify. It can be supported in some interesting cases. For example, in the solution of partial differential equations in a Euclidean space, the grid points can be divided among the processors so that the local memory of a processor stores all data items associated with a set of spatially nearby grid points. The computations for this set of grid points would be done by the processor having data for those points in its local memory. At the interfaces of spatial domains where computations at a grid point require information from grid points stored in other memories, messages are sent and received to communicate the required information. The amount of computation is proportional to the volume or area (in grid points) of the region assigned to a processor while the amount of communication is proportional to the region's surface or perimeter. A large area to perimeter ratio supports the principle of partitionable locality in this so-called *domain decomposition* approach to physical simulation in Euclidean space.

Determining a partitioning that exhibits locality, or even verifying that such a partitioning exists, in an arbitrary multiprocessor program can be very difficult, although such decompositions have been done for many computationally intensive scientific computations to obtain speed benefit from large numbers of simply connected processors. Even with domain decomposition, problems arise in scaling up the number of processors in the system. As more domains are fit into the same total volume, each one becomes smaller, and, thus, its perimeter to volume ratio increases. At the limit of one point per domain, information must be communicated to at least four neighboring processors, for a two-dimensional domain, for each unit of computation at the grid point.

We will develop the discussion of distributed memory architectures starting from a low level of support for data placement and movement among processors to establish the problems that need to be solved by either software or hardware. At the bottom level, parallel aspects of distributed memory program execution are dominated by the transmission of messages among individual processors and their local memories. For this reason, such architectures are sometimes called message passing multiprocessors.

5.2 Programming with Message Passing

The nature of programming with explicit message passing is established by the characteristics of the operations that transmit and receive messages. We have seen that in shared memory multiprocessors, the key to sharing computations among several processors is to maintain the proper precedence among processors in accessing data. Various synchronization mechanisms are used for this purpose. In distributed memory multiprocessors, the key to sharing computations is making data computed by one processor available to another processor that will use it. When each processor has a different address space, explicit operations are required to transfer data from one address space to another. These explicit transfers of data are commonly done by the message passing operations, *send* and *receive*. These operations have built in synchronization because the contents of the receiver's address space cannot be modified without it issuing an explicit receive instruction. This means that data sharing and synchronization are tied together in distributed memory multiprocessors much as they are by *produce/consume* in shared memory.

There is some flexibility in the type of synchronization provided by *send* and *receive*. The minimum property satisfied by all systems is that a specific message cannot be received before it is sent. A *send* operation cannot be entirely completed until the corresponding *receive* is executed, but if messages can be queued without involving the receiver, several messages may be sent before one is received. Both *send* and *receive* can have variable execution time, blocking progress to the next instruction until the other process involved in the communication completes its part of the operation. Synchronization is imposed on communicating processes depending on the blocking properties of *send* and *receive*.

A simple situation is nonblocking send and blocking receive. This assumes buffering, so that a sending process may issue a *send* and continue. It also assumes that the receiving process needs the message to make further progress. The buffering is done outside the address space of the receiving process. Once the contents of the receiver's address space can be changed without its cooperation, the synchronization properties of the message passing operations disappear, and *send* simply becomes a remote write into the address space of another processor. If there is no buffering, the sending process must wait for the receiver to accept the message. With just one unit of buffering, it cannot send a second message until the first one has been received. This corresponds closely to the effect of *produce/consume* in shared memory. Just as *send* may or may not block progress until the receiver has responded, *receive* need not necessarily block the process executing it. It can return a failure indication, and let the receiving process do other work, trying the *receive* again later.

One way to look at the synchronization implicit in *send* and *receive* is that these operations impose precedence relations on parallel operations occurring in their respective processes.

Figure 5-1 shows the activity in two processes communicating by means of *send*, *S*, and *receive*, *R*. The capital letters *A*, *B*, *C*, and *D* denote actions, while *S* and *R* mark send and receive points respectively. If $x \to y$ denotes precedence in the sense that action *x* must occur before action *y*, then $A \to C$ and $B \to D$ simply because individual processes are sequential, but $C \to D$ because sending a message precedes its reception. In the mutually blocking case, where send and receive both wait and occur together, it is also true that $A \to B$ because the send in Process 2 will not complete and allow *B* to be executed until the receive, and, therefore, *A*, have been completed in Process 1.

These precedence relations on actions constitute the constraints placed on the order of occurrence of actions in a distributed memory multiprocessor. Those relating actions in different processes represent the interprocess synchronization imposed by messages. The relation is a partial order, so a precedence relation can be shown by a diagram of its covering relation, as in Figure 5-2. If send is nonblocking, then *A* and *B* are unordered as shown in Figure 5-2(a). The most constrained synchronization is as shown in Figure 5-2(b) when both send and receive wait and complete together, that is, the processes *rendezvous* at a message transmission.

All four combinations of blocking properties of send and receive can occur, and all lead to different sets of precedence constraints. Table 5-1 gives a summary of the different blocking possibilities and their implications for message synchronization. For send to be nonblocking, there must be buffering of messages in the system. The size of a buffer determines how many nonblocking sends can successfully occur before a corresponding receive. A nonblocking receive must have an interface that allows for a failure return, because a message may not be available. If either send or receive is blocking, there should be some way for the system to determine if a blocked operation is waiting on a process that has terminated. Perhaps the most commonly used form of message transmission has nonblocking send and blocking receive. Buffering is usually needed at the receiver for hardware reasons, and a receive operation is not usually executed until the result is needed to proceed.

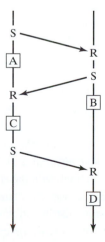

Figure 5-1 Precedence imposed by interprocess communication.

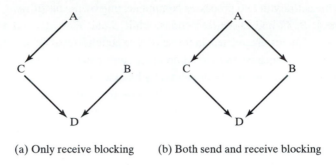

(a) Only receive blocking   (b) Both send and receive blocking

Figure 5-2   Covering relations for the precedence constraints.

Table 5-1   Implications of blocking properties of send and receive.

Message synchronization	System requirements	Precedence constraints
Send: nonblocking Receive: nonblocking	Message buffering Failure return from receive	None, unless message is received successfully.
Send: nonblocking Receive: blocking	Message buffering Termination detection	Actions preceding send occur before those following receive.
Send: blocking Receive: nonblocking	Termination detection Failure return from receive	Actions preceding receive occur before those following send.
Send: blocking Receive: blocking	Termination detection Termination detection	Actions preceding rendezvous occur before those following it in both processes.

5.2.1   The Communicating Sequential Processes (CSP) Language

The language CSP is a formally defined language with a minimal set of parallel features that is suitable for distributed memory multiprocessors. CSP was proposed by C. A. R. Hoare. OCCAM, a commercial language for the Inmos Transputer, is based directly on it. CSP extends ordinary sequential programming by adding only the most basic features of multiprocessors, namely the concepts of *parallelism*, *communication*, and *indeterminacy*. The communication in CSP is done using send and receive operations with the rendezvous type of blocking. Send and receive operations and the lack of sharing of variables among processes make CSP suitable as a pseudocode like notation for discussing distributed memory multiprocessor programming. Although we do not use it in this way, CSP is also designed to allow formal proofs of correctness for algorithms expressed in the language. The concept of a statement failing is introduced to assign a precise, formal outcome, failure, to cases in which program cannot proceed correctly.

CSP is explained below using a BNF description of the syntax. We use the Backus Naur Form (BNF) notation described in Table 5-2, where ::= is the BNF definition symbol, | denotes alternative choice, names in ⟨⟩ are meta symbols, and {y} denotes one or more repetitions of y. In addition, ⟨x list⟩ denotes one or more x separated by semicolons.

Parallelism in CSP is introduced at the top of the program hierarchy. A program in CSP consists of a group of sequential processes, executing in parallel. The syntax for this is:

⟨process⟩ ‖ ⟨process⟩ ‖ ...‖ ⟨process⟩

A process consists of a name and list of commands.

⟨process⟩ ::= ⟨label⟩ :: ⟨command list⟩

There are *no* shared variables in CSP. The name spaces of different processes are completely disjoint. All information shared among processes must be communicated by messages.

Communication in CSP is by blocking send and receive. Each command waits for the other, and both complete together. A send operation is written:

⟨process label⟩ ! ⟨expr⟩

where ⟨expr⟩ is an expression with a value of the correct type. A receive operation is written:

⟨process label⟩ ? ⟨target variable⟩

where ⟨target variable⟩ is a receiving process variable that is set to the value received. Send and receive wait until a corresponding operation, on a message of the same type, occurs in the other process named in the command. Only then do both proceed. If a process attempts to send to, or receive from, a process that has terminated, the command fails. Failure of a command results in the failure of any program containing the command and is an important concept for the use of CSP to prove correctness of communications protocols. For example, the program fragment:

    proc1 :: ... proc2 ! (4+x); ...‖
    proc2 :: ... proc1 ? q; ...

is similar to the assignment q := 4 + x. Note that the assignment statement could not be written in CSP because no process can access both q and x.

Table 5-2 Summary of BNF notation used in describing CSP.

Notation	Meaning
⟨lhs⟩::= rhs	The ⟨lhs⟩ meta symbol is defined by the rhs BNF expression
		Separates alternative choices in a BNF expression
⟨name⟩	Indicates that name is a BNF meta symbol
{y}	Denotes one or more repetitions of y
⟨x list⟩	List of one or more x separated by semicolons

Indeterminacy is handled in CSP by guarded commands. Guarded commands were introduced by E. Dijkstra and are a form of conditional. The guard is a condition and a command list is the consequence:

⟨guard⟩ → ⟨command list⟩

The power of guards is seen when they are used in alternative commands. An alternative command is written:

[⟨guard 1⟩ → ⟨command list 1⟩ ❑ ⟨guard 2⟩ → ⟨command list 2⟩ ❑ ...]

If one or more guards in an alternative command are true, the command list corresponding to one true guard is executed. In the case of more than one true guard, it is indeterminate which command list is executed. If all guards are false, the alternative command fails. A related command is the repetitive command, written:

*[⟨guard 1⟩ → ⟨command list 1⟩ ❑ ⟨guard 2⟩ → ⟨command list 2⟩ ❑ ...]

This command repeatedly executes a command list associated with a true guard until all guards are false, when it successfully terminates. Thus, the repetitive command exits when all guards are false, while the nonrepeating alternative command fails if all guards are false.

Guards may contain input commands as well as boolean conditions. The detailed structure of a guard is given by the BNF definitions:

⟨guard⟩ ::= ⟨guard list⟩ | ⟨guard list⟩; ⟨input command⟩
⟨guard list⟩ ::= ⟨guard element⟩{; ⟨guard element⟩}
⟨guard element⟩ ::= ⟨boolean expression⟩ | ⟨declaration⟩

There can be at most one input command per guard. The inclusion of input commands in the guards of an alternative command allows a process to respond to one of a set of different inputs nondeterministically with respect to the code of the process. Thus, the response may be determined by the order of arrival of the inputs. For example, consider the three processes A, B, and X, shown below:

A :: ... X ! 8; ...||
B :: ... X ! 5; ...||
X :: ... [c=0; A?p → c := 1 ❑ c=0; B?p → c := 2] ...

In this example, if c = 0, the command waits for either A or B to send a message; if c ≠ 0, the command fails; and if both A and B have terminated, the command also fails. A repetitive command with input statements in one or more guards continues to attempt to receive as long as any of the sending processes is still running. This assumes that any ⟨boolean expression⟩ in the same guard as an input command from a running process evaluates to true. Thus, a guard fails either if its input command (if any) refers to a terminated process or if its ⟨boolean expression⟩ (if any) is false. All guards being false terminates a repetitive command but causes an alternative command to fail.

To understand the synchronization properties of send and receive, we use them to model the semaphore synchronization mechanism. To shorten the writing, we introduce another bit of notation:

(i : 1..100) X(i) :: … defines 100 processes X(1), X(2), …

The iteration notation can be used on other statements as well. Another useful idea is the *signal*. A signal is a message with a type but no value. It is used to separate message synchronization from value transmission. Signals of types P and V are written P() and V(), respectively. A semaphore accessed by all 100 X processes is modeled as the process S with code shown in Program 5-1, and the primitive operations P and V are modeled by signals sent to this process.

S :: val: **integer**; val := 0;
*[(i : 1..100) X(i)?V() → val := val + 1 ❑
    (i : 1..100) val > 0; X(i)?P() → val := val − 1]

Program 5-1   CSP program for a semaphore, S.

To wait for semaphore S, a process, say X(17), would execute S!P(), and to release the semaphore, it would do S!V(). Neither send allows X(17) to proceed until the corresponding semaphore operation is done. Nothing delays the X(17)?V() receive operation in the process S, while the X(17)?P() may be delayed until some other process causes val to be greater than zero.

A semaphore would not be used in a distributed memory machine to control access to a shared data structure as it is in shared memory MIMD but might be used to manage a shared resource, such as an I/O device. However, its implementation illustrates several important points about CSP.

1. Because there are no shared variables, the semaphore value must be owned and updated by one process.

2. P() and V() are signals, so no value information is being passed between processes. Messages do nothing but provide synchronization.

3. The second guard has a boolean condition as well as an input command to prevent any response to a P() signal unless the semaphore is positive.

4. The atomicity, or mutual exclusion, required by P and V is provided by sequentialization of operations on a semaphore through one process.

The CSP semaphore implementation uses a distributed memory multiprocessor programming paradigm related to the *remote procedure call*. A *client* process sends a message to a *server* running on another machine and, on receipt of a reply, continues with the assurance that the requested service is complete. In this case, the service is a synchronization resulting in a delay.

5.2.2   A Distributed Memory Programming Example: Matrix Multiply

As a more substantive example of a distributed memory multiprocessor program, we consider matrix multiply. The first step, as with SIMD, is to determine how to lay out the matrix data in the different memories belonging to each processor. Let the operation be $C = A \times B$, where A, B, and C are $n \times n$ matrices. To do a large problem, the operand matrices should be distributed over the processors so that only a portion of each is in any one processor, and the result matrix, C, should also be partitioned. Because matrix multiply involves dot products of rows of A with columns of B, it is tempting to partition A by row and B by column over the processors. The problem with this approach is that matrix multiply is usually only a part of a computation, and it is not clear whether A, B, or C is the first or second operand in a subsequent matrix multiply. If A, say, is stored by row and is needed as the second operand of another matrix multiply, it has to be transposed so that it is stored by column, involving much interprocessor communication. A preferable partitioning is to divide all of the matrices similarly into nearly square submatrices. We assume that $n = b \times N$ and that each matrix is distributed over $p = N^2$ processors with a $b \times b$ block of the matrix in each processor. In addition to making the storage of all matrices consistent, this scheme allows us to simplify the problem to that of designing a matrix multiply algorithm for the case of one element of each matrix per processor. When the design is complete, it is only necessary to replace scalar element multiply by sequential matrix multiply of $b \times b$ blocks and scalar addition by element wise addition of matrices.

Let the processors be labeled $P(i, j)$, $0 \le i, j < N$. We use round brackets to enclose row and column numbers for processors to distinguish them from matrix elements. Processor $P(i, j)$ stores element (or block) $[i, j]$ of A and B and computes the same element of C. Focusing on the processor doing the computation, processor $P(i, j)$ must get elements $A[i, k]$ and $B[k, j]$, multiply them, and add the result to an accumulated $C[i, j]$. This must be done for all $0 \le k < N$. To get $A[i, k]$, processor $P(i, j)$ must engage in a communication with processor $P(i, k)$, which stores this value in its memory. We, therefore, must also view the computation from the position of the processor that must send the value. If the processors are thought of as arranged into a square array by their two subscripts, then the element $A[i, k]$ from processor $P(i, k)$ is needed by all processors in row i. Similarly, element $B[k, j]$ is needed by all processors in column j. Formulated in terms of the high-level communication concept of broadcasting a value from one processor to a specific subset of processors, the algorithm can be represented by the relatively simple pseudocode of Program 5-2.

The high-level concept is easy to understand, but it is not general because it depends on the organization of processors into rows and columns. Broadcast to a limited subset of processors is not likely to be supported directly in the hardware of a distributed system, so it has to be done by software. If we split up the jobs of the sending and receiving processors, the pseudocode for processor $P(i, j)$ executing one of the broadcasts using point-to-point, nonblocking send and blocking receive operations would appear as in Program 5-3. In this code, only processors in row q take part in either sending or receiving. With N^2 processors, this could take place for all rows simultaneously by removing the $i = q$ condition in both **if**s. The broadcast code works even if both send and receive are blocking, as in CSP, because for each send to processor $P(i, m)$ there is a processor $P(i, j)$ with $j = m \neq k$ that executes a corresponding receive operation. Program 5-3 supports broadcast in any distributed memory multiprocessor that supports point-to-point communication from any source to any destination. Given a particular interconnection topology among processors, however, there may be a more efficient way to organize the broadcast. We will defer the discussion of high-performance communication on specific topologies to Chapter 6 on interconnection networks.

```
Initialize C[i, j];
for k := 0 step 1 until N-1
begin
        Processor P(i,k) broadcasts A[i,k] to all processors in row i;
        Processor P(k,j) broadcasts B[k,j] to all processors in column j;
        C[i,j] := C[i,j] + A[i,k]×B[k,j];
end
```

Program 5-2   Matrix multiply pseudocode using high-level communication concept.

```
if i = q and j = k then
        for m := 0 step 1 until N-1
                if m ≠ k then send A to P(i,m);
if i = q and j ≠ k then receive A from P(q,k);
```

Program 5-3   Broadcast from P(q, k) to all P(q, m) for m ≠ k.

Program 5-4 is a distributed memory MIMD matrix multiply program using blocking send and receive instructions of the type defined in Hoare's CSP language. The program is written to multiply two $N \times N$ matrices using $p = N^2$ processors. A trivial modification allows it to multiply $bN \times bN$ matrices by having each processor deal with $b \times b$ blocks instead of scalar real elements. The code is for processor $P(i, j)$, $0 \leq i, j \leq N - 1$ of N^2 processors and is written in pseudocode with the addition of CSP send (!) and receive (?) statements. There are only $N = \sqrt{p}$ message transmissions going on in parallel, placing a fairly light load on the interconnection network between processors. With block partitioning, each processor only requires an extra $2b^2$ storage elements for temporary blocks of A and B in addition to the $3b^2$ elements required for its own blocks of A, B, and C.

Another version of matrix multiply that separates communication and computation is based on processor $P(i, j)$ collecting row i of A and column j of B from other processors in a communication phase and then combining them to get $C[i, j]$ in a computation phase. Pseudocode for this version is shown in Program 5-5. The elements of A, B, and C are identified by global matrix element notation in the pseudocode, but any one processor only needs one row of A, one column of B, and one element of C. This form of distributed matrix multiply requires nonblocking send and blocking receive. It deadlocks if both send and receive are blocking. Furthermore, each processor requires an additional $(2N - 2)b^2$ storage elements for communicated blocks of A and B. The order N additional storage can be a distinct drawback for very large matrix multiplies.

```
real myC, myA, myB, tmpA, tmpB;
integer i, j, m, k, N;
myC := 0;
for k := 0 step 1 until N - 1          /* Loop over inner product terms. */
begin
      for m := 0 step 1 until N - 1   /* Loop over receivers. */
      begin
          if k ≠ m then
              { if j = k then P(i,m)!myA;       /* P(i, k) sends A[i, k] */
                if j = m then P(i,k)?tmpA;      /*   to P(i, m), for all i. */
                if i = k then P(m,j)!myB;       /* P(k, j) sends B[k, j] */
                if i = m then P(k,j)?tmpB; } /*   to P(m, j), for all j. */
      end
      if j = k then tmpA := myA;      /* Copy when sender and receiver */
      if i = k then tmpB := myB;      /*     would be the same.        */
      myC := myC + tmpA×tmpB;
end
```

Program 5-4   Distributed memory matrix multiply using CSP blocking communication.

```
for m := 0 step 1 until N-1
    if m ≠ j then send A[i, j] to P(i, m);
for m := 0 step 1 until N-1
    if m ≠ j then receive A[i, m] from P(i, m);
for m := 0 step 1 until N-1
    if m ≠ i then send B[i, j] to P(m, j);
for m := 0 step 1 until N-1
    if m ≠ i then receive B[m, j] from P(m, j);
C[i, j] := 0;
for m := 0 step 1 until N-1
        c[i, j] := c[i, j] + A[i, m]×B[m, j];
```

Program 5-5   Distributed matrix multiply with split communication and computation.

From the matrix multiply example, we can see several steps to be taken in parallelizing a computation for a distributed memory multiprocessor. First, computation input and result data must be partitioned among the memories of different processors. Second, a strategy must be formulated for communicating data originally mapped onto or produced by one processor to all others that need it. Next, the send and receive portions of the communications must be isolated and assigned to the correct processors. Finally, the send and receive operations must be written in terms of specific communication primitives supported by the system software and hardware, for example, point-to-point, blocking, or nonblocking, etc. If data are used as received, less temporary storage is needed in each processor. In many systems, however, overheads in communication make the transmission of many short messages less efficient than collecting communications into long messages. The bias towards long messages competes with the reduction of temporary storage in the receivers.

5.3 Characterization of Communication

Having seen an example of programming with message passing, it is useful to abstract some characteristics of the process of moving data from where it is produced to where it is used. Programs are often conceived and organized in terms of high-level operations like "broadcast to all processors in a row (column)" as was used in the matrix multiply program. The high-level operations are ultimately realized by lower-level, point-to-point communications, so it is important to characterize these before dealing with high-level operations.

5.3.1   Point-to-Point Communications

There are five important characteristics of the transmission of data from a source to a destination. They are *initiation* of the operation, *synchronization*, *binding* of a source-destination pair, *buffering* of data, and *latency* control. Initiation of the transmission is almost always by the sender in a message passing environment. Although it is possible for a receiver to make a request for data and have the sender respond, this indirect process is seldom used when a single programmer writes both sending and receiving parts of the program. Synchronization must be understood to write even the simplest deadlock-free, distributed memory program and has already been discussed and summarized in Table 5-1.

In the examples, we assumed the simplest form of source-destination binding, namely that of designating the sender and receiver by their process identifiers. This is also the binding concept used in CSP, a language that takes a minimalist approach to distributed memory programming extensions. Other binding concepts are both useful and common in other languages. One of these is the message channel. A channel is opened by both sender and receiver, using a designator selected from the channel name space. Send and receive operations then specify the name of the channel instead of a process name. Channels may be unidirectional or bidirectional, and an *open* operation can specify send or receive capability as well as the channel name. Channels are usually limited in number, and there may be an additional restriction on the number of channels that are open at a time. A *close* operation is used to terminate channel binding.

Another common form of binding involves a receiver process and tag pair. The tag is an item sent with the message that identifies its role in the computation. It is attached to a message by the send operation and a receive operation then specifies a particular tag instead of a specific sending process. The tag may or may not identify the sending process, and a receive for a message with a given tag may return the sending process identifier as a side effect. By managing tags, a distributed memory programmer can organize messages on the basis of their purpose in the computation rather than by source process. Because a tag is part of a message, retrieval by tag can be considered to be a form of content, or associative, addressing. An extreme form of associative binding is found in the language Linda [66]. In this language, messages are sent to an area not associated with any processor and are retrieved by a consumer strictly on the basis of their content. Though this language has been implemented through message passing on many distributed memory machines, its concept is nearer to that of including an associative shared memory.

A specific binding of any of the three types is associated with an ordered sequence of messages, with the order established by the execution times of the sends with that binding. Order is preserved so that the k-th message received is the k-th message sent with a given binding. The idea of an ordered sequence of data is important to correct interpretation of the received data and can also be applied to the values taken on by a cell in shared memory. In shared memory, however, the idea is less important because there is usually a tight binding of all processes to a global clock. In that case, identifying the correct member of a sequence of data values occupying the same memory cell reduces to the idea of the "current" value.

The concept of an ordered sequence of messages associated with a binding leads naturally to the consideration of a message buffer where part of this sequence may reside. On their way to a destination, messages may be moved from the sender's address space through one or more first-in first-out (FIFO) buffers. Buffers have finite capacity and may limit the number of messages sent but not yet received for a given binding. Buffers may be located in user or system memory at either the sending or receiving processor and may be associated with I/O processors that perform communication. Buffering is closely tied to the blocking or non-blocking nature of send. A nonblocking send usually copies message data from the sender's space to a buffer, allowing the sender to assemble the next message in the same memory while the transmission is completed. If combined buffers are used for different bindings, one type of message may block another that is not logically associated with it. For example, a common receive buffer for all sends might become full and allow messages sent early to block the receipt of a message required for the receiver to make progress. Rendezvous communication, as used in CSP, can be accomplished with no buffering. Nonblocking send requires buffering somewhere in the system and ultimately blocks when the data sent but not yet received exceeds the buffer capacity.

Message latency is the time from the execution of a send operation until the message data arrives at the receiver. The control of latency is a performance issue that is so important that it affects the overall organization of distributed memory programs. Delivery time for a message is roughly characterized by

$$T = T_S + LT_B, \tag{5.1}$$

where T_S is a start-up time required for any message to arrive at the receiver, T_B is a time associated with each byte of the message, and L is the message length in bytes. The key performance concern is that, in many message passing environments, T_S greatly dominates the delivery time, $T_S \gg T_B$. This means that very long messages are favored because only one T_S penalty is paid rather than several start-up times that would be needed if the long message were sent in shorter parts. Each level of buffering adds to both T_S and T_B. To control latency, many distributed memory programs are written to aggregate many data items, sometimes fairly unrelated, into one long message before sending it to its destination. The receiver must dissect the message into its several parts for use in different computations.

Table 5-3   Summary of point-to-point communication characteristics.

Initiation	sender; rarely: receiver request

Synchronization	blocking/nonblocking send/receive (Table 5-1)

Binding	Type	Associated operations
	(source ID, destination ID)	send(destination ID); receive(source ID)
	channel number	open(channel); close(channel) send(channel); receive(channel)
	(tag, destination ID)	send(tag, destination ID); receive(tag)

Buffer	Type	Location		Capacity
	One per source for each destination	Sender:	user space	byte limit
	One per channel		system space	message limit
	One per tag for each destination		I/O processor	
		Receiver:	user space	
			system space	
			I/O processor	

Latency	Time parameters	Transfer through an additional buffer
	Start-up time	Adds to start-up time
	Time per byte	Adds to time per byte unless pipelined

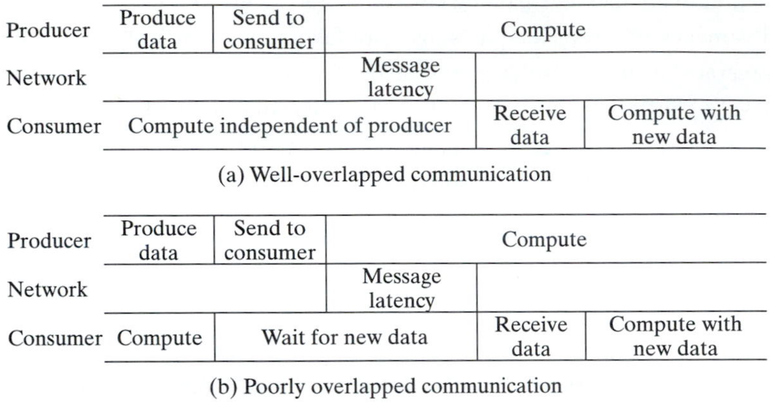

Producer	Produce data	Send to consumer	Compute	
Network			Message latency	
Consumer	Compute independent of producer		Receive data	Compute with new data

(a) Well-overlapped communication

Producer	Produce data	Send to consumer	Compute	
Network			Message latency	
Consumer	Compute	Wait for new data	Receive data	Compute with new data

(b) Poorly overlapped communication

Figure 5-3　Overlapping communication with computation.

A summary of the five characteristics of point-to-point communication is shown in Table 5-3. Message latency, buffering, and nonblocking send all contribute to the potential overlap of communication and computation. The ability of the producer of information to proceed while that information is being sent is very important for maximizing parallel activity. Even if send is nonblocking, the effectiveness of overlapping communication with computation depends on when the receiver must have the transmitted data to proceed. Figure 5-3 shows two situations, one where computation and communication are well overlapped and one where they are not. To overlap more effectively, messages should be sent as soon as possible and computation should be made as independent of communication as possible. If the sender needs to recompute values in a message area just used in a send, it is helpful to have the message in the user's space copied to a buffer in either system space or an I/O processor. Then the sender can immediately start to construct a new message in the same area. On the other hand, each copy of message data between buffers adds time to the producer's send operation, the message latency, or the consumer's receive operation. The correct choice of buffering depends on software overheads in send and receive and on the performance characteristics of the interconnection network. The naive, processor-centric idea that at most a factor of two speedup could be obtained by perfect overlap of equal length computation and communication misses a major point. The initiation of new sends, perhaps to other processes, is one result of further computation. Thus, the overlap of many simultaneous communications is enabled by communication/computation overlap, assuming the processor interconnect supports multiple concurrent messages. The overlap of communications between many pairs of processes can also be designed into the high-level communication operations that we consider in Section 5.3.3.

5.3.2　Variable Classes in a Distributed Memory Program

We now begin to consider higher level communications operations. A useful way to introduce this topic is to consider the way variables are shared among processes in a distributed memory program. This corresponds to the parallelism classes, shared and private, that we discussed in the programming of shared memory multiprocessors. At the low level, the parallelism class of variables in distributed memory multiprocessors is trivial. Each variable resides in some processor's local memory and is, thus, private to the process running on that processor. This view, however, is not very useful in formulating distributed memory programs. In an SPMD style program for a distributed memory machine, the same variable may have representatives in different processors, and these representatives may be updated so as to represent the same value in all processors. A possible classification distinguishes the parallelism class of a variable in an SPMD-style distributed memory program as *private*, *unique*, *cooperative update*, *replicated*, or *partitioned*.

Private variables are the same as in the shared memory case. A single name refers to a different memory cell and value in each processor. The variables tmpA, tmpB, i, and j are private in Program 5-4. While tmpA and tmpB are temporary values, i and j are private read-only values that give the row and column number of a specific processor. If a variable and its value are only defined for one processor, the variable is called *unique*. A *unique* simple variable would have algorithmic meaning if one processor had unique capabilities, as in the case of a special I/O processor. Structured variables may have individual components that are unique to a single processor. The best example in Program 5-4 is myC, representing $C(i, j)$ in processor $P(i, j)$.

Data considered shared in an abstract parallel algorithm are treated in several different ways in actual distributed memory multiprocessor programs. The first case is that of a variable with a single value available to all processors. It must be represented by one cell in each processor's memory. To keep the values of all the representatives the same, any update must be performed cooperatively by all the processors. We call such variables *cooperative update* shared variables. The special case of a read-only shared variable fits well here. The alternative of having a single processor "own" a shared variable and supply its value to others upon request can have severe performance penalty in the many processor case as a result of the sequential bottleneck of repeated transmissions. In Program 5-4, N represents the trivial case of a read-only shared variable. In the broadcast of Program 5-3, $A[q, k]$ can be seen as cooperatively updated across all processors, $P(q, j)$, $0 \leq j < N$. We will see that cooperative update variables are often supported by high level, and sometimes complex, communication operations.

Another type of "shared" variable is sometimes used in distributed memory multiprocessor programs. It is often more efficient to make a value available to many processors by carrying out redundant computations rather than by communicating its value. The simplest example is that of a loop index that should step through the same range in each processor. Its value should surely be incremented independently by each processor rather than being broadcast from a single processor which calculates it. We call such variables *replicated*. Note that, although a replicated variable takes on the same sequence of values in every processor, a given update to the representative in one processor may occur at a somewhat different time than the corresponding update in a different processor, because processor speeds may vary. This is in contrast to changes to a cooperative update variable, which are done simultaneously by all processes cooperating by way of message passing. The loop indices m and k in Program 5-4 are examples of replicated variables.

Structured variables, vectors, arrays, etc., bring up a different aspect of the parallel storage class of variables. Each component of a structure has one of the above classes, but the structure as a whole may present a different aspect. *Private* structures are straightforward, and the simple case of a *shared* structure, where all elements of the structure are *shared* is useful. Large arrays, however, are probably distributed in such a way that only a fraction of the structure is stored in any one processor. An array distributed by rows, for example, might be considered to have each element of class *unique*. The indexed row A[I,] of an array distributed across processes by row could be considered to have parallel class *unique*, but the entire structure A is known to more than one processor, so the array as a whole is in some sense shared. A parallel loop over the row index involving A in the loop body should, ideally, distribute the work over the processors so that each processor handles index values for its own rows. Of course, this is only possible when the loop does not specify combining elements from different rows in an arithmetic operation. We name the storage class of such variables *partitioned*. Various partition patterns are possible for a structure, and a language providing high-level support for distributed memory programming should attempt to suppress or simplify these details as much as possible. At the minimum, there should be automatic translation of algorithm-level indexing into an address in the correct processor's memory. Note that the specific partition strongly influences the way in which parallel operations on the structure are allocated to different processors. In Program 5-4, the partitioned structures are A, B, and C, where myA in processor $P(i, j)$ is $A[i, j]$, and similarly for B and C.

The concept of parallelism class of a variable in a distributed memory program leads naturally to the subject of high-level communication operations in which more than two processes participate. Such collective communications are needed whenever a variable of one of the shared classes is updated. For example, a broadcast allows a single processor to give a new value to a cooperative update variable. The next section surveys high-level collective communications and relates them to variables of different parallelism classes.

5.3.3   High-Level Communication Operations

In addition to using a broadcast to assign a new value to a cooperative update variable, communication operations that combine values from different processes and distribute the result can also be used for cooperative update. A summation, or more generally any reduction, can combine a value from each process and either pass the sum to a single root process or distribute it to all processes. A prefix computation across values from different processes can return different but related values to each process in the group. For example, a sum prefix receiving a one from each of p processes returns to each process an integer in the range 0 to $p - 1$. The results might be private or components of a partitioned vector. For partitioned variables, a remapping of the structure into a different partition over the processes corresponds to a permutation of structure components among processes. We mentioned in connection with matrix multiply that a matrix partitioned across processes by row might need to be partitioned by column in subsequent computations. A summary of distributed parallelism classes and update methods is shown in Table 5-4.

Table 5-4   Distributed variable classes and methods of updating them.

Variable class	Update methods
unique	assignment by one processor
private	parallel assignment of different values by all processes
	prefix computation
cooperative update	broadcast from a single processor
	reduction
replicated	parallel assignment of same value by all processes
partitioned	each process assigns to its own components
	prefix computation
	permutation for remapping

Many of the useful collective communication operations can be characterized by the source(s) of their input and the destination(s) for their output. In *broadcast*, input comes from a single source process and the result (a copy of the input) is delivered to each process in the participating group. For arithmetic data types, reductions over many associative binary operators are useful: sum, product, maximum, minimum, logical and, logical or, etc. A *reduction* takes inputs from all processes, combines them arithmetically and delivers the result to a single process. The useful combination of reduce with broadcast does reduce and then distributes a copy of the result to each process. The combined operation can often be implemented more efficiently than just doing the two communications in sequence. The *prefix* operation is closely related to reduction, but instead of a single result, it produces a different value for each destination process. It is useful with many of the arithmetic operations that can be used in reduction. A *scatter* operation takes a vector of P items, where P is the number of processes, from one process and distributes it, one item to each process. The reverse operation is *gather*, which collects an item from each process and concatenates them into a vector result delivered to a single destination process. A *permutation*, often used for remapping a partitioned structure, is done by a combined gather/scatter operation, where a vector of P source items, one for each destination process, is taken from each process, the collection is reorganized as a vector of items for each destination, and those vectors are delivered to their respective processes. Figure 5-4 gives a schematic representation of some of the collective communication operations.

Table 5-5 summarizes the different choices for the source(s) of items to be communicated and for the destination(s) of the messages. The specific choices of source and destination for the communications identified so far are summarized in Table 5-6. Any specific language or library of communication functions may exhibit a number of variations on the communication operations of Table 5-6. A major source of variation is in the data type associated with a source or destination item. Vectors of values are often supported as sources and results, and unified communication systems may support the definition and use of general structures for items. The utility of aggregating multiple values into an item for transmission is based on the need to control message latency by forming long messages.

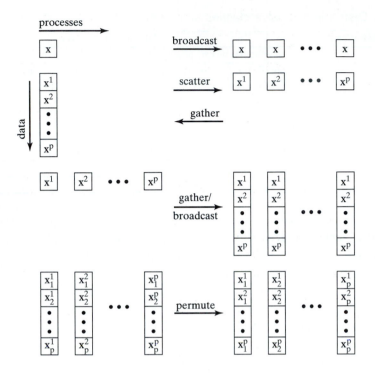

Figure 5-4   Behavior of some collective communication operations.

Table 5-5   Characterizing source and destination of collective communications.

	Source		Destination
one process:	single item multiple items	one process:	single item multiple items
all processes:	concatenation arithmetic combining	all processes:	single item per process multiple items per process

Table 5-6   Communication operations and their source and destination types.

Communication	Source	Destination
point-to-point	one process	one process
broadcast	one process: one item	all processes: item per process
gather	all processes: item per process	one process: P items
scatter	one process: P items	all processes: item per process
gather/broadcast	all processes: item per process	all processes: P items per process
gather/scatter	all processes: P items per process	all processes: P items per process
reduce	all processes: arithmetic combining	one process: one item
reduce/broadcast	all processes: arithmetic combining	all processes: same item in each
prefix	all processes: arithmetic combining	all processes: different item in each

Defining a data type is useful when a particular arrangement of data forms a meaningful unit or is used repeatedly in different communications, but latency control also leads to the aggregation of only loosely related, or even unrelated, data for a specific communication. The situation is similar to that in I/O, where many data items may be merged into an output file which, when read, may be decomposed into individual items by file specific input code. The corresponding communication ideas are *packing* and *unpacking* a message buffer. In packing, items of different types and sizes are concatenated into one long message, to be separated at the destination by unpacking. A lowest common denominator unit of length is needed for all data types, usually the byte; therefore, the items referred to in the discussion of communication operations may be message buffers packed with more or less related data values. The motivation for packing and unpacking long messages is message start-up overhead, an irreducible amount of time taken to start sending a message of any length. The start-up time, or latency, varies with the system, but it can be very long. The need for packing is reduced or absent in a system that supports low latency transmission of short messages. When building long messages is important, it applies equally to collective and point-to-point communications, except that nonnumeric types like packed cannot be used in communications that do arithmetic combining.

5.3.4   Distributed Gauss Elimination with High-Level Communications

As a substantive example of a distributed memory program, we treat the solving of a system of linear equations using Gaussian elimination. We will not go to the level of actual code, but the program is a real one, written originally for an Intel iPSC Hypercube computer, and some characteristics of the specific machine are reflected in the program design. The machine has one host processor that does all I/O and p worker processors that are all identical. One process runs on each processor, and all worker processes execute the same program. The machine has a communications library that supports the high-level, collective operations broadcast and sum reduce, as well as point-to-point communications. It is expected that the order, n, of the linear system satisfies $n \gg p$.

Without giving detailed performance numbers, some abstract characterizations of performance that affect the program design can be stated. Communication latency is large compared to floating-point operation time, so it is advantageous to minimize communication and to make messages as long as possible. Each worker computes efficiently with stride one vectors. This could result either from worker processors including vector operations or from efficient cache behavior with contiguous data. The program was written in a version of Fortran, which stores two-dimensional matrices in column major order. Thus, vector operations on columns are particularly efficient. Each worker process has a unique identifier, $0 \le id < p$, and the host process id is outside this range. The only aspect of communications topology important to the program design is that process id communicates efficiently in point-to-point mode with processes $(id + 1) \bmod p$ and $(id - 1) \bmod p$. The example is a test program for performance measurement, so it generates its own system of linear equations to solve instead of reading it from input.

The mathematical formulation of the problem is to solve $Ax = b$ by first factoring $A = LU$ into lower, L, and upper, U, triangular matrices. The solution can then be obtained by solving two recurrence systems—forward substitution, $Ly = b$, followed by back substitution, $Ux = y$. The matrix A, which is replaced by L and U, is partitioned cyclically over processors by column with process $P_r, 0 \le r < p$, owning columns $A[,kp + r + 1], 0 \le k < m$, where m is the largest integer such that $mp + r + 1 \le n$. Specifically, $m = \lfloor n/p \rfloor + 1$ for $r < n \bmod p$ and $m = \lfloor n/p \rfloor$ for $r \ge n \bmod p$. That is, column j is owned by processor $r = (j - 1) \bmod p$. The cyclic partitioning establishes for each process r a successor, $(r + 1) \bmod p$, and a predecessor, $(r - 1) \bmod p$. The mapping of an 8×8 matrix to three processors is shown in Figure 5-5.

The order n^3 work of factorization is done by stepping sequentially through diagonal elements. The processor owning the current pivot column does partial pivoting by finding the index of the maximum absolute value below the diagonal in the column, recording the index, and swapping the element to the diagonal. The pivot index is stored in the local part of a cyclically partitioned pivot vector v. The pivot column process then scales the L portion of the column by the pivot to get a vector of multipliers that is broadcast to all workers. All workers then do vector multiply-adds in parallel to update the columns they own that lie to the right of the pivot column. Note that the order n^2 work of searching for all pivots is done sequentially unless there is a vector maximum search operation.

The order n^2 work of forward and backward substitution is done sequentially in the absence of vector operations. The right-hand-side b vector is initialized by process zero and then passed cyclically to successor processes to be updated by each for forward substitution. After n updates, it is transformed into the vector y that solves $Ly = b$. This vector is then updated and passed backward cyclically through predecessors until n back substitution updates transform it into the solution x of $Ux = y$. During the solution phase, worker processes spend most of their time waiting at receive operations for the current version of the solution vector to arrive. This is a result of the column partitioning, which is done to utilize the efficient column vector operations of the workers.

The overall structure of the program is shown in Figure 5-6. The host program is unique. It does I/O and communicates with the workers by broadcast and point-to-point communication with process zero. The same program is executed by all worker processes. It calls separate procedures to factor A (PGEFA), to solve the system for a given right hand side (PGESL), and to do the matrix-vector multiply (PGEMUL) to check the solution by comparing Ax to b. The worker processes receive the host's broadcast, and process zero sends results to the host for output. The procedures combine floating point computation and communication to do the majority of the program's work. PGEFA needs only broadcast to communicate the pivot column multipliers, PGESL uses point-to-point communications to send a developing solution vector to successor or predecessor processes. PGEMUL uses broadcast to send all workers the x vector and then uses an element wise sum reduction over vectors to get the product vector Ax.

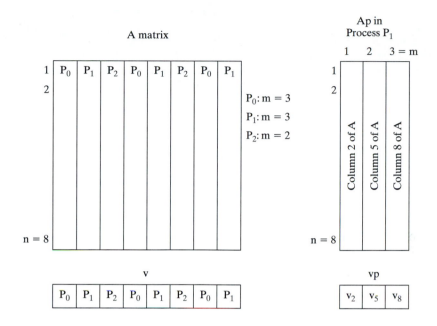

Figure 5-5 Partition of Gauss elimination problem over processes.

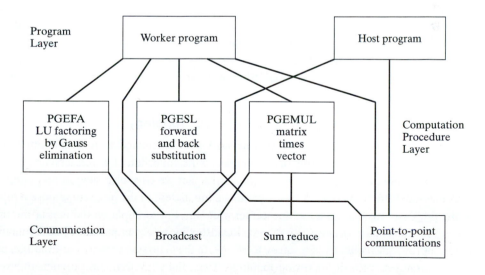

Figure 5-6 Program structure for distributed Gauss elimination.

Host program:
    Input number p of processes and order n of the linear system;
    Broadcast p and n to all workers;
    Receive time to generate test case from process zero and print it;
    Receive time for LU factorization from process zero and print time and rate;
    Receive solution time for test b vector from process zero and print time and rate;
    Receive residual from process zero, check and print it;
    End

Worker program (process number id):
    Receive p and n from host;
    Compute the number m of matrix columns for this processor;
    Generate m columns of the test matrix, $A[i, j] = 1/(i - j + 0.5)$, for Ap of process id;
    Process zero sends time for generation to host;
    Call the PGEFA procedure to factor A into the matrix product LU;
    Process zero sends time for factorization to host;
    Process zero computes test right hand side vector, $b[i] = i, i = 1, ..., n$;
    Call the PGESL procedure to solve equations, leaving solution vector in process zero;
    Process zero sends time for solving to host;
    Call PGEMUL to compute Ax and leave result in process zero;
    Process zero computes residual, $\sum_i |(Ax)[i] - b[i]|$ and sends it to host;
    End

Program 5-6   Host and worker programs for distributed Gauss elimination.

Program 5-6 gives a step by step description of the host and worker main programs, and Program 5-7 gives the same type of description for the computational procedures. The right side of Figure 5-5 shows the partitioned variables in a worker process. We distinguish the A matrix and v vector portions in one processor as Ap and vp, respectively. Borrowing Fortran 90 like array notation, the A matrix would be $A[1..n, 1..n]$ if it existed in any one processor, while a given process' portion of A is $Ap[1..n, 1..m]$. Similarly, each process has portion $vp[1..m]$ of the pivot index vector.

5.3.5   Process Topology Versus Processor Topology

We saw in Chapter 4 that the interconnection network of a distributed memory multiprocessor could impose a topology, such as a ring or hypercube, on the collection of processors, and we will treat this topic in more detail in Chapter 6 on networks. But we have also seen in programming examples that the distribution of data and communication pattern in the program impose a topology on the processes making up a multiprocessor program. For example, in the matrix multiply example of Section 5.2.2 processes $P(i, j)$ were identified by an index pair and communication was done over rows and columns of a square topology. In the Gaussian elimination example, processes were arranged cyclically in a ring topology. Thus, the algorithm and program impose a process topology that may be different from the processor topology imposed by the interconnection network, even if one and only one process runs on each processor. Communication software

PGEFA procedure: —does *LU* factorization
  Initialize pointer to current column for this process, $q = 1$;
  Begin loop over pivot position, $k = 1, ..., n$;
       Identify root process *r* as owner of the *k*-th column (the pivot column);
       Begin if process $id = r$
            Find position of maximum absolute value in $Ap[k..n, q]$, record 0 if singular;
            Swap pivot and diagonal elements, and scale column to get multipliers;
            Build message containing pivot column multipliers and pivot index;
            Increment $q := q + 1$ to next column in process r;
       End of execution by process *r*;
       Cooperatively execute broadcast so all workers have multipliers and pivot index;
       Begin if matrix is not singular (pivot index $\neq 0$)
            Loop over columns to right of pivot, $j = q, ..., m$;
                 Swap pivot row element to diagonal in column *j*;
                 Scale multipliers by *j*-th pivot row element and add to $Ap[k + 1...n, j]$;
            End of loop over columns;
       End of if not singular;
  End of loop over pivot position;
  Return;

PGESL procedure: —does forward and back substitution
  Identify predecessor, $(id - 1) \bmod p$, and successor, $(id + 1) \bmod p$, processes;
  $k := id + 1$; index of 1st column owned by this process;
  Begin forward substitution loop over columns owned by this process, $q = 1, ..., m$;
       If $k > 1$ receive *b* vector from predecessor;
       Swap $vp[q]$ element of *b* with *k*-th element of *b*;
       Multiply $b[k]$ times $Ap[k + 1...n, q]$ and add to $b[k + 1..n]$;
       If $k < n$, send *b* vector to successor;
       $k := k + p$ to get index of next column owned by this process;
  End of forward loop, owner of column *n* has forward substitution result $y = b$;
  Reverse back substitution loop over columns owned by this process, $q = m, ..., 1$;
       $k := k - p$ for index of next column in reverse order owned by this process;
       If $k < n$, receive *b* vector from successor;
       $b[k] := b[k]/Ap[k, q]$ (globally, $b[k]/A[k, k]$) and $T := -b[k]$;
       $b[1..k - 1] := b[1..k - 1] + T \times Ap[1..k - 1, q]$;
       If $k > 1$, send *b* vector to predecessor;
  End of reverse loop over columns, process 0 (owner of column 1) has solution $x = b$;
  Return;

PGEMUL procedure:
  Process 0 broadcasts solution vector *x* to all processes;
  Each process sets private vector $z[1..n] := 0$ and $k = id + 1$;
  Begin loop over columns owned by this process, $q = 1, ..., m$;
       $z[1..n] := z[1..n] + x[k] \times Ap[1..n, q]$;
       $k := k + p$;
  End of loop over columns owned;
  Sum reduce private *z* vectors component wise to $y[i] := \sum_{id=0}^{p-1} z[i], i = 1, ..., n$ in process 0;
  Return;

Program 5-7   Computational procedures for distributed Gauss elimination.

can make any network topology support arbitrary source/destination pair messages by forwarding them from point to point in the network, but the performance is determined by how well message paths match physical links. A program with a given process topology may run very inefficiently on a machine with a very different processor topology.

Careful mapping of processes to processors can improve the efficiency of communication in a distributed memory program. For this reason, many program libraries that support high-level communications allow the programmer to specify a process topology but leave it to the library to map the processes onto the underlying processor topology. The library programs for a particular distributed memory machine can then tailor the communications on the abstract process topology to the actual message transfers allowed by the machine's network. Even with clever mapping algorithms, however, programs may communicate much more efficiently when mapped onto one processor topology than another. For example, the square mesh process topology of the matrix multiply Program 5-4 is much more efficiently supported by a hypercube interconnection network, into which a square mesh can be embedded, than by a ring network, where either rows or columns have to be distributed around the whole ring.

It is fairly common to find algorithms designed for specific process topologies and meant to be run on machines with an identical processor topology. One example is *Cannon's algorithm* for matrix multiply. This algorithm is written for a square mesh topology, in which processors communicate only with nearest neighbors to the top, bottom, left, and right. The mesh has wrap around connections so that the left column adjoins the right column and the top row adjoins the bottom one. Process and processor topologies are taken to be identical. As in Program 5-4, each process computes a block of the matrix $C = A \times B$, but the blocks of A and B are initially distributed to make subsequent communication efficient. We again write the algorithm in terms of one element per process, understanding that an element stands for a square subblock of its matrix. Initially, processor $P(i, j)$ has element $A[i, (j + i)\bmod N]$, $0 \le i, j < N$, of the A matrix and element $B[(i + j)\bmod N, j]$, $0 \le i, j < N$, of the B matrix. This initial placement of blocks of A and B can either be done by a host processor or by initial communication among the $p = N^2$ processors of the mesh. After this initial placement, blocks of A are passed to left neighbors and blocks of B are passed upward at each step of the algorithm. The initial layout and communication paths are shown in Figure 5-7.

Program 5-8 shows how Cannon's algorithm multiplies A and B starting from the initial mapping of Figure 5-7. $C[i, j]$ is initialized to zero, and then an N step computation and communication loop is executed. At each pass through the loop, processor $P(i, j)$ multiplies the local elements (blocks) of A and B and adds the product to $C[i, j]$. The local block of A is sent left and a new one is received from the right, while the local block of B is sent upwards and a new one is received from below. Nonblocking send and blocking receive are used. The communication in the last pass is not needed to compute C, but it leaves the blocks of A and B distributed as they were at the start of the computation. Communication latency can easily be equivalent to thousands of floating point operation times. Because matrix multiply has $2n^3$

floating point operations, on the order of 10×10 blocks would balance communication and computation. Communication efficiency might be improved by exchanging the 6th and 7th lines of Program 5-8 to start both sends before waiting for either receive.

One way to accomplish the initial distribution of A and B, assuming $A[i, j]$ and $B[i, j]$ are originally owned by process $P(i, j)$, is shown in Program 5-9. With this code, the entire algorithm is executed efficiently if all processes can simultaneously transmit to the left and then simultaneously receive from the right and, correspondingly, send upwards and receive from below. No other communications paths are required by the program. The initial distribution of blocks of A and B can be made more efficient if left, right, up, and down transmissions can all be done in parallel. In this case, only $N/2 - 1$ row (column) shifts need to be done in sequence rather than the $N - 1$ shown in Program 5-9. If simultaneous shifts of rows and columns by more than one unit are supported by the hardware, the initial distribution can be made even faster.

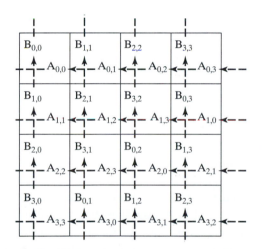

Figure 5-7 Cannon's matrix multiply, initial layout, and communication paths.

```
myC := 0;
for k := 0 step 1 until N - 1
begin
        myC := myC + myAxmyB;
        send myB to P((i-1)mod N, j);
        receive myB from P((i+1)mod N, j);
        send myA to P(i, (j-1)mod N);
        receive myA from P(i, (j+1)mod N);
end
```

Program 5-8 Computational core of Cannon's algorithm for processor $P(i, j)$.

```
if j ≠ 0 then
begin
    for k := 0 step 1 until j-1
    begin
        send myB to P((i-1)mod N, j);
        receive myB from P((i+1)mod N, j);
    end
end
if i ≠ 0 then
begin
    for k := 0 step 1 until i-1
    begin
        send myA to P(i, (j-1)mod N);
        receive myA from P(i, (j+1)mod N);
    end
end
```

Program 5-9   Initial distribution using one step left and upward transmissions.

5.4   The Message Passing Interface, MPI

SIMD computers require programming language support for new operations in the instruction set of a processor. Fortran 90 supports them with new data types and extended expression evaluation rules. A shared memory MIMD machine involves fewer new operations in the instruction sets of its processors. OpenMP supports the new operations as a language extension, without requiring low-level changes in expression evaluation or new data types. The processor instruction sets in a distributed memory MIMD computer are nearly identical to those of uniprocessors. If interprocessor communication is made a form of I/O, the instructions may be entirely identical. As a consequence, one way of providing high-level support for distributed memory programming is to provide a communications subroutine package for an existing sequential language. The message passing interface, MPI is such a subroutine package.

This approach implies that concepts like cooperative update or partitioned variables can be used to design distributed programs, but they are not represented directly in the code. Specifically, automated support for partitioning of variables and operations on them are not provided by the programming language. The advantage of such an approach is that no new compiler is required for a machine to support distributed memory programming in this way, and the low cost of supporting the MPI subroutine package makes programs written with it more portable across machines from different vendors. Programmers may also feel that they have less new information to acquire to program with MPI. MPI has subroutines to do both point-to-point sends and receives as well as high-level communications like those described in Section 5.3.3, which it calls *collective communications*.

The MPI-1 standard does not include any process management operations. Processes must be assigned to processors, associated with programs to execute, started, and stopped by a mechanism that is not part of MPI-1. A more recent standard, MPI-2, supports process management operations. As it is our purpose to focus on communications in distributed memory programming, we treat MPI-1 but not MPI-2. MPI is defined as an extension to Fortran, C, and C++. We refer to the Fortran 77 version whenever specific MPI calls are described. Because one of our purposes in this book is to compare and contrast programs for different parallel architectures, using the Fortran version of MPI allows us to easily compare algorithms written in the SIMD Fortran 90 language, the shared memory OpenMP Fortran language, and the distributed memory MPI Fortran language. Also, because two-dimensional arrays are a basic data type in Fortran, less effort is spent on the matrix algorithms we have been using as examples than would be the case in C.

When MPI-1 is initialized simultaneously by all processes in the system, it identifies a fixed group of processes that will communicate, and this basic group does not change during the program. MPI does not directly support hierarchical parallelism, where a process may consist of subprocesses, or threads, but it is designed not to prevent threads from being used. Mainly, this amounts to ensuring that the blocking of one thread on a pending communication does not prevent other threads of the same process from completing independent communications. Such a design is called *thread-safe*.

A comprehensive list of MPI routines is given in Appendix A. This detailed listing of the routines of the MPI library is meant to give an idea of the scope of the communications package and the detailed facilities needed to implement the overall concepts of the language extension. It is probably not sufficient to write and debug MPI programs for a specific machine. For that purpose, it is necessary to refer to the standard [220]. By seeing what routines have been provided in MPI, it can be discovered what kind of facilities the writers of message passing programs have found useful in real applications. As with any subroutine library, useful programs can be written without invoking or knowing all the facilities supported by the package.

5.4.1 Basic Concepts in MPI

MPI introduces the idea of a communication environment, within which source and destination processes are identified and which defines the group of processes taking part in a collective communication. Such an environment is called a *communicator*. The internal structure of a communicator cannot be directly accessed by the user of MPI. It is a so-called *opaque object* allocated in system space by MPI routines and manipulated only through calls to the MPI library. The user refers to an opaque object by a *handle*, which is returned to the user by an MPI program creating the object and passed by the user to MPI routines that need to access or modify the object. A communicator handle is passed to every MPI routine that sends or receives any kind of message to identify the process group and environment within which a communication is done.

5.4.1.1 Communicator Structure

The internal structure of a communicator includes a *process group*, a *context*, a *process topology*, and attributes associated with the communicator by the user. The attributes and their key values are said to be *cached* in the communicator. Within a group of p processes, each process is identified by an integer *rank*, $0 \le id \le p - 1$. The context is not accessed or manipulated by the user but is attached like another tag to each message sent using its communicator to guide the receiver's interpretation of the message. Point-to-point messages are sent with a different context than collective communications so that a message of one type does not block the receipt of a message of the other type. MPI starts with a built-in communicator, MPI_COMM_WORLD, that includes all processes in the system and assigns a rank to each. Any other communicator is built from processes belonging to MPI_COMM_WORLD, and a process may belong to several different communicators.

The numbering of processes in a group imposes a linear topology on them, but a user can also explicitly impose a cartesian grid or general graph topology. An MPI call that imposes a topology on a process group can allow the MPI system to reorder processes of the group to make communication between neighbors in the virtual process topology efficient on the physical network connecting processors of the machine. A process topology can be thought of as an attribute cached with its communicator. Various MPI calls map a process rank to or from a specified position in an associated topology. User-defined attributes can be paired with key values obtained from MPI and then used in storing or retrieving associated attributes cached with a communicator. The interpretation of user-defined cached attributes is the user's responsibility. Attributes can be pointers (integers in Fortran) or handles to MPI objects.

The communicator described above is actually an *intracommunicator*. There is also an *intercommunicator*, which is an association of two intracommunicators with nonoverlapping process groups. In MPI-1, intercommunicators only support point-to-point communication from a process in one group to a process in the other. Collective communications can only be done through intracommunicators. For an intercommunicator, there must be two processes, one in each group and called *local leader* and *remote leader*, that can communicate with each other through a third, *peer*, communicator. The local leader belongs to both the local and peer communicators, and the remote leader belongs to the remote and peer communicators. Other processes may, or may not, belong to the peer communicator. The actual MPI communicator routines and their parameters are described in Appendix A.4.

5.4.1.2 The Envelope

Send and receive calls require several parameters that can be grouped into envelope and data parameters of the message. The communicator is the foundation of the message envelope. The *envelope* consists of a communicator, source, destination, and tag. *Source* and *destination* are ranks within the process group of the communicator (or within the local and remote groups of an inter-communicator). The *tag* is an integer that partitions messages into different classes so that a receiver can choose to pay attention only to messages of a particular class (tag value) at some point in the program. A specific source (the sender), destination, and tag are associated with the message envelope by a send operation, and a receive obtains the next message with source and tag matching its specifications. A receive operation can either specify unique source and tag values, or it can replace either or both with one of two "wild cards" that match any source or any tag. A receive specifying any source and any tag simply returns the next message destined for the process calling the receive routine.

5.4.1.3   The Data

The *data* portion of a message consists of a buffer, a data type, and a count. A *buffer* is the starting address of a block of memory that contains the data to be sent or received. The *data type* is a handle to an opaque MPI object describing the length and interpretation of an individual data item in the message. The *count* gives the number of data items. The data type specified is an MPI type, but binding to a specific host language, C or Fortran, is supported by providing MPI types that correspond directly to each basic type of the host language. MPI_LONG for C long int and MPI_DOUBLE_PRECISION for Fortran DOUBLE PRECISION are examples of corresponding MPI and host language types. MPI also provides support for uninterpreted byte and packed data and for user-defined types derived from basic MPI types.

User-defined data types allow the description of a send or receive buffer, or a portion of it, as containing mixed data of different basic types, or data dispersed in the buffer and separated by gaps. Dispersed data is useful, for example, if the buffer is declared as an array with dimensions larger than those of an array transmitted to or from the buffer. We will see in connection with the discussion of MPI-IO in Chapter 11 that user-defined data types are also useful in describing the data structure of a record in a file and in allowing different processes to access different file data elements in parallel read and write operations. The MPI routines and their parameters to deal with data types are described more completely in Appendix A.3.

5.4.1.4   Point-to-Point Communication Concepts

From the previous discussion, we see that the essential parameters for send and receive routines are buffer, count, data type, source, destination, tag, and communicator. Of course, send does not need the source nor receive the destination. Point-to-point sends and receives in MPI can be blocking or nonblocking, in more than one sense. In Section 5.2, we described blocking send and receive operations as those that did not complete until the corresponding receive or send, respectively, completed on the remote process. MPI uses a different sense for blocking. A *blocking MPI* send call does not return to the calling program until the buffer specified in the call has been completely read and is available to be overwritten with new data. A *blocking receive call* returns to the caller only when the data of a message matching the receive specifications has been completely copied into the receive buffer. Although a blocking receive call does not return until the corresponding send is substantially complete (but may not have returned to the caller), a blocking send call, in the MPI sense, may return before any part of a corresponding receive takes place. This would happen, for example, if the MPI implementation copied a message from the user's send buffer to a system buffer and returned to the application program before any message transmission. Return from a blocking MPI call only means that the buffer named in the call is available for reuse.

MPI has both blocking and nonblocking send and receive calls (in the buffer available sense). Within these two types of send calls, there are ways to control message buffering by the MPI system and obtain blocking or nonblocking message transmission in the sense of Section 5.2. There are four *modes* of send operation—standard, buffered, synchronous, and ready. A corresponding *synchronous* send and blocking receive perform a rendezvous communication, as in CSP. A *buffered* send, even when it is blocking in the MPI sense, is nonblocking in the sense of Section 5.2. A buffered send call returns after copying the send buffer into MPI buffer space associated with the sending process. The MPI buffer is supplied by the user through separate calls to MPI and is shared by all buffered sends in a process. A *standard* mode send is either synchronous or buffered by choice of a particular MPI implementation. If it is buffered, the MPI system rather than the user supplies the buffer space. The return from a standard send call may be blocked when this buffer fills up, to be unblocked only after some pending message is received. A user should not invoke a *ready* mode send unless it is guaranteed that a matching receive has been started in the destination process. Ready mode send is erroneous if this is not the case.

A *nonblocking MPI* send or receive call merely starts a communication and returns immediately to the caller with no guarantee about the contents of a buffer. A handle for an opaque MPI *request object* is returned to the caller to be used in determining the completion of the send or receive. Nonblocking sends may be initiated in any of the four modes—standard, buffered, synchronous, or ready. Completion of a request can be determined either by a *wait* operation, which specifies a request handle and does not return until the associated buffer is available, or by a *test* operation, which returns a true or false for buffer availability. For either blocking or nonblocking operations, the transmission mode is specified only in the send call. There are only two receive calls, one blocking and one nonblocking. Table 5-7 summarizes the different types of point-to-point communication calls in MPI. The specific MPI routines for point-to-point communication are described in Appendix A.1.

5.4.1.5   Collective Communications Concepts

Concepts associated with collective communications follow from the discussion of high-level communications in Section 5.3.3 Collective communications are not required by the standard to synchronize all participating processes (except for the barrier operation), but an implementation may do so. When a collective operation synchronizes, no process returns from the collective communication call until all processes have made the call. This is the only function of the barrier procedure, and it, thus, requires only a communicator argument to identify the processes to be synchronized. Other procedures have parameters in addition to the communicator.

Some collective communications have a distinguished process that is either a source (broadcast, scatter) or a destination (gather, reduce). This single process is designated as *root* because these operations are usually done using a binary tree communication pattern with the distinguished process at the root of the tree. All collective procedures other than barrier specify data buffers and describe their contents. A call to the MPI broadcast procedure specifies a single buffer that contains the data to be sent in the root process and the received data in all other processes. All other collective communications procedures use two buffer arguments, one for the data to be sent and the other for the received data. Buffer contents in collective communications are described by the same sort of data type and count parameters that are used for the data portion of a message in point-to-point communications. The routines provided by MPI for collective communications are presented in Appendix A.2.

Table 5-7   Types of point-to-point MPI calls.

Send			
Blocking	Nonblocking	Mode	Nonblocking completion
Send	Isend	Standard	
Bsend	Ibsend	Buffered	Wait, Test
Ssend	Issend	Synchronous	
Rsend	Irsend	Ready	
Receive			
Blocking	Nonblocking initiation		Nonblocking completion
Recv	Irecv		Wait, Test

Table 5-8   Representative MPI routines.

MPI routines used in matrix multiply program	
environment control (Table A-13)	`MPI_INIT(IERR)`
	`MPI_FINALIZE(IERR)`
communicators (Table A-9)	`MPI_COMM_RANK(COM, RNK, IERR)`
collective communication (Table A-3)	`MPI_BCAST(BUF, CNT, TYPE, ROOT, COM, IERR)`
	`MPI_BARRIER(COM, IERR)`
point-to-point communication (Table A-1)	`MPI_ISEND(BUF, CNT, TYPE, DST, TAG, COM, REQ, IERR)`
	`MPI_RECV(BUF, CNT, TYPE, SRC, TAG, COM, STAT, IERR)`
	`MPI_REQUEST_FREE(REQ, IERR)`
communicator topology (Table A-11)	`MPI_CART_CREATE(COM, NDIMS, DIMS, PERS, REORD, NEWCOM, IERR)`
	`MPI_CART_SUB(COM, REMAIN, NEWCOM, IERR)`

5.4.2   An Example MPI Program—Matrix Multiplication

The MPI library has very many functions and subroutines. To present them without over-whelming the reader with the sheer number, we start with an example program that uses a selection of them. Table 5-8 shows the MPI routines that are used in the distributed matrix mul-tiply program based on Program 5-2. It is important to note that only a handful of the numerous routines supplied by MPI-1 was used to write the program. Appendix A gives a comprehensive list of MPI routines. A language must supply a set of basic and essential features for writing parallel programs. Many additional features are supplied by the language that add to both the complexity of the language and to its functionality, providing the programmers with functions that would otherwise have to be part of the programming task. In studying MPI, the reader is encouraged to keep in mind which routines are essential and which ones are desirable and what additional features are needed, keeping in mind that MPI-2 provides many more routines than MPI-1. Table 5-9 describes the parameters that are used in the MPI routines of Table 5-8.

Table 5-9   Parameters for MPI routines of Table 5-8.

`IERR`	MPI error return code
`COM`	Handle for the communicator used in transmission
`RNK`	Rank of calling process in group or communicator
`BUF`	Starting address of a buffer for a message to be sent or received
`CNT`	Number of items of the specified type in the buffer—space on receive
`TYPE`	Handle for MPI type of the data in a send buffer or type to be received
`ROOT`	Rank of the distinguished process when source or destination is one process
`DST`	Rank of the destination process in the specified communicator
`TAG`	Tag for the message, specific on send—may be `MPI_ANY_TAG` on receive
`REQ`	Handle used to refer to an initialized request
`SRC`	Rank of source process in the communicator—may be `MPI_ANY_SOURCE`
`STAT`	Array of 3 integers containing return status: source, tag, and error
`NDIMS`	Number of dimensions in a Cartesian grid
`DIMS`	List of extents of each dimension
`PERS`	Logical flags telling if each dimension is periodic or not
`REORD`	Logical flag allowing reordering of processes for efficient implementation if true
`NEWCOM`	New communicator created with a specified topology
`REMAIN`	True/false value for whether each dimension remains in a Cartesian subgrid
`NDIMS`	Number of dimensions in a Cartesian grid

We look at the main program and two subroutines for matrix multiplication. Loading and starting the program on all N^2 processors is done by process management operations not specified in MPI. The main program uses interprocess communications to send input data to all processors and to collect output data at the process with rank zero, which is presumed to be the one attached to the reader and printer. One of the subroutines organizes the processes into a grid topology so broadcasts along rows and columns can be done conveniently. The other does the distributed matrix multiply in which $Nb \times Nb$ matrices are distributed over N^2 processors with one $b \times b$ block of each matrix in each processor.

The input section of the main program and its call to the distributed matrix multiply procedure is shown in Program 5-10. There are assumed to be N^2 processors in the process group of the `MPI_COMM_WORLD` communicator. Because process management is not a part of MPI, the code to start N^2 processes, all executing this same code, is not shown. The `INCLUDE 'mpif.h'` statement imports the definitions of MPI routines and constants. Each process stores its sub-blocks of the matrices A and B to be multiplied along with a block of the result matrix C. These private blocks are called `Ap`, `Bp`, and `Cp`. The indices, `myrow` and `mycol` represent the position of the private blocks within the full matrices. They are established by the `procgrid` routine that forms communicators with Cartesian grid topologies. The dimension statements impose the limit $b \leq 50$. It is assumed that the process with rank 0 in MPI_COMM_WORLD does all input and output, so it reads b and N and broadcasts them to all other processes. To prepare for this, MPI is initialized, which must precede any other MPI call, and a call to MPI_COMM_RANK returns the rank of each calling process. The last argument of a Fortran MPI subroutine is an error flag returned to the caller. In the C binding for MPI the error is the returned value of the function. As in the current example, the error flag is often ignored. The returned value, myrank, is an integer between 0 and $N^2 - 1$.

```
      PROGRAM main
      INCLUDE 'mpif.h'
      INTEGER b, N
      REAL Ap(50, 50), Bp(50, 50), Cp(50, 50)
      REAL blockbuf(50,50), printbuf(50, 500)
      INTEGER comsq, comrow, comcol, myrow, mycol
      INTEGER ierr, request, myrank, ii, jj, i, j
      INTEGER ibuf(2), status(MPI_STATUS_SIZE)
C Initialize MPI and determine process ranks.
      CALL MPI_INIT(ierr)
      CALL MPI_COMM_RANK(MPI_COMM_WORLD, myrank, ierr)
C Process 0 reads b and N and broadcasts them to all others.
      IF (myrank .EQ. 0) THEN
        READ *, b, N
        ibuf(1) = b
        ibuf(2) = N
      ENDIF
      CALL MPI_BCAST(ibuf, 2, MPI_INTEGER, 0, MPI_COMM_WORLD,
     &                                                  ierr)
      b = ibuf(1)
      N = ibuf(2)
C Establish the topology and obtain this process' blocks of A and B.
      CALL procgrid(N, comsq, comrow, comcol, myrow, mycol)
      DO i = 1, b
        DO j = 1, b
          Ap(i, j) = getA(myrow*b+i, mycol*b+j)
          Bp(i, j) = getB(myrow*b+i, mycol*b+j)
        ENDDO
      ENDDO
C Do the block wise distributed matrix multiply.
      CALL distmult(b, N, comrow, comcol, myrow, mycol, Ap, Bp, Cp)
```

Program 5-10   Input, grid setup, and matrix multiply in main program.

The broadcast of b and N illustrates the technique of packing items into a buffer for transmission to avoid the penalty of multiple communications with high software overhead and

```
C Send blocks of C to process 0 for printing.
      DO ii = 0, N-1
        DO jj = 0, N-1
          IF ((ii .EQ. myrow) .AND. (jj .EQ. mycol)) THEN
            CALL MPI_ISEND(Cp, 2500, MPI_REAL, 0, 1,
     &                            MPI_COMM_WORLD, request, ierr)
          ENDIF
          IF (myrank .EQ. 0) THEN
            CALL MPI_RECV(blockbuf, 2500, MPI_REAL, MPI_ANY_SOURCE,
     &                            1, MPI_COMM_WORLD, ierr)
            DO i = 1, b
              DO j = 1, b
                printbuf(i, jj*b+j) = blockbuf(i, j)
              ENDDO
            ENDDO
          ENDIF
C Wait for send and receive completion for this (ii, jj) pair.
          CALL MPI_BARRIER(MPI_COMM_WORLD, ierr)
        ENDDO
        IF (myrank .EQ. 0) THEN
          CALL printrow(printbuf, b, N)
        ENDIF
      ENDDO
C Release unchecked requests and terminate.
      CALL MPI_REQUEST_FREE(request, ierr)
      CALL MPI_FINALIZE(ierr)
      END
```

Program 5-11   Output section and completion of distributed matrix multiply main program.

start-up latency. Only process zero loads b and N into its buffer. The fourth argument of MPI_BCAST identifies the root (or sender) as process zero. On completion, all N^2 buffers will be identical, and all processes can extract b and N, although it is unnecessary for process zero. The procgrid subroutine uses MPI routines to form communicators for the $N \times N$ processor grid and for each row and column. The comsq communicator contains all processes with an $N \times N$ grid topology imposed on them. There are N versions each of the communicators com-row and comcol. The current process and all others in its row belong to its version of comrow, while the current and all others in its column belong to its version of comcol. The functions getA and getB complete the input section by taking arguments i and j and returning the (i, j)-th element of the corresponding matrix. We do not specify these subroutines further. They may either calculate or input the matrix element values. Finally, the subroutine distmult is called to compute the private block Cp of C for each process.

The output section of the main program is shown in Program 5-11. It illustrates the use of point-to-point transmissions to send rows of N blocks of C to process zero, which then prints out the result in row-major order using an unspecified routine printrow. The send has the form

```
    MPI_ISEND(buf, count, type, dest, tag, comm, request, ierr)
```

This initiates a nonblocking send from the buffer `buf` containing `count` values of data type `type` to destination process with rank `dest` in the communicator `comm` and returns a handle, `request`, that can be used to check the completion status of the send. Blocks are sent with their maximum dimensioned size so that they can be used as arrays without unpacking when received. The matching receive is executed by process zero, which may send to itself. After each receive, a barrier synchronization is done on the `MPI_COMM_WORLD` communicator to ensure that the blocks of a process row arrive in order at process zero. When a row of blocks has arrived, process zero prints the row using the `printrow` subroutine. This is done for all N rows of N blocks each. Either `MPI_WAIT` or `MPI_TEST` could check the completion of `request`, but in this instance the fact that the barrier includes the receiver process guarantees that the corresponding send-receive pair is done. Thus, the request can simply be discarded by the call to `MPI_REQUEST_FREE`. The call to `MPI_FINALIZE` must be the last MPI call in a program.

The `procgrid` subroutine shown in Program 5-12 forms a communicator `comsq` consisting of the same N^2 processes as are in `MPI_COMM_WORLD` but now having a two-dimensional Cartesian topology associated with them. The MPI routine that does this has the form

```
      SUBROUTINE procgrid(N, comsq, comrow, comcol, myrow, mycol)
      INCLUDE 'mpif.h'
      INTEGER N, comsq, comrow, comcol, myrow, mycol
      INTEGER dims(2)
      LOGICAL periodic(2), remain(2), reorder
C
      dims(1) = N
      dims(2) = N
      periodic(1) = .FALSE.
      periodic(2) = .FALSE.
      reorder = .TRUE.
      CALL MPI_CART_CREATE(MPI_COMM_WORLD, 2, dims, periodic,
     &                                    reorder, comsq, ierr)
C
      remain(1) = .FALSE.
      remain(2) = .TRUE.
      CALL MPI_CART_SUB(comsq, remain, comrow, ierr)
      remain(1) = .TRUE.
      remain(2) = .FALSE.
      CALL MPI_CART_SUB(comsq, remain, comcol, ierr)
      CALL MPI_COMM_RANK(comcol, myrow, ierr)
      CALL MPI_COMM_RANK(comrow, mycol, ierr)
      END
```

Program 5-12   Construction of communicators for the process grid.

```
MPI_CART_CREATE(oldcomm, ndims, dims, wraps, reorder, newcomm, ierr)
```

The communicator `newcomm` is formed from the processes of the communicator `oldcomm` by arranging them in an array of `ndims` dimensions with extents from the integer array `dims()`. The logical array `wraps()` specifies for each dimension whether the topology is periodic, or wrap-around, in that dimension. The periodic property affects whether shifts are circular or end-off, but is not used in this program. If the logical value `reorder` is true, MPI is allowed to reorder the ranks of the processes to make communications with processes that are neighbors in the new topology efficient on the underlying machine hardware. The `MPI_CART_SUB` routine is used to form new communicators from `comsq` having topologies that are sub-grids of the $N \times N$ grid. With the form

```
MPI_CART_SUB(oldcomm, remain, newcomm, ierr)
```

the routine creates communicators `newcomm` from a Cartesian `oldcomm` by suppressing dimensions associated with false values in the logical array `remain()`. Each calling process receives a handle for the new communicator of which it is a member. Suppressing the first dimension gives row communicators, while suppressing the second dimension gives column communicators. After the two calls to `MPI_CART_SUB` there is one communicator, `comsq`, N communicators called `myrow` and N called `mycol`, so each process belongs to four communicators, including `MPI_COMM_WORLD`. The row number of a process is obtained by determining the process' rank in its column and its column number is determined from rank in row.

Using the row and column communicators, the MPI subroutine of Program 5-13 does the distributed matrix multiply using the outline of Program 5-2 that was implemented with point-to-point CSP communications in Program 5-4. The processor with row index `ii` and column index `jj` computes the corresponding block of the C matrix by first initializing the block to zero and then successively adding inner product terms consisting of $b \times b$ matrix products of the (`ii`, `kk`) block of A times the (`kk`, `jj`) block of B. The outer loop steps through inner product terms. For each value of `kk`, processors in the `kk`-th column in every row transmit their blocks of A to all other processors in their respective rows. Processors in the `kk`-th row of every column also transmit their blocks of B to all other processes in their respective columns. At the end of these communication steps, process (`ii`, `jj`) has the (`ii`, `kk`) block of A in `tmpA` and the (`kk`, `jj`) block of B in `tmpB`. The last triply nested loop multiplies the $b \times b$ blocks `tmpA` and `tmpB` and adds the result to the private block (`ii`, `jj`) of C.

It is clear from the example that constructing communicators with topologies that match the requirements of an algorithm can be a powerful way of enabling collective communications to make the computational core of a distributed program straightforward. Because processes are identified by their rank with respect to a communicator, there may be several "identifiers" for a process in a computation that makes use of different communicators. The software overhead in doing a subroutine call is dominated by the transmission latency in many distributed systems, but the combined effect of the two means that as few separate transmissions as possible should be done. This concern was only seen in the broadcast of b and N in this example because other transmissions sent full matrix blocks. On the other hand, if b is less than its upper limit of 50

```
      SUBROUTINE distmult(b, N, comrow, comcol, myrow, mycol, Ap, Bp, Cp)
      INCLUDE 'mpif.h'
      INTEGER b, N, comrow, comcol, myrow, mycol
      REAL Ap(50, 50), Bp(50, 50), Cp(50,50)
      REAL tmpA(50, 50), tmpB(50, 50)
      INTEGER i, j, k, kk
C
      DO i = 1, b
        DO j = 1, b
          Cp(i, j) = 0.0
        ENDDO
      ENDDO
C Processes in the kk-th column broadcast their blocks over rows.
      DO kk = 0, N-1
        IF (mycol .EQ. kk) THEN
          DO i = 1, b
            DO j = 1, b
              tmpA(i, j) = Ap(i, j)
            ENDDO
          ENDDO
        ENDIF
        CALL MPI_BCAST(tmpA, 2500, MPI_REAL, kk, comrow, ierr)
C Processes in the kk-th row broadcast their blocks over columns.
        IF (myrow .EQ. kk) THEN
          DO i = 1, b
            DO j = 1, b
              tmpB(i, j) = Bp(i, j)
            ENDDO
          ENDDO
        ENDIF
        CALL MPI_BCAST(tmpB, 2500, MPI_REAL, kk, comcol, ierr)
C Processor (ii, jj) adds product of A and B block to C block.
        DO i = 1, b
          DO j = 1, b
            DO k = 1, b
              Cp(i, j) = Cp(i, j) + tmpA(i, k)*tmpB(k, j)
            ENDDO
          ENDDO
        ENDDO
      ENDDO
      END
```

Program 5-13   MPI distributed matrix multiply using row and column broadcasts.

imposed by the dimension declarations, many unused elements may be transmitted with a $b \times b$ block. The problem could be solved by defining b with a PARAMETER statement and dimensioning the arrays with it.

5.5 Hardware Managed Communication—Distributed Cache

All of the point-to-point communications discussed, and to a lesser extent, the collective communications, are initiated by the process producing the data that must be shared with other processes. The characterization of data sharing as *producer initiated* is a property closely identified with message passing systems. In shared memory computers, the initiation of transfers is more symmetric, with the producer initiating the transfer into shared memory and one or more consumers initiating retrieval of the stored data. In distributed memory multiprocessors, it is possible to have the consumer of the data initiate the transfer by making a request of the producer. This consumer initiated paradigm is not common in explicitly programmed communications because it requires two communications, but it is the norm in distributed memory systems in which hardware manages the local memories as caches. In a simple form of this scheme, sometimes called *distributed shared memory*, the local memory of each processor is treated as a cache with a directory indicating whether a copy of a main memory cache line is present in the cache or not. A cache hit allows a processor to access the information locally while a miss requires a remote access to the shared memory.

A variation on using local memories as caches is to eliminate the shared memory altogether and treat the aggregate of all the processors' caches as a distributed form of shared memory, or more precisely, a shared address space. In this scheme, called *cache only memory architecture* (COMA), a cache miss causes a request for the appropriate line to be sent to the cache of the processor that currently "owns" the information, giving a truly consumer initiated sharing paradigm. Both COMA and architectures with caches backed up by a shared memory are nonuniform memory access (NUMA), architectures, in which memory access completion time varies with the address in shared memory.

5.5.1 Cache Coherence

Any shared memory multiprocessor with caches must address the problem of cache coherence. Consider a two-processor system P_1 and P_2 with local cache C_1 and C_2, respectively, sharing memory M. Initially, assume C_1, C_2, and M contain a copy of shared variable x. If later P_1 updates its own copy of x to x', then the three copies of x in C_1, C_2, and M become inconsistent. There are two general policies for implementing coherent caches. Write invalidate, also known as dynamic coherence policy, invalidates all other cache copies of a block containing the data every time a processor modifies its local copy of the data. Write update updates all other cache copies of the data when a process writes it rather than invalidating them. Write update gains back some of the efficiency of producer initiated data sharing, because not all reads of remotely produced data require a round trip request and response. However, the hardware update protocols cannot predict which processes will actually read newly written data but can only update the caches of those processes that used the written memory address recently. Thus, some network bandwidth is wasted on unused communication with write update.

The protocol used to implement write update or write invalidate depends on the interconnection network. When an efficient broadcast can be supported, for example using a bus, the write invalidate or update commands can be broadcast to all caches. In this case, each cache must listen to, or "snoop" on, every command to see if it addresses any data item the cache is holding. All protocols based on this technique are known as snoopy cache. The requirement that a snoopy cache see all memory requests makes it more appropriate for some interconnection networks than others. A bus interconnection naturally makes all transactions available to every processor attached to it. With a ring interconnection, all remote memory transactions can be sent around the ring and not considered complete until they return to the originating processor and all other processors on the ring have seen them. The ring has a longer latency than the bus but can process multiple transactions at a time compared to one at a time for the bus.

Although broadcasting memory transactions so that all caches can see them is natural for bus or ring interconnections, P processors broadcasting to P destinations produces order P^2 traffic in more general interconnection networks. This limits the practical number of processors, or scalability, for a system using snoopy caches. To overcome this problem, a system can use a *directory-based* cache coherence mechanism where a central directory for each cacheable line of main memory contains information about all caches currently sharing the data in the line. This restricts messages about transactions on that line to just those caches that need them. A PMS diagram of a multiprocessor system with directory-based cache is shown in Figure 5-8. For every line in a particular shared memory cache, the cache directory needs to have more state information than just the valid/invalid indicator required for a line in a uniprocessor cache. Important states are *invalid*, *shared*, and *exclusive*. In the invalid state, memory or another cache must be contacted to supply a copy of the line. In the shared state, a line that is written must be either invalidated or updated in the other caches that share it. In the exclusive state, only main memory needs to be notified on a write. With write back rather than write through caches, some performance can be gained by splitting the exclusive state into *modified exclusive* and *unmodified exclusive* states. When another cache wants to share a modified exclusive line, the cache holding the line in the modified state, rather than the memory, must supply the data, but memory can supply the data for an unmodified exclusive line. Multiprocessor caches add a fourth type of cache miss to the "three Cs," compulsory, capacity, and conflict, misses found in uniprocessor caches. The *coherence miss* occurs when a line that was invalidated by a write from another processor is again referenced by the processor whose copy became invalid.

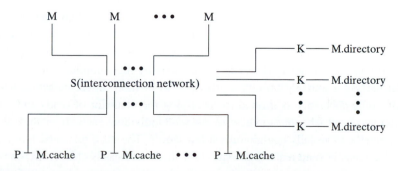

Figure 5-8   Shared memory multiprocessor with directory-based cache coherence.

Both the broadcasts needed by snoopy cache coherence and the update or invalidate messages needed by a directory based mechanism require messages to be passed around the system, even if no actual data is transferred. For example, writing to a shared cache line may send invalidate messages to all caches sharing that line even though no data is transferred. Further, because cache lines are usually larger than one word, two processes writing different words of the same line may cause the line to move back and forth between their caches even if neither reads what the other writes. This so-called *false sharing* increases communication traffic in the system. False sharing overhead decreases with the size of a cache line, to disappear for one word lines. As one word lines make impractical demands on directory size and data transfer overhead, some false sharing is inevitable. Thus, the use of caches with shared memory reduces the number of remote data accesses at the expense of the extra messages among processors and memory that are required to maintain cache coherence.

From the point of view of system behavior, cache coherence can be defined in terms of the results of a program execution with respect to each memory location.

Definition: Cache coherence is maintained if the results of a multiprocessor program behave as if there were a total ordering of accesses to each particular memory location satisfying:

(a) The total order is consistent with the program order for accesses to that memory location from any single processor.

(b) The value returned by a read is the last value written in the total ordering. ■

Numerous directory structures and protocols have been developed to ensure that a shared memory multiprocessor is cache coherent. Write atomicity is important to cache coherent behavior. A write to a location must complete by doing all invalidates and updates associated with that location before another write to that location starts, and a load cannot return the value of a write until the write has completed. This is the standard definition of an atomic operation. Any other operation (on the same location) sees the shared value either as it was before the write started or as it became after the write completed.

5.5.2   Shared Memory Consistency

More than cache coherence is required for a shared memory to behave in a way that is predictable and usable by a multiprocessor programmer. Also, caches are not the only reason for inconsistent behavior of data accesses in a multiprocessor program. Inconsistency can arise any time a data item has more than one representative in a system. This can happen as a result of processor write buffers, copies of data kept in registers by the compiler, and even data copies contained in messages moving through a processor to memory interconnection network. The definition of cache coherence is limited to specifying the behavior of reads and writes to the same location because cache management works with individual cache lines that, as a result of false sharing overhead, usually contain only a few words. The need for consistency in memory behavior that extends beyond reads and writes to a single address is clear from the two process Dekker's algorithm for mutual exclusion for a critical section shown in Program 5-14. Dekker's algorithm will be discussed in more detail in Chapter 8, Section 8.4. The expectation that both

Initially F1 = F2 = 0

Process P1

```
F1 := 1;
if (F2 = 0) then
        ⟨enter critical section⟩;
```

Process P2

```
F2 := 1;
if (F1 = 0) then
        ⟨enter critical section⟩;
```

Program 5-14 Algorithm expecting consistency in access to different locations.

P1 and P2 cannot simultaneously enter the critical section is not implied by cache coherence because it involves restrictions on the order of access to two different locations, F1 and F2. The example also shows how inconsistency can arise without caches by considering what would happen if the writes to F1 and F2 were delayed in write buffers or the interconnection network while the reads (to different locations than the corresponding writes) completed quickly.

The cache coherence definition can be extended to a notion of shared memory consistency, called *sequential consistency*, with the following definition.

Definition: A multiprocessor system is sequentially consistent if the results of any execution appear as if there were a single total order on all memory accesses that is consistent with the program order for each processor. ∎

The total order in the definition is often thought of as a random interleaving of the program orders of all processes. The fact that all processes observe the same total order on memory accesses again implies atomicity of accesses and rules out the possibility of process P3 of Program 5-15 observing B = 1 while still seeing A = 0. Sequentially consistent behavior of a multiprocessor program execution can be ensured by several conditions on the operation of the system formulated in terms of the completion of memory operations. A memory operation is said to be complete when all invalidates and updates that it causes are done. Necessary conditions for sequential consistency are then

Initially A = 0, B = 0

Process P1	Process P2	Process P3

```
A := 1;       B := A;       if (B = 1) then
                                if (A = 0) then
                                    ⟨consistency failure⟩
```

Program 5-15 Different memory access orders observed by different processes.

1. Each process issues memory requests in program order.

2. A process issuing a write waits for it to complete with respect to all processes before issuing another memory request.

3. A process issuing a read waits for it to complete and for the write producing the value that the read returns to complete before issuing another memory request.

The requirements of sequential consistency are demanding and can negate performance gains from techniques as diverse as compiler register allocation and processor write buffers. These stringent requirements are more than is needed for the type of shared memory programming discussed in Chapter 4. Clearly, private data stored in a shared memory need only behave consistently with the program order of its processor. Further, the update of shared data shown in Program 5-16 does not require that the writes to the shared variables A and B be seen in the same order by all processes. It only requires that both writes complete before **unlock** L is performed by P1 and that the synchronizing **lock** and **unlock** operations behave consistently. Then processes other than P1 that only access A and B after obtaining lock L will see A and B as they both were before the update or as they both become after the update. Recognizing the importance of synchronization in data sharing, relaxed memory consistency models have been proposed and applied that distinguish synchronization operations from ordinary operations on shared variables. One such model is that of *weak ordering*. In weak ordering, operations on shared variables are distinguished as *ordinary* or *synchronization* operations.

```
        Process P1                        Processes P2 through PN
    shared A, B, L;                        shared A, B, L;
    private x, y;                          private z;
    lock L;                                lock L;
        A := x;                                z := f(A, B);
        B := y;                            unlock L;
    unlock L;
```

Program 5-16   Maintaining consistency through synchronization.

Definition: A multiprocessor system conforms to the weak ordering model if

1. An ordinary shared memory access cannot be issued until all preceding synchronization operations complete with respect to all processes.
2. A synchronization operation cannot be issued until all preceding ordinary accesses to shared memory complete with respect to all processors.
3. Synchronization operations are sequentially consistent among themselves. ■

The definition is still satisfied when ordinary operations are rearranged among themselves by hardware or compiler optimizations.

Synchronization constructs in high-level languages such as critical sections, lock/unlock, produce/consume, barrier, etc. are implemented in such a way that they perform their expected function with the memory consistency model implemented in the system. This, in addition to the difficulty of reasoning about synchronizations using only reads and writes on shared variables, demands that well-written shared memory multiprocessor programs communicate data among processes only by way of properly synchronized constructs. This happens automatically, but in a restricted manner, with send and receive in message passing multiprocessors.

5.6   Conclusion—Shared Versus Distributed Memory Multiprocessors

With both shared address space and message passing, large scale multiprocessors are programmed in the SPMD style because it is impractical to write hundreds of separate programs for different processors. For a message passing program, a number of program design steps are needed to produce a computationally correct program.

- Major program data structures must be partitioned over the processors of the system.
- Work must be distributed so that most required data is local to the process doing a task and so that the computational load is balanced over the processors.
- Process topology must be related to processor topology to avoid serious communication inefficiency.
- Variables must be identified with the various sharing classes: private, cooperative update, replicated, and partitioned.
- Communication should be planned to enhance its overlap with computation.
- Message wait loops leading to deadlock must be avoided.

For a shared memory program at the same level of design, there are fewer concerns.

- Shared and private data must be identified.
- Work is distributed for computational load balance with no data access concerns.
- The sharing of data among processes must be synchronized.

For hardware managed distributed shared memory with caches, a computationally correct program can be obtained by only addressing the three concerns of a shared memory program. However, to get even a moderately efficient program, all of the message passing planning steps except the last two that relate to explicit message operations should be followed. Because the hardware cache coherence and memory consistency mechanisms manage data transfer among processors, it is not necessary to handle data transmission explicitly, but it is also not possible to do so to gain performance either, unless cache prefetch or similar operations are explicitly available to the programmer.

The most negative performance impact in distributed memory multiprocessors, and in shared memory also, comes from latency in data transmission. Latency can be reduced in distributed memory systems by using partitionable locality inherent in an application or by a distributed shared memory caching scheme that has a high hit rate and that does not introduce too much extra latency in the communications necessary to maintain coherence. Latency can also be addressed by masking its effect. Overlapping communication with computation and with other communication can be a powerful technique for maintaining high performance in spite of latency. A problem with controlling latency using overlap is that it is difficult to organize a program so that all processes are able to proceed with computation in spite of delays in obtaining shared data. This is especially true in parallel programs with fine granularity where data sharing is frequent. One very effective way to address this problem is to have more processes than processors and time multiplex (or multiprogram) several processes on the same physical processor. Then when one process is delayed by latency in data transmission, the computation cycles can be used by another process rather than being wasted.

Figure 5-9 shows a time line for data transmission from a process P1 running on one processor to a process P2 time multiplexed with a process P3 on a second processor. The sharing is consumer initiated, so it requires a round trip communication from consumer to producer and back. To support this latency hiding technique efficiently, processors should provide fast context switching between processes, a wait queue for processes waiting on message arrival, and a run queue for processes that are ready to use the processor, as shown in Figure 5-10. Communications processors to buffer messages and manage queues can enhance performance considerably in such a system. With this system, part of the parallelism in a program is used to exploit multiple processors, and part is used to mask latency. The number of processes, P, required for efficient operation in a system with C time multiplexed processors is on the order of

Producer processor	P1: Produce shared data and compute	Send to P2	P1: Compute	
Network		Message latency		Message latency	
Consumer processor	P2: request data	P3: Compute		P2: Compute with new data

time ⟶

Figure 5-9   Consumer-initiated data sharing latency masked by multiprogramming.

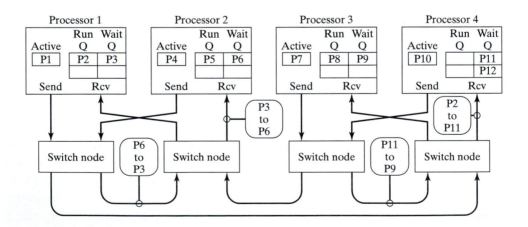

Figure 5-10   Messages in a distributed memory system with time multiplexed processors.

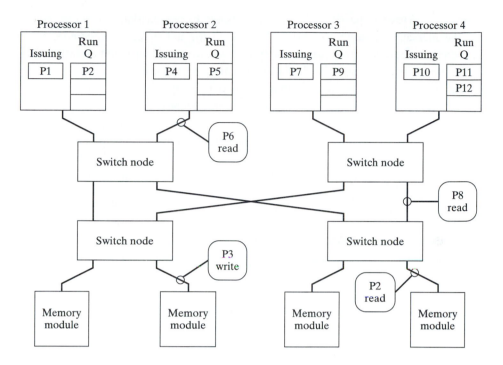

Figure 5-11   Shared memory latency masked by MIMD multithreading.

$$P = C/p_r \tag{5.2}$$

where p_r is the probability that a process is ready to run, or

$$p_r = 1 - p_w \tag{5.3}$$

where p_w is the probability that a process is waiting on a data item.

Equation (5.2) should be compared with Eq. (4.2) of Section 4.5, where time multiplexing in an MIMD pipeline is used to mask the latency of access to a shared memory. The similarity of the systems is emphasized by the diagram of Figure 5-11 that shows shared memory reads and writes in a pipelined MIMD systems as messages moving through the network connecting processors and modules of the shared memory. The extra parallelism required to support latency hiding for either pipelined shared memory machines or distributed memory machines with time multiplexed processors is typically available in applications large enough to warrant using a many processor machine. Exceptions are very sequential programs that do not parallelize well on any type of system. Fine granularity programs that lead to a high probability of waiting for data can also usually be broken down into a large number of processes, so programs that need the latency hiding most are also amenable to the multiplexing used to do it.

Even though message passing and shared memory programs may seem very different, it can be seen that the same issues need to be addressed by both shared and distributed memory multiprocessors. Message passing programs can always be run on shared memory systems by passing the messages through memory buffers. With the aid of cache coherence hardware, shared memory programs can be run on a system with a very distributed architecture. Small shared memory multiprocessors, or clusters, can communicate through a second level interconnection network using message passing in the fairly popular symmetric multiprocessor, or *SMP cluster*, style architecture. Management of latency is important in all parallel systems, either by latency reduction, latency hiding, or a combination of the two. All high performance parallel systems use a mixture of techniques to increase the number of parallel operations and to manage latency, so although it is useful to present the fundamentals of shared and distributed memory multiprocessors separately, it is difficult and often futile to try to separate them in practice.

5.7 Bibliographic Notes

Several parallel algorithm books, for example [49, 187] focus almost exclusively on distributed memory multiprocessing models. Distributed memory multiprocessor architectures are often tightly bound to their interconnection network topology. In addition to comparisons of distributed memory architectures, for example, [30], there are numerous, for example, [136, 256], discussions of machines with a particular interconnection topology. MPI-1 is treated in [265], and recent standards information is on the World Wide Web at [220]. Because MPI does not include process control operations, it is used with machine specific process control or with another language extension that supports process control. One such extension is PVM [271], which has support for process control, synchronization, and point-to-point communications, but not collective communications. Cache coherent distributed memory machines are treated thoroughly in [80], and the memory consistency models they use are well surveyed in [3]. Specific cache coherent machines are also described in detail, for example [171, 199].

Problems

5.1   In the program below, written in Hoare's Communicating Sequential Processes language, CSP, there are three processes, *P1*, *P2*, and *P3*. Upper case letters represent statements, and lower case letters are variable names.

[*P1* :: *A*; *P2* ! *u*; *B*; *P3* ! *v*; *C* ‖

P2 :: *D*; *P3* ? *w*; *E*; *P1* ? *x*; *F* ‖

P3 :: *G*; *P2* ! *y*; *H*; *P1* ? *z*; *K*]

(a)   The sequential processes of CSP, along with the send (!) and receive (?) commands, impose a partial order on the statements. Diagram the covering relation for the partial order on *A*, *B*, *C*, *D*, *E*, *F*, *G*, *H*, and *K*. The covering relation is the order with all relations implied by transitivity removed. No arrows that are implied by transitivity are to be included in the diagram.

(b)   What happens if *P2!y* is exchanged with *P1?z* in process *P3*?

5.2   Eight parallel CSP processes *X(i: 0..7)* all compute partial results. It is required that *X(0)* obtain the sum of all the partial results. In the questions below, which require you to write CSP, do not worry too much about correct syntax, but be sure to use the correct semantics for parallelism, indeterminacy and interprocess communication. Explain your notation in English if you are in doubt about how to write a CSP construct.

(a) Show CSP program fragments for $X(0)$ and $X(i: 1..7)$ to do the summation in a "linear time" of eight steps.

(b) Show CSP code to do the summation in a "logarithmic time" of three steps.

5.3 In a multiprocessor, a number 'n' of worker processes W(i) execute the same code. The programmer wants to specify 'k' different code sections that are each to be executed by one and only one process, but by whichever is available "first." He conceptualizes this by adding a new statement to Hoare's CSP and writes pseudocode for the workers as:

W(i:1..'n') :: ... doeach case <sect. 1> case <sect. 2> case ... endeach ...

where 'n' and 'k' are fixed integers for any specific execution. He then proceeds to implement this construct using the primitives available in CSP.

(a) Show how to do this if 'k' ≤ 'n'. Be sure to use the correct semantics for parallelism, indeterminacy, and interprocess communication in CSP. Use sequential pseudocode style for sequential aspects of CSP programming of which you may be uncertain.

(b) Extend the solution to the case 'n' < 'k'. As in (a) work should be started as soon as there is a process available to do it, and the entire doeach should be exited by each process as soon as there is no more work it can do.

5.4 Three processors in a distributed memory multiprocessor communicate by *send* and *receive* running the code sketched below, where upper case letters represent local activities.

Process P1	**Process P2**	**Process P3**
A	D	G
receive(P3)	send(P1)	receive(P2)
B	E	H
receive(P2)	send(P3)	send(P1)
C	F	I

(a) If *send* is nonblocking and *receive* is blocking, draw a diagram of the precedence relation on the local activities.

(b) What is the longest chain of activities that must be executed in sequence?

(c) If both *send* and *receive* were blocking, what would happen to the program and how would it relate to the precedence diagram?

5.5 The three processes below run on three processors of a distributed memory multiprocessor in which all data movement between processors is by means of nonblocking *send* and blocking *receive*. Show the partial order imposed on the statements *X1-X5*, *Y1-Y5*, and *Z1-Z5* by the three process program below. Assume that message transmission takes two time units and that statements take one time unit each except for *send* and *receive*, which take no time except for transmission. How many time units are required for program completion?

Process X	Process Y	Process Z
X1	Y1	Z1
receive i from Y	send p to Z	send a to X
X2	Y2	Z2
receive j from Z	receive q from Z	receive b from Y
X3	Y3	Z3
send k to Y	send r to X	send c to Y
X4	Y4	Z4
send n to Z	receive s from X	receive d from X
X5	Y5	Z5

5.6 $N = 2^d$ processors are connected in a hypercube topology. Processor p can only transmit to, or receive from, processors $p \oplus 2^k$, $k = 0,1,..., d - 1$.

Give an algorithm in SPMD pseudocode for all processes of a message processing multiprocessor that sends a message from source processor S to destination processor D.

5.7   The discussion of Program 5-4 claims that single real numbers can be replaced by $b \times b$ matrix blocks, multiply replaced by matrix multiply, and add replaced by matrix add to obtain a correct matrix multiply program in which each process computes a $b \times b$ block of matrix C instead of a single element.

(a)   Show mathematically that this procedure gives the correct result for the matrix $C = A \times B$.

(b)   Elaborate Program 5-4 for $b \times b$ blocks of A, B, and C in each process. Assume blocking operations `send(buf, d, P)` and `recv(buf, d, S)` that send a buffer, buf, of length d to process P and receive the buffer from process S, respectively. Handle the details of packing and unpacking the buffer and multiplying the blocks of the matrices.

5.8   Consider the Gauss elimination solution of $Ax = b$ where rows of A are distributed over p processors of a machine that does not favor operations on contiguous vectors. The maximum absolute value search for a pivot can then be done in parallel over processors. The pivot row is scaled sequentially by the process owning it and then broadcast to all processes, which update the rows they own by row wise Gauss elimination. The forward and back substitution can now be done in parallel by the column sweep method, with individual solution vector elements being broadcast one at a time to all processes as they are produced.

5.12 The function below is called in parallel by $N = 2^K$ processors of a distributed n. processor. Processes run on separate processors and communicate using:

Send(processor_number, value)   Send the value to the specified processor and do not wait for a response.

Receive(processor_number, value)   Wait for a message to arrive from the specified processor and return its value.

```
REAL FUNCTION Q(K,VALUE,ME)
INTEGER K,ME
C = VALUE
DO 10 L = 1,K
NB = IXOR(ME-1,2**(L-1))+1
Send (NB,C)
Receive (NB,C1)
C = C+C1
10   CONTINUE
Q =C
RETURN
END
```

K is the same constant in all processors. ME is the unique number of each processor, $1 \leq ME \leq N$. The function IXOR performs the bit wise exclusive or on its two integer arguments, and ** is the Fortran exponentiation operator.

   (a) What function is performed by Q when called by all N processors?
   (b) Describe the synchronization properties of the statement S = Q(K, V, ME) performed in parallel by N = 2**K processors.

5.13 Suppose that processors of a machine executing Cannon's algorithm can transmit left or upward by any power of two steps. sendl(v, k) sends v to the processor 2^k steps to the left, and recvr(v, k) receives v from the processor 2^k steps to the right. sendu(v, k) and recvb(v, k) operate similarly for upwards transmission.

Rewrite Program 5-9 using these operations to reduce the number of sequential transmission steps needed to get elements of A and B to their starting positions for Cannon's matrix multiply. No more than $\log_2 N$ transmissions should be used to get an element to its destination.

5.14 Modify Program 5-11 to use MPI collective communication to gather the blocks of a row for output. Start by considering a simple case where all processes can output to the same printer. Then consider the case in which only the process with rank zero in MPI_COMM_WORLD can do output. Reordering processes in building the comsq communicator could be reconsidered, causing a modification in the procgrid subroutine.

Write the distributed program at the same level as the column wise Gauss elimina
text. Assume that communication is fairly efficient compared to computation so tha
long messages is less important than maximizing parallel computation.

5.9   A computation on two length N vectors A and B, defined by the sequential pseudoco
is to be done on a distributed memory multiprocessor.

```
B[1]  := A[1];
for i := 2 step 1 until N
      B[i]  := ( A[i] + A[i-1] )/2. ;
```

The machine has P processors, where $N = m \times P$, and communication is by means
blocking `send(proc, expr)` and blocking `recv(proc, var)`. The paramete
is a processor number, `expr` is an expression giving the value to be sent, and `var` is th
of a variable into which the received value is stored.

Assume that in processor i, $0 \le i \le P-1$, the values of $A[i \times m+1 : i \times m+m]$ are stor
vector $a[1:m]$ and that $B[]$ is similarly mapped to $b[]$ in each processor. Write disti
memory multiprocessor pseudocode that will work for any processor i in the system to
above computation. Structure the code to minimize completion time in view of m
latency.

5.10 The pseudocode below represents a sequential version of odd/even transposition sort. It
an N element array, $a[0:N-1]$, for N even.

```
while notsorted do
begin
      for i := 0 step 2 until N-2 do
            compare&swap(a[i], a[i+1]);
      for i := 1 step 2 until N-3 do
            compare&swap(a[i], a[i+1]);
end;
```

It is assumed that *compare&swap* is a subroutine that compares its two arguments and sw
them if they are not in order. It is also assumed that *notsorted* will be changed from *true*
false when sorting is complete.

(a) How should the array $a[0:N-1]$ be spread over the memories of a P processor distri
uted memory multiprocessor to implement a parallel version of this program? Assun
that P divides N evenly, so $N = Pm$, where m is an integer.

(b) Write pseudocode for processor i of the P processors assuming i is neither the first n
the last processor. Assume a nonblocking *send(⟨process⟩,⟨value⟩)* and a blockin
receive(⟨process⟩,⟨variable⟩) for communication.

5.11 $x = Ax + y$ is a general recurrence system, where x and y are N element vectors and A is an
$N \times N$ lower triangular matrix, with $a_{ij} = 0$ for all $1 \le i \le j \le N$. It is to be solved on an N
processor distributed memory multiprocessor where processors communicate only by
send(dest, value) and *receive(source, value)*.

(a) How should elements of x, y, and A be stored in the separate memories M_i of processors
P_i, $1 \le i \le N$, for solution using the column sweep method?

(b) Write a single MIMD pseudocode program for any processor P_i using *send* and *receive*
to accomplish the column sweep solution.

Interconnection Networks

SIMD and MIMD computers all use some form of interconnection network to facilitate communication and cooperation among their processing elements. Each of the parallel computer architecture types uses the interconnection network in a different way. In the distributed memory SIMD architecture, the interconnection network physically connects the processing elements so that the PEs can permute data stored in their registers. In shared memory SIMD, the alignment network provides access to data stored in different memory modules to different PEs directly. The interconnection networks in distributed memory MIMD architectures physically connect the system CPUs to provide explicit send and receive communications directly between the CPUs. In shared memory MIMD systems, the interconnection network provides access by the system CPUs to all system memory modules. Processors communicate by reading and writing shared memory locations. Although there are major differences between these architectures, the role of the interconnection network in all cases is to deliver information to the right place reliably. Important issues are the cost, how much information can be delivered at a given time, and how fast and efficient is the delivery.

The following questions may provide a useful perspective in reading the chapter. Transmissions from any processor to any other may be supported at a basic hardware or software level, but does the topology of the network make the overhead depend significantly on the identities of the source and destination? Does the network topology allow efficient implementation of common collective communications? How does the network respond to concurrent transmissions between multiple disjoint pairs of processes, that is, what is the effect of contention for network resources? Is the system in which the network is used such that multiple transmissions can be scheduled together to reduce contention, or is there randomness in the timing that requires a different form of contention reduction?

6.1 Network Characteristics

Interconnection networks can be characterized based on several design choices and their band-width, latency, and concurrency. The topology of interconnection networks is either static or dynamic. In *static* networks, processors are connected to each other directly, and, hence, they are also known as *direct* networks. The nodes are connected using point-to-point links that do not change during program execution. In *dynamic* networks also known as *indirect* or *switching* net-works, the processing elements are connected with switches that can be configured to meet the communication requirements of the executing programs. Dynamic networks provide a higher degree of interconnection flexibility in hardware. Static networks may need to use software to provide the routing mechanisms available in hardware in dynamic networks. Software may have higher overhead and degraded performance. Some examples of static networks are mesh, ring, binary tree, and fully connected nodes. Examples of dynamic networks include buses, crossbar switches, and multistage networks. Figure 6-1 shows some example static interconnection net-works and Figure 6-2 shows some dynamic interconnection networks.

Major performance metrics for characterizing a network are *latency, bandwidth, diameter, distance, concurrency, functionality, cost,* and *scalability.*

- Latency: *Latency, L*, is defined as transmission time of a single message. In general we can distinguish four components of latency. In many systems one must account for the *soft-ware overhead* associated with sending and receiving messages. The second component is the length of time that the communication channel is occupied by the message, called the *channel delay* (message length divided by the channel bandwidth). In the context of the interconnection networks, a *channel* is defined as a physical link between switch elements or hosts and a buffer to hold the data while it is being transferred. A *link* is a group of wires. The time to establish a route, including the setting of the switches, is referred to as the *switching delay* or *routing delay*, and, finally, there is *contention time*, which is caused by more than one message needing a single network resource at the same time. The con-tention delay and the software overhead are dependent on the program behavior. The sum of switching and channel delays constitutes the network latency, which is determined by the network hardware and is independent of program behavior and network traffic.

- Bandwidth: The network *bandwidth, B*, is usually measured as the *bisection bandwidth* defined as the maximum number of bytes per second that the network can transport across a bisection plane dividing the network into two equal halves.

- Diameter: The *diameter, r*, of a network is defined as the longest path between any two nodes. The path length, or number of links between nodes at the ends of the diameter, uses the maximum number of hops between one node to the next as a simple estimate for com-munication delay of the interconnection network.

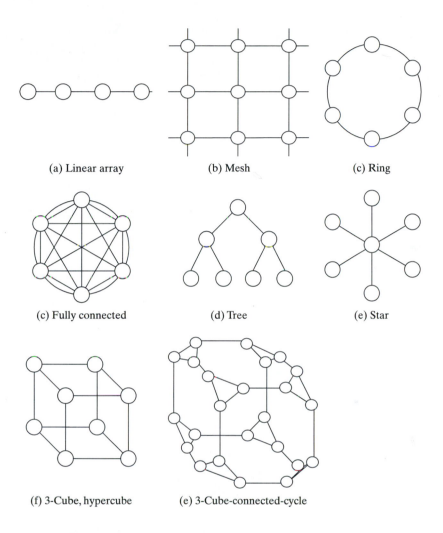

(a) Linear array   (b) Mesh   (c) Ring

(c) Fully connected   (d) Tree   (e) Star

(f) 3-Cube, hypercube   (e) 3-Cube-connected-cycle

Figure 6-1   Static interconnection networks.

- Average distance: *Distance, d*, between two nodes is defined as the number of links in the shortest path between the nodes. *Average distance, d_a*, is defined as:

$$d_a = \frac{1}{N-1} \sum_{d=1}^{r} d \cdot N_d \qquad (6.1)$$

where r is the network diameter, N is the total number of nodes, and N_d is the number of nodes with a distance d from a given node. Networks with low average distances are desirable, but this could lead to a high node degree, which would be expensive to implement. The number of communication ports per node divided by the average distance is a useful measure.

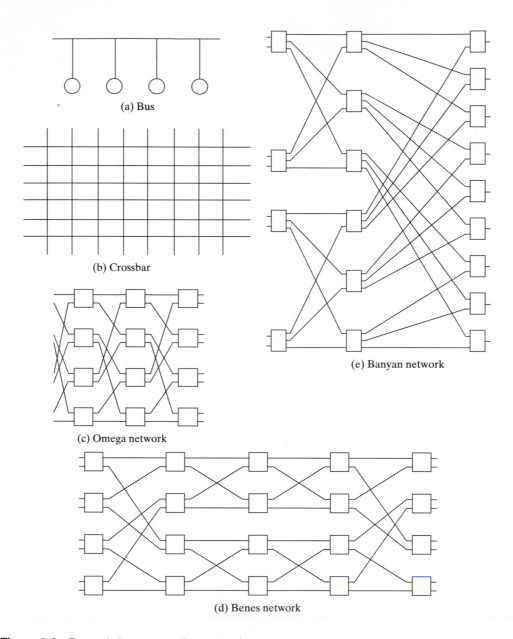

Figure 6-2 Dynamic interconnection networks.

• Connectivity: *Connectivity* or *node degree*, P, is the number of nodes that can be reached from a given node in one hop. Node degree divided by average distance, P/d_a, is the maximum number of new messages that can, on the average, be inserted into the network by each node in a cycle representing one hop from a node to the next.

- Concurrency: *Concurrency* is the number of independent connections that a network can make between source-destination pairs at a given time. Using a bus, a node can be connected to any other node but with concurrency of one. In a hypercube, a node is directly connected to $\log_2 N$ other nodes and the network can provide concurrency of N provided a processor can send one message and receive another at the same time; concurrency is $N/2$ otherwise.

- *Functionality*: Some networks may perform functions in addition to transporting data among resources they connect. Additional features to deal with packet routing, message combination, fault tolerance, switch and channel conflict handling, and others may be added to an interconnection network to enhance its functionality and performance.

- *Hardware cost*: The cost of implementing an interconnection network must include the cost of the total hardware and the performance gains resulting from its implementation. This includes the cost of switches, interface logic, connectors, wires, and any additional functionality that the network implements.

- Scalability: A network that can be expanded in a modular fashion to yield performance that increases, or scales, approximately as the number of processes is a *scalable network*. While a hypercube interconnection network is considered scalable, buses are not.

Interconnection networks may operate in a synchronous or an asynchronous mode. In a *synchronous* mode like CSP rendezvous communication, the path between the source and destination is established synchronously. Synchronous mode is used in SIMD computers in which all PEs operate in lock-step. Requests submitted to the network are satisfied synchronously. In this case, the source delays (blocks) until the destination has received the data. In *asynchronous* networks, buffers are required so that a source can send data to its destination without having to wait, or block, for the destination to receive it. Asynchronous networks are mainly used in multiprocessors in which network requests are issued dynamically by the parallel processors. The same network topology and even the same network can allow for both modes of operation.

A switching strategy is needed to determine the routing path between a source-destination pair or among multiple nodes for broadcast communication. In *circuit switching*, a circuit consisting of a path from source to destination is established prior to any communication. The circuit is maintained for the duration of the transmission providing a contention-free and low-latency communication. The time to transfer a message of length l over a distance d is $l/b + d\delta$, where δ is an individual switch delay on the distance d route from source to destination node and b is the raw bandwidth of the channel. Circuit switching works well for long message communication, where the setup time is short compared to the actual data transmission time. In *packet switching*, messages containing data and address are routed through the network. The address field is read at each node, and the message is forwarded to the next node according to some established control scheme. This process is repeated at each node on the path until the message reaches its destination. Packet switching is economical when the interconnection network is used for communicating short messages.

There are two main strategies for routing messages in a packet switched network, namely store-and-forward and cut-through, or wormhole, routing. In *store-and-forward*, a buffer large enough to hold the entire message is associated with each node. The entire message is stored at each node on the path between the source and destination before it is sent to the next node on the path. The successive packets are sent sequentially without any overlap. This scheme increases the network bandwidth over circuit switching; however, it also increases the network latency. The time to transfer a message of length l from a source node to a destination node at a distance d is $d(l/b + \delta)$. *Wormhole routing* combines the advantages of circuit switching and store-and-forward switching. The messages are divided into fixed sized cells called *flits* for flow control unit. Each node has a *flit buffer* to hold one flit at a time. Data flits belonging to the same packet follow the header on the source-destination path. As the header reaches a node, it is decoded by the node. The subsequent flits are automatically forwarded to the next node on the path, one flit per unit time in a pipeline fashion. Because subsequent flits do not contain routing information, the input and output ports for a message must be reserved at each node until the last flit is routed. This method improves the network latency over store-and-forward switching due to pipelining. In fact, the latency is basically the same as that of circuit switching if the same route is used and can be expressed as $l/\hat{b} + d\delta$, where $\hat{b}$ is link bandwidth adjusted for router logic and flit buffer. Strategies to handle the case where a link is busy at message arrival time must be implemented.

6.2 Permutations

Assuming that data to be accessed in parallel is stored in different memory modules or processor registers, such as the routing registers in SIMD architectures, the problem of moving it in parallel to its destination is that of doing a permutation on the data. An interconnection network provides the means by which data is permuted in its traversal from sources to destinations. Using the network to do a permutation represents a coordinated transfer of data from multiple sources to the same number of destinations in parallel. It contrasts with sending many unsynchronized messages through the network, as would be the case in an MIMD architecture. The ability to do all possible permutations, $N!$ total permutations, is expensive, either in terms of time or equipment. Interconnection networks can be built to support all possible permutations (not practical for large systems) or more commonly, a subset of all possible permutations. For clarity of presentation in this section, we will consider a true SIMD architecture with processor-memory pairs that can communicate through an interconnection network. The following discussion applies equally well to an SIMD architecture with an alignment network between the processors and memories if some of the software steps are shifted into hardware.

The simplest representation of an arbitrary permutation is as a list of source-destination pairs. The list could be sorted either by source number or by destination number. A permutation can also be represented as a product of cycles. A permutation consisting of the one cycle (A, B, C, D) stands for the mapping: $B \leftarrow A, C \leftarrow B, D \leftarrow C, A \leftarrow D$. For example, consider permutation of data in an architecture with 8 PEs numbered 0, 1, ..., 7. A circular shift of all data to the next higher processor is represented as:

$$\text{Route}(+1) = (0, 1, 2, ..., 7)$$

and means:

$$R_i \leftarrow R_{i-1}, \; i = 1, 2, ..., 7, \qquad R_0 \leftarrow R_7.$$

A shift of 2 places is represented as product of 2 cycles as:

$$\text{Route}(+2) = (0, 2, 4, 6)(1, 3, 5, 7)$$

and means:

$$R_i \leftarrow R_{i-2}, \; i = 2, 3, ..., 7, \qquad R_0 \leftarrow R_6, \; R_1 \leftarrow R_7.$$

For an example of an 8 PE system with a simple routing network capable of Route(+1), Route(+2), and Route(+4) operations, refer to the network operations needed by the parallel sum prefix program in Chapter 3, Program 3-12.

Cyclic shifts of 2^h places for $0 \le h < m$, where $N = 2^m$, can be done with $N\log_2 N$ switches and $\log_2 N$ control signals. Each source, S, has m switches connecting it to destinations, $(S + 2^h) \bmod N$, for $0 \le h < m$, see Figure 6-3. To maintain a readable diagram, output connections are only shown for nodes 0, 3, and 5. A shift of any length from 1 to N can be done by $\log_2 N$ or fewer of these shifts. The set of permutations for different values of h constitutes the *m-dimensional hypercube routing* functions that are supported by the hypercube networks.

An interesting permutation that is used by magicians performing card tricks is the *perfect shuffle*. Figure 6-4 shows the perfect shuffle permutation of 8 elements. As bidirectional interconnections can be supported with little cost, such networks can efficiently implement an *inverse perfect shuffle* permutation. The inverse perfect shuffle permutation can be obtained by reversing the arrows in Figure 6-4. Many parallel algorithms such as matrix transpose, Fast Fourier Transforms (FFTs), and sorting make use of perfect shuffle permutation. The two permutations can be represented mathematically as follows:

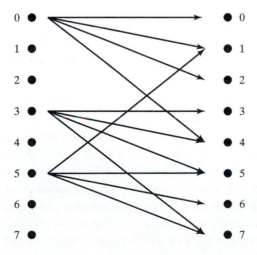

Figure 6-3 Cyclic shifts of 2^h places (not all connections are shown).

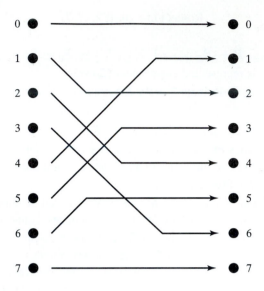

Figure 6-4   Perfect shuffle permutation.

As a permutation of $N = 2^k$ integers, $0 \leq i \leq N - 1$, the *perfect shuffle* maps input i into:

$$P(i) = \begin{array}{ll} 2i & \text{for } i < N/2 \\ 2i - N + 1 & \text{for } i \geq N/2 \end{array}$$

The inverse perfect shuffle is mathematically represented as:

$$P^{-1}(i) = \begin{array}{ll} i/2 & \text{for } i \text{ even and } 0 \leq i \leq N - 2 \\ (i - 1)/2 + N/2 & \text{for } i \text{ odd and } 1 \leq i \leq N - 1 \end{array}$$

An example of using the inverse perfect shuffle permutation and a one-step shift to do sum prefix is shown in Program 6-1. In this example, the vector add operation is performed if the corresponding mask bit is one, otherwise it is skipped. The loop must only be executed $\log_2 N$ times in order to complete the algorithm. The prefix results appear in all processors. The data dependence graphs and mask for the three steps needed for calculating the prefix on a vector of 8 elements is shown in Figure 6-5. When N processors are connected using a perfect shuffle pattern and a left shift of one can also be done, a reduction operation can be performed among all PEs in $\log_2 N$ steps. The summation of the elements of vector A is shown in Program 6-2. Here again, the summation is performed by the PEs with corresponding mask bits of one. The final result appears only in PE_0. In the remainder of this chapter we will study static and dynamic interconnection networks capable of permutations discussed in this section.

```
Y[i] := A[i], (0 ≤ i ≤ N-1);
n := log₂N;
for j := 1 step 1 until n
    begin
        mask[i] := i mod 2^(n-j+1) ≠ 0, (0 ≤ i ≤ N-1);
        Y[i] := Y[i] + shift(Y[i-1], 1), (mask| 0 ≤ i ≤ N-1);
        inverse perfect shuffle(Y);
    end
```

Program 6-1 Sum prefix using inverse perfect shuffle and shift.

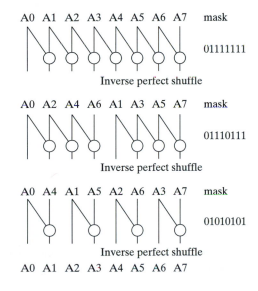

Figure 6-5 Data dependence for Program 6-1.

```
Y[i] := A[i], (0 ≤ i ≤ N-1);
for j:= 1 step 1 until log₂N
    begin
        mask<i> := (i mod 2^j = 0), (0 ≤ i ≤ N-1);
        Perfect shuffle(Y);
        Y[i] := Y[i] + Shift(Y[i+1], 1),(mask| 0 ≤ i ≤ N-1);
    end
```

Program 6-2 Reduction operation using perfect shuffle and shift permutations.

6.3 Static Networks

A number of static network topologies are shown in Figure 6-1. As can be seen from the figure, a wide range of connectivity patterns can be built into a static network from a simple ring topology to a fully connected one. Once the network is built, however, the connections are fixed. A fully connected network provides the best performance, as every node is connected to every other node with a distance of one. This topology works efficiently for all applications with all types of communication pattern needs. Such a network is not practical in highly parallel computers because network cost grows as the square of the number of PEs and quickly dominates the cost of the computer. One must note that the best computational performance obtainable grows only linearly with the number of PEs.

The fixed communication topology of static networks makes them most appropriate and yields the best performance for problems with predictable communication patterns involving mostly neighboring PEs. For this reason, static networks are most commonly used with SIMD computers. Shared memory MIMD computers often use dynamic networks to provide a more uniform time for memory access operations. We will next study a number of static networks with topologies in between the two extremes of a simple ring and a fully connected network.

6.3.1   Mesh

Several topologies can be listed under the general mesh topology. The simplest one is a *linear array*, or a one-dimensional mesh, which simply connects N nodes using $N-1$ links on a line. The two boundary nodes have a degree of one while all the interior nodes have a degree of two and are connected to two neighboring nodes. The diameter of this structure is $N-1$. It is important to note the difference between a linear array and a *bus* interconnection. A bus is a single means of communication and is time-shared among all nodes connected to it. Switching is used to establish links between two nodes connected by a bus. A bus can do any source to any destination routing in one step but can only route one message at a time. In the linear array network, nodes can use disjoint sections of the network concurrently, but it will take multiple steps to route messages between nonadjacent processors. Therefore, a shift of +1 can be done by all nodes concurrently except at the last node on the line.

Higher dimensional meshes can similarly be constructed. In a general k-dimensional mesh with N nodes, all interior nodes have degree $2k$ connecting them to their $2k$ nearest neighbors. In a k-dimensional network with $\sqrt[k]{N}$ nodes on each dimension, the diameter is $k(\sqrt[k]{N}-1)$. In a generalized mesh with N PEs, an arbitrary shift requires $\sqrt[k]{N}-1$ or fewer shifts along a coordinate. Two-dimensional meshes are the most common topology implemented. Illiac IV, Goodyear Massively Parallel Processor (MPP), ICL Distributed Array Processor (DAP), IBM Wire Routing Machine (WRM), and Intel Paragon are some examples of architectures implementing different versions of a two-dimensional mesh interconnection network. The difference between these interconnection networks is in the way the boundary nodes are connected to the neighboring nodes. For example, WRM uses a pure mesh in which the boundary nodes have degree three and the corner nodes have degree two. Illiac IV on the other hand uses a torus-like topology where the right-most node in each row is connected to the left-most node of the next row and the bottom node in each column is connected to the top node in the same column. Every node in Illiac IV has degree four as shown in Figure 6-6. The network diameter of an $n \times n$ Illiac IV mesh is $n - 1$. This early SIMD machine was built with 64 PEs attached to a single control unit. The PEs were connected as an 8×8 mesh. Shift routings of $+1$, -1, $+8$, and -8 all modulo 64, could be done by single routing instructions. This meant that any shift of length 0 –63 could be done with 7 or fewer shifts of the above type. The extra wraparound connections help reduce the network latency. A *torus* has about half the latency of a general mesh and combines the mesh and ring topologies. Examples of a higher dimensional mesh are the MIT J-machine and Cray T3D and T3E series that implement a three-dimensional torus. The Tera MTA implements a three-dimensional torus with half the connectivity in two of the dimensions.

The common routing strategy used in a k-dimensional mesh is to traverse along one dimension at a time from the source node to the destination until the final address is reached. Therefore, to route a message from the node at network address $(s_1, s_2, ..., s_k)$ to the destination address $(d_1, d_2, ..., d_k)$ the message is sent through the following path:

```
for i := 1 step 1 until k

    traverse the i-th dimension if s_i ≠ d_i;
```

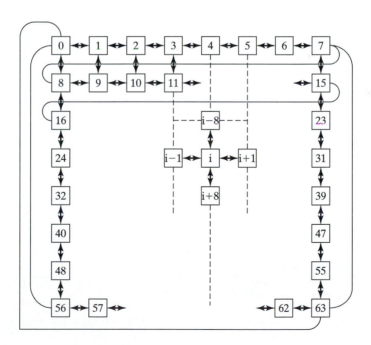

Figure 6-6   Illiac IV.

In Chapter 5 we discussed the all-to-all broadcast operation. Given an N-node square mesh with wrap around topology the all-to-all broadcast can be performed as shown in Figure 6-7. The operation is performed in two phases. First processors on the same row performs an all-to-all broadcast concurrently. Next, processors on the same column do an all-to-all broadcast. The row or column all-to-all broadcast is simply the all-to-all broadcast on a ring. This is done by processors participating in $\sqrt{N}-1$ circular shifts of one step, collecting data from other processors in the row or column, after which all processors have exchanged values. In the first stage, the processors are transmitting messages of length L. Given message start-up time, t_S, and time to transfer a byte of the message, T_B, it takes $(t_S + LT_B)(\sqrt{N}-1)$ time to complete the $\sqrt{N}$ concurrent all-to-all row broadcasts. The size of the messages for the second phase is now $L\sqrt{N}$. The $\sqrt{N}$ all-to-all column broadcast completes in time $(t_S + LT_B\sqrt{N})(\sqrt{N}-1)$. The total time to do the all-to-all broadcast in this architecture is given by Equation (6.2).

$$2t_S(\sqrt{N}-1) + LT_B(N-1) \tag{6.2}$$

A common computation that can readily be mapped on the mesh topology is the solution of discretized differential equations. For a function u on a grid indexed by $[i, j]$, the common operation

$$\frac{\partial^2 u}{\partial x^2} + \frac{\partial^2 u}{\partial y^2}$$

is approximated on a discretized two-dimensional grid by

$$f(u[i-1, j], u[i, j-1], u[i, j], u[i, j+1], u[i+1, j]).$$

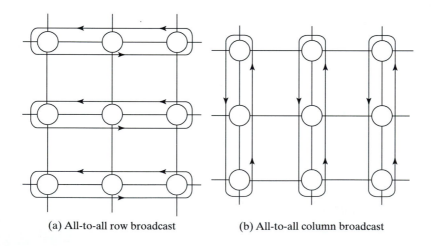

(a) All-to-all row broadcast   (b) All-to-all column broadcast

Figure 6-7   All-to-all broadcast on a mesh.

A mesh topology provides concurrent access to PEs computing this function by supporting the shift operation. If the array is stored in column major order and successive memory locations are assigned to successive PEs, then shifts of one, route(± 1), on the i index amount to linear shift by the number of elements in a column.

6.3.2   Ring

A *ring* topology is obtained by connecting the two terminal nodes of a linear array. *Ring* networks have often been used to interconnect a number of computers at different geographical locations for the purpose of transferring files among them. In a unidirectional ring, each node is connected to one source and one destination neighbor and, hence, has a node degree of two. In a N-node unidirectional ring, where messages travel in one direction from source to destination processor, the diameter is $N - 1$. A bidirectional ring is a symmetric network where the longest path a message would travel to reach its destination is no longer than $N/2$. When rings are used in an SIMD computer, the message transfer between PEs connected through the ring is simultaneous. The transfer takes place as a result of instructions such as *shift* or *rotate*.

Ring networks have simple logic in which a node must be able to initiate a message to be sent over the network to a destination node, recognize and receive a message destined to it, and act as a hub that relays a message not destined to itself to the next node. The *IBM token ring* is an example of this topology. Messages travel along the ring until the destination processor with a matching token (address) is reached. *CDC Cyberplus* (1985) [67] and *Kendall Square's KSR-I* (1992) [171] multiprocessors implemented pipelined ring networks with more sophisticated operations and packet switching. The KSR-I implemented a two-level hierarchy of unidirectional rings. Rings at level zero contain 8 to 32 processor cache pairs and a ring interface. The level-1 ring connects the level-0 rings. It consists of 2 to 34 ring interfaces, one for each level-0 ring.

The memory system of the KSR-I, called ALLCACHE, has the COMA structure and consists of local cache memories, one per processor. The system provides a global address space by implementing cache directories to keep track of data location throughout the system. Each processor/cache pair is connected to a level-0 ring via an interface that contains a directory of data blocks stored in the local cache. The interface at each level-0 ring then contains a directory of every data block stored in every cache in the ring. Each level-1 ring interface holds a copy of the corresponding level-0 directory. A reference to location l by processor P results in a search in P's cache first. The cache memory of the processors on the same ring as P are searched next. Finally, the caches of all the other processors on other level-0 rings are searched through the directory information on the level-1 ring. To keep local cache information up-to-date and consistent, KSR-I uses a read broadcast operation. A read broadcast results in all nodes on the path of the message updating their cache memories with the contents of the new message and relaying it to the next node. This addresses the *cache coherence* problem that exists when shared writable data is cached in shared memory multiprocessor systems with local processor caches.

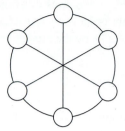   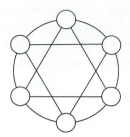

(a) Chordal ring with node degree 3   (b) Chordal ring with node degree 4

Figure 6-8   Chordal rings.

In a unidirectional ring, failure of one link breaks the network communication. In a bidirectional ring, one link failure does not break the communication while two link failures divide the network into two disjoint sub nets. Adding redundant paths improves the fault tolerance of ring networks. Figure 6-8 shows two *chordal rings* with node degree three and four, respectively. The extra links provide not only better fault tolerance for the network but also higher node degree and shorter network diameter. Another variation of the ring is the *barrel shifter* connection where each node on the ring is connected to those whose indices are different by 2^r. Here, r is an integer between 0 to $n - 1$ and N is the total number of nodes in the network such that $N = 2^n$. The node degree therefore is $2n - 1$ and the diameter is n.

6.3.3   Tree

A *tree* topology provides parent-child connections between nodes so that two nodes may communicate by finding a path ascending from the source to a common parent node and then descending to the destination. The root node is the most congested node and must handle the largest amount of traffic. In a *binary tree*, interior nodes have degree three, the root node has degree two, and the leaf nodes have degree one. A *m*-level binary tree has $N = 2^m - 1$ nodes and a diameter of $2(m - 1)$. A *k-way tree* of *m* levels has $k^m - 1$ nodes. Binary trees have mapping properties that make them suitable for VLSI and other planar layouts. The *H-layout* of the binary tree of Figure 6-9(a) is shown in Figure 6-9(b). The area for the H-layout grows linearly in N, number of nodes in the tree, instead of $N\log_2 N$ as in Figure 6-9(a). Figure 6-9(c) shows the building block used in recursive construction of larger tree networks. A free node with left and right connections is used to connect the block to other modules. Figure 6-9(d) shows the connection of four modules. A 1023-node binary tree with ten levels was implemented in the DADO multiprocessor at Columbia University in 1987.

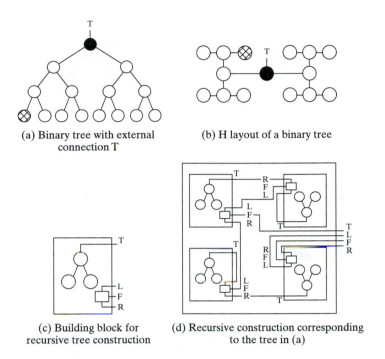

(a) Binary tree with external connection T

(b) H layout of a binary tree

(c) Building block for recursive tree construction

(d) Recursive construction corresponding to the tree in (a)

Figure 6-9 Binary tree and H-layout.

Leiserson introduced the *fat tree* as a solution to the congestion problem toward the root. In fat trees the communication channels between nodes increases in width as we get closer to the root. Figure 6-10 represents this concept. The increase in the communication link width in each channel is determined by the amount of hardware available. In Figure 6-10, the number of communication links in each channel is increased by one from one level to the next. The interconnection network in the Connection Machine CM5 is based on a *dynamic fat tree* where the internal nodes of the tree are switches and the leaf nodes are the processing elements; see Figure 6-11. Each switch node contains several routers. A router is connected as a parent to either four child routers or four leaf processing nodes and is connected to either two or four parent routers. The routers in the first two levels of the data network use only two parent connections to the next higher level. The routers at the higher levels use four parent connections to handle higher bandwidth requirements. A data network chip is implemented as a crossbar connecting eight input ports to eight output ports, but certain input/output connections are blocked to support the routing algorithm. A message may have several choices as to which parent connection to take. A link is chosen pseudorandomly from among all available unobstructed links.

A *star* can be viewed as a special multiway tree in which the root node has degree $N - 1$ with a network diameter of two. Fault tolerance in star network is very low, failure of the root breaks all communication.

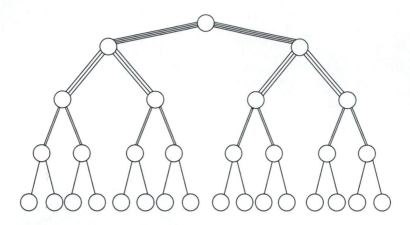

Figure 6-10   Binary fat tree.

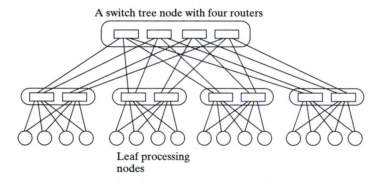

Figure 6-11   The 4-ary dynamic fat tree structure of CM5 data network.

The routing algorithm for a binary tree network is simple and follows the method used in numbering the nodes. We number the nodes using a binary representation and the node level in the tree. A node number at level n consists of n bits. Let the root number at level one be 1. The binary number of a left child is obtained by appending a 0 to the right most bit of the parent node. The right child number is similarly obtained by appending a 1 to the parent node number, see Figure 6-12. The algorithm to route a message from node S to node D, first finds the common parent node, P, of the two nodes S and D and then ascends from S to P and descends from P to D as shown in Figure 6-13.

6.3.4   Cube Networks

K-ary n-cube networks are the most general of the cube networks. Rings, meshes, tori, hyper-cubes, and omega networks are topologically isomorphic to a family of *K*-ary *n*-cube networks.

In this network n is the dimension and K, radix, is the number of nodes forming a cycle along each dimension. There are a total of $N = K^n$ nodes in a K-ary n-cube. Nodes are addressed by a n-digit radix K number of the form $a_0, a_1, ..., a_{n-1}$. Each digit, $0 \le a_i < K$, represents the position of the node in the corresponding i-th dimension, $0 \le i \le n - 1$. A neighbor node to $a_0, a_1 ... a_{n-1}$ at dimension i can be reached by $a_0 a_1 ... a_{(i \pm 1)} \bmod k ... a_{n-1}$. In this network the node degree is $2n$ and the network diameter is $n \lfloor \frac{k}{2} \rfloor$; see Figure 6-14.

A topology related to the K-ary n-cube is the *cube connected cycles* network. A general *n-cube connected cycles* can be constructed from a binary n-cube with 2^n vertices where each vertex is made up of a cycle of n nodes. Therefore, there are a total of $n2^n$ nodes in the network. The network diameter in this case is reduced to $2n - 1 + \lfloor n/2 \rfloor$, and the node degree is a constant three. A *3-cube connected cycles (3-CCC)* is shown in Figure 6-1(e).

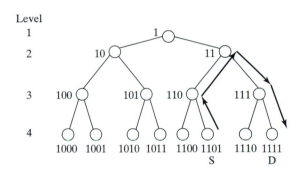

Figure 6-12 Addressing and routing in a binary tree topology.

```
—        Let the binary representation of a source node S at
         level i and a destination node D at level j be
         S_iS_{i-1}...S_1 and D_jD_{j-1}...D_1 respectively.

—        Find the leftmost common bits of D and S such that
         parent node P = D_jD_{j-1}...D_x = S_iS_{i-1}...S_{(i - j + x)}.

—        From S ascend (i - j + x) levels to reach P.

—        for k = x - 1 step 1 until 0 (* reach D from P*)
             {descend to left if D_k = 0
              descend to right if D_k = 1};
```

Figure 6-13 Routing algorithm in the tree topology.

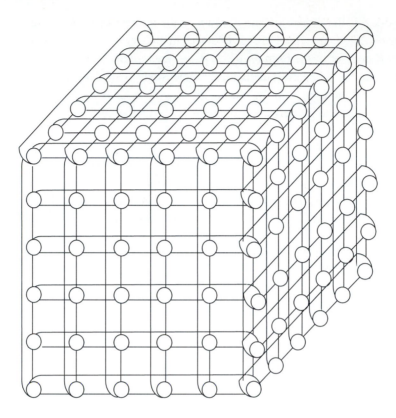

Figure 6-14   6-ary-3-cube.

A *hypercube* or a *binary n-cube* is a special form of a *K*-ary *n*-cube that has been imple-mented in many computers such as iPSC, ncube, and CM-2. An *n-cube* consists of $N = 2^n$ nodes along *n* dimensions of the hypercube. A three-dimensional cube or *3-cube* with 8 nodes labeled from 000 to 111 is shown in Figure 6-15. The labeling is done such that nodes that are connected via one edge have labels that are different in one bit position only. Node that are distant by two edges (two hops) are different in two bit positions and so on. The far-thest that a message has to travel in an *n-cube* is $n = \log_2 N$. The total number of bit posi-tions at which two labels differ is called the *Hammimg distance*. The Hamming distance between processors labeled 110 and 101 is two, which is the number of hops a message must travel for the two processors to communicate. A *n-dimensional hypercube* has a node degree of *n*. A *4-cube* can be constructed by connecting corresponding nodes of two 3-cubes as shown in Figure 6-16.

Broadcast communication in an *N*-processor distributed memory MIMD computer with hypercube interconnection topology is implemented cooperatively by all processors. Broadcast takes $\log_2 N$ steps in an N-node hypercube. The algorithm configures a *spanning tree* of the hypercube rooted at the source processor. A *spanning tree* of a graph is defined as a tree whose nodes correspond one-to-one to the nodes of the graph and its edges are a subset of those of the graph. The broadcast procedure in Program 6-3 is executed by all processors. Here `source` and `myid` are $\log_2 N$-bit binary numbers representing the processor numbers in the hypercube topology as was described earlier. Variable `dist`, which is calculated from the bitwise exclusive or, $\oplus$, of each process id and the `source` is used to identify the position of each processor in the tree with respect to the root processor. When a processor has received the message, it becomes a source and sends the message to its children in a particular spanning tree. Figure 6-17 shows the communication steps in a 3-cube network. In Chapter 5, Eq. (5.1) characterized the message delivery time by $T = T_S + L T_B$, where T_S is start-up time or total message overhead and T_B is the time associated with each byte of a message of length L. The broadcast algorithm of Program 6-3 takes $\log_2 N$ steps and uses at most $N/2$ of the total $N\log_2 N$ bidirectional communication links available. Associated with each step is a message start-up time, t_s, so that $T_S = \sum_{i=1}^{\log_2 N} t_s$. The complete time to broadcast is therefore given in Equation (6.3).

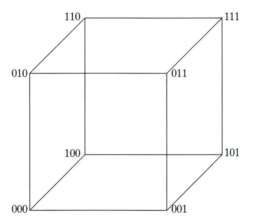

Figure 6-15   3-dimensional cube.

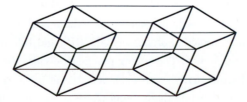

Figure 6-16   Construction of higher dimensional cube from lower dimensional.

```
procedure broadcast(source, message);
        dist := myid ⊕ source;
        for i:= 0 step 1 until log₂N-1
            begin
                if (myid = source) then send(myid ⊕ 2ⁱ, message);
                if (2ⁱ ≤ dist < 2ⁱ⁺¹) then
                    begin
                        receive(myid ⊕ 2ⁱ, message);
                        source := myid;
                    end;
            end;
    end procedure
```

Program 6-3 One-to-all broadcast algorithm in a hypercube.

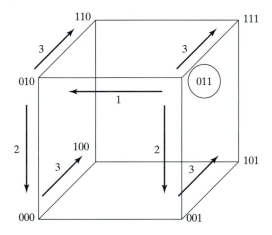

Figure 6-17 Source 011 broadcasts to all other processors.

$$T_{Broadcast} = (t_s + LT_B)\log_2 N \qquad\qquad (6.3)$$

If we assume that processors can send and receive simultaneously, and that bidirectional links are available, then a more complex broadcast algorithm can be implemented that makes more effective use of all of the communication links [158]. The algorithm uses the property that there are $\log_2 N$ edge-disjoint spanning trees with the same root node in an N-node hypercube. Figure 6-18 shows the three spanning trees rooted at processors 001, 010, and 100, respectively, as subtrees to the source processor 000 in a 3-cube. The source processor divides the message to be broadcast into $\log_2 N$ equal parts and sequentially sends each part to a different spanning tree root over the $\log_2 N$ communication links connecting them. Figure 6-19 shows the routing of the three parts of the message A, B, and C with their time steps on the hypercube for each spanning tree separately. These trees, called *rotated spanning trees*, are constructed so that there are no conflicts involving messages travelling in the same direction at the same time step on any of the hypercube links. Breaking up the message into equal parts and sending them sequentially is similar to the pipelining idea of cut-through routing. In this case the flit size is dictated by the hypercube dimension. In cut-through routing, flits follow the header, here each part of the message is routed through different paths although they may share the same link at different time steps. The analogy can be made between this method and pipelining where the links play the role of pipeline stages and the objective is to get as much overlap as possible. The source processor takes $\log_2 N$ steps to sequentially send the $\log_2 N$ parts of the message to its neighbors. The last part of the message takes an additional $\log_2 N$ steps to reach the leaf processors of its spanning tree. Therefore, this algorithm takes $2\log_2 N$ steps to complete the broadcast. Each step takes $t_s + \dfrac{LT_B}{\log_2 N}$. Time to complete the broadcast in this algorithm is given in Equation (6.4).

$$T_{Broadcast} = \left(t_s + \frac{LT_B}{\log_2 N}\right)(2\log_2 N) \tag{6.4}$$

The message transfer time is reduced by a factor of $\log_2 N\,/2$ while the message start-up time is increased by a factor of 2. This algorithm would perform better than the first one only if the messages are long enough to mask the additional overhead and if the communication is performed synchronously. It is not effective if the start-up time makes the transmission time negligible, just as a pipeline is no good if the pipeline is so long that the vector length does not count. In a distributed MIMD architecture, the fact that some of the links are not utilized by a given communication operation such as broadcast is not necessarily undesirable. The asynchronous nature of operations in this architecture enables the use of the available links by the processors connected to them for other communication operations. In short, when implementing a communication operation, one must consider whether it must be designed to perform well under a special circumstance or to perform well for an average case behavior.

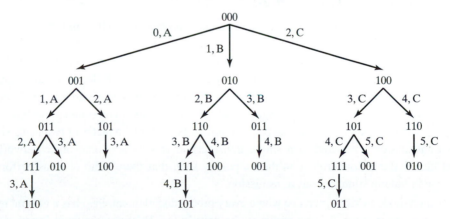

Figure 6-18 Three edge-disjoint spanning trees in a 3-cube. The original message is broken into three parts A, B, and C and broadcast from processor 0 to others.

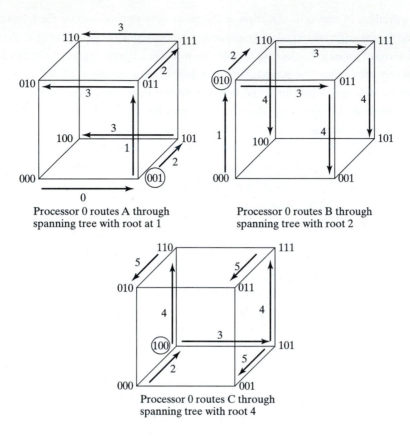

Processor 0 routes A through
spanning tree with root at 1

Processor 0 routes B through
spanning tree with root 2

Processor 0 routes C through
spanning tree with root 4

Figure 6-19 Broadcast of a message divided into three parts A, B, C from processor 0 using three rotated edge-disjoint spanning trees.

Throughout this chapter, we have assumed that a processor can transmit data on one of its ports at a time. The ability to simultaneously transmit messages on all ports can have performance advantages in certain situations. In the above broadcast algorithm for example, the message transmission time can be further reduced by a factor of $\log_2 N$. It does not, however, affect the start-up overhead. Hardware such as DMA or I/O processors can be used to implement the ability to transmit simultaneous messages on all of a processor's communication links. Some topologies, such as the binary tree, can perform broadcast faster by a factor of two using simultaneous transmission compared to a single transmission at a time. Some other networks can exploit the available concurrency in their topology such that there is no obvious performance advantage in having simultaneous transmission.

In an N-node SIMD hypercube where every processing element, PE_k, has a general register, A_k, and a routing register, R_k, sum prefix can be done in $\log_2 N$ step as shown in Program 6-4. In this algorithm, the synchronous communication is done one axis at a time using a *transfer* operation. $transfer_j(R_i)$ transfers the contents of R_i to the routing register R_k of PE_k, $0 \leq k \leq N-1$

such that the k and i indices only differ in the j-th bit position and $i < k$. $transfer_{-j}(R_i)$ does the same operation in the opposite direction. $transfer_j(R_i)$ shifts by 2^j positions and should be distinguished from the *shift* permutation where j gives the number of positions shifted. The sum prefix is done over the N elements of array X, where PE_i holds X_i. The method used in this algorithm is known as *recursive doubling*. Figure 6-20 shows the contents of the registers at the completion of each iteration. Register R_k carries the sum of all values of X in a group of 2^j containing k while A_k sums only those elements X_m in the group for which $m \le k$.

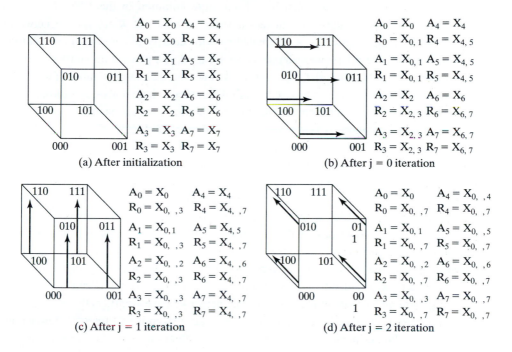

Figure 6-20   Steps of the sum prefix algorithm on a hypercube.

```
/* initialization*/
Ak  = Xk  ,(0 ≤ k ≤ N-1);
Rk  = Ak  ,(0 ≤ k ≤ N-1);
for j = 0 step 1 until log₂N -1
    begin
        /* bit position 0 is the least significant bit */
        /* communicate over the j-th axis, i.e. j-th bit position */
        Ak = Ak + transferj (Ri), (all k such that bit j of k = 1);
        Rk = Rk + transferj (Ri), (all k such that bit j of k = 1);
        Ri = transfer-j (Ri),(all i such that bit j of i = 0);
    end;
```

Program 6-4   Sum prefix in an SIMD hypercube architecture.

6.3.5   Performance

High-performance interconnection networks are at the core of parallel computer architectures. A performance-cost model that can accurately model the performance of the network under various conditions is complex. There are many design trade-offs that must be considered driven by factors such as technology, cost, performance requirements under certain conditions, and applications.

Binary hypercube architectures that have been quite common in the 1980s have been replaced by lower dimension topologies in recent years. A study of K-ary n-cube networks shows that the cost of most networks is dominated by wire density required to implement the topology. The K-ary n-cube interconnection networks are used as a general framework to evaluate the performance of static networks. These networks encompass a large number of technologies from simple two-dimensional meshes to high-dimensional hypercubes. Performance of low-dimensional networks are then compared to those of higher dimensions under certain criteria. If the total number of nodes is kept constant, study shows that higher dimension networks scale better than those of lower dimension. However, high-dimension networks require more wires, pins, and larger switches. To factor in the high cost of high-dimension networks, other models have considered keeping the total number of wires constant. Clearly, given a constant number of wires, a high-dimensional network must use narrower channels, which results in increased latency. Another difficulty in implementation of high-dimension networks is in the way the network layout must be designed. The number of wires crossing the network bisection to be laid out in a two-dimensional space plays a significant role in the design decisions. Additional dimensions also add to the length of wires. It appears that the above argument favors the low-dimensional networks under fixed cost. However, one must study the performance of the networks in a system under load. Higher dimensional networks have significantly lower latency under load compared to those of lower dimension. The main reason is that there are fewer routing options in lower dimensional networks, and therefore contention for channels increases.

6.4 Dynamic Networks

The interconnection networks presented in Section 6.3 are known as direct networks, where a host is connected to every node in the network. These networks perform well for applications that can exploit the regular fixed topology that they offer. For applications where the communication patterns are variable and not regular, dynamic interconnection networks are more suitable. Dynamic networks are indirect networks that provide greater flexibility in communication patterns and are most often used in MIMD architectures providing asynchronous communication. Some examples of these networks are shown in Figure 6-2. We will study some of these networks and their properties next. Any of the networks presented can become a direct network provided every switch element in the network topology is replaced with a processing element. The indirect networks normally connect processors to either processors or memory modules at the two ends (inputs and outputs) of the interconnection network.

6.4.1   Bus

The simplest dynamic interconnection network that can be implemented with existing technology is the bus. It is shared by the processors that it connects. A bus can perform one data transmission at a time, but it can route a message from any source to any destination in one step. Broadcast also takes one step in the bus network and is very efficient.

The bus bandwidth is defined as the product of its clocking frequency, f, and the number of data lines in the bus, w. This bandwidth dictates the maximum number of processors that the system can support. The bus bandwidth must be matched to the product of the number of processors and their speed. As buses become faster through technology changes, so do processors, and in general, only a small number of processors connected through a bus can provide effective performance. To reduce bus traffic and increase the overall performance, the bus-based multiprocessors use cache memories with protocols for cache consistency. A split-phase bus protocol is often used in multiprocessors. This protocol releases the bus after a request by a processor to reference the memory is transmitted. When memory is ready to respond to the request, it acquires the bus. The split phase allows other processors to use the bus in between the two parts of the memory reference, provided that memory interleaving or pipelining is available.

6.4.2   Crossbar

The crossbar, Figure 6-21, is a fully connected network that enables all possible permutations of the N items that it connects. The ability to do all possible $N!$ permutations is expensive for any parallel computer system, either in terms of equipment or time. The crossbar requires N^2 switches, which is excessive if N is large. However, a permutation is completed in constant time, and the control of the network switches is easy. A unique switch corresponds to a source/destination pair, so the representation of a permutation as a list of such pairs leads directly to the correct switch settings. Therefore, broadcast and multicast operations can efficiently be performed in one step. In a crossbar network, the connections among source and destination pairs can take place incrementally as needed. A switch setting only must change if a source needs to communicate with a destination different from the previously established connection.

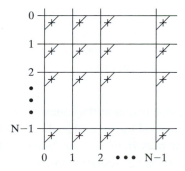

Figure 6-21   Crossbar network.

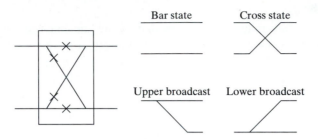

Figure 6-22   An exchange element and its functions.

Due to the high cost and number of cross points, fully connected networks such as the crossbar are not practical for complete network implementation. However, crossbar switches of reasonable size are often used as the basic building blocks in larger networks. IBM SP2, Cray YMP/816, and IBM GF11 are some examples of parallel computers that use smaller crossbar switches to implement larger interconnection networks of different topologies.

6.4.3   Multistage Interconnection Networks (MINs)

Multistage interconnection networks are compromise solutions that lie between the low performance of the simple bus and the high cost of the crossbar. In general, MINs support many interesting permutations with a longer latency, $O(\log_2 N)$, than the constant time for the crossbar. The cost of the network, however, is reduced to be on the order of $N\log_2 N$ in comparison to N^2 for the crossbar.

All MINs make use of 2×2 or larger crossbar switches as their building block. A 2×2 switch is called an exchange element, and its four functions are shown in Figure 6-22. In the figure, $\times$ represents a contact that may be open or closed. A 2×2 exchange element can perform two possible permutations: route upper and lower inputs to the corresponding output or exchange them. The two permutations are indicated as bar state and cross state in Figure 6-22. The other two states, upper and lower broadcasts, can be used in switching applications where broadcast is desired.

Useful MIN topologies can connect any source to any destination. They mainly differ in the number of permutations they can support. The Benes network is capable of all the functionality of the crossbar. A Benes network that is implemented using 2×2 exchange switches can do any permutation in $2\log_2 N - 1$ steps. Both the crossbar and the Benes network are said to *pass* any permutation. The omega network can do many interesting permutations but not all without conflict. We will study these networks in more detail in the remainder of this section.

6.4.3.1   Benes Network

We present the Benes network as the first multistage interconnection network because it is powerful enough to do any permutation and has fewer than the N^2 switches required by the crossbar. The network is constructed recursively from 2×2 exchange switches as shown in Figure 6-23. In this network the interconnection pattern between the two $N/2$ permutation boxes and the output exchange elements is a perfect shuffle. The interconnection pattern between the input exchange elements and the two $N/2$ permutation boxes is the inverse perfect shuffle.

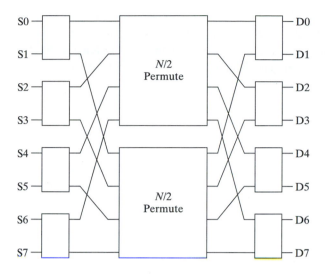

Figure 6-23   Structure of the Benes network.

This construction is continued recursively by expanding each of the $N/2 \times N/2$ Permute boxes into two $N/4 \times N/4$ Permute boxes, preceded and followed by columns of exchange switches. Continuing until all Permute boxes have only two inputs and two outputs, those boxes also become simple exchange switches. The result is a general permutation network constructed of columns of exchange switches. An 8×8 network requires two recursive steps to arrive at an array of five columns of four exchange switches per column, as shown in Figure 6-24.

In general, the Benes network has $2\log_2 N - 1$ columns of $N/2$ exchange elements each. With 4 switches in each exchange box, this makes about $4N\log_2 N$ switches, which is many fewer than N^2 for large N. The Benes network can do all permutations, as can the crossbar, but it is harder to control. In the crossbar, a given (source, destination) pair corresponds to one unique switch, making it clear that the connections are independent. Thus, reconnecting a small subset of the sources and destinations involves changing only a few switches. In the Benes network, the reconnection of a few pairs generally requires a complete reconfiguration of the switch settings.

Given any one-to-one mapping, π, of N inputs to N outputs, $N = 2^m$, one can find a set of edge disjoint paths from the inputs to the outputs connecting every source S to its destination $D = \pi(S)$. A demonstration that the Benes network can perform any permutation of N inputs proceeds as follows. A general permutation can be described as a set of N (source, destination) pairs. Pick one input and set the connected exchange box to send it to the upper $N/2$ permutation. Using the upper permutation, connect it to the output exchange box, which is associated with the correct destination. Set the output exchange box to connect the correct destination. Now this leaves the paired destination connected to the lower $N/2$ permutation. Find the (source, destination) pair for this destination, and set the lower $N/2$ permutation to connect it to the correct input exchange box. Set the input exchange box to connect to the correct input. There are two possibilities for the other input to the same input exchange box: either it has already been connected, in which case we start over with any unconnected (source, destination) pair, or we continue as before to make its connection using the upper $N/2$ permutation. Routing in the Benes network requires accessing the set of (source, destination) pairs both by source and by destination.

The only constraint for a path to use the upper or lower $N/2$ permutation networks is that paths from inputs to the same exchange box must use different $N/2$ permutation networks. The construction of edge disjoint paths for permutation $\pi = (1,3,7,6,2,4,0,5)$ is shown in Figure 6-25. π represents the permutation:

$$(S_0, D_5), (S_4, D_0), (S_2, D_4), (S_6, D_2), (S_7, D_6), (S_3, D_7), (S_1, D_3), (S_5, D_1).$$

We start by connecting the first pair (S_0, D_5) through the upper $N/2$ network. We then satisfy the above constraint by establishing the connection for (S_2, D_4) pair through the lower $N/2$ network. Then we route the (S_3, D_7) connection through the upper $N/2$ network. The construction continues in this order until at the last stage the connection (S_5, D_1) establishes the last route.

A large Benes network was used in the IBM GF11 SIMD computer. It implemented a three stage Benes network using 24×24 crossbar switches instead of the 2×2 exchange switches to connect 566 PEs and ten disk units together.

6.4.3.2   Butterfly Network

Networks without the complete generality of the Benes are more common. They are often constructed from exchange elements and use interconnection patterns that are similar to those of the Benes network. The butterfly network, implemented in BBN T2000, has interesting communication patterns inherent to many problems such as the FFT and the Batcher odd-even merge sort. The network is best described as having $N = 2^m$ processing nodes and is organized in $N/2$ rows and m columns of 2×2 exchange elements as shown in Figure 6-26.

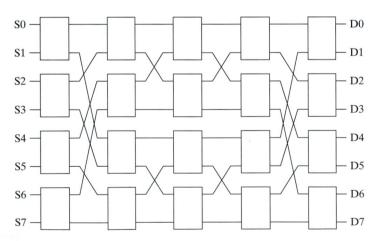

Figure 6-24   An 8×8 Benes network.

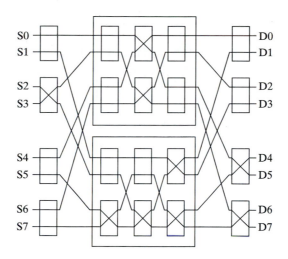

Figure 6-25   Construction of disjoint paths for $\pi = (1,3,7,6,2,4,0,5)$ in Benes network.

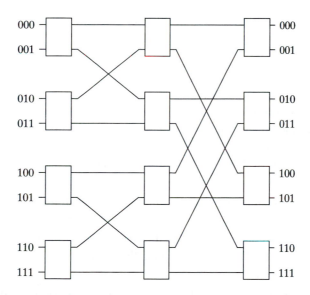

Figure 6-26   An 8×8 butterfly network.

Let us identify the $m2^{m-1}$ exchange elements by their binary number $r = r_{m-2}r_{m-3}...r_0$ corresponding to the row index and their column number i where $0 \leq r \leq N/2-1$ and $0 \leq i \leq m-1$. In this network, the output of the exchange node r at column i is connected to nodes r and $q = r_{m-2}...\bar{r}_{i+1}\bar{r}_i...r_0$ both at column $i+1$.

The cross state, control $= 1$, is

$$P_e^1(s) = (s_{m-1}s_{m-2}...s_2s_1\overline{s_0})_2. \tag{6.9}$$

Omega network routing is done by the destination tag method. Although we know that an omega network cannot perform all $N!$ permutations, we want to verify that it can at least route every source to every destination. The verification is given by the theorem below. The proof of the theorem is constructive and shows how to set the exchange elements. The procedure is called the *destination tag method*.

THEOREM

For an m stage omega network with $N = 2^m$ inputs, there is a way of setting the exchange elements so that any one source $s = (s_{m-1}s_{m-2}...s_1s_0)_2$ can be connected to any one destination $d = (d_{m-1}d_{m-2}...d_1d_0)_2$.

PROOF

Let the inputs and outputs for each column of exchange elements be numbered 0 through $N-1$ from top to bottom, and let the $mN/2$ exchange elements be indexed by row and column,

$$E_{r,c}, 0 \le r < N/2, 1 \le c \le m. \tag{6.10}$$

Let $E_{r,c} = 0$ mean the element is in the bar state and $E_{r,c} = 1$ mean it is in the cross state. Using their binary representations, define the m numbers

$$r_i = (s_{m-1-i}s_{m-2-i}...s_1s_0d_{m-1}d_{m-2}...d_{m+1-i})_2. \tag{6.11}$$

Setting $E_{r_i,i} = s_{m-i} \oplus d_{m-i}$, where $\oplus$ represents exclusive or, connects input s to output d.

The reasoning is as follows:

The first shuffle connects input s to the s_{m-1} input of the exchange box

$$E_{r_1,1}, r_1 = (s_{m-2}s_{m-3}...s_1s_0)_2. \tag{6.12}$$

The setting specified for this box connects the s_{m-1} input to the d_{m-1} output by exchanging if $s_{m-1} \ne d_{m-1}$. This leaves s connected to $(s_{m-2}s_{m-3}...s_1s_0d_{m-1})_2$ after the first stage. An induction over the m stages whose induction step is essentially the same as the above argument completes the proof. ■

The omega network is capable of many useful permutations. Not only can any one input be connected to any one output at a time, but many permutations of interest in vector processing are also possible. The omega network can perform cyclic shifts of any length from 1 to N. It can also do matrix transpose-type permutations, and the perfect shuffle is useful in the fast Fourier transform algorithm.

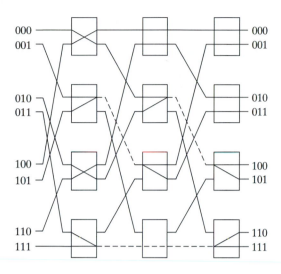

Figure 6-29 Omega network blocks on permutation p = (1,3,7,6,2,4,0,5).

For multistage interconnection networks, a broadcast is implemented simply by using the two upper and lower broadcast functions of the exchange elements described in Figure 6-22. A second control bit must be used to set the state of the exchange element to either upper or lower broadcast. A broadcast to a subset of destinations or to all is accomplished in log_2N steps in these networks.

The omega network and the butterfly networks cannot perform all possible input-to-output permutations. The permutation $\pi = (1,3,7,6,2,4,0,5)$ that was shown as an example to construct the Benes network, Figure 6-25, cannot be performed by the omega network. As shown in Figure 6-29, the pairs of source/destinations $[(S_0, D_5), (S_2, D_4)]$, $[(S_5, D_1), (S_1, D_3)]$, and $[(S_3, D_7), (S_7, D_6)]$ all must share a path in the network for a simultaneous transfer. Networks with this property are called blocking networks. The Benes network is a nonblocking network.

6.4.4   Combining Networks—Mutual Exclusion Free Synchronization

Synchronization by mutual exclusion extends poorly to very many processes. Many processes can be waiting for access to the mutually excluded code region, potentially wasting a large amount of processor resources. Not only is explicit mutual exclusion a problem, but the atomicity required by every synchronization is usually done at low level by mutual exclusion. The resulting mutual exclusion delay is proportional to the number of processors. Jacob Schwartz [255] proposed an idealized multiprocessor model, called the para computer, with a synchronization that could be executed by an arbitrary number of processors simultaneously in unit time. To approximate this ideal, the NYU Ultra computer designers proposed a parallel synchronization that could be executed by many processors with only logarithmic delay. The secret is implementing it within the switching network interconnecting multiple processors to multiple memory modules. In the Ultra computer, this switch is an omega network.

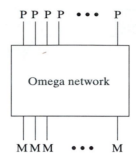

P P P P • • • P

Omega network

M M M • • • M

Figure 6-30   Structure of the NYU Ultra computer.

A key concept is that if N processes compete for a resource, the expected waiting time is $N - 1$ units. However, if $N = k \times m$ and groups of size k compete, followed by a competition among the m winners, the expected delay time is $k + m - 1$ units. Thus, if 64 processors compete, the expected waiting time is 63 units while breaking the 64 into two groups of 32 gives an expected waiting time for the two level competition of 33 units. By synchronizing two by two in the omega network, the Ultra computer synchronization has delay proportional to $\log_2 N$.

The structure of the NYU Ultra computer is that of a shared memory MIMD machine with a "Dance Hall" architecture, and an omega network connecting processors to memories, as shown in Figure 6-30. There are two implementations of this architecture, an eight processor prototype NYU Ultra computer at New York University and the 512 processor RP^3[237], which IBM T. J. Watson Research Center built with this architecture.

The feature of the Ultra computer architecture that interests us is its basic synchronization mechanism. It is called fetch&add and is a data-based synchronization operating on any cell of the shared memory. The form is: `fetch&add(X, e)` where X is a variable and e is an integer expression. The interpretation of a single fetch&add is: "Return the current value of x, and then replace x by x+e in memory." If multiple fetch&adds are done simultaneously, results are returned to processors as if they had been done in some sequential order. This order is unspecified and need not be deterministic. At this level, fetch&add appears similar to other atomic read-modify-write operations and could be implemented by mutual exclusion among the processors. The important feature of the Ultra computer fetch&add is that it exploits the latitude in the phrase, "*as if* the operations had been done in some sequential order," by doing a parallel implementation of the computation performed by many simultaneous fetch&adds.

It is not surprising that a parallel implementation is possible because the problem can be viewed as a parallel prefix computation, where the first input vector element is the original contents of the memory cell and subsequent elements are the expression arguments of the multiple fetch&add operations. Each processor receives as a result one of the outputs of the prefix computation, and the memory cell holds the last result. The only difference is that the order of the components of the prefix vector is unspecified. The implementation of fetch&add is partly in the memory and partly in the switch. The simple part of the implementation is an adder in each memory. The more important part is an interconnecting switch that does N fetch&adds in no more time than it takes to do one.

The network to do this is called a *combining network*. It is an omega network built of nodes that do fetch&add combining as shown in Figure 6-31. Using a network of such nodes, multiple fetch&adds issued simultaneously by different processors are combined pairwise, as shown in Figure 6-32. Examining the figure, it can be seen that each node does two adds, one to send a combined request on to memory and one to generate one of two replies when the reply to the combined request returns. It is important to note that combining works in both synchronous and asynchronous modes. It is easier to see the benefits of combining in synchronous networks, where all network requests are issued at the same time. In this case, requests to the same address submitted in a given cycle meet pairwise at one of the switch nodes on their path to their destination and are combined. Combining can occur in the asynchronous mode as well. Processors in MIMD computers operate independently and generate network requests and references asynchronously. Thus, interconnection networks for MIMD computers mostly operate in an asynchronous mode. It is important to recognize that combining of references is needed and most beneficial when requests occur at the same cycle time. To enhance the combining ability, combining networks may implement input buffers at each switch port. At every cycle, all entries present in the input buffers are searched for a matching address and are combined if a match is found.

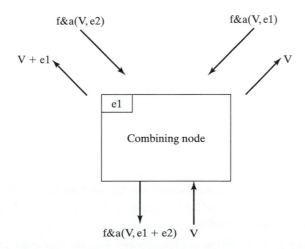

Figure 6-31   Fetch&add combining at one switch node.

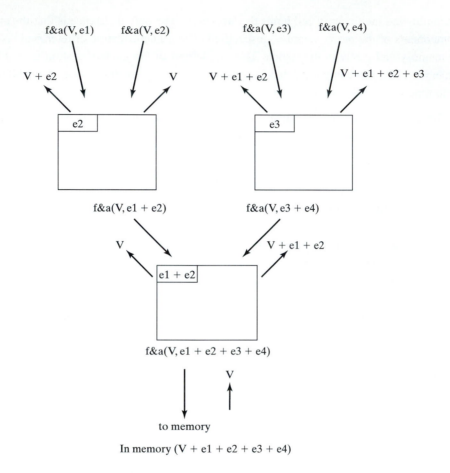

Figure 6-32 Fetch&add combining in the network.

We can get an understanding of some of the properties of fetch&add by using it to implement another synchronization. The semaphore, well known from the operating system's literature, is a good example. A semaphore S is an integer valued variable with two synchronization operations called *wait*, *P(S)*, and *signal*, *V(S)*. They are defined as:

P(S) - Wait for $S > 0$, subtract one and proceed;

V(S) - Add one to S.

Each semaphore operation is atomic with respect to all other operations by other processors on the same semaphore. Using fetch&add, the semaphore primitives could be implemented in the form of procedures shown in Program 6-5.

There are several features of the implementation that are important and illustrate aspects of fetch&add to be noted. Test and change on the semaphore must be atomic when they finally succeed, but fetch&add makes the change as it returns the value to be tested. Thus, a change takes place even if S is not greater than zero and must be undone. For this reason, the body of the outer `if` in the `P(S)` procedure generates pairs of fetch&add operations: `fetch&add(S,-1)`, `fetch&add(S,+1)`. If many processes generate pairs simultaneously, the apparent execution order might be such that S never attains its maximum value, and, therefore, no process finds it greater than zero even though there are enough outstanding increment operations to make it so if they were all completed. This is the reason for the $S-1 \geq 0$ condition. It prevents `fetch&add(S,-1)` from being issued until it is at least possible that it finds $S > 0$. Of course, the test may succeed and the `fetch&add(S,-1)` still finds $S \leq 0$ because another process has decremented it first.

```
procedure P(S);
    repeat
        if (S-1 ≥ 0) then
        begin
            if fetch&add(S,-1) > 0 then ok := true
            else
            begin
                fetch&add(S,1);
                ok := false;
            end;
        end;
    until ok;
end procedure;

procedure V(S);
    fetch&add(S,1);
end procedure;
```

Program 6-5 Wait and signal implemented with fetch&add.

```
shared integer x, P;
procedure barrier()
        boolean wasless;
        wasless := (x < P);
        if (fetch&add(x, 1) = 2P - 1 then x := 0;
        while ((x < P) = wasless) ;
end procedure;
```

Program 6-6 Reusable barrier implemented with fetch&add.

Another example of using fetch&add to implement mutual exclusion free synchronization is the implementation of barrier synchronization given in [15]. Barriers used repeatedly, say in a loop executed by all processes, need to use different counters to record the arrival of processes at successive barriers to avoid confusion between the count that releases processes from the first barrier and the count that is incremented as processes arrive at the second barrier, possibly before all have exited the first. The code of Program 6-6 cleverly combines two counters into one to implement a reusable barrier for P processes using fetch&add. The combined counter, x, is initialized to zero. This solution is a hardware version of a barrier that is tree structured to reduce contention among processes, but the tree is embodied in the hardware of the combining network for fetch&add. This implementation is very near to the logic diagrammed in Figure 4-15 of Section 4.3.4 where we first argued that atomicity does not require mutual exclusion.

6.4.5   Performance

Design of a parallel computer can be achieved at a low cost if one uses a simple bus to interconnect the processors. In this case only a few processors can be interconnected to exploit the bus bandwidth for effective concurrency. Bus interconnection supports broadcast in one step, but the processors must use it one at a time to communicate. On the other hand, the crossbar network allows all permutations in constant time at the high cost of the number of switches it requires.

The multistage interconnection networks are interesting solutions between the low cost/performance of the bus and the high cost/performance of the crossbar. When these networks are implemented as indirect networks, the latency of every communication is of the order of $\log_2 N$. Computer systems that use these networks must be designed such that long latency associated with every reference that must go through the network can be tolerated. Pipelined processors are often used in these parallel computers to achieve a greater degree of overlap execution. A problem associated with MINs that must be addressed in the computer system is that of a *hot spot* in the network. In a multiprocessor interconnection network, a hot spot refers to a node, typically a memory module, that is referenced heavily by many/all processors and becomes overloaded. This phenomenon typically happens due to nonuniform references to the node in question. The effect of a burst of references to the hot spot is that it backs up the network traffic all the way to the input nodes and affects the messages entering the network, as shown in Figure 6-33. In networks where the switch nodes have buffers to queue messages that contend for the same output port, the hot spot problem can be remedied by providing message combining at each switch node if most messages are combinable references to the same address. We will now investigate the effectiveness of combining in a network.

Consider modeling a 2×2 combining node similar to the one shown in Figure 6-31 with the following added features. Associated with each output port of a node is a combining queue. Messages are only enqueued when a succeeding node cannot accept further messages, no queueing takes place otherwise. Only those messages that have been enqueued are compared for possible combination, therefore, with low traffic, no queueing or combining occurs. An output queue can accept two messages simultaneously to handle the arrival of simultaneous messages destined for the same output port. An input buffer is provided to hold a message in case the destination output queue is full. The entire network operation is pipelined so that the arrival of a message at a node overlaps with combining of messages already in the combining queues, which overlaps in turn with the departure of messages from the node. A wait buffer is used to record the combination of messages in the output queues so replies can be generated correctly by the node. Figure 6-34 shows the overall structure of the combing node with input buffers, output buffer, and the wait queue.

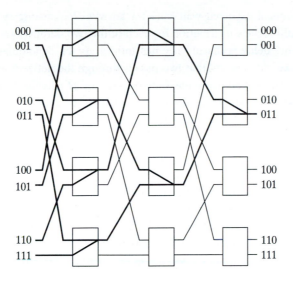

Figure 6-33   Effect of hot spot in an omega network.

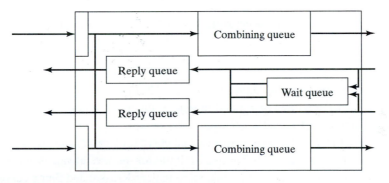

Figure 6-34   Structure of the simulated combining node.

To understand the performance of the omega network, we use a model developed by Kruskal and Snir [181] for the banyan network, which is isomorphic to the omega network. P processors are connected to P memory modules by an omega network of 2×2 switching nodes. Each processor has a probability of r of making a memory request on each cycle, and the addresses requested are uniformly distributed over the P modules. Kruskal and Snir find that the average delay through the omega network is

$$T_r = \log_2 P\left(t_\tau + \frac{t_c r}{4(1-r)}\right),$$ (6.13)

where t_τ is the contention free transit time through a node and t_c is the node cycle time. The term

$$T_W = \frac{r}{4(1-r)},$$ (6.14)

is the queueing theoretical expected wait time for an M/G/1 queueing system having Poisson arrivals and a Bernoulli service distribution for each of the two output ports [173]. An important feature of the queueing delay is that it becomes infinite as the denominator goes to zero as r tends to one. Now take into account that two passes through the network are necessary to complete a memory request, assume that a message consists of M parcels for a pipeline start up of $M - 1$ cycles, and assume one cycle to enter the network for each pass. Taking $t_\tau = t_c = 1$ gives an average delay in cycles for a reference traveling from processor to memory and back of

$$T_r = 2\left[\log_2 P\left(1 + \frac{Mr}{4(1-r)}\right) + (M-1) + 1\right].$$

(6.15)

Now to model the situation where some hot spot gets more than an equal share of references, assume a single hot spot address receives a fraction f of all references, with the rest of the references uniformly distributed over modules. The hot memory module receives $rfP + r(1-f)$ references per cycle while any other module receives $r(1-f)$ references per cycle. The queueing theory result of Eq. (6.14) implies a delay at the input to the hot module of

$$T_f = \frac{r(1-f) + rfP}{4(1 - r(1-f) - rfP)},$$

(6.16)

in addition to any other delays in the network. This delay becomes infinite for

$$r = \frac{1}{1 + f(P-1)},$$

(6.17)

causing the tree saturation back up shown in Figure 6-33. Pfister and Norton [238] simulated an omega network with $P = 64$ and $M = 4$ and measured the average delay in cycles for different values of r, the number of requests per cycle, and several values of the hot spot fraction f. Figure 6-35 shows their results, along with a dashed curve for Kruskal and Snir's model and vertical asymptotes where the wait should become infinite for the several values of f. It is clear that the simulations behave as the models predict, starting near Kruskal and Snir's curve for small r increasing rapidly as the vertical asymptote for the associated f is approached, and indicating unstable simulation results near the asymptote.

Now suppose that the hot spot is a memory cell used for fetch&add synchronization and that the omega network includes combining of fetch&add operations. Then it is no longer true that an average of $rfP + r(1-f)$ requests per cycle reach the hot module. Instead, the average number of fetch&add requests to the hot spot is between rf and rfP, depending on the amount of combining that occurs. Pfister and Norton's results for the omega network with combining are shown in Figure 6-36. The infinite wait behavior is no longer in evidence, although there is extra delay for large hot spot fractions, f. The r values for which the simulation results begin to indicate instability do not depend strongly on f but now all occur in the range $0.6 \leq r \leq 0.7$. Combining substantially reduces the average memory response time and is an effective solution to the hot spot problem. Combining has been used in NYU Ultra computer, IBM RP3, and the Columbia Homogeneous Parallel Processor (CHoPP) [211].

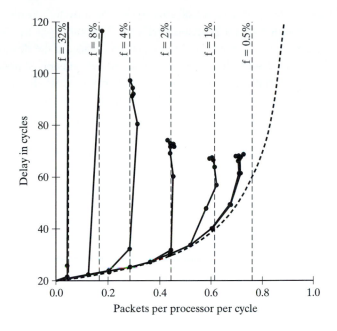

Figure 6-35 Simulated omega network delay with hot spot probability f.

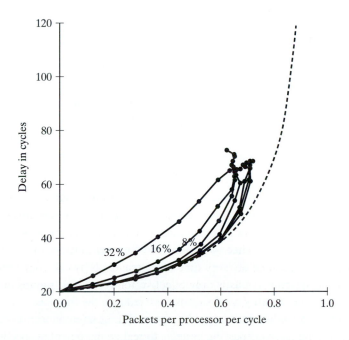

Figure 6-36 Simulated delay in an omega network with fetch&add combining.

One way to look at the performance of a network would be to consider the ratio of data movement to the computation that a program performs. This ratio places a constraint on the bandwidth that the network must deliver to the processors to sustain the desired computational rate. This approach, although sensible, is not easy to accurately model. Memory hierarchy and operating systems play a significant role in the data delivery process. Furthermore, programs have different data movement requirements and the amount of data and time required will vary significantly. Bursty behavior places a significantly higher bandwidth requirement on the network than a nicely distributed data movement over the execution time of the program with the same total data movement requirements. We will study this approach to performance modeling in Chapter 10.

6.5 Conclusion

Often the topology of an interconnection network is considered to be its most important feature and the major determiner of performance. In reality, the mode of operation of the network can have a greater effect on performance. Whether the network is used synchronously or asynchronously, has store and forward or cut-through routing, includes combining of synchronization operations, etc. may be more important to its effectiveness than its topology. Cost is also a major concern. It is easy to build very capable interconnection networks if cost is no object. Building a network with order P^2 hardware for a P processor system that yields a speedup of less than P is not a good alternative. Therefore, the combination of cost and performance must be taken into account in any design.

Scalability is also a major concern in the design of interconnection networks. A topology that is quite suitable for a small system may lose all its cost effectiveness when the system size is increased. Even the simple fact that the number of communication ports for every node of a hypercube network increases by one when the system size is doubled may be a reason not to use them in a system that is required to scale smoothly to increasingly larger numbers of processors. Hierarchical topologies have some advantage in this regard, but they may lead to programming complexity if the topology or operating mode of the network changes radically with level of the hierarchy.

The interconnection network is the heart of a parallel processor, and many systems have failed to meet their design goals for reasons connected with the design of this essential component. Managing latency in a network by pipelining communications can be very important. Cut-through routing was a major advance over store and forward networks in systems that had a strong dependence on end-to-end delivery time of messages. Network concurrency is essential to all but the smallest systems. A bus is only effective for very small groups of processors and only when caching or other locality mechanisms have reduced the frequency of communications to a minimum. Careful attention must be paid to the design of interconnection networks in both shared address space and message passing systems to realize the potential speedup of the multiple processors employed in the system.

6.6 Bibliographic Notes

An interesting survey by Feng [106] represents an interconnection space as a function of intersection of four design choices, namely topology (static or dynamic, each with its own category), operation mode (synchronous or asynchronous), switching strategy (circuit, store-forward, or cut-through), and control strategy (centralized or distributed). Cube connected cycles (CCC) was proposed by Preparata and Vuillemin [240] where they showed that many of the properties of a hypercube topology can be maintained by CCC without the node-degree growth that occurs with the increase in dimension of the cube. An in depth analysis of K-ary n-cube networks and some reasons for choosing mesh over hypercube topologies is presented in [85]. More detailed discussion on static topologies is covered in [139]. Cut-through and wormhole routings are described in [172] and [83], respectively.

Multistage networks and their properties are covered in [195] and [258]. Many of these networks have been shown to be topologically equivalent [291]. The communication properties of interconnection networks are studied in [158]. The omega network was proposed by Lawrie as described in [193]. The single-stage shuffle network equivalent to one stage of the omega network was first proposed by Stone in [268] along with several applications of perfect shuffle permutation. Analysis of hot spots through simulations is presented in [238], where it is shown that a relatively small number of hot spot references can seriously degrade the performance of all paths in the network. In [196], it is shown that a fat tree of a given size is almost the best possible network of that size.

Problems

6.1   A network implements one property from each of the following three categories:
   (a) Circuit or packet switched
   (b) Central or distributed control
   (c) Synchronous or asynchronous mode of operation
   Describe the implications of all possible combinations.

6.2   Design an efficient prefix sum algorithm for a m-level binary tree network. What is the complexity of your algorithm?

6.3   Design and implement an all-to-all broadcast algorithm for a $N = 2^m$ node hypercube network. Use MIMD pseudocode with one *send* or one *receive* at a time. What is the time complexity of your algorithm?

6.4   Design and implement a multicast algorithm, that is, a single input can be broadcast to any subset of outputs, for a $N = 2^m$ node hypercube network.

6.5   Describe a routing algorithm for the butterfly network similar to the destination tag method described for the omega network in Section 6.4.3.3.

6.6   We know that any single source in an omega network, $s = s_{n-1}s_{n-2}\cdots s_1 s_0$, can be routed to any destination. If s is routed to the destination, $d = \overline{s_{n-1}}\,\overline{s_{n-2}}\cdots\overline{s_1}\,\overline{s_0}$ with destination tag equal to the complement of the source tag, then exhibit some other source-destination pair that cannot be connected simultaneously and prove that it cannot be.

6.7   Consider using "exchange" boxes with three inputs and three outputs each to build a multistage switching network. Assume initially that a box can connect inputs to outputs in any permuted order. (There is no broadcast capability.)

(a) Using these elements and a three-way "perfect shuffle" interconnection, show how to build a two-stage network connecting nine inputs to nine outputs that is analogous to the omega network.

(b) Define the three-way perfect shuffle permutation of $n = 3^k$ elements mathematically.

(c) Use your definition to prove that a k stage "ternary omega network" can connect any specific one of $n = 3^k$ inputs to any one of n outputs.

(d) Is it necessary that the three input, three output "exchange" boxes be able to perform all permutations of three elements for the proof of part c to work? If not, give a minimal set of permutations which is sufficient.

6.8 An N input multistage cube interconnection network consists of $m = \log_2 N$ exchange networks (each network is a column of $N/2$ two function exchange elements) each followed by a permutation interconnection P_k, $k = 1, 2, ..., m$ reading from left to right across the network, with inputs at the left. The permutation interconnections transform the binary representations of their input indices as follows:

for $1 \le k < m$, $\quad P_k(i_{m-1}, ..., i_{k+1}, i_k, i_{k-1}, ..., i_1, i_0) = i_{m-1}, ..., i_{k+1}, i_0, i_{k-1}, ..., i_1, i_k$,

for $k = m$, P_m is an inverse shuffle $P_m(i_{m-1}, i_{m-2}, ..., i_2, i_1, i_0) = i_0, i_{m-1}, i_{m-2}, ..., i_2, i_1$.

(a) Draw an 8 input multistage cube network.

(b) Prove that any input $S = s_{m-1}, s_{m-2}, ..., s_1, s_0$ can be connected to any output $D = d_{m-1}, d_{m-2}, ..., d_1, d_0$ by a proper setting of exchange boxes.

(c) Assume input $S = s_{m-1}, ..., s_{k+1}, s_k, s_{k-1}, ..., s_1, s_0$ is connected to output $S = s_{m-1}, ..., s_{k+1}, \bar{s}_k, s_{k-1}, ..., s_1, s_0$, where $\bar{s}_k = 1 - s_k$ is the complement of the bit. Exhibit an input/output pair that *cannot* also be connected at the same time.

6.9 Consider an omega network with N inputs and N outputs, where $N = 2^m$. Describe how to set the exchange switches so that every input i is connected to output j, where j differs from i by 2^k, for some fixed $k < m$, $0 \le i \le N - 1$.

6.10 Can the switching network below, built of 2×2 exchange elements perform all permutations from inputs to outputs? Prove or disprove as simply as possible.

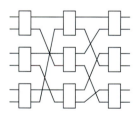

6.11 A switching network connecting N processors to N memories has queueing at the nodes so that a message that cannot be switched to the correct node output is delayed for a cycle time Δ. The omega network has 2-input, 2-output switching elements and depth $\log_2 N$. This network has k-input, k-output nodes, and depth $\log_k N$. We assume a simplified operation model in which, at some initial time, all processors make memory requests simultaneously, and the requests are then satisfied before anything else occurs. A request, thus, takes a minimum of $2\Delta \log_k N$ time units to be satisfied. Conflicts on the way to memory may cause the time to be longer. (There are no conflicts on the return path.) Assume that the expected waiting time at a node, $E(wait) = pk\Delta$, is proportional to the number of inputs k and the probability p of collision with one other input. Derive an equation for the number of inputs (and outputs) k that will minimize the expected time for a request to be satisfied. Discuss qualitatively the behavior of the optimal value of k for very small and very large collision probability p.

6.12 Give a mathematical description of the perfect shuffle permutation on $N = 2^k$ inputs.

6.13 Can an N-input m-stage omega network, $N = 2^m$, pass a perfect shuffle? Show your work.

6.14 Consider an N-input multistage omega network where each switch cell is individually controlled and $N = 2^n$.

   (a) How many different permutation functions (one-to-one and onto mappings) can be defined over N inputs?

   (b) How many different permutation functions can be performed by the omega network in one pass? If $N = 8$, what is the percentage of permutation functions that can be performed in one pass?

   (c) Given any source-destination $(S - D)$ pair, the routing path can be uniquely controlled by the destination address. Instead of using the destination address D as the routing tag, we define $T = S \oplus D$ as the routing tag. Show that T alone can be used to determine the routing path. What is the advantage of using T as the routing tag?

   (d) If the 2×2 switches have all 4 functions, the omega network is capable of performing broadcasting (one source and multiple destinations). If the number of destination PEs is a power of two, can you give a simple routing algorithm to achieve this capability?

6.15 Prove or disprove that the multistage omega network can perform any shift permutation in one pass. The *shift permutation* is defined as follows: given $N = 2^n$ inputs, a shift permutation is either a circular left shift or a circular right shift of k positions, where $0 \le k \le N$.

7.1 Discovering Parallel Operations in (Sequential) Code

We start by considering a set $P_1, P_2, \ldots, P_k$ of program fragments described by sequential code. The code fragments may consist of one or more statements. The Bernstein conditions describe when two different program fragments P_i and P_j are independent and can, thus, be executed in parallel. Let I_i be the set of all variables read by P_i, called the *input set* of P_i. Let O_i be the set of all variables written by P_i — the *output set* of P_i. Then P_i and P_j are independent and can execute in parallel if the input and output sets satisfy *Bernstein's conditions*

$$I_j \cap O_i = \varnothing,$$
$$I_i \cap O_j = \varnothing, \text{ and}$$
$$O_i \cap O_j = \varnothing,$$

which specify null set intersections on pairs of the input and output sets. In words, these equations specify that no input can be the output of another program fragment running in parallel and that outputs of fragments running in parallel must be different.

The individual conditions are related to different types of data dependence. Data dependences are often analyzed taking each of the program fragments as a single statement, but all that is really necessary is that the sequential program determine an execution order for the fragments. If program fragment P_i precedes P_j in a sequential program, then the following correspondences between data dependence types and the individual Bernstein conditions hold. Violation of the condition $I_j \cap O_i = \varnothing$ is called a *flow dependence*. It corresponds to the first statement producing a result that is used by the second statement. Violation of $I_i \cap O_j = \varnothing$ is called an *antidependence*. It occurs when the second statement overwrites a variable needed to execute the first statement. Violation of the condition $O_i \cap O_j = \varnothing$ is an *output dependence*. Here both statements write the same variable, and the rules of sequential execution say that the final value must be that written by the second statement.

Examples of each of the types of data dependence follow. In the pair of single statements

$$
\begin{array}{llll}
S_1: & \text{A = B + C} & & I_1 = \{B, C\}, O_1 = \{A\} \\
S_2: & \text{D = 2.5*A} & & I_2 = \{A\}, O_2 = \{D\}
\end{array}
$$

$I_2 \cap O_1 = \{A\} \neq \varnothing$ implies a flow dependence. Concurrent execution of the two statements could result in the old value of A being used by S_2 instead of the value produced by S_1. In the statement pair

$$
\begin{array}{llll}
S_1: & \text{A = B + C} & & I_1 = \{B, C\}, O_1 = \{A\} \\
S_2: & \text{B = 3.14*D} & & I_2 = \{D\}, O_2 = \{B\}
\end{array}
$$

$I_1 \cap O_2 = \{B\} \neq \varnothing$ implies an antidependence. Concurrent execution of S_1 and S_2 could result in the new value of B produced by S_2 being used in S_1, contrary to the specification. Lastly, in the statement pair

$$S_1: \qquad \mathtt{A\ =\ B\ +\ C} \qquad I_1 = \{B, C\}, O_1 = \{A\}$$
$$S_2: \qquad \mathtt{A\ =\ 7.5*D} \qquad I_2 = \{D\}, O_2 = \{A\}$$

$O_1 \cap O_2 = \{A\} \neq \emptyset$ implies an output dependence. The final value of A should be the value produced by S_2 but could be that produced by S_1 if the two statements are executed concurrently. The relations are often expressed by a δ operator as summarized in Table 7-1.

If we do dependence analysis among individual statements in a high-level language, several relationships can hold among a set of statements. The *data dependence diagram* is a graph that expresses the collection of dependences and can be used to give a visual representation of the overall interdependences. Individual statements are represented by vertices (circles) in the graph, and dependences between statements are represented by edges marked according to the type of dependence. The program fragment

$$S_1: \qquad \mathtt{A\ =\ B\ +\ C}$$
$$S_2: \qquad \mathtt{B\ =\ A*D}$$
$$S_3: \qquad \mathtt{C\ =\ 7.5*B}$$
$$S_4: \qquad \mathtt{A\ =\ A\ +\ 1}$$

corresponds to the dependence diagram of Figure 7-1.

Table 7-1   Relations assuming S_i precedes S_j in sequential code.

Bernstein condition		Dependence type	Notation
$I_j \cap O_i \neq \emptyset$	$\Rightarrow$	flow dependence	$S_i \, \delta \, S_j$
$I_i \cap O_j \neq \emptyset$	$\Rightarrow$	antidependence	$S_i \, \bar{\delta} \, S_j$
$O_i \cap O_j \neq \emptyset$	$\Rightarrow$	output dependence	$S_i \, \delta^o \, S_j$

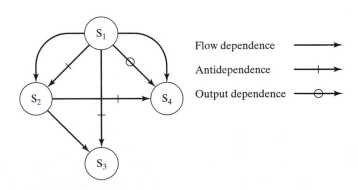

Flow dependence

Antidependence

Output dependence

Figure 7-1   Data dependence diagram.

Data-dependent flow of control introduces some complexity into the analysis of data dependences. The effect can be represented by the *control dependence*. A statement S_j is control dependent on a statement S_i, written $S_i \, \delta^c \, S_j$, if an output variable of S_i appears in the condition of an **if** statement or other statement that controls whether S_j is executed. As an example consider the code fragment containing an **if** statement.

$$
\begin{aligned}
&S_1: \quad & \mathtt{Q\ =\ sin(Z)} \\
&   & \mathtt{if\ \ (Q\ >\ 0)} \\
&S_2: \quad & \mathtt{then\ A\ =\ B\ +\ C} \\
&S_3: \quad & \mathtt{else\ A\ =\ 2*Z}
\end{aligned}
$$

In this case S_2 and S_3 are control dependent on S_1, written $S_1 \, \delta^c \, S_2$ and $S_1 \, \delta^c \, S_3$.

Control dependences can be reduced to the data dependences already treated if the controlling conditions are propagated to the controlled statements by the use of conditional assignment. Conditional assignments can be expressed by if-then, but the concept useful here is more like masked execution in SIMD machines. Both Fortran 90 and High Performance Fortran use a WHERE construct for conditional assignment. We adopt it in the pseudocode form

$$\mathbf{where} \quad (\langle\text{condition}\rangle) \ \langle\text{assignment}\rangle$$

Then the if-then-else example above becomes

$$
\begin{aligned}
&S_1: \quad & \mathtt{Q\ =\ sin(Z)} \\
&S_2: \quad & \mathbf{where} \quad \mathtt{(Q\ >\ 0)} \qquad \mathtt{A\ =\ B\ +\ C} \\
&S_3: \quad & \mathbf{where} \quad \mathtt{(Q\ \le\ 0)} \qquad \mathtt{A\ =\ 2*Z}
\end{aligned}
$$

and the variable Q becomes an input variable for statements S_2 and S_3. This transforms the control dependences into flow dependences. If several conditions must hold for a statement to be executed, as for example with a statement enclosed in nested **if**s, the controlling condition becomes the logical and of the individual conditions.

A different type of dependence arises when several program fragments make use of the same scarce resource. Data and control dependences are independent of machine hardware while the *resource dependence* is not. For example, on a machine with only one divider, the statements

$$
\begin{aligned}
&S_1: \quad \mathtt{A\ =\ B/C} \\
&S_2: \quad \mathtt{X\ =\ Y/Z}
\end{aligned}
$$

are resource dependent. This type of dependence does not imply an execution order on the statements, but only that S_1 and S_2 are mutually exclusive. Resource dependence is usually resolved in a scheduling phase that takes place after a complete analysis of data and control dependences. This separates the machine independent and dependent parts of the process.

The job of dependence analysis is to prove pairs of statements independent. If an analysis cannot explicitly show independence, a parallelizing compiler cannot execute statements in parallel. Automatic parallelization of sequential code must, therefore, take the pessimistic viewpoint that statements must be executed in the original sequential order unless they can explicitly be shown to be independent.

7.2 Variables with Complex Names

We have been discussing dependences as if the name of a variable uniquely designates a memory location with the name binding occurring at compile time. Names are not always that simple. The extreme of a name bound at run-time is a pointer variable. For example, in the C code fragment

```
real *p;
p = f(x);
```
S_1: `y = *p;`
S_2: `*p = z;`

it is not possible for a compile time analysis to determine the dependence relation of S_1 and S_2 to each other, or to any other statement in the program because the variable read by S_1 and written by S_2 is unknown until $f(x)$ is computed. These statements would have to be scheduled strictly sequentially by a parallelizing compiler, which must assume dependence if independence cannot be proven. Only if the range of a pointer variable is restricted in some way is there any hope of showing independence when one of two statements contains a pointer.

The pointer is an extreme case of a computable address, but many common cases involve addresses that are partially computable at run-time. The most common, and the one with the most potential for parallelism impact, is a subscripted array element. Because loop code offers the most opportunity for parallelism, and because loop bodies usually involve array references, it is important to be able to do dependence analysis on array references. The array name is bound at compile time, and it is easy for the compiler to determine that references to different arrays are independent (provided that array bounds are not exceeded). Thus, the hard part of the problem is determining whether two indexed references to the same array refer to the same element. This task is called *disambiguating* array references.

The problem should be analyzed in the most common and potentially most useful case for parallelism extraction, the counted loop. The array references in a counted loop have indices that are usually simple functions of the loop variable, which has a limited range and varies in a known way. Consider the counted loop

```
for j := k step s until m
```

with lower limit k, step size s, and upper limit m. We change variables to make the analysis simpler by transforming the loop variable to a unit step form by the transformation $i = (j - k)/s$. We use the **do** keyword to indicate that we treat simple counted loops as used in Fortran. Using $u = (m - k)/s$, we write

```
do i = 0, u
```

```
                    do i = 0, u
        S₁:                A(f(i)) = ...
        S₂:                ... = A(g(i))
                    end do
```

Figure 7-2 Schema for a loop carried dependence.

The dependence analysis we want to consider involves two statements in a loop body that reference the same array. The loop of Figure 7-2 really represents the following sequence of 2u + 2 statements with subscripts corresponding to the statement number in Figure 7-2 and superscripts corresponding to the loop iteration.

S_1^0 : A(f(0)) = ...

S_2^0 :   ...   = A(g(0))

S_1^1 : A(f(1)) = ...

S_2^1 :   ...   = A(g(1))

   ...

The question of whether there is a flow dependence of S_2 on S_1 can be formulated as follows. Do there exist two integers κ and λ, $0 \le \kappa$, $\lambda \le u$ such that $\kappa \le \lambda$ and $f(\kappa) = g(\lambda)$? Such equations having solutions constrained to be integers are called Diophantine equations. The solution of such equations is computationally hard, even when f and g are linear functions.

If there is a dependence, the *dependence distance* is defined to be $D = \lambda - \kappa$. In a simple loop, the dependence distance must be positive or zero. We see negative dependence distances later in connection with nested loops. If the distance is zero, the dependence is an ordinary one between statements S_1 and S_2 and would exist even without the loop. If the dependence distance is nonzero, the dependence is *loop carried*.

As a concrete example of the ideas, the loop

```
                do i = 0, u
        S₁:              A(i) = ...
        S₂:              ... = A(i-3) ...
                end do
```

has a loop carried flow dependence from S_1 to S_2. For $\kappa = 0$, $\lambda = 3$, in fact for any $\kappa = \lambda - 3$, where both κ and λ are in the index range, we have $S_1^{i-3} \delta S_2^i$ or $S_1 \delta_3 S_2$, where the subscript on δ is the dependence distance.

```
            do i₁ = 0, u₁
               do i₂ = 0, u₂
                 ...
                  do iₙ = 0, uₙ
   Sₚ:            ... A(f₁(I), f₂(I), ..., fₘ(I)) ...
   Sq:            ... A(g₁(I), g₂(I), ..., gₘ(I)) ...
                  end do
                 ...
               end do
            end do
```

Figure 7-3   General loop nest schema.

There may also be loop carried output or antidependence. In the general loop of Figure 7-2, S_1 is antidependent on S_2 if and only if there exist integers $0 \leq \kappa < \lambda \leq u$ such that $g(\kappa) = f(\lambda)$. The change from $\kappa \leq \lambda$ for flow dependence of S_2 on S_1 to $\kappa < \lambda$ for antidependence of S_1 on S_2 comes about because S_1 precedes S_2 in sequential program order. The subscript of the array in the dependent statement is a function of λ while the array subscript on which it depends is a function of κ. As an example of antidependence, the loop

```
            do i = 0, u
   S₁:          A(i) = ...
   S₂:          ...   = A(i+2) ...
            end do
```

has a loop carried antidependence with dependence distance two. It is expressed as $S_2^i \bar{\delta} S_1^{i+2}$ or $S_2 \bar{\delta}_2 S_1$.

Note that there are two distinct types of integers connected with loop carried dependence, both of which are connected with the word index. One is a loop index variable that starts at its lower bound and counts to its upper bound. The other type of index is an array index designating which element of an array is being referenced. It is important to distinguish these. The array indices, or subscripts, are functions, $f(i)$ and $g(i)$, of the loop index i.

7.2.1   Nested Loops

In general, we are interested in nested loops and multiple index arrays. We study a loop nest in the standardized form of Figure 7-3. In the figure, I is the vector of loop indices $I = (i_1, i_2, ..., i_n)$ and at least one of the two references to array A is an output variable of its statement. The nested loop is a compact representation of $\prod_{k=1}^{n} 2(u_k + 1)$ statements. There are m array subscripts, each of which is a function of up to n loop variables.

Each instance of S_p (or S_q) is associated with a particular value of the vector I of loop variables, and they are ordered by the rules of loop execution in *lexicographic order* on I. Values of I appear in the order

$$(0, 0, ..., 0)(0, 0, ..., 1)...(0, 0, ..., u_n)...(0, u_2, ..., u_n)(1, 0, ..., 0)...(u_1, u_2, ..., u_n).$$

Mathematically, the lexicographic order can be defined as follows. Let $\kappa = (i_1, i_2, \ldots, i_n)$ and $\lambda = (j_1, j_2, \ldots, j_n)$ be two values of I. Then $\kappa < \lambda$ lexicographically if and only if there exists an l, $1 \leq l \leq n$ such that $i_k = j_k$, $1 \leq k \leq l - 1$ and $i_l < j_l$. That is, κ is lexicographically less than λ if, reading from left to right, the first component of κ, which differs from the corresponding component of λ is smaller than that component of λ.

In the loop nest of Figure 7-3, there is a dependence from S_p to S_q if and only if there exist vectors of integers $\kappa = (i_1, i_2, \ldots, i_n)$ and $\lambda = (j_1, j_2, \ldots, j_n)$ where $0 \leq i_k, j_k \leq u_k$ for all $1 \leq k \leq n$, $\kappa \leq \lambda$ lexicographically, and $f_k(\kappa) = g_k(\lambda)$ for all $1 \leq k \leq m$. The statements are independent and can run in parallel only if no such index vectors exist. If there is a dependence, the *dependence distance vector* is

$$D = \lambda - \kappa = (D_1, D_2, \ldots, D_n) = (j_1 - i_1, j_2 - i_2, \ldots, j_n - i_n).$$

The *dependence direction vector* is $d = (d_1, d_2, \ldots, d_n)$, where

$$d_k = \begin{cases} < & \text{if } (D_k > 0), \\ = & \text{if } (D_k = 0), \\ > & \text{if } (D_k < 0). \end{cases} \tag{7.1}$$

The dependence is carried by the outermost loop for which d_k is not $=$, that is, d_k is $<$. The statement that $\kappa \leq \lambda$ lexicographically implies that the leftmost nonzero component of the distance vector cannot be negative or that the leftmost component of the direction vector that is not $=$ cannot be $>$.

As an example of a loop carried dependence in a loop nest consider

```
        do i = 0, u₁
            do j = 0, u₂
                do k = 0, u₃
S₁:                 A(i+1, j, k-1) = A(i, j, k) + B
                end do
            end do
        end do
```

In this example, $S_1^\kappa \delta S_1^\lambda$, where $\kappa = (i - 1, j, k + 1)$ and $\lambda = (i, j, k)$. Remember the distinction between the set of loop variable values and the array index triples. When κ is substituted for the loop variable triple (i, j, k), S_1 becomes $A(i, j, k) = A(i - 1, j, k + 1)$. Element $A(i, j, k)$ is written, and when λ is substituted for the loop variables, S_1 becomes $A(i + 1, j, k - 1) = A(i, j, k)$, which reads the same element of A. The distance vector is $D = \lambda - \kappa = (1, 0, -1)$, and the direction vector is $d = (<, =, >)$. The dependence $S_1 \, \delta_{<=>} \, S_1$ is carried by the outer loop on i.

Dependence graphs like that of Figure 7-1 can be extended to the case of loop carried dependences by labeling each edge of the graph of dependences among loop body statements with the distance vector of the dependence. For example, the doubly nested loop

```
do i = 0, u₁
    do j = 0, u₂
S₁:         A(i, j+1) = B(i, j) + C(i+1, j)
S₂:         D(i, j-1) = 2*A(i, j) - 1
S₃:         C(i, j+1) = 3.14*(D(i, j) - C(i, j))
    end do
end do
```

corresponds to the dependence graph of Figure 7-4. The loop carried flow-dependence of S_2 on S_1 results from a reference to A, the antidependence of S_3 on S_1 results from C, the antidependence of S_2 on S_3 is due to D, and the loop carried flow-dependence of S_3 on itself is a result of references to C on both the left and right sides of the assignment.

Another type of dependence graph is sometimes useful in analyzing nested loops. It diagrams dependences in the iteration space of the loops, consisting of a point for each distinct vector of loop variable values. Any loop carried dependences among statements of the loop body are represented by distance vectors between points of the iteration space. The doubly nested loop example has the iteration space dependence diagram of Figure 7-5. The diagonal arrows represent the antidependence of S_3 on S_1 with respect to C while each horizontal arrow represents the three dependences, $S_1 \, \delta_{(0,1)} \, S_2$, $S_3 \, \delta_{(0,1)} \, S_2$, and $S_3 \, \delta_{(0,1)} \, S_3$, all of which have the same distance vector.

7.2.2   Variations on the Array Reference Disambiguation Problem

In the general loop nest of Figure 7-3, a dependence is implied by a solution to the following system of Diophantine equalities and inequalities.

$$f_k(\kappa) = g_k(\lambda), \ 1 \leq k \leq m, \qquad (7.2)$$

$$0 \leq i_k, j_k \leq u_k, \ 1 \leq k \leq n,$$

Either $\exists l, \ 1 \leq l \leq n$, such that $i_k = j_k, \ 1 \leq k \leq l - 1$, and $i_l < j_l$,

or $i_k = j_k, \ 1 \leq k \leq n$.

There are several interesting variations on the general problem posed by these equations.

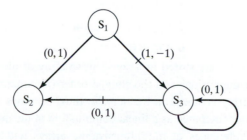

Figure 7-4   Loop carried data dependence diagram.

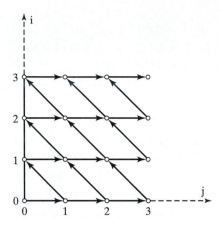

Figure 7-5   Nested loop dependence diagram in iteration space.

1. It is usually assumed that $f_k(I)$ and $g_k(I)$ are linear functions of the loop variables i_r, $1 \le r \le n$. This covers most cases of interest in array subscripting and makes the equalities and inequalities in the Diophantine equation set linear functions of the problem variables. Usually no more than one or two loop indices appear in a given array subscript position, and some analyses make use of this.

2. u_k is independent of the loop variables of enclosing loops. This is the case of *rectangular loops*, so called because the iteration domain is a rectangle in n-dimensional space. The more general case in which u_k can depend on variables of enclosing loops is called the *trapezoidal loops* case.

3. The loop bounds are unknown at the time that dependencies are analyzed. This removes the loop bound inequalities from the set of Diophantine equations and forces a dependence to be assumed by the analysis if one exists anywhere in the n-dimensional space of integers.

4. In reordering loops for parallel execution, it is sometimes useful to ask if there is a dependence with a given direction vector. To analyze this case, for every specified component of the direction vector, add to the equation set (7.2) the equation

$$i_k < j_k, \text{ if } d_k \text{ is } <, \tag{7.3}$$
$$i_k > j_k, \text{ if } d_k \text{ is } >, \text{ and}$$
$$i_k = j_k, \text{ if } d_k \text{ is } =,$$

5. Multidimensional arrays are stored in a consecutive array of memory cells with a layout determined by their dimensions and the storage order (row major, column major). When an m-dimensional array is stored in memory, it, thus, becomes a one-dimensional array with a single subscript computed as a linear combination of the m subscripts for individual dimensions. Thus, references to multidimensional arrays within the loop nest can be reduced to references to one-dimensional arrays by replacing $A(f_1(I), f_2(I), ..., f_m(I)) ...$ by $A(f(I))$, where

$$f(I) = \cdots + w_{m-1}w_m f_{m-2}(I) + w_m f_{m-1}(I) + f_m(I),$$ (7.4)

$$= \sum_{k=1}^{m} \prod_{l=k+1}^{m} w_l f_k(I).$$

The w_l are the m-dimensions of the array, and the index origins are all zero. A similar formula holds for $g(I)$.

Reduction to a one-dimensional array is only valid, however, if array bounds are not violated. For example, consider the transformation of the two-loop nest

```
      real  A(5, 10)
      do 10 i = 1, 5
          do 10 j = 1, 5
              A(i, 2*j) = ...
                  ... = ... A(i, 2*j-1) ...
10    continue
```

into the nest involving a one-dimensional version a of A

```
      real a(50)
      do 10 i = 1, 5
          do 10 j = 1, 5
              a(5*(i-1) + 2*j) = ...
                  ... = ... a(5*(i-1) + 2*j - 1) ...
10    continue
```

This transformation is fine if the loop bounds are known, but if they are unknown, taking $i = 1, j = 6$ in the first reference and $i = 2, j = 4$ in the second results in two references to $a(12)$. The original references to A were distinct, and one was out of bounds on the second index, resulting in an ambiguous reference to an in-bounds element of a.

The most common case, and one for which several approaches lead to more or less efficient and complete dependence analysis procedures, is that in which each array index is a linear function of one or more loop indices.

To illustrate the type of analysis that can be done, we make the general assumption that each array index is a linear function of any number of loop indices. Because the index to the one-dimensional version of the array is a linear function of the multidimensional array indices, the functions $f(I)$ and $g(I)$ are linear in the loop indices also:

$$f(I) = a_0 + \sum_{k=1}^{n} a_k i_k,$$

$$g(I) = b_0 + \sum_{k=1}^{n} b_k i_k.$$

In this case, Banerjee has shown the following result.

THEOREM

In the loop nest of Figure 7-3 with one-dimensional array references, if S_q is dependent on S_p caused by the references $A(f(I))$ and $A(g(I))$ then the following two conditions hold.

1. The greatest common divisor, gcd $(a_1, a_2, \ldots, a_n, b_1, b_2, \ldots, b_n)$, divides $b_0 - a_0$, provided the gcd is not zero (which can only happen if all arguments are zero).
2. There exists an l, with $1 \le l \le n$ if $p < q$ but with $1 \le l \le n + 1$ if $p \ge q$, such that

$$-b_l - \sum_{k=1}^{l-1}(a_k - b_k)^- u_k - (a_l^- + b_l)^+(u_l - 1) - \sum_{k=l+1}^{n}(a_k^- + b_k^+)u_k \qquad (7.5)$$

$$\le b_0 - a_0 \le$$

$$-b_l + \sum_{k=1}^{l-1}(a_k - b_k)^+ u_k - (a_l^+ - b_l)^+(u_l - 1) + \sum_{k=l+1}^{n}(a_k^+ + b_k^-)u_k,$$

where $x^+ = \max(x, 0)$ and $x^- = \max(-x, 0)$, and by definition $a_{n+1} = b_{n+1} = u_{n+1} = 0$.

PROOF

See reference [35]. Condition (1) must hold if the Diophantine equation $f(\kappa) = g(\lambda)$ is to hold for any two points κ and λ in the unbounded n-dimensional space of integers. It is, thus, a necessary condition but does not take the loop bounds into account. Condition (2) holds if there is a solution for real κ and λ within the bounds of the loops. It does not mean that there is a solution for integer values of κ and λ. Thus, condition (2) is also necessary but not sufficient. ∎

To understand the application of Banerjee's result, let us specialize it to the case of a single loop and array indices linear in the loop index

```
        do i = L, U
S₁:         A(a₁·i + a₀)  = ...
S₂:             ...  = A(b₁·i + b₀) ...
        end do
```

There is a dependence of S_2 on S_1 if there are integer values $L \le \kappa \le \lambda \le U$ such that $a_1\kappa + a_0 = b_1\lambda + b_0$, and there is a dependence of S_1 on S_2 if there are integer values $L \le \kappa < \lambda \le U$ such that $b_1\kappa + b_0 = a_1\lambda + a_0$. Banerjee's result says this cannot happen unless condition (1) of the theorem, called the GCD test, and condition (2) are both satisfied. Violation of either condition proves independence.

The importance of the GCD test is shown by the following loop

```
do i = 1, u
    A(2*i) = A(2*i - 1)*B + C
end do
```

Here we have $f(I) = 2i$ or $a_0 = 0$, $a_1 = 2$ and $g(I) = 2i - 1$ or $b_0 = -1$, $b_1 = 2$. Thus, $\gcd(a_1, b_1) = 2$ but $b_0 - a_0 = -1$, which is not divisible by the GCD. Thus, there is no loop carried dependence. The odd versus even nature of the subscripts is fairly easy to see in this example. It would be harder to see that all $f(I)$ were 1 modulo 7 and all $g(I)$ were 4 modulo 7, but the GCD test would prove independence in that case also.

The GCD test is independent of the loop limits. Violation of the GCD test says that the two array subscripts cannot be equal for any values of i, in the loop range or not. The second condition depends on the range of the loop index and covers some cases in which subscript values could be equal but not within the loop index range. In the example

```
do i = 0, u
    A(i) = A(i + u + 1)
end do
```

we have $a_0 = 0$, $a_1 = 1$, $b_0 = u + 1$, and $b_1 = 1$. With one nested loop, only $l = 1$ is possible in the second Banerjee condition, and for this we get the inequality

$$-b_1 - (u - 1) \le b_0 - a_0 \le -b_1 , \text{ or } -u \le u + 1 \le -1. \qquad (7.6)$$

This condition cannot hold for any nonnegative u, confirming the evident disjointness of the array portions referenced on the left and right hand sides for positive u.

If the loop limits are not known at the time of dependence analysis, then Banerjee's second condition cannot be evaluated and only the GCD test is applicable. In this case the reduction of the problem to the case of a one-dimensional array is not a good idea because, as mentioned above, the reduced problem is not equivalent to the original if array bounds are exceeded. In this case there is a generalized GCD test that determines whether a solution exists for the set of Diophantine linear equations, one for each array dimension. It does so by transforming the set of equations to an easily solved set by a procedure similar to Gaussian elimination. If the transformed equations have no solution in integers, then neither has the original set. The mechanics of the generalized GCD test are described in [36].

Two other general approaches to sharpening the approximate analysis of loop carried dependences are to develop algorithms for the general Diophantine equations (7.2), or to develop algorithms for common cases having restricted forms of array subscripts that are simpler to analyze. An example of the first approach is the Omega test, described in [241]. The second approach is taken, for example, in [122].

7.3 Sample Compiler Techniques

Parallelizing compilers use many techniques to optimize the performance of a program. The most performance gain is obtained from optimizing the most time consuming sections of the code that are normally iterative loops. We have already seen several methods that can be used to test for dependence in counted loops. In this section we focus on some common transformation techniques to optimize counted loops. In restructuring loops, one must consider both the *legality* and the *benefit* of the transformation. The benefits of a transformation are normally tied to the target computer architecture for which the program is being compiled. The legality of a transformation is related to the language semantics and is derived from the data and flow dependence analyses that was discussed in detail in the previous sections.

7.3.1 Loop Transformations

Some optimizations require global data flow information while others need only local information. A multiple statement loop can sometimes be broken into smaller loops so that several of the loops may be executed concurrently. This is referred to as *loop distribution*. The principle of loop distribution can be best described by identifying all of the strongly connected components of the dependence graph corresponding to the original loop and determining the partial ordering that exists between the strongly connected components as described next.

Consider a dependence graph G corresponding to statements $S_1, S_2, ..., S_N$ of a loop L. The graph G is *cyclic* if it contains at least one cycle. A *maximal cycle* is defined to be a cycle that is not a proper subset of any cycle in G. An *isolated point* is a node not belonging to any cycle. A strongly connected component of a dependence graph is called a π-*block* and is either a maximal cycle or the set consisting of an isolated point. The π-*block*s partition the loop statements into disjoint subsets with a partial ordering that represents the existence of any dependence between the blocks. The following example illustrates the loop distribution transformation using π-block analysis. The dependence graph corresponding to the loop is shown in Figure 7-6.

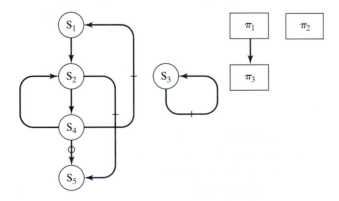

Figure 7-6   Data dependence graph and corresponding π partition.

```
          do i = 0, u
S₁:            A(i)   = G(i)+2*Z
S₂:            B(i+1) = A(i)/C(i+2)
S₃:            L(i)   = L(i+3) + 2*L(i+1)
S₄:            C(i+5) = B(i)*A(i+1)
S₅:            C(i+2) = G(i+1) + X
          end do
```

There are two maximal cycles $\{S_1, S_2, S_4\}$ and $\{S_3\}$ in the graph G, and there are three π-blocks $\pi_1 = \{S_1, S_2, S_4\}$, $\pi_2 = \{S_3\}$, and $\pi_3 = \{S_5\}$. $\{S_5\}$ is the isolated node. Figure 7-6 also shows the partial ordering that exists between the π-blocks. This graph indicates that the above loop can be distributed over three loops each corresponding to one of the π-blocks. Loops corresponding to π_1 and π_2 can be executed concurrently, but the loop corresponding to π_3 can only be executed after the execution of π_1 is complete.

The distribution of the above loop becomes

```
          do i = 0, u
S₁:            A(i)   = G(i)+2*Z
S₂:            B(i+1) = A(i)/C(i+2)
S₄:            C(i+5) = B(i)*A(i+1)
          end do
          do i = 0, u
S₃:            L(i)   = L(i+3) + 2*L(i+1)
          end do
          do i = 0, u
S₅:            C(i+2) = G(i+1) + X
          end do
```

Loop distribution, also referred to as *loop fission*, can improve the locality of references by referencing all of the elements of an array that are accessed in one of the distributed loops before executing the next distributed loop. In a machine with a small instruction cache, loop distribution can be used to break up a large loop, that does not fit in the cache, into several smaller loops that do.

Loop fusion is the transformation that is dual to loop distribution. Loop fusion is used to reduce the overhead and start-up cost of loops. More significantly, it is beneficial in reducing the memory to register traffic in register to register machines when fused loops can share references to variables or when the individual loops are small and do not reference enough variables to take advantage of the available machine registers. Care must be taken in compilers that perform both loop distribution and fusion so that loop fusion is not performed on loops created by the distribution transformation. The following two loops

```
          do i = 1, u
S₁:            A(i) = A(i) + B(i)
          end do
          do i = 1, u
S₂:            C(i) = A(i-1)
          end do
```

can be fused into a single loop because the dependence relation $S_1 \delta S_2$ is not violated by the fusion.

```
        do i = 1, u
S₁:           A(i) = A(i) + B(i)
S₂:           C(i) = A(i-1)
        end do
```

If S_2 had referred to A(i + 1) instead of A(i − 1), the transformation would not have been correct. In this case however, a *loop reversal* transformation followed by loop fusion would yield the desired form. Loop reversal changes the direction in which loop iteration is traversed.

```
        do i = u-1, 0
S₁:           A(i) = A(i) + B(i)
S₂:           C(i) = A(i+1)
        end do
```

Loop reversal of a loop with independent body instances is always legal because they are independent of the order of the index range. Loop reversal is legal when the loop carries no dependence relation. We call such loops doalls instead of foralls in this chapter to emphasize the restricted Fortran like nature of the loops considered.

One of the most important loop transformations is *loop interchanging*. Loop interchange can be applied to nested loops by switching the inner and the outer loop positions provided that the transformation does not violate any data dependence relation. This transformation was initially developed to help in automatic detection of parallelism in sequential programs. Loop interchange is now used as a powerful optimization technique to improve the performance of a program in several ways. Interchanging an outer loop that iterates many times with an inner loop that has only few iterations results in a significant reduction in the start-up overhead of the inner loop. It can be used to increase the number of loop-invariant expressions in the newly formed inner loop. Interchange can also be used to change the stride of array accesses in the inner loop. In the following code

```
    do i = 1, u
        do j = 1, u
            A(i) = A(i) + 2*B(i,j)
        end do
    end do
```

array *B* is being accessed with stride *u* if *B* is stored with the Fortran convention of column-major order. Interchanging the two loops results in stride-1 access to *B* and the possibility of parallelizing the inner loop.

```
do j = 1, u
    do i = 1, u
        A(i) = A(i) + 2*B(i,j)
    end do
end do
```

In computers with caches, when B is large and one column of B does not fit in the cache, this optimization reduces the cache misses significantly. However, one must note that in the original loop, $A(i)$ would have remained in a register while the computation of the inner loop for each index i was being carried out. In the transformed version, elements of A must be stored and fetched repeatedly. The savings in the cache misses is from u^2 to $u^2 \times \frac{\text{element size}}{\text{line size}}$, while the increase in the number of load/store operations for A is from $2u$ to $2u^2$. Therefore, if array B fits in the cache, the original loop would perform better, provided inner loop parallelization is not required.

Interchanged loops must preserve the original dependence relations. Dependence relations that are loop independent do not prevent the interchange and remain loop independent after the transformation. A dependence relation is said to be *interchange sensitive* if the dependence distance is nonzero in both loops. An interchange-sensitive dependence relation remains the same if the original inner loop has a positive dependence distance or the direction is <. The outer loop must also have a positive dependence distance or < direction. Remember that the original outer loop carried the interchange sensitive dependence. Therefore, loop interchange only violates dependence relations with direction vector of (<,>).

7.3.2   Loop Restructuring

Loop restructuring refers to those transformations that leave the computations performed by a loop iteration and their relative order unchanged but change the structure of the loop.

Loop unrolling is an important example of loop restructuring. It replicates the body of the original loop r times, called the *unrolling factor*, and changes the step size by r. The example below shows how loop unrolling can be used to improve the locality of references in terms of register, cache, or translation lookaside buffer (TLB) accesses, improve instruction level parallelism, and further reduce the loop overhead cost.

```
do i = 1, u                          do i = 1, u-1, 2
    X(i) = X(i-1) + X(i+1)               X(i) = X(i-1) + X(i+1)
end do                                   X(i+1) = X(i) + X(i+2)
                                     end do
                                     if (mod(u, 2) = 1) then
                                         X(u) = X(u-1) + X(u+1)
                                     end if
```

Loop collapsing is intended to improve the performance by increasing the effective length of vector operations in vector computers. It transforms two nested loops into a single loop of a larger range. Therefore,

```
do i = 1, u₁
      do j = 1, u₁
            A(i,j) = B(i,j) + C(i,j)
      end do
end do
```

transforms into

```
do ij= 1, u₁**2
      A(ij) = B(ij) + C(ij)
end do
```

The array declarations for A, B, and C must be changed accordingly. On parallel computers where only a single level of doall loops is supported, loop collapsing can be used to generate the maximum amount of parallelism. When the loop limits do not match the array limit or when the strides are not constant, nested loops can still be coalesced. *Loop coalescing* may incur some overhead due to some extra computation within the body of the loop and, therefore, its advantage must be carefully weighed. The following nested loop

```
do i = k₁, u₁
      do j = k₂, u₂
            A(i,j) = B(i,j) + C(i,j)
      end do
end do
```

can be coalesced into one loop by calculating the i and j indices within the body as follows:

```
h₁ = u₁ - k₁ + 1
h₂ = u₂ - k₂ + 1
do ij = 0, h₁*h₂ -1
      i = ij/h₂ + k₁
      j = mod(ij, h₂) + k₂
      A(i,j) = B(i,j) + C(i,j)
end do
```

Sometimes moving one or more of the first or last iterations of the loop into separate code sections can result in a highly parallel loop, which otherwise could not have been detected. A first glance at the following example where array B is referenced in a circular fashion using the i and j indices, suggests that the code must be executed sequentially to ensure correctness.

```
    j = u
    do i = 1, u
          A(i) = 2*B(i) + B(j)/3
          j = i
    end do
```

However, by *peeling* off the first iteration of the loop we can remove the dependences:

```
    if (u ≥ 1) then
          A(1) =  2*B(1) + B(u)/3
          do i = 2, u
                A(i) = 2*B(i) + B(i-1)/3
          end do
    end if
```

Loop spreading is used to move some computations from one sequential loop into another one so that they can both be executed in parallel. The two sequential loops below cannot be fused because there is a data dependence between statements S_1 and S_2.

```
          do i = 1, u/4
S₁:             A(i) = A(i) + A(i+1)
          end do
          do i = 1, u-2
S₂:             C(i) = C(i+1) + A(i+2)
          end do
```

The first loop can be changed to include S_2 so that both statements can be executed in parallel. After spreading is applied the following two loops can be done concurrently:

```
          do i = 1, u/4
S₁:             A(i) = A(i) + A(i+1)
                if (i > 2) then
S'₂:                  C(i-2) = C(i-1) + A(i)
                end if
          end do
          do i = u/4-1, u-2
S₂:             C(i) = C(i+1) + A(i+2)
          end do
```

7.3.3   Loop Replacement Transformations

Transformations that operate on an entire loop and completely change its structure are known as *loop replacement transformations*. One of the most common replacement transformation is the *reduction* operation. Reduction reduces a vector of values to a scalar value as the result of some operation such as maximum, minimum, summation, etc. While a loop performing a reduction operation contains dependences that must normally be executed sequentially, it can be parallelized if the operation being performed is associative and commutative. The sequential loop to find the maximum element of the array *A*

```
amax = 0.0
do i = 1, u
      if (A(i) > amax) then
            amax = A(i)
      end if
end do
```

can be transformed into the following:

```
shared amax, u, P
private pmax, i, ip
pmax = 0.0
do i = ip, u, P
      if (A(i) > pmax) then
            pmax = A(i)
      end if
end do
critical
      if (pmax > amax) then
            amax = pmax
      end if
end critical
```

P is the number of parallel processes executing the parallel code. pmax is a private variable, so every process has its own copy of pmax. amax is the shared maximum. In the do loop, every process with an ip number from 1 to P computes the maximum value of its portion of the array *A*. Finally, all processes compare their private maximum values to compute the shared maximum over the entire array in the critical section code. Some SIMD architectures provide special hardware to perform reduction operations directly in the processor interconnection network. For example, the Connection Machine, CM-2, in addition to hardware reduction, provided hardware support for parallel prefix operations. The dot product is another common reduction operation that compilers can recognize and vectorize. Therefore, the dot product of the vectors *A* and *B*:

```
S = 0.0
do i = 1, u
      S = S + A(i)*B(i)
end do
```

is transformed into the following vector loop assuming a vector register length of *V*.

```
S = 0.0
temp(1:V) = 0.0
do i = 1, u, V
      temp(1:V) = temp(1:V) + A(i:i+V-1)*B(i:i+V-1)
end do
do i = 1, V
      S = S + temp(i)
end do
```

A loop restructuring technique known as *strip mining* is commonly used to set the granularity of a parallel operation and memory management. It is usually selected depending on some characteristics of the target computer system such as the cache size or the length of the vector registers. Strip mining is usually applied after other transformations such as loop distribution and loop interchange have been applied. Strip mining by itself is always legal and is used to decompose a single loop into a nested loop so that the outer loop steps between strips of the desired size. The inner loop iterates within the strips. Most commonly, strip mining is used to choose the number of independent computations in the inner loop. For example, in an SIMD computer with vector registers of size 64, the loop

```
do i = 1, u
      A(i) = 2*A(i)
end do
```

is transformed using strip size of 64 to the following nested loop:

```
do j = 1, u, 64
      do i = j, min(j+63, u)
            A(i) = 2*A(i)
      end do
end do
```

A multidimensional generalization of strip mining is *loop tiling*. Tiling or blocking is used to improve locality of data in cache, processor, register, TLB, or a page. Matrix transpose is a good example to illustrate the need for tiling:

```
do i = 1, u
      do j = 1, u
            A(i,j) = B(j,i)
      end do
end do
```

In the innermost loop, *B* is being accessed with stride 1 while accesses to A are with stride u. In this case loop interchange does not help. Tiling divides the iteration space into rectangular blocks of size s, which should be chosen based on the characteristics of the target computer system.

```
do it = 1, u, s
    do jt = 1, u, s
        do i = it, min(it+s-1, u)
            do j = jt, min(jt+s-1, u)
                A(i,j) = B(j,i)
            end do
        end do
    end do
end do
```

After tiling, the pair of outer loops or the pair of inner loops may be interchanged to improve locality across tiles or to improve parallelism and register locality. The legality of interchanging the tiled loops is the same as that described for the loop interchange transformation earlier.

Parallelizing one or both of the outer loops results in a specific processor working on one or more $s \times s$ blocks of A and B. In nonuniform memory access multiprocessors, tiling can result in great performance improvements by distributing the blocks of data to memories closest to processors that need to access them.

7.3.4   Anti- and Output Dependence Removal Transformations

Data dependence testing procedures are helpful in detecting the existence of data dependence in the code. However, some of the data dependence can be detected and removed from the data-dependence graphs to enhance the potential for parallelism. Antidependence and output-dependence relations can be removed from the code by simply using extra temporary variables where a conflict is detected. Compilers perform this transformation, *scalar renaming*, whenever possible by generating compiler temporary variables. For example, to remove the output dependence with respect to X and the antidependence with respect to Y in the following code the new variables temp1 and temp2 are introduced:

S_1:	X = 2*Y + 3*A		S_1:	temp1 = 2*Y + 3*A
S_2:	Y = A + B*C		S_2:	temp2 = A + B*C
S_3:	X = B + 2* Y		S_3:	X = B + 2* temp2

The forward dependence between statements S_2 and S_3, however, cannot be removed. These dependence relations can also be detected in several other forms and removed to enhance the potential for parallelism. *Scalar expansion*, *constant* and *copy propagation*, *forward substitution* and *induction variable substitution* are some of the most common techniques to remove some existing dependences from the code to enhance parallelism.

Scalars that are assigned and later used in a loop introduce not only a flow dependence in the dependence graph but also introduce a loop-carried antidependence relation from each use of the scalar back to its assignment. *Scalar expansion* or *promotion* is used to break the antidependence by replacing the scalar with a compiler generated array with one element for each loop iteration. Therefore, scalar z in the loop

```
do i = 1, u
      Z = B(i) + 2*C(i)
      A(i) = 2*Z + 1/Z
end do
```

is replaced with a temporary array so that each loop statement can be vectorized:

```
do i = 1, u
      ZT(i) = B(i) + 2*C(i)
      A(i) = 2*ZT(i) + 1/ZT(i)
end do
```

In multiprocessors Z in the first loop would be declared as a private scalar. This is also known as *array contraction* where an array that is assigned and used with no loop carried dependences, and not used after the loop, is replaced with *privatized* scalars. This is beneficial in reducing the amount of storage used by temporary arrays and when loop fusion has resulted in the removal of the need to save all of the array elements across the fused loops.

Constants are normally used freely and in abundance by most programmers. *Constant propagation* is an important compiler optimization. Compilers can perform a significant amount of precomputation by propagating the constant values throughout the program. In addition to optimizations common to all compilers such as dead-code elimination, loop optimizations are affected by constants that appear in loop induction ranges. Loops can be optimized best when the loop range is known. In the following example, the value of the upper loop limit, u, can be derived from its constant definition prior to its use:

```
       u = 32
       up = u + 1
       C = 4
       do i = 1, u
S₁:          B(i) = B(i) + 2*C
S₂:          A(up) = A(i) + C*A(up)
       end do
```

An optimizing compiler would perform *constant propagation* by replacing 32 for u in the loop limit and 4 for C in S_2. It would perform *constant folding* by computing 8 for $2*C$ in S_1. The compiler would also perform *forward substitution* by replacing up in S_2 with 33 and distribute the do loop into two loops, one containing statement S_1 and the other containing S_2:

```
       do i = 1, 32
S₁:          B(i) = B(i) + 8
       end do
       do i = 1, 32
S₂:          A(33) = A(i) + 4*A(33)
       end do
```

In the new form, the first loop can clearly be vectorized, while without the constant propagation it had to be strip mined. The constant folding has resulted in improved execution time because the multiplication is no longer performed for each loop iteration. In the second loop, it is obvious that the forward substitution of up with 33 has clarified the dependence relations between the array element A(i) and A(up) being accessed in the loop. The compiler can recognize the second loop as a reduction operation and implement it as a parallel reduction.

An *induction variable* is a scalar that has its value incremented by some constant on each iteration of a loop. Induction variables are often used in array subscript expressions. In most compilers, it is a common optimization technique to find induction variables and remove them from the loops and to optimize array address calculations when they are used in subscript expressions. For data dependence tests, it is important to find the induction variables because the array subscripts must be known as a function of the loop index variables. By substituting a linear function of the index variable for the right-hand side of an induction variable statement, dependence testing is simplified without increasing the execution time. Most compilers recognize that next and last are induction variables in the loop:

```
last = u
do i = 1, u
      next = 3*i - 2
      A(last) = B(next) + C(i)
      last = last -1
end do
```

and transform the loop into:

```
do i = 1, u
      A(u-i+1) = B(3*i-2) + C(i)
end do
```

The two loops above are equivalent if the last values of last and next are not used later in the program. The induction variable substitution is the inverse of *strength reduction* where a more expensive operator such as multiplication is replaced with a less expensive but equivalent operator such as addition. Reduction in strength may be used for architectures where multiplication is slower than addition and the linear recurrence that is generated can be evaluated serially with no performance penalty. Most pipelined processors, however, take advantage of sophisticated memory interface hardware indexing for efficient access.

7.4 Data Flow Principles

A set of concepts for specifying computations without saying anything about scheduling operations or allocating storage to data has been developed under the name of *data flow*. Some have said that data flow programs are inherently parallel, but that is not accurate. Such representations of a computation simply do not specify any control flow or other constraint on the order of operation beyond what is inherent in the flow dependences among the data. In this sense, data flow is parallelism neutral. A computation specified in a data flow representation allows the implementation to use as much or as little parallelism in its execution as desired. Data flow ideas have led to the construction of data flow computers and data flow languages to be executed on computers of other types, but it is probably the concepts themselves that are most important to the study of parallel processing. The removal of artificial sequentiality in the specification of a computation can reveal opportunities for parallel implementation that might be masked by a sequential representation.

7.4.1 Data Flow Concepts

One way to look at data flow is that it eliminates output and antidependences by restricting attention to *values* and not considering where the values are stored. No data flow representation of a computation specifies locations of values in any memory. It is, therefore, impossible to talk about the wrong order of overwriting one value by another that could result from output dependence or the overwriting of a value before it is used that is the problem in antidependence. Because storage is not represented in the data flow program that specifies the computation, all storage management is left to the system that implements the data flow computation. The implementation may assign more than one value to a storage location, but it must be done so that the result is the same as if the two values were stored in different locations.

Thus, in a data flow language for a serial or parallel machine, the entire burden of placing values in storage is shifted from the user to the compiler. The size of this burden can be appreciated by considering Gaussian elimination. A large part of the structure of that algorithm is concerned with updating a matrix in place and cleverly overwriting its upper and lower triangles with the results of the elimination. Several variants of Gaussian elimination important to numerical analysts differ only in their storage management aspects.

Another aspect of a data flow representation is that it does not explicitly schedule operations at particular times or in any particular order. Of course the flow of data among operations specifies that some operations must be performed before or after others, and any particular implementation must schedule operations in a way consistent with the data flow constraints, but this is the only restriction on scheduling. These restrictions can be summed up by saying that there is no flow of control in a data flow representation of a computation. Control sequencing is a property of the implementation used to achieve performance within the constraints of the data flow specified order of operations.

A data flow program consists of three parts

1. A collection of input values;
2. A set of operations, partially ordered by flow dependences;
3. One or more results.

The results are simply functions of the inputs. Because there is no concept of storage location, a program cannot have a change in some stored data structure as an outcome. For this reason, data flow languages are *functional languages*, where a program can have no *side effects* apart from computing its results as functions of its inputs. Thus, a data flow program could not solve the linear equations $Ax = b$ and as a side effect replace A by its LU decomposition. It could solve the equations and return both x and LU as results.

In summary, some of the features that distinguish a data flow program from one written in a procedural language are

1. There is no flow of control in a data flow program;
2. There are no named storage locations;
3. Programs have no side effects;
4. The only type of procedure or program is the function.

One could say that the main thing missing in data flow is the idea of stored state. Because there is no named storage, no state can be referred to, and because procedures have no side effects, the state cannot be modified. Finally, because there is no control flow, there can be no concept of *current* state.

Names are still important in data flow, even though they cannot name storage locations. Names in data flow refer to values. If x and y are input values and the output value of a function is described by

$$F = (x*(x + y) - (x + y)/y)/(x*(x + y)*(x + y)), \tag{7.7}$$

then F names the value computed from the input values x and y. The repeated subexpressions in the function description make intermediate names useful in describing F. This can be done in data flow provided that it is understood that the names name values and not locations where values are stored. Some data flow languages handle the introduction of intermediate names by the use of a **let** expression. Using the SISAL 1.2 data flow language, for example, the right hand side of the function F could be written using intermediate names P and Q as

```
let
        P = x + y;
        Q = x*P;
in
        (Q - P/y)/(Q*P)
end let
```

The names P and Q name the values of the subexpressions. A name may only name one value, so it can appear only once on the left hand side of the = assignment symbol. Data flow languages are referred to as *single assignment* languages for this reason.

The name P can be viewed as a connection from the output of the x + y computation to an input of the computation whose output is Q and to two different input points in the final **let** expression result. Names may only appear in expressions following the one in which they are defined. No circularity is allowed.

7.4.2   Graphical Representation of Data Flow Computations

Because only data flow dependences constrain the behavior of data flow computations, the data dependence graph we used informally to describe data flow computations as early as Chapter 1 gives a language-independent form for specifying such a computation. The dependence graphs that we used informally need to be given a more precise form and semantics to yield data flow graphs that accurately describe a computation. Data flow graphs consist of edges, nodes, and tokens. *Tokens* represent values and move over directed edges to be transformed at nodes into other values. Figure 7-7 shows two important types of node, or *actors*. Part (a) shows a dyadic operator and its firing rule as an actor. When value tokens are available on both of its input edges the actor may *fire*, whereby both input tokens are deleted and their values combined by the dyadic operator to produce a new value token on the output edge. Figure 7-7(b) shows the replication actor, or link, which fires by absorbing the token on its single input edge and producing tokens with the same value on each of its output edges. The firing of an actor, consisting of deleting a token from each of its input edges and producing a token on each of its output edges, is atomic with respect to all other firings.

Dyadic operators, replication actors, and edges can be combined into data flow graphs for simple functions. The data flow graph for Equation (7.7) is shown in Figure 7-8. The firing rule for an actor in the graph under the rules of *static data flow*, the simplest version of data flow, is that an actor may fire only if all of its input edges contain tokens and none of its output edges contain tokens. This rule prevents more than one token from occupying an edge at a time.

Relating the graph to the SISAL **let** expression associated with Equation (7.7) in the last section, the output of the + actor could be named P and the output of the leftmost × actor could be named Q. This illustrates that names in a data flow language play the role of connections in a data flow graph.

The graphical format in Figure 7-8(a) can be represented as a linear data structure as shown in Figure 7-8(b). Note that the replication actors are encoded by specifying multiple destinations for the output of a dyadic operator. The firing rule for static data flow allows output values to be immediately written to the dyadic operator inputs constituting their destinations. As shown, the data flow graph represents a function of its two inputs. With specific value tokens at both inputs, it represents a specific computation of a result value. An assignment of value tokens to edges of a data flow graph is called a *marking* of the graph.

The linear memory representation of the data flow graph must have a state associated with each input value location to indicate whether a token has arrived or not. It is also useful to be able to mark an input as constant. This could be used, for example, to turn a two-input add actor into a one-input actor that increments by three (+3). Arrived and constant markings and the corresponding graphical symbols are shown in Figure 7-9(a) and (b), respectively.

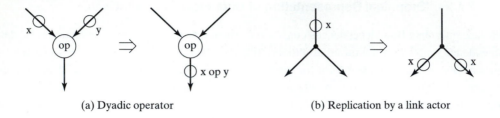

(a) Dyadic operator   (b) Replication by a link actor

Figure 7-7   Elementary data flow actors and their behavior.

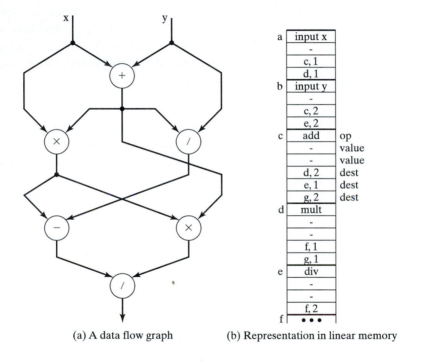

a	input x	
	-	
	c, 1	
	d, 1	
b	input y	
	-	
	c, 2	
	e, 2	
c	add	op
	-	value
	-	value
	d, 2	dest
	e, 1	dest
	g, 2	dest
d	mult	
	-	
	-	
	f, 1	
	g, 1	
e	div	
	-	
	-	
	f, 2	
f	• • •	

(a) A data flow graph   (b) Representation in linear memory

Figure 7-8   A data flow graph and its representation.

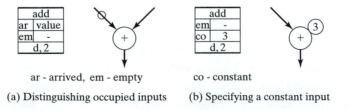

ar - arrived, em - empty   co - constant

(a) Distinguishing occupied inputs   (b) Specifying a constant input

Figure 7-9   Input state markings and graphical equivalents.

7.4.3   Data Flow Conditionals

Because there is no flow of control in a data flow program, there can be no conditional branch. As in SIMD operation, data-dependent conditionals must be handled by conditional values instead of conditional control transfer. Figure 7-10 shows some actors that can be used to support conditional computation. Figure 7-10(a) is a predicate that accepts numeric inputs, compares them, and outputs a Boolean token with a value of **true** or **false** representing the outcome of the comparison. Using open arrowheads for Boolean inputs and open circles for replication of Boolean values improves the readability of a data flow graph by making its control structure evident. Figure 7-10(b) introduces the concept and representation for a *sink* actor that absorbs any token at its input and produces no output. This concept is used in the *true* and *false* actors of Figure 7-10(c) that accept a Boolean input and another input of any type. Each behaves as a sink if the token on the Boolean input does not match the actor's name and copies the non-Boolean input token to the output if actor name and Boolean input do match. Finally, Figure 7-10(d) shows an elementary *merge* operator that requires a token on only one of its inputs to fire, copying that token to the output. It can only be used in a data flow graph that guarantees only one of its inputs have a token at a time. This form of merge is nondeterministic in the sense that the choice of which input to absorb depends on the order of arrival of input tokens.

The elementary actors of Figure 7-10 can be combined into the somewhat higher level conditional operations of Figure 7-11. The *multiplex* operation of Figure 7-11(a) outputs the token on the input corresponding to the Boolean control value and discards the token at the other input. The multiplex actor requires tokens on all three inputs to fire. An alternative form of conditional only requires tokens on the Boolean input and the selected input. We call such an actor a select actor and use the same symbol shape as for multiplex. The *switch* actor of Figure 7-11(b) routes its single input to the T or F output according as its Boolean input token is true or false, respectively.

Note that several of the conditional actors modify the simple firing rule that an actor may fire only if there are tokens on all of its inputs; it deletes a token from each input and places tokens on each output. The merge, true, false, and switch actors either consume tokens on only some of the inputs or produce them only on some outputs, depending on the value of some input token. Constraining actors to obey the simple firing rule can make it easier to show that the computation performed by a data flow diagram is deterministic, that is, independent of the order in which actors fire. The practical expressive power of the conditional actors is great enough, however, that almost all data flow treatments allow them.

The conditional actors can be used to represent the data flow computation of the conditional expression for an output y in terms of an input x. A data flow graph for the SISAL 1.2 conditional expression

$$y := 4*(\textbf{if } x > 3 \textbf{ then } x + 2 \textbf{ else } x - 1 \textbf{ end if})$$

is shown in Figure 7-12. Two representations are shown. The one in part (a) uses the simplified merge because the semantics of the switch actor guarantee that only one merge input can have a token at a time. Part (b) does both computations and uses the multiplex actor to select the correct value.

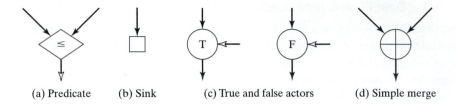

(a) Predicate   (b) Sink   (c) True and false actors   (d) Simple merge

Figure 7-10   Some elementary actors associated with conditionals.

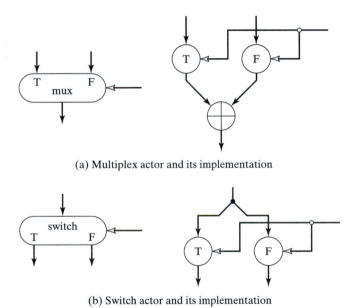

(a) Multiplex actor and its implementation

(b) Switch actor and its implementation

Figure 7-11   Higher level conditional actors.

Because operation scheduling is not specified by a data flow program but is left to the system that interprets it, the interpreter may choose to fire an actor as soon as tokens are available at its inputs. This corresponds to *data driven* evaluation. It is also possible to delay scheduling an operation until its result is needed. This results in a *demand driven* evaluation order. The conditional computation version of Figure 7-12(a) would be preferred for data driven scheduling and that of Figure 7-12(b) for demand driven scheduling. Information is available from the high-level merge operation in Figure 7-12(b) about which of its inputs is demanded, while the switch of Figure 7-12(a) sends data to only one of its outputs so that only one of the + and − actors fires under data driven scheduling. Replacing the merge actor of in Figure 7-12(a) by a select actor whose Boolean input is a copy of that going to the switch results in a diagram that is equally suited to data driven or demand driven execution. An extensive discussion of data driven and demand driven evaluation is beyond the scope of this text.

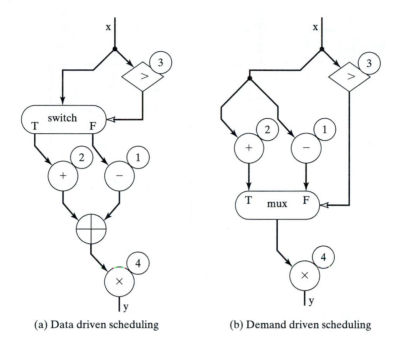

(a) Data driven scheduling   (b) Demand driven scheduling

Figure 7-12 Data flow diagrams for a conditional expression.

7.4.4 Data Flow Iteration

With conditional operations, cycles in data flow graphs can be used to express iteration. Because the cycles are based on flow dependences, they represent true iterations that cannot be trivially transformed into doalls. An example is the data flow diagram of Figure 7-13 representing the iteration

```
f := a;
for i := 0 step 1 until n - 1
      f:= 1 + 1/(i + f);
```

where n is a constant.

Because this diagram is for a counted loop, it exhibits two fairly independent parts, one for the index generation and the other for the loop body computation. They are connected by two edges, one of which carries a stream of Boolean control tokens and the other carrying successive values of the loop index. This partitioning would not be evident in a **while** or **until** loop with termination based on some aspect of the loop body computation. The data flow graph of Figure 7-14 represents the loop

```
do x := f(x) until p(x);
```

for some function $f(\cdot)$ and predicate $p(\cdot)$.

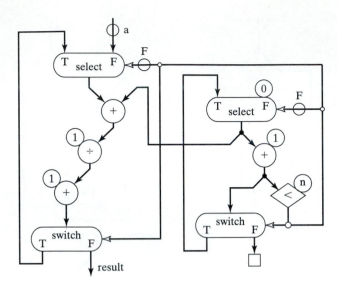

Figure 7-13   Data flow graph for a counted loop.

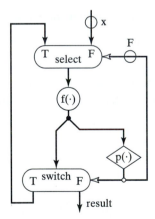

Figure 7-14   Skeleton of a **do until** loop as a data flow graph.

Note that the control inputs to the select actors at the top of Figures 7-13 and Figure 7-14 initially contain false tokens. The last test, for which the index value is n or the predicate is false, restores these two control tokens so that the computation can be restarted when the next token arrives on the input. With the restriction that the final marking of the graph is the same as its initial marking, the iteration has no saved state, and, thus, the result is a side-effect-free function of the input. The side effect freedom of a data flow graph is an important characteristic. It holds trivially for unmarked graphs without cycles.

In a data flow language, graph edges that are not implicitly specified by the structure of an expression are represented by naming values and using those names in other expressions. In addition to the feed-forward, expression to expression connections already illustrated by the **let** statement, names in loops specify two additional kinds of connections:

1. They specify the feedback loops that connect an output of one instance of the loop body to one or more inputs of the next instance.
2. They are the basis for specifying the result of the iteration.

SISAL 1.2 has a sequential **for** construct that can be used to express the counted loop of Figure 7-13 as

```
for initial
        f := a;
        i := 0;
    repeat
        f := 1 + 1/(old i + old f);
        i := old i + 1;
    until
        i = n
    returns
        value of f
end for
```

The keyword **old** in front of a value name specifies the value computed in the previous loop body instance, or in the **initial** section if this is the first instance. The first line of the loop body, following the **repeat** keyword, defines f in terms of **old** f and represents the loop on the left side of the Figure 7-13 graph. In the **returns** clause, **value of** f specifies that the result of the iteration is the last value computed for f. This result is treated in the SISAL language as the value of the **for** construct, which is just a type of expression.

7.4.5   Data Flow Function Application and Recursion

Because properly formed data flow graphs are free of side effects, their overall operation should result in absorbing tokens from the graph inputs and producing on the outputs result tokens that are memoryless functions of the input tokens. This is essentially the operation of a data flow actor. Thus, a function corresponding to a nontrivial data flow graph, such as in Figure 7-13, may be represented in a data flow graph that uses it by an actor with the corresponding number of inputs and outputs. For example, the function $f(\cdot)$ in Figure 7-14 might actually be the one input, one output function of Figure 7-13. The firing of the $f(\cdot)$ actor then represents the application of the function of Figure 7-13 to a token on its input.

In many cases it is useful to be able to apply a variable function. We have seen that a function can be represented by a data flow graph or its representation in a linear memory. A function can, thus, be viewed as a data item with complex structure. As a data item, it can be represented by a token in a data flow graph and serve as input to an actor that applies the function to other inputs of the actor. The role of the apply actor shown in Figure 7-15 is to copy its inputs (other than the function input) to the inputs of the function token and copy the function's outputs to the outputs of the apply actor. Data flow languages use the standard mechanism of a parenthesized list of actual parameters following the function name in its invocation to correspond to the parenthesized list of formal parameters in its definition.

If one of the inputs to the function (and the apply actor) is a copy of the function token being applied, then recursion can be expressed. Recursion can be used as an alternative to iteration expressed by cycles in a data flow graph. The recursive factorial function of Figure 7-16 is free of cycles, while an iterative factorial would require them.

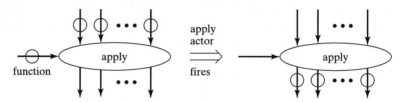

Figure 7-15   Representation of a data flow apply actor.

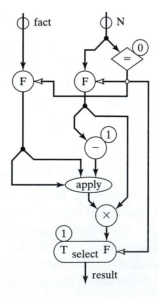

Figure 7-16   Data flow graph for a recursive factorial function.

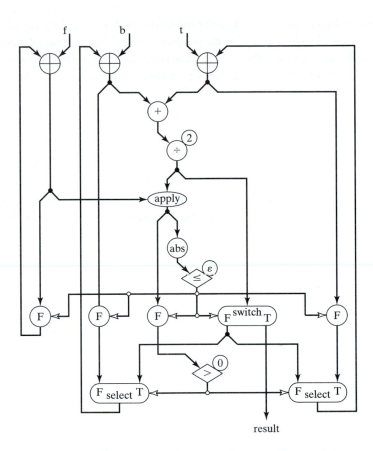

Figure 7-17   Data flow diagram for finding a root of a variable function.

As a substantive example involving many of the concepts introduced, we design a data flow implementation of the algorithm that finds the root of a function by binary chopping. A sequential pseudocode function to do this computation would appear as

```
function chop(function: f; real: b,t)
     repeat    begin
                    m := (b + t)/2;
                    if f(m) > 0 then b := m
                                   else t := m;
           end
        until abs(f(m)) ≤ ε;
  end function;
```

Here f is an arbitrary real function of a real argument, $b < t$, and it is guaranteed that $f(b) > 0$ and $f(t) < 0$. The function abs($\cdot$) takes the absolute value, and ε is assumed to be a constant.

The data flow graph for the function chop is shown in Figure 7-17. The four false gates and the switch in a row across the diagram are all controlled by the abs($f(m)) \leq \varepsilon$ test and determine whether tokens are fed back to the top of the diagram to repeat the loop or whether feedback tokens are absorbed and a result produced. Note that the use of nondeterministic merge gates on the inputs means that the diagram only work correctly if no new inputs arrive until a result token has been produced. Removing this restriction is left as a problem for the reader.

7.4.6   Structured Values in Data Flow—Arrays

The discussion of variable function application introduced the idea that a token may have complex structure. A function token can only serve as input to an apply actor or another function and is treated as a single unit. Another set of issues arise for tokens representing structured data such as records or arrays, where access to individual components of the structure is important. A token representing a structured value not only carries the values of its components but also information about the structure itself. For records, this may be the number and structure of fields, and for arrays, it is the number of dimensions and their extent. We focus the discussion on arrays, remembering that records and other structures present similar problems.

The elements of an array may need to be individually read or produced one at a time in a computation partially serialized by dependences. In the case of element-by-element computation of an array, the semantics of data flow must be preserved. In particular, the single assignment property must hold. An array representing a previous array with one element changed must behave as a new array token with all elements but one equal to those of a previous array token. A naive implementation of a data flow computation could achieve correct semantics whenever a single element is added or changed by copying all other elements of the previous array token and including the new one. The problem with this approach, of course, is poor performance resulting from excess copying in the case of large arrays. Copying is not necessary. Any implementation that behaves as if it uses copying is correct. For example, an array equal to another with an added element could be represented by the new element, its index, and a pointer to the other array token. The problem is essentially that of storage management, which is left entirely to the implementation because data flow programs cannot represent memory cells. A good implementation of data flow arrays must efficiently support incremental changes to arrays and identify array tokens that can no longer be accessed so that their storage space can be reclaimed.

Another issue is parallel access to multiple components of a structured value so they can be operated on in parallel. Of course, data flow does not specify parallel operation but only the absence of any flow dependences that would force sequentiality. For arrays, much of the problem of parallel access can be addressed by extending primitive actors. An addition actor could be defined to accept two arrays of the same dimension and add them elementwise to produce an output array of the same dimension. An indexing actor that takes a vector token on one input and a vector of integer indices on the other could output a vector of values of the first token at positions indicated by the second.

We use arrays to give some examples of data flow computation with structured values. A minimal set of actors to deal with one dimensional arrays, or vectors, is shown in Figure 7-18. The *create* actor of Figure 7-18(a) outputs a vector with one element at index position zero. The *extend* actor of Figure 7-18(b) outputs a vector identical to its input vector but with one more element at the first index past the upper limit of the input vector. The *index* actor of Figure 7-18(c) returns the value of the vector element at an integer index position, and the *replace* actor of Figure 7-18(d) returns a vector identical to its input vector except that the value at the specified index position is replaced by the input scalar. The *limh* actor of Figure 7-18(e) outputs the index value of the last element of its array input. For simplicity, we will assume that the first element always has index zero, so limh is also the array size minus one. The primitive actors of Figure 7-18 are also sufficient to handle multidimensional arrays if a d-dimensional array is treated as a one-dimensional array with elements of type $d - 1$ dimensional array.

In SISAL, the indexing operation is simply represented by A[i], where A is an array and i an integer index. The replace operation A[i:v] produces an array identical to A but with the ith element replaced by the value v. Create and extend operations are also available in SISAL, but arrays are more often created in the **returns** clause of a **for** iteration. If v is a value defined in the iteration body of a for construct, a **returns array of** v clause makes the value of the **for** construct a one-dimensional array consisting of all the values of v defined by the iteration. SISAL is a language that builds multidimensional arrays as one-dimensional arrays of lower dimensional arrays, so a one-dimensional **array of** construct is sufficient. The **for** construct has two forms, one with inherently sequential and the other with inherently parallel semantics. Either form can return an array.

The dot product of two n + 1 element vectors can be represented by the data flow graph of Figure 7-19. The top left portion of the diagram produces indices running from n down to zero. The top center and top right portions produce $n + 1$ copies of the input vectors so that individual elements can be selected from them by indexing. The lower part of the diagram is an iteration that sums the products of corresponding pairs of vector elements. The SISAL code for Figure 7-19 uses the sequential **for**, the limh($\cdot$) operation and indexing.

```
for initial
        i := limh(v);
        d := 0;
    repeat
        d := old d + v[old i]*w[old i];
        i := old i + 1;
    until
        i < 0
    returns
        value of d
end for
```

It is clear that the data flow graph of Figure 7-19 contains much artificial sequentialization of operations. The element by element sequentiality might be required in some computations but is certainly unnecessary for the dot product. If the upper bound n is a constant, a parallel data flow graph for the dot product can be represented as in Figure 7-20. The ellipsis symbols (…) indicate that the complete graph cannot be drawn without knowing the value of n. The value of n also determines the shape of the summation tree, which must be performed differently depending on the relation between n and the next power of two.

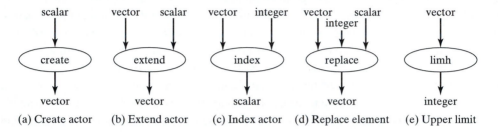

Figure 7-18   A set of actors to manipulate vectors by component.

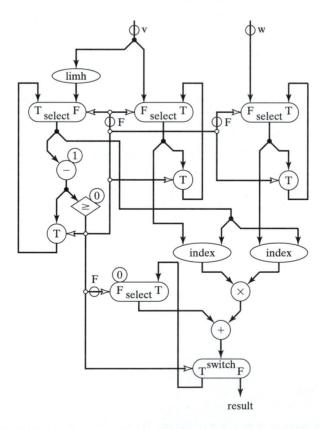

Figure 7-19   Iterative version of dot product as a data flow graph.

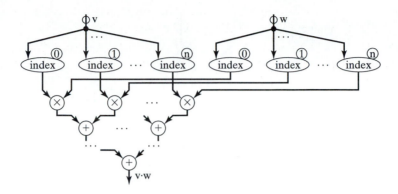

Figure 7-20 Parallel data flow graph for the dot product.

The parallel version of the **for** construct in SISAL 1.2 is called the product form and is used to express iteration without artificial sequentiality. A product form **for** that computes the dot product is

```
for i in 0, n
        d := v[i]*w[i];
    returns
        sum of d
end for
```

The pair $0, n$ represents an integer range vector starting at 0 and ending with n. The scalar d is defined for each index in this range, and the **returns** clause uses the **sum of** operation to add up the d values.

Another way of eliminating artificial sequentiality in array computation is to extend the low-level primitive actors. The two operand arithmetic actors, $+$, $-$, $\times$, and $\div$, can easily be extended to do element-wise arithmetic on conforming vector tokens at their inputs. If one input is a scalar and the other a vector, the scalar is replicated and combined with each vector element. New primitive actors for arrays can also be defined. For dot product, sum reduction is clearly indicated. We borrow APL notation and label the sum reduction actor $+/$. With the new primitives, the dot product takes on the simple form of Figure 7-21, and the question of parallel versus serial operation is left to the implementation.

The closest SISAL equivalent for Figure 7-21 eliminates the artificial index value i and uses the **dot** combination of two sets of values in a **for** list to indicate that each value of one set is to be paired with the corresponding value of the other. The dot product code then becomes

```
for vv in v dot ww in w
        d := vv*ww;
    returns
        sum of d
end for
```

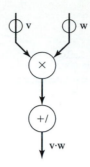

Figure 7-21   Dot product using vector primitive actors.

With the introduction of the reduction actor, a new degree of freedom is given to the data flow implementation. In addition to managing storage and scheduling operations, the implementation may choose between left-to-right, right-to-left, and various forms of tree summation. This algorithm choice does not affect the answer for infinite precision real arithmetic but may influence round off error with finite precision floating point add. Leaving such algorithmic choices to the implementation of a primitive operation may result in better performance, but it does so at the expense of precise user control of the computation.

Some vector primitives are shown in Figure 7-22. The *range* primitive of Figure 7-22(a) is an *index* generator that outputs a vector of integers starting with its left input value and increasing by one to its left input value. The index actor of Figure 7-22(b) extends the semantics of the simple index of Figure 7-18(c) by allowing the index input to be a vector of integers. It outputs a vector consisting of the elements of the input vector at the positions indicated by the integers of the index input. Figure 7-22(c) shows a *concatenation* operator that appends its right input vector to its left input vector to make a vector with size equal to the sum of the sizes of its inputs.

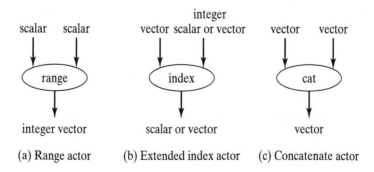

Figure 7-22   Primitive actors dealing with complete vectors.

We can use the vector primitive actors to construct the recursive upper/lower sum prefix algorithm of Figure 7-23. Index range generators and extended index actors extract the upper and lower halves of the input vector. After the prefix function is recursively applied to both halves, the top element of the lower half prefix vector is selected by an index actor having the upper limit of the vector as its scalar index input. The + operator takes a scalar left input and a vector right input to add the last element of the lower prefix vector to all elements of the upper prefix vector. The lower and upper prefix vectors are then concatenated to form the final result. In the case of a one element input vector, having an upper index limit of zero, the output is just the single element input vector, and the input prefix function token is discarded instead of being applied recursively.

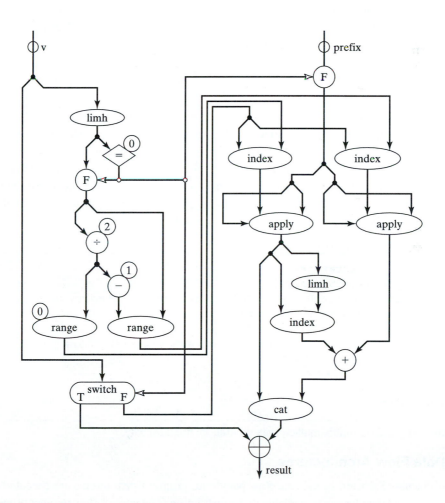

Figure 7-23   Data flow diagram for computing sum prefix by the recursive upper/lower algorithm.

```
        for ⟨in_exp⟩ [cross ⟨in_exp⟩] ...              % Two product form
        for ⟨in_exp⟩ [dot ⟨in_exp⟩] ...               %    for constructs.
             ⟨in_exp⟩ := ⟨int_var⟩ in ⟨int⟩, ⟨int⟩    % Two types of
             ⟨in_exp⟩ := ⟨var⟩ in ⟨array⟩ [at ⟨int_var⟩]  %    in expression.
        returns value of ⟨reduction_op⟩ ⟨exp⟩         % Scalar returned value.
        returns array of ⟨exp⟩                        % Array returned value.
             ⟨reduction_op⟩ := sum|product|greatest|least
        end for
```

Figure 7-24   Product form **for** constructs in SISAL.

The best illustration of SISAL's ability to express an algorithm without artificial sequentiality is probably matrix multiply written using parallel **for** constructs. A **for initial** is a sequential construct; other **for** constructs are parallel and are called product form **for** constructs. The formats of the two types of product form **for** are summarized in Figure 7-24. A complete parallel **for** construct starts with one of the two **for** lines, followed by an optional declaration/definition part (as in the **let** construct), followed by a **returns** line, followed by **end for**.

Using these constructs, matrix multiply can be written as in Program 7-1 where there is no sequentiality in the code itself. The code simply specifies that the dot product be computed for all pairs of i and j in their respective ranges, in any order, and the results assembled into an array. The dot product specifies that all A[i,k]*B[k,j] be evaluated and summed up, in any order. Of course, eliminating sequentiality does not automatically achieve parallelism. It becomes the job of the SISAL implementation to assign and schedule potentially parallel operations on whatever processors or functional units are available.

```
    type OneD = array[real];
    type TwoD = array[OneD];
    function MatMul(A,B: TwoD; M,N,L: integer returns TwoD)
        for i in 1, M cross j in 1, N
            c :=        for k in 1, L
                            returns value of sum A[i,k]*B[k,j];
                        end for
        returns array of c
        end for
    end function
```

Program 7-1   SISAL matrix multiply with no artificial sequentiality.

7.5 Data Flow Architectures

As was discussed earlier, in the data flow paradigm, program instructions are executed (fired) when the needed data becomes available to the instruction. The control flow in other programing paradigms is, therefore, replaced by data flow. The conventional Von Neumann models, where a program counter in the processor is used to address and fetch instructions to be executed from memory, does not fit the data flow paradigm. Mapping the data flow graph concept to an architecture that is capable of executing the represented program leads to the design of a processing element that must receive input data tokens (operands), perform the intended operation upon receipt of the operands, form new result token(s), and send them to the destination actor (instruction) in the graph. The underlying machine architecture is also impacted by the type of data flow representation adopted. In the static data flow approach, only one token is allowed to reside on any one arc. Under static data flow, an actor is enabled as soon as tokens are present on all its input arcs and there is no token on any of the output arcs. The dynamic data flow achieves more flexibility and increased parallelism by allowing multiple tokens to reside on each arc. Tokens belonging to different instances are distinguished by tags associated with each instance of the tokens and their activity. Under dynamic data flow, an actor is enabled as soon as tokens with identical tags are present on all its input arcs. The MIT static data flow architecture and the Manchester data flow machine are two key computer designs for static and dynamic data flow respectively and are described next.

7.5.1 The MIT Static Data Flow Architecture

The fundamental concepts of data flow were originated and developed by Dennis in 1973. His work lead to the development of static data flow architectures and has served as the basis for subsequent development of dynamic data flow. A data flow graph is represented as a collection of activity templates. Each activity template contains an operation code, slots to hold the input operands, and destination address fields for referencing the activity templates that must receive the result values. These fields are the fixed part of each activity template. Receiver fields are the dynamic part of each template. A receiver has a value and a state that may be full or empty. Receivers are used to indicate the firing state of the template.

```
operation code
receiver          state      (full/empty)
                  value
receiver          state      (full/empty)
                  value
destination       template address
                  input
```

Using this concept, the implementation of the data flow graph for the conditional expression of Figure 7-12 is as shown in Figure 7-25. For very simple graphs these fields are enough to support the static firing rules. However, this implementation is not enough to guarantee one token/arc requirement of the static firing rule for graphs containing loops. Acknowledgment fields are added to each activity template that receives token(s) to send replies to the token producing activities reporting the receipt of the input token(s). The graph and implementation of the loop

while X>0 **do** X:= X-1;

is shown in Figure 7-26.

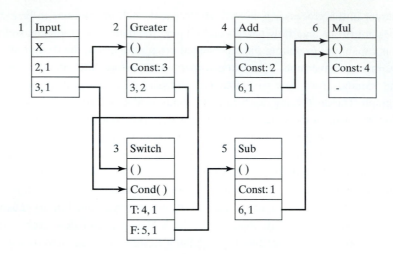

Figure 7-25   Implementation of the data flow graph of Figure 7-12.

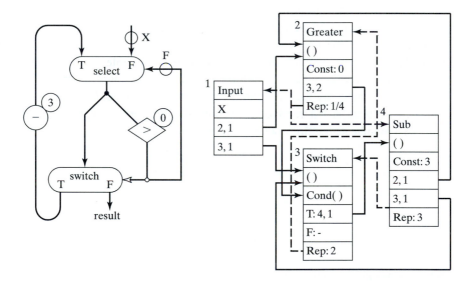

Figure 7-26   Using acknowledge fields in static data flow implementation.

Data flow computers have a pipelined ring structure design. The major components of a typical static data flow computer are shown in Figure 7-27. In general, a data flow program is stored in the activity store as a collection of activity templates of the form described earlier. Each activity template has a unique address. An activity template is ready to be executed when all of its receiver fields are set to full. When an activity template is ready its address is entered in the instruction queue, a FIFO buffer. The fetch unit takes an instruction address from the instruction queue, reads its activity template from the activity store, forms it into an operation packet with data operands and passes it on to the operation unit. The operation unit performs the intended operation on operand values and produces a result packet for each of the destinations specified in the operation packet. The update unit receives the result packets and enters the value they carry into the operand fields of the activity templates specified in the destination address fields of the result packets. The update unit also checks whether all operands and acknowledge packets required to activate the destination instruction have been received, if so it enters the instruction address in the instruction queue. From this architecture, it should be clear that during a program execution, the number of entries in the instruction queue measures the degree of concurrency that is present in the program.

The MIT static data flow architecture, the first of its kind, was pioneered by Dennis. The block diagram of the MIT architecture is presented in Figure 7-28. The memory modules hold the activity templates and their operand values. The processing elements (PEs) perform the operations on the data tokens. The arbitration network, R2, delivers the operation packets from the memory modules to the PEs. The distribution network, R1, delivers the data tokens from the PEs to the memory. A small prototype of the MIT static data flow with four microcoded processors was built.

The addition of acknowledgment arcs to the static data flow to guarantee one token/arc requirement introduces several drawbacks. Not only is the underlying machine architecture more complex to design, but also the acknowledgment signals double the token traffic in the machine. Parallelism is limited to partially overlapping consecutive iterations of a loop as opposed to executing them concurrently even in the absence of loop carried dependencies. The requirement of the acknowledgment signals enforces a pipelining effect in the execution of the loop iterations, where the pipeline length is bounded by the critical path through the loop body. Similar problems exist in the case of subprogram invocations.

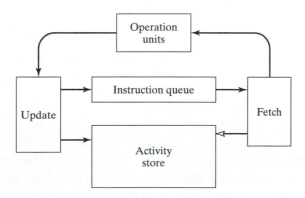

Figure 7-27 A typical static data flow architecture.

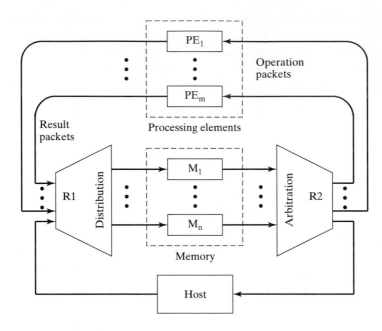

Figure 7-28   The MIT Static Data Flow architecture.

Static data flow machines do not produce a satisfactory solution for the problem of storing and handling structured values such as arrays. A practical solution to the problem of excessive copying of the entire structure for simple updates is a special store where structures are represented as acyclic directed graphs. This allows substructures to be shared. Only pointers to structure elements are carried between nodes. Using this approach a simple operation does not need to destroy the array and make a new copy; it only copies the desired element.

7.5.2   Dynamic Data Flow Computers

In dynamic data flow machines data tokens are tagged, sometimes referred to as labeled or colored, to allow for multiple tokens on any input arc of an actor node. Dynamic data flow models allow for concurrent execution of loop iterations and subprogram invocations. This is possible if each loop iteration or subprogram invocation can be executed as a separate instance of a reentrant subgraph. At the implementation level, only one copy of any data flow graph is stored. Instructions are fetched and executed independent of iteration numbers and procedure context. The only rule for executing an instruction is that as soon as tokens with identical tags are present at each of its input arcs it is enabled. Dynamic data flow machines are also referred to as *tagged-token*. Figure 7-29 represents the tagged-token operation, where each activity is identified by a tag consisting of a context field, C, to identify the procedure invocation, an activity name or the instruction number, and an iteration number, I, to identify the iteration instance. When actor N fires, it consumes the two tokens ($C.N.I$, *value1*) and ($C.N.I$, *value2*) and produces the result packet ($C.S.I$, *value1*vlaue2*) to be consumed by the next node S. One can imagine an unordered bag of mixed tokens on inputs of an actor that may belong to different invocations and/or loop iterations that must be matched for identical tags and operated upon. This results in more complex hardware requirements as is illustrated by the Manchester data flow computer next.

7.5.2.1   Manchester Data Flow Computer

Dynamic data flow computers have a ring structure similar to their static counterparts. However, in place of the activity store, there is an instruction store and a matching store. Figure 7-30 shows the block diagram of a single-ring Manchester data flow architecture, which is the first actual hardware implementation of a dynamic data flow computer built in 1981. To distinguish instances of target instructions, arrived operands are no longer held in a single activity template for an instruction. Instructions are divided into two groups of one-operand (unary) and two-operand instructions. Result packets include a count of how many operands the target instruction requires. For one-operand instructions, the result packet is sent directly to the instruction store where the instruction is fetched and an operation packet is constructed. For two-operand instructions, the first result packet to arrive at the matching store is held until the second result packet of the same tag arrives. The information from the two result packets is then combined and sent on to the instruction store. The matching store is an associative memory that uses the tag fields of a result packet as its search key. Figure 7-31 represents a more detailed view of the Manchester architecture. The contents of operation, result, and destination packets are shown in Figure 7-32.

The format of the instruction and data tokens are presented in Figure 7-33. The combined token has two values for the two operands of the same tag and a destination address for an instance of an instruction. The matching unit performs hardware hashing and has eight hash tables of $2K \times 96$ bits per table.

7.5.2.2   The MIT Tagged-Token Data Flow Machine

The Manchester Data Flow computer provided no explicit storage. All data structures, including arrays, are stored in the matching unit. The MIT tagged-token data flow machine has a ring structure similar to the Manchester machine with a special feature for handling data structures. It consists of a number of processing elements connected through a hypercube packet-switched network to a set of I-structure storage units that are provided to handle large data structures. Figure 7-34 illustrates the organization of the MIT tagged-token architecture.

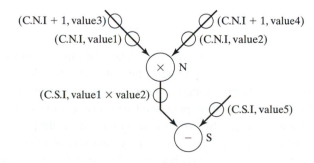

Figure 7-29   The tagged-token principle of dynamic data flow.

Allocate: Reserves a specified number of elements with their state initialized to empty.

I-fetch: Reads the value and forwards it to the requesting instruction if its state is full. The state is changed to waiting if it was empty. If the state was waiting when the I-fetch occurred, the read request is deferred and the tag of the destination instruction is entered into the queue associated with the I-structure element.

I-store: Write a value into an element if its state is empty. As a result, the state is changed to full. If the state before the I-store operation is waiting, in addition to the latter action all pending read requests for this I-structure element are processed. An I-store operation attempted on an element in full state results in an error.

The I-fetch operation as described above is implemented as a "split-phase" memory operation so that requests issued to an I-structure storage are time independent from the responses received. This way the requesting processing element does not need to wait for the response. The MIT tagged-token data flow machine was the first to implement the concept of I-structures. It has been simulated on a multiprocessor consisting of 32 TI Explorer Lisp machines, which led to the development of the Monsoon architecture.

The Monsoon architecture uses Explicitly Addressed Token Store (ETS) to alleviate the problems associated with the waiting-matching unit. The basic idea behind ETS is to use a separate memory for code and data. An activity frame, which contains slots for instruction operands, is associated with each instance of a loop iteration or a subprogram activation. The slots in the frame are directly addressable by instructions using an offset relative to the beginning of the frame corresponding to the current loop iteration. Full/empty synchronization is associated with each slot to indicate presence or absence of the data. To make this implementation practical, the number of concurrently active loop iterations is limited to a constant, K, referred to as K-bounded loops. The Monsoon architecture also uses the I-structure concept to implement large shared data structures, but it does not provide a separate memory for this purpose. It uses the local tagged memories of each PE.

7.5.3   Issues to Be Addressed by Data Flow Machines

Data flow computers need to solve the storage problem without the help from software. Efficient allocation of storage for large data structures such as arrays is difficult when only part of the structure is updated. Another major concern is efficient scheduling of operations for execution. Because a data flow formulation of an algorithm has no control flow, operations that are simultaneously ready must be scheduled by the hardware. Dynamic data flow architectures can identify the ready instructions using waiting-matching stores. Performance can be gained by implementing the waiting-matching store as an associative memory. Unfortunately, the amount of memory needed to store operands for a match tends to be very large. Large, fast associative memories are expensive. Hashing methods can be used with associative memory; however, they result in slow operations. The amount of parallelism in data flow is unpredictable. Some applications may generate amounts of concurrent activities that exceed the available parallel hardware resources. The decision as to which of the ready operations to run on fewer hardware units is algorithmically difficult. Furthermore, for each dyadic operation a new entry must be created in the matching store. Efficient management of the matching store due to the lack of enough memory is difficult.

7.6 Systolic Arrays

Systolic arrays are special-purpose architectures that take advantage of the use of VLSI technology. Simple, regular, and modular layouts are best suited for VLSI implementations. Systolic arrays are designs that lay out well in two dimensions and consist of simple cells with regular design patterns. Cells perform specific regular operations. The concept of systolic architectures was first developed by Kung and Leiserson [188] in the late 1970s.

Systolic arrays are globally structured cellular arrays of computing units. The arrays can be one, two, or even many dimensional, and cells connect to others around them in the array topology. Data is pumped through these computing arrays in a pipeline fashion that is analogous to pumping blood through a heart. A one-dimensional array corresponds directly to a pipeline, others correspond to more complex pipeline structures. Cells can have varying degrees of complexity, from simple logic gates in very fine grain arrays up to full programmable processors in coarse grain systolic systems.

In the literature, several properties are commonly associated with systolic arrays that may differ somewhat from the most general definitions. For example, cells are usually not too fine grain and at least do arithmetic, say, 32-bit multiply-add. Most cells of an array are identical, except those on array edges, which may differ from the interior ones. The design of the array is geometrically regular. Although the degree of regularity is not specified, a systolic array would definitely not be considered to be randomly interconnected. The regular structure extends to the synchronization, communication, and control within the array. Data communication is local, involving array neighbors separated from each other plus or minus one in one or more array indices. Some systolic arrays have a limited amount of broadcasting to all cells in parallel, but because local communication is considered one of the advantages of systolic design, broadcasting is considered a negative feature. Most of the array geometries presented as systolic in the literature are two dimensional. This applies to the overall structure and does not imply local planarity with no crossovers at all.

Systolic arrays are effective computational structures for "compute bound" jobs. The term *compute bound* refers to a job for which many operations are performed on intermediate data for each new operand that is introduced into the computation and for each final result that is output. For example, matrix add is not compute bound because it requires n^2 operations and $3n^2$ I/O operations. On the other hand, matrix multiply with $O(n^3)$ operations and $O(n^2)$ I/O operations is compute bound.

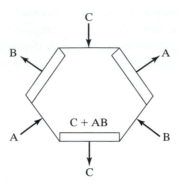

Figure 7-35   A typical multiply-add systolic cell with three inputs.

If we consider systolic arrays to be two-dimensional pipelines, then their individual cells have two functions. A cell transforms data by arithmetic operations and moves it to and from other cells of the array. A typical cell might do multiply-add on three inputs, as shown in Figure 7-35. The communication function of the cell is done by latching the A and B inputs in the cell's registers, so that the A and B outputs are equal to the inputs delayed by one clock step. The C output becomes the C input plus the A input times the B input. The connection associated with C, thus, both communicates the C input and updates it according to the cell's function. Systolic arrays are considered control driven because the execution of operations is based on a schedule that is determined by the array design and not by the arrival of data. Even so, there are many similarities between systolic arrays and dataflow. Algorithms in systolic arrays are designed to schedule computations in such a way that data are latched as they enter a cell, operated on, and reused as they move through the array pipelines. Because systolic arrays have highly regular structures, only algorithms with regular and repetitive computations perform well on them. Signal processing and similar number crunching applications are particularly suitable to systolic processing. Algorithms with nested loops often exhibit the regular characteristics needed for proper implementation on systolic arrays. Dependence analysis techniques and distance vectors discussed in this chapter for dataflow are used to map these algorithms onto systolic arrays for high performance [217].

A linear array of multiply-add cells can perform matrix-vector multiply. Consider computing $y = Ax$ where the matrix A is banded; i.e., $A_{ij} = 0$ for $i \leq j - p$ and for $i \geq j + q$. p and q are called the half bandwidths of the matrix. For $p = 2$ and $q = 3$, the matrix is shown in Figure 7-36. If the bandwidth is fixed, A can be any size, because it is input by diagonals into the systolic array. The length of the vectors x and y is also arbitrary, because they are input sequentially. The linear array of multiply-add cells and its inputs are shown in Figure 7-37. An important feature of systolic processing is timing. It must be done so that the operand pairs meet at the right time in the right cell. Here, elements of x enter the right end every other step, and an element of y is produced at the right on every other step. The inputs and the C output of each cell for the first five time steps are shown in Table 7-2. The C output of cell 1 corresponds to the final computed y component of the product vector. At time step t_1, the A and B inputs of cell 2, a_{11} and x_1, respectively, are multiplied and added to the C input, which is zero at this time, to produce the partially computed y_1 output. At the next time step, this y value flows to the C input of cell 1, where it is added to the result of A times B inputs to produce the first y_1 value, $a_{11}x_1 + a_{12}x_2$, of the matrix-vector multiply. Notice that at time t_2, a_{21} and x_1 have reached the A and B inputs of cell 3 to produce $a_{21}x_1$. As Table 7-2 shows, at every time step only half of the cells participate in the computation, and a result is produced at every other step. An element of y is computed in time $w = p + q - 1$, where p and q are half bandwidths of A. For length n vectors and $n \times n$ matrices, the complete multiply takes $2n + w$ steps. In this design, one of a pair of adjacent cells is idle at each step. The idle hardware can be eliminated by combining pairs of adjacent cells. A combined cell with one multiply-add unit can do the work of two. It needs registers to delay the x and y values for two steps and a small amount of sequencing logic. Call the B input and output x_{in} and x_{out}, and call the C input and output y_{in} and y_{out}, respectively. There are two internal registers called R_x and R_y, see Figure 7-38. The cell has the following two step behavior:

$$
\begin{array}{cccccc}
A11 & A12 & 0 & 0 & 0 & 0 & . \\
A21 & A22 & A23 & 0 & 0 & 0 & . \\
A31 & A32 & A33 & A34 & 0 & 0 & . \\
0 & A42 & A43 & A44 & A45 & 0 & . \\
0 & 0 & A53 & A54 & A55 & A56 & . \\
. & . & . & . & . & . & . \\
\end{array}
$$

Figure 7-36   Matrix A with half bandwidths $p = 2$ and $q = 3$.

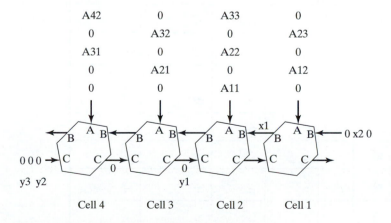

Figure 7-37   Linear array of multiply-add cells and its inputs.

Table 7-2   Computation steps of the matrix-vector multiply systolic array.

Time Step	Cell 4				Cell 3				Cell 2				Cell 1			
	A_i	B_i	C_i	C_o	A_i	B_i	C_i	C_o	A_i	B_i	C_i	C_o	A_i	B_i	C_i	C_o
t_1	0	0	0	0	0	0	0	0	a_{11}	x_1	0	$a_{11}x_1$	0	0	0	0
t_2	0	0	0	0	a_{21}	x_1	0	$a_{21}x_1$	0	0	0	0	a_{12}	x_2	$a_{11}x_1$	$a_{11}x_1$ $+a_{12}x_2$
t_3	a_{31}	x_1	0	$a_{31}x_1$	0	0	0	0	a_{22}	x_2	$a_{21}x_1$	$a_{21}x_1$ $+a_{22}x_2$	0	0	0	0
t_4	0	0	0	0	a_{32}	x_2	$a_{31}x_1$	$a_{31}x_1$ $+a_{32}x_2$	0	0	0	0	a_{23}	x_3	$a_{21}x_1$ $+a_{22}x_2$	$a_{21}x_1$ $+a_{22}x_2$ $+a_{23}x_3$
t_5	a_{42}	x_2	0	$a_{42}a_{42}$	0	0	0	0	a_{33}	x_3	$a_{31}x_1$ $+a_{32}x_2$	$a_{31}x_1$ $+a_{32}x_2$ $+a_{33}x_3$	0	0	0	0

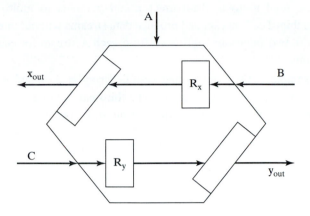

Figure 7-38 Combined multiply-add systolic cell with internal registers.

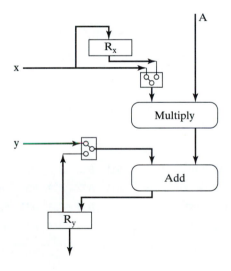

Figure 7-39 Combined multiply-add systolic cell design.

$$Step \ 1: R_y \leftarrow y_{in} + AR_x; \quad R_x \leftarrow R_x$$
$$Step \ 2: R_y \leftarrow R_y + Ax_{in}; \quad R_x \leftarrow x_{in}$$

y_{in} and x_{in} are read on different steps, one x and one y each cycle. Two A values are used per cycle, one on each step. The internal design of this multiply-add cell is shown in Figure 7-39.

The multiplexers are used to route the correct x and y inputs to multiply and add units, respectively. The combined cells accept and produce data streams without interspersed zeros. As shown in Figure 7-40, two values are consumed from each A stream for each value consumed from the x or y streams.

As another example, a two-dimensional systolic array is designed to do matrix-matrix multiply. Two banded matrices are multiplied to get a third banded matrix, $C = AB$, as shown in Figure 7-41. If upper and lower half bandwidths of A are q_1 and p_1, respectively, and those of B are q_2 and p_2, then the upper half bandwidth of C is $q = q_1 + q_2 - 1$, and the lower is $p = p_1 + p_2 - 1$. Four steps of the matrix-matrix multiply are shown in Figure 7-42(a) through Figure 7-42(d).

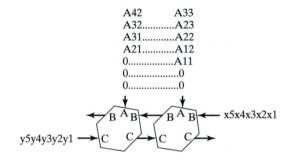

Figure 7-40   Combined multiply-add cells eliminates the idle steps.

$A11$	$A12$	0	.
$A21$	$A22$	$A23$	.
$A31$	$A32$	$A33$	.
0	$A42$	$A43$	.
.	.	.	.

$B11$	$B12$	$B13$	0	0	.
$B21$	$B22$	$B23$	$B24$	0	.
0	$B32$	$B33$	$B34$	$B35$	.
0	0	$B43$	$B44$	$B45$	.
.	.	.	.	.	.

$C11$	$C12$	$C13$	$C14$	0	.
$C21$	$C22$	$C23$	$C24$	$C25$	.
$C31$	$C32$	$C33$	$C34$	$C35$	.
$C41$	$C42$	$C43$	$C44$	$C44$	.
0	$C52$	$C53$	$C54$	$C54$	.
.	.	.	.	.	.

Figure 7-41   Multiplication of two banded matrices A and B results in C.

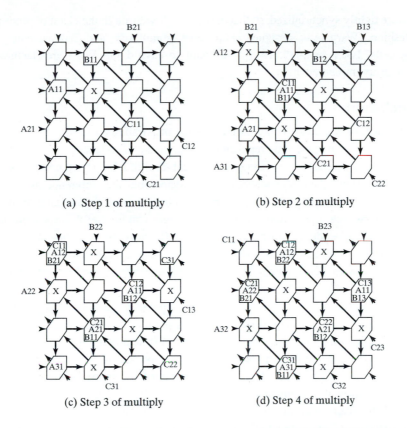

(a) Step 1 of multiply

(b) Step 2 of multiply

(c) Step 3 of multiply

(d) Step 4 of multiply

Figure 7-42 Four steps of matrix-matrix multiply in a two-dimensional systolic array.

Systolic arrays can do many matrix algorithms such as produce L and U factors of a matrix A, invert a triangular matrix, solve a linear recurrence system, and do filtering and other signal processing operations. A way to arrive at systolic array design is to start from a nested loop representation of a matrix algorithm and use two indices for position in the two-dimensional systolic array, leaving the other index(ices) sequential in time. Dependence vectors must be such that they do not point backward over indices stepped through sequentially in time. Methods exist to transform nested iterations so that iteration axes move from time to space dimensions [216]. Several parallel computers have architectures related to systolic arrays. SIMD architectures with arrays of processing elements, such as Illiac IV, MPP, DAP, and CM-2 can execute systolic algorithms efficiently. Special purpose computers for signal processing have been based on the systolic array idea. A general purpose computer whose design is based on the systolic array was the Warp built in the mid-1980s [19]. A Warp system consisted of a linear chain of ten or more processors connected to a host. The host supplied inputs to and received outputs from the ends of the chain. Each processor was capable of up to 10 MFLOPS execution rate, so that the total capacity of a 10-processor system was 100 MFLOPS peak. Input and output from processors in the chain were tightly synchronized, so that data could flow through the chain of processors in the systolic fashion. Warp was designed with large granularity and independently operating processing cells. Later in 1989, iWarp was built to extend the Warp architecture to a two dimensional array implementation.

7.7 Conclusion

Data dependence, or the lack thereof, is the essence of parallelism in algorithms or programs. Compiler analysis, languages, and graphical tools that make data dependences evident are, thus, a fundamental part of parallel processing. At the local level of a loop nest, compilers can be very effective at identifying data dependences among statements that reference arrays. Replacing indexing by pointer manipulation can prevent the compiler from recognizing array references and defeat automatic parallelization. Data flow languages can be useful in focusing attention on the essential flow dependences in an algorithm uninfluenced by the anti- and output dependences introduced by memory management. Data flow diagrams can give a graphical view of the flow dependences in an algorithm and by choosing the appropriate level for the actors in the diagram, hierarchical designs can be represented.

Data flow machines have not enjoyed wide popularity. Considerable intellectual effort goes into the storage management aspects of current parallel algorithms, and considerable performance can be gained by carefully integrating control flow and memory access portions of an algorithm. Data flow machines must solve the general problems of storage management and scheduling and can seldom take advantage of aspects of the computation that a user might invoke to get an efficient implementation. The study of data flow machines, however, has made clear many of the issues that must be addressed to implement data flow languages, or even to realize the performance gains enabled by the transformations performed by a parallelizing compiler for a sequential language.

Finally, systolic arrays embody data dependences in hardware interconnections and can be very efficient for implementing special purpose algorithms. Systolic arrays find important application in the area of signal processing, where continuous streams of values flow through and are transformed by a computational unit. General purpose systolic architectures suffer from the conflict between the high performance of interconnects arranged to fit a particular algorithm and the flexibility of interconnection required for general application.

7.8 Bibliographic Notes

Compiler requirements for parallel computers are reported in detail in [239, 288, and 294]. Data dependence analysis, compiler techniques and optimizations for automatic parallelizing compilers are described well in [13, 14, and 231]. The concepts of data dependence was introduced by Bernstein [47]. Data dependence distance vectors have been used in systolic arrays to generate regular communication patterns [170]. Kuck [183] and Allen [13] showed how to use dependence graphs for parallelization and optimization of sequential programs. Banerjee [35] developed the extreme value test, which was the first major attempt in using mathematics for solving problems of data dependence between general array references. Later in [36], he extended his work to triangular loop limits and introduced the generalized GCD test for dependence testing. The Omega test for data dependence is described in [241] and was used in [122]. A general discussion of automatic loop interchange in presented in [37]. Loop coalescing was introduced by Polychronopoulos [239] to simplify code generation and scheduling for parallel computers.

A historical perspective on data flow models can be found in [6]. The paper by Dennis [90] motivates the arguments behind data flow. Data flow graphs as programs are described in [87]. A comprehensive critique of the data flow idea is presented in [116]. Ackerman [2] described the criteria that a data flow language must satisfy. A thorough critique of the VAL data flow language can be found in [210]. A discussion of the relationship between functional languages and data flow is given in [102].

Data flow architectures are described in [117]. Dennis [90] introduced the static data flow architectures. The dynamic data flow architectures and the MIT tagged-token architectures are described in [26] and [28]. The description of the Manchester data flow machine can be found in [130]. Other data flow architectures are described in [141, 227, and 252].

Systolic array research was initiated by Kung and Leiseron [188] and is described in detail in [189]. Partitioning and mapping algorithms for systolic arrays are covered in [217]. The Warp and iWarp general purpose architectures are presented in [19 and 54].

Problems

7.1 Suppose the upper loop limit n in Figure 7-13 were not constant but represented by an incoming token. Expand the data flow diagram to make the number of copies of this token needed by the n termination tests.

7.2 Revise the data flow graph of Figure 7-17 to protect against erroneous computation if new inputs arrive before a previous computation is complete. New inputs should only be accepted after iterations for a previous computation are finished.

7.3 Draw a data flow diagram that accepts an integer input n and constructs a one-dimensional array of the first $n + 1$ Fibonacci numbers, $F(0), F(1), ..., F(n)$, where $F(0) = 0, F(1) = 1$, and $F(i) = F(i - 1) + F(i - 2)$ for $i \geq 2$.

7.4 Consider the following Fortran program fragment.

```
    DO 20   K = 1, N
          DO 10   J = K, M
                C(K)  =  C(K) + A(K, J)*B(K, J)
10        CONTINUE
20 CONTINUE
```

(a) Draw dependence graphs, both for the assignment to show loop carried dependence and in iteration space to show how statements for different (K, J) pairs are dependent.

(b) Take the program from part (a) and interchange the K and J loops. Draw the two dependency graphs of the resulting program.

(c) If the goal is vectorization, which of the two preceding programs would you prefer? What if the goal is parallelization for a shared-memory MIMD computer? Explain your answer.

7.5   Identify the basic blocks in the following C program:

```
void f(int x) {
    int a, b, c;
    a = x + 3;
    b = a + x;
    if (b > a) {
        c = x + b;
        b += c;
    } else {
        c = x - b;
        b *= c;
    }
    while (x > b) {
        x -= a*a + 1;
    }
    printf ("x is %d\n", x);
}
```

7.6   Show the dependence graphs among statements of each of the following Fortran program frag-
      ments, with justification.

   (a)   S1:   A = B + D
                S2:   C = A*3
                S3:   A = A + C
                S4:   E = A/2

   (b)   S1:   X = SIN(Y)
                S2:   Z = X + W
                S3:   Y = -2.5*W
                S4:   X = COS(Z)

   (c)   Determine the dependences in the following Do-loop. Distinguish dependences within
            the same iteration from those between iterations.

```
              do 10 I = 1, N
S1:               A(I+1) = B(I-1) + C(I)
S2:               B(I)   = A(I)*K
S3:               C(I)   = B(I) - 1
         10   continue
```

7.7   Determine the dependence relations among the three statements in the following loop nest.
      Give the direction vector and distance vector for all dependence relations.

```
         do I = 1, N
             do J = 2, N
S1:              A(I, J) = A(I, J-1) + B(I, J)
S2:              C(I, J) = A(I, J) + D(I+1, J)
S3:              D(I, J) = 0.1
             end do
         end do
```

7.8   Draw data flow graphs to represent the following computations:

   (a) if ((a=b) and (c<d)) then c := c-a
                                 else c := c+a;

(b) $Z = N! = N \times (N-1) \times (N-2) \times \cdots \times 2 \times 1$

Use the **merge** operator, the **true** gate, the **false** gate, the **multiply**, **add** and **subtract** operators, the logical **and**, and the **compare** operator in your graph construction.

7.9 The function below is written in SISAL.

function f(x: **real**, a: **array**[..] **of real**, i,j: **integer returns real**, **real**)
    if i = j **then** x, a[i]
    else

        let

            m : **integer** := (i + j)/2;
            x1, r1 : **real** := f(x, a, i, m);
            x2, r2 : **real** := f(x, a, m+1, j);

        in

            x1*x2, x1*r2 + r1

        end let

    end if
end function

Note that division of integers yields the integer part of the quotient.

(a) If a[0..n − 1] is a vector of reals, what is the pair of real values returned by f(x, a, 0, n − 1)?

(b) If only add and multiply operations on real numbers are counted, what are the depth and size of the computation done by f(x, a, 0, n − 1)?

7.10 A sequential algorithm for finding a root x of a function f(x) = 0 is the binary chopping method shown below assuming that we start with two real numbers b and u such that b < u, f(b) < 0, and f(u) > 0.

```
until u-b < e do
    begin m := (b+u)/2;
        if f(m) > 0 then u := m else b := m;
    end;
x := m;
```

Show how this algorithm would appear in SISAL. Write it as a procedure with inputs b, u, and ε and output x.

7.11 Given a sequence of weights $\{\omega_0, \omega_1, \ldots, \omega_{k-1}\}$ and a sequence of input signals $\{x_1, x_2, \ldots, x_n\}$, design two linear systolic arrays with k processing cells to solve the convolution problem

$$y_i = \omega_0 x_i + \omega_1 x_{i-1} + \cdots + \omega_{k-1} x_{i-k+1}.$$

The length n of the input stream is much larger than k, and it is the steady state behavior of the computation that is of interest.

(a) In the first design, you are to use the unidirectional cells that compute $y_{out} \leftarrow y_{in} + \omega \cdot x_{in}$ as shown below.

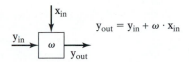

Explain your design, the distribution of the inputs, and the systolic flow of the partial results y_i's from left to right.

(b) In the second design, you are given the bidirectional cells that compute $y_{out} \leftarrow y_{in} + \omega \cdot x_{in}$ and $x_{out} \leftarrow x_{in}$, as shown below.

$$y_{out} \leftarrow y_{in} + \omega \cdot x_{in}$$

$$x_{out} \leftarrow x_{in}$$

Explain the design and operation of this systolic convolution array. Why might it be a better design than that of part (a) in terms of data movement?

CHAPTER 8

Implementing Synchronization and Data Sharing

A high-level language programmer may only use the synchronization operations supported by the language, but it is important to be aware of implementation details of synchronization constructs. Synchronizations often have a major impact on performance. The ease of implementing a synchronization by serializing execution means that synchronization operations with terrible performance on large-scale multiprocessors are readily available. Better implementations lead to better performance. Low-level libraries can often be made available to several languages for improved performance and functionality. A unique pattern of data sharing in an application may benefit from a special synchronization uniquely designed to support it.

Synchronization and data sharing among processes are closely related. Synchronization can be viewed as the communication of information about shared data. It is, thus, related to data transmission by one level of indirection. The distinction between data based and control-based synchronization was pointed out in Chapter 4. Data-based synchronization is directly associated with data communicated among processes, whereas control-based synchronization communicates information about the state of some other process' execution. Information about the state of an execution is used to infer information about data items another process may have written before the synchronization point or about data it may reference in the future but has not yet accessed. Control-based synchronization requires a memory consistency model to deduce information about data that was written before, or may be written after, a specific synchronization point in the program. An initial understanding of synchronizations can usually be based on sequential consistency, but many are easily extendable to relaxed consistency models like weak or release consistency. The understanding of sequential consistency as a total order on memory operations consisting of some interleaving of the program orders of individual processes implies that all data accesses of a process prior to one of its synchronization points are complete, and no data accesses after that point have started.

In striving to understand the role and behavior of synchronization in a shared or distributed multiprocessor computation, the reader should keep several questions in mind. What is the relationship of a synchronization construct to the specific type of data sharing it is used to coordinate? Are processes, perhaps uninvolved in the data sharing, made to wait unnecessarily by a synchronization? How can a programmer guarantee a synchronization is correct without testing all possible relative timings of hundreds of synchronized processes? What mathematical or other tools are available to analyze a synchronization? What is the role of testing in eliminating synchronization errors?

8.1 The Character of Information Conveyed by Synchronization

Several distinct types of information about data or the progress of processes are conveyed by synchronizations that are common in parallel programming. Some of the different types are given in the following list.

1. Data item x has been written. Additional information may include this being the k-th write and the identity of the writing process. This synchronization is used to satisfy a flow dependence on the variable x. A shared memory example is a produce operation on a full/empty variable. In distributed memory, the k-th transmission of a message of type x to a designated receiver, perhaps identifying the sender, serves a similar purpose.

2. The variable x or its associated message buffer has been read and may be rewritten. This synchronization handles antidependence. The standard shared memory example is the consume of a full/empty variable. In distributed memory, a rendezvous communication accomplishes both type 1 and type 2 synchronizations simultaneously, while with nonblocking send, a return message from the receiver may be necessary to convey type 2 information.

3. Process i has progressed to a specific point L in its program, and, by extension, all data operations prior to that point are done. In shared memory, a shared flag could be set on reaching point L, or a specific lock could be set or cleared. In distributed memory, a unique message associated with point L could be sent.

4. All processes have reached a designated point in their code (the same point in SPMD programs), and all previous data accesses in all processes are complete. This describes the barrier in either shared or distributed memory.

5. Another process is not, or no other process is, within any of one or more designated sections of code. By extension through the memory consistency model, none of the set of shared variables that are only accessed within one of the designated sections of code is currently being accessed. The prototypical example synchronization in shared memory is the critical section. Though not directly corresponding, an analogous instance in distributed memory is the remote procedure call used in the CSP implementation of a semaphore in Section 5.2.1 of Chapter 5.

6. At least one item of a limited shared resource is not in use by some other process. The shared memory example of this synchronization is the P operation on a semaphore. In distributed memory with nonblocking send, a request message to a resource manager and its response usually conveys information of this type.

Another useful characterization of control-based synchronizations is on the basis of the identity of processes with which synchronization information is exchanged. With a large number of processes, and especially with the SPMD programming style, including specific process identifiers in synchronization operations is impractical. Useful operations are those characterized as *generic synchronizations* that do not specify processes by name. Barrier blocks the progress of any process until all have arrived while critical section blocks execution if any other process is in a corresponding critical section. Both depend on nonspecific quantifiers over the set of all processes: *all* in the case of barrier and *any* for the critical section. Some process management operations can also be characterized as generic. The completion of a cobegin/coend construct or of an OpenMP parallel region waits for all processes forked at the beginning of the construct before allowing the master process to continue. Data-based synchronizations are naturally generic because synchronizing conditions are based on the state of data and not on the progress of processes.

If there is a topology associated with processes, then quantifying generic synchronizations with respect to process groups other than the universe of all processes can make sense. Drawing a parallel with the matrix multiply of Program 5-13 suggests that barriers or critical sections involving only processes in the same row or column in a process set with a two-dimensional grid topology might find application. The most common topology on processes, however, is a parent/child hierarchy. Defining a parent as a level-zero grandparent, it could be useful to have barriers or critical sections over the set of all children of the same level-k grandparent. Few parallel languages supply such synchronizations. They introduce added complexity not only in their implementation but also in the reasoning required to argue correctness of a parallel program using them.

8.2 Synchronizing Different Kinds of Cooperative Computations

Another way to look at synchronizations is in terms of the specific types of cooperative computations that they support. In this context, a cooperative computation is one in which two or more processes access the same data. This view is somewhat ambiguous because, as we saw in Chapter 4, many synchronizations can be implemented in terms of others. Nevertheless, some synchronizations are ideally suited for specific cooperative computations. Most synchronizations have analogous versions in both shared and distributed memory. One ubiquitous difference between the two environments is that, while the receipt of a message guarantees that the sending process must have reached the point of sending it, reading a shared variable always returns a value, even if it has not been written yet. With nonblocking send, however, completion of a send says nothing about the receiver having gotten a previous message.

8.2.1   One Producer with One or More Consumers

The basic mechanism for one process to notify others that it has made new data available for further computation is to supply them with a unique bit of synchronizing information indicating that the associated data has been newly produced. In distributed memory, this bit may just be implied by the presence of a message at a receiver. In shared memory, it may be encoded as a lock, a full/empty state, or the value of a shared logical flag variable. Finding the value of this synchronizing bit true implies that a read of the associated data returns the newly produced value. In shared memory, this requires that a memory consistency model be in force. For the simple writing of a shared flag to convey information about the value in a different memory location, sequential consistency is needed. If the data available bit is associated with a distinct synchronizing operation, as with a lock or full/empty bit, then it may be enough to require weak consistency, which demands only that synchronization operations are observed in proper order with respect to data operations and other synchronization operations performed by the same process.

Synchronizing the use of data with its prior production satisfies flow dependence, but antidependence can be viewed as producing an empty space for new data. In message passing systems with nonblocking send, antidependence is often ignored. This amounts to a tacit assumption that the compiler, run-time system, and operating system combination solves the storage management problem for shared data by providing sufficient message buffers.

With multiple consumers for the same data, the situation becomes less symmetric. For message passing, the produced data must be replicated, either explicitly by the producer or implicitly by the communication system, and a copy sent to each consumer. In shared memory, a data available flag can be read by many processes as well as by one, but with synchronizations that include a wait (lock or consume), multiple and single use become different. With full/empty variables, the copy operation, which waits for full but does not set empty, is used instead of consume. With lock synchronization, only one process succeeds at a time, so the sequence shown in Program 8-1 is necessary. The lock is initially set, and when the producer finishes writing the associated data, it clears the lock. Each consumer executes lock to wait for the data, copies the data to private variables, and then clears the lock so another consumer can access the data. If antidependence information is needed, the last consumer may need to explicitly empty the full/empty cell or use another lock or flag to report completion to the producer. More frequently, however, a control-based synchronization such as the barrier is used to indicate that all consumers have finished the code region in which they consume the data.

8.2.2   Global Reduction

In a reduction operation, multiple producers contribute to a single result that may then be used by one or more processes. The reduction over multiple processes may be preceded by a reduction over private or partitioned variables in each process. If there are only a few processes, the reduction may be synchronized by mutual exclusion, as shown in Program 8-2. If the number, P, of processes is large, the order P sequential execution imposed by mutual exclusion can have a large performance penalty. The ideal hardware support for integer sum reduction would be fetch&add, preferably with combining in the processor/memory interconnection network. Without such hardware, or when doing reductions other than integer sum, a recursive reduction based on hierarchical groups of size k will have better performance than the critical section synchronized version for a large number of processes. The hierarchical group reduction is sketched in the pseudocode of Program 8-3 and has a delay proportional to $k\log_k P$. Each process, distinguished by a unique identifier, id, is associated with a specific group of k at every level, from the leaves of a base k tree to the root. While this association could be computed from k, P, and id, we show it as an array, mygroup$[0:P-1, 0:\log_k P]$.

```
shared data;
lock L;
⟨Initialize L to locked.⟩
```

Producer	One of several consumers
`data := ... ;`	`lock L;   /* Wait for L unlocked. */`
`unlock L;`	`    ... := data; /* Read data. */`
	`unlock L; /* Allow other reads. */`

```
/* Test counter or execute barrier to determine that access to data is complete. */
lock L;
```

Program 8-1   One producer sharing data with multiple consumers.

```
loop over private variables or elements of this process' partition
        reduce into private_result;
end loop over private part of computation;
critical
        reduce private_result into shared variable;
end critical;
```

Program 8-2   Critical section synchronized reduction for few processes.

In a message passing system, the role of the critical section can be played by a designated process that receives all private results and performs the reductions. If the result is required by all processes, the designated process must do a broadcast after performing the reduction. Send and receive overhead makes it even more important to use a tree structured reduction algorithm to reduce the order P execution time to order $k\log_k P$. This requires that the interconnection network has sufficient concurrency. A bus or ring, for example, would prevent the network communication time from reaching order $k\log_k P$, even if the software overhead were reduced that much. Program 8-4 shows a recursive reduction procedure for a message passing system in which all processes require the result of the reduction. The recursive calls form a base k tree (for groups of size k) that does the reduction on the way to the root, while the recursive returns broadcast the result through the tree from the root.

```
call group_reduce(private_result, 0);    Recursive call at level 0.

procedure group_reduce(value, level)
    lock(lk[mygroup[id, level]]);
        reduce value into group_result;
        if (last process of group and not top level) then
            call group_reduce(group_result, level + 1);
        end if;
    unlock(lk[mygroup[id, level]]);
end procedure;
```

Program 8-3 Hierarchical global reduction with a base k tree.

```
real procedure group_reduce(value, level)
    if (not designated group head at level) then
        send value to this group's head at level;
        receive return_value from group head;
    else
        for other processes, i, in group
            begin
                receive value from i;
                reduce into group_value;
            end;
        if (not top level) then
            return_value := group_reduce(group_value, level+1);
          else
            return_value := group_value;
        end if;
        if (level ≠ 0) then
            for other processes, i, in group
                send return_value to i;
        end if;
    end if;
    return(return_value);
end procedure;
```

Program 8-4 Recursive reduction and result broadcast in a message passing system.

8.2.3   Global Prefix

The global prefix problem has several variations based on whether the prefix calculation is over one or many items per process and whether processes participate in the prefix calculation in an ordered or unordered way. We start with the case of one item per process. If the value contributed to a sum prefix calculation by each process is one and the computation is unordered, the result is the "take a number" algorithm used in meat markets and bakeries to assign a unique number to each of many randomly arriving customers. The prototype synchronization for this calculation is fetch&add, although critical section synchronization can also be used. Many of the reduction algorithms also apply to prefix with only minor modifications. For an ordered prefix algorithm, neither fetch&add nor critical sections can be used because their definitions do not specify process ordering. The message passing reduction algorithm of Program 8-4 extends easily to ordered prefix, provided the correct ordering is used in the for loops over members of a group. For both prefix and reduction with distribution of the result, the logarithmic algorithms have the form of two trees joined at their roots. One collects input values and the other distributes results from the root. The diagram of the recursive odd/even prefix algorithm, $P^{oe}(16)$, described in Chapter 2, is shown in Figure 8-1. It also suggests the form of root to root binary trees.

When a prefix calculation is to be done over many items in each process, it is usually an ordered prefix, in which a vector of values is partitioned over multiple processes and the prefix done on the partitioned vector. As shown in Problem 8-5 for a shared memory multiprocessor, the computation on a $N = m \cdot P$ element vector using P processes takes place in three stages. First, each process independently computes the prefix on its partition of the vector. Second, the last elements of these computed prefixes, VP[m-1], VP[2m-1], ..., VP[N-1], are globally combined using one of the single element per process prefix algorithms to produce final values for VP[m-1], VP[2m-1], ..., VP[N-1]. Each of these values is then added to the following m-1 values of VP by all but the first process in parallel to get final values for all VP elements. The size of this algorithm is $S = 2N + \alpha P$ and the depth is $D = 2m - 1 + \beta \log_2 P$, where $1 \le \alpha \le \log_2 P$ and $1 \le \beta \le 2$, depending on the parallel prefix algorithm used across processes. If m dominates P, the speedup is about $P/2$.

```
shared real V[0:N-1], VP[0:N-1];
shared integer N, P, m;
private integer id, i;
VP[id*m] := V[id*m];
for i := id*m + 1 step 1 until (id+1)*m - 1
    VP[i] := V[i] + VP[i-1];
VP[(id+1)*m - 1] := ordered_prefix(id, VP[(id+1)*m - 1]);
if (id ≠ 0) then
    for i := id*m step 1 until (id + 1)*m - 2
        VP[i] := VP[i] + VP[id*m - 1];
end if;
```

Program 8-5 Sum prefix on an $N = m \cdot P$ element vector for process *id* of *P* processors.

The prefix computation is a special case of a bounded recurrence. Callahan [64] gives a general treatment of the computation of bounded recurrences in a shared memory multiprocessor.

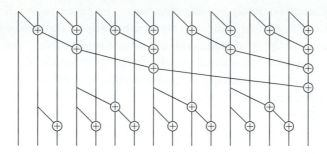

Figure 8-1   Tree patterns in the dependence diagram for $P^{oe}(16)$.

8.2.4   Cooperative Update of a Partitioned Structure

Many computations involve a large structure, say an array, being updated by multiple processes. In shared memory, the partitioning of the structure over the processes may not be fixed but may be determined by self-scheduling or other dynamic assignment of work to processes. It is possible to set a lock associated with the entire structure on entry to a parallel section that updates it and clear the lock on exit, but by far the most common synchronization in this case is the barrier. As with OpenMP, many shared memory languages terminate parallel loops with an implicit barrier. The loops typically operate on arrays that are either statically or dynamically partitioned over processes. Completion of the barrier at the end of the parallel loop guarantees the satisfaction of flow dependences or antidependences between array writes or reads in the loop and subsequent reads or writes of the same array. Because barrier is a generic synchronization, it is very appropriate for this purpose, because with self-scheduling, the identity of the process dealing with a specific array element may not be known. The inclusion of barrier synchronization in the collective communications of MPI supports this method of synchronizing cooperative update of a partitioned structure in the distributed memory environment.

The barrier is, thus, a very coarse-grained way of simultaneously satisfying a large number of produce/consume or consume/produce orderings on operations before and after the barrier. Of course, it may also enforce unnecessary orderings, the removal of which might potentially speed up the computation. Gaussian elimination, as done in Program 4-13 of Chapter 4, is a good example of barrier synchronized update of an array, and Problem 4.22 shows how to gain performance by using finer-grained synchronization for solving the same problem.

8.2.5   Managing a Shared Task Set

A type of cooperative computation closely related to the self-scheduled parallel loop is that where a set of processes access an ordered or unordered set of tasks, each task being done by one process. Here, *task* is used in its common sense as a piece of work, not in a technical sense associated with some specific system. This is the situation that was illustrated in Section 4.3.3 by the adaptive quadrature example. Fundamental differences between this and the self-scheduled loop include the fact that the tasks may be unordered and the possibility that performing a task may involve adding new tasks to the set. The integer nature of a loop index is a minor difference, for while several parameters may be required to define a task, they can be represented by an integer index into a table of tasks. It may be convenient to separate the synchronization necessary to sharing the set of tasks into two parts: managing the task set by claiming a task or adding a new one and the actual reading or writing of task definitions in the set.

To access tasks, a hash table could be used for an unordered set of tasks, but the most common case is an ordered set arranged either as a LIFO or FIFO queue, depending on the preferred order for handling newly created tasks. We treat task access from queues or linked lists as a separate problem from managing processes with respect to task availability. The usual synchronization to manage availability of a limited resource with discrete units is the counting semaphore. However, the blocking of a process on the P operation assumes that the resource eventually becomes available, while here the task set should eventually become empty and processes should proceed to other work. The task set can only be considered empty when all processes have finished their last task, as the execution of a task can add new ones to the set. The Force shared memory language [10], which observes the principle that a language primitive should do only one thing, supplies an *Askfor do* construct that just manages a task set. The beginning of an *Askfor do n* specifies an initial number, n, of tasks, or executions of the "loop" body. A *Morework k* operation executed in the loop body increases the size of the task set by k. A process finding the task set empty waits until either the task set becomes nonempty or all processes complete their executions of the body and find the set empty. Processes exit the construct when all become idle and the task set is empty. Most languages that supply a similar construct combine claiming a task or adding a new task with access to the task itself, usually from a LIFO or FIFO queue. The ASKFOR construct in the P4 macro set [208] not only uses the latter model but also includes a way for one process to indicate that the overall computation of the task set has completed early, before all tasks are exhausted, and cause processes to exit the construct the next time they request a task.

8.2.6 Cooperative List Manipulation

The parallel manipulation of shared linked lists is an important cooperative computation with one application being to LIFO or FIFO task queues implemented as linked lists. A synchronization directly suited to this job and implemented in hardware in the IBM System 370 series of machines is *compare&swap*. Compare&swap has three parameters. It reads the memory value at the address given in the first parameter and compares it against the value of the second parameter (a register). If the values are equal, the value of the third parameter (also a register) replaces the memory cell contents; if not, the value of the second parameter is replaced by the contents of the memory cell. This can be written

```
if (var = R1) then var := R2; else R1 := var;
```

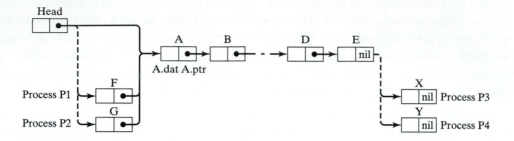

Figure 8-2   Linked list with parallel element insertions.

```
procedure add_head(F)                    procedure add_tail(X)
    private pointer Q;                        private pointer E, R;
    until (Q = F.ptr) do                      until (R = nil) do
        begin                                     begin
            Q := Head.ptr;                            Find tail E  (E.ptr = nil);
            F.ptr := Q;                               R := nil;
            CS(Head.ptr, Q, F);                       CS(E.ptr, R, X);
        end;                                      end;
end procedure                            end procedure


procedure delete_head(F)
    private pointer Q, Next;
    until (F = Q) do
        begin
            F := Head.ptr;
            Q := F;
            Next := F.ptr;
            CS(Head.ptr, F, Next);
        end;
end procedure
```

Program 8-6   Add and delete procedures for linked lists using compare&swap.

All of this is done atomically with respect to other accesses to the same memory location. Consider the linked list shown in Figure 8-2 with processes P1 and P2 attempting to add elements F and G, respectively, at the head of the list and processes P3 and P4 attempting to add elements X and Y, respectively, to the tail of the list, which is identified by a list element with a null pointer. A list element, say A, is a structure with data and pointer components, A.dat and A.ptr, respectively. The order of competing additions to the list is not important, but the link changes must be done atomically. Program 8-6 shows pseudocode for procedures built around the compare&swap (CS) operation to add elements to the head and tail and to delete an element from the head of the list. Using the right pair of procedures, either a FIFO or LIFO queue can be manipulated by parallel processes.

8.2.7 Parallel Access Queue Using Fetch&add

An important operation that often has its performance hampered by a mutual exclusion approach to synchronization is the manipulation of queues by parallel processes. Gottlieb, et al. [123] showed that pointers to FIFO queues can be manipulated in parallel with fetch&add to eliminate the necessity for mutual exclusion. Queue manipulation with fetch&add requires a passive test followed by a test and change, as in the semaphore implementation of Section 6.4.4. The test-decrement-retest procedure of Program 8-7 is used to decrement a pointer and test underflow. Similarly, a test-increment-retest procedure is used to increment pointers and test overflow, as shown in Program 8-8. Both procedures attempt to change an integer by an increment delta and return false if the change would put the integer out of range as determined either by the pretest or by the result of the atomic test and change operation.

```
boolean procedure TDR(S, delta)
    if (s - delta ≥ 0) then
        begin
            if (fetch&add(S,-delta)≥ delta) then TDR := true;
            else
                begin
                    fetch&add(S,delta);
                    TDR := false;
                end;
        end
    else TDR := false;
end procedure;
```

Program 8-7 Test-decrement-retest procedure.

```
boolean procedure TIR(S, delta, bound)
    if (S + delta ≤ bound) then
        begin
            if (fetch&add(S,delta) ≤ bound -delta) then TIR := true;
            else
                begin
                    fetch&add(S,-delta);
                    TIR := false;
                end;
        end
    else TIR := false;
end procedure;
```

Program 8-8 Test-increment-retest.

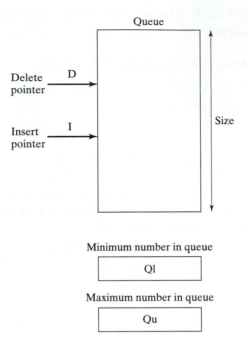

Figure 8-3   Structure of a parallel access queue.

The structure of a parallel access queue is somewhat different than that of a queue used sequentially by one process. With parallel accesses going on, the size of the queue is not a single number but ranges between a lower and upper bound. The lower bound can be thought of as the number of elements that would be in the queue if all outstanding deletes were to complete before any insert. Similarly, the upper bound would be the number of elements if all outstanding inserts completed first. A diagram of the queue structure is shown in Figure 8-3. The insert procedure for parallel queue access must handle possible overflow. This is interpreted as occurring if the maximum number of items possible in the queue with some execution order of outstanding requests exceeds the size. The insert procedure of Program 8-9 obtains space in the queue by incrementing the upper bound, gets a pointer to a free location, inserts the data, and then reports an increased lower bound. Insertion and deletion of the actual values is synchronized separately from access to the data structure defining the queue, as indicated by `wait_turn_at_myI`. An insert may have to wait for a delete that is in progress to actually free the data location. Produce/ consume synchronization is the right concept to use for this, although it might be implemented using another mechanism.

The delete procedure shown in Program 8-10 reports underflow if the minimum number of items in the queue, assuming all outstanding deletes completed, would fall below zero. The TDR and TIR routines do no waiting if they are unable to obtain a pointer value. Instead, queue overflow and underflow are handled by the routines invoking insert and delete. It may mean retrying after a delay, if activity of other processes eventually remove the underflow or overflow.

```
procedure insert(data, Q, ov)
    if TIR(Qu, 1, size) then
        begin
            myI := fetch&add(I,1) mod size;
            wait_turn_at_myI;
            Q[myI] := data;
            fetch&add(Ql, 1);
            ov := false;
        end
    else ov := true;
end procedure;
```

Program 8-9   Insert procedure for parallel access queue using fetch&add.

The parallel access queue is a very important mechanism for MIMD systems with a very large number of processors. Synchronizing queues with mutually exclusive access to the insert and delete pointers introduces a significant sequential bottleneck into an otherwise parallel program. The common case in which the queue is used to keep track of tasks to be performed by self-scheduling processes is a common source of sequential overhead in large parallel systems.

```
procedure delete(data, Q, un)
    if TDR(Q1,1) then
        begin
            myD := fetch&add(D,1) mod size;
            wait_turn_at_myD;
            data := Q[myD];
            fetch&add(Qu,-1);
            un := false;
        end
    else un := true;
end procedure;
```

Program 8-10   Delete procedure for parallel access queue using fetch&add.

8.2.8   Histogram—Fine Granularity, Data Dependent Synchronization

The parallel computation of a histogram, discussed in Problem 4.17 of Chapter 4, is the prototype for an important class of computations that place special demands on synchronization. A process selects a histogram element on the basis of the value of a data item and then increments that element. Increments must be atomic with respect to increments of the same histogram element by other processes. Although the computation would yield the same result if all increments were atomic with respect to each other, performance would be little better than sequential, because only the selection of the histogram element could be done in parallel. Data-based synchronization is more natural for this problem than control based. Fetch&add is an ideal atomic increment operation. If any cell may have a full/empty state, then using consume and produce to increment histogram elements solves the problem. With lock/unlock as the synchronization mechanism, a vector of locks, one for each histogram element, can provide the fine-grained atomicity required. The control-based synchronization that comes closest to satisfying the needs of the histogram problem is the named critical section, which is atomic only with respect to critical sections of the same name. However, to be useful in synchronizing the histogram computation, the name would have to be indexed by a run-time variable. Such a critical section naming facility is unlikely to be provided by a parallel language, especially because the alternative array of locks is equally convenient and would probably be used to implement the named critical sections anyway.

The performance improvement in synchronizing element by element compared to using mutual exclusion over the whole histogram is a complex function of the distribution of the data. To get a rudimentary idea of the behavior, we can calculate the average number of different elements accessed by simultaneous requests from P processes in a simple case. Let there be H elements in the histogram and a uniform probability of $1/H$ that any specific element is accessed. Then the probability that an element is not accessed by any of the P requests is

$$p_N = (1 - 1/H)^P. \tag{8.1}$$

Computing the probability, $p_A = 1 - p_N$, that an element is accessed at least once gives the average number of elements accessed by P simultaneous requests as

$$N_A = Hp_A = H(1 - (1 - 1/H)^P). \tag{8.2}$$

Using the first few terms of the binomial expansion for this result gives the approximation,

$$N_A = P - \frac{P(P-1)}{2H} + \frac{P(P-1)(P-2)}{6H^2} - \cdots. \tag{8.3}$$

If H is distinctly greater than P^2, then keeping only the first two terms is a good approximation. For $P = 10$ and $H = 1,000$, this yields $N_A \approx 9.955$, so there is less than half a percent probability of more than one reference to any element. With $H = 1,000$ and $P = 50$, an average of $N_A = 48.8$ different elements are accessed by 50 simultaneous requests; thus, for large histograms, the gain of fine-grained synchronization with respect to each element over mutual exclusion with respect to the entire shared histogram is significant.

8.3 Waiting Mechanisms

In a uniprocessor operating system or other uniprocessor program using time multiplexed parallel processes, all waiting involves releasing the processor to another process. Otherwise the system would stop. In an MIMD computer, it is quite feasible to delay a process on one processor while other processors continue to execute processes, one or more of which can remove the condition causing the delay. In a multiprocessing system having more processes than processors, processors are time multiplexed among several processes, and waiting may involve either delaying a processor or reallocating it to another process. Delaying a processor gives better performance than reallocating it if reallocation takes longer than the expected delay. The general term for a wait in which the processor is not reallocated is a *busy wait*.

Two parts of a wait can be distinguished, its beginning and its termination. In a uniprocessor or other system where certain processes can only make progress by processor reallocation, say through an interrupt, the progress of a process or class of processes may be delayed by another process disabling a particular interrupt. In a multiprocessor, however, the delay of a process is almost always initiated by the process itself executing some synchronization operation rather than by the activity of another process. The termination of a wait can come about in two distinct ways. The delayed process may periodically reexamine the synchronizing condition and terminate its own wait when the condition changes, or another process that changes the condition may actively terminate the wait of a process blocked on that condition. Passive termination of a wait through retesting by the waiting process and active termination of the wait by another process may have the same behavior with respect to synchronization constraints and deadlock but very different behavior with respect to fairness and livelock.

8.3.1   Hardware Waiting

Waiting mechanisms may also be distinguished by whether the wait is supported by hardware or implemented in software. One hardware delay mechanism is for an instruction testing a synchronization condition not to advance the program counter if the condition dictates a wait. The instruction would then be reissued, leading to a passive self-termination of the wait when the condition is changed by another process. As with any passive termination, there is no guarantee that any specific process will be restarted by a change in the synchronization condition. If several processes are waiting, any of them may detect a release condition first and atomically reset it before another waiting process detects that the condition has changed. Thus, there is no fairness guarantee for multiple processes terminating their own waits.

There may also be hardware support for processor reallocation on a wait. A synchronization condition dictating a wait may cause a process testing it to trap and yield the processor to the operating system, run-time system, or another process that is time multiplexed on the same processor. Depending on the amount of support for multiplexed processes, say multiple register sets, a minimal amount of process state is saved, to be restored at the end of the wait. The waiting process may be reactivated in two ways. An autonomous, periodic reactivation allows the process to retest its own wait condition and yield the processor again if the wait must continue. More software overhead at the time of yielding the processor can add the process to a queue of waiting processes, to be reactivated in response to another process' synchronization operation that terminates the wait. This probably requires setting an interrupt trigger associated with the specific synchronization condition at the start of the wait.

In pipelined MIMD computers, hardware support for limited time waiting is particularly simple. The process ID of the waiting process can simply be taken out of the execution queue and reinserted when the wait is complete. According to the hardware sketch of Figure 4-18 in Section 4.5, this happens automatically when the wait is a result of a memory reference. If a synchronization condition is associated with the memory access, say a wait on a full/empty bit, the process can recirculate in the memory access queue, retrying the access until the bit is in the right state. It is even possible for a device attached to the memory interface to remove a process ID from the memory access queue as well as the execution queue by not replying to an access request until some synchronization condition is satisfied. Process ID removal is not good for very long waits because, although no dynamic execution resources are used, the process still occupies static resources in the processor: program counter, registers, etc.

8.3.2   Software Waiting

The simplest software waiting mechanism is the *spinlock* shown in Figure 4-17 of Section 4.3.4. Processes executing a lock operation "spin" in a short loop waiting for an originally clear lock value to be returned indicating that the value was actually changed by the test&set. Both dynamic and static processor resources are occupied during a spinlock operation, but it may be very efficient when waits are expected to be short, as with critical sections that are used infrequently and/or are very short.

For longer waits when multiple processes share a processor, a process starting a synchronization wait may *sleep*, or yield the processor to another process. The required context switch may be invoked by a call to either the run-time system or operating system, depending on the protection level required for user process (thread) management. Termination of a wait started by a system call to yield the processor may, as in other cases, be passive or active. The sleeping process may be periodically reactivated by a timer, when it retests the condition on which it is waiting and may sleep again, or it may be actively restarted by the system in response to the change of a synchronization condition. The system may awaken all processes waiting on a particular condition and let them manage any further competition, say for a lock or a full/empty cell, or it may do synchronization specific process management, say by waking up only that process to which a released lock is allocated next. In operating systems for uniprocessors, a queue of waiting processes is a very common data structure. In parallel processing, centrally managed, sequentially accessed queues can have a severe performance penalty. In general, the better a synchronization operation is distributed over the processes taking part in it, the higher the performance. The extreme of synchronizing by serializing operations through a single master process, as was illustrated by the CSP implementation of a semaphore in Program 5-1 of Section 5.2.1, delivers very poor performance on a system with many processors.

8.3.3   Multilevel Waiting

To tune performance, several of the above waiting mechanisms can be combined. Busy waits can be limited by counting the number of retrys, either by hardware or software, and yielding the processor when a specified retry count is exceeded. As an example of a multilevel waiting mechanism, consider a consume operation on the Cray, Inc. (formerly Tera) MTA pipelined multiprocessor [16]. A consume operation is removed from the processor execution queue and placed in the memory access queue of its processor. If the consume request sent through the interconnection network finds the memory cell empty, it returns to the processor, increments a retry count, and is reissued. If the retry count is exhausted without finding the cell full, a trap occurs for the process issuing the consume. It is placed in a wait list associated with the memory cell, the contents of the cell is replaced with a pointer to the wait list, and a trap bit in the memory cell is set. Any subsequent reference to this cell causes a trap. If the reference is another consume, the process issuing it is added to the wait list. If it is a produce, the new value and a full state are written into the cell and all processes on the wait list are reactivated. Note that a produce trapping on a full cell must copy the value to the wait list before replacing it with a pointer. Thus, the effect is that the first process accessing a cell that is in the wrong state busy waits for a limited time in hardware, using only dynamic resources of the memory access unit. Accesses subsequent to a time-out immediately trap and are added to the wait queue. A releasing access modifies the memory cell and releases all waiting processes.

8.4 Mutual Exclusion Using Atomic Read and Write

It has been mentioned that it is possible to implement synchronization using only atomic read and write in shared memory. The atomicity of read and write implies a memory consistency model, which we take to be sequential consistency for the duration of this discussion. This problem is not of practical interest because the complexity of the required code gives poor synchronization performance, and it is very easy to supply inexpensive hardware synchronization support that improves the performance significantly. The purpose of the discussion, therefore, is primarily theoretical. Showing that mutual exclusion synchronization in the form of critical sections can be implemented using only atomic read and write and the ability to build other synchronization mechanisms by using critical sections gives a Turing machine-like feel for how much support for synchronization is absolutely necessary. Also, some of the problems encountered in implementing mutual exclusion give insight into how tricky a correct implementation using weak primitive synchronization operations can be. The problem was first solved by Dekker [91].

Two problems are addressed in algorithms that accomplish mutual exclusion between processes using only atomic read and write operations. The first is the simple guarantee that no two processes can simultaneously be executing the mutually exclusive region, or critical section. The second is that no process should be prevented from accessing the critical section for a long time as a result of multiple accesses by other processes, a situation called *starvation* or *livelock*. The elimination of livelock requires that synchronizations implement the idea of fairness, discussed in Section 4.3.4 of Chapter 4. As noted in that section, fairness may not be an issue in a tightly coupled parallel program, but it is considered to be part of the theoretical mutual exclusion problem. Fairness implies that if there are P processes waiting to enter a critical section, a

```
shared y[0:n-1], turn, n;      /* y is Boolean, turn and n integers */
private i, j;                  /* i is process index, j integer */
/* Process i code */
repeat
        y[i] := 1;                     /* request (1st time) or release claim (2nd time) */
        j := turn;                     /* scan starting at turn pointer */
        while (j ≠ i) do               /* and ending at this process */
              if (y[j] = 0) then j := (j+1) mod n /* advance circularly */
                      else j := turn;;            /* or reset to beginning */
        /* loop continues until no process between turn and i is requesting*/
        y[i] := 2;                     /* tentatively claim critical section */
        j := 0;                        /* scan all others for a conflicting claim */
        while (j < n and (j = i or y[j] ≠2)) do j := j+1;
    until (j ≥ n);                     /* this process has priority and no conflict */
    turn := i;                         /* advance the turn pointer */
    ⟨critical section⟩
    y[i] := 0;                         /* release the request */
    j := (i+1) mod n;                  /* pass the pointer to the next requester, if any */
    while (j ≠ i and y[j] = 0) do j := (j+1) mod n;
    turn := j;
```

Program 8-14   Mutual exclusion for process i of n processes using only atomic read and write.

A common reaction to the code for mutual exclusion using only atomic read and write is, "Is all that really necessary?" The answer is yes. Several papers from good authors and good referees appeared in the 1960s purporting to solve the mutual exclusion problem but having subtle errors that were subsequently pointed out. One reason for presenting the code is to make the point that it is difficult to reason about synchronizations based on weak atomic primitive operations. The appropriate way to do multiprocessor synchronization is to use a small set of synchronizations, each tailored to the computation type it is to synchronize, with each implementation supplied with a proof of correctness. The implementations and correctness proofs generally are easier the higher the level of the hardware synchronization used to support the implementation. It is worth reiterating that the correctness proof is essential. Because the errors introduced by an incorrect synchronization are timing dependent, no program of testing is at all likely to expose an error before the code is released to a production environment, where a synchronization error can do real damage.

8.5 Proving a Synchronization Implementation Correct

Because no amount of testing can exhaust all process execution orderings in a program with many processes, proving that a synchronization is correct replaces testing it in debugging. One can rely on synchronization primitives from a library, but only if there is confidence that the author of the library has done the correctness proof. Mathematical tools are available to support such proofs. As an example of a proof of correctness for an implementation of one synchronization in terms of another, we consider implementing the Produce, Consume, and Copy operations on full/empty variables using lock/unlock operations already available in a system. Locks are a plausible basic synchronization because most multiprocessor systems supply an atomic test&set operation and lock combines test&set with a wait. The correctness proof uses the ideas of temporal logic, a formal way of reasoning about future behaviors of a system. Temporal logic extends ordinary logic with the assertion that a statement is true forever and the assertion that a statement holds until a second statement is true. This rudimentary model of time in a system is sufficient to prove correctness of the synchronization implementation. Once the implementations of Produce, Consume, and Copy, along with the properties of lock and unlock, have been expressed as statements in temporal logic, the proof of correctness is not difficult.

8.5.1   Implementing Produce/Consume Using Locks

In the implementation we use, each variable is associated with two locks that together encode the full/empty state of the variable. Without loss of generality, we confine the discussion to a single variable, var, with associated locks, A and B. The encoding of variable states by the locks is summarized in Table 8-1. The implementations of Produce, Consume, and Copy are shown as procedures in Program 8-15. Normally, a shared full/empty variable would be set from or read into a private variable, but this is not essential to the implementation or the proof of correctness. The bodies of Produce, Consume, and Copy could equally well read or write a multiple item data structure instead of a single shared memory location. The use of two locks per full/empty variable is practical when locks are not a scarce resource in the system. The complexity of the synchronizations is very low, but note that, except for Copy, they do not use matched pairs of lock and unlock operations on the same item, as is done in implementing mutual exclusion with a lock. A lock set by one process in a Produce may be unlocked by another process doing a Consume.

Figure 8-4 shows a state transition diagram for the full/empty states of the shared variable and their encodings in terms of the states of locks A and B. An intuitive understanding of the correctness of the implementation can be gained from observing that each state transition is realized by an atomic operation on a lock and that none of the three operations can be entered from the reserved state. Thus, if a process succeeds in putting the variable into the reserved state by a lock(A) or a lock(B) operation, it can proceed to manipulate the variable without interference from other processes doing Produce, Consume, or Copy.

Table 8-1   Encoding of variable state by lock states.

Variable state	Lock A	Lock B
empty	unlocked	locked
full	locked	unlocked
reserved	locked	locked
undefined	unlocked	unlocked

```
procedure Produce(var, priv)
    lock(A);
    var := priv;
    unlock(B);
end procedure;

procedure Consume(var, priv)
    lock(B);
    priv := var;
    unlock(A);
end procedure;

procedure Copy(var, priv)
    lock(B);
    priv := var;
    unlock(B);
end procedure;
```

Program 8-15   Implementation of `Produce`, `Consume`, and `Copy`.

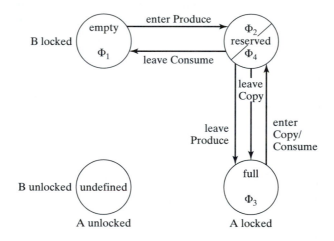

Figure 8-4   State transition diagram for full/empty variable implementation.

8.5.2   Temporal Logic

Our proof of correctness follows the Manna-Pneuli temporal logic [180]. The familiar logic operations of and ($\wedge$), or ($\vee$), not ($^-$), and exclusive or ($\oplus$) are extended by a few, less familiar primitives. For a statement P, $\models P$ asserts that the statement is true in the temporal logic system. Given a predicate P, $\square P$ asserts that the predicate P always holds. For two predicates, P_1 and P_2, $P_1 \cup P_2$ asserts that P_1 holds until a point in time at which P_2 holds. The simple temporal concepts of a statement always being true and of a statement being true until another is true is a sufficient characterization of behavior over time for the purpose of our correctness proof.

Table 8-2 summarizes temporal logic operators and definitions that characterize our synchronization operations. A large part of the work is in formulating definitions and statements that represent the behavior of the lock/unlock operations in the implementation as temporal logic statements. The assertion that a process is within a Produce, Consume, or Copy operation means that it has succeeded in executing the atomic lock operation at the beginning of the procedure and has not yet executed the atomic unlock operation at the end. Before and during the execution of a normal program, the sets π and γ of processes able to do a Produce or a Consume/Copy, respectively, contain most processes but become empty as processes complete their portion of the parallel program. These sets becoming empty allows statements about behavior for the duration of program execution to be extended to statements holding for all time.

Table 8-2 Temporal logic operations and definitions.

Symbol	Meaning
$\Box P$	predicate P always holds
$P_a \cup P_b$	P_a holds until a time when P_b holds
$\models P$	P is true in the temporal logic system
$\overline{P}$	not P
$P_a \rightarrow P_b$	P_a implies P_b
$P_a \oplus P_b$	exclusive or of P_a and P_b
L_p^i	process i is within a Produce
L_c^i	process i is within a Consume or Copy
$L^i = L_p^i \vee L_c^i$	process i is within a Produce, Consume, or Copy
$L^i \wedge L^j$	processes i and j are both within a Produce, Consume, or Copy
$A(\overline{A})$	A is locked (unlocked)
$B(\overline{B})$	B is locked (unlocked)
π	set of processes able to do a Produce
S_π	set π of processes is nonempty
γ	set of processes able to do a Consume or Copy
S_γ	set γ of processes is nonempty

Six premises, formulated in terms of the operations and definitions of Table 8-2, character-ize the behavior of Produce, Consume, and Copy.

$$P_1: \quad \models \overline{L}_p^i \to \overline{L}_p^i \cup \overline{A}$$

Process i cannot enter Produce until A is unlocked.

$$P_2: \quad \models \overline{L}_c^i \to \overline{L}_c^i \cup \overline{B}$$

Process i cannot enter Consume/Copy until B is unlocked.

$$P_3: \quad \models \overline{A} \wedge S_\pi \to \overline{A} \cup (A \wedge \exists_{i \in \pi} L_p^i)$$

Process $i \in \pi$ enters Produce by locking A.

$$P_4: \quad \models \overline{B} \wedge S_\gamma \to \overline{B} \cup (B \wedge \exists_{i \in \gamma} L_c^i)$$

Process $i \in \gamma$ enters Consume or Copy by locking B.

$$P_5: \quad \models L_p^i \to L_p^i \cup (\overline{B} \wedge \overline{L}^i)$$

Process i leaves Produce by unlocking B.

$$P_6: \quad \models L_c^i \to L_c^i \cup ((\overline{A} \oplus \overline{B}) \wedge \overline{L}^i)$$

Process i leaves Consume (Copy) by unlocking A (B).

The atomicity of lock and unlock and the definition of entry to and exit from the synchronization operations are consistent with the use of the until ($\cup$) temporal operator to characterize the behavior of entry and exit. The first two premises represent conditions for entry to a synchronization, the second two the result of entry, and the third two the result of exiting one of the implemented synchronizations.

We also define four disjoint states, Φ_1, Φ_2, Φ_3, and Φ_4, of the system, one each for the empty and full states of the variable and two in which the variable is reserved.

$$\Phi_1 = (\forall_i \overline{L}^i) \wedge \overline{A} \wedge B \tag{8.4}$$

represents the empty state of the variable with no process executing a synchronization.

$$\Phi_2 = (\exists_i L_p^i) \wedge (\forall_{j \neq i} \overline{L}^j) \wedge A \wedge B \tag{8.5}$$

is true if some process is executing Produce, no other process is executing a synchroniza-tion, and the variable is reserved.

$$\Phi_3 = (\forall_i \overline{L}^i) \wedge A \wedge \overline{B} \tag{8.6}$$

represents the full state of the variable with no process executing a synchronization.

$$\Phi_4 = (\exists_i L_c^i) \wedge (\forall_{j \neq i} \overline{L^j}) \wedge A \wedge B \tag{8.7}$$

is true if some process is doing either a Consume or Copy, no other process is executing a synchronization, and the variable is reserved.

The transitions between these states are also shown in Figure 8-4. The initial state of the system is Φ_1, in which the variable is empty and no process is executing a synchronization.

8.5.3   Proof of Correctness

Proving correctness of the implementation amounts to showing that Produce, Consume, and Copy behave atomically with respect to one another. In this implementation, they are mutually exclusive, which implies atomicity. Mutual exclusion is expressed by

$$\Psi = (\forall_i \ \forall_{j \neq i})(\overline{L^i \wedge L^j}), \tag{8.8}$$

and we can prove correctness by showing that this condition holds in any reachable state of the system. A set of lemmas characterizes the reachable states.

Lemma 1
$\vDash \Phi_1 \rightarrow (\Phi_1 \cup \Phi_2) \vee \square \Phi_1.$

PROOF
$\vDash \Phi_1 \wedge S_\pi \rightarrow \Phi_1 \cup \Phi_2$ by P_3 for $i \in \pi$ and by P_1, P_2 for $j \neq i$. $\vDash \Phi_1 \wedge \overline{S_\pi} \rightarrow \square \Phi_1$ by P_2. ∎

Lemma 2
$\vDash \Phi_2 \rightarrow \Phi_2 \cup \Phi_3.$

PROOF
The result holds by P_5 for $i \in \pi$ and by P_1, P_2 for $j \neq i$. ∎

Lemma 3
$\vDash \Phi_3 \rightarrow (\Phi_3 \cup \Phi_4) \vee \square \Phi_3.$

PROOF
$\vDash \Phi_3 \wedge S_\gamma \rightarrow \Phi_3 \cup \Phi_4$ by P_4 for $i \in \gamma$ and by P_1, P_2 for $j \neq i$. $\vDash \Phi_3 \wedge \overline{S_\gamma} \rightarrow \square \Phi_3$ by P_1. ∎

Lemma 4
$\vDash \Phi_4 \rightarrow \Phi_4 \cup (\Phi_1 \oplus \Phi_3).$

PROOF

The result holds by P_6 for $i \in \gamma$ and by P_1, P_2 for $j \neq i$. ∎

From lemmas 1 to 4, it can be seen that the union of disjoint states, $\Phi = \Phi_1 \oplus \Phi_2 \oplus \Phi_3 \oplus \Phi_4$, exhausts the set of reachable states.

Lemma 5

$\vDash \Phi \rightarrow \Box \Phi$.

PROOF

$\vDash \Phi_1 \rightarrow \Phi_1 \cup \Phi$ by lemma 1. $\vDash \Phi_2 \rightarrow \Phi_2 \cup \Phi$ by lemma 2. $\vDash \Phi_3 \rightarrow \Phi_3 \cup \Phi$ by lemma 3. $\vDash \Phi_4 \rightarrow \Phi_4 \cup \Phi$ by lemma 4. ∎

Correctness of the implementation is then established by the theorem showing that, starting in the initial state, Φ_1, mutual exclusion among the synchronization operations always holds.

THEOREM

$\vDash \Phi_1 \rightarrow \Box \Psi$.

PROOF

Ψ is satisfied in each of the four states of Φ, and by lemma 5, $\vDash \Phi_1 \rightarrow \Box \Phi$; thus, $\vDash \Phi_1 \rightarrow \Box \Psi$. ∎

The degree of subjective conviction one gains from such a correctness proof depends on one's familiarity with temporal logic, but correctness proofs are the only sort of evidence that is valid for understanding synchronizations. No amount of testing should give any degree of confidence whatever for synchronization correctness. The number of different timings and interactions among processes in a multiprocessor system is so large that no test sequence can cover a large enough fraction of the possibilities to have any meaning for the whole.

8.6 Alternative Implementations of Synchronization—Barrier

There are numerous different ways of implementing a given synchronization operation in terms of others that are directly supported by the hardware or system. The barrier is a good example for alternative implementations for several reasons. First, it is a global synchronization over all processes, while hardware synchronizations that may be used to implement it are often data based or synchronize two specific processes. It is possible to supply direct hardware support for barriers, but few systems do so. Several distinct choices for structuring individual process synchronizations into the globally acting barrier can be identified and combined in different ways. In addition, the barrier can be applied equally well to both shared and distributed memory multiprocessor systems.

8.6.1 Features of Barrier Synchronization

Some features of barrier synchronization apply to most of its implementations. When treated as an ideal primitive operation, a barrier requires all processes to reach it, at which point all immediately exit to perform the next operation. When the barrier is implemented using other synchronizations, there will be some program logic to be executed by each process. If the barrier is packaged as a procedure, the semantics are modified to require all processes to enter the procedure before any process exits. In addition, variation in the speed and scheduling of processes mean that not every process necessarily exits the barrier immediately after the conditions for it to do so have been satisfied. This means that processes not only arrive at a barrier at different times but may also leave the barrier at times that vary with interrupt handling, preemption, and other factors. Analogous features of entry and exit apply if the barrier is expanded as a macro or as an inlined procedure.

The skewed exit of processes from a barrier leads to the general problem of barrier reuse. If processes encounter successive barriers, either in straight line code or because a barrier is contained in a loop executed by all processes, it is possible that some process enter the second barrier before all have exited the first. The code used to implement the barrier must often take this into account when assuring correct interaction of processes executing the barrier code.

```
shared arrived[1:P-1];
Initially: arrived[i] = false, 1 ≤ i ≤ P-1;
```

Master process	Slave process k
for i := 1 **step** 1 **until** P-1	arrived[k] := **true**;
while (**not** arrived[i]) ;	**while** (arrived[k]) ;
for i := 1 **step** 1 **until** P-1	
arrived[i] := **false**;	

Program 8-16   A simple master/slave barrier.

Program 8-16 shows a simple barrier implementation where one process plays the role of a master controller and the others are subordinate to it. It has some drawbacks and inefficiencies. In addition to being asymmetric, there are two sequential loops over processes, with time linearly proportional to the number of processors, that must be executed by the master after it arrives at the barrier and could cause significant delays for large numbers of processes. The second loop could be replaced by a single shared Boolean flag that is written by the master and waited for by each of the slaves. This broadcast style release, however, brings up the problem of barrier reuse. If the master sets a `release` flag to **true** to signal completion of the barrier, when will `release` be returned to **false** in preparation for the next barrier? No one process knows that all others have seen and responded to the **true** value of `release`. Program 8-17 shows a master/slave style barrier with broadcast release that solves the problem of reuse by alternating the sense of the `arrived[]` and `release` flags from one barrier to the next.

```
shared arrived[1:P-1], release;
private alt;
Initially: arrived[1:P-1] = release = false; alt = true;

        Master process                          Slave process  k
for i := 1 step 1 until P-1              arrived[k] := alt;
    while (arrived[i] ≠ alt) ;           while (release ≠ alt) ;
release := alt;                          alt := not alt;
alt := not alt;
```

Program 8-17   Master/slave barrier with broadcast release.

```
        Master process(process 0)               Slave process  k
for i := 1 step 1 until P-1              send true to 0;
    receive arrived from i;              receive release from 0;
for i := 1 step 1 until P-1
        send true to i;
```

Program 8-18   Linear time, master/slave, message passing barrier.

In message passing systems, process interaction is by way of send and receive operations rather than shared memory variables. Program 8-18 shows a message passing barrier equivalent to the shared memory barrier of Program 8-16. The barrier is of the master/slave type with time linear in the number of processes. Note that the value of a transmitted message is irrelevant. The synchronization depends only on using blocking receive, where the presence or absence of a message does the synchronization.

8.6.2   Characterization of Barrier Implementations

An idea of the kind of variation possible in barrier implementation can be obtained by listing a set of two way alternatives for an implementation that are relatively independent of one another and can be mixed arbitrarily, with some exceptions. Table 8-3 shows six such implementation alternatives. An understanding of several of the alternatives can be obtained by looking at the barriers of the last section. Program 8-16 differs from Program 8-18 only on the shared memory versus message passing alternative. Both are of the master/slave type because one process, the master, executes distinctly different code from the other processes. A symmetric, shared memory barrier, in which each of P processes executes the same code, is shown in Program 8-19. This barrier also illustrates some of the other alternatives. In addition to being symmetric, it is also self-scheduled. The barrier of Program 8-16 is prescheduled because process arrivals are checked in a fixed order. If process one arrives last, the master still must check all the other processes after it receives the report of process one's arrival, even if they had arrived earlier. In Program 8-19, processes increment the arrival count as soon as they reach the barrier, so if the last arriving process is very late, all of the other processes may have executed their check in code, and only one more execution of the critical section on `inlock` by the last process completes the barrier entry. The check in is still characterized as having an execution time that is linear in the number of processes because if all processes do arrive at the same time, they all must go through the critical sections on `inlock` and `outlock` one at a time to satisfy the barrier synchronization. The timing diagram of Figure 8-5 shows a possible arrival order of processes at the barrier of Program 8-19 and the subsequent behavior imposed by the critical sections of the implementation. Processes are arranged left to right in the order in which they obtain the exit critical section and not by process number.

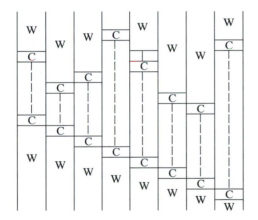

W – per process work
C – entry or exit critical section

Figure 8-5   Temporal behavior of processes passing the barrier of Program 8-19.

Table 8-3   Alternatives for barrier implementation.

Shared memory	—	Message passing
Master/slave	—	Symmetric
Prescheduled	—	Self-scheduled
Test&set	—	Read/write
Logarithmic structure	—	Linear structure
Distributed exit	—	Broadcast exit

Another feature of the barrier of Program 8-19 is that all of the synchronization is done using the lock/unlock primitives. In contrast, the barrier of Program 8-16 uses only read and write on shared memory variables to do the synchronization. If a shared memory multiprocessor implements a relaxed model of memory consistency, it may be necessary to use a system supported primitive synchronization rather than relying on simple read and write of shared data in order to get correct memory behavior. Finally, the barrier of Program 8-19 uses a distributed exit because each process separately contributes to the exit condition, in contrast to the release flag of Program 8-17 that is broadcast to all processes and checked simultaneously. Thus, the barrier of Program 8-19 can be characterized in terms of the six alternatives as a shared memory, symmetric, self-scheduled, lock/unlock, linear structured, distributed exit barrier. It can be seen that the fourth alternative of Table 8-3 is really not a two-way choice but a specification of the basic synchronization to be used in the implementation. The most important distinction, however, is between a system supported synchronization such as test&set or lock/unlock and shared memory read/write, where the memory consistency model must be taken into account to reason about the correctness of the implementation.

```
shared lock inlock, outlock;
shared integer count, P;
Initially: inlock = clear; outlock = set; count = 0;

lock(inlock);                    Atomically report
    count := count + 1;              a new arrival, and
    if (count = P) then             if it is the last process,
        unlock(outlock);            enable the checkout mechanism.
    else                            If it is not the last, release
        unlock(inlock);             the checkin mechanism.
lock(outlock);                   Atomically report
    count := count - 1;             another exiting process, and
    if (count = 0) then             if it is the last one,
        unlock(inlock);             enable checkin for the next barrier.
    else                            If it is not the last one,
        unlock(outlock);            release the checkout mechanism.
```

Program 8-19 Symmetric, shared memory barrier with lock/unlock synchronization.

Program 8-20 shows a shared memory, symmetric, self-scheduled, produce/consume/copy, linear structured barrier with broadcast exit. Because all shared variables are accessed using produce, consume, or copy, memory consistency only needs to be argued with respect to these specific synchronizations. Processes arriving before the last one wait for the shared value of phase to change. Detection of a changed phase can, in principle, be done in parallel by all processes using copy, although a specific machine may sequentialize accesses to the single shared memory cell at the hardware level. The concept of phase goes back to the general problem of barrier reuse discussed in Section 8.6.1. The fetch&add barrier presented in

```
shared P, count, phase;
private test, alt, temp;
Initially: count = 0; phase = false, alt = false;

consume count into test;
if (test = P - 1) then
    begin
            consume phase into temp;
            produce count := 0;
            produce phase := not temp;
    end;
else produce count := test + 1;
do copy phase into temp;
    until (temp ≠ alt);
alt := not alt;
```

Program 8-20   Symmetric, self-scheduled barrier with broadcast exit.

Program 6-6 on page 259 encodes the phase idea by doubling the range of the counter and associating counts less than P with one phase and those greater than or equal to P with the other.

The code of the fetch&add barrier of Program 6-6 would lead to a linear structured barrier if fetch&adds were mutually exclusive. The combining network implementation of fetch&add in an Omega network gives it an implicit logarithmic structure. Explicitly logarithmic barriers can be programmed in numerous ways. By dividing processes into groups of k, processes can report arrival within their group and have one representative of the group report completion for the group to a higher level group of k groups. The simplest situation is for $k = 2$, giving a binary reporting tree for arrivals. If the group representatives are fixed in advance, the barrier is prescheduled, if not, it is self-scheduled. Once the root of the tree detects that all processes have arrived, a completion message may be passed back down the tree, eventually informing all processes, or if support for broadcast is available, the completion signal may be broadcast to all processes simultaneously. As for any barrier, the reuse problem must be addressed.

Program 8-21 shows symmetric, self-scheduled barriers with explicit logarithmic structure for both message passing and shared memory machines. Although no process exits until all have arrived, there is no separation of entry and exit phases. The code shown is for process myid of P processes, $0 \leq \text{myid} < P$. P is not necessarily a power of two, and $p = \lceil \log_2 P \rceil$. The shared memory version has an array of $P \times p$ cells for pair wise synchronization. Only the full/empty bit of each is used; the value is ignored. This storage does not appear explicitly in the message passing version. Instead, it is implicit in the received message buffers for each process. A process arriving after all the others can have up to p messages waiting on it, so there is implicit storage for $P \times p$ messages. As with the shared memory version, the message passing barrier ignores the value of the message and uses only its existence for synchronization. The synchronization pattern of the barriers in Program 8-21 is shown in Figure 8-6 for $P = 11$ processes. The pairwise synchronization patterns justify the name, *butterfly barrier*, for this algorithm.

Initially: No pending messages.	```shared P, p, flag[0:P-1, 0:p-1];```
	```private myid, j, nbr, dummy;```
	Initially: ```flag[:, :] = empty;```

```
for j := 0 step 1 until p-1;       for j := 0 step 1 until p-1;
begin                              begin
  nbr := 2^j ⊕ myid;                 nbr := 2^j ⊕ myid;
  if (nbr < P) then                  if (nbr < P) then
  begin                              begin
    send true to nbr;                  produce flag[myid, j] := true;
    receive dummy from nbr;            consume flag[nbr, j] into dummy;
  end;                               end;
end;                               end;
    (a) Message passing version        (b) Shared memory version
```

Program 8-21   Symmetric, self-scheduled, logarithmic structured barriers.

The different implementations of barriers lead to performance differences. In addition to the interaction between the implementation algorithm and the basic hardware supported synchronizations, different implementations may perform better if the number of processes is very large or very small. With message passing implementations, the latency and bandwidth of the interconnection network in relation to the processor cycle time can have a big influence on the performance of different implementations. Chapter 9 will give some examples of barrier performance measurements.

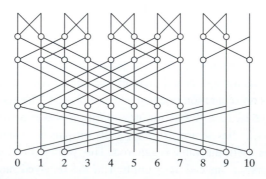

Figure 8-6   Synchronization pattern for a butterfly barrier on 11 processes.

8.7 Conclusion

Many different synchronization operations have been proposed and/or implemented for different parallel computer systems. A list of the more common ones can be found in Appendix B. The forms of different synchronizations have been influenced not only by the tasks they are designed to perform, as outlined in Section 8.2, but also by historical evolution and convenience of hardware and software implementation. Thus, in many cases, structure and classification have been imposed after the fact on a haphazard collection of synchronization primitives.

The roots of many synchronization operations are in uniprocessor operating systems design, where the only parallelism is among processes that are time multiplexed on a single processor. This origin has influenced the characteristics of such synchronizations. They emphasize fairness because the delay of one process represents a delay for all processes through the one shared processor. Operating system derived synchronizations often include fairly complex process management because, once a context switch has been initiated to cooperate with another process, high-level, software-based process management is easily incorporated. Synchronizations developed specifically for multiprocessors tend to be simpler, require minimal communication between processes, and deemphasize fairness. It is probably not useful, however, to try to characterize each synchronization as a multiprocessor or uniprocessor based operation. Much cross-fertilization has taken place in the evolution of the current set of synchronizations.

8.8 Bibliographic Notes

One of the earliest associations of a specific type of synchronization with a particular data sharing problem was the readers/writers problem [75]. Early surveys of synchronization, for example, [22], took a point of view heavily influenced by operating systems. More parallel processing oriented treatments have often focused on a set of different machines [93] or a range of implementations on a specific machine, such as the treatment of spin locks on the Sequent system in [124]. Spin lock comparisons are also treated by Anderson [20]. The starvation-free mutual exclusion problem was first solved by Dekker [91]. It has been generalized and discussed by others, for example, [192], including textbook presentations, for example, [236]. The proof of parallel program and synchronization correctness has been treated by Hoare [142]. The implications of various barrier implementations have been treated in general [24, 31] and in connection with specific hardware, such as the Ultra computer fetch&add operation [15].

Problems

8.1   This problem assumes a computer that does all synchronization using full/empty variables. The operations on them are defined as:

produce(a, x)—waits for a to be empty, stores the value of x into it, sets a full and proceeds, all in an atomic manner.

consume(a, $priv$)—atomically waits for a to be full, copies its value into the private variable $priv$, sets a empty and proceeds.

It is required to have synchronized access to two word variables considered as a unit. For the purposes of this problem, assume a representation by two element vectors $a2[1{:}2]$, $x2[1{:}2]$, and $priv2[1{:}2]$.

     (a) Using only **produce** and **consume** for synchronization, write procedures **produce2**($a2$, $x2$) and **consume2**($a2$, $priv2$) which treat $a2$ as a single synchronized unit.

     (b) Does your solution extend to multiple word variables of more than two words? Why or why not?

8.2   Assume a multiprocessor with P processes running on different processors. The set of processes is divided into K disjoint subsets, 0, 1, ..., $K-1$, by assigning a color to each process. For example, the process with index ME could be assigned color, color $(ME) = ME$ mod K.

        Define a control-oriented synchronization called a rainbow section that has an entry, **begin rsect**, and an exit, **end rsect**. It imposes the synchronization condition that no two processes of the same color can occupy a rainbow section simultaneously. Processes of different colors can overlap their executions of the section.

        Implement rainbow sections for a shared memory multiprocessor having only unconditional critical sections for synchronization. That is, using only **begin critical** and **end critical** as synchronization operations, write pseudocode to implement **begin rsect** and **end rsect**. Comment well, and describe the purpose of any auxiliary variables introduced.

8.3   A k-restricted section is like a critical section except that, instead of only one process, no more than k processes can be inside the section simultaneously.

     (a) Extend Amdahl's law to give the execution time with N processors for a program containing S seconds of strictly sequential work, L seconds of perfectly parallelizable work, and a k-restricted section of length R seconds that must be executed by all processes.

     (b) Show how to implement k-restricted sections using only critical section synchronization by writing MIMD pseudocode for the entry, **ksect**, and the exit, **end ksect**, statements of a k-restricted section. Specify shared and private variables and initial conditions.

8.4   The IBM370 multiprocessors had a compare and swap synchronization instruction, which did the following atomically with respect to all other accesses to Var:

        CAS(old, new, Var, match)—If old=Var, set match:=**true** and Var:=new. Otherwise, replace old:=Var and set match:=**false**.

        Other synchronizations were implemented in terms of this assembly language primitive.

        Show how to implement critical sections with pseudocode using CAS as the only primitive synchronization operation.

8.5   Consider implementing a barrier synchronization on a machine that has only produce/consume operations as its basic synchronization mechanism. For simplicity, assume that the barrier is executed only once so that only one blocking variable, called `outlock` below, is needed. Ignore the lock needed to prevent processes from executing the barrier a second time before all have completed the first. Pseudocode for the barrier could be:

```
consume count into c
c := c + 1 ;
if c ≠ numproc then produce count := c
     else produce  outlock := true ;
waitfull(outlock) ;
```

        The problem is that a potentially large number of processes may be accessing count or reading `outlock` to test its state in competition with the one process which wants to write it. The solution to this problem is to divide up the competition and have each process synchronize with a limited number of others.

Let the processes be broken up into groups of size G. When all processes of a group have arrived at the barrier, a single process reports for that group to the next higher level group of G. P processors require $\log_G P$ levels of reporting.

Write MIMD pseudocode similar to the above to show how this solution for the barrier competition can be implemented. You may assume a language with recursive procedures, but use only the full/empty data mechanism for synchronization.

8.6 Consider the atomic fetch&add operation. `fetch&add(x, e)` returns the old value of x and replaces its value with `x + e` in one memory cycle. As an example, if the initial value of x is one, then `fetch&add(x, 2)` returns a one and replaces x with three in memory.

The following is an attempt to implement the semaphore operations P and V using the fetch&add operation. What is wrong with the implementation? show a scenario that demonstrates your answer clearly. Provide the necessary correction.

```
shared integer S;
private boolean OK;
S := 1;
OK := false;

procedure P(S)
      repeat
           begin
                if (fetch&add(S, -1) > 0) then OK := true;
                     else
                          begin
                               OK := false;
                               fetch&add(S, 1);
                          end;
           end;
        until OK;
end procedure;

procedure V(S)
        fetch&add(S, 1);
end procedure;
```

8.7 Suppose you are given a machine in which a memory word has three distinct atomic operations, read, write, and an increment instruction, INC, that in one memory cycle increments the integer in a word by one, and, if the word contains the maximum representable integer, the word is not altered but a testable overflow bit is set.

   (a) Show how the **lock** and **unlock** synchronizations can be implemented using the INC instruction.

   (b) How important is the fact that incrementing the largest integer does not change its value?

CHAPTER 9

Parallel Processor Performance

Modeling the performance of a computer system accurately is complex. Too many factors from a variety of sources play significant roles in the performance of a computer system, not least of which are the memory hierarchy, operating systems, interconnection networks, processor design, cache and memory management, latency tolerance mechanisms, algorithm design, and programming languages. A complete model including all these influences is not feasible to build. However, performance measures have been introduced to provide insight into the behavior of a computer system, some more successfully than others. It is quite common to represent the performance of a computer system in terms of its peak operation rate. Floating point operations per second (FLOPS) is a poor indicator of system performance for all but the simplest code sequences. While this processor-centered performance measure represents a start in characterizing the performance of compute bound problems that fit in the lowest level of the memory hierarchy, it is inadequate for large problems or for those with even moderate complexity in data access patterns. It is completely meaningless for non-numeric problems such as sorting and database queries. Performance measures must be derived to represent the program execution reasonably and to correctly explain the reason behind the obtained performance. Such measures must include overall system factors affecting the performance and not only the speed of the processor.

Observing program execution time while varying some parameters can give fairly detailed information about parallel program behavior. For example, we can observe the effects of different synchronization mechanisms and the divisibility of parallel work and its mapping on the parallel units. A better measure of computer performance than FLOPS is data transfer capacity. This applies not only to the processor but throughout a computer system. Data transfer capacity is primarily measured by bandwidth and latency. This performance measure does not ignore FLOPS but includes it. The data transfer capacity of a pipelined floating point unit is characterized by its bandwidth, which corresponds to peak FLOPS, and its latency, which is the pipeline start up time.

Bandwidth and latency are standard for characterizing disk I/O, and they also have been used to describe communication overhead in distributed memory multiprocessors. It is a natural measure for load and store behavior in superscalar processors and for the interface between cache and main memory. Many of the reasons for derating peak FLOPS in determining performance on real problems are related to the movement of data within a system. Inability to keep cache hit ratio high because successive data accesses are not unit stride, or not predictable at all, can be a problem even in a scalar uniprocessor. In vector processors, the need to move large vectors piecewise into the lowest level of storage hierarchy supplying the vector unit, for example vector registers, is a major reason for failure to achieve the peak vector processing rate. In a distributed memory multiprocessor, the movement of messages containing intermediate results is the primary reason for not obtaining peak operation rate in the processors. In a shared memory multiprocessor, processing is slowed when the processor is forced to wait for large shared memory access latency, either for the transmission of data or of cache coherence information.

In this chapter, we build parameterized execution models to reflect the behavior of executing parallel programs on parallel architectures, the focus being on coupling the physical parallelism of the architecture with the parallelism and synchronization needs of the executing program. We then explore various implementations of barrier synchronization and study their performance and efficiency for certain systems. Finally, we design analytical models for dynamically and statically scheduled parallel loops, concentrating on the effects of synchronization, workload, the size of the parallel work, and conditional executions.

Among the questions to keep in mind while reading this chapter are the following. Can a performance model give insight into the efficacy of a particular architectural feature? Can a performance model be sufficiently general to predict the best code structure over a variety of architectures? Can performance analysis predict the best implementation of a high overhead synchronization? Which work scheduling mechanisms give the best performance under different conditions?

9.1 Amdahl's Law Revisited

Recall from Section 2.7 of Chapter 2 the discussion of Amdahl's law as a general model of parallel processor performance. We took f as the fraction of the program that must be executed sequentially and assumed that the remaining fraction $(1 - f)$ can be executed in parallel with 100% efficiency. With P representing the number of parallel hardware units, we modeled the execution time $T(P)$ as

$$T(P) = f \cdot T(1) + (1-f)\frac{T(1)}{P}. \tag{9.1}$$

This oversimplified model of parallel computation is surprisingly informative and can be modified and extended to give precise information about several types of parallel systems.

9.1.1   The Effect of Work Granularity on Amdahl's Law

One of the oversimplifications is the assumption that the parallel work, $(1-f)T(1)$, can be evenly divided over an arbitrary number P of processors. The simplest case that occurs in practice is that the parallel work consists of N units of work of a fixed size, t_u, so that $(1-f)T(1) = Nt_u$. Each unit of work, t_u, may be executed in parallel with others but cannot be subdivided. A parallel loop, **doall**, with N iterations would have this kind of behavior. Executing such a program on a multi-processor with P processors results in $\lceil N/P \rceil$ steps, during the first $\lfloor N/P \rfloor$ steps all P processors execute a unit of work, and during the last step fewer than P processors execute the remaining number of units. Thus, execution time is given by

$$T(P) = fT(1) + \left\lceil \frac{N}{P} \right\rceil t_u.$$ (9.2)

Clearly the execution time can only decrease when P becomes large enough to divide N one fewer times. For example, with $N = 100$, the same execution time of $fT(1) + 3t_u$ is obtained with 34–49 processors. A graph of the execution time versus number of processors gives useful insight. For $N = 50$, $f = 0$, and $T(1) = 100$ time units ($t_u = 2$), the curve would appear as in Figure 9-1. The graph does not represent measured data but values from the model with the specified parameters. The discontinuities in the graph are at points where the amount of work, N, divides the number of processors evenly. The execution remains flat between two consecutive discontinuity points, illustrating the fact that no increased performance is obtained by adding processors unless enough processors are added to achieve one fewer units of work for all pro-cesses. Comparison of this graph with the continuous curve given by Equation (9.1) shows the execution time differences resulting from the fixed granularity of the parallel work.

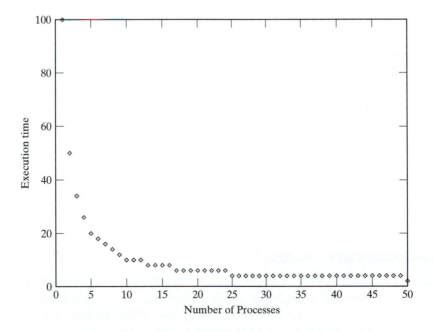

Figure 9-1   Execution time versus processors for fixed granularity work.

9.1.2   Least Squares Estimation of Amdahl's Law Parameters

It is often useful to estimate the parameters of an Amdahl's law model of execution time from measurements on an actual program. In tuning an application for high performance on a specific parallel architecture, for example, estimates of the sequential fraction of code before and after a modification can give an idea of its value. If a series of k measurements of execution time, T_i, for differing numbers of processors, P_i, $i = 1, \ldots, k$, are taken, then the Amdahl's law prediction, $T(P_i)$, should correspond to T_i. A least squares estimate of the parameters in the Amdahl's model comes from minimizing the sum, S, of the squared deviations of the measured values from the model values, where

$$S = \sum_{i=1}^{k} (T_i - T(P_i))^2 = \sum_{i=1}^{k} \left(T_i - fT(1) - \frac{(1-f)T(1)}{P_i} \right)^2. \tag{9.3}$$

There are two cases of interest. In the first case, the time for one process is explicitly measured and assumed to be exact, say $P_0 = 1$, $T_0 = T(1)$. Then the only free parameter in Amdahl's law is the fraction, f, of sequential work, and it is estimated by minimizing S with respect to f. This is done by solving $\partial S/\partial f = 0$ for f and using the measured value for $T(1)$. The second case arises when either the time for one process execution is not measured or is not considered exact. In this case, both $T(1)$ and f can be estimated by simultaneously solving $\partial S/\partial f = 0$ and $\partial S/\partial T(1) = 0$. After some algebra, the results can be simplified by defining

$$t_1 = \sum_{i=1}^{k} T_i, \quad t_2 = \sum_{i=1}^{k} T_i/P_i, \quad r_1 = \sum_{i=1}^{k} P_i^{-1}, \text{ and } r_2 = \sum_{i=1}^{k} P_i^{-2}. \tag{9.4}$$

Then for the first case with one free parameter

$$f = \frac{(t_1 - t_2)/T(1) - r_1 + r_2}{k - 2r_1 + r_2}. \tag{9.5}$$

In the second case with two free parameters

$$T(1) = \frac{r_1(t_1 + t_2) - t_1 r_2 - kt_2}{r_1^2 - kr_2}, \text{ and} \tag{9.6}$$

$$f = \frac{t_1}{T(1)(k - r_2)} - \frac{r_1}{k - r_1}. \tag{9.7}$$

9.2 Parameterized Execution Time

Two measures of performance have frequently been used in characterizing computations; execution time and its reciprocal, speed. Speed, that is, rate of execution of operations, has the disadvantage of suppressing the total number of operations needed to complete a job. It only represents how fast the operations are being executed. An algorithm and its implementation can exhibit a high rate of executing operations while, at the same time, requiring far more operations than a better algorithm or implementation. Even more questionable is the use of speedup $S = T_1/T_P$, or the ratio of operation rate on a parallel computer to the operation rate of a "similar" sequential machine R_P/R_1. Speedup is only accurate if the terms R_1 and R_P actually belong to comparable parallel and sequential computers. Imagining a sequential machine that forms a meaningful basis for R_1 is extremely tenuous. The utility of speedup curves is a result of the fact that they characterize performance over a range of variation in a system parameter, yielding much more information than a single value of the (suspect) ratio. As we saw in Section 9.1, fairly detailed information was obtained by observing performance while varying the number of processors. This idea of tracking a performance measure over the variation of a parameter of the computation is quite powerful when applied to the total execution time, which is the direct characterization of the performance.

A significant advantage of execution time as a measure of performance is that it is noninvasive. Measuring start and stop times is simple and does not affect or change the performance of the program. Execution time, however, represents a combination of influences from all the levels of the computation from algorithm to the architecture listed in Table 2-2 of Chapter 2. Valuable information can be obtained if the execution time is measured as a function of some parameter that can be varied to demonstrate the influence of one or more aspects of overall performance. Some examples of parameters whose variation can give significant information about performance are:

- Vector length—on either a pipelined or a true SIMD machine
- Number of processes—on a multiprocessor
- Address stride—on a machine needing regular access patterns
- Data placement—in private or shared memories
- Virtual process ratio—on a massively parallel virtualized SIMD machine

Parameterized execution time can be modeled to explore the ability of the architecture to handle a particular kind of parallelism, the effectiveness of the compiler in exploiting the architecture, and the efficiency of the run-time/operating system in handling certain control or synchronization structures in the program.

9.2.1   Pipelined Vector Machine Performance

An important example is the characterization of the performance of pipelined vector computers by expressing the time to complete a simple vector operation as a function of vector length. Assume that vectors of length N are processed in strips of R components at a time. The strips can arise from machines with vector registers or from a limitation on the size of a vector length specifier.

The key parameters in characterizing a vector operation are listed in Table 9-1. Using these parameters, the execution time can be expressed by Equation (9.8).

Table 9-1   Parameters characterizing a vector operation.

N	Vector length
T_S	Time to start a full vector operation
T_r	Time to start a strip
T_e	Time to deliver one result at full pipeline speed
R	Length of strip (size of vector registers)

$$T(N) = T_S + NT_e + T_r \left\lceil \frac{N}{R} \right\rceil. \tag{9.8}$$

This equation can be rearranged as in Equation (9.9) to better describe the behavior of a vector pipeline.

$$T(N) = T_S + N\left(T_e + \frac{T_r}{R}\right) + T_r\left(1 - \frac{N \bmod R}{R}\right)\left(\left\lceil \frac{N}{R} \right\rceil - \left\lfloor \frac{N}{R} \right\rfloor\right). \tag{9.9}$$

The first two terms represent the behavior of an ideal pipeline that takes strips into account only in an average way. The last term is the "granularity correction" term. It corrects for the fraction of the startup time for the last strip that is not included in the second term. The last term is zero when N divides R evenly, otherwise it is the fraction that is needed to make a complete last sweep over the vector operation. Taking hardware values of the parameters of Table 9-1 for a Cray 1 computer performing $A = A + b$, where A is a vector and b is a scalar, results in the execution time versus vector length graph of Figure 9-2. The parameter values are $T_S = 900$ ns, $T_r = 275$ ns, $T_e = 25$ ns, and $R = 64$. In this figure the execution time is divided by N, which makes the curve approach an asymptote of $T_e + \frac{T_r}{R}$. This asymptotic rate is the maximum pipeline delivery rate with the strip startup time amortized over the R vector components in a strip. The positions of the discontinuities correspond to multiples of the strip length, 64. The height of the discontinuities at the strip boundaries gives a good estimate of the time to start a strip, T_r.

The parameters characterizing a vector operation are influenced by both hardware and software. In particular, the compiler can have a significant influence. A vector operation is specified by the user either as a sequential loop for an autovectorizing compiler or as an explicit vector operation, as in Fortran 90 for example. The compiler produces the code that strip mines the operation and attempts to recognize special cases where more efficient code than the general case can be used. T_S and T_r are influenced by the type of code produced, as well as the vector unit hardware. The use of such a parameterized execution time measurement, along with its describing model, can give valuable insight into system performance. Even in a complex program, it is possible that the strip character of a major vector operation will have a visible effect on the overall execution time. If the hardware values are known, the model can help to understand the quality of compiler generated vector code as well.

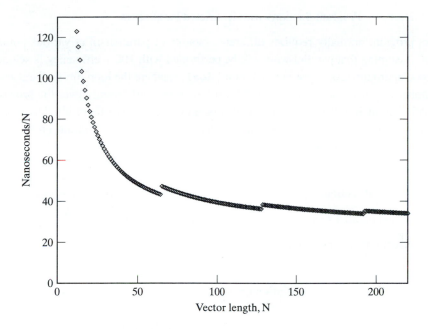

Figure 9-2 Execution time per component for a V = V + S operation.

9.2.2 Pipelined Multiprocessor Performance

The object in getting maximum performance from a pipelined multiprocessor is to execute enough processes simultaneously to keep pipelines full of independent operations. There may be different pipelines for different operations and a limit on the number of operations that can be issued in a cycle. These limitations can be summarized by an average pipeline length and issue rate that lead to an upper limit, say U, on the number of processes that can execute in parallel. Running a number of processes $P > U$ will only result in more processes waiting in the queues of Figure 4-18 of Section 4.5, but no more operations per second. If there is overhead associated with additional processes, execution time increases with more processes when $P > U$. For $P < U$, however, a pipelined multiprocessor effectively behaves like a true multiprocessor made up of CPUs that execute at the rate of a single process running on the pipelined machine.

The performance studies of this and the next sections refer to the Denelcor HEP pipelined multiprocessor. This machine had the advantage of following a fairly pure pipelined MIMD execution model. A processor issued one instruction per clock cycle and had an average pipeline length of 10–15, depending on system size and instruction mix. The principles illustrated by the studies apply to shared memory multiprocessors in general, with some easily distinguishable features resulting from pipelined or multithreaded operation.

9.2.2.1   Program Sections with Restricted Parallelism

A parallel program normally requires different amounts of parallelism at various points of its execution. Assuming that parallel work can be performed with 100% efficiency is seldom justified. A good approximation is for parallel loops, doalls, where the loop limit is large compared to the number of processors. In this case the work divides nearly evenly over the processors. A doall with a limit less than the number of processors cannot use them all. Therefore, some parts of a program may limit the possible parallelism. Suppose the program breaks into three fractions with different characteristics:

- f_1 - Sequential section.

- f_2 - Limited parallel section.   doall $I = 1, K, K \approx P$

- f_3 - Perfectly parallel section.   doall $I = 1, N, N >> P$

Then, ignoring granularity, the execution time with P processors is given by Equation (9.10).

$$T(P) = f_1 T(1) + \frac{f_2 T(1)}{\min(K, P)} + \frac{f_3 T(1)}{P}. \qquad (9.10)$$

In this case, a speedup curve gives insight into performance. The speedup with P processors is

$$S(P) = \frac{1}{f_1 + \dfrac{f_2}{\min(K, P)} + \dfrac{f_3}{P}}. \qquad (9.11)$$

In this case, the speedup is computed relative to one processor executing the same parallel program, and it is the relative values of speedup for $P > 1$ that are important, so the concern about a good single processor comparison is not an issue. A close look at Equation (9.11) shows that the slope of the speedup curve versus the number of processors changes at the point where P becomes larger than the limited parallelism K. If f_1 and f_2/K are both small, the slope of the speedup curve is about $\frac{1}{f_2+f_3}$ for $P \le K$ and about $\frac{1}{f_3}$ for $P \ge K$. Execution of a sparse LU decomposition program consisting of several thousand lines of code with a known section limiting speedup at $P = 6$ resulted in the speedup curve of Figure 9-3. The program was run on the Denelcor HEP computer. The limited parallelism is accounted for by the fact that the sparse matrix had approximately six nonzero elements per row and column. A sharp change in slope of the speedup versus P curve indicates limited parallelism. One can imagine optimizing the performance of a parallel program by observing the position of such a slope change and searching for the code section limiting speedup at that point.

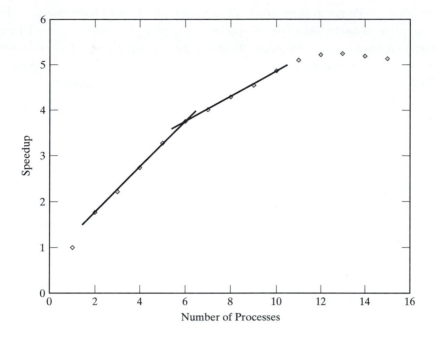

Figure 9-3   Speedup of a program with a limited parallelism section.

There can also be a hardware limit on the amount of parallelism. This effect is observed when more parallelism can be exploited by the program than the hardware can actually support. It has some similarity to program limited parallelism and occurs when more processes can be created than there are processors. It also happens for pipelined multiprocessors, where more processes are active than can be in the pipeline at any time. Let U be the number of parallel hardware units, processors or pipeline stages. The execution time of a parallel program can be expressed by

$$T(P) = fT(1) + \frac{(1-f)T(1)}{\min(U, P)}.$$
(9.12)

This implies that in a machine with hardware parallelism, U, the execution time reaches a lower limit, beyond which the use of more processes can give no more speedup. The limit is given by

$$T(P) = fT(1) + \frac{(1-f)T(1)}{U}.$$
(9.13)

This limit is clearly seen in the speedup curve of Figure 9-3, starting at about $P = 12$, and the execution actually slows beyond this point due to the overhead of adding unproductive processes.

9.2.2.2   Programs Requiring Critical Sections for Parallel Execution

It is also possible to model the effect of synchronizing critical sections on parallel execution time. Synchronization has an important effect on the execution time of parallel programs. Mutual exclusion, or critical sections, form a simple model of synchronizing behavior. Assume that of the $T(1)$ work in a program a fraction f is strictly sequential, a fraction $(1-f)$ is perfectly parallel, but parallelizing the fraction $(1-f)$ requires adding a critical section of length t_c in each process, as shown in Figure 9-4.

The effect of the critical section on performance depends on the order of execution. If all of the processes arrive simultaneously at the critical section, one of them must wait for $P-1$ others to complete it before entering. This is the worst case behavior. If the amount of work for each process is larger than $(P-1)t_c$, then it is possible that while one process is executing its critical section, all others are doing useful work. This is the best case behavior. When $(P-1)t_c > \frac{(1-f)T(1)}{P}$ then, even in the best case, all critical section delay cannot be masked by useful work. Therefore, a process needs at least $(P-1)t_c$ units of parallel work to mask the critical section delay as other processes serially execute work of length t_c each. In practice, the best case analysis corresponds to actual program behavior. This happens because the parallel work section in each process is usually in the form of a loop of, say m, iterations. The critical section time t_c is actually m sections of length t_c/m in the loop. On the first loop iteration, all processes arrive at the critical section simultaneously. Each process is delayed by a different amount so that they arrive at the critical section at times separated by t_c/m on the second and subsequent iterations and, thus, obtain the best case behavior.

We write the execution time model assuming best case arrival times at the critical section. For the case where the parallel work for a process is greater than the total critical section delay, $\frac{(1-f)T(1)}{P} \geq (P-1)t_c$, the execution time of the program is given by

$$T(P) = fT(1) + \frac{(1-f)T(1)}{P} + t_c. \tag{9.14}$$

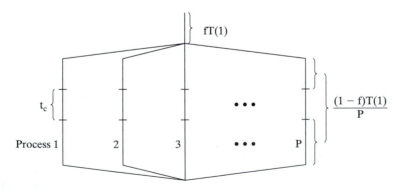

Figure 9-4   Program for which parallelization requires a critical section.

When the sum of the sequentially executed critical sections is larger than the parallel work, $\frac{(1-f)T(1)}{P} < (P-1)t_c$, the program execution time becomes

$$T(P) = fT(1) + Pt_c. \tag{9.15}$$

Combining the two cases for large and small parallel work results in the unified form of

$$T(P) = fT(1) + t_c + \max\left(\frac{(1-f)T(1)}{P}, (P-1)t_c\right). \tag{9.16}$$

Taking the hardware parallelism limit into account, we obtain the execution time model

$$T(P) = fT(1) + t_c + \max\left(\frac{(1-f)T(1)}{\min(P, U)}, (P-1)t_c\right). \tag{9.17}$$

We use the measurements made for a successive over-relaxation (SOR) program on the Denelcor HEP computer to show the accuracy of the execution time model of Equation (9.17). The parallelism limit in the HEP and the critical section overhead are seen in the measurements of execution time of the SOR program versus the number of processes shown in Figure 9-5. A fit to the execution time model equation matches the measurements well, as shown by Figure 9-6. The continuous line in the figure represents the equation,

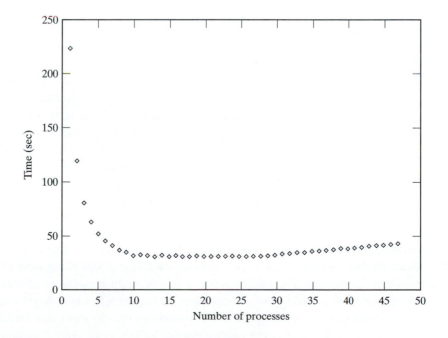

Figure 9-5 Execution time measurements for an SOR program.

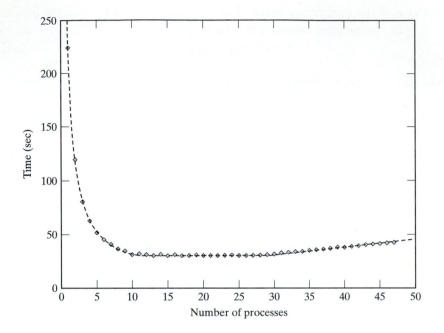

Figure 9-6 Measured data and fitted execution time model equation.

$$T(P) = 9.15 + 0.73 + \max\left(\frac{215.10}{\min(P,\ 10.51)},\ 0.73(P-1)\right).$$ (9.18)

From the fitted equation, we can gain an understanding of the parallel program. The amount of strictly sequential work in the program is about 9.15 seconds. The amount of parallelizable work is about 215.10 seconds. The slope of linear rise for $P > 30$ gives a critical section time of 0.73 seconds. The onset of the flat bottom to the curve is at the hardware parallelism limit of $U = 10.51$. This represents the effective MIMD pipeline length in the specific HEP system for which this experiment was run. All of the time parameters are consistent with time estimates derived directly from the program code. The hardware parallelism limit is also consistent with that measured on other programs run on the same pipelined MIMD computer.

9.2.2.3   Granularity Correction to the Critical Section Model

There seem to be some small deviations, like noise, in the measurements. In fact it is not noise, but can be understood mathematically. We refine the execution time model of Equation (9.17) to include a granularity correction. The parallel work of this program is made up of indivisible units of work derived from a parallel loop, as discussed in Section 9.1, where N units of work each of size t_u can be done in parallel. Equation (9.2) would describe the execution time if there were separate, complete processors in the multiprocessor. Including the critical section effect and the hardware parallelism limit of a pipelined multiprocessor results in

$$T(P) = fT(1) + t_c + \max\left(\frac{P\lfloor N/P \rfloor t_u}{\min(P, U)} + \frac{(N \bmod P)t_u}{\min(N \bmod P, U)}, (P-1)t_c\right). \tag{9.19}$$

If we rewrite Equation (9.17) using Nt_u for the amount of parallel work $(1-f)T(1)$, we obtain

$$\hat{T}(P) = fT(1) + t_c + \max\left(\frac{Nt_u}{\min(P, U)}, (P-1)t_c\right) \tag{9.20}$$

for the continuous execution time model, without the effects of discrete work units. The difference $T(P) - \hat{T}(P)$ can be viewed as a small correction term, $\delta(P)$, to adjust the continuous model to its correct discrete form and is given by

$$\begin{aligned}
\delta(P) &= \frac{P\lfloor N/P \rfloor t_u}{\min(P, U)} + \frac{(N \bmod P)t_u}{\min(N \bmod P, U)} - \left(\frac{P\lfloor N/P \rfloor t_u}{\min(P, U)} + \frac{(N \bmod P)t_u}{\min(P, U)}\right) \\
&= \frac{N \bmod P t_u}{\min(N \bmod P, U)} - \frac{N \bmod P t_u}{\min(P, U)}
\end{aligned} \tag{9.21}$$

provided $(P-1)t_c \le \frac{P\lfloor N/P \rfloor t_u}{\min(P, U)}$. For $(P-1)t_c \ge \frac{P\lfloor N/P \rfloor t_u}{\min(P, U)}$, Equations (9.20) and (9.19) are both dominated by $(P-1)t_c$ in the maximum function, and $\delta(P) = 0$.

Thus, we can write an execution time model with granularity correction as

$$T(P) = fT(1) + t_c + \max\left(\frac{Nt_u}{\min(P, U)}, (P-1)t_c\right) + \delta(P), \text{ where} \tag{9.22}$$

P: number of processes,
$fT(1)$: amount of sequential work,
N: range of parallel loop,
t_u: work for one instance of the loop body,
U: average length of multiprocessor pipeline,
t_c: work for single critical section execution, and
$\delta(P)$: granularity correction when P does not divide N evenly.

The behavior of $\delta(P)$ is characterized in several separate cases. First, $\delta(P) = 0$ for $(P-1)t_c \ge \frac{P\lceil N/P \rceil t_u}{\min(P, U)}$. This is the case when execution time is dominated by processes serially executing their critical sections. The granularity correction is always zero if P divides N evenly. For the condition under which Equation (9.21) holds, $\delta(P) = 0$ if $N \bmod P \ge U$, while if $P \le U$, Equation (9.21) can be rewritten in the form,

$$\delta(P) = t_u\left(1 - \frac{N \bmod P}{P}\right). \tag{9.23}$$

$\delta(P)$ vanishes in three cases, when P evenly divides N, when the critical section dominates execution time, and when the parallelism limit is smaller than the number of processes active for

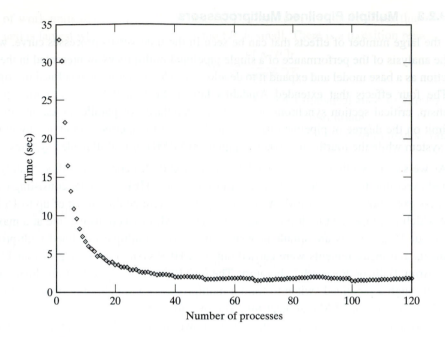

Figure 9-8   200×200 matrix multiply on a 4 PEM HEP.

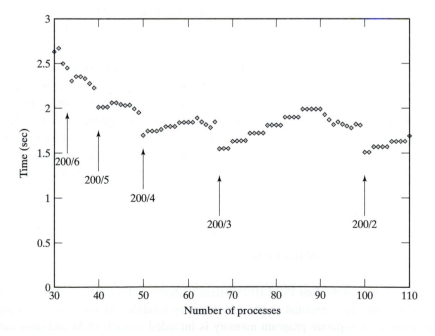

Figure 9-9   Granularity discontinuities and fine structure.

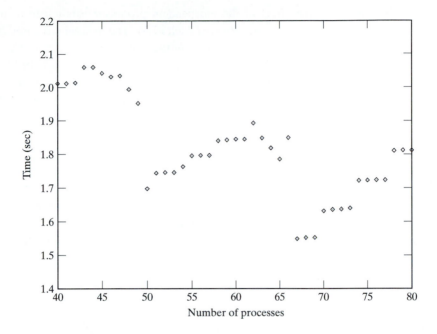

Figure 9-10 Details of the matrix multiply performance fine structure.

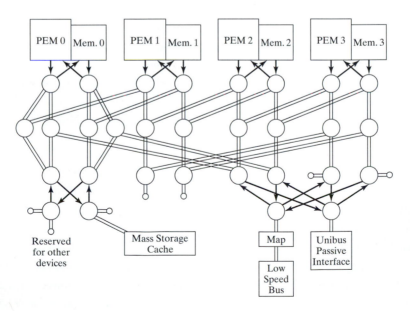

Figure 9-11 Architecture of a four PEM HEP computer.

We start by explaining the effect of the independent processor parallelism of the four PEMs, superimposed on the pipelined parallelism of each PEM. The parallel processes of a single job in this system are managed by the program rather than the operating system. This matrix multiply program divides the processes evenly among the four PEMs. On a single PEM, adding processes decreases the overall execution time until the pipeline parallelism limit has been reached. After this point addition of a process results in increase in the execution time. The execution time increases until the addition of a process reduces the maximum number of work units per process, $\lceil \frac{N}{P} \rceil$. In the case of working with four PEMs and distributing the processes evenly among them, the addition of a process to the first one of the four increases the total execution time, which is the maximum over each of the PEMs. Addition of three more processes does not increase the total execution time, as the execution time of the PEMs with more work units is the overall completion time. This argument predicts a jump in execution time for each P such that $P \bmod 4 = 1$. This effect is best seen in Figure 9-10 between 70 and 80 processes. Using the above argument, the jump in the execution time should be observed at $P = 69$, $P = 73$, and $P = 77$ respectively. A closer look at Figure 9-10, however, reveals that the jumps are occurring at $P = 70$, $P = 74$, and $P = 78$. This is the result of the way this version of the program was implemented. Rather than assign one process to each PEM in a round robin fashion so that we would have assigned process 0 to PEM0, process 1 to PEM1, process 2 to PEM2, process 3 to PEM3, process 4 to PEM0, and so on, the assignment was done differently. In this version, the original process, process 0, was used to assign process 1 to PEM0, process 2 to PEM1, process 3 to PEM2, process 4 to PEM3, process 5 to PEM0, and so on. At the end of this process assignment, process 0 itself participated in the matrix multiply by picking up work and executing on PEM0. As a result of this distribution, when $P \bmod 4 = 1$, PEM0 should have exactly one more process than the other PEMs. The increases in execution time, therefore, occur at $P \bmod 4 = 2$, where four divides $P - 2$ PEMs evenly but the two remainder processes are assigned to PEM0.

The fine structure in Figure 9-10 can almost be explained by superimposing the above four PEM effect on the granularity correction of Equation (9.25). However, there are still some unexplained decreases in the execution time, most obvious between 62 and 65 processes. To explain this final feature of the execution time versus processes curve, it is necessary to understand the lookahead feature installed on each of the PEMs of the HEP computer.

The primary use of the execution pipeline in a pipelined multiprocessor is to overlap the execution of the instructions from independent streams. Figure 9-12(a) shows a four-stage pipeline executing the jth instruction of four independent instruction streams, I_0, I_1, I_2, and I_4. The instruction execution rate for each process is $r = \frac{1}{\text{pipeline latency}}$. If more instruction streams are active than there are pipeline stages, then the time between instruction issues from the same stream is increased by the ratio of the number of active processes to the length of the pipeline, $\frac{4}{6}r$ for the example shown in Figure 9-12(b). Finally, some successive instructions in a single process may be independent. In this case, a limited number of simultaneous executions may be obtained by placing such instructions together in the pipeline if lookahead is available. The lookahead feature of a HEP PEM only takes effect if the process queue is empty at issue time. In that case, it checks some simple sufficient conditions for independence of the next instruction in the stream just serviced and, if they are satisfied, issues that instruction immediately. Two consecutive instructions belonging to one process are shown to be executing in a four-stage pipeline in Figure 9-12(c). In this case, the instruction rate is $f_l r$, where f_l is the average number of instructions in the execution pipeline.

In a HEP PEM, the execution pipeline is eight stages long and lookahead does not apply to the memory access pipeline. Thus, lookahead has an effect only when fewer than eight processes are active on a PEM, and it is quite sensitive to the actual instruction sequence. The effect of lookahead on matrix multiply is observed when a small number, 200 mod P, of rows of the product matrix remain to be done after $\left\lfloor \frac{200}{P} \right\rfloor$ parallel steps with all of the processes are completed. When fewer than eight processes are active on a PEM in the remainder phase, lookahead is used more and more efficiently as the number of active processes decreases.

Specifically, between $P = 62$ and $P = 65$ in Figure 9-10, the number of active processes in the remainder phase decreases by three for each increase of P by one, that is, 14, 11, 8, and 5, respectively. The allocation of processes to PEMs and the assignment of the remainder work to processes implies that the PEM having the most work, PEM0, executes 5, 4, 3, and 2 processes in the remainder phase for $P = 62$, 63, 64, and 65, respectively. The speedup resulting from increasing use of lookahead on this PEM accounts for the decreasing execution time.

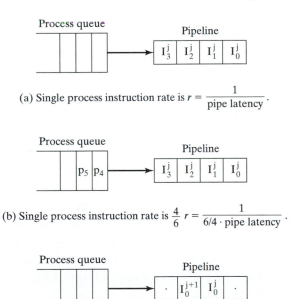

(a) Single process instruction rate is $r = \dfrac{1}{\text{pipe latency}}$.

(b) Single process instruction rate is $\dfrac{4}{6} r = \dfrac{1}{6/4 \cdot \text{pipe latency}}$.

(c) Instruction rate is $f_l r$, where f_l = average number of instructions in pipe.

Figure 9-12   Load cases for a multiprocessor pipeline.

With the final addition of the lookahead understanding, the nature of the fine structure is completely explained. While at first glance it was tempting to explain the fine structure as measurement noise, its apparent randomness comes from the superimposition of effects with an underlying period of P mod 4 related to the remainder of 200 divided by P.

9.3 Performance of Barrier Synchronization

The models developed in the previous sections describe execution behavior of a program as a whole on a parallel architecture focusing on hardware and software parallelism limits, divisibility of work, and effects of synchronization on performance. We now turn our attention to a specific synchronization, barrier, and study its performance influence on the execution of parallel programs. The barrier is a synchronization among all executing processes, all of which encounter a barrier construct at some point in their execution. The synchronization requires that all processes execute the barrier construct before any process can proceed past it to the next executable statement. Since its introduction in connection with hardware support for global synchronization, it has been used in various parallel languages and incorporated in parallel language standards proposals. We have seen in Section 8.6 that several implementations of barrier synchronization are possible. A particular implementation may perform well on some systems and poorly on others. To understand its behavior, we must identify the key components influencing a barrier's performance and investigate the effects of alternative implementations in various environments.

The barrier is usually used to satisfy a number of data dependences simultaneously by imposing sequentiality on the production and use of data items. We discussed its use in the cooperative update of a partitioned structure in Section 8.2.4. The barrier is one of a class of synchronizations that can be called "generic," to indicate that processes are not identified by name. The synchronization condition is specified by the quantifier "all."

Of several variations on the semantics of the barrier, perhaps the most important is the way in which the set of processes quantified by "all" is defined. In some systems, implicit knowledge of a parallel execution environment defines the set, while in other systems a simple count of the number of processes to arrive before the barrier is satisfied is used. It is also possible to modify the semantics by including a section of sequential code to be executed by one process between the beginning and end of a barrier construct. This code is executed after all processors have arrived at the barrier and before any process leaves it. Even an ideal barrier with no implementation overhead has a performance impact resulting from processes that arrive early becoming idle while waiting for the latest arriving process, as shown in Figure 9-13.

9.3.1 Accounting for Barrier Performance

The barrier implementation choices listed in Table 8-3 all have their own impacts on performance, but regardless of implementation, there are several different influences on time accounting in measurements of barrier performance. The major ones are:

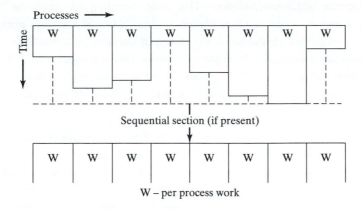

Figure 9-13 Execution time profile of an ideal barrier.

- Delays in arrival of processes;
- Waiting mechanism;
- Swapped processes, perhaps due to interrupts;
- Code of the barrier implementation;
- Synchronization delays, i.e., critical sections.

Delays in arrival of processes: The purpose of the barrier is to synchronize processes arriving at different times, so the ideal performance is to wait for the latest arriving process with no other overhead. In addition to the ideal behavior, a differential delay among the arriving processes can mask some of the barrier code execution. This masking is most effective for a self-scheduled barrier that uses a critical section to update a shared count of arriving processes. If a prescheduled, master-slave barrier implementation is used, then the order of arrival of processes makes a large difference in the amount of barrier code that can be masked by the arrival time differential. Thus, in measuring the performance of such barriers, either a fixed arrival order must be specified and guaranteed, or a sufficiently large sample of random arrival orders must be taken to obtain average performance. The arrival order for self-scheduled, symmetric barriers is irrelevant, and no measurement precautions need be taken with respect to arrival order.

Waiting mechanism and swapped processes: Once processes start arriving at the barrier, the early arrivals must be caused to wait for the later ones. The waiting mechanism may be busy waiting, virtualization of processes (swapping them out), or something intermediate between the two. Busy waiting wastes processor cycles during long delays, while virtualization is associated with an irreducible minimum overhead, which is often quite long. Intermediate positions are possible in systems that support a lightweight process model or by giving up the processor only after an initial busy waiting period, the duration of which is determined by the swapping overhead of the particular system. Measurements reported later are for tightly coupled parallel scientific codes, and process virtualization has been avoided wherever the underlying system has allowed.

Code of the barrier implementation: The code executed by processes in a barrier depends on the structure of the implementation chosen and on the system primitives used to implement it. The major code influence is the choice of linear or logarithmic organization. The logarithmic organization requires somewhat more code. This can make it slightly slower than a linear barrier when used with only a few processes, but the code increase is more than compensated for by the increased parallelism possible in executing the code for even a modest number of processes.

Synchronization delays: Much more important than the amount of code is the nature of the synchronization primitives on which the barrier is built. For tightly coupled parallel processing, it is important to avoid operating system overhead wherever possible. Hardware locks used to support critical sections or to implement interprocess synchronization directly are one good choice. Another is to use a master-slave implementation based on shared variables capable of atomic read and write. The time processes spend waiting for synchronization messages from other processes or for a critical section to be released is a major factor in barrier time accounting.

9.3.2   Instrumentation for Barrier Measurement

The most important instrument for measuring performance in a parallel system is a low overhead timer. Of course, timers are important in measuring sequential systems also, but the effect of their overhead is much easier to subtract out of a strictly serial execution history. The key components of a timer are listed in Table 9-2. In considering the structure of timers, there are two main aspects to take into account: the timer update mechanism and the timer sampling mechanism.

Table 9-2   Possible configurations of a timer.

	Update	Hardware	Transparent to processes	Processor cycle stealing
Timer Structure		Software	Independent process to do software updates	Periodic interrupts
	Sampling	Shared variable		
		System call		
	Single clock accessible by all processors			
	Single clock per processor			

Update mechanism: The time may be updated by a mechanism that is completely transparent to the processes involved in the parallel computation. This is usually done by a hardware mechanism, but it is possible to allocate an independent process to do a transparent software update in some systems. The timer update can involve processor cycle stealing, in which case it is nearly, but not entirely transparent. It can also be done by a periodic interrupt, which usually performs other periodic operating systems functions in addition to updating a timer.

Sampling mechanism: Timer sampling can either be done by simply reading a shared variable, or it may require the more substantial overhead of a call to the run-time or operating system.

Number of clocks in the system: Another important aspect of timers for multiprocessors is whether there is a single system clock, which is accessible to all processors, or whether each processor maintains a separate hardware or software timer. Having separate timers for each processor eliminates competition when many processors try to sample the time simultaneously, but a single timer gives a more coherent measure across the processors. If it is important to keep track of the distinction between system time and user time on a per processor basis, then a timer for each processor may well be a natural choice. Systems range from having a single hardware timer, which is readable by any processor as a shared memory location, as in the Encore Multimax, to having a software timer per processor, which is updated by a periodic kernel interrupt, as in the Flexible Computer Systems Flex/32.

An important parameter for a software timer is the uncertainty introduced by the time spent in the timer interrupt handler. This uncertainty can be expressed as

$$\Delta H = \frac{\text{Interrupt service time}}{\text{Interupt interval}}. \tag{9.26}$$

Because the timer interrupt may support periodic operating system functions of different frequencies, ΔH may vary, so that it may be appropriate to use an average value.

There are several aspects of barrier performance that may be measured. Most obvious is the effect of an ideal barrier, one with no overhead, on the behavior of a section of a parallel program. In a simple case, the effect of delaying all processes until the last one arrives can be calculated analytically, but in more complex situations, especially data dependent ones, it may be necessary to measure the effect. In addition to the ideal synchronization performed by the barrier as a synchronization tool, there are synchronization delays introduced by interprocessor synchronizing communications used to implement the barrier itself. Typical would be critical section delay protecting the update of a shared arrival mechanism. Finally, there are the processor cycles used to execute code associated with a particular barrier implementation. If it is assumed that barriers are the right synchronization to use for a particular parallel algorithm, then the important thing to measure is the difference between the ideal barrier behavior and one that includes the synchronization and code of the real implementation. In short, the goal of measuring the performance of a barrier might be either of the following:

1. Compare the use of a barrier versus another synchronization construct:

Given a specific parallel applications program, some simple probes of barrier behavior are possible using only an elapsed time measurement. This assumes a system dedicated to the applications program so that no substantial time is used for systems functions or time multiplexed users during the course of program execution. If the flow of program control is not altered by the violation of data dependences imposed by barriers (only the answers are wrong), then a program can be run and timed both with and without barriers to get a measure of their total effect. Another possibility is to change the barrier implementation in a known way, say by doubling the processor cycles used in the barrier code, and to measure the effect of this change on the overall execution time. These methods are primarily useful to measure the influence of barrier synchronization on a specific parallel program to determine whether it is important to try to find a less costly synchronization method.

2. Compare the performance of various barrier implementations:

If measurements are made for the purpose of comparing different barrier implementations for the best performance, then barriers should be measured independently of surrounding code. It is not possible to separate barriers completely from their execution environment as a result of the dependence of implementation overheads on skew and order of arrival times for different processes. A careful set of measurements on barriers with such dependence includes different types of arrival loading. A common arrival pattern occurs when two successive barriers are separated by a fixed amount of computation that is the same for each process. The order of arrival at the second barrier is determined by the order of their release from the first. A configuration having two barriers, separated by random, and different, amounts of work for each process, represents another useful measurement. Enough samples must be taken to average both the latest arrival time and the effects of different arrival orders, if any. Another common form of arrival loading corresponds to two barriers separated by fixed length work containing a critical section. The time skew introduced by processes waiting to enter the critical section may influence barrier performance. For example, a self-scheduled, linear barrier can do a good job of masking critical section skew.

The nature of timers used to measure barrier performance is important and, in at least one case, has a drastic effect on the reliability of the measurement. Because barriers synchronize all processes, a single clock per system is most natural to their measurement. This assumes, however, that the whole system is used for the measurement. In multiprogrammed systems the situation is more complicated. A case presenting considerable difficulty is a dedicated system, but one that has one software timer per processor. In addition, the timer interrupts in different processors are asynchronous. The measurement uncertainty ΔH interacts with the synchronization function of the barrier in an unpleasant way. A worst case situation can occur in which all processors are interrupted while executing a barrier in a sequential order which causes the other processors to wait on the return of each interrupted processor to complete the barrier. Thus, with P processors, the uncertainty of the measurement of barrier completion is not just ΔH but can be as large as $P \times \Delta H$. An example of this situation will be reported in the next section.

9.3.3   Examples of Barrier Performance Measurement

We present examples to illustrate the various performance effects of the factors discussed in the previous sections on barrier synchronization and its implementation on platforms with specific characteristics. The major points demonstrated by the experiments are:

1. Using program specific changes to understand performance of barrier synchronization;
2. Measuring barrier performance in a system with timer uncertainty;
3. Effects of multiprogrammed multiprocessors on barrier synchronized programs.

1. Using program specific changes to understand performance of barrier synchronization:

Barrier performance measurements were done on the Denelcor HEP shared memory multiprocessor, which consisted of four pipelined multiprocessor modules (PEMs). Each PEM could obtain a speed of 10 MIPS (or MFLOPS) by executing 12–15 processes in parallel. The system could support up to 200 processes executing in parallel, but the pipelined structure implied that improved performance could not result, even theoretically, for more than about 64 processes. Each PEM was equipped with a hardware performance monitor known as the System Performance Indicator (SPI). The SPI kept track of clock cycles of 10^{-7} second along with numbers of completed instructions in several categories. The instruction categories were floating point instructions, other register-to-register instructions, memory reference instructions, and wave-offs (instructions that could not be issued because of synchronization).

The barrier measurements made on the HEP system were with respect to a parallel Gaussian elimination program that used barriers for its synchronization. The flow of control in Gaussian elimination is not influenced by the correctness of the floating point computations, which are the operations synchronized by the barriers. At most, the time for pivoting could be influenced, but this was not the case in this program. Figure 9-14 shows the execution rate versus number of parallel processes for the Gaussian elimination program run on a 500×500 matrix with and without its synchronizing barriers. A summary of the results is that the synchronized version obtained a maximum speed of 7.5 MFLOPS, corresponding to 32 MIPS, while the program with barriers removed ran 9.5 MFLOPS, or 40 MIPS, which is the maximum speed for a four PEM HEP. A decrease in execution speed is observed as the number of processes increases. This decrease begins when all pipelines are filled and is a result of process contention for shared synchronization variables in the barriers and of the increase in barrier complexity with number of processes.

Measurements were also done by making changes in the barrier implementation. The initial implementation used in the HEP Gaussian elimination program counted processes entering the barrier and blocked them with a single shared memory locking variable until the last process had arrived. The compiled code for this implementation amounted to about 20 instructions per process. Because four PEMs could generate memory reference retries at four times the rate that a single memory module could handle them, it was suspected that memory access congestion made this implementation inefficient on the four PEM system. An alternate implementation of the barrier, which suspended processes as they arrived and used the last one to restart them, executed about 50 instructions per process but reduced execution time by 31.8%, verifying the memory contention effect. In the final Gaussian elimination program about 14% of the time is spent in barrier synchronization. This illustrates how program specific changes in a well-understood code can be used to examine barrier performance.

2. Measuring barrier performance in a system with timer uncertainty:

Barrier measurements were done on the Flexible Computer Corporation's Flex/32 running under the MMOS multiprocessor operating system. This system consists of 20 single board microprocessors associated with a combination of shared and private memories. The particular system used allocated two processors to run in a single processor mode, leaving 18 processors available under MMOS. The experiments were run with a fixed mapping of one process per processor with no multiprogramming. The operating system is distributed over the processors, and in particular, has a software timer per processor. The measurements compared several different implementations of the barrier for performance in different environments, but of most interest here is the effect of the software timers running asynchronously on each processor.

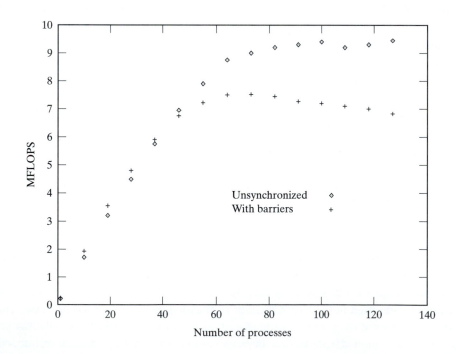

Figure 9-14 Performance impact of removing barriers in a 500 × 500 Gaussian elimination.

The Flex/32 system measurements exhibit the problem, mentioned earlier, of multiplying the measurement uncertainty ΔH due to the service time for timer interrupts by the number P of processes. The standard configuration of the MMOS operating system uses a 20 ms interrupt interval with a service time of 0.3 ms. The resulting $\Delta H = 1.5\%$ is acceptable for timing single stream phenomena, but using 18 processors synchronized by barriers, it presents a significant problem. In the worst case sequence of timer interrupts using all 18 processors, some processor is unavailable to satisfy the barrier synchronization 27% of the time. The resulting uncertainty in barrier measurements is not a result of inaccurately sampling the value of the time but of overheads involved in updating the time. The problem of obtaining accurate times was solved by increasing the timer interval to one second, thus reducing ΔH to 0.03% and the worst case influence on barrier measurements to 0.54%. Of course, it was necessary to make very long timing runs to reduce the effect of the one second accuracy of the time to an acceptable percentage of the measurement.

3. Effects of multiprogrammed multiprocessors on barrier synchronized programs:

Another example of a major performance effect and corresponding execution time model comes from the class of multiprogrammed multiprocessors. Multiprogramming involves the operating system in process management to optimize the use of system resources, primarily I/O devices and memory occupancy. If multiple processes are used within a single job, the operating system often becomes the mechanism chosen to manage process interactions unique to parallel programming: process creation, termination, and synchronization. Even if the operating system is not directly involved in synchronizations, process management by the operating system for the purpose of multiprogramming may interact strongly with the process control involved in parallel process synchronization. Such an effect was measured on the Encore Multimax and Sequent Balance multiprocessors. Barrier synchronization measured in a multiprogrammed environment constitutes an interesting example of operating system interaction with parallel programs. Understanding the effect of multiprogramming is virtually independent of barrier implementation given the relation of instruction execution times to swap overhead. The basic effect results from the tacit assumption that parallel processes working on a single job are coscheduled and the contradictory multiprogramming assumption that processes are independent of one another, except in so far as they compete for resources.

If the number of processes assumed for execution is fixed, then it is possible that the multiprogramming load prevents their coscheduling on physical processors, even if the system contains that many physical processors. The nature of a process barrier demands participation of all processes in reporting that they have reached the barrier and in acknowledging the barrier release signal. If some processes are swapped out at any given time, and if the operating system does not take explicit account of the barrier synchronization in its scheduling, the barrier may take several process swap times to complete. To remove the complications introduced by an arbitrary multiprogramming load, Figure 9-15 shows the situation when a parallel program, run alone on a 20-processor Encore Multimax, uses more processes than there are physical processors.

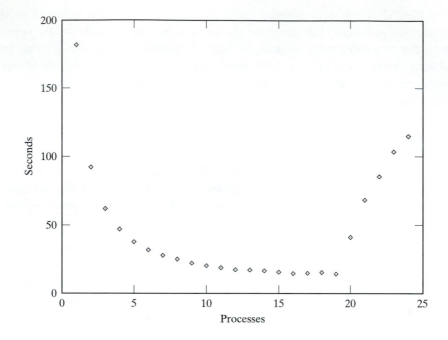

Figure 9-15   Barrier synchronized Gauss elimination on a 20 processor system.

The specific program is a barrier synchronized Gaussian elimination on a 200×200 matrix. Three barrier synchronizations are done in processing each of the 200 pivots. Using more processes gives the expected drop in execution time up to 19 processes. The Umax® operating system keeps one processor occupied with system functions, so 20 processes is already more than can be coscheduled on a 20-processor system. The sharp rise in execution time beginning at 20 processes is qualitatively the result of adding to the barrier delay, caused by small variations in process arrival times, the effects of operating system process management, which involve a much larger time scale.

To model the effect, assume that P processes are running on a smaller number Q of physical processors. Assume that the operating system scheduler runs processes for a time quantum T_q before making a new scheduling decision in the absence of other explicit operating system interaction by the program. It is also assumed that the barrier is implemented directly with hardware supported lock/unlock to make it efficient in the normal coscheduled case. When a barrier is reached, $P - Q$ processes are swapped out. After an expected wait of T_q/Q, one of the Q running processes reaches the end of its time quantum and is swapped out, thereby starting one of the suspended processes that quickly satisfies its part of the barrier synchronization. When this has happened $P - Q$ times, assuming first come first served scheduling, the barrier is satisfied. The expected wait at a barrier resulting from the lack of coscheduling is thus:

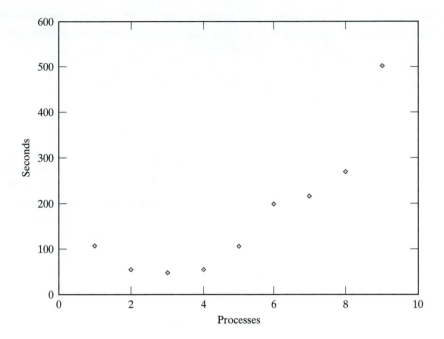

Figure 9-16 Barrier synchronized Gauss elimination with multiprogramming load.

$$\hat{W}_b = \frac{P-Q}{Q}T_q. \tag{9.27}$$

If the time to execute the program with coscheduled processes is T_{prog} and the number of barriers in the program is N_b, then the total execution time with $P > Q$ processes is:

$$T(P) = T_{prog}(Q) + N_b\hat{W}_b = T_{prog}(Q) + N_b\frac{P-Q}{Q}T_q. \tag{9.28}$$

With 600 barriers in the measured program and 19 processors, a linear fit to the rising tail of the graph of Figure 9-15 gives an operating system time quantum of about 0.6 second. The fit is not particularly good, because the extra time per process apparently decreases as $P - Q$ increases. The example, thus, shows that parametrized measurements of execution time can give insight into operating system parameters as well as architecture and program structure. Figure 9-16 shows that the presence of multiprogramming load on the system merely causes the effect to be seen for fewer processes and to increase in magnitude. The curve suggests that only three or four processors were available to run the program given the other workload on the system.

9.4 Statistical Models for Static and Dynamic Parallel Loops

Loops are a main source of parallelism in most applications. Analytical models to measure parallel loop performance are needed to give insight into program performance and to select an optimal scheduling strategy and optimal number of processes to execute the program. The information can also be used by a parallelizing compiler to optimize program performance. A sequential loop of the form

```
do I = 1 , N
    A(I) = K * B(I) * C(I)
end do
```

may be parallelized in different ways depending on how the loop work is assigned to processes. The two scheduling policies considered are static scheduling, where work is scheduled at compile time, and dynamic scheduling, where iterations are assigned to processes at run-time.

Static scheduling minimizes the run-time overhead because the mapping of processes to iterations is completely done at compile time. Each process is assigned an equal number of iterations to execute. If the number of processes divides the number of iterations evenly and if the loop iterations are of the same size (same execution time), the load is perfectly balanced among processes. In many applications, however, the time to execute an iteration is not constant due to program, system, and architectural issues and, thus, load imbalance may occur. A program example would be an "`if then else`" inside the loop body, which generates two different possible execution times for each iteration. System level issues such as contention for resources in multi-user environments and architectural issues such as variation in memory latency due to cache misses or memory faults and conflicts are also causes for load imbalance.

Dynamic scheduling assigns work to processes at run-time and, therefore, better balances the work when the execution times of iterations vary. However, this better balance is obtained at the expense of an increase in run-time overhead resulting from the need for each process to execute a critical section to assign iterations to processes at run-time. We discussed a model of a computation that is parallelized by the inclusion of a critical section in Section 9.2.2.2 and alluded to its use with parallel loops. We will see similarities between the performance models of that section and those to be developed specifically for loops. Beckman and Polychronopoulos[41] have developed models for the execution time of parallel loops combined with barrier synchronization when the execution time of an iteration is normally distributed. We treat the simple case of two different execution times for the loop body that would result from a single conditional statement in the loop.

9.4.1   Dynamic Scheduling Model

A dynamically scheduled or self-scheduled parallel loop is used to achieve better load balance. We use the following format to refer to a self-scheduling forall loop discussed in Chapter 4, Section 4.3.3.

```
selfsched do I = 1 , N
    A(I) = K * B(I) * C(I)
end selfsched do
```

Upon arrival at the `selfsched do`, each process atomically obtains a loop index. As processes complete execution of an iteration they obtain the next available loop index until the loop is completely executed. The obtaining of an index value and updating the shared index variable for the next iteration is done in a critical section of code. Only one process at a time can be inside this critical section, so in certain situations processes have to wait to enter it. We refer to this critical section as the *scheduling critical section* (SCS). The SCS code and the waiting time to enter it is the run-time overhead required to obtain the load balancing advantages of dynamic scheduling.

A critical section in the body of a parallel loop might contain operations not used for scheduling, such as code for a global reduction operation. The discussion of Section 9.2.2.2 treated an arbitrary calculation, probably, but not necessarily, containing a loop that was parallelized by the introduction of critical section time into each process. Here, the critical section is strictly devoted to dynamic scheduling of loop iterations and does not appear in the static scheduling model of Section 9.4.2.

9.4.1.1   Dynamically Scheduled Iterations of Equal Length

We first consider the execution time of a self-scheduled loop with equal iterations to understand the behavior of the loop and the run-time overhead effects. This can be abstracted through the queuing model in Figure 9-17. The figure shows that processes trying to execute the loop first enter a waiting queue, QS, from which they execute the SCS one at a time to obtain a loop index. After each process has completed execution of its iteration, it returns to the SCS. Here T_i is the time to execute an iteration of the loop, and T_S is the time to execute the SCS.

We assume that T_S is independent of the number of processes, N_q, waiting to enter the critical section and the execution of the loop iterations. We also assume that T_i is independent of N_q and the execution of the critical section code. In general, these independence assumptions are not guaranteed, as the synchronization implementation and the memory traffic may slow down the execution of the SCS and the loop body. When many processes busy wait in the queue by repeatedly accessing a synchronizing variable, the resulting network traffic and memory contention slows down processes in the system that are not waiting for the critical section.

Two cases must be considered depending on the number of processes, P, the length, T_S, of the SCS, and the length of each iteration T_i. The cases correspond to conditions discussed in Section 9.2.2.2 and are referred to here as saturated and unsaturated loops.

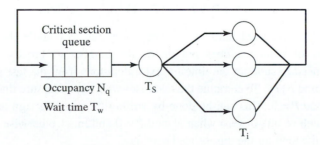

Figure 9-17   Queueing model for dynamically scheduled loop iterations.

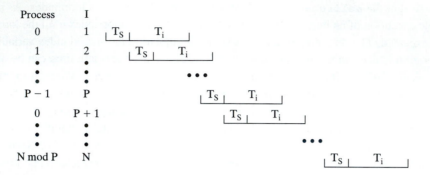

Figure 9-18   Saturated dynamic loop timing.

Saturated Loop: A process must wait to enter the critical section when the time to execute an iteration of the loop, T_i, is not large enough to schedule the rest of processes, or

$$T_i < (P-1)T_S. \tag{9.29}$$

This scenario is depicted in Figure 9-18. In this case all processes have to wait in the SCS queue before they can execute a loop iteration. Therefore, the total execution time of the loop, T_e, is

$$T_e = T_i + N \cdot T_S, \tag{9.30}$$

where N is the total number of loop iterations.

Unsaturated Loop: When the time to execute a loop iteration is large enough so that the rest of the processes can execute the SCS while one process is executing a loop iteration, that is, $T_i > (P-1)T_S$, the processes leave the critical section one after another skewed by a time equal to T_S. Figure 9-19 illustrates this situation. The first P iterations are done at a rate of $1/T_S$. The $P+1$st iteration completes at time $2T_i + 2T_S$. In general one complete sweep takes a time equal to $T_i + PT_S$. If the number of processes divides the number of iterations evenly, that is, $N \bmod P = 0$, the complete execution time of the loop is

$$R_c(T_i + T_S) + (P-1)T_S, \tag{9.31}$$

where $R_c = \lceil N/P \rceil$ is the total number of sweeps required to completely execute the loop. When the number of iterations does not divide the number of processes evenly, that is, $N \bmod P \neq 0$, we need to subtract the time for extra iterations from the last sweep. This corresponds to $(P - N \bmod P)T_S$. To combine the two cases we must make sure that this term is equal to zero when $N \bmod P = 0$. This can be done by writing the negative sign as $(R_f - R_c)$, where $R_f = \lfloor N/P \rfloor$, which results in zero when $N \bmod P = 0$ and in -1 otherwise. Thus T_e, the total execution time of the loop for the unsaturated case, is

$$T_e = R_c(T_i + T_S) + (P-1)T_S + (R_f - R_c)PT_S + (N \bmod P)T_S. \tag{9.32}$$

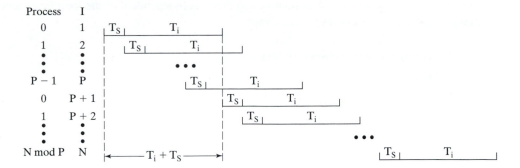

Figure 9-19 Unsaturated dynamic loop timing.

Equation (9.32) can be cast in the form of a continuous approximation plus a granularity correction to give insight into the overall and local behavior of performance with a varying number of processes. The continuous approximation, N/P for R_c can be introduced by

$$R_c = \frac{N}{P} + (R_c - R_f) - \frac{N \bmod P}{P}. \tag{9.33}$$

This yields the continuous model plus granularity correction form

$$T_e = (N/P)(T_i + T_S) + (P - 1)T_S + \delta(P), \tag{9.34}$$

where the granularity correction is

$$\delta(P) = \left(R_c - R_f - \frac{(N \bmod P)}{P} \right)(T_i - (P - 1)T_S). \tag{9.35}$$

The first factor in (9.35) is zero if $N \bmod P = 0$ and less than one otherwise. The second factor is an upper bound on the size of the granularity correction and is the excess time in a loop iteration after subtracting the critical section time for $P - 1$ other processes.

9.4.1.2 Dynamically Scheduled Iterations of Different Lengths

Now consider a loop where the code executed in each iteration is dependent on some condition tested by an **if** statement inside the loop. Then a process executing the code may execute either of the two code sections depending on the result of the **if** test, as shown.

```
selfsched do I = 1, N
    if test(i) then ⟨code 1⟩
        else ⟨code 2⟩
end selfsched do
```

If the two sections are of different lengths, the time needed to complete the iteration depends on the path taken. To reflect this possibility in our model, we consider two possible lengths for an iteration of the parallel loop, l_1 and l_2. Assuming that the probability of an iteration being of length l_1 or l_2 is constant and can be estimated, and that it is independent of the loop index and of the previous iterations, we can define the terms:

p_1 : Probability that an iteration is of length l_1.

p_2 : Probability that an iteration is of length l_2, $(p_2 = 1 - p_1)$.

T_1 : Time to execute an iteration of length l_1.

T_2 : Time to execute an iteration of length l_2.

The expected execution time of an iteration $E(T_i)$ is given by

$$E(T_i) = p_1 T_1 + p_2 T_2 \text{ for } N/P \gg 1. \tag{9.36}$$

The analysis with fixed loop body execution time suggests that we distinguish saturated and unsaturated cases. When $\max(T_1, T_2) \leq (P-1)T_S$, the loop is saturated for any set of outcomes of the test, and a process always must wait for the SCS to become free before obtaining a new index value. In this *completely saturated* case, the expected value of the execution time is

$$E(T_e) = E(T_i) + NT_S. \tag{9.37}$$

In an analogous *completely unsaturated* case, where $\min(T_1, T_2) \geq (P-1)T_S$, processes never wait to enter the SCS, except perhaps the first time. In this case, the performance model is obtained by replacing T_i in Equations (9.34) and (9.35) by $E(T_i)$ to obtain

$$E(T_e) = (N/P)(E(T_i) + T_S) + (P-1)T_S + \delta(P), \text{ and} \tag{9.38}$$

$$\delta(P) = \left(R_c - R_f - \frac{N \bmod P}{P}\right)(E(T_i) - (P-1)T_S). \tag{9.39}$$

If we assume $T_1 > T_2$ is the longer execution time, the transition case, is the region where $T_1 \geq (P-1)T_S$ but $T_2 \leq (P-1)T_S$. A simple approximation is to assume that the saturated model holds if $E(T_i) < (P-1)T_S$ and that the unsaturated model holds if $E(T_i) \geq (P-1)T_S$. The combined model is continuous at the splice point, $E(T_i) = (P-1)T_S$, but has a change in slope there.

A more accurate model for execution time in the transition region requires a more detailed analysis of the queueing model of Figure 9-17. There is no guarantee that either the SCS is in use when a process needs to enter it, as is the case for a saturated loop, or that it is free, as for an unsaturated loop. We use the results from queueing theory (see for example [173]) to analyze the system as a closed queue. In the absence of any queueing delay, each process requests the SCS at a rate of

$$\lambda = \frac{1}{E(T_i) + T_S}. \tag{9.40}$$

If P is large, we can approximate the request distribution as Poisson with an offered rate of

$$\lambda_o = \frac{P}{E(T_i) + T_S}. \tag{9.41}$$

The system can then be analyzed as an M/D/1 closed queue, as has been done for a single memory module or a single disk serving multiple processors. See, for example, Chapters 6 and 9 of [111]. The achieved request rate is

$$\lambda_a = \frac{P}{E(T_i) + T_S + T_W},$$ (9.42)

where T_W is the wait time in the queue. A Markov chain analysis [173] gives as a second equation for T_W,

$$T_W = \frac{\lambda_a T_S^2}{2(1 - \lambda_a T_S)} = \frac{P T_S^2}{2(T_W + E(T_i) - (P-1)T_S)}.$$ (9.43)

Equations (9.42) and (9.43) can be solved for T_W to obtain

$$T_W = \frac{1}{2}(\sqrt{(E(T_i) - (P-1)T_S)^2 + 2P T_S^2} - (E(T_i) - (P-1)T_S)).$$ (9.44)

The expected execution time for N iterations follows from the achieved request rate, λ_a, as

$$E(T_e) = \frac{N}{\lambda_a} = \frac{N}{P}(E(T_i) + T_S + T_W).$$ (9.45)

The Poisson request distribution does not take into account the fact that $T_2 \leq T_i \leq T_1$, so the fully saturated and fully unsaturated models do not match the queueing model in their regions of validity. The unlimited range of intervals between requests in the Poisson distribution does not support a guarantee either that the critical section is occupied or that it is free, as required in the saturated and unsaturated cases, respectively. There is always a nonzero wait time in the queueing model.

9.4.2 Static Scheduling Model

A statically scheduled or prescheduled parallel loop has the best performance when the loop iterations are of the same size. We use the following format to refer to a cyclic prescheduled `forall` loop, as discussed in Chapter 4, Section 4.3.3.

```
presched do I=1, N
    A(I)=K * B(I) * C(I)
end presched do
```

Prescheduling is done at compile time, with each process doing N/P iterations in parallel, starting with an index based on its process index and stepping by P times the stride. There is no need for an SCS so a prescheduled loop has the advantage of not having the scheduling overhead of a self-scheduled loop. There are two load balancing issues to be considered with prescheduled loops. The first is the assignment of equal number of iterations to each process. If the number of processes does not divide the number of iterations evenly, then some of the processes must execute one extra iteration to complete the loop execution. The second issue is whether all iterations are of equal length. When this is true, the work is balanced among processes, but if iterations have different execution times, processes could be assigned significantly different amounts of work.

9.4.2.1 Prescheduled Iterations of Equal Length

Assuming that all processes arrive at the loop simultaneously, the total time to completely execute the loop, T_e, is determined by the iteration time, T_i, and the maximum number, $R_c = \lceil N/P \rceil$, of iterations executed by any process and is given by

$$T_e = R_c T_i. \tag{9.46}$$

9.4.2.2 Prescheduled Iterations of Different Lengths

As with the dynamic scheduling policy two possible iteration times, T_1 and T_2 are considered, as would result from code of the form

```
presched do I = 1, N
      if test(i) then ⟨code 1⟩
           else ⟨code 2⟩;
end presched do;
```

We assume without loss of generality that $T_1 > T_2$. The execution time of the prescheduled loop is equal to the execution time of the process that is assigned the most iterations of time T_1. We refer to the maximum number of iterations of time T_1 assigned to any process as max_1. If we assume that the number of iterations divides the number of processes evenly, then T_e is given by

$$T_e = T_1 max_1 + T_2(R_c - max_1). \tag{9.47}$$

The expected loop execution time is

$$E(T_e) = T_1 E(max_1) + T_2(R_c - E(max_1)) = E(max_1)(T_1 - T_2) + R_c T_2, \tag{9.48}$$

where $E(max_1)$ is the expected maximum number of long iterations assigned to any process. A model for the expected execution time is based on an evaluation of $E(max_1)$.

Each process is preassigned $R = N/P$ iterations, each of which is of time T_1 with probability p_1 and of time T_2 with probability $p_2 = (1 - p_1)$. The probability that a process gets $n_1 = k$ iterations of time T_1 and $R - k$ iterations of time T_2 is given by the binomial distribution,

$$P(n_1 = k) = \binom{R}{k} p_1^k p_2^{R-k}. \tag{9.49}$$

The probability that the maximum number of iterations of time T_1 assigned to one of the P processes is j is the probability that the number is less than or equal to j but not less than or equal to $j - 1$. Assuming the assignments to different processes are independent events, we find

$$P(max_1 = j) = \left(\sum_{k=0}^{j} \binom{R}{k} p_1^k p_2^{R-k} \right)^P - \left(\sum_{k=0}^{j-1} \binom{R}{k} p_1^k p_2^{R-k} \right)^P. \tag{9.50}$$

The expected value of the maximum number of time T_1 iterations that are assigned to a process is

$$E(max_1) = \sum_{j=0}^{R} j \left(\left(\sum_{k=0}^{j} \binom{R}{k} p_1^k p_2^{R-k} \right)^P - \left(\sum_{k=0}^{j-1} \binom{R}{k} p_1^k p_2^{R-k} \right)^P \right). \tag{9.51}$$

To simplify the equations, the sums over the binomial distribution can be written in terms of the incomplete beta function, $I_x(a, b)$, as

$$I_{1-p_1}(R-j, j+1) = \sum_{k=0}^{j} \binom{R}{k} p_1^k p_2^{R-k}, \tag{9.52}$$

so (9.50) becomes

$$P(max_1 = j) = I_{1-p_1}^{P}(R-j, j+1) - I_{1-p_1}^{P}(R-j+1, j). \tag{9.53}$$

The above analysis is only exact if R is an integer. If P does not divide N evenly, then there is a little more complexity. Some processes are assigned $R_c = \lceil N/P \rceil$ iterations, while others get only $R_f = \lfloor N/P \rfloor$ iterations. Specifically, $P_c = N \bmod P$ processes get R_c iterations, while $P_f = P - P_c$ processes get R_f iterations. The probability that no process is assigned more than j iterations of time T_1 is then

$$P(n_1 \le j) = I_{1-p_1}^{P_c}(R_c - j, j+1) I_{1-p_1}^{P_f}(R_f - j, j+1). \tag{9.54}$$

Thus, in both cases of even and uneven divisibility of N by P, we have

$E(max_1) =$

$$\tag{9.55}$$

$$\sum_{j=0}^{R_c} j[I_{1-p_1}^{P_c}(R_c - j, j+1) I_{1-p_1}^{P_f}(R_f - j, j+1) - I_{1-p_1}^{P_c}(R_c - j+1, j) I_{1-p_1}^{P_f}(R_f - j+1, j)]$$

Using this expression in Equation (9.48) gives a correct theoretical model when P does not divide N evenly.

9.4.3   Comparison with Experimental Results

Two simple program segments using prescheduled and self-scheduled loops, respectively, are used to compare and verify the models developed in the two previous sections.

```
presched (or selfsched) do I = 1, N
    if (probability = p₁) then
        Iterate = 10000;
    else
        Iterate = 1000;
    do J = 1, Iterate
        ⟨Compute⟩
    end do
end presched (or selfsched) do;
```

As the code shows, the sequential do loop is executed 10,000 times with probability of p_1, resulting in a long iteration of time T_1. The same loop is executed 1000 times with probability p_2 yielding a short iteration time T_2.

The code was implemented and run on a 20-processor Encore Multimax, a shared memory bus–based architecture. In this architecture, each processor has a direct mapped instruction/data cache. The above example was carefully designed and sized to fit into the cache completely to avoid cache misses. This way, no caching effects were visible. For the self-scheduled loops, the long, T1, and short, T2, loop iterations were intentionally decreased with respect to the Scheduling Critical Section execution time, T_S, so that the loop saturation effects could be observed during run-time. On a computer such as Encore Multimax with only few processors and relatively small synchronization cost relative to instruction execution time, the loop saturation effects can only be seen for very small loops. On machines such as Cray Y-MP, where a lock acquisition takes about 2000 cycles, or machines capable of running thousands of processes such as the Cray multithreaded architecture, the loop saturation becomes more important and a larger factor in the performance.

The Encore Multimax used to run the experiments was a multiprogrammed system but was run with only a single user, so the only interference was from possible execution of background system functions. The number of processes used was kept below 18, so two processes were always available to perform operating system functions without interfering with the experiments. The execution times presented are the mean values of the execution times of 50 runs.

Figure 9-20 shows the expected execution time of prescheduled and self-scheduled loops for different numbers of processes. In this figure the number of loop iterations, $N = 100$, and T_S is 4 ms. A long iteration takes $T_1 = 1.199$ sec. and has probability $p_1 = 30\%$, and a short iteration takes $T_2 = 0.12$ sec. The loop is completely unsaturated over the range from two to 18 processors because saturation for the shorter loop time, T_2, would require 31 processes. The figure shows the advantage of self-scheduled execution for 30% long loop probability resulting from the ability to dynamically balance the load rather than execute a fixed set of loop instances assigned at compile time with no knowledge of the instance length. The theoretical model for the prescheduled loop shown in Figure 9-20 is that of Equation (9.55). The agreement is very good, but the model slightly overestimates the execution time, probably because the 50 runs did not sample large values of the maximum number of long iterations assigned to a process, while these large values do affect the theoretical model. The theoretical model for the self-scheduled loop shown in Figure 9-20 is based on the completely unsaturated case using Equations (9.38) and (9.39). Again there is very good agreement, but this time the model slightly underestimates the experiments. This is probably a result of the assumption of zero queueing delay in the unsaturated model. The randomness introduced by the choice of one of two loop lengths probably introduces some small queueing delay for $p_1 = 30\%$.

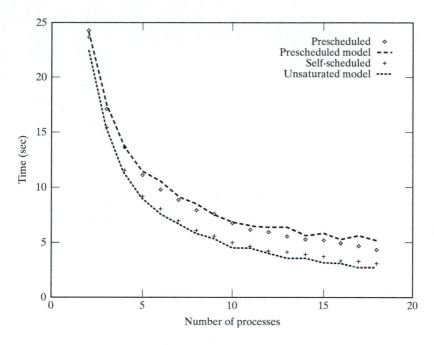

Figure 9-20   Static and dynamic loops with two iteration lengths versus number of processes.

Figure 9-21 shows the static and dynamic execution times for the same loop illustrated in Figure 9-20, but varying the probability of a long loop iteration instead of the number of processes. Thus, the parameters of the loop are $N = 100$, $T_1 = 1.199$ sec., $T_2 = 0.12$ sec., and $T_S = 4$ ms. The number of processes is now fixed at $P = 10$ and the probability of a long iteration, p_1, varies from 0% to 100%. The prescheduled and self-scheduled loops perform equally well, and also match the theoretical models, for $p_1 = 0$% and 100%, that is, the cases in which there is only one loop body length. The performance advantage of dynamic scheduling is maximized for $p_1 = 50$%, which represents the maximum variability of loop body time. The theoretical model for prescheduled execution (Equation (9.55)) matches the measurements surprisingly well. The match of prescheduled theory and experiment in Figure 9-20 is also particularly good at $P = 10$, possibly because there is no granularity correction there. Two theoretical models for the dynamically scheduled loop are shown in Figure 9-21, the one based on saturated and unsaturated loops and the one based on queueing theory. The saturation model uses only Equations (9.38) and (9.39) because the loop is completely unsaturated for either choice of iteration length. The queueing theory model uses Equations (9.44) and (9.45). The two theoretical curves are indistinguishable because the SCS time, $T_S = 0.004$ sec., is so small with respect to either $T_1 = 1.199$ sec. or $T_2 = 0.12$ sec. Although the match to experiment is quite good, both of the theoretical models underestimate the experimental results, perhaps because neither model takes into account the deviation from expected iteration time that occurs when the last process to schedule an iteration happens to get a long one.

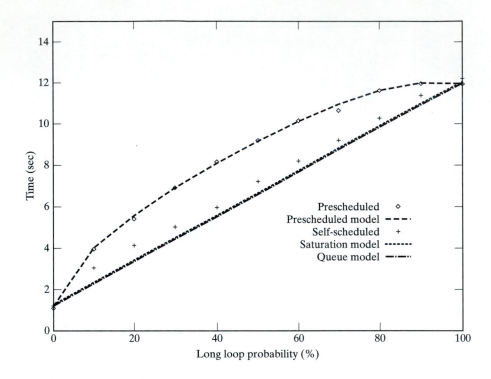

Figure 9-21   Static and dynamic loop time versus the probability of a long iteration.

In Figure 9-22 both the long and short iteration times have been reduced to make them closer to the SCS time of $T_S = 0.004$ sec. Specifically, $T_1 = 0.121$ sec. and $T_2 = 0.012$ sec. The number of iterations is $N = 1000$ and the number of processes is $P = 10$. The saturation condition based on $E(T_i)$ is $p_1 = 22\%$, corresponding to $E(T_i) < (P-1)T_S$. Between 30% and 90% probability of a long iteration both static and dynamic scheduling perform about equally well. The difference between T_1 and T_2 for one of the $N = 1000$ loop iterations is fairly small compared to total execution time, with the approximately 100 iterations assigned to each process giving a fairly accurate average performance. Saturation of the dynamically scheduled loop is clearly seen for $p_1 < 22\%$. The prescheduled model equation based on Equation (9.55) matches extremely well, as it did in Figure 9-21. The saturation model for the self-scheduled loop now corresponds to using Equations (9.36) and (9.37) for $E(T_i) < (P-1)T_S$ and Equations (9.38) and (9.39) for $E(T_i) \geq (P-1)T_S$. As would be expected, the queueing model fits better in the region of transition from saturated to unsaturated behavior, where the queueing delay, T_w, becomes a significant portion of the execution time. The saturation model is quite a reasonable fit away from the transition.

We see that quite accurate models can be developed for the restricted case of dynamically and statically scheduled loops of two different execution times. The theoretical models accurately predict the performance obtained and could certainly be used to decide whether to use a self-scheduled or a prescheduled `forall` given a specific set of loop parameters.

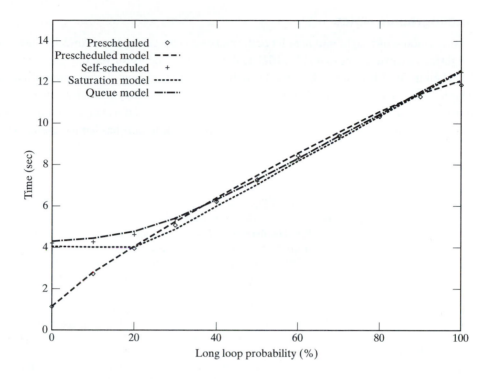

Figure 9-22 Loop showing saturation effects for dynamic scheduling.

9.5 Conclusions

We have shown several examples of performance impacts arising from different levels of the computation. In each case, a parametrized performance measure can be related to a model that gives insight into policies and characteristics of the architecture, operating system, language, or program. The real power of parametrized execution time measurements comes from the identification of the correct model in a specific case. The case of the matrix multiply fine structure shows, however, that even very complex seeming variations in measurements yield to this kind of analysis.

Some performance effects are, of course, specific to individual systems. But if a sufficiently general model is developed, it can give insight into all systems of a general class. The classes of pipelined vector processors, parallel/pipelined multiprocessors, and multiprogrammed multiprocessors were explicitly covered here. The combination of parametrized performance measurement with models based on the parameters offers a powerful mechanism for understanding performance for the purposes of extrapolating the performance of long production runs, discovering beneficial program modifications, optimizing architectural parameters, and determining operating system policies.

9.6 Bibliographic Notes

A surprising amount of insight into parallel performance can be gained from Amdahl's law [18] and straightforward extensions to it [131, 162]. Quite accurate models for vector processors have been based on it [58, 144], and architectural insights were derived from the variation of performance with a parameter in an extended Amdahl's law model [161, 162]. Numerous papers have treated the impact of synchronization on performance, with barrier performance playing a major role [24, 31, 41]. The dominance of loop parallelism in many programs has led to several analyses of loop performance [41, 162, 208].

Problems

9.1   Write Equation (9.2) in the form of Equation (9.1) plus a granularity correction. Describe the behavior of the correction term as P varies for fixed N.

9.2   Study the performance predicted by the static and dynamic models for two loop iteration execution times as a function of the ratio of the two times. Assume equal probabilities of execution of the two `if` branches. Give the asymptotic behavior for both extremes of the ratio of T_1 to T_2, and draw graphs similar to Figure 9-21 and Figure 9-22 but with the horizontal axis being the T_1/T_2 ratio.

Let the length, T_S, of the scheduling critical section be 10% of the length of the short iteration, and let $N = 1000$ and $P = 10$. Normalize the execution time so that the graphs illustrate the behavior of the performance as a function of the T_1/T_2 ratio and not a variation in the total work of the loop.

9.3   Adapt the performance time model for a loop with a critical section developed for a pipelined MIMD computer in Section 9.2.2.2 to a true MIMD machine with P processors. Plot a comparison graph of time versus P for your model with the model of Section 9.2.2.2. Choose model parameters and graph range to clearly show the difference between the two models.

9.4   Develop an execution time model for a loop with a critical section for an architecture having K pipelined MIMD processors sharing memory. That is, adapt the execution time model of Section 9.2.2.2 to an architecture like that of Section 9.2.3 but having K PEMs instead of four. Take the hardware parallelism limit in each pipelined MIMD processor to be U, and distribute P processes over K processors as evenly as possible.

Temporal Behavior of Parallel Programs

To obtain optimal performance, several factors must work well together to achieve a balance between all levels of a computer system involved in the execution of a program. A balance between program execution demands and the underlying systems delivery capabilities such as bandwidth, latency mechanism, system scalability, and memory hierarchy implies an understanding of not only the system architecture but also the behavior of the program structure.

Characterizing computer system performance in terms of data transport capacity gives important insight into the issue of scalability. Of the two parameters specifying data transport capacity, bandwidth is not directly affected by increasing the system size. Latency, however, is surely increased as system size increases, unless it is artificially long in the smaller system. Arguments that data accesses can be made local, only make sense over a limited time and cannot apply to the entire problem. After all, data must reach the local area originally. Latency in current technology is somewhat more strongly influenced by less fundamental principles. Increased fan-in and fan-out as system size is increased also adds to latency. Latency changes significantly at the VLSI chip boundary, and a large system has more signals traveling in the slower environment.

A scalable computer system is one in which all aspects of data transport performance, not only that of the arithmetic unit, depend to first order only on bandwidth and not on latency. There are two primary methods for reducing the dependence of system performance on data transport latency, latency reduction and latency tolerance by overlap operation. Cacheing and cut through routing of interprocessor messages are both examples of latency reduction. Pipelined vector arithmetic units and multiprogramming at virtual memory page faults are both examples of latency tolerance. The system architecture that most effectively reduces the dependence of performance on latency through one or a combination of these techniques is the most scalable architecture.

When the program also has control over data transport, its structure can affect scalability. This is certainly the case at the machine language level, and much optimization in compiler code generation is based on latency reduction through proper use of registers and caches. In processors with pipelines exposed to the code generator, latency tolerance by code restructuring also plays a major role. Application programmers spend much effort on restructuring parallel programs for both distributed memory multiprocessors and for nonuniform access time shared memory systems to reduce data movement or overlap it with processing. It is, thus, sensible to talk about a correctly structured program as being scalable, in the sense that the size of its data can be increased along with the size of the system executing it without suffering a decrease in the usable bandwidth of individual system components.

In a hierarchical memory system, that might consist of registers, cache, private main memory, global memory, disk storage, and network file system, the optimal balance occurs when the bandwidths above and below a given level differ by the amount of data reuse at that level. If traffic were uniform, such a balance would imply good system performance. Because traffic is bursty and hard to predict, the latency from the time a request is issued until it is satisfied by the next higher level may prevent the bandwidth at a particular level from being fully utilized. Thus, data movement demands vary with time, and peak demands may cause slowing, even though the system speed exceeds the average program requirements. In general, the most precise way to analyze the capability of an architecture is to characterize its components using both parameters of data movement. In simple cases, such an analysis of even a single unit can give an excellent match between performance model and experiment. Complexities arise when multiple interacting components of an architecture are considered, but even in this case, tractable and predictive architectural models can be constructed. For a complete understanding of performance, however, the data transport capacities of the architecture must match the demands for data movement of the program it executes. Characterizing those demands is the subject of this chapter.

A careful structuring of programs can result in improved overall execution performance. We distinguish between the two stages of design of an algorithm and design of the program that implements the algorithm. The order of executing the operations of a program can significantly influence the speed in which the program is executed on the target computer system. We study and present program metrics based on the temporal characterization of program performance from three different but related points of view. First, we measure the temporal data locality of two implementations of an algorithm on an SISD architecture with cache memory. Next, we examine the relationship of temporal data movement demands of parallel programs with the latency tolerance mechanisms of the interconnection network of a given computer system. Last, we look into scheduling send and receive operations in a distributed memory multiprocessor system so that message transmission latency is overlapped with computation in individual processors.

It will be helpful to contemplate some questions while reading this chapter. How important is it for a software programmer to understand the underlying computer architecture? Are program restructuring and algorithm design the same thing? Does program structure affect its performance? Do all correctly executing programs perform well? Can you describe the execution of a program as it relates to the movement of data it needs? Can program characteristics be changed to match the capabilities of the machine executing it? Do performance data based on an analysis of average execution rate give a reasonable measure of how well a program performs on a given parallel computer? Can program characteristics be used as an indication of what characteristics a computer architecture must have for it to perform well? Can we form an idea of what type of performance to expect from executing a parallel program on different architectures by analyzing the program's expected behavior independent from the underlying machine? Is it enough for a message passing program to be deadlock free? Does execution performance of a program depend on the overall number of communications? Does it matter how much data is needed at an execution point and when and how it is made available?

10.1 Temporal Characterization of Cache Behavior

Just as different system architectures supply different data transport capacities, including high bandwidth devices and high degrees of overlap, different program structures make different demands on data movement within a system. A uniprocessor program that accesses all elements of a large data structure several different times in sequence is more poorly supported by a cache than one that clusters multiple accesses to subsets of the large structure. In many cases the same algorithm can be restructured to improve its temporal locality and, thus, its performance in a system with cache. The analysis of such situations can be aided by metrics that reveal the data locality of programs.

We start with a measure of the temporal data locality of a uniprocessor program and see how it applies to two versions of an algorithm, one of which is intentionally structured to perform well with cache memory. The relationship between temporal data locality and the amount of data movement helps us understand the importance of restructuring programs to reduce the cache-memory traffic, increase data reuse, and, hence, obtain faster execution. The discussion assumes independent handling of instructions and data, as is done in machines with separate instruction and data caches. The program structures are simple enough that known techniques for instruction lookahead are sufficient to make data cacheing the only concern. We consider bubble sort, not because it is a good sorting algorithm, but because it directs attention away from floating point arithmetic to data movement and has a structure that mimics the access patterns in other programs dealing with linear array data.

The naive bubble sort program, which performs well if all data can be contained in the lowest level of the memory hierarchy, is shown in Program 10-1. For brevity we denote the operations in lines 3 through 6 by cswap(a[j], a[j+1]) in what follows. The program sweeps repeatedly through the N word array $a[1:N]$, stopping one item earlier each time. This is illustrated by the data dependence diagram in Figure 10-1 for $N = 10$. If this program is run on a machine with cache of size much smaller than N, a large number of cache misses occur regardless of the replacement strategy used. For example, it can be verified from Figure 10-1 that with a four word data cache having one word cache lines, the optimal replacement strategy gives 33

10.1.1 A Temporal Locality Metric for Cache Behavior

Let us generalize the discussion of the two versions of bubble sort by considering any sequence of two operand operations. In the bubble sort programs, these are compare/swap operations. Let r_{1i} and r_{2i} be the memory references for the first and second operands, respectively, for operation i. We make use of ideas similar to those developed for paged virtual memories. Define the working set over the last h operations at the time of performing operation k as:

$$W_k(h) = \bigcup_{i=k-h+1}^{k} \{r_{1i}\} \bigcup \{r_{2i}\}$$

Then the number of items referenced at operation k that are new with respect to those referenced within the last h operations is:

$$\delta_k(h) = \left| W_k(h+1) \bigcap \overline{W_{k-1}(h)} \right|.$$

For operations with two or fewer operands, $\delta_k(h)$ can be 0, 1, or 2. The average size of δ_k over a number of operations gives a measure of the temporal locality of an algorithm (or more precisely, of the program having the specific reference string). Locality is thus:

$$L(h) = \frac{1}{T} \sum_{k=1}^{T} \delta_k(h),$$

where T is the total number of operations in the reference string considered. This measure of locality applies to a time window h that should be viewed as being related to the cache size. The larger the time window, the larger the cache required to capture the working set over that window.

In both of the bubble sort algorithms, if h is zero, then every operation references two new operands and $L(h) = 2$. If h is as large as the number of operations, T, in the program, $L(T)$ becomes the size N of the data set divided by the total number of operations. Because the number of compare/swap operations is $(N(N-1))/2$, the metric $L(T)$ goes to zero as $1/N$ for large data sets. This sort of single operation and whole program limiting behavior can be expected for the locality metric applied to any algorithm.

10.1.2 Example Application of the Locality Metric to Bubble Sort

We compute and compare the locality metric, $L(h)$, for the two bubble sort programs. The comparison confirms that the naive bubble sort has a much larger locality metric than the cache-oriented one corresponding to the fact that unless the cache size is very large, execution of the naive bubble sort results in a cache miss for most of the operations. On the other hand, execution of the cache-oriented version results in a cache miss every K operations for data sets much larger than the cache size. To apply this locality measure to bubble sort, we look at the behavior of δ_k over the operations of each algorithm for various window sizes, h. The doubly nested loop of the naive bubble sort can be considered to consist of multiple sweeps over the data set, while the triply nested loop of the cache oriented bubble sort can be viewed as major sweeps over the data containing minor sweeps over the portion in the cache. The number of new operands for a given compare/swap operation and window size depends on the position of the operation within a sweep, or within major and minor sweeps. Therefore, we distinguish operations and the number of new operands they need on the basis of window size and relative position within a sweep.

For the naive bubble sort, the algorithm starts new sweeps at operation numbers

$$b(m) \ = \ mN - m\frac{(m+1)}{2} + 1, \qquad 0 \le m \le N - 2.$$

If the size of the window is zero, then two new operands are referenced at each step, so

$$\delta_k(0) \ = \ 2, \quad \text{for all } k.$$

For $h > 0$ and h small with respect to N, two new items must be referenced at the beginning of most new sweeps. This fails to be true for the last few sweeps that are short enough that the small window h begins to cover a full sweep. In general,

$$\delta_{b(m)}(h) \ = \ 2, \qquad 0 \le m \le N - h - 2.$$

At the beginning of sweep $N - h - 1$, or operation $b(N - h - 1)$, only one new operand is accessed because the previous sweep had h operations and $h + 1$ operands. Thus,

$$\delta_k(h) \ = \ 1, \qquad \text{for } k = b(N - h - 1).$$

For $k > b(N - h - 1)$, all operands that are referenced up to the end of the algorithm have been referenced in the last h operations, so

$$\delta_k(h) \ = \ 0, \qquad \text{for } k > b(N - h - 1).$$

It remains only to note that in the initial sweeps, after the first operation, one new operand is referenced per compare/swap. Thus, a complete definition of $\delta_k(h)$, $h > 0$, for the naive bubble sort is:

$$\delta_k(h) \ = \ \begin{cases} 2, & k = b(m), \quad 0 \le m \le N - h - 2; \\ 1, & 2 \le k \le b(N - h - 1), \quad k \ne b(m);\ . \\ 0, & k > b(N - h - 1) \end{cases}$$

From this equation, we can see that for $h \ll N$, the measure δ of new information used at each step becomes zero only near the end of the algorithm. It is usually one, being two only at the beginning of each sweep ($j = 1$). A small value of the locality metric, $L(h)$, represents good locality. For the naive bubble sort $L(h)$ is greater than but near one for values of T less than $b(N - h - 1)$. The point $b(N - h - 1)$ occurs $h(h + 1)/2$ operations before the end of the algorithm, which consists of a total of $N(N - 1)/2$ operations. Therefore, the locality for the naive bubble sort is as follows:

$$L(h) \ = \ \frac{1}{T}(min(T, b(N - h - 1)) + min(N - h - 1, 1 + \lfloor R \rfloor)),$$

where $b(N-h-1) = \frac{N(N-1)}{2} - \frac{h(h+1)}{2}$ and $R = \frac{2N-1-\sqrt{4N^2-4N-9-8T}}{2}$. Note that the locality metric, $L(h)$, is not dependent on the cache replacement strategy. For an appropriate window size, if fewer new items are referenced, any replacement policy should result in fewer misses.

The cache-oriented bubble sort consists of $\left\lceil \frac{(N-1)}{K} \right\rceil$ major sweeps, one for each value of m. A major sweep consists of a series of reverse sweeps. The general reverse sweep is of length K, with exceptions occurring near the beginning of each major sweep. The m-th major sweep begins at operation number

$$c(m) = 1 + mK\left(N - \frac{1}{2} - \frac{mK}{2}\right), \quad 0 \le m \le \left\lceil \frac{N-1}{K} \right\rceil - 1.$$

The q-th minor sweep within the m-th major sweep begins at

$$s(m, q) = \left(mKN - \frac{1-mK}{2}\right) + min\left(\frac{q(q+1)}{2}, \frac{K(K+1)}{2}\right) + max(0, K(q-K)) + 1,$$

$$0 \le q \le N - mK - 1.$$

If the time window h is small with respect to K, then the working set changes frequently, but if $h \ge K + 1$ then δ is zero except at the beginning of minor sweeps, which is consistent with the miss behavior shown in Table 10-2. If k is an operation preceding the tail of the computation,

$$\delta_k(h) = \begin{array}{ll} 2 \text{ if } k = s(m, 0), \\ 1 \text{ if } k = s(m, q), & 1 \le q \le N - mK - 2, \\ 0 \text{ if } k \ne s(m, q), & 1 \le q \le N - mK - 2. \end{array}$$

The calculation of $\delta_k(h)$ changes when k enters the tail of the computation that occurs $h(h + 1)/2$ operations before the end. The above is sufficient to compute the locality measure $L_T(h)$ for $h \ll N$, where

$$T < \frac{N(N-1)}{2} - \frac{h(h+1)}{2}$$

covers most of the algorithm.

In terms of major sweeps, the number of the sweep beginning the tail is

$$m = 1 + w, \quad \text{where } w = \left\lceil \frac{N-1-h}{K} \right\rceil.$$

The number of operations in major sweeps 0 through m is

$$c(m) - 1 = (1 + w)K\left(N - \frac{1}{2}(1 + (1 + w)K)\right),$$

and the number of new elements added to the window h working set is

$$\sum_{k=0}^{c(m)-1} \delta_k(h) = \sum_{m=0}^{w} (N - mK), \quad = N(1 + w) - \frac{K}{2}(1 + w)w.$$

Some calculation shows that over the part of the algorithm preceding the tail

$$L(h) < \frac{1}{K}\left(1 + \frac{K+1}{N(1-r)}\right).$$

where $r = K\frac{w}{2N}$ is a number near one half. Thus, the metric confirms the intuition from the diagram that if h is large enough to cover a minor sweep, one out of K operations causes a cache miss.

The locality metric introduced in this section is independent of the cache replacement strategy used. Replacement strategies are used to reduce the total number of cache misses by taking advantage of locality of references that are generated by the program. The locality metric, $L(h)$, is used for restructuring the programs to cluster references to the data items to reduce cache misses by maximizing the amount of data reuse. The two bubble sort programs access the data memory the same number of times, but have a very different temporal behavior within the programs. The locality metric for the same window size is about one for the naive bubble sort and about $1/K$ for the cache oriented bubble sort. A small locality metric for reasonable window size, h, implies few cache misses, while a large locality metric implies many misses.

10.2 Read Sharing in Multiprocessors with Distributed Caches

Having introduced the idea of a temporal metric for data references in the context of a uniprocessor with cache, we now move to a distributed shared memory environment with multiple processors and coherent caches. In this section, we expand on the working set idea and introduce a metric to demonstrate the importance of a latency tolerance mechanism of a particular interconnection network. A global address space multiprocessor is the underlying architecture for this discussion. In contrast to the previous case, it is assumed that programs and data fit in the local cache memories associated with each processor system so there is no main memory, making this a cache-only memory architecture (COMA). Data is distributed among the system caches, so when a processor references a data item not in its local cache, it must obtain it from the cache of another processor, resulting in an interprocessor communication. We consider programs, or sections of code, where each process executes the same number of operations. This scenario is an approximation of single program multiple data (SPMD) codes, such as parallel loops and iterative algorithms. We also assume that all processors execute operations at about the same speed, so that at a given time, on the average, all processors have executed the same number of operations. The *read multiplicity* metric measures the average number of reads that occur in a program at a given time scale. The metric applies only to read accesses preceded by a single write-invalidate that leads to the demand for interprocessor data movement on read. The write-invalidate protocol, as was described in Section 5.5.1, is one that invalidates all cache copies of a data item when a processor modifies its copy of the same data. In this case, processors must obtain an updated copy of the datum from the processor that owns the modified version (owner) before a valid access is allowed. To capture temporal information about read sharing, we use a varying size operation window similar to the previous section to compute a metric that gives a temporal characterization of the way data is accessed by a single execution stream.

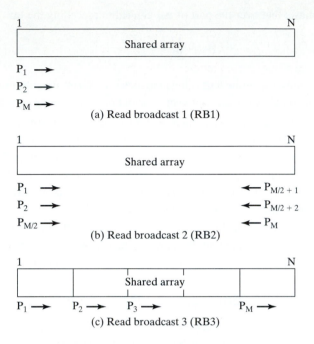

Figure 10-3   Three implementations of shared vector read.

A parallel program defines a sequence of operations to be executed in each processor. The read multiplicity metric is calculated over all possible strings of operations of length h, the operation window size, in the sequence. By varying h, we obtain information about the temporal separation of the data accesses that define the read multiplicity metric. For example, if the metric shows no read sharing for $h = 4$, we can conclude that accesses to a data item, executed by distinct processors, are separated at least by four operations. The operation execution rate relates this number to real time, giving time-dependent demands on data transport among processors.

10.2.1   A Simple Example of Read Sharing

Let us use a simple example to introduce the read multiplicity metric and its relationship to the latency tolerance mechanism of a multiprocessor system. Consider a program where M parallel processes (readers) read a shared array of N data items written by a writer process other than the M readers. Three implementations of this program are presented in Figure 10-3. We use this simple program as a working example to show how a metric can be used to predict the benefits of read broadcast, a latency tolerance mechanism used in some multiprocessors with caches and described in the next section. Therefore, the three implementations are called read broadcasts, RB1, RB2, and RB3. In the first implementation, all M processes read the vector of shared data at the same time and in the same order. In the second implementation, processes are divided into two groups, each half reading the shared vector sequentially but starting at different ends. The third implementation allows each process to start reading the vector from a different starting point. Processes read the array in a circular fashion to completely read the entire vector. Although the three implementations require the same number of operations to be performed by each of the reader processes, their performances vary significantly due to the temporal load they put on the network to satisfy their data movement requirements.

Qualitatively, in RB1 all M readers read the same set of data at the same time, regardless of how small the time window h is. In RB2, only about $M/2$ processes read the same data if h is less than the time to read half the array. And in RB3, only one process reads a data item until h becomes large enough to cover the time it takes a processor to read $1/M$ of the vector. The read multiplicity metric provides this characterization independent of the architecture. The characterization can then be related to a specific architecture to determine the ability of the architecture to deliver the data movement requirements of a program within the required time window. Conversely, the program can be restructured, as above, to better match the data transport capabilities of the underlying computer system.

10.2.2 The KSR-1 Architecture

We use the KSR-1 global address space multiprocessor to show the influence of program restructuring on the performance. KSR-1 was chosen because it supports a variety of network latency reduction techniques. The KSR multiprocessor is composed of a hierarchical ring interconnection network. The lowest level, Ring 0, consists of 32 cells for processing elements and two cells for routing to the next higher level ring, Ring 1. A completely configured Ring 1 consists of 32 Rings 0's. A general KSR architecture provides a third ring, Ring 2, consisting of 32 ring 1's. This study presents results on a KSR-1 with a single ring 0 installed. Each node on Ring 0 consists of a 64-bit superscalar processor with a 0.5 Mbytes of cache and 32 Mbytes of local memory. An interesting feature of the KSR is its memory management, the ALLCACHE scheme. The sum of the local memories forms the total memory of the system. Addresses are mapped to local memories dynamically and are managed like caches. Therefore, the KSR has a COMA[171]. Data items are not bound to specific memory locations, and to be accessible by a processor, a valid copy of the data must migrate to, and/or exist in, the processor's local memory. Data moves between local memories on demand, controlled by a write-invalidate coherence protocol. When a processor writes into its local cache it marks it valid. All other copies of the data item in other processors caches are then marked as invalid. In this section we adopt the KSR terminology and refer to local memory as cache, and to the processor's cache as subcache. Data is stored in units of pages and subpages in the memory. A page is 16 Kbytes and is divided into 128 subpages of 128 bytes each. The local caches share data in units of subpages. Therefore, the unit of ring transmission, and cache block, is a 128-byte subpage. The ring bandwidth is 8 Msubpages/sec. The processor cycle is 50 nanoseconds. The subcache contains 0.5 Mbytes of storage with an access latency of 2 cycles. The nominal latency to local cache is 20 cycles, to remote cache on the same ring, 150 cycles, and to remote cache on a different ring, 570 cycles.

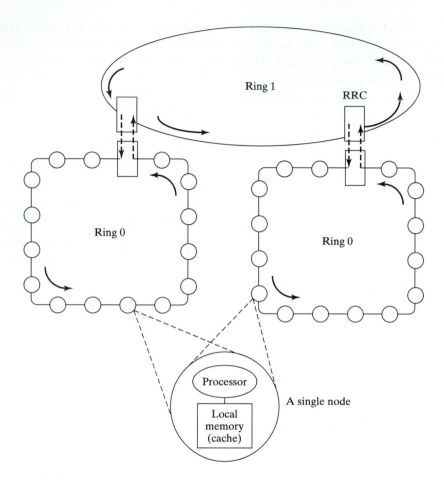

Figure 10-4 The KSR-1 ring hierarchy and routing.

A search procedure is used to accomplish the communication between processors. When a processor references an item that is not in its local cache (read miss) but is in the local cache of a processor in the same ring, only the Ring 0 containing the source and destination processors is searched. The local cache directories show what addresses are found in the local caches connected by the ring. Each Ring 0, a unidirectional slotted ring designed for pipelined fashion searching, is searched until the destination is reached. Figure 10-4 shows how a search in a multilevel ring is done. Ring 1 consists entirely of *Ring Routing Cells*, *RRC*s. Each RRC contains a directory for the Ring 0 connected to it. When a packet reaches an RRC, the directory is checked. If the corresponding Ring 0 does not contain the requested address the packet is sent to the next RRC on the Ring. Otherwise, the packet is routed down to the RRC on Ring 0 containing the address. KSR-1 provides three mechanisms for overlapping interprocessor access latency with execution, *read broadcast*, *prefetch*, and *poststore*.

A read miss causes a remote request through the interconnection network. The data is transferred from a remote cache to the local cache that originated the request. Using read-broadcast, during the transfer of the data through the interconnection network caused by a read to remote data, the data is copied in read only state into any cache that has a descriptor for the page containing the data and is not "busy," using the KSR terminology. If a processor accesses a broadcast data item after it has been copied into its cache, the reference is a hit unless an invalidation occurs before the access. Notice that consecutive accesses to a data item need to be separated in time at least by the network latency, so that the second access can benefit from the broadcast initiated by the first. The mechanism effectively hides the latency of the data move for all the processors that receive and later access a broadcast datum.

We can associate two states with a data request packet in the KSR-1 ring: empty and full. The packet is empty before it reaches the cache with the valid data and full after it has copied the valid data. Only the caches in the path of the full packet benefit from read broadcast. On the average, the mechanism is effectively a half broadcast.

Poststore and prefetch operations are provided to the programmer to enhance the program execution time by overlapping data movement latency with execution. Poststore allows a processor to broadcast a copy of data to all caches with a descriptor for the page containing that data before it is needed. The processor issuing the poststore must be the owner of the data, as defined by the coherence protocol. A packet containing the poststore data circulates around the ring, all caches that are not busy and have the correct descriptor acquire a copy of the data. A processor issues a prefetch to request a remote data item before it is needed. The processor continues execution, effectively overlapping future local execution with the remote data transfer. Only up to three prefetches can be outstanding in the KSR-1 architecture. If a fourth prefetch is issued, the processor stalls until one of the previously issued prefetches completes.

10.2.3 Read Multiplicity Metric

Define o_{in} to be the nth operation executed by processor i. Let $a(o_{in})$ be the set of all the operands read by operation o_{in}. We define the *read set* for processor i, at operation k, during the last h operations, as,

$$r_{ik}(h) = \bigcup_{n = k - h + 1}^{k} a(o_{in})$$

and the *global read set* during the last h operations at operation k for all P processors, as,

$$R_k(h) = \bigcup_{i = 1}^{P} r_{ik}(h).$$

Over the whole computation, the average sum of the read set sizes with window h is

$$F(h) = \frac{1}{N - h + 1} \sum_{k = h}^{N} \sum_{i = 1}^{P} |r_{ik}(h)|. \tag{10.1}$$

The corresponding average size of the global read set with window h is

$$G(h) = \frac{1}{N-h+1} \sum_{k=h}^{N} |R_k(h)|. \tag{10.2}$$

An estimate of the average number of processes that read the same data item within a time window h is the read multiplicity, $\rho(h)$, defined by

$$\rho(h) = \frac{F(h)}{G(h)}. \tag{10.3}$$

The read multiplicity quantifies the amount of read sharing that occurs on a particular operation window. If the read multiplicity is studied for different window sizes, h, a temporal characterization of the amount of read sharing can be obtained. A read multiplicity that is similar for small and large operation windows indicates that the reads to the same data item by different processors occur close in time (tight sharing). A read multiplicity that is much larger for large operation windows than for small ones indicates the read sharing occurs over long periods of time (loose sharing). We will see, for the three implementations of the example in Section 10.2.1, how read multiplicity can be used to predict, semi-quantitatively, the effectiveness of read-broadcast on a single ring KSR-1 multiprocessor. Qualitatively, read-broadcast mechanisms are effective for programs with loose sharing and ineffective for programs with tight sharing.

10.2.4 Experiments

The M readers read the same elements of a vector of 40,960 64-bit floating point numbers. The vector is previously written by a processor, different from any of the readers, so the only valid copy of the vector is in the writer's cache. The read is performed with a stride of 16, accessing only one element per subpage, so the expected number of coherence data moves per reader is the number of elements accessed, $N = 2560$.

The three read broadcast programs (see Figure 10-3) differ in the temporal relation in which the different readers access the data. In RB1 all the readers access the vector in the same order, from 1 to 40,960. In RB2 half of the readers access the vector from 1 to 40,960, and the other half in inverse order, from 40,960 to 1. In RB3 each reader starts reading the vector at a different point and, at the end of the vector, continues reading from the first element until reaching the element before the starting point. The starting point for a reader i is given by $(i-1)\frac{40,960}{M}+1$, for M readers.

The total number of misses per reader for each of the programs is shown in Figure 10-5. The expected number of misses without the benefit of read-broadcast, poststore, or prefetch, is 2,560. (Other experiments showed that, for the runs considered here, the call to the performance monitor was responsible, on the average, for 100 cache misses.) The effectiveness of read-broadcast in overlapping remote data moves is reflected in the number of coherence misses avoided. The total read time is shown in Figure 10-6. The results are the average of ten runs. The synchronization overhead is not included. Because the amount of data to be read per processor is constant, the read time should ideally be constant. However, due to the increase in remote access latency, the total read time increases with the number of readers. Read-broadcast tolerates this latency by overlapping it with computation.

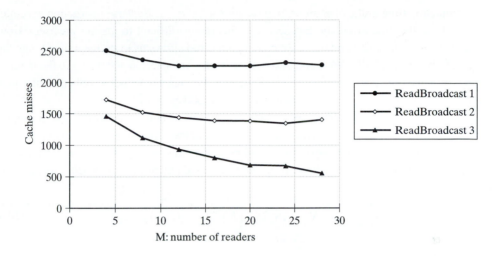

Figure 10-5 Number of cache misses/reader for RB1, RB2, RB3.

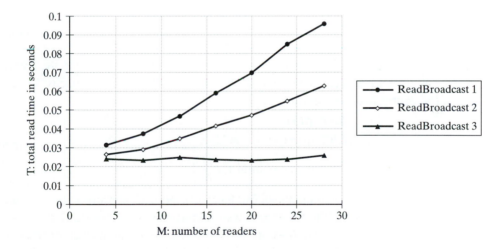

Figure 10-6 Total read time for the RB1, RB2, RB3 (processor cycle = 50 nanosec.)

The read multiplicity in Equation (10.3) is calculated by counting operations on a given operation window throughout the programs. The operations are counted in average units of time required to reference a data item, so for the programs considered there are N operations, the number of data accesses. The operation count used as the size h of the operation window is related to time. This time is determined from the instruction execution rate for the sequence of operations considered. For example, in the term $R_k(h)$ of Equation (10.2), the relation of h to time depends on the completion time of the operations $k - h, k - h + 1, ..., k - 1$. Because instruction execution rate depends on the time to satisfy data accesses, this rate is difficult to predict precisely. However, an analysis of the worst and best case completion times allows us to define a time range that corresponds to a particular h. Worst and best case scenarios are selected according to the memory hierarchy architecture. For example, on the KSR-1, a data read is satisfied either on the local cache (20 cycles) or in a remote cache (between 150 and 600 cycles).

The simplicity of the programs makes it possible to write equations for the read multiplicity. In RB1, all the M readers access the same data at about the same time, so the read multiplicity is M for all h. In RB2, in an operation window much smaller than $N/2$, about $M/2$ readers access any datum. The exact multiplicity for RB2 is obtained from $F(h) = Mh$ and the more complex

$$G(h) = \frac{1}{N-h+1}\left[2h(N-2h+2) + \left(h + 2\left\lfloor\frac{h}{2}\right\rfloor\right)(h-1) - 2\left\lfloor\frac{h}{2}\right\rfloor^2\right], \tag{10.4}$$

which if h is even, simplifies to

$$G(h) = 2h - \frac{h^2}{2(N-h+1)}. \tag{10.5}$$

If $h \ll N$, the read multiplicity for RB2 is about

$$\rho(h) = \frac{F(h)}{G(h)} \cong \frac{M}{2} \tag{10.6}$$

In RB3, for $h < \frac{N}{M}$, only one reader accesses a datum, but as h increases above N/M, the average number of readers that access a data item increases linearly to M. The read multiplicity for the 3 programs can be written in closed form as:

$$\begin{aligned}
RB1: \rho(h) &= \quad M, \\
RB2: \rho(h) &\approx \quad M/2 \\
RB3: \rho(h) &= \min\left(1, h\frac{M}{N}\right)
\end{aligned} \tag{10.7}$$

For the programs considered, the multiplicity can be associated with network traffic, some of which, can be tolerated by the KSR-1 read-broadcast mechanism. Read-broadcast is effective when data items are read by multiple processors, and these accesses occur at intervals separated in time by at least the latency of the network. Equation (10.7) characterizes temporally the way read sharing occurs in the three vector read programs. In a program that has high multiplicity for small h (tight sharing), the reads to shared data by different processors occur too closely in time for read-broadcast to be effective, and the network traffic is high. If a program has low multiplicity for small h, but high multiplicity for large h (loose sharing), the network traffic is reduced by the read-broadcast mechanism. As can be seen from Equation (10.7) all the programs have multiplicity M for $h = N$, which means that at the program scale, the three programs have identical demands. RB1 has multiplicity of M for small h and, therefore, all shared accesses should result in cache misses. The graph of Figure 10-5 shows fewer misses because processes become skewed, and the assumption of equal rate of progress that was adopted does not accurately apply. RB2 and RB3 have multiplicities of $M/2$ and 1 respectively, for small h, indicating that read-broadcast should be more effective in RB3 than in RB2, and that both use it better than RB1.

10.2.5 Programmed Poststore and Prefetch

There has been considerable work on building compilers and preprocessors to generate automatic prefetch and poststore operations to overlap data transfer time with execution. Because KSR-1 provides poststore and prefetch instructions as well as the hardware managed read broadcast, we modify our simple RB1 experiment to exploit poststore and prefetch and compare the effectiveness and overheads of the three latency tolerance mechanisms.

Two new programs, Poststore and Prefetch, are constructed from modifications to RB1. In Poststore, the write that invalidates the reader data poststores all the data before any processor starts to read it. In Prefetch, every reader prefetches all the data before it is referenced. RB2, RB3, Poststore, and Prefetch have resulted from four different optimizations to RB1. In the first two, we used program restructuring to reduce $\rho(h)$ for small h, so that the hardware managed read broadcast can deliver data to the processors cache by the time they need it. In the other two, we are using software instructions to control data movement. The cache misses for the five programs are shown in Figure 10-7. All figures in this section represent an average of 10 runs. The figure shows that Prefetch and Poststore almost entirely eliminate the cache misses (misses shown are caused by the call to the performance monitor). Poststore and prefetch, as opposed to the read broadcast, do not depend on the processor's position on the ring. Prefetch succeeds regardless of the busy condition of the receiving processor. Poststore fails if the receiving cache is busy. However, for the Poststore program, the poststore data is the only traffic on the ring during the poststore phase and, therefore, all poststores will succeed.

In contrast to RB1, RB2, and RB3 that take advantage of the hardware managed read broadcast for latency tolerance, the execution of poststore and prefetch instructions by Poststore and Prefetch programs respectively adds an overhead to the program execution time. The reduction in coherence cache misses shown Figure 10-7 comes at the cost of executing the poststore and prefetch instructions. The poststores are executed by the writer process and the prefetch instructions are executed by the reader processes. Figure 10-8 shows the sum of the write time and the average read time to include the poststore and prefetch overheads. Synchronization overheads are not included. We observe a linear increase in total time for RB1, where there is essentially no overlap of data moves. It is important to note that, although the number of reads per processor is kept constant, the execution time increases because the remote latency increases. RB3 exhibits the best performance. The total execution time is constant in RB3 as the number of processors increases, which is expected in a scalable program-architecture system. The overhead associated with Poststore and Prefetch is quite high. Prefetch is always better than RB1, but Poststore is only better than RB1 for more than eight readers. The read broadcast with no extra associated overhead seems to be the most effective technique in programs that can be restructured to have low reference multiplicity for small h.

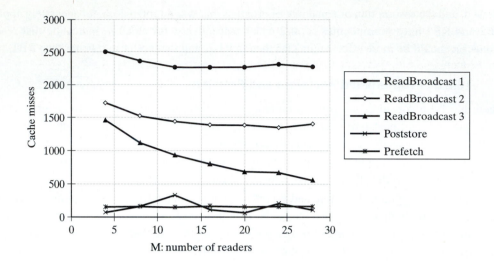

Figure 10-7 Number of read misses/reader for RB1, RB2, RB3, Poststore, Prefetch.

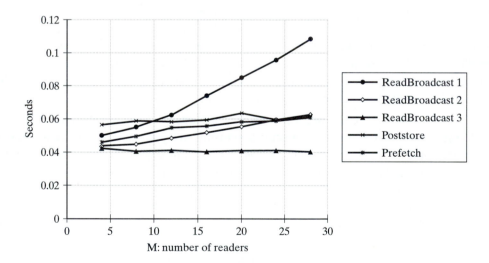

Figure 10-8 Average read time plus write time for RB programs; average read time plus write time plus poststore time for Poststore; average read plus prefetch time plus write time.

10.3 Message Waiting in Message Passing Multiprocessors

In the single processor with cache system of Section 10.1, we studied the importance of scheduling operations of a program so that data loaded resides in cache longest by grouping as many required references to the cache contents as possible, hence minimizing the number of cache misses and program execution time. In Section 10.2, where data is distributed among cache memories in a global address space multiprocessor system, we use the single processor-cache techniques to maximize data reuse in cache. However, we learned that we must distribute the interprocess cache references in time to avoid network delays due to traffic congestion that may result from bursty program reference behavior. Where in the first case we attempt to keep references to data close together to prevent cache misses, in the second case we attempt to separate in time references that cause interprocess communication. In this section, we study the effect of scheduling send and receive operations in a distributed memory multiprocessor. The amount of time a distributed memory multiprocessor program spends waiting at receive operations for messages to arrive is one of the most difficult parts of communication overhead to characterize. This discussion is closer in concept to the way poststore operations are used to overlap data transfer with execution; poststore is done as soon as data needed by other processors is produced.

We specify a message between processes by sender and receiver process numbers and by the serial index of the message in the sequence of N_{pq} messages from process p to process q. Process p, thus, executes send operations $s_i(p,q)$, $0 \leq i < N_{pq}$, and process q executes corresponding receive instructions $r_i(p,q)$, $0 \leq i < N_{pq}$. We assume a correct program in which the pairing of sends and receives is determined, recognizing that a program trace may be necessary to do this in nondeterministic cases such as multiple client–server situations.

We assume a nonblocking send with a corresponding blocking receive for communication. The time for delivery of a message is broken into four parts:

1. The deterministic time associated with the execution of a nonblocking send.
2. The deterministic time associated with the execution of a blocking receive when a message is present at the beginning of the receive execution.
3. The delivery time, or network latency $L_i(p,q)$ for the i-th message sent from process p to q. The delivery time has some fixed minimum but may vary as a result of network routing and contention. Although we retain the precise notation as long as feasible, we tend to think in terms of a fixed delivery time that is independent of the source, destination, and message number.
4. The wait that occurs when no message is present at the time of execution of a blocking receive. This receive wait time is what we wish to characterize in the remainder of this section.

Assume a collection of processors p_k, $0 \leq k < P$ with completely independent memories communicating intermediate results only by way of messages. A source p_k and destination p_m uniquely identify a communication channel. The i-th message over that channel is $c_i(k,m)$, $0 \leq i < N_{km}$. Each processor p_k executes an instruction stream E_j^k, $0 \leq j < M_k$, where j is an instruction number in the instruction execution stream and M_k is the total number of instructions in the stream of processor k. The position of a given instruction instance in that stream is given by an integer valued function $I^k(.)$. Because an instruction instance can belong to only one process, the superscript on I is suppressed. Thus, a send instruction $s_i(p,q)$ occupies position $I(s_i(p,q))$ in the instruction stream of processor p, and its corresponding receive is instruction $I(r_i(p,q))$ of process q.

Every instruction is associated with a deterministic execution time. For send and receive instructions these are assumed to be the nonblocking send execution time and the time for receive execution with a message waiting; that is, no additional waiting time for receiving the message is included. We denote the (deterministic) time to execute instructions E_i^k through E_j^k by $T^k(i,j)$. With these assumptions, the execution time of a process p_k is $T^k(0,M_k)$ plus some possible waiting time at each receive. A measure of the cumulative waiting time for a process gives a useful tool for organizing a program to reduce communication overhead.

To get a measure of the "unavoidable" waiting time at the time of execution of receive operations we introduce the notion of an *external dependence* between a send and a subsequent receive in the same process. There is an external dependence between $s_{m_1}(p_1, p_2)$ and $r_{m_n}(p_n, p_1)$ if and only if

1. $I(s_{m_1}(p_1, p_2)) < I(r_{m_n}(p_n, p_1))$ and
2. there exists a chain $p_1, p_2, ..., p_n, p_{n+1} = p_1$ of processes and messages
   $c_{m_k}(p_k, p_{k+1}), \ 1 \le k \le n$ such that $I(r_{m_k}(p_{k-1}, p_k)) < I(s_{m_{k+1}}(p_k, p_{k+1})), 2 \le k \le n$.

For each external dependence, two time separations between $s_{m_1}(p_1, p_2)$ and $r_{m_n}(p_n, p_1)$ can be computed. The first is the deterministic part of the execution time for p_1. This internal time is

$$\tau_i = T^1(I(s_{m_1}(p_1, p_2)), I(r_{m_n}(p_n, p_1))).$$

There is also an external time consisting of the deterministic message transmission times and the execution times between the receives and sends for the chain passing through the other processes, see Figure 10-9 for an example. This external time is

$$\tau_e = \sum_{k=1}^{n} L_{m_k}(p_k, p_{k+1}) + \sum_{k=2}^{n} T^k(I(r_{m_{k-1}}(p_{k-1}, p_k)), I(s_{m_k}(p_k, p_{k+1}))).$$

If $\tau_i \ge \tau_e$, then process p_1 does not have to wait at the receive $r_{m_n}(p_n, p_1)$ unless other receive delays or network traffic increase τ_e above its nominal deterministic value. Thus, the nominal wait at $r_{m_n}(p_n, p_1)$ resulting from the single external dependence on $s_{m_1}(p_1, p_2)$ is

$$W(r_{m_n}(p_n, p_1), s_{m_1}(p_1, p_2)) = max(0, \tau_e - \tau_i).$$

The nominal wait at a particular receive is the maximum of the above wait over all sends on which that receive is externally dependent. If the nominal waits at all receives in a program are zero, then the processors can be started and terminated in such a way that all actual waits are zero. If some nominal wait is nonzero, then the interaction between the external dependences needs to be taken into account. Minimizing the waiting times resulting from external dependence over all the receives of a program is one way to reduce communication overhead in a distributed memory multiprocessor program by most effectively overlapping computation and communication.

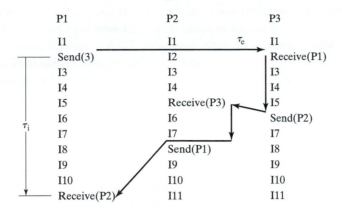

Figure 10-9 External dependence of a receive on a send.

Process p_i

Process p_i

```
1        send(p_{i-1}, a[i×m]);
2        receive(p_{i-1}, t);
3        a[i×m] := max(t, a[i×m]);
4        send(p_{i+1}, a[(i+1)×m-1]);
5        receive(p_{i+1}, t);
6        a[(i+1)×m-1] := min(t,a[(i+1)×m-1]);
7        for j := i×m step 2 until (i+1)×m-2
                cswap(a[j], a[j+1]);
m/2+7    for j := i×m+1 step 2 until (i+1)×m-3
                cswap(a[j], a[j+1]);
```

```
m+6      send(p_{i-1}, a[i×m]);
m+7      receive(p_{i-1}, t);
m+8      a[i×m] := max(t, a[i×m]);
m+9      send(p_{i+1}, a[(i+1)×m-1]);
m+10     receive(p_{i+1}, t);
m+11     a[(i+1)×m-1] := min(t, a[(i+1)×m-1]);
              . . .
```

Program 10-3 Code for process p_i of transposition sort.

As an illustration of the application of this measure, Program 10-3 shows a simplistic version of a distributed memory multiprocessor program for odd/even transposition sort, which is in some sense the distributed version of the bubble sort discussed in Section 10.1. Transposition sort first does compare/swap on adjacent data items with the first of the pair being an odd numbered item. All of these can be done in parallel. Then it does the same for pairs with the first being an even-numbered item, again all in parallel. We assume that the N word array to be sorted is divided into blocks of m words, each of which is handled by one of the processors. Only the inner loop code for an arbitrary process internal to a linear chain of processes is shown. The processors at the end of the chain and the iteration and termination code are ignored. A complete inner loop execution is shown between the horizontal lines. A few instructions from the next instance of the loop are shown to clarify the externally dependent instructions. The data dependence diagram for $m = 8$ is shown in Figure 10-10 with the portions allocated to processors p_i and p_{i+1} shown between horizontal dashed lines. The operations associated with the execution of one inner loop execution are between the vertical dashed lines. The compare/swap operations intersected by horizontal lines are those requiring interprocessor communication.

It is sufficient to focus on the messages between p_i and p_{i+1}. In the simplistic version of Program 10-3, there is an external dependence of the receive in instruction E^i_{m+10} on the send in instruction E^i_4 in process p_i. The internal time between the two dependent send and receive operations is:

$$\tau_i = (m + 10) - 4 = m + 6.$$

For external time, we note that p_i sends a message to p_{i+1} in instruction E^i_4 where p_{i+1} receives in instruction E^{i+1}_2. p_{i+1} then sends a message to p_i in instruction E^{i+1}_{m+6} to be received in E^i_{m+10}:

$$\tau_e = 2L + (m + 6) - 2 = 2L + m + 4$$

Therefore, the nominal wait time is $W = max(0, 2L - 2)$ assuming the latency for any message is L. This wait is almost sure to be nonzero unless L is very small. A similar calculation for the external dependence of receive E^{i+1}_{m+7} on send E^{i+1}_1 in process p_{i+1} by way of process p_i gives the same nominal wait time.

Program 10-4 shows an optimized version of the distributed multiprocessor odd/even transposition sort. In this version, the sends and receives are placed in the code so that the amount of computation between the external sends and receives for a given process is reduced. As soon as a process receives a message, it computes what needs to be sent to another process in the dependent chain and sends it. In process p_i the receive $E^i_{3m/2+3}$ is externally dependent on the send $E^i_{m/2+4}$, but here the internal and external times are given by

$$\tau_i = \frac{3m}{2} + 3 - \left(\frac{m}{2} + 4\right) = m - 1 \text{ and}$$

$$\tau_e = 2L + ((m + 6) - (m + 3)) = 3 + 2L.$$

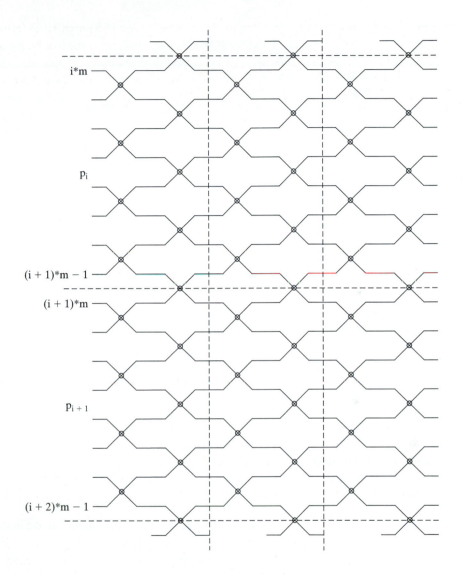

Figure 10-10   Data dependence for odd/even transposition.

This makes the nominal wait $W = max(0, 2L + 4 - m)$, which is much more likely to be zero for interesting values of m and L. The result was essentially achieved by reducing the amount of code between the receive and the send in the external process p_{i+1} to a minimum resulting in smaller τ_e. In other words, receive a message when it is needed, send a message as soon as possible. Again the external dependence of E^{i+1}_{m+3} on E^{i+1}_2 in process p_{i+1} gives the same nominal wait.

Process p_i

1	`cswap(a[i×m], a[i×m+1]);`
2	`send(p_{i-1}, a[i×m]);`
3	`for j := i×m+2 step 2 until (i+1)×m-4`
	`    cswap(a[j], a[j+1]);`
m/2+1	`receive(p_{i+1}, t);`
m/2+2	`a[(i+1)×m-1] := min(t, a[(i+1)×m-1]);`
m/2+3	`cswap(a[(i+1)×m-2], a[(i+1)*×m-1]);`
m/2+4	`send(p_{i+1}, a[(i+1)×m-1]);`
m/2+5	`for j := i×m+1 step 2 until (i+1)×m-3`
	`    cswap(a[j], a[j+1]);`
m+3	`receive(p_{i-1}, t);`
m+4	`a[i×m] := max(t, a[i×m]);`
m+5	`cswap(a[i×m], a[i×m+1]);`
m+6	`send(p_{i-1}, a[i×m]);`
m+7	`for j := i×m+2 step 2 until (i+1)×m-4`
	`    cswap(a[j], a[j+1]);`
3m/2+3	`receive(p_{i+1}, t);`
3m/2+4	`a[(i+1)×m-1] := min(t, a[(i+1)×m-1]);`
3m/2+5	`cswap(a[(i+1)×m-2], a[(i+1)×m-1]);`
3m/2+6	`send(p_{i+1}, a[(i+1)×m-1]);`
	`. . .`

Program 10-4   Communication optimized transposition sort.

10.4 Conclusion

By focusing on the capacities of architectural components for data transport and on the demands of programs for such transport, high-performance systems can be better designed and utilized. The two parameters of data transport, bandwidth and latency, considered for the important components of an architecture, give a much better measure of its performance than bandwidth of the arithmetic unit alone measured in FLOPS.

Given an architecture, an analysis of the data transport requirements of an algorithm can be used to select the best program structure for it. The idea of latency is also an important concept at the program level. After bandwidth has been addressed by reducing operation count, the latency properties of a program are of primary importance. We have presented three program metrics based on latency and shown how they can be used to optimize program structure.

Considering programs as series of computations and data movements, data movement demands of programs defined by data sharing may be characterized in an architecture independent fashion. These demands may be estimated statically for program execution by a fixed number of processes on general classes of multiprocessors. Time can be characterized by the number of operations within certain window size. One possible use of such information is to guide program restructuring that lowers the data movement requirements. The number of interprocess data movements within a window size corresponding to network response is directly related to the underlying interconnection network's ability to handle remote requests. The interprocess data movement demands are not architecture dependent, and regardless of the cache and memory organization, they eventually involve the interconnection network. Once the program characterization for data movement is known, its performance over different network architectures can be predicted.

Many characterizations of program demands for data movement, like coherence miss ratio on global address space multiprocessors or ratio of communication to computation in message passing architectures, have been based on program averages. Whole program averages do not, however, effectively predict the performance impact of latency, resource contention, and bandwidth limitations in the data transport resources of parallel architectures.

We have studied the temporal characterization of parallel programs and presented experimental results to validate the usefulness of an architecture independent temporal metric. The time scale of program requirements for data movement is important, especially at small time scales. The most common of these characterizations include the coherence miss ratio on global address space multiprocessors and the communication to computation ratio on message passing machines. It is important to characterize demands for data movement at the scale of remote latency, and for many programs the demands at this scale are much higher (usually an order of magnitude) than those measured at the program scale. Predictions of contention for network resources are underestimated by program scale metrics. Temporal characterization of program behavior opens new opportunities for future research in parallel performance modeling.

10.5 Bibliographic Notes

Proper use of registers and caches to optimize compiler code generation to reduce latency is investigated in [168]. Restructuring of parallel application programs to reduce data movement and to overlap it with processing have been studied in [177] for distributed memory multiprocessors and in [244] for nonuniform access time shared memory multiprocessors. Masking of long message latency in distributed memory multiprocessors by scheduling nonblocking sends early has been proposed in [164]. Tolerating communication latency was raised as a fundamental architectural issue in [27]. Active messages described in [101] attempt to reduce the communication layer functionality to the minimum required. Some multithreaded computer architectures manage data movement latency primarily by overlapping it with computation as described in [4, 16, 198, and 264]. Performance of latency tolerance techniques are presented in [285] and [128]. Development of metrics to evaluate coherence protocols by parameterizing simulated runs are described in [99]. A model to characterize the efficiency of a general class of multithreaded architectures is reported in [250]. Temporal characterization of program behavior has been extensively studied in [165, 167, 246, and 247].

Problems

10.1 This program and its cache-oriented version compute a pairing between numbers in one array and the nearest number in a second array. Use the techniques of Section 10.1 to analyze the advantage of the cache-oriented version in terms of the locality metric. Assuming one-word lines, what size cache is needed to get the advantage of the cache-oriented version. The parameter K in the cache-oriented version divides M evenly.

Naive version

```
real x[1:M], y[1:M], c;
integer n[1:M], i, j, nn;
for i := 1 step 1 until M
begin
    c := maxreal;
    nn := 0;
    for j := 1 step 1 until M
        if (|y[j] - x[i]| < c) then
        begin
            c := |y[j] - x[i]|;
            nn := j;
        end
    n[i] := nn;
end;
```

Cache-oriented version

```
real x[1:M], y[1:M], c[1:M];
integer n[1:M], i, j, jj;
for i := 1 step 1 until M
begin   c[i] := maxreal;
        n[i] := 0;
end;
for j := 1 step 1 until M/K
    for i := 1 step 1 until M
        for jj := 1 step 1 until K
        if (|y[j*K+jj] - x[i]| < c[i]) then
        begin
            c[i] := |y[j] - x[i]|;
            n[i] := j*K+jj;
        end;
```

10.2 Two processes on a distributed memory multiprocessor communicate by nonblocking *send* and blocking *receive* while executing the code below. Execution time for this program uses the following information. Arithmetic assignments take time t_a; *send* takes t_s in the sender plus t_L for message delivery to the receiver; and *receive* takes t_s to prepare for the receive plus any waiting time for the message to arrive from the sender.

P1	P2
a := b+c	q := r+s
c := c×a	*receive* t from P1
send c to P2	q := q×t
b := b–4	r := r–q
d := b×b	*send* q to P1
receive a from P2	s := r×t

(a) Calculate the waiting time at each *receive*.

(b) Is there a program restructuring that reduces the waiting time, and what are the minimal assumptions on t_a, t_s, and t_L that guarantee a reduction?

10.3 Assume we have a global address space multiprocessor similar to the KSR-1 architecture presented in Section 10.2.2. Consider the following two program segments.

Segment 1
```
low  :=  (me - 1)*N/P + 1;
high := low + N/P - 1;
for i := low + 1 step 1 until high
     v[i] := v[i] + v[i-1];
sum[me] := v[high];
barrier;
start := 0;
for j := (me - 1) step -1 until 1
     start := start + sum[j];
for i := low step 1 until high
     v[i] := start + v[i];
```
Segment 2
```
low  := (me - 1)*N/P + 1;
high := low + N/P - 1;
for i := low + 1 step 1 until high
     v[i] := v[i] + v[i-1];
sum[me] := v[high];
barrier;
start := 0;
for j := 1 step 1 until (me - 1)
     start := start + sum[j];
for i := low step 1 until high
     v[i] := start + v[i];
```

The vector size, N, and the number of processors, P, are powers of two and N >> P. Assume the entire vector is initially in the memory of a processor other than the P processors doing the computation. Use the same memory hierarchy and access times as in Section 10.2.2, that is, a local cache access takes 20 processor cycles, a remote access in the same ring takes 150 cycles, and an access to a different ring takes 570 cycles. Also assume processors execute the code at the same rate in lock-step.

(a) What operation is being performed by the two program segments?

(b) Draw a graph that shows the communication between the processors at different time steps for each program segment.

(c) What are the total number of communications needed in each implementation?

(d) Compare the efficiency and performance of the two implementation.

10.4 Given are a vector of N distinct integers, V[N], and P distinct integer values, search[P], where N and P are powers of two and N >> P. We want to search the vector, V, for each of the values in search[P] and return the index of the value in V. Assume a shared address space multiprocessor similar to the KSR-1 architecture presented in Section 10.2.2 and that processes execute the code at the same rate in lock-step. Assume the vector, V, is initially in the memory of a processor other than the P processors doing the search and that every processor's cache is large enough to hold the entire vector. For simplicity, we ignore the search stop condition and assume each search value can definitely be found in V. Consider two implementations.

Implementation 1

```
myvalue := search[me];
index[me] := 0;
for i := 1 step 1 until N
      if (myvalue = V[i]) then index[me] := i;
```

Implementation 2

```
low := (me - 1)*N/P + 1;
high := low + N/P - 1;
for j := 1 step 1 until P
      begin
            myvalue := search[j];
            for i := low step 1 until high
                  if (myvalue = V[i]) then index := i;
      end;
```

(a) Compare the performance and efficiency of the two implementations for the KSR-1 style machine.

(b) If the vector is stored in increasing order, can you implement a search with better overall performance than either of the above two implementations?

10.5 Consider the solution of a discretized partial differential equation where at each step every point on a two-dimensional grid indexed by [i, j] is approximated as a function of itself and its four neighbors, f(A[i-1, j], A[i, j-1], A[i, j], A[i, j+1], A[i+1, j]). The sequential pseudocode for the heart of the solver for an NxN grid is given below.

```
alpha := 0.1;
allpoints := N*N;
done := false;
while (not done) do
    begin
        change := 0.0;
        i := 1 step 1 until N
            j := 1 step 1 until N
                begin
                    oldval := A[i, j];
                    A[i, j] := alpha*f(A[i-1, j], A[i, j-1],
                        A[i, j], A[i, j+1],A[i+1, j]);
                    change := change + abs(A[i, j] - oldval;
                end;
        if (change/allpoints < tolerance) then done := true;
    end;
```

(a) Assume a uniprocessor with a separate data cache memory, and describe how well the above algorithm exploits temporal locality.

(b) Describe a method to increase the temporal locality of the solver in the uniprocessor of part (a).

(c) Now consider a shared address space multiprocessor like the KSR-1 described in Section 10.2.2. Assume 64 processors, $N = 1024$, and row major allocation for the two dimensional arrays. Discuss and compare locality and the amount of communication for the following two partitioning strategies:

    i. Partition the grid into square blocks.

    ii. Partition the grid into N/64 contiguous rows per processor.

Parallel I/O

The parallel I/O problem involves multiple processes doing a combination of I/O or computational tasks in parallel. Overlapping I/O with a single computational task has been studied for a long time in connection with uniprocessors. Running multiple I/O tasks on multiple processors and I/O devices in support of a single computation has a shorter history. Following our algorithms, languages, and architectures approach, we discuss the I/O needs of applications and to what extent the required operations can be done in parallel, the ways of specifying parallel I/O operations on a parallel system, and the hardware architectures needed to accomplish parallel I/O.

11.1 The Parallel I/O Problem

The I/O needs in support of an application can usefully be separated into three types: mandatory I/O, checkpoint I/O, and out-of-core I/O. *Mandatory I/O* does the input of data required by the computation and the output of results. *Checkpoint I/O* allows the computation to be suspended, taken off the machine, and then later reloaded and restarted where it left off. *Out-of-core I/O* uses disks or other direct access storage devices (DASDs) as secondary memory to hold problem data that do not fit in primary memory. Virtual memory is an automatic way of extending memory usage to secondary storage devices while out-of-core techniques are user controlled and application specific uses of I/O devices for secondary storage.

Three subtasks can be associated with an I/O operation. Foremost is the physical movement of data between primary memory and a device. This subtask is most directly influenced by I/O hardware, not only by the devices themselves but also by the interconnections and support for primary memory access: processors, direct memory access (DMA), and/or I/O processors (IOPs). The second subtask is format conversion of the I/O data. There are two distinct types of format conversion, with the simplest only involving a change in blocking of the data bits, say from memory words to fixed length records of bytes on a disk. The second type of format conversion is more computationally intensive and can be illustrated by the conversion between a memory word stored in floating point format and a human readable character string that represents the same real value (to some round-off error). We may call this second type of format conversion *interpreted I/O* because it involves an interpretation of the meaning of the data. The third subtask arises when large data structures are moved into or out of primary memory. Movement of an array requires knowledge of its dimensions that may come from a previous input operation as well as from a computation. Access to subarrays requires even more structural information about the data and can be very important in distributed memory parallel systems where processors operate on disjoint portions of a large array.

11.1.1 Data Dependence and I/O

The idea of using data dependence analysis to identify parallelism in a problem also applies to I/O. A data-dependence graph can show input operations as sources of operands for computations and output operations as sinks for results. Inputs are needed and outputs are generated at different points in the dependence graph. An input operation can also produce structural information for a subsequent input or output operation on a data structure, so it can be useful to identify *structural dependence* between operations. There may also be obscured dependences in I/O operations involving file names and file pointers. A file pointer is often updated by an I/O operation and, thus, appears in both the operation's input set and output set used to identify dependences using Bernstein's conditions.

As a simplistic but representative example of a data dependence diagram involving I/O, consider a matrix multiply program. The program reads two matrices, $A[N, L]$ and $B[L, M]$, from a single input file, computes the matrix product $C = A \times B$, and writes $C[N, M]$ to a separate output file. Each matrix is represented in its file by a header containing its dimensions followed by the data, and matrix B follows matrix A in the input file. Figure 11-1 shows a dependence graph for the program. Input operations are identified by I, computations by C, and output operations by O. Three types of dependence arcs are distinguished: data dependence (no label), structural dependence (struct), and *file pointer dependence* (fp). The I_{Adim} input operation reads the dimensions of A and advances the input file pointer while I_{Adat} reads the data values for A and advances the pointer to B. The I_{Bdim} and I_{Bdat} operations behave similarly. The read operations for the data of each matrix depend structurally on the dimensions read from the matrix header, and all input file reads depend on the previous read through the file pointer. The C_{conf} operation determines whether A and B are conformable and outputs the dimensions of C. The C_{mmul} operation computes the actual matrix product, and the two output operations write the header and data of C into the output file. It can be seen from the diagram that the reading of data for A or B cannot begin until the corresponding dimension information is available, and B cannot be read until the file pointer has been advanced past A in the input file.

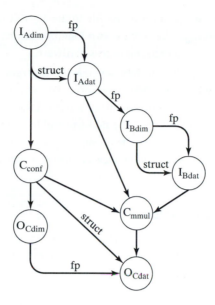

Figure 11-1   Dependence graph for a problem involving I/O.

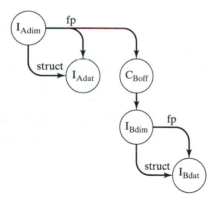

Figure 11-2   Enabling parallel data input for the A and B matrices.

Suppose that there is potential parallelism in file input. The input file may be cached in a random access memory or spread over multiple disk files that can be accessed simultaneously. For large A and B matrices, it would be desirable to read the data for A and B in parallel, but the diagram of Figure 11-1 shows that this is inhibited by the file pointer dependences. This dependence can be eliminated by computing an offset into the input file for the matrix B as soon as the dimensions of A are known and using it for the input of B. The changed part of the dependence diagram is shown in Figure 11-2. The new computation node, C_{Boff}, uses the information about the dimensions of A to compute the offset in the file to the start of matrix B. Now the lack of a dependence between I_{Adat} and I_{Bdat} allows these two long operations to be done in parallel, in so far as is permitted by parallel file storage and access hardware.

Checkpoint I/O would appear in a data dependence diagram as a large output operation with a dependence arc leading to a large input operation. This input-output pair would divide the dependence graph of the computation into two disjoint parts, that before the checkpoint and that following it. For out-of-core computations, it could be useful to distinguish dependences on secondary memory data that give rise to arcs from output to subsequent input operations from dependences on primary memory data with arcs connecting input, output, and computation operations.

11.1.2 I/O Format Conversion

Movement of data between primary memory and any I/O device almost surely involves some format conversion. The storage unit in primary memory is a multibyte word while on a disk, for example, the storage unit is a record consisting of a number of bytes that is a multiple of the number in a memory word. Even if the data bits are unchanged between memory and disk, these blocking factors vary. In addition, the disk contains sector and track header information and error control bits that differ from those used to control memory errors. Many of these minimal format transformations are done by I/O device hardware and occur naturally in parallel when multiple devices are used for parallel I/O.

Interpreted I/O may require significant computation for format conversion. For example, it can take hundreds of instructions to convert a floating point number in memory to a character representation for output in human readable form. If large arrays of real numbers are to be converted, the importance of doing this work in parallel on a parallel computer is clear. The argument that humans are slow readers and writers of character oriented formats, making high performance on this task unimportant, ignores the fact that human readable files are often used as intermediaries, say between a vector field computation and a data visualization program, to support debugging and spot checking of intermediate results. An I/O model such as the one often used in Unix-based systems that standardizes all I/O as accesses to a sequential stream of bytes not only serializes the I/O itself but inhibits the use of parallel computation for format conversion.

Interpreting data for a visual display device can involve significant amounts of computation. From the simple rasterization of grey scale data to complex color rendering algorithms, there is a wide range of computational complexity in such interpretations. The potential for parallelism in visual rendering and interpretation is large. Disjoint image portions may be independent as may different image frames of a movie. Display devices are often built around multiported random access memories, from which the display is updated by hardware using a dedicated port. Parallel access to the display memory is a natural way to address the high bandwidth requirements of a display in a parallel system and to allow the format interpretation computations to be spread over multiple processing units.

11.1.3   Numerical Examples of I/O Latency and Bandwidth Requirements

All forms of I/O, mandatory, checkpoint, and out-of-core, are limited by the characteristics of hardware devices, including processors, memory, interconnections, and I/O devices. In addition, mandatory I/O may have real-time constraints, as is the case with audio and video, or longer term constraints, such as the requirement that a five-day weather forecast, along with all of its intermediate I/O, must complete in considerably less than five days. I/O demands involve transferred data volume and time. Bandwidth and latency are the parameters most often used to express these demands. Common I/O devices with high bandwidth requirements are magnetic tapes, disks, color displays, and local or wide area network ports. Sometimes system balance involves supplying enough I/O capacity to keep the processor from becoming idle. Then it is the rate at which an application program generates I/O that becomes important for system design and configuration.

One specific example computation is the finite difference time domain (FDTD) calculation of the electric and magnetic fields in three dimensions, evolving in time according to Maxwell's equations. A program using this method on a $200 \times 200 \times 200$ point spatial grid required about 2.3×10^9 floating point operations per time step, 285 floating point operations per grid point per time step. Suppose the mandatory output is to drive a 3D display processor at 1% resolution in each space dimension, updated once every five time steps. 1% resolution corresponds to a $100 \times 100 \times 100$ spatial grid, so with four-byte floating point numbers, a frame requires $100^3 \times 6 \times 4 = 24$ MB of I/O and $5 \times 2.3 \times 10^9$ floating point operations, or about 479 floating point operations per byte of I/O. The example demonstrates the plausibility of a common rule of thumb that scientific applications generate about one byte of I/O for every 500 floating point operations. It also demonstrates the large variability of this estimate. Even for this single computation, the number of operations varies as the cube of the space resolution times the time resolution and can change greatly with result requirements.

The most common real time I/O requirements are imposed by audio and video. A stereo audio standard requires 44,100 samples of 16 bits per second for each of two channels, for 176 KB per second of I/O bandwidth. Video is much more demanding. A color video sample is often eight bits for each of three colors, or 24 bits per sample. High resolution displays are reaching about 1,500 points in each of two dimensions and are refreshed 60 times per second for a 405 MB per second I/O bandwidth requirement. This large bandwidth requirement is reduced in several ways. Interleaving updates only half the frame every 1/60 of a second, and dedicated display hardware can refresh the display, making it only necessary to transmit changes from frame to frame. Display devices are usually built around a dual ported random access memory, with one port dedicated to the display refresh hardware and the other accessed through an output port to change the display. Even with compression, several tens of megabytes per second of I/O bandwidth are required for real-time video.

Disk, tape, and networks are high-performance I/O devices most likely to be accessed in parallel in a parallel computing system. Thus, the performance parameters for these individual devices underlie any discussion of their use in parallel configurations. Little parallelism is incorporated

memory of a high performance video display device. For data to actually move in parallel between multiple memory modules and multiple I/O devices, the interconnection network between them must have a concurrency greater than one. This concurrency might be obtained by time multiplexing a high-speed I/O connection, or *channel*, over several devices, but with high speed devices such as disks, where parallel I/O is important to performance, multiple physical channels in the network supply the concurrency.

Given parallelism in the memory modules, I/O network, and I/O devices, a parallel I/O operation can be accomplished. A prototypical operation to keep in mind in the discussion is a read or write access to a file on disk using *file striping*. In this scheme, a logically contiguous file is partitioned over several disks by cyclically allocating physically contiguous *stripes* of the file to different disks. A striped file can then be accessed in parallel with a concurrency that is the smaller of the number of memory modules, the number of I/O channels (the concurrency of the I/O switching network), and the number of independent disk drives. In practice, the limiting factor is usually the number of disks.

11.2.1 Control of the Primary Memory Side of the Transfer

In a shared memory multiprocessor, there is already a high concurrency network connecting processors and memory modules. DMA devices or, more likely, *I/O processors* (IOPs) can be attached to this network to access memory in parallel. Several IOPs can then collectively access the memory modules simultaneously and move data to or from parallel I/O devices through the same network or a specialized I/O network. The computational processors need not be directly involved in the parallel I/O operation, although one or more of them initiate the operation and supply its parameters to the IOPs. If the shared memory technique of address randomization is used to support parallel access to memory modules, the IOPs need to have a buffer to assemble enough data so that module contention does not inhibit efficient I/O data transfer. This type of configuration is sketched in Figure 11-3(a). This figure and the next use the PMS notation summarized in Table 3-1, "Summary of PMS notation.," on page 60.

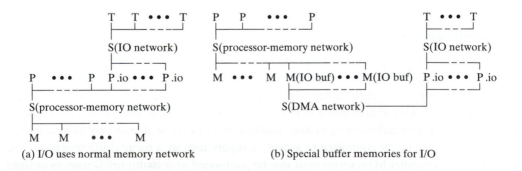

Figure 11-3 I/O connections to modules of a shared memory.

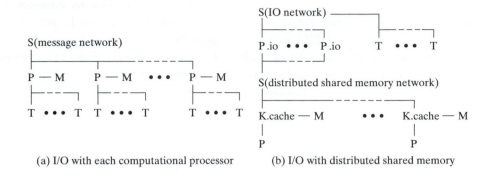

(a) I/O with each computational processor   (b) I/O with distributed shared memory

Figure 11-4   I/O connections in distributed memory multiprocessors.

Another possibility in a shared memory multiprocessor is for a subset of the memory modules to have an extra access port, or "back door," that is attached to DMA devices or I/O processors. These memory modules would be used for I/O buffers and could be interleaved in such a way as to support parallel I/O transfers effectively. This configuration is shown in Figure 11-3(b). The scheme requires I/O buffers to be placed in a specific portion of the address space where they are accessed on one side by the computational processors, sometimes called *clients*, and through the back door by IOPs, sometimes called *servers*. There may also be a low bandwidth control connection, not shown in Figure 11-3, through which the computational processors specify and initiate the I/O data transfers carried out by the IOPs.

A minimal hardware configuration for parallel I/O in a distributed memory multiprocessor is shown in Figure 11-4(a). Here the computational processors double as I/O processors, and each is connected to its own I/O devices. In this simplistic configuration, a disk "file" could be considered to be made up of stripes of data from the disks associated with the different processors. The stripes can easily be transferred in parallel, but would have to be read from disk by the same processor configuration that wrote them. A file could not be written by, say, P processors and then later read by the same or a different program using $P/2$ processors. A more flexible hardware configuration would supply another interconnection network between processors and I/O devices. This network of I/O channels would allow any processor to access any device and would, among other things, allow a file to be striped across a number of disks that is independent of the number of processors. It is also possible that not all processors connect to I/O devices. With a square array processor topology, for example, it might be decided that only processors at the ends of rows have I/O access. These distinguished processors might also do computation but could well be specialized IOPs. The specialized IOP configuration corresponds well to the client-server model, with the client computational processors sending messages to obtain service from the server IOPs. The clear physical distinction between the two types of processors implies a performance difference between assembling small I/O requests into larger ones in the clients' memories, *client buffering*, and assembling the long requests in the servers' memories, *server buffering*.

Another sort of system structure emerges with distributed shared memory machines that manage local memories as caches. The structure shown in Figure 11-4(b) could be used in such a machine. The figure shows the IOPs accessing memory through the cache controllers. Some bandwidth might be gained by accessing the memories directly, but the cache and I/O coherence problem, which is also present in uniprocessors when I/O bypasses cache, is formidable in the multiprocessor environment. In this configuration, the unit of data transfer between memories and IOPs almost surely is a multiple of the cache line size.

11.2.2 I/O Channel Concurrency

The possible I/O interconnection topologies are covered in Chapter 6, but there is some specialization resulting from the character of I/O devices. Distances between processor and I/O device cabinets are longer than processor to memory module distances within a cabinet, so densely connected switching topologies like, say, the Omega network would involve impractical numbers of wires and connectors. A bus, chain, or ring topology requires only one or two I/O connections, or *ports*, per device. A star topology has one central device with multiple ports, but all the rest have only one. Parallel I/O over a bus is only possible if the bus is so much faster than the devices it interconnects that time multiplexing can be used to support effective concurrency. A ring connecting N hardware modules can have up to N data transmissions in progress at a time, $2N$ if the ring is bidirectional. A star topology on N devices with parallel port-to-port connecting hardware in the hub could also support $O(N)$ concurrent transmissions, with lower latency but larger contention than in a ring. The importance of standards for supporting I/O devices from many vendors has already been noted, and although the topologies used in the standards are influenced by the above considerations, the I/O interconnect topology of a specific machine will probably be determined by the standard adopted.

Another characteristic of the demand placed on an I/O network is uninterrupted transmission of long blocks of data. This demand is influenced by the degree of buffering within individual I/O devices and is becoming less stringent as disks and tape drives are supplied with more and more RAM. In a specialized I/O network, the techniques of circuit switching or cut-through routing, discussed in Chapter 6, can be used to support uninterrupted transmission, but these methods can interfere with the flexibility needed in a standardized network supporting devices from many vendors. These networks are often based on short packets of data that provide fine-grained time multiplexing and frequent error checking. When long transmissions are divided into short packets for a network using a packet protocol, errors, lost packets, and buffer overflow are all addressed by *flow control* methods. In its simplest form, such a protocol requires an acknowledgement of the receipt of a packet before another is sent. The round-trip delay for the acknowledgement of every packet interferes with the need for uninterrupted transmission of long data blocks, so more elaborate flow control protocols address this concern. One technique is for the receiver to issue *credits* to the sender representing available packet buffer space. The sender can then transmit packets without waiting for a reply until the credits are exhausted.

A reply from the receiver that indicates no transmission errors increase the number of sender credits by the amount of newly available buffer space.

11.2.3 Peripheral Device Parallelism

Peripheral devices can be roughly divided into three types on the basis of the way they are accessed. They may be random access, direct access, or sequential access. A naturally random access device is a video display with multiported display memory, but more and more devices of all types are being supplied with I/O cache that has random cache line access regardless of the device type. DASDs are typified by disk. Any sector can be accessed directly at the cost of some seek and rotational latency. The DASD class used to include drums, but this technology is no longer used. Magnetic tape is the major representative of the sequential access class. Accessing an arbitrary point on the tape may involve winding through the entire length of a tape reel.

Parallel I/O access to random access devices is feasible at virtually any granularity of interleaving. It only requires that multiple access ports be available. Parallel access to DASDs requires interleaving in multiples of a sector. Various ways of using multiple disk drives to provide parallel file access are discussed in the next section on RAID technology. It is possible to use multiple tape drives to store files in distributed configurations similar to those of RAID for disks, but the removability of the tape media makes distributing files over multiple media inconvenient. The interleaving granularity for tape is also much larger than for disk. While disk sectors are typically 512 B, record sizes of 32 KB or more are recommended for efficient use of modern tape drives. A large tape cache can modify all these access considerations, making the tape appear more like a random access device or DASD.

11.3 Parallel Access Disk Arrays—RAID

As already mentioned, modern disks are characterized by high areal density, which means both high track density and high linear bit density along a track. High linear density implies expensive, precision head and read/write electronics design. A high track density gives rise to an active track following servomechanism. The servomechanism driven actuators and arm assemblies that carry the heads are also expensive items. These factors tend to favor disk drives with serial by bit access to one track at a time, using one actuator and arm carrying one head per surface. Thus, at this stage of technological evolution, cost-effective disk drives tend to be very sequential devices.

On the other hand, current technology makes it economical to place significant processor power and data storage buffers on a board mounted on the disk drive. Locating buffers and control intelligence at the drive can reduce I/O channel bandwidth requirements, but more significantly, it reduces contention for a channel connected to multiple drives. If the controller is remote from the drive, seek request, seek response, sector arrival, and data transfer must use the channel in a time critical sequence with variable and perhaps long time gaps between events. The loss of performance when a disk cannot obtain use of the channel at a time-critical point, such as sector arrival can put a high cost on contention. Placing low-level control at the disk eliminates this problem.

The currently favored technique for parallel disk I/O is to use arrays of independent disks to obtain parallelism rather than to incorporate parallelism into a single drive unit. As the number of drives in a disk system increases, the probability of failure of one of the drives also increases, implying that, even if the mean time to failure (MTTF) of a single disk is sufficiently long, the MTTF of the whole array may be unacceptably short. It, thus, becomes important to consider the whole disk failure mode in designing parallel disk arrays, and almost all proposed schemes with a high degree of parallelism incorporate some redundancy to allow for failed drives, in addition to the redundancy represented by error correcting codes recorded with the serial data on a single drive.

A fairly thorough study and taxonomy of techniques for parallel access to arrays of disks, including the redundancy required by error control, has been done under the name of RAID [235]. The acronym, RAID, originally denoted redundant arrays of inexpensive disks, but because disk cost was only of concern because it enabled the assembly of multiple disks into a system, the I is now usually taken to denote independent. As the first word in the acronym suggests, a major concern of this work was error control through various forms of redundancy, but our major concern in a parallel processing text is the parallel transfer of information between memory and disks. RAID consists of a collection of numbered schemes that address error control and/or parallelism in different ways. RAID 0 and RAID 1 are conceptually simplest and address pure parallel transfer and pure error control separately, but the numbering scheme becomes less transparent thereafter.

RAID 0 is pure *file striping*, in which a file is partitioned into equal length blocks, called stripes, and stripes are cyclically allocated across a set of independent disk drives, as shown in Figure 11-5(a). Assuming that there are sufficient physical I/O channels from memory to a set of k disks, k stripe transfers can be done in parallel in an I/O operation, except perhaps at the end of the file, where the number of remaining stripes may be less than k. The increase in transfer bandwidth over that for a file stored on a single disk is clearly a factor of k. The reduction in access latency is less clear, because a file could be arranged on a single disk so as to minimize access latency to successive blocks, whereas this is more difficult for striped files. The expected rotational latency for accessing a set of k stripes, one for each disk, increases from half the rotation time, $T_r/2$, to $kT_r/(k+1)$, because k randomly placed stripes are, on the average, $j/(k+1)$, $j = 1, 2, ..., k$ of a revolution away from the current head position, and the longest access dominates. This increased average rotational latency can be avoided at the cost of using synchronized disks that are controlled by hardware to have their heads over the same sector at the same time.

RAID 1 is called disk mirroring and is a pure redundancy technique used for error control. Two copies of each block of a file are written to two independent disks, as shown in Figure 11-5(b), so that in the event of failure of one of the disks, the data can be recovered from the other. The anticipated mode of failure is that of an entire disk drive because error control for individual sector data is separately incorporated into each drive, and the focus of RAID is on the behavior of the array rather than one drive. In both RAID 1 and RAID 0, no restructuring of the file data is required other than partitioning it into blocks, each of which naturally correspond to an integral number of sectors, the basic transfer unit of a disk.

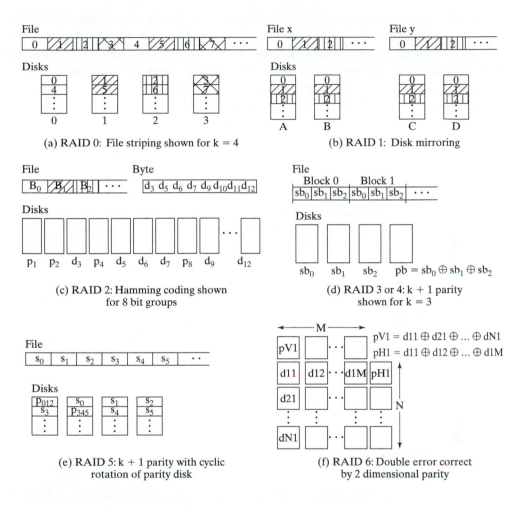

Figure 11-5 The elementary RAID storage schemes for disk arrays.

RAID 2 applies the Hamming code scheme to allow single bit errors over groups of bits to be corrected. In this scheme, groups of bits (bytes or words) are spread over a set of disk drives so that the bit position in the group corresponds to the drive on which that bit is recorded. A system of parity checks, with an extra drive for recording each parity bit, allows the determination of the bit position in error, assuming only a single bit error in the group. This word by word determination of the position of an error is not very useful in a RAID system, where the primary failure mode is that of an inaccessible drive. Inability to access a drive establishes the failed bit position without resorting to the multiple parity check information. Further, the overhead of the scheme is proportional to the base two logarithm of the number of data plus parity bits and is 50% for 8-bit data bytes, reducing to about 12% for 64-bit memory words, where the scheme is very popular in its SECDED (single error correct, double error detect) form. Finally, the transfer unit is large, being at least the number of data bits in a group times the sector size. For these reasons, RAID 2 is seldom used. Figure 11-5(c) shows the RAID 2 scheme for 8-bit bytes with the data bits numbered $d_3\, d_5\, d_6\, d_7\, d_9\, d_{10}\, d_{11}\, d_{12}$ and the parity bits occupying positions numbered with powers of two.

RAID 3 uses an extra parity disk to record a single parity bit for each group of data bits spread across a set of disks. If the identity of a single failed disk is known, this is sufficient to reconstruct the original data. File data is partitioned into blocks consisting of k sub-blocks, each of which is a multiple of the disk sector size. A parity subblock is computed by exclusive ORing the k sub blocks, and the resulting $k + 1$ subblocks are striped across $k + 1$ disks, as shown in Figure 11-5(d). The figure shows the subblocks as contiguous in the file to stress the relationship to RAID 4, but in RAID 3 the subblocks are interleaved by byte or word within the file. If a single disk out of the $k + 1$ fails, the data can be reconstructed from the other k disks and a knowledge of the parity, odd or even, used in the recording. Writing a block involves writing all $k + 1$ disks, and the block size is large, a multiple of k sectors. RAID 2 and 3 are natural applications for synchronized disks that all have their heads reaching the same sector at the same time because the buffer space required for assembly and disassembly of interleaved data for transfer to memory is minimized by having a low time skew from disk between data items that must move to memory together.

RAID 4 is RAID 3 with the unit of transfer reduced to a single subblock, usually one sector, and no interleaving of sector data. The distinction between blocks and subblocks disappears, and writing becomes a five-step process accessing two disks with both a read and a write.

1. The sector data being overwritten is read.
2. The corresponding parity sector is read.
3. The parity sector is updated by subtracting the old data and adding the new.
4. The new data is written.
5. The new parity sector is written.

In the absence of errors, single sector reads access only one disk. If one disk fails, all k good disks must be read and the missing data (or parity) reconstructed. Figure 11-5(d) also describes RAID 4, which behaves well for short transfers, except that all transfers access the same parity disk, making it a bottleneck if the system would otherwise support parallel transfers.

The solution to this bottleneck is RAID 5, shown in Figure 11-5(e). In this scheme, parity is stored on a different disk for each group of k successive sectors, with cyclic allocation of parity sectors to the $k + 1$ disks. RAID 5 is almost always used instead of RAID 4, and for long write requests, some accesses to the parity sector may be suppressed because rewriting all k sectors in a group makes it unnecessary to read the old parity information, making RAID 5 act more like RAID 3. The addition of random access disk cache to the system can allow data and parity sectors to be updated in cache instead of being read and written anew on every sector write request. When a group of k sectors and their parity sector become idle in the cache, they can all be written to disks in a RAID 3 mode.

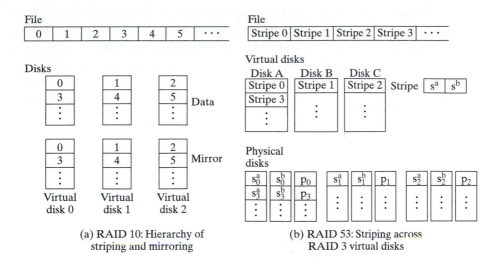

Figure 11-6 Two composite RAID disk organizations.

RAID 6 is a collection of techniques for correcting more than one error. The most commonly described technique is two-dimensional parity. In this scheme, MN data disks are logically arranged into a matrix of M rows and N columns, and $M + N$ parity disks are included, one for each row and one for each column. If the position of a failed disk $D_{ij}, 1 \leq i \leq M, 1 \leq j \leq N$, is known, its data can be reconstructed from either row or column parity information, provided that either row i or column j contains no other failed disk. This is guaranteed if no more than two disks fail, because either their row or column numbers must be distinct, so the information on any two disks that fail simultaneously can be recovered using the two-dimensional parity scheme. The space overhead of the scheme is $(M + N)/(MN)$, and a write requires updating the data disk and two parity disks. The RAID 6 storage scheme is illustrated in Figure 11-5(f).

Two other RAID organizations are composites, made up of a two-level hierarchy of elementary RAID schemes already discussed. RAID 10 uses RAID 1 to form a number of virtual disks, each consisting of a data disk and its mirror. A file is then striped using RAID 0 across the set of mirrored virtual disks. The lower level of the hierarchy supplies the redundancy for error control while the upper level supplies the access parallelism. RAID 10 is illustrated in Figure 11-6(a). There is 100% overhead for redundancy in RAID 10, but separate disks are accessed for each stripe, up to the number of virtual disks. RAID 53 is also a two-level scheme consisting of a RAID 0 collection of virtual disks, each of which is a RAID 3 array of three or more disks. In spite of the number designation, the RAID 5 scheme does not appear in RAID 53, illustrated in Figure 11-6(b) for RAID 3 virtual disks of three drives each. For k drive RAID 3 virtual disks, the overhead for error correcting redundancy is $1/(k-1)$. For $k = 2$, RAID 53 becomes RAID 10 with 50% of the total capacity used for redundancy. The minimum request size for RAID 53 is $k - 1$ sectors on one of the virtual disks.

A RAID system available in 2001 [103] supports RAID 0, RAID 1, RAID 10, RAID 3, and RAID 5. Each can use up to 16 disk drives except for RAID 3, which can use five or nine drives. The length of a stripe can be 4, 16, 64, 128, or 256 sectors, and different subsets of disks can be assigned to different RAID configurations. Two internal storage processors manage the disks, which can be 18 Gb, 36 GB, or 73 GB in capacity, with transfer rates of 40–50 MB per second and internal buffers of 4–16 MB. The RAID system connects to the I/O network through four Fibre Channel ports of 100 MB per second each. At maximum transfer rate, 16 disks could access their buffers at an aggregate rate of 800 MB per second. Taking latency and idle time into account, the maximum 400 MB per second through the storage processors and onto the four ports of the I/O network is sufficient to supply the bandwidth requirements of the disks. A 400 MB per second access rate to main memory can be expressed as a 16-B cache line every 40 ns. This would necessarily require parallel access to multiple memory modules.

11.4 Parallel Formatted I/O in Shared Memory Multiprocessors

Input and output have mixed characteristics for parallel implementation. On the one hand, the ideas behind I/O to a file are very sequential. Especially if a file is to be read or written by a human, the sequential nature is inherent. On the other hand, much of the work done in output involves formatting and assembling independent data items into lines that are then output in order. For input, it is possible that every item read might influence the interpretation of all subsequent items, but this is seldom the case. For large input files that are the real opportunity for speedup through parallel processing, many lines of the same format are read to fill large data arrays, with each line having the same format and conversion specifications. If the beginnings of these lines can be located without scanning each one sequentially, they can all be processed and their data converted in parallel. Even if bytes were transferred sequentially to or from a file, parallelizing the computational work of scanning or constructing formatted data can have a large impact on the speed of I/O on a parallel processor.

Conceptually, I/O is done on files handled by a file system in the lowest common denominator format of a string of bytes. The ubiquitous case of formatted I/O interprets the bytes as characters and gives structure to files through line breaks and/or white space between words. This human-oriented formatting is frequently used even for temporary files both written and read by the machine, either for debugging and spot check purposes or to maintain consistency between internal and output files. The general parallel I/O input or output process for such a file consists of three parts. First, there is a transformation between a serial character string view of the file on secondary storage and a random access, and, thus, parallel, representation of it in memory. Second, a parallel interpretation of the internal file structure must be made to identify starting points and lengths of items in the file that can be processed in parallel. Third, the independent items are formatted or interpreted concurrently.

The actual movement of the file between primary and secondary memory can be done in parallel only to the extent that the file is partitioned, or striped, across multiple disks, or other devices that can be accessed simultaneously. Several RAID designs support such parallel physical

I/O transfers. The size of the file and the parameters of the striping are needed to accomplish the parallel read or write. The simplest case occurs when there is sufficient memory space for the entire file and any intermediate buffers required. Buffering the file in several sections to save space only entails some fix-up processing at the partition points, so we assume sufficient buffer space. We discuss the shared memory multiprocessor case for simplicity. With distributed memory, partitioning and communication at partition boundaries must also be taken into account.

Parallelism in the internal structure of a file differs significantly between input and output. The structure of an output file is deterministic on the basis of application data in the random access memory while an input file may contain header data, such as array dimensions, that must be read before the structure of subsequent portions of the file, say array data, is known. A consecutive set of input items can also have a terminator that determines the number of items in the set, thus, posing a problem for a nonsequential interpretation of the items. Of course, it is possible for an application to structure memory data as sequences with headers and/or terminators so the problem of nonsequential interpretation of file structure can occur for output from artificially sequential applications as well as for the much more common case of sequentially structured input. After the determination of structure from dimension data residing in memory or interpreted from header information, much of the parallelism in I/O is associated with counted loops with known bounds, as is true for parallelism in computation. A typical case is the input or output of arrays with known dimensions.

The formatting or interpretation of individual data items in I/O is the most computationally intensive of the three tasks and has significant potential for speedup using parallelism. Assuming the substructure of a file, or a portion of it, is known, integers, reals, and other data types can be converted between ASCII and internal representations concurrently. Although it is possible to prespecify detailed ASCII field lengths for input and output, it is normal for the number of characters in a data item to be determined by separator characters on input and to depend both on the data and the conversion algorithm on output. For input, a parallel computation of the positions of all the separator characters in the random access version of the input file identifies the starting points and lengths for individual items that are then scanned and interpreted in parallel. For output, individual ASCII items, say lines, are formatted into an array of separate buffers of sufficient sizes, and a character count is computed for each. A parallel prefix computation on the counts then identifies the starting position of the ASCII string for each item in the random access file buffer, and the items' strings are then written to the buffer in parallel.

A parallel prefix computation is important to determining the starting positions of items in the character string file buffer both for input and output, but it appears in two somewhat different forms. Output starts with an array of line lengths and applies sum prefix to generate an equal size array of starting points for the lines. If nl is the number of lines, one auxiliary array of nl starting positions is required to assemble the file buffer from the nl line strings and the nl lengths that serve as input to the process. For input, parallel computation on individual characters consumes considerable extra space to achieve parallelism. First, characters of the length nch file are tested for line separators, and a marker array of length nch with ones corresponding to separators and zeros corresponding to nonseparators is built. Applying sum prefix to this array yields a second array of nch integers that gives a line number for each character in the file buffer. This array is then used to construct a length nl array of integers representing starting character positions for each line. The progression of the computation is shown in Figure 11-7. The length nch array of line numbers can replace the marker array, and each line number requires only $\log_2(nl - 1)$ bits. However, if multiple line number entries are stored in a single memory word, care must be taken to control unsynchronized simultaneous access to different line number fields of a word.

11.4.1 Parallel Input Using C I/O Routines fread() and sscanf()

As a fairly typical example consider reading a file containing initial electric and magnetic field vector values in three dimensions for a Maxwell's equation simulation. Each x, y, or z component of each field is stored in a separate three-dimensional matrix, Ex, Ey, Ez, Bx, By, and Bz. The file includes in its header the dimensions NX, NY, and NZ for six three-dimensional matrices and the matrix data, six elements per line, one for each matrix, arranged in row major order by line. The integers NX, NY, and NZ are contained in that order on a line started by the keyword "DIMENSIONS:". White space separates items on a line. The lines containing the floating point matrix data are preceded by the keyword "FIELD_DATA:" on a separate line.

The general structure of the input process is an application independent portion that reads the file into random access memory and identifies starting positions and lengths for all lines and an application dependent part that converts file data according to the specified format. The application dependent part has a sequential portion that scans header lines for items, including those that specify the structure of the matrix data. Once the dimensions of the matrices are known, the lines of matrix data can be converted in parallel.

11.4.1.1   Application Independent Input Operations

The application independent part of the process can be formulated as a function

```
int maplines( char *name, char **buffer, int **start, int *nl)
```

that reads a file, name, returns the number of characters, say flen, in it, allocates and returns a pointer to a character string buffer for the file, and constructs a vector of line starting points, start[], for nl lines. In point form, the algorithm for maplines() is:

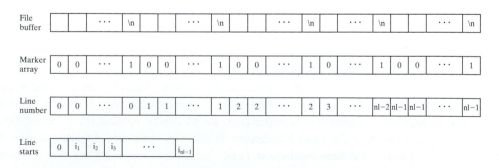

Figure 11-7   Arrays for parallel computation of line start positions on input.

1. Read the file into main memory using `stat()` and `fread()` with whatever parallel input facilities, for example, RAID, are available.

2. A **forall** over the `flen` characters of the file replaces each newline with `\0` to properly terminate `sscanf()` when it is used to interpret the line and builds a length `flen` marker vector with a one in the position of each newline and zeros elsewhere.

3. Use a parallel prefix to turn the marker vector into a vector giving the line number for each character. Each processor first does an independent serial sum prefix on a disjoint contiguous segment of the vector. The processors then cooperatively compute the sum prefix on the last elements of each of their segments. The new last elements are then independently added to each element in the next segment to form the final sum prefix vector.

4. The last element of the prefix vector is `nl − 1`, where `nl` is the number of lines. A **forall** over the prefix vector then builds a length `nl` vector containing for each line number the character position at which that line starts.

5. Return the number of lines in the input file, the file buffer in memory, and the vector of starting character positions in the buffer for each line.

Recognizing end of line characters in the RAM character array is clearly a parallel operation over all characters. Replacing end of line by "`\0`" characters is parallel except when two "`\0`" characters share a memory word. If the minimum line length is greater than the number of characters in a word, this does not occur. In any case, write conflicts to the same word are rare, so if producer/consumer synchronization on memory words is available, it can be used to synchronize character replacements in a word. If a serial prefix computation on the marker vector requires $\alpha \cdot$`flen` operations, the parallel prefix computation with P processors requires $2\alpha \cdot$`flen` $+ O(\log_2 P)$ operations, for a parallel efficiency of about 50% if `flen` $\gg P$. A **forall** over the length `flen` line number and marker vector suffices to compute the elements of the length `nl` start vector. The marker and line number vector is needed only within the `maplines()` function and can be released on its completion. The long character string file buffer of length `flen` and the line start vector of length `nl` are allocated and returned by `maplines()`.

11.4.1.2   Application Dependent Input Operations

The reading of the header in the application dependent part of the file read process is most easily formulated as a sequential scan by line searching for keywords marking appropriate header items. Once the size and structure information for parallel access data, say matrices, has been extracted from the header, the data may be read in parallel over the range of lines occupied by it. The code for the current example is sketched in Program 11-1. Because C only supports one-dimensional arrays directly, the row major order field matrices are referenced by a single linearized index related to row i, column j, and plane k indices by `matline = i +j*NX + k*NX*NY`. If the overhead of three levels of pointers is acceptable, then three-level recursive arrays can be used, with i, j, and k indices computed from the linear, row major index `matline` by

```
flen = maplines("filename", &buffer, &start, &nl);
line = 0;
for( ; line < nl; line++);
{    sscanf(&buffer[start[line]], "%s %n", &keywd, &nxtchar);
     if(strcmp(keywd, "DIMENSIONS:") == 0)
     {    sscanf(&buffer[start[line]+nxtchar], "%d %d %d",
                                                 NX, NY, NZ);
          line++;
          break;
     }
}
for( ; line < nl; line++)
{    sscanf(&buffer[start[line]], "%s", &keywd);
     if(strcmp(keywd, "FIELD_DATA:") == 0) { line++; break; }
}
matstart = line;
forall matline = 0 step 1 until NX*NY*NZ - 1
{/* Compute indices for 3D matrices from line number if needed. */
     matindices(matline, NX, NY, NZ, &i, &j, &k);
     sscanf(&buffer[start[matstart+matline]],
          "%lf, %lf, %lf, %lf, %lf, %lf",&Ex[matline],
          &Ey[matline], &Ez[matline], &Bx[matline],
          &By[matline], &Bz[matline]);
}
```

Program 11-1   Application-dependent part of file read example.

```
k = matline/(NY*NX);
j = (matline%(NY*NX))/NX;
i = (matline%(NY*NX))%NX;
```

and replacements of Ex[matline] by Ex[k][j][i], etc. made in Program 11-1.

For input, reading the file and partitioning it on line terminators or other item separators forms a mostly application independent part of I/O, and the techniques used to parallelize this part are application dependent only in the choice of separator character and considerations connected with the file size. As described, this part can use considerable extra space to make the item separator identification parallel. Once the application dependent operations of bringing the file into RAM and partitioning it are complete, the application dependent part of the process involves interpreting the formatted items. This is parallelizable to the extent that it does not involve sequential search through the file.

11.4.2 Parallel Output Using C I/O Routines sprintf() and fwrite()

This example writes an output file consisting of header information giving the three dimensions of six field arrays, Ex, Ey, Ez, Bx, By, and Bz, an error estimate, and field array data. For output, the application specific part is done first by using sprintf() to format and store separate output records (lines) in an array, `lines[]`, of nl strings in parallel. Recording the lengths of the strings in an array, `lngs[]`, gives the information needed to write an application independent output section that assembles the line strings in parallel into a long character string in memory for output to the file using `fwrite()`. Parallelism in `fwrite()` depends on parallel hardware, such as RAID, available for writing to disk.

11.4.2.1   Application Dependent Output Code

The application specific code for output is executed first to interpret output values into individual character strings for each output line. The code for this example could take the form shown in Program 11-2. It is assumed that all output data, both structural (array dimensions) and data values, are available when this point in the program is reached. The first three lines of the file constitute the header information and are formatted as individual cases. The rest of the lines hold array data. The matrices are again assumed to be packed three-dimensional matrices stored in row major order. Because all output data and formats are known, all lines can be formatted concurrently in a **forall**.

```
forall line = 0 step 1 until nl-1
{switch(line)
    {case 0: lngs[line] = sprintf(lines[line],
            "DIMENSIONS: %d %d %d\n", NX, NY, NZ);
            break;
    case 1: lngs[line] = sprintf(lines[line],
            "ERROR: %g\n", error);
            break;
    case 2: lngs[line] = sprintf(lines[line],
            "FIELD_DATA: \n");
            break;
    default: matline = line - 3
            lngs[line] = sprintf(lines[line],
            %.10f %.10f %.10f %.10f %.10f %.10f\n",
            Ex[matline], Ey[matline], Ez[matline],
            Bx[matline], By[matline], Bz[matline]);
    }
}
fsize = buildfile("filename", nl, lines, lngs);
```

Program 11-2   Application-dependent portion of parallel output example.

11.4.2.2   Application Independent Part of the Output Code

The application independent function used to assemble and output the file has the form

```
int buildfile(char *name, int nl, char **lines, int *lngs);
```

This routine takes a file name, an array, `lines[]`, consisting of one character string for each output line, and a vector, `lngs[]`, of line lengths. It assembles the individual lines into a single character string for the file and writes it to the disk file identified by name using as much parallelism as possible. The function returns the length of the file written. The algorithm for build-file() can be summarized as:

1. Do a parallel prefix computation on the vector of line lengths to form a vector of line starting positions in the file.
2. Use a **forall** over lines to assemble them into one contiguous character string in memory representing the file. Prevent or synchronize simultaneous access to different characters in the same memory word.
3. Use whatever parallel disk access hardware is available to output the file.
4. Return the number of characters in the output file.

The parallel prefix operation in step 1 is about 50% efficient, as described for the input algorithm, but it is only over nl line lengths rather than over flen character positions. The parallel copy operation to move lines into the file is complicated by the fact that adjacent sets of characters are resource dependent because they share memory words. Several ways to synchronize the dependence are possible. If the minimum number of characters per line is greater than the number of characters in a word, then only consecutive lines can share words. This allows writing all even numbered lines in parallel, followed by all odd numbered lines as a second parallel group, with no resource dependence within either group. If low overhead producer/consumer synchronization is available on whole memory words, it can be used to synchronize partial word writes with little chance of concurrent access by more than one process.

For shared memory multiprocessor output, formatting individual output items, say lines, forms the application dependent part of the output process and precedes the assembly and output operations that form the application independent part. The application dependent part is usually easily parallelized because the file structure is represented by random access data in memory. The actual writing of the file is parallel if there is striping over independent secondary storage devices, while the assembly of the file from separate items can be parallelized using a parallel prefix computation and properly synchronizing the accesses to characters sharing a memory word.

11.5 Collective I/O in Multiprocessors—MPI-IO

In software support for parallel I/O operations, a major step is in going from a collection of distinct I/O commands on separate processors with explicit synchronization to specifying a collective I/O operation over a coherent set of processors. This is especially important in distributed memory systems where, although memories may be private, the I/O system is probably shared. The typical collective operation is multiple processor access to a shared file, with each processor reading or writing a distinct portion of the file. Recognizing the similarity between the transmission of messages and of I/O data, the designers of the message passing interface standard MPI-1, which we discussed in Chapter 5, extended the standard to include individual and collective I/O operations in MPI-2. We now discuss the I/O facilities provided by MPI-2, focusing on the collective, parallel operations.

11.5.1 MPI-2 I/O Concepts

The specification of a set of processes to participate in a parallel I/O operation is already well supported in MPI-1 by intracommunicators and groups. There also needs to be a way to describe the format of a file and what portion of it should be accessed by each processor. MPI-2 bases this capability on complex data types. Data types in MPI-1 describe how sequences of message bytes in a target buffer are interpreted as language data types, integers, reals, etc. The job of describing the format of a buffer is similar to that of describing a file. The major difference is that a buffer has finite size while a file, at least on write, may have indeterminate length. MPI-2 extends the user defined data type capabilities to be convenient for I/O and introduces some new concepts explicitly associated with files.

One new concept introduced in MPI-IO is that of a *file handle*. This references an opaque MPI object representing a file. A file handle is returned by MPI on open, freed on close, and identifies a file in reads, writes, and other file specific operations. Each process has a *view* associated with each open file that may differ from another process' view of the same file. The file view is based on MPI derived data types. A general data type in MPI consists of a sequence of predefined data types and a sequence of byte displacements. The *type signature* consists of the sequence of basic data types, $type\_signature = \{type_0, type_1, \ldots, type_{n-1}\}$, while the *type map* has both sequences, $type\_map = \{(type_0, disp_0), (type_1, disp_1), \ldots, (type_{n-1}, disp_{n-1})\}$. When generalized data types are used in I/O, they must satisfy the additional restrictions that all displacements are nonnegative and the sequence of displacements is nondecreasing. A file view then consists of an etype, a filetype, and a displacement. The *etype* is the unit of access and positioning for the file and corresponds to the idea of a record. It is a generalized data type that obeys the above restriction on displacements. A *filetype* is either one etype or a derived data type consisting only of etypes. The file is described as an indefinite number of repetitions of the filetype. The *file displacement* is a byte position where the repetitions of the filetype begin. It is used to allow a file view to skip some header portion of the file.

Reads and writes transfer integral numbers of etypes to or from a buffer in memory starting at a file position given either by an explicit offset or implicitly by a file pointer. Both offsets and file pointers are integral numbers of etypes from the beginning of the current view. The memory buffer is also described by an MPI data type that must satisfy the restriction that its type signature matches some number of contiguous copies of the etype of the view. Because displacements of etypes in a filetype may be adjusted to leave "holes" in the file where data are not accessible to a specific process, and because other processes may have different views of the same file, a group of processes can read or write the same file and access different data. As a simple example, a group of P processes might access a file of 8 byte real numbers with process i, $0 \le i \le P - 1$, having a view with the filetype map $\{(\text{MPI\_LB}, 0), (\text{MPI\_REAL8}, 8i), (\text{MPI\_UB}, 8P)\}$, where MPI_LB and MPI_UB are special types for the lower and upper bounds, respectively, of a derived type. All processes' views would have the same etype, MPI_REAL8, and the same starting displacement. With these views, the P processes could do a collective read of 10 etypes into a buffer consisting of 10 contiguous MPI_REAL8 numbers. The read would transfer a total of $10P$ numbers, with 10 going to each process using cyclic interleaving of reals in the file. The pictorial view of this operation is shown in Figure 11-8.

Three independent choices of read or write behavior are supported by MPI-IO, making 12 different types of read or write. There are three choices for specifying the starting position in the file, two for collective or one process operation, and two for blocking or nonblocking behavior. The initial file position can be specified by giving an explicit offset in the read/write call, using a shared file pointer maintained by MPI, or using separate file pointers for each process, also maintained by MPI. All of these methods specify the file position in terms of the number of visible etype elements from the beginning of the current view. A collective read or write is done in parallel by all processes in the group of the communicator specified in the collective file open operation. Noncollective operations by a group of processes on the same file behave as if performed in some sequential order. If the specific order is important, it must be imposed by explicit synchronizations. Processes doing noncollective operations on the same file using the shared pointer are required to have the same view of the file. As with MPI message routines, blocking MPI-IO calls return when new data is available in the read buffer or when the write buffer is available for its next use. Nonblocking and noncollective reads and writes return a request handle, and operation completion is checked by using this handle in an `MPI_TEST` or `MPI_WAIT` call, as done for nonblocking sends and receives. Nonblocking collective calls are somewhat different. A nonblocking collective I/O operation is split into two collective subroutine calls, one to begin the operation and one to end it. Buffers are available at the completion of the end operation. Completion of a split collective operation is, thus, communicated synchronously to all participating processes.

To maintain portability, MPI-IO makes no assumptions about the structure or interconnection of I/O hardware. MPI-IO does, however, give the user a mechanism to supply hints about file and system organization that can be used by MPI routines to optimize I/O operations. Hints are supplied by way of an `MPI_INFO` object associated with each file. The latter consists of a set of key and value pairs, both represented as character strings. Hints may be ignored by the MPI system without changing its specified semantics, but use of the hints may improve performance. There are a set of reserved hints in MPI-IO that, by their character and interrelations, define a model for the I/O system such as is sketched in Figure 11-9. I/O is performed on behalf of a group of user processes by a set of *target nodes* that can be thought of as IOPs. These target nodes connect to a group of *I/O nodes* that can be thought of as disks. Reserved hints describe file striping by giving the number of disks across which a file is striped, `striping_factor`, and the length of each stripe, `striping_unit`. Buffering of collective accesses in the target nodes is described by hints that tell whether collective buffering is beneficial, the size of a file unit accessed by a target node, `cb_block_size`, the number of these units in a buffer, `cb_buffer_size`, and the number of target nodes, `cb_nodes`. Another group of reserved hints allows the specification of a multidimensional array that is accessed in chunks consisting of specific sized subarrays. Hints give the size of array elements, the dimensions of the array, and the dimensions of a subarray chunk.

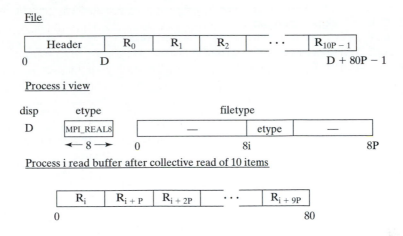

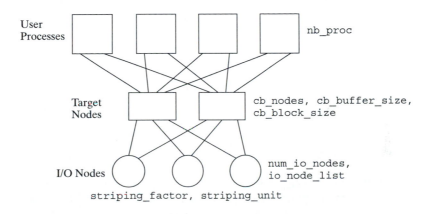

Figure 11-8 Interleaved access to a file by P processes.

Figure 11-9 Conceptual I/O model embodied in MPI-IO reserved hints.

11.5.2 MPI-IO Examples

11.5.2.1   Cyclically Mapped Read from a Striped Disk Array

Assume that there is a file of real numbers striped across an array of eight disks. A program for P processors is to read the file and distribute the reals cyclically to the processors using a collective read. The cyclic distribution to processors follows the picture in Figure 11-8 except that we assume a header of length $D = 0$. The striped nature of the file is described by hints supplied to MPI-IO through an info object. The cyclic distribution of reals to processes is governed by the file views in force during the collective read. An MPI Fortran code fragment to do this job is shown in Program 11-3.

```
      INTEGER P, rank, realsz
      INTEGER ierr, finfo, fh, filetype, stat
      INTEGER len(3), disp(3), type(3)
      REAL buf(10)

      CALL MPI_INFO_CREATE(finfo, ierr)
      CALL MPI_INFO_SET(finfo, "striping_factor", "8", ierr)
      CALL MPI_INFO_SET(finfo, "striping_unit", "512", ierr)
      CALL MPI_FILE_OPEN(MPI_COMM_WORLD, "infile", MPI_MODE_RDONLY,
     &                                             finfo, fh, ierr)

      CALL MPI_COMM_SIZE(MPI_COMM_WORLD, P, ierr)
      CALL MPI_COMM_RANK(MPI_COMM_WORLD, rank, ierr)
      CALL MPI_TYPE_SIZE(MPI_REAL, realsz, ierr)
      len(1) = 1
      len(2) = 1
      len(3) = 1
      disp(1) = 0
      disp(2) = rank*realsz
      disp(3) = P*realsz
      type(1) = MPI_LB
      type(2) = MPI_REAL
      type(3) = MPI_UB
      CALL MPI_TYPE_CREATE_STRUCT(3, len, disp, type, filetype, ierr)
      CALL MPI_TYPE_COMMIT(filetype, ierr)
      CALL MPI_FILE_SET_VIEW(fh, 0, MPI_REAL, filetype, "native",
     &                                             finfo, ierr)

      CALL MPI_FILE_READ_AT_ALL(fh, 0, buf, 10, MPI_REAL, stat, ierr)
                            ...
      CALL MPI_CLOSE(fh, ierr)
      CALL MPI_INFO_FREE(finfo, ierr)
      CALL MPI_TYPE_FREE(filetype, ierr)
                            ...
```

Program 11-3 Cyclic distribution of a striped file in MPI-IO.

First, an empty info object is created, and then two calls to MPI_INFO_SET insert (key, value) pairs, ("striping_factor", "8") and ("striping_unit", "512") respectively. The completed info object is supplied to the file open call. The above information is likely only to be effective on file open. Although an info object is supplied as a parameter to MPI_FILE_SET_VIEW, that is likely too late for striping information. If the system can make use of these hints to optimize performance, they are probably needed at file open time and would be ignored in subsequent uses of the info object. The parameters for the call to MPI_FILE_OPEN are a communicator containing the processes collectively opening the file, the file name, a mode field allowing one or more file access modes to be specified, the info object handle, and the error code.

The elementary type to be used in the read is MPI_REAL. The filetype used in the different process' views are built by creating STRUCT data types that start with a special, zero length MPI_LB lower bound place holder, leave a gap of rank real elements for the process corresponding to rank, and end with the special, zero length MPI_UB place holder P reals away from the lower bound. The number of bytes in an MPI_REAL is established by a call to MPI_TYPE_SIZE, and the parameters to the call to MPI_TYPE_CREATE_STRUCT are the number of distinct types, the number of repetitions of each type, an array of offsets from the beginning of the new type, an array of elementary or defined types, the new returned type, and the error code. The new type is committed before it is used, allowing MPI to compile an efficient representation for a type that will be used repeatedly. This file type is then used in the call to MPI_FILE_SET_VIEW, whose parameters are the file handle, the byte displacement of the view from the file start (to skip a header), the etype for the view, the file type, a specification of one of a few standard representations for file data, the info object, and the error code. If the view is not set, the subsequent read acts on a default view of the file consisting as a sequence of bytes starting at a zero displacement.

The collective call to MPI_FILE_READ_AT_ALL has as parameters the file handle, a displacement in etype elements from the beginning of the view, the address of the buffer to receive the data, the number of etype elements to be read into the buffer (for each process), the etype, the handle of a status object to return information including the actual number of items read, and the error code. If the 10-element per process collective read were contained in a counted loop on I, the displacement parameter could be set to 10*I to advance each process by 10 etypes in its distinct view of the file. When the use of the file is completed, it may be closed and the info object and the filetype freed. The MPI routines used in this example are summarized in Table 11-2 and their parameters are described in Table 11-3.

Table 11-2 MPI routines used in the cyclic mapped read example.

MPI_INFO_CREATE(INFO, IERR)
MPI_INFO_FREE(INFO, IERR)
MPI_INFO_SET(INFO, KEY, VALUE, IERR)
MPI_COMM_SIZE(COM, CSIZE, IERR)
MPI_COMM_RANK(COM, RANK, IERR)
MPI_TYPE_SIZE(TYPE, TSIZE, IERR)
MPI_TYPE_CREATE_STRUCT(COUNT, LENS, DISPS, TYPES, NEWTYPE, IERR)
MPI_TYPE_COMMIT(TYPE, IERR)
MPI_TYPE_FREE(TYPE, IERR)
MPI_FILE_OPEN(COMM, FILENAME, AMODE, INFO, FH, IERR)
MPI_FILE_SET_VIEW(FH, DISP, ETYPE, FILETYPE, DATAREP, INFO, IERR)
MPI_FILE_READ_AT_ALL(FH, OFFSET, BUF, NUM, TYPE, STAT, IERR)
MPI_FILE_CLOSE(FH, IERR)

Table 11-3   Parameters for the MPI routines of the cyclic read example.

INFO	Handle for an opaque info object.
IERR	MPI error return code.
KEY	String representing a key for an info object entry.
VALUE	String representing the value of a key in an info object entry.
COM	Communicator handle.
CSIZE	Size of the process group of the communicator.
RANK	Rank of the calling process in the group of the communicator.
TYPE	Handle for an MPI basic or defined data type.
TSIZE	Number of bytes occupied by the data type.
COUNT	Number of previously defined types in the new struct type.
LENS	Vector of repetitions of each of COUNT types in the new type.
DISPS	Vector of byte displacements to blocks of old types.
TYPES	Vector of old types making up the struct.
NEWTYPE	Returned handle for newly created type.
FILENAME	String representing the name of a file or a path in the file system.
AMODE	Access mode. Bit vector OR or sum of disjoint access modes.
FH	File handle returned by open and used by all operations on the file.
DISP	Byte displacement to the beginning of a file view.
ETYPE	Elementary type (record) from which the file type is constructed.
FILETYPE	Defined data type consisting of ETYPEs describing the file view of a process.
DATAREP	String describing the representation of data in the file.
OFFSET	Number of ETYPEs from the beginning of the file view where read will start.
BUF	Buffer into which file data is read.
NUM	Number of items of data type, TYPE, to read.
TYPE	Buffer data type consisting of some number of copies of ETYPE.
STAT	Handle for status object returned by read.

11.5.2.2   MPI-IO for Distributed Matrix Multiply

As an example of using MPI-IO in a distributed memory multiprocessor computation supported by MPI message passing, we will supply MPI-IO file access for the distributed matrix multiply program discussed in Section 5.4.2 of Chapter 5. The file access interface assumes that two $Nb \times Nb$ input matrices, A and B, are written using the processors' *native* format on an input file named "infile" in column major order, with B following A. The input file also has a header containing the integers b and N specifying the sizes of the $b \times b$ blocks distributed to each of the $N \times N$ processors. The result matrix, C, is written as an $Nb \times Nb$ matrix in column major order on a newly created file, "outfile," also in native format with a header of the integers b and N. The input and output are done in the main program, which continues to use the subroutines procgrid of Program 5-12 and distmult of Program 5-13.

The input file header is read, the process topology is set up, and the file type is defined for distribution of an $Nb \times Nb$ matrix to $N \times N$ processes by the code given in Program 11-4. After initializing MPI, all processes in MPI_COMM_WORLD open the input file and set a common file

```
      PROGRAM main
      INCLUDE 'mpif.h'
      REAL Ap(50,50), Bp(50,50), Cp(50,50)
      INTEGER b, N, comsq, comrow, comcol, myrank, myrow, mycol
      INTEGER fh, filetype, bin50, ierr, status(MPI_STATUS_SIZE)
      INTEGER ibuf(2), gsizes(2), distribs(2), dargs(2), psizes(2)
      INTEGER starts(2), intsz

      CALL MPI_INIT(ierr)
C Open file to read header b and N.
      CALL MPI_FILE_OPEN(MPI_COMM_WORLD, "infile", MPI_MODE_RDONLY,
     &                                  MPI_INFO_NULL, fh, ierr)
C Set file view for all processes to read b and N from header.
      CALL MPI_FILE_SET_VIEW(fh, 0, MPI_INTEGER, MPI_INTEGER,
     &                              "native", MPI_INFO_NULL, ierr)
      CALL MPI_FILE_READ_AT_ALL(fh, 0, ibuf, 2, MPI_INTEGER,
     &                                           status, ierr)
      b = ibuf(1)
      N = ibuf(2)
C Establish a 2D topology on NxN processes of MPI_COMM_WORLD.
      CALL procgrid(N, comsq, comrow, comcol, myrow, mycol)
C Reopen the input file with a communicator having correct topology.
      CALL MPI_FILE_CLOSE(fh, ierr)
      CALL MPI_FILE_OPEN(comsq, "infile", MPI_MODE_RDONLY,
     &                                  MPI_INFO_NULL, fh, ierr)
      CALL MPI_COMM_RANK(comsq, myrank, ierr)
C Set views to distribute bxb blocks of NbxNb matrices to processes.
      gsizes(1) = N*b
      gsizes(2) = N*b
      distribs(1) = MPI_DISTRIBUTE_BLOCK
      distribs(2) = MPI_DISTRIBUTE_BLOCK
      dargs(1) = b
      dargs(2) = b
      psizes(1) = N
      psizes(2) = N
      CALL MPI_TYPE_CREATE_DARRAY(N*N, myrank, 2, gsizes, distribs,
     &   dargs, psizes, MPI_ORDER_FORTRAN, MPI_REAL, filetype, ierr)
      CALL MPI_TYPE_COMMIT(filetype, ierr)
      CALL MPI_TYPE_SIZE(MPI_INTEGER, intsz, ierr)
      CALL MPI_FILE_SET_VIEW(fh, 2*intsz, MPI_REAL, filetype,
     &                              "native", MPI_INFO_NULL, ierr)
```

Program 11-4   Set-up to do distributed read and write of $Nb \times Nb$ matrices.

view interpreting it as consisting of integers. All processes then read the same two integers, b and N, from the file. Knowing N, the same procgrid subroutine given by Program 5-12 can be used to construct the 2D topology on the processes. The major issue of constructing a file view such that each process sees only its own $b \times b$ block of reals out of an $Nb \times Nb$ sequence of reals representing a matrix written in the Fortran standard column major order is made much simpler by an MPI-2 subroutine that constructs a data type representing a distributed array. Refer to Table 11-4 for new MPI subroutines used in this example and to Table 11-5 for the description of their parameters.

Table 11-4   New MPI-2 routines used in the distributed matrix multiply.

MPI_TYPE_CREATE_DARRAY(SIZE, RANK, NDIMS, GSIZES, DISTRIBS, DARGS,   PSIZES, ORDER, OLDTYPE, NEWTYPE, IERR)
MPI_TYPE_CREATE_SUBARRAY(NDIMS, SIZES, SUBSIZES, STARTS, ORDER,   OLDTYPE, SBTYPE, IERR)
MPI_FILE_WRITE_AT(FH, OFFSET, BUF, CNT, TYPE, STAT, IERR)
MPI_FILE_WRITE_AT_ALL(FH, OFFSET, BUF, CNT, TYPE, STAT, IERR)

Table 11-5   Parameters for new MPI-2 routines used in matrix multiply.

SIZE	Size of process group.
RANK	Rank of calling process in process group.
NDIMS	Number of array dimensions as well as process grid dimensions.
GSIZES	Number of elements of type OLDTYPE in each dimension of the global array.
DISTRIBS	Array of methods of distribution of the array in each dimension.
DARGS	Array of arguments for the distribution method in each dimension.
PSIZES	Array of sizes of process grid in each dimension.
ORDER	Flag indicating row major or column major array storage order.
OLDTYPE	Array element type.
NEWTYPE	Returned handle for new type for file view of process RANK.
IERR	MPI error return code.
SIZES	Array of number of elements of OLDTYPE in each dimension of full array.
SUBSIZES	Array of number of elements of OLDTYPE in each dimension of the subarray.
STARTS	Starting position of the subarray in each dimension of the full array.
SBTYPE	Returned type handle for the subarray type.
FH	File handle.
OFFSET	Offset in ETYPE elements from beginning of file view where write begins.
BUF	Buffer from which write data is taken.
CNT	Number of elements to be written.
TYPE	Type of each buffer element. Must match some number of ETYPEs.
STAT	Handle for returned status object.

MPI_TYPE_CREATE_DARRAY builds a data type representing a distributed portion of a global array for the process of rank, RANK, in a process group of size, SIZE, assumed to represent an NDIMS array in row major order. The use of row major order for the process group matches the convention used in establishing the topology associated with a communicator, as discussed in Chapter 5, while the ordering of the distributed matrix can be specified as column major for Fortran or row major for C or C++ by the parameter ORDER. The extent of each dimension of the global matrix is given in an array of integers, GSIZES(NDIMS), and the extent of each dimension in the process group by PSIZES(NDIMS). In the general case, if the number of dimensions of the process group is smaller than the number of dimensions in the global array, some entries in PSIZES(NDIMS) are one. The distribution of each dimension of the global array over the process array is controlled by the corresponding entries in the DISTRIBS(NDIMS) and DARGS(NDIMS) arrays. Each DISTRIBS entry can specify block, cyclic, or no distribution, while the corresponding entry in DARGS is the size of a block or a default argument. In this example, both dimensions are distributed as blocks of size b. The data type of each matrix element is specified by OLDTYPE and the returned data type is NEWTYPE. The type creation routine is not collective but is called by all processes and returns to process, RANK, a data type describing its portion of the array, which is then committed and used as the filetype for this process' file view, skipping two integers for the header.

The read and write buffer structure is set up, the A and B matrices are read, the distributed matrix multiply is done, and the result matrix written by the code of Program 11-5. The private sections of the matrices, Ap, Bp, and Cp, are allocated as 50×50 Fortran arrays. If the $b \times b$ elements read, say, for Ap can be placed correctly in the 2500 element memory space, the array can be accessed with standard Fortran indexing. Another MPI-2 data type construction routine, MPI_TYPE_CREATE_SUBARRAY, can be used to describe the data type of a read buffer to accomplish this. From an array of NDIMS with each dimension size given in by an entry in the integer array, SIZES(NDIMS), a subarray with dimension sizes given by the array, SUBSIZES(NDIMS), is formed. The subarray begins in each dimension at the position given by the corresponding element of the integer array, STARTS(NDIMS), and row major or column major ordering can be specified by the ORDER parameter. Each matrix element is of type OLDTYPE and the returned type is SBTYPE. In this use of the subroutine, a $b \times b$ subarray of reals is constructed that starts at the beginning of both row and column index ranges in a 50×50 array of reals.

Using the subarray data type to describe the read buffer, a collective read of the matrix A is performed. The view skips the header, and the type signature of the buffer data type matches $b \times b$ repetitions of the etype of the view. One submatrix is read into each process representing its private portion Ap of A. In the same way, each process reads its portion Bp of B from an offset of $b \times b$ etypes from the start of its file view. At this point, the input file is closed, the distributed matrix multiply is done, and an output file is created and opened collectively by all processes. Process zero sets an integer view of the file and writes b and N in the header. All processes then set their distributed matrix views of the output file and collectively write C using the $b \times b$ subarray type for Cp. The output file is closed, the defined types are freed, and MPI is finalized.

The conceptual structure of MPI-IO makes it possible to distribute an array by associating specific parts of the array written in a file with specific processes using the filetype. Construction of the filetype, however, would be quite laborious without the subroutine specifically designed to create the distributed array filetype. A similar comment applies to the subarray situated in a read or

```
C Make a type to map a bxb array into a 50x50 array.
      gsizes(1) = 50
      gsizes(2) = 50
      psizes(1) = b
      psizes(2) = b
      starts(1) = 0
      starts(2) = 0
      CALL MPI_TYPE_CREATE_SUBARRAY(2, gsizes, psizes, starts,
     &                  MPI_ORDER_FORTRAN, MPI_REAL, bin50, ierr)
      CALL MPI_TYPE_COMMIT(bin50, ierr)
C Read one bxb submatrix into each process, partitioning A into Ap.
      CALL MPI_FILE_READ_AT_ALL(fh, 0, Ap, 1, bin50, status, ierr)
C Read Bp into each process from an offset of bxb in the file view.
      CALL MPI_FILE_READ_AT_ALL(fh, b*b, Bp, 1, bin50, status, ierr)
      CALL MPI_CLOSE(fh, ierr)
C Do the block distributed matrix multiply.
      CALL distmult(b, N, comrow, comcol, myrow, mycol, Ap, Bp, Cp)

C Write an output file with header and result matrix.
      CALL MPI_FILE_OPEN(comsq, "outfile", MPI_MODE_CREATE +
     &                  MPI_MODE_WRONLY, MPI_INFO_NULL, fh, ierr)
C Process zero writes the header information.
      IF (myrank .EQ. 0) THEN
          CALL MPI_FILE_SET_VIEW(fh, 0, MPI_INTEGER, MPI_INTEGER,
     &                      "native", MPI_INFO_NULL, ierr)
          CALL MPI_FILE_WRITE_AT(fh, 0, ibuf, 2, MPI_INTEGER,
     &                                        status, ierr)
      ENDIF
      CALL MPI_FILE_SET_VIEW(fh, 2*intsz, MPI_REAL, filetype,
     &                  "native", MPI_FILE_INFO_NULL, ierr)
      CALL MPI_FILE_WRITE_AT_ALL(fh, 0, Cp, 1, bin50, status, ierr)
      CALL MPI_FILE_CLOSE(fh, ierr)
      CALL MPI_TYPE_FREE(filetype, ierr)
      CALL MPI_TYPE_FREE(bin50, ierr)
      CALL MPI_FINALIZE(ierr)
      END
```

Program 11-5   Buffer structuring, input, matrix multiply, and result output.

write buffer array of larger dimensions. The latter capability is not only useful for I/O but can also be used to transmit messages consisting of arrays with dimensions smaller than the dimensions of the array represented by the buffer from which they are sent or into which they are received.

11.6 Conclusions

I/O operations are usually locally independent of computations but interact with them on a global basis. Overlap of I/O and computation is very important for achieving high performance in any application. Parallelizing computation without parallelizing I/O rapidly turns a compute bound application into an I/O bound one. In addition to the normal data dependence restrictions on parallelism, I/O also suffers from resource dependences. Parallel I/O devices and high concurrency networks to access them are required to actually exploit parallelism that might exist in an application's I/O. RAID technology addresses this in connection with disks.

The formatting that goes on in I/O operations, especially with a byte stream model of I/O, can have a strong serializing influence on an application. Developing parallel methods for format conversion can be of prime importance in such cases. The ability to specify I/O operations, especially collective operations, at a high level gives the system an opportunity to effectively introduce parallelism in ways that would be difficult if the operations had already been decomposed into a collection of low-level operations. Systems with high-level operations can also shield the user from the need to know about some of the architectural details to obtain acceptable I/O performance. MPI-I/O has a moderately high-level interface and supports collective operations well. Higher level interfaces exist in scientific data libraries, but these are far less available and standardized.

11.7 Bibliographic Notes

An excellent, up-to-date book by John May [212] treats the subject of parallel I/O in general. The I/O requirements of applications have been characterized by several papers, for example, [156, 214, 259, 263]. Separate characterizations of specific types of parallel I/O, checkpointing [203, 289] and out-of-core methods [1, 169], have also been done. An overview of parallel I/O subsystems to satisfy the demands of applications has appeared in [105]. Physical components of the subsystems, including networks [145, 155, 221, 275], disks [29, 103], and tape drives [213, 242] have been treated in numerous places. The RAID style of organization of disk systems [235] has become widespread for parallel disk I/O. Several parallel file system organizations [73, 214, 222] have been built on parallel disk and tape networks. Parallel I/O format conversion is particularly important for large-scale, fine-grained multiprocessors such as the Cray MTA [16], and several applications have been adapted for the MTA prototypes using the techniques described. Collective I/O operations moved from the research literature to more widespread support with MPI-IO [126] and High Performance Fortran (HPF) [176]. Reference [169] describes out-of-core methods written in the HPF style.

Problems

11.1 In the discussion of RAID 4 on page 452, step 3 of the update process specifies updating the parity sector by "subtracting the old data and adding the new." Give a precise mathematical description of this process.

11.2 Estimate the number of processors, P, for which the parallel input format conversion of Section 11.4.1 becomes advantageous in spite of its extra overhead. Assume $NX = NY = NZ = 100$. You need to make and justify several assumptions about execution times. To concentrate on the advantage of parallel formatting, it can be assumed that the actual file read operations take the same time for both the parallel and serial versions. Thus, you can assume that the number of elementary operations for equivalent `fscanf()`, for direct serial file read, and `sscanf()`, for in-memory format conversion, are the same and ignore the time for `stat()` and `fread()`.

An elementary operation time should probably be some basic idea of a C assignment statement execution. In such units, a format scan time is probably proportional to the number of characters scanned. Judging from the `%.10f` formats specified in the example output program, Program 11-2, floating point numbers probably require about 12 characters each. Make and justify the same style assumptions for the other operations used by the parallel input formatting to complete the estimate of P.

11.3 Using similar techniques and assumptions to those of Problem 11.2, estimate the number of processors, P, for which the parallel output formatting of Section 11.4.2 becomes advantageous for $NX = NY = NZ = 100$.

11.4 Rewrite the `distmult` subroutine of Program 5-13 using the subarray data type constructed in Program 11-5 so that only $b \times b$ elements are transmitted in each broadcast instead of the 2500 elements that constitute the full buffer.

Routines of the MPI Message Passing Library

This appendix presents the message passing interface (MPI) library routines and their attributes. We do not attempt to give a complete treatment of the routines but list almost all of them to give a feel for the extent of the system. In fact, the only section that is completely left out is the profiling support. The fairly exhaustive list is given on the principle that knowing what is not in a language is nearly as important to understanding its character as knowing what is in it. For a complete specification of the MPI standard see [220]. There are about 128 procedures in the MPI library, divided among the classifications of point-to-point communications, collective communications, data type procedures, communicator operations, environment procedures, error handling, and profiling.

A.1 Point-to-Point Communications Routines

There are 35 procedures dealing with point-to-point communication: 8 send procedures, 2 receive procedures, 1 combined send/receive, 7 persistent request procedures, and 16 other procedures. The calling sequences for the Fortran versions of these procedures are shown in Table A-1. All MPI library procedures begin with MPI_ to avoid possible collision with user defined names. The meanings of the parameters used in the point-to-point procedures are given in Table A-2. As described in Section 5.4.1, sends and receives can be blocking or nonblocking in the sense of buffer availability. The standard, buffered, synchronous, and ready modes of send are done by the procedures SEND, BSEND, SSEND, and RSEND, respectively. All sends specify the start of a buffer, BUF, that contains CNT items of MPI data type, TYPE. Messages are sent to the process with rank DST in the group of the communicator COM. A TAG, which in Fortran is an integer, is associated with the message so that receive operations can distinguish it from messages of other types. All Fortran MPI procedures return an error code, IERR, that specifies success of the procedure call or one of a number of predefined error codes. In C, the return code is the value of the function that is the C counterpart of the Fortran subroutine for the MPI procedure. It is very often ignored. For all send modes, receive is done by the RECV procedure. It specifies a source, SRC, and a TAG that are used to match source process' rank and the specified tag in a received message. Wild card specifiers, MPI_ANY_SOURCE and MPI_ANY_TAG can be used to ignore either or both specifications in a received message. Nonblocking operations are initiated by the ISEND, IBSEND, ISSEND, IRSEND, and IRECV procedures. These procedures have calling sequences identical to their blocking counterparts but also return a request handle that can be used in testing for completion of the initiating request.

Table A-1 MPI procedures related to point-to-point communications.

Send proce- dures	`MPI_SEND(BUF, CNT, TYPE, DST, TAG, COM, IERR)`
	`MPI_BSEND(BUF, CNT, TYPE, DST, TAG, COM, IERR)`
	`MPI_SSEND(BUF, CNT, TYPE, DST, TAG, COM, IERR)`
	`MPI_RSEND(BUF, CNT, TYPE, DST, TAG, COM, IERR)`
	`MPI_ISEND(BUF, CNT, TYPE, DST, TAG, COM, REQ, IERR)`
	`MPI_IBSEND(BUF, CNT, TYPE, DST, TAG, COM, REQ, IERR)`
	`MPI_ISSEND(BUF, CNT, TYPE, DST, TAG, COM, REQ, IERR)`
	`MPI_IRSEND(BUF, CNT, TYPE, DST, TAG, COM, REQ, IERR)`
Receive pro- cedures	`MPI_RECV(BUF, CNT, TYPE, SRC, TAG, COM, STAT, IERR)`
	`MPI_IRECV(BUF, CNT, TYPE, SRC, TAG, COM, STAT, REQ, IERR)`
Send/receive	`MPI_SENDRECV(SBUF, SCNT, STYPE, DST, STAG, RBUF,` `        RCNT, RTYPE, SRC, RTAG, COM, STAT, IERR)`
	`MPI_SENDRECV_REPLACE(BUF, CNT, TYPE, DST, STAG,` `        SRC, RTAG, COM, STAT, IERR)`
Persistent requests	`MPI_SEND_INIT(BUF, CNT, TYPE, DST, TAG, COM, REQ, IERR)`
	`MPI_BSEND_INIT(BUF, CNT, TYPE, DST, TAG, COM, REQ, IERR)`
	`MPI_SSEND_INIT(BUF, CNT, TYPE, DST, TAG, COM, REQ, IERR)`
	`MPI_RSEND_INIT(BUF, CNT, TYPE, DST, TAG, COM, REQ, IERR)`
	`MPI_RECV_INIT(BUF, CNT, TYPE, SRC, TAG, COM, REQ, IERR)`
	`MPI_START(REQ, IERR)`
	`MPI_STARTALL(REQCNT, REQ_ARR, IERR)`
Other	`MPI_GET_COUNT(STAT, TYPE, RCVCNT, IERR)`
	`MPI_BUFFER_ATTACH(BUF, SIZE, IERR)`
	`MPI_BUFFER_DETACH(BUF, SIZE, IERR)`
	`MPI_PROBE(SRC, TAG, COM, STAT, IERR)`
	`MPI_IPROBE(SRC, TAG, COM, FLAG, STAT, IERR)`
	`MPI_WAIT(REQ, STAT, IERR)`
	`MPI_TEST(REQ, FLAG, STAT, IERR)`
	`MPI_WAITANY(CNT, REQ_ARR, IDX, STAT, IERR)`
	`MPI_TESTANY(CNT, REQ_ARR, IDX, FLAG, STAT, IERR)`
	`MPI_WAITALL(CNT, REQ_ARR, STAT_ARR, IERR)`
	`MPI_TESTALL(CNT, REQ_ARR, FLAG, STAT_ARR, IERR)`
	`MPI_WAITSOME(ICNT, REQ_ARR, OCNT, IDX_ARR, STAT_ARR, IERR)`
	`MPI_TESTSOME(ICNT, REQ_ARR, OCNT, IDX_ARR, STAT_ARR, IERR)`
	`MPI_CANCEL(REQ, IERR)`
	`MPI_TEST_CANCELLED(STAT, FLAG, IERR)`
	`MPI_REQUEST_FREE(REQ, IERR)`

Table A-2   Parameters for point-to-point communications procedures.

BUF	Starting address of a buffer for a message to be sent or received.
CNT	Number of items of the specified type in the buffer—space on receive.
TYPE	Handle for MPI type of the data in a send buffer or type to be received.
DST	Rank of the destination process in the specified communicator.
TAG	Tag for the message, specific on send—may be MPI_ANY_TAG on receive.
COM	Handle for the communicator used in transmission.
IERR	MPI error return code.
REQ	Handle used to refer to an initialized request.
SRC	Rank of source process in the communicator—may be MPI_ANY_SOURCE.
STAT	Array of 3 integers containing return status: source, tag, and error.
SBUF	Start of source buffer when 2 buffers used in call.
SCNT	Number of items of the specified type to be sent.
STYPE	Handle for the MPI type of the data items to be sent.
STAG	Tag specified by the sender for the message.
RBUF	Start of receive buffer when 2 buffers used in call.
RCNT	Number of items of the specified type that can be held in the receive buffer.
RTYPE	Handle for the MPI type of the data items to be received.
RTAG	Tag to be matched at the receiver—may be MPI_ANY_TAG.
REQCNT	Number of request handles held in a request array.
REQ_ARR	Address of an array of requests.
RCVCNT	Number of items of the specified type actually received—associated with status.
SIZE	Size in bytes of buffer used by buffered send operations.
FLAG	Logical flag returned by probe indicating message with matching source and tag.
IDX	Index of handle in an array of requests.
STAT_ARR	Array of statuses returned by completed receive requests.
ICNT	Length of array of requests.
OCNT	Number of completed requests in a request array.
IDX_ARR	Array of indices in a request array of requests that completed.

Two procedures do simultaneous send and receive. SENDRECV uses separate send and receive buffers while SENDRECV_REPLACE uses only one buffer for both sent and received data. There are also persistent requests that allow the parameters of a send or receive to be specified only once and then requests may be started repeatedly without respecifying parameters. The procedures, SEND_INIT, BSEND_INIT, SSEND_INIT, RSEND_INIT, and RECV_INIT initialize an operations and return a request handle. Given a request handle or an array of them, the procedures START and STARTALL are used to start new requests with the specified parameters.

The status returned by receive operations is an array of three integers, indexed by MPI_SOURCE, MPI_TAG, and MPI_ERROR. The source and tag elements can be used to get the specific source or tag when a wild card was used in the receive operation. The error element is important when multiple requests are completed by a single MPI procedure. The number of items received is also associated with the status, but must be accessed by the GET_COUNT procedure, which, given the status and data type, returns the number of items of that type that were received. The buffer used by the buffered send mode must be supplied by the user by calling the BUFFER_ATTACH procedure. BUFFER_DETACH releases the buffer space. The existence of a message matching a given source and tag specification can be tested using PROBE or IPROBE. PROBE is a blocking routine that returns only when a matching message is available while IPROBE returns immediately with a true or false flag value that tells of the presence of a matching message.

A group of routines are used with the requests returned either by nonblocking or persistent sends and receives. WAIT blocks and returns with a status only when the specified request has completed while TEST returns a flag and a status if the flag is true. Arrays of requests can be specified and tested or awaited in a number of ways by WAITANY, WAITALL, WAITSOME, TESTANY, TESTALL, and TESTSOME. A request may be cancelled using the CANCEL procedure and the status returned by a request can be tested to see if the corresponding request was cancelled by the TEST_CANCELLED procedure. Finally, a request can be freed for reuse by the REQUEST_FREE procedure.

A.2 Collective Communications Routines

Procedures dealing with collective communications can be classified as synchronization, communication, or reduction and are listed in Table A-3. The parameters for these procedures are summarized in Table A-4. The IERR and COM parameters are as in point-to-point communications, except that COM must be an intracommunicator, whereas in point-to-point communications it may also be an intercommunicator. The communicator defines the group of processes over which the collective operations act and underlies all such communications. The MPI procedures correspond to the discussion of Section 5.3.3 with some differences. The Section 5.3.3 discussion suggested single numbers were communicated or combined, but all MPI routines assume that items are vectors. This is a concession to start up overhead that usually makes the transmission of small messages inefficient. Routines that deal with multiple data items, either at the source or destination or both, have two versions. One assumes that all data have the same length, while the other, ending with V, allows variable lengths for the items.

The logic of many collective communications operations is closely related to the communications that would be necessary to synchronize the communicating processes. The specification of an MPI collective operation allows it to synchronize processes, but does not require it to do so. The only collective operation guaranteed to synchronize processes is MPI_BARRIER, from which no process may return until all have called it. The MPI_BARRIER call uses only the two ubiquitous parameters, COM and IERR.

tine, MPI_BCAST, has the fewest parameters of any collective operation
ates data. The first parameter, BUF, is a buffer, in which CNT items of MPI
stored. The parameter, ROOT, is the rank of the broadcast source processor,
e usual communication pattern for broadcast is that of a tree with the source
ot, the buffer contains CNT items to be broadcast, while in other processes, the
T items to make their contents the same as that of the buffer in the root. The
d TYPE should be the same across all processes. As with other collective com-
tines using these parameters, ROOT and COM must be the same for all processes.

r and scatter operations, different items are sent than received, so there are both a
parameter, SBUF, and a receive buffer parameter, RBUF, for these routines. SCNT and
T and RTYPE) are the count and data type parameters associated with SBUF (RBUF).
parameter designates the destination for gather and the source for scatter. In gather, the
uffer is meaningful only for the root process, SCNT is the number of items in the send
nd RCNT, only meaningful at the root, is the number of items received from any one pro-
he data sent by all processes is concatenated in order of process rank in the communicator
laced in RBUF at the root. In scatter, $P \times$ SCNT items, where P is the number of processes,
xtracted from SBUF and partitioned into groups of SCNT items that are sent to individual pro-
ses in rank order. The routines MPI_GATHERV and MPI_SCATTERV allow varying amounts of
ata to be received from, or sent to, different processes, respectively. The RCNT, respectively
SCNT, parameter is replaced by a vector of P counts, one for each sender or receiver. In addition,
a vector of P displacements, giving independent offsets from the beginning of the buffer in the
root to the data received from or sent to each process allows blocks of data for each process to be
flexibly placed in the buffer, perhaps with intervening gaps.

The routines MPI_ALLGATHER and MPI_ALLGATHERV behave identically to MPI_GATHER
and MPI_GATHERV, respectively, except that the result is delivered to all processes instead of being
confined to one root process. Thus, the calls to these routines do not need the parameter, ROOT. In
MPI_ALLTOALL and MPI_ALLTOALLV, each process sends a set of P different messages, one for
each destination process. They are stored in order of the rank of the destination process in each
send buffer. The receive buffer in each process gets all P messages destined for that process, stored
in rank order of the sending process. The MPI_ALLTOALLV routine allows the blocks of both the
information to be sent and the received information to be stored at specified offsets from the beginning of the send and receive buffers. Thus, the integer RCNT and SCNT parameters are replaced by
vectors, SCNTS and SDISPS, and RCNTS and RDISPS, respectively.

The collective communications that do arithmetic on the transmitted data allow not only
standard, predefined operations to be used for arithmetic combining, but also make it possible
for the user to define an operation, supplying the name of a function to perform it, that is used
in a reduction or prefix computation. The standard operators that can be used for the OP
parameter in a reduce or prefix, called *scan*, communication are given in Table A-5. Both the
MPI types corresponding to Fortran REAL and DOUBLE PRECISION are classed as floating
point types. The MAX and MIN operators operate on integer or floating point types. SUM and

Table A-3   MPI procedures for coll

Synchroniza-tion	MPI_BARRIER(CO
Communica-tion	MPI_BCAST(
	MPI_GATHER(S
	MPI_GATHERV(SBU
	MPI_SCATTER(SBUF, S
	MPI_SCATTERV(SBUF, SCN
	MPI_ALLGATHER(SBUF, SCNT,
	MPI_ALLGATHERV(SBUF, SCNT, STY
	MPI_ALLTOALL(SBUF, SCNT, STYPE, RE
	MPI_ALLTOALLV(SBUF, SCNTS, SDISPS, ST.
	RCNTS, RDISPS,
Reduction (cooperative arithmetic)	MPI_REDUCE(SBUF, RBUF, CNT, TYPE, OP, ROO
	MPI_OP_CREATE(FUNCT, COMMUTE, OP, IERR)
	MPI_OP_FREE(OP, IERR)
	MPI_ALLREDUCE(SBUF, RBUF, CNT, TYPE, OP, COM,
	MPI_REDUCE_SCATTER(SBUF, RBUF, RCNTS, TYPE, OP,
	MPI_SCAN(SBUF, RBUF, CNT, TYPE, OP, COM, IERR)

Table A-4   Parameters for collective communications procedures.

COM	Handle for the communicator whose group does the collective communication.
IERR	MPI error return code.
BUF	Starting address of buffer for data to be sent or received.
CNT	Number of items of type TYPE to send, or spaces in receive buffer.
TYPE	Handle for MPI type of data to be sent or received.
ROOT	Rank of the distinguished process when source or destination is one process.
SBUF	Address of send buffer when both send and receive buffers used in call.
SCNT	Number of items of type STYPE to be sent.
STYPE	Handle of MPI type of data to be sent.
RBUF	Address of receive buffer when call uses two buffers.
RCNT	Number of items of type RTYPE that can fit in receive buffer.
RTYPE	Handle of MPI type of received data items.
RCNTS	Array of numbers of items of buffer space for data from each source.
RDISPS	Array of displacements from start of receive buffer to data from each source.
SCNTS	Array of numbers of items of type STYPE for each receiver.
SDISPS	Array of displacements from start of send buffer to data for each destination.
OP	Handle for predefined or user defined associative operation for reduction or scan.
FUNCT	Function (Fortran subroutine) associated with a user-defined reduction operation.
COMMUTE	True if user-defined operation is commutative, false otherwise.

PROD act on integer, floating point, or complex data. LAND, LOR, and LXOR operate on logical variables, and BAND, BOR, and BXOR operate on integers or bytes. MINLOC and MAXLOC operate on a pair of numeric values to get both the value and position of a minimum or maximum. MPI supplies special types consisting of a pair of values for these operations. In the Fortran binding, these are MPI_2REAL, MPI_2DOUBLE_PRECISION, and MPI_2INTEGER. For a user-defined operation, the parameter, FUNCT, is the name of a subroutine called by the Fortran statement

$$CALL\ FUNCT(VEC1,\ VEC2,\ LEN,\ TYPE)$$

which performs the operation VEC2(i) = VEC2(i) op VEC1(i), i = 1, ..., LEN. VEC1(*) and VEC2(*) are assumed size arrays. The OP parameter of the MPI_OP_CREATE call is a handle for an opaque object representing the defined operation. All operators are assumed to be associative, and if the COMMUTE parameter is true, MPI may use commutativity to optimize the communication.

Table A-5 Standard operators for reduction or scan communications.

Name	Meaning	Name	Meaning
MPI_MAX	Maximum	MPI_LOR	Logical or
MPI_MIN	Minimum	MPI_BOR	Bit wise or
MPI_SUM	Sum	MPI_LXOR	Logical exclusive or
MPI_PROD	Product	MPI_BXOR	Bit wise exclusive or
MPI_LAND	Logical and	MPI_MAXLOC	Value and location of maximum
MPI_BAND	Bit wise and	MPI_MINLOC	Value and location of minimum

Both MPI_REDUCE and MPI_ALLREDUCE start with a send buffer, SBUF, containing a vector of CNT items of type, TYPE. Reduction is performed componentwise across the vectors from all processes. The CNT resulting components are then stored in the receiving buffer, RBUF, of the root process (for MPI_REDUCE) or of all processes (for MPI_ALLREDUCE). For MPI_REDUCE_SCATTER, the length of the vector in each send buffer is the sum of the vector of receive counts, RCNTS. The vector result of the reduction is then partitioned into P segments, with RCNTS(i) values delivered to the receive buffer, RBUF, of the process with rank i. The MPI_SCAN operation performs the prefix computation with operator, OP, with the order inherent in the prefix computation supplied by the rank ordering of processes in COM. As in reduce, prefix is performed component wise on vectors of CNT values from each process. Process i receives the result of reduction on the vectors from processes 0 through i, inclusive.

A.3 MPI Data Types and Constructors

There are basic MPI data types that correspond to basic types in the host language. The basic types used with Fortran are given in Table A-6. Two MPI types, MPI_BYTE and MPI_PACKED, are not language specific and provide for low-level message structuring. The MPI routines that deal with data types can be divided into four categories, as shown in Table A-7. There are type constructors that build user-defined types from basic types, interrogation routines to obtain sizes and other characteristics, two routines to establish and free handles for types, and routines to deal with the type `MPI_PACKED`. The parameters for the MPI data type routines are listed in Table A-8.

Table A-6   Basic MPI types used with Fortran.

MPI data type	Fortran data type
MPI_INTEGER	INTEGER
MPI_REAL	REAL
MPI_DOUBLE_PRECISION	DOUBLE PRECISION
MPI_COMPLEX	COMPLEX
MPI_LOGICAL	LOGICAL
MPI_CHARACTER	CHARACTER
MPI_BYTE	
MPI_PACKED	

Table A-7   MPI routines that deal with data types.

Type constructors	MPI_TYPE_CONTIGUOUS(CNT, OLDTYP, NEWTYP, IERR)
	MPI_TYPE_VECTOR(CNT, BLKLEN, STRIDE, OLDTYP, NEWTYP, IERR)
	MPI_TYPE_HVECTOR(CNT, BLKLEN, STRIDE, OLDTYP, NEWTYP, IERR)
	MPI_TYPE_INDEXED(CNT, BLKLENS, DISPS, OLDTYP, NEWTYP, IERR)
	MPI_TYPE_HINDEXED(CNT, BLKLENS, DISPS, OLDTYP, NEWTYP, IERR)
	MPI_TYPE_STRUCT(CNT, BLKLENS, DISPS, TYPES, NEWTYP, IERR)
Interrogation	MPI_ADDRESS(LOC, ADDR, IERR)
	MPI_TYPE_SIZE(TYPE, SIZE, IERR)
	MPI_TYPE_LB(TYPE, DISP, IERR)
	MPI_TYPE_UB(TYPE, DISP, IERR)
	MPI_TYPE_EXTENT(TYPE, EXTENT, IERR)
	MPI_GET_ELEMENTS(STATUS, TYPE, ELCNT, IERR)
Type management	MPI_TYPE_COMMIT(TYPE, IERR)
	MPI_TYPE_FREE(TYPE, IERR)
Packing and unpacking	MPI_PACK(INBF, INCNT, TYPE, OUTBF, OUTSZ, POS, COM, IERR)
	MPI_UNPACK(INBF, INSZ, POS, OUTBF, OUTCNT, TYPE, COM, IERR)
	MPI_PACK_SIZE(INCNT, TYPE, COM, PKSIZE, IERR)

Table A-8   Parameters for routines dealing with MPI data types.

CNT	Number of elements or number of blocks of the old type or types.
OLDTYP	Type to be replicated to form new type.
NEWTYP	Type formed from multiple copies of the old type or types.
IERR	MPI error return code.
BLKLEN	Number of OLDTYP in a block.
STRIDE	Separation between blocks, number of OLDTYP elements or bytes.
BLKLENS	Vector of block lengths.
DISPS	Vector of displacements.
TYPES	Vector of types.
LOC	Location of variable in memory.
ADDR	Byte address of LOC as an integer.
TYPE	MPI type being interrogated or managed.
SIZE	Size of MPI data type in bytes.
DISP	Displacement from origin in bytes of lower or upper bound.
EXTENT	Difference between upper and lower bounds of type.
STATUS	Status of a read operation being interrogated.
ELCNT	Count of basic type elements received.
INBF	Address of buffer to pack or unpack from.
INCNT	Number of items to pack.
OUTBF	Address of buffer to pack or unpack into.
OUTSZ	Size of OUTBF.
POS	Current position in packed buffer.
COM	Communicator to be used in sending packed information.
INSZ	Size of INBF.
OUTCNT	Number of items to be unpacked.
PKSIZE	Upper bound on size of packed message, in bytes.

The routines that construct new types do so by assembling multiple copies of an old type or, in the case of MPI_TYPE_STRUCT, of several old types. The simplest constructor is MPI_TYPE_CONTIGUOUS, which simply concatenates CNT copies of the old type to form the new one. To handle separations between elements or blocks of elements, MPI_TYPE_VECTOR builds a new type consisting of CNT blocks of BLKLEN elements of the old type with each block starting STRIDE elements after the start of the previous block. This routine could be used, for example, to define a row vector in a matrix stored in column major order. In this application, the block length would be one, and the stride would be the column dimension of the matrix. Separations between blocks of elements are also used in the parallel I/O operations supported by MPI-2 where a user-defined data type describes the subset of a file's data that is "seen" by a given process participating in a parallel I/O operation. If the stride is not a multiple of the size of the old type, MPI_TYPE_HVECTOR (H for heterogeneous) takes the stride specified in bytes. The routines, MPI_TYPE_INDEXED and MPI_TYPE_HINDEXED allow CNT blocks to have different numbers of elements of the old type, specified by the integer array BLKLENS, and starting at different displacements from the beginning, given in elements or bytes, respectively, in the array, DISPS. Finally MPI_TYPE_STRUCT allows each of the CNT blocks to have elements of a different type, with the number of elements per block given in the array, BLKLENS, and the byte displacements from the beginning given in the array, DISPS. The old types are specified by the array, TYPES.

In several of the type constructors, displacements relative to a starting buffer address are used. An item's address in memory can be obtained by a call to MPI_ADDRESS. This routine returns the byte address, ADDR, of the item at location, LOC, relative to an origin given by the predefined constant, MPI_BOTTOM. Address differences can then be used as displacements, or MPI_BOTTOM can be used as the buffer address and absolute addresses used as displacements. MPI_TYPE_SIZE returns the size, in bytes, of a data type while MPI_TYPE_LB, MPI_TYPE_UB, and MPI_EXTENT return byte values of lower bound, upper bound, and the difference between them, called the extent, respectively. The upper and lower bounds can be artificially adjusted in defining a type so that it contains "holes" or extends past the upper or lower bound. The size, however, gives the actual number of bytes used to transmit an item of that type in a message. The routine MPI_GET_ELEMENTS returns the number of basic elements obtained by a receive operation whose return status is the STATUS parameter. A receive operation using a derived type may not match a send of an integral number of elements of that high-level type. If it does, MPI_GET_COUNT returns that number, but if not, MPI_GET_ELEMENTS returns in ELCNT the number of elements of a basic type received.

Handles for derived types are managed by MPI_TYPE_COMMIT and MPI_TYPE_FREE. Before a derived type is used in communication, it is committed. This allows a compact representation or an efficient transfer mechanism to be associated with it. It may then be used for multiple sends from the same or different buffers. MPI_TYPE_FREE deallocates a data type after all pending transmissions using this type are complete.

The packed data type is used by packing and unpacking routines that place information into, or extract it from, a message buffer, much the way formatted write and read construct and analyze an I/O buffer. The packed buffer, which is OUTBF for the routine MPI_PACK and INBF for MPI_UNPACK, is associated with a byte position, POS, to which the next item is packed or from which it is unpacked. The position is updated by each pack or unpack call to reflect the operation. In MPI_PACK, INCNT items of data type, TYPE, are taken from INBF and packed into the buffer, OUTBF, of size, OUTSZ, starting at position, POS, which is then advanced by the number of bytes packed. MPI_UNPACK unpacks items from INBUF, of size, INSZ, starting at POS and places the resulting OUTCNT items of type, TYPE, into OUTBF. POS is advanced to the first byte of INBF past the unpacked items. The amount of space needed to pack INCNT items of type, TYPE, is returned in PKSIZE by a call to MPI_PACK_SIZE. In all three pack routines, the parameter COM identifies the communicator used to send and receive the packed message.

A.4 Communicators, Process Groups, and Topologies

A large number of MPI routines deal with communicators and the groups and topologies associated with them. Those that manage communicators and the process groups associated with them are categorized and summarized in Table A-9. The parameters for these routines are summarized in Table A-10. Process groups are fundamental to communicators, and they may be formed, released, and queried. The communicators themselves may also be formed, released, and queried, with a group forming the basis of a new communicator or obtained from an old one. Both groups and communicators are opaque MPI objects and are referred to by handles in calls to MPI routines.

A group may be obtained from a communicator by MPI_COMM_GROUP and its handle freed by MPI_GROUP_FREE. New groups can be formed from old ones by applying a set operation to two original groups. The operations of union, intersection, and difference are supported. A new group can also be formed by including specified processes in, or excluding specified processes from the group. The processes come from an old group and are specified either by listing their ranks or giving ranges of rank numbers. Each range is a vector of three integers specifying first rank, last rank, and stride. Several ranges can be specified for inclusion, respectively exclusion, in a call. Routines are supplied to query the size of a group and rank of the calling process within the group. Other routines map ranks from one group to another and compare two groups.

Table A-9   MPI routines for communicators and their process groups.

Groups: form and release	`MPI_COMM_GROUP(COM, GRP, IERR)`
	`MPI_GROUP_UNION(GRP1, GRP2, NEWGRP, IERR)`
	`MPI_GROUP_INTERSECTION(GRP1, GRP2, NEWGRP, IERR)`
	`MPI_GROUP_DIFFERENCE(GRP1, GRP2, NEWGRP, IERR)`
	`MPI_GROUP_INCL(GRP, N, RNKS, NEWGRP, IERR)`
	`MPI_GROUP_EXCL(GRP, N, RNKS, NEWGRP, IERR)`
	`MPI_RANGE_INCL(GRP, N, RANGES, NEWGRP, IERR)`
	`MPI_RANGE_EXCL(GRP, N, RANGES, NEWGRP, IERR)`
	`MPI_GROUP_FREE(GRP, IERR)`
Groups: query	`MPI_GROUP_SIZE(GRP, SIZE, IERR)`
	`MPI_GROUP_RANK(GRP, RNK, IERR)`
	`MPI_GROUP_TRANSLATE_RANKS(GRP1, N, RNKS1, GRP2, RNKS2, IERR)`
	`MPI_GROUP_COMPARE(GRP1, GRP2, RESULT, IERR)`
Form and release communicators	`MPI_COMM_CREATE(COM, GRP, NEWCOM, IERR)`
	`MPI_COMM_DUP(COM, NEWCOM, IERR)`
	`MPI_COMM_SPLIT(COM, COLOR, ORDR, NEWCOM, IERR)`
	`MPI_COMM_FREE(COM, IERR)`
Query communicators	`MPI_COMM_SIZE(COM, SIZE, IERR)`
	`MPI_COMM_RANK(COM, RNK, IERR)`
	`MPI_COMM_COMPARE(COM1, COM2, RESULT, IERR)`
Inter-communicators	`MPI_INTERCOMM_CREATE(LCOM, LLDR, PCOM, RLDR,` `                              TAG, NEWCOM, IERR)`
	`MPI_INTERCOMM_MERGE(INTERCOM, HIGH, NEWCOM, IERR)`
	`MPI_COMM_TEST_INTER(COM, FLAG, IERR)`
	`MPI_COMM_REMOTE_SIZE(COM, SIZE, IERR)`
	`MPI_COMM_REMOTE_GROUP(COM, GRP, IERR)`

Table A-10   Parameters for MPI communicator and process group routines.

COM	Sole or old communicator referred to in call.
GRP	Process group.
GRP1	First process group to be combined, compared, or translated.
GRP2	Second process group to be combined, compared, or translated.
NEWGRP	New process group formed by operation.
N	Number of processes or ranges to be included or excluded.
RNKS	Ranks of processes to be included or excluded.
RANGES	Ranges of processes to include or exclude; first, last, and stride for each range.
SIZE	Size of group.
RNK	Rank of calling process in group or communicator.
RNKS1	Ranks of processes in GRP1 input to translation.
RNKS2	Ranks of processes in GRP2 output from translation.
RESULT	Compare result: MPI_IDENT, MPI_SIMILAR, MPI_UNEQUAL, or MPI_CONGRUENT.
NEWCOM	New communicator resulting from operation.
COLOR	Integer number of subset occupied by process after split.
ORDR	Control of rank order in subset.
COM1	First communicator in comparison.
COM2	Second communicator in comparison.
LCOM	Local communicator for intercommunicator.
LLDR	Rank of leader for local group of intercommunicator.
PCOM	Peer communicator for intercommunicator, containing local and remote leaders.
RLDR	Rank of leader of remote group of intercommunicator.
TAG	Tag for communication between leaders using peer communicator.
INTERCOM	Intercommunicator to be merged into an intracommunicator.
HIGH	Logical value that is true for processes in group getting higher ranks on merge.
FLAG	True/false result from test for an intercommunicator.

A new communicator can be formed from an old one and a new group. In practice, the old communicator is often MPI_COMM_WORLD. An old communicator can also be duplicated to form a new one. New communicators can also result from splitting an old one. In a split, each process has an integer number, COLOR, identifying to which subset communicator it belongs after the split. An ordering parameter is also supplied for the split to determine the ranking of processes within each subset, with ties resolved by the ranking within the original group. Communicator handles are freed by MPI_COMM_FREE. A communicator query returns the size of the communicator's group and another returns the rank of the calling process in that group. There is also a routine to compare two communicators. Group comparison results in MPI_IDENT if groups have the same members and ranking, but communicator comparison gives MPI_IDENT only if the two communicators are handles for the same object. Communicators with identical groups give MPI_CONGRUENT on comparison. Comparison of communicators or groups gives MPI_SIMILAR if the groups have the same members but a different rank ordering.

Routines dealing with intercommunicators involve the local group, local leader, remote group, remote leader, and peer communicator. An intercommunicator is created cooperatively by two groups of processes that each specify one of two local intracommunicators. The create call also specifies local and remote leaders with respect to the peer communicator through which they communicate using an otherwise unused tag supplied in the call. An intercommunicator can create an intracommunicator by merging its two process groups by `MPI_INTERCOMM_MERGE`. Query routines test whether a communicator is an intercommunicator and obtain the size and group for the remote group. The local group is queried using the size and group queries defined for intracommunicators.

Routines that deal with the topologies and cached information associated with a communicator are summarized in Table A-11. The parameters for these routines are summarized in Table A-12. Two types of topologies can be associated with a communicator, Cartesian grid and general graph topologies. The definition of a Cartesian grid topology requires a number of dimensions, the extent of each dimension, whether shifts are periodic in each dimension, and whether the `MPI_CART_CREATE` routine is allowed to reorder process ranks for efficient implementation. `MPI_GRAPH_CREATE` requires an index, `IDX`, for the number of neighbors for each node, an edge list, `EDGS`, with `IDX(i)` entries for each node, i. Communicators with grid topologies can also be created by dividing a grid into subgrids by suppressing the indices of certain dimensions in the grid and returning a new communicator to each calling process according to its values for the indices that remain.

Table A-11   MPI routines for topologies and other cached values of a communicator.

Topology: create	`MPI_CART_CREATE(COM, NDIMS, DIMS, PERS, REORD, NEWCOM, IERR)`
	`MPI_CART_SUB(COM, REMAIN, NEWCOM, IERR)`
	`MPI_GRAPH_CREATE(COM, NNODES, IDX, EDGS, REORD, NEWCOM, IERR)`
Topology: query	`MPI_CARTDIM_GET(COM, NDIMS, IERR)`
	`MPI_CART_GET(COM, MAXDIMS, DIMS, PERS, COORDS, IERR)`
	`MPI_CART_RANK(COM, COORDS, RANK, IERR)`
	`MPI_CART_COORDS(COM, RANK, MAXDIMS, COORDS, IERR)`
	`MPI_CART_SHIFT(COM, DIR, DIST, SRCRNK, DSTRNK, IERR)`
	`MPI_DIMS_CREATE(NNODES, NDIMS, DIMS, IERR)`
	`MPI_CART_MAP(COM, NDIMS, DIMS, PERS, NEWRNK, IERR)`
	`MPI_GRAPHDIMS_GET(COM, NNODES, NEDGS, IERR)`
	`MPI_GRAPH_GET(COM, MAXIX, MAXEDGS, IDX, EDGS, IERR)`
	`MPI_GRAPH_NEIGHBORS_COUNT(COM, RANK, NNBRS, IERR)`
	`MPI_GRAPH_NEIGHBORS(COM, RANK, MAXNBRS, NBRS, IERR)`
	`MPI_GRAPH_MAP(COM, NNODES, IDX, EDGS, NEWRNK, IERR)`
	`MPI_TOPO_TEST(COM, STATUS, IERR)`
Caching: key values	`MPI_KEYVAL_CREATE(CPYFN, DELFN, KEY, STATE, IERR)`
	`MPI_KEYVAL_FREE(KEY, IERR)`
Caching: attributes	`MPI_ATTR_PUT(COM, KEY, ATTR, IERR)`
	`MPI_ATTR_GET(COM, KEY, ATTR, FLAG, IERR)`
	`MPI_ATTR_DELETE(COM, KEY, IERR)`

Table A-12   Parameters for MPI topology and caching routines.

COM	Old communicator being queried or from which new one is built.
NDIMS	Number of dimensions in a Cartesian grid.
DIMS	List of extents of each dimension.
PERS	Logical flags telling if each dimension is periodic or not.
REORD	Logical flag allowing reordering of processes for efficient implementation if true.
NEWCOM	New communicator created with a specified topology.
REMAIN	True/false value for whether each dimension remains in a Cartesian sub-grid.
NNODES	Number of nodes (processes) in a topology.
IDX	List of graph node degrees.
EDGS	List of graph edges.
MAXDIMS	Length of vectors supplied for Cartesian grid query.
COORDS	Coordinates of specified process in grid.
RANK	Rank of process for which topology information is queried.
DIR	Cartesian coordinate of shift.
DIST	Shift distance, positive or negative.
SRCRNK	Rank of source process in SENDRECV used for shift.
DSTRNK	Rank of destination process in SENDRECV used for shift.
NEWRNK	Reordered rank of calling process for topology optimization.
NEDGS	Number of edges in a graph.
MAXIX	Length of index vector supplied for graph node degrees.
MAXEDGS	Length of vector supplied for edge list.
NNBRS	Number of neighbors of process of specified rank.
MAXNBRS	Length of vector supplied to receive neighbor ranks.
NBRS	Vector of neighbor ranks.
STATUS	Outcome of topology test: MPI_CART, MPI_GRAPH, or MPI_UNDEFINED.
CPYFN	Function called for each cache key when MPI_COMM_DUP is used on communicator.
DELFN	Function called for each cache key when communicator is deleted.
KEY	Integer key value for accessing associated attribute.
STATE	Extra state that may be used by copy and delete functions.
ATTR	Attribute value associated with a key.
FLAG	True/false flag telling whether attribute is successfully obtained.

Numerous query routines are available to obtain attributes of a communicator's topology, sometimes associated with the calling process' place in the structure. In addition to a routine that returns the parameters of a grid, there are routines that map in both directions between coordinates and rank in a grid topology. The routine MPI_DIMS_CREATE recommends extents for each unspecified dimension to make a "balanced" grid with a given number of processes. The low-level routine, MPI_CART_MAP is usually not called by the user but is invoked on grid creation if the reorder parameter is true to optimize rank ordering. Another routine associated with a grid topology is MPI_CART_SHIFT. This routine uses a coordinate direction, a positive or negative distance, and the periodic nature of the dimension to return source and destination process ranks for use with MPI_SENDRECV in order to shift information among processes of the grid along the specified coordinate. Query routines can also get either the numbers of nodes and edges in a graph or the entire graph structure. Graph access by a given process often involves discovering the number of its neighbors and their ranks using `MPI_GRAPH_NEIGHBORS_COUNT`, and `MPI_GRAPH_NEIGHBORS`, respectively. `MPI_GRAPH_MAP` is also a low-level routine used for reordering in creation of a graph topology but not usually called directly by the user. The topology associated with a communicator can also be queried using `MPI_TOPO_TEST`. The possible results are `MPI_CART`, `MPI_GRAPH`, or `MPI_UNDEFINED`.

Topologies can be thought of as extra information associated with a communicator. User-defined information can also be associated with a communicator through caching. A cached item of information consists of a key value and a corresponding attribute. Keys are integers managed by `MPI_KEYVAL_CREATE` and `MPI_KEYVAL_FREE`. Once a key value is available, an attribute may be associated with it using `MPI_ATTR_PUT`, retrieved using `MPI_ATTR_GET`, or deleted using `MPI_ATTR_DELETE`. When key values are created, two functions are associated with each. One is called whenever a copy is made of the communicator with which that key value is associated, and the other is called whenever the communicator associated with that key value is deleted.

A.5 MPI Environment and Error Handling

The rest of the routines of the MPI library deal with error handling, the MPI environment, and profiling. We omit a discussion of profiling. The error handler and environment routines are listed in Table A-13. Briefly, a user-defined function can be associated with a handle for an error handler, which is an MPI opaque object, and this error handler can then be associated with a communicator. We omit the details of the interaction between user and MPI error handling, except to note that each error code is associated with an identifying string and that errors are grouped into classes.

Table A-13   MPI error handling and environment routines.

Error handler routines	`MPI_ERRHANDLER_CREATE(FUNCT, HANDLER, IERR)`
	`MPI_ERRHANDLER_SET(COM, HANDLER, IERR)`
	`MPI_ERRHANDLER_GET(COM, HANDLER, IERR)`
	`MPI_ERRHANDLER_FREE(HANDLER, IERR)`
	`MPI_ERROR_STRING(ERRCODE, STRNG, LEN, IERR)`
	`MPI_ERROR_CLASS(ERRCODE, CLASS, IERR)`
Environment query	`MPI_GET_PROCESSOR_NAME(NAME, LEN, IERR)`
	`DOUBLE PRECISION MPI_WTIME()`
	`DOUBLE PRECISION MPI_WTICK()`
Environment control	`MPI_INIT(IERR)`
	`MPI_FINALIZE(IERR)`
	`MPI_INITIALIZED(FLAG, IERR)`
	`MPI_ABORT(COM, ERRCODE, IERR)`

Table A-14   Environment attributes cached with `MPI_COMM_WORLD`.

`MPI_TAG_UB`	Upper bound for integer tag value.
`MPI_HOST`	Rank of host process if there is one, otherwise `MPI_PROC_NULL`.
`MPI_IO`	Rank of a process that has regular I/O facilities.
`MPI_WTIME_IS_GLOBAL`	True if clocks in all processes are synchronized.

The environment in which MPI operates has several features. The alphanumeric name of the calling processor can be obtained by calling `MPI_GET_PROCESSOR_NAME`. The current time in seconds and the resolution of the timer in seconds are obtained from the Fortran functions, `MPI_WTIME()` and `MPI_WTICK()`, respectively. When `MPI_INIT` is called, once and only once by all processes before any other MPI calls, it sets up some predefined attributes associated with `MPI_COMM_WORLD`, as defined in Table A-14. The last MPI routine called by all processes is `MPI_FINALIZE`. It should not be called until all pending communications are complete for the process calling it. A call to `MPI_INITIALIZED` returns a true or false flag. Finally, `MPI_ABORT` attempts to cleanly abort all processes in the group of the communicator, `COM`.

A.6 Summary and MPI-2 Extensions

The main goal of MPI has been to develop standards for writing message passing programs for distributed memory multiprocessors. With standards come not only portability and ease of use but also well-defined definitions that computer companies can use to provide efficient implementations and design hardware to support them. While MPI-1 provides an interface where processes within a parallel program can communicate, it does not provide support for process creation and establishing communication between them. MPI-1 supports a static application model where processes cannot be added or deleted from an application once it has been started.

MPI-2 has added several features to MPI-1, mainly dynamic process management, one-sided communication, extended collective operations, external interfaces, parallel I/O, and C++ and Fortran 90 language bindings. These features are incorporated so that the main objectives of MPI are preserved. To preserve portability, the MPI process model must encompass many parallel environments ranging from tightly coupled distributed systems to heterogeneous networks of loosely connected workstations. In so doing, MPI-2 cannot manage the parallel environment in which programs execute. It provides an interface between the application and the system software as a layer above the operating system. MPI-2 uses Remote Memory Access (RMA) to extend the communication mechanism of MPI-1. This allows a process to identify all communication parameters for both the sending and the receiving sides through the use of `MPI-PUT`, `MPI-GET`, and `MPI-ACCUMULATE` operations. In this model, a process may not know what data in its memory may be accessed by another process. The transfer parameters are only available on one side as opposed to regular send/receive operations where both sides must have complete transfer information. Use of RMA can add to efficiency in message passing as some platforms provide efficient RMA support through DMA, communication coprocessors, hardware supported put/get, etc.

The parallel I/O features supported by MPI-2 are discussed in Chapter 11. They build on intracommunicators and groups to define a set of processes involved in a parallel I/O operation and employ user-defined data types to describe the data content of a file. By having each process associate a related, but different, data type with a file using a file *view*, processes can read or write different parts of the file data in a parallel operation. The MPI-1 concept of collective communications extends well to parallel I/O operations, which are collective operations in the MPI-1 sense.

Synchronization Mechanisms

There are a large number of proposed and implemented synchronization mechanisms, some suitable for hardware implementation and some with enough complexity that software is routinely used in their implementations. Even with clever implementations that avoid the use of mutual exclusion to ensure atomicity, synchronizations can have significant performance impact. For this reason, many synchronization mechanisms have been developed that are tailored to specific jobs. Section 8.2 associated specific synchronizations with the data sharing jobs that they naturally support, and Section 8.1 characterized the types of information that different synchronizations might convey. Historically, synchronization operations have not been coherently developed and organized. The attempts of Chapter 8 to impose structure on them should be taken as only a first step. The number and diversity of synchronization operations used at this time in various systems justifies giving an overview of the subject by simply listing them and briefly defining their operation. Table B-1 presents a list of common synchronizations, and the remainder of this appendix is devoted to brief descriptions of the individual operations.

B.1 Hardware Level Synchronization

Machine level synchronization mechanisms are structurally simple enough that they can be implemented directly in hardware. In some, but not all, cases this means that code may need to be added to them to achieve some software level synchronization, which is natural to use in a program. The following is a fairly complete sampling of hardware synchronizations.

Read/write   Synchronization using only atomic read and write on a shared memory is possible but quite complex as the discussion of Chapter 8 makes clear. Typically, only mutual exclusion is implemented using the atomic read/write operations and all other synchronizations are built on top of it.

Table B-1   List of synchronizations and waiting mechanisms.

Hardware level	Software level
Read/write	Lock/unlock
Test-and-set	Critical section
Compare-and-swap	Named
Fetch-and-add	Conditional
Produce/consume: (memory cell)	Semaphores
	Binary
	Counting
Waiting mechanisms	Retry
Hardware	With wait queue
Reissue instruction	Active or passive signal
Set interrupt trigger	Events
Software	Messages
Spinlocks	Connection
Sleep/retest	(source, dest) pair
Sleep/wakeup	Channel
	Destination/tag
	Synchronization
	Rendezvous (CSP !/?)
	Blocking send
	Blocking receive
	Produce/consume: (data type)
	Monitors
	Cobegin/coend
	Join (fork)
	Barriers

Test-and-set   Test-and-set is an atomic memory transaction, which tests a bit for zero (clear) and if it is, sets it to one. The result of the test is returned so that the program may implement a wait and retest if the bit is already set. The discussion of Chapter 8 shows that implementation of mutual exclusion is fairly direct with this primitive available in hardware.

Compare-and-swap   This instruction was implemented on multiprocessing versions of the IBM System 370. It is also an atomic operation on the memory that includes a test as well as a possible change in the contents of the location referenced. The instruction tests the contents of the memory location against the contents of a register, and, if the two are equal, replaces the contents of the memory cell with the contents of a second register. If the contents of the memory cell is not equal to that of the first register, that register is loaded with the contents of the memory cell. This fairly complex instruction can be understood as a command to "store this value in memory provided I know what is there now, but if I don't know what is there, tell me so I can decide what to do." The instruction is particularly useful for managing linked lists that are shared by several processors.

Fetch-and-add   This instruction has both a defined action and a tacit assumption associated with it. The action is to return the contents of a memory cell and replace it with the sum of its original contents and an increment specified in the instruction. If multiple processors issue this instruction simultaneously for the same memory cell the results are defined to be the same as if the operations were all executed atomically in some serial order. The tacit assumption is that they are not, in fact, executed serially, but a clever interconnection network between the memory and the processors combines and processes the operations so as to give the effect of serial execution without requiring the time that serial execution would require. Other operations have been proposed in place of the add, fetch-and-replace, fetch-and-set, fetch-and-multiply, etc.

Produce/consume (memory cell)   This pair of operations combines both a synchronization state and a data value. The atomic Produce operation waits until the state of the memory cell is empty, writes a data value into it, and sets it full. The consume operation waits for the cell to be full, reads its value, and sets it empty. The "wait" operation is part of both primitives and was supported in hardware on the Denelcor HEP and Cray MTA supercomputers, which used these operations as their basic hardware synchronization mechanism. If waiting is not supported in hardware, similar operations that return a failure indication so that waiting can be done in software are possible. A key feature of these primitives is that the state test and change are atomic with the transfer of data. The operations are very similar to one-word send and receive message operations. The memory is required to have a one-bit full/empty indicator for each location.

B.2 Language Level Synchronization

At the language level, synchronization operations are built on top of the hardware primitives. They may reflect the hardware operations directly, with slight differences arising from the software and language environment, or they may be complex, using one or more hardware primitives and auxiliary variables with code to accomplish their purpose.

Lock/unlock   These two primitives are often used in matched pairs within a single process to begin and terminate a critical section and could be considered low-level features used to implement critical sections. The fact that they take an argument, usually thought of as a memory location, gives them some of the character of data oriented synchronizations. But there is no data *value* associated with the operations; the argument has only a two-valued *state*, locked or unlocked. It is possible to use these primitives for rudimentary signaling between processes so that they do not appear in matched pairs. In this case, the nature of the signal sent is also that of a pure *state*, lacking any *value*.

Critical section   The critical section is a control oriented synchronization primitive, which can be implemented easily by a matched lock/unlock pair. A critical section is a sequential code block with the property that no two critical section code blocks can be executed simultaneously by two different processes. This mutual exclusion also holds in the sense that a process may not be suspended in the middle of a critical section, another process allowed to execute code in a critical section, and the first process then allowed to continue. The code sections in critical sections are said to be mutually exclusive. The mutual exclusion is usually implemented by focusing on the entry to, and exit from, the critical section. A process must determine that no critical section is already occupied, report that it is now occupying a critical section, and proceed into the code body, all in an atomic manner that ensures that two processes cannot enter critical sections simultaneously. The lock/unlock operations are a natural way to implement the entry and exit. The state of the lock encodes the occupied or unoccupied state of the critical section.

Named critical sections   It is possible to associate a name with one or more critical sections. Mutual exclusion then applies only between critical sections with the same name. This makes the critical section even closer to lock/unlock, which have a named lock variable as their argument. It is not valid to nest unnamed critical sections or critical sections with the same name, but critical sections with different names may be nested meaningfully in some cases.

Conditional critical sections   The critical section is often used to manipulate some shared data structure. Sometimes the updating of a shared structure requires that it be in a particular state. An overly simple example is a shared list from which an element is to be removed. The element can only be removed if the list is nonempty. Instead of having a process enter a critical section protecting access to the shared structure and then finding that the structure is not in the correct state for the intended operation (by testing some condition on the shared variables), one can make entry to the critical section depend on the condition to be tested. The conditional critical section is made for this purpose. A conditional critical section may or may not have a name but always has a condition that must be satisfied before the process can enter the critical section. This condition should be constructed so that it can only be changed by another process in a critical section (of the same name). Entry to the critical section is, thus, controlled by an atomic determination that no other process is in its critical section (of the same name) and that the condition is satisfied.

Semaphores   The semaphore is a synchronization mechanism introduced by E. W. Dijkstra to support mutual exclusion and synchronized access to shared resources. A semaphore S is a special type of variable that may be initialized and then operated on by two atomic synchronization primitives *wait* and *signal*, called P(S) and V(S). Semaphores were first introduced in connection with multiprogrammed operating systems running on a single processor. They are usually thought of as having an associated queue of waiting processes, managed in either a FIFO or priority fashion. The shared queue is easily managed in the multiprogrammed uniprocessor environment but must be supported by some other synchronization mechanism in a true multiprocessor. Thus, there are also discussions of

semaphores that attempt to separate their synchronization action of causing certain processes to be delayed from the specific process management scheme used to implement and
terminate the delay.

Binary semaphores   A binary semaphore S can take the values one and zero. The
operation P(S) applied to a semaphore with value one will set S to zero and proceed.
If S = 0 then P(S) causes the process executing it to wait until S = 1. The test for the
waiting condition and the setting of S to zero are atomic, so two processes cannot
decide to proceed simultaneously. The operation V(S) simply sets S to one and never
causes the process executing V(S) to wait. If a shared queue of waiting processes is
associated with S, then V(S) removes one of the waiting processes from the queue
and makes it ready to run (perhaps by entering it into a ready queue).

Counting semaphores   A counting semaphore S may take on any nonnegative integer value. The P(S) operation tests the value, and if it is greater than zero, decrements
it by one and proceeds. If S is zero when tested by P(S) the process executing P(S) is
caused to wait (and perhaps enrolled on a wait queue). V(S) increments S by one and
does not block the process executing it. If S is zero and a nonempty wait queue is
present then V(S) does not change S but instead makes one of the waiting processes
ready to run.

Semaphores with retry   One way to think of implementing semaphores in a true multiprocessor environment is to have processes blocked by a P(S) operation repeatedly
testing the semaphore to see when it becomes greater than zero. An atomic test and
change operation can then decrement S and allow one blocked process to proceed.
V(S) would then simply increment S regardless of whether or not it was zero. In this
case there is no shared queue of waiting processes. The waiting processes "know
who they are" without a shared data structure to record them. Note that a process that
executes a V(S) on a zero semaphore and then immediately executes P(S) may find S
equal to one, even though other processes were already waiting when it executed
V(S).

Semaphores with wait queue   This is the usual assumption for semaphores used in
operating systems. There is a queue of waiting processes associated with each semaphore and a queue of processes that are ready to run. In a multiprocessor system,
these queues must be shared by the processors and synchronized by some lower level
mechanism. In this case it is often useful to allow the semaphore to take on negative
integer values, where the magnitude of the negative integer represents the current
length of the wait queue. The P(S) operation then decrements S, tests it for negative
and, if so, blocks the current process and puts it at the end of the wait queue for S. It
then resumes the next (highest priority) process that is ready to run. V(S) always
increments S and does not block the process executing V(S), but it also checks to see
if S is less than or equal to zero and, if so, removes the next process from the wait

queue for S and places it on the ready queue. Note that the accesses to the shared queue sequentialize operations on S to the extent that a process executing V(S) when other processes are waiting on S always makes one of these other processes ready, even if it proceeds to immediately execute a P(S) itself. This makes P and V with a wait queue a somewhat stronger synchronization than P and V with retry waiting, but of course, another form of synchronization must be added to synchronize access to the shared queue in the multiprocessor case.

Active or passive semaphore signaling   The key to the stronger synchronization in the case of the wait queue does not really depend on the existence of a queue. Instead, the issue is whether the V(S) operation is active or passive with respect to process scheduling. If V actively causes the change of state of a waiting process to ready, then the synchronization is strong. If V(S) merely records its occurrence (by incrementing S) and some other, asynchronous process monitoring S is responsible for changing the state of a waiting process, then there is no way to determine that the process made ready was actually waiting at the time V(S) occurred; it may have entered the wait queue immediately after the V(S) but before the test by the monitoring process.

Events   An event can also be considered a data type on which two operations, *post* and *await*, are defined. Multiple processes may *await* the occurrence of an event that another process will *post*. The posting of an event releases all processes that are awaiting it, in contrast to a V operation on a semaphore, which can release at most one waiting process. If several post operations occur in the course of a calculation, the implementation must ensure that every waiting process is released from only one *await* by a single occurrence of the event, even if it executes another *await* on the same event before all of the other waiting processes have been notified. Processes that have not executed an *await* are not affected by a *post*, implying that if a process executes *await* concurrently with another process' *post*, it is indeterminate whether it is immediately released or waits for the next *post* operation.

Messages   Messages consist of one or more data values explicitly transmitted by one process and explicitly recieved by another. A message may consist of a fixed number of information units (often bytes), a length and the specified number of units, or a record-like structure described by a given pattern. In the case of a number of uninterpreted i-units, the sender and receiver are assumed to agree on the structure of the message, and no checking is done.

Message connection   There are several ways to establish the path from the source of the message to its destination. The simplest is to have named processes and include the source and destination names as part of the message, but channels may be associated with the transmission path or message types may help establish a connection.

(Source, dest) pair connection In this case the send operation is of the form "send to process dest," and the receive of the form "receive from process source." It is also possible to broadcast or send a message to multiple receivers, but it is not possible to receive a message from multiple sources. Thus, source is a single process(or) designator while dest might specify one or a group of processes(ors).

Channel connection Message delivery can also be through a "channel" or mailbox. In this case send and receive operations are connected because they both specify the same channel. A channel holds a sequence of messages limited by the channel capacity. The ordering of messages from a given sender may, or may not, be preserved.

Destination/tag connection To facilitate a receiver handling messages from several sources, a sender can specify a type for the message by a unique tag and the receiver ask for the next message with that tag. The source is then not explicitly specified by the receiver but may be supplied to the receiver as part of the message.

Synchronization with messages Message transmission is a method for synchronization because the receipt of a message implicitly tells the receiver that the sender has reached the send instruction. The produce/consume synchronization discussed earlier under machine level primitives could be looked at as a one-word message mechanism where the connection is through a channel consisting of the memory cell. Produce corresponds to a send operation and consume to a receive.

Rendezvous synchronization (CSP !/?) C. A. R. Hoare proposed specific versions of send (!) and receive (?) as the only way in which communicating processes may exchange information. Both ! and ? are blocking in his Communicating Sequential Processes (CSP) language, and messages must be directed to, and received from, specific process names. The blocking nature of ! and ? makes the synchronization very tight; they must occur simultaneously in matched pairs. One can think of the message delivery system as having zero buffering capacity, with messages received simultaneously with their transmission. One of the important aspects of the CSP language is that, because processes can only communicate in this very tightly synchronized way, and because other nondeterministic aspects of the system are carefully defined and limited, there are systems for proving CSP algorithms correct. The large number of sources of nondeterminism in systems with shared memory or less restrictive communications makes formal proof of parallel algorithm correctness more difficult.

Synchronization with blocking or nonblocking send The synchronization properties of message passing operations are enhanced by the association of a process delay with the transmission of the message. A send operation may block the process doing the send until the message is actually received, or it may merely send the message and proceed with other work. The ability to send several messages before the first one is received is an immediate consequence of nonblocking send, and this implies that implementation of this type of send must include buffering of messages. Message queues can be associated with the sender, the receiver or both. If a message channel is used, it may be restricted to a maximum capacity of one or more messages that can be simultaneously buffered in the channel.

Synchronization with blocking or nonblocking receive   A receive operation may either wait until a message is available or may return a failure indication if no message is available from the specified source or channel. If there is a nonempty queue of messages at the receiver, a receive operation typically delivers the next message in order of receipt. Blocking receive is quite common and probably most often combined with nonblocking send on the principle that, because message transmission takes some time, a message should be sent as soon as possible, while there is still other work to do, but received only when it is definitely needed to proceed.

Produce/consume — data type   As a language-level synchronization mechanism, produce and consume function essentially the same as described for the machine level. The difference is that the data item dealt with is no longer a memory cell but a data type of the language, that might occupy more than one word of memory. A single full/empty indicator suffices for the entire data element, but the transfer of all the memory words involved must be atomic with the change of indicator state.

Monitors   Monitors bind synchronization to the data structures whose manipulation requires it. A monitor consists of a collection of variables forming the storage for the data structure, some code initializing the variables, and a set of procedures that are the only means for modifying the variables of the monitor (other than the initialization). Monitors are defined for use in a parallel environment, and the specification of what happens when multiple processes call procedures of the monitor simultaneously constitutes the associated synchronization. Execution of the same or different monitor procedures by parallel processes is guaranteed to be mutually exclusive, or atomic. Interesting issues in implementing monitors are how to do as much work as possible concurrently while still maintaining the effect of mutual exclusion and what to do about nested invocation of monitors.

Cobegin/coend   This control-oriented mechanism is primarily concerned with process management rather than synchronization, but a synchronization is implied. The cobegin/coend statements bracket the specification of several instruction streams to be executed in parallel. The implied synchronization occurs in connection with coend because it is assumed that all parallel instruction streams have completed before a single process proceeds to the statement following coend.

Join (fork)   A fork/join pair can be used for the same purpose as cobegin/coend. The synchronization, however, is explicitly associated with join, which may specify a number of processes (instruction streams) that must complete to satisfy the join or even a set of processes to participate in the operation.

Barriers   A barrier synchronizes a fixed set of processes. All processes must arrive at the barrier before any process proceeds past the barrier. One form of the barrier includes a block of sequential code that is executed by one process after all processes have arrived at the barrier and which is complete before any process proceeds past the barrier.

B.3 Waiting Mechanism

Because all synchronization is connected with coordinating the times of two or more events, a key feature is how the earlier one(s) is(are) caused to wait. The type and amount of system resources consumed by waiting processes is key to the effectiveness (or even usability) of an implementation of a synchronization mechanism.

Hardware waiting   If synchronization operations are issued with a frequency comparable to the rate of computation (fine-grained synchronization), then hardware support for the waiting mechanism is essential. Two lengths of time are important, the average and the worst case delay. With critical sections, for example, the average delay may be very small as a result of an extremely low collision probability while the worst case delay in the event of simultaneous requests for critical section entry may be fairly large.

  Reissue instruction   In the situation when average and worst case delays are small, a processor may simply reissue the instruction causing the wait. Care must be taken that the repeated issuing of synchronization instructions does not overload some part of the system. This mechanism makes most sense in connection with hardware supported multiprogramming, where other processes make use of the processor hardware between successive issues of the synchronization instruction.

  Set interrupt trigger   Failure in the attempt to obtain a lock may arm an interrupt to be sent to the attempting processor whenever that lock is released. The processor may then be given to another process and attempt to obtain the lock again only after it has been released. Of course, it may fail again because other processors may also be waiting for the same interrupt. Description in terms of locks is only an example; other synchronizations with a well-defined release condition can use the same mechanism.

Software waiting   The software implementation of a synchronization may include the instructions necessary to support waiting. Delay loops, operating system calls, or a combination of the two may be used.

  Spinlocks   The "spin" method for waiting involves an explicitly coded waiting loop and is usually used in waiting for a lock to be cleared. The loop can usually be accomplished with two or three instructions (test-and-set, conditional branch) so that, as with the hardware reissue, a heavy load may be placed on some system resources.

  Sleep/retest   A waiting loop may include an operating system call to reallocate the processor for some delay period to increase the probability that the waiting condition has been satisfied when the test is issued again. The length of the delay (or sleep) time is important to the smooth operation of synchronized processes.

Sleep/wakeup In this case, the synchronization command that may cause another process to proceed also invokes the operating system, which, by means of an interprocessor interrupt or similar method, explicitly reschedules one or more delayed processes.

Bibliography

1. J. M. Abelo and J. S. Vitter, eds., *External Memory Algorithms*, Vol. 50 of *DIMACS: Series in Discrete Mathematics and Theoretical Computer Science*, American Mathematical Society, Providence, RI (1999).

2. W. B. Ackerman, "Dataflow languages," *IEEE Computer*, Vol. 15, No. 2, pp. 15–25 (Feb. 1982).

3. S. Adve and K. Gharachorloo, "Shared memory consistency models: A tutorial," *IEEE Computer*, Vol. 29, No. 12, pp. 66–76 (Dec. 1996).

4. A. Agarwal et al., "The MIT Alewife Machine: A large-scale distributed memory multiprocessor," in *Scalable Shared Memory Multiprocessors*, M. Dubois and S. Thakkar, eds., Kluwer Academic Publishers, Norwell, MA (1992).

5. A. Agarwal, "Performance tradeoffs in multithreaded processors," *IEEE Transactions on Parallel and Distributed Systems*, Vol. 3, No. 5 (Oct. 1992).

6. T. Agerwala and Arvind, "Data flow systems: Guest editor's introduction," *Computer*, Vol. 15, No. 2, pp. 10–13 (Feb. 1982).

7. S. Ahuja, N. Carriero, and D. Gelernter, "Linda and friends," *IEEE Computer*, Vol. 19, No. 8, pp. 16–34 (1986).

8. M. M. Ajmone, G. Balbo, and G. Conte, *Performance Models for Multiprocessor Systems*, McGraw-Hill, New York (1989).

9. S. G. Akl, *The Design and Analysis of Parallel Algorithms*, Prentice Hall Inc. (1989).

10. G. Alaghband and H. F. Jordan, "Overview of the Force scientific parallel language," *Scientific Programming*, Vol. 3, pp. 33–47 (1994).

11. S. Allan and R. Oldehoeft, "HEP SISAL: Parallel functional programming," in Kowalik, ed., *Parallel and MIMD Computation: HEP Supercomputers and Applications*, MIT Press, Cambridge, MA (1985).

12. J. R. Allen and K. Kennedy, "PCF: A program to convert Fortran to parallel Fortran," in Hwang, ed., *Supercomputers: Design and Applications*, IEEE Computer Society Press, Los Alamitos, CA (1984).

13. J. R. Allen and K. Kennedy, "Automatic translation of Fortran programs to vector form," *ACM Transactions on Programming Languages and Systems*, pp. 491–542 (Oct. 1987).

14. J. R. Allen and K. Kennedy, *Optimizing Compilers for Modern Architectures*, Morgan Kaufmann Publishers San Francisco, CA (2001).

15. G. S. Almasi and A. Gottlieb, *Highly Parallel Computing*, 2nd edition, Benjamin Cummings, Redwood City, CA (1994).

16. R. Alverson, D. Callahan, D. Cummings, B. Koblenz, A. Poterfield, and B. Smith, "The Tera computer system," *Proceedings of the ACM International Conference on Supercomputing,* Amsterdam pp. 1–6 The Netherlands (June. 1990).

17. S. Amarasinghe and M. Lam, "Communication optimization and code generation for distributed memory machines," *Proceedings of the ACM SIGPLAN '93 Conference on Programming Language Design and Implementation,* Albuquerque, NM (June 1993).

18. G. M. Amdahl, "Validity of the single processor approach of achieving large scale computing capabilities," *AFIPS Conference Proceedings*, Vol. 30, pp. 483–485 (1967).

19. M. Anaratone, E. Arnould, T. Gross, H. T. Kung, M. S. Lam, O. Mezilcioglu, K. Sarocky, and J. A. Webb, "Warp architecture and implementation," *Proceedings of the 13th Annual International Symposium on Computer Architecture*, Computer Science Press, Tokyo, pp. 346–356 (June 1986).

20. T. E. Anderson, "The performance of spin lock alternatives for shared-memory multiprocessors," *IEEE Transactions on Parallel and Distributed Systems,* Vol. 1, No. 1 (Jan. 1990).

21. G. R. Andrews, *Concurrent Programming: Principles and Practices*, Benjamin/Cummings, Redwood, CA (1991).

22. G. R. Andrews and F. B. Schneider, "Concepts and notations for concurrent programming," *Computing Surveys*, Vol. 15, No. 1, pp. 3–43 (March 1983).

23. J. Archibald and J. L. Baer, "Cache coherence protocols: Evaluation using a multiprocessor simulation model," *ACM Transactions Computer Systems*, Vol. 4, No. 4, pp. 273–298 (Nov. 1986).

24. N. S. Arenstorf and H. F. Jordan, "Comparing barrier algorithms," *Parallel Computing*, Vol. 12, pp. 157–170 (1989).

25. B. W. Arden and H. Lee, "Analysis of chordal ring network," *IEEE Transactions on Computers,* Vol. 30, No. 4, pp. 291–294 (April 1981).

26. Arvind and D. E. Culler, "Dataflow architectures," *Annual Review of Computer Science,* Vol. 1, pp. 225–253 (1986).

27. Arvind and R. A. Iannucci, "Two fundamental issues in multiprocessing," *Proceedings of DFVLR Conference of 1987 on Parallel Processing in Science and Engineering*, Bonn-Bad Godesberg, West Germany (June 1987).

28. Arvind and R. S. Nikhil, "Executing a program on the MIT Tagged-Token dataflow architecture," *IEEE Transactions on Computers*, Vol. 39, No. 3, pp. 300–318 (March 1990).

29. K. G. Ashar, *Magnetic Disk Drive Technology: Heads, Media, Channel, Interfaces, and Integration*, IEEE Press, New York (1997).

30. W. C. Athas and C. L. Seitz, "Multicomputers: Message-passing concurrent computers," *IEEE Computer*, Vol. 21, No. 8, pp. 9–24 (Aug. 1988).

31. T. Axelrod, "Effects of synchronization barriers on multiprocessor performance," *Parallel Computing,* Vol. 3, No. 2, pp. 129–140 (1986).

32. D. F. Bacon, S. L. Graham, O. J. Sharp, "Compiler transformations for high-performance computing," *ACM Computing Surveys*, Vol. 26, No. 4, pp. 345–420 (Dec. 1994).

33. J. L. Baer and D. P. Bovet, "Compilation of arithmetic expressions for parallel computations," *Proceedings IFIP Congress 1968*, North Holland, Amsterdam, pp. 340–346 (1968).

34. J. L. Baer, *Computer Systems Architecture*, Computer Science Press, Rockville, MD (1980).

35. U. Banerjee, S. C. Chen, D. J. Kuck, and R. A. Towle, "Time and parallel processor bounds for Fortran-like loops," *IEEE Transactions on Computers*, Vol. C-28, No. 9 (Sept. 1979).

36. U. Banerjee, *Dependence Analysis for Supercomputing*, Kluwer Academic Press, Boston, MA (1988).

37. U. Banerjee, *Loop Transformations for Restructuring Compilers: The Foundations*, Kluwer Academic Publishers, Norwell, MA (1993).

38. G. H. Barnes, R. M. Brown, M. Kato, D. J. Kuck, D. L. Slotnick, and R. A. Stokes, "The ILLIAC IV computer," *IEEE Transactions on Computers*, Vol. 17, No. 8, pp. 746–757 (Aug. 1968).

39. K. Batcher, "Design of a massively parallel processor," *IEEE Transactions on Computers*, Vol. 29, No. 9, pp. 836–840 (Sept. 1980).

40. K. Batcher, "The Flip network in STARAN," *Proceedings of International Conference on Parallel Processing*, pp. 65–71 (1976).

41. C. J. Beckman and C. D. Polychronopoulos, "The effect of barrier synchronization and scheduling overhead on parallel loops," *International Conference on Parallel and Distributed Processing,* IEEE Computer Society (1989).

42. J. Beetem, M. Denneau, and D. Weingarten, "The GF11 supercomputer," *Proceedings of the 12th Annual International Symposium on Computer Architecture*, pp. 363–376, Boston, MA (May 1985).

43. G. Bell, "Ultracomputer: A teraflop before its time," *Communications of the ACM*, Vol. 35, No. 8, pp. 27–47 (1992).

44. G. Bell and A. Newell, *Computer Structures: Readings and Examples*, McGraw-Hill, New York (1970).

45. M. S. Benten and H. F. Jordan, "Multiprogramming and the performance of parallel programs," *Proceedings of the 3rd SIAM Conference on Parallel Processing for Scientific Computing,* Los Angeles, CA (Dec. 1987).

46. M. Ben-Ari, *Principles of Concurrent and Distributed Programming*, Prentice-Hall, Englewood Cliffs, NJ (1990).

47. A. J. Bernstein, "Analysis of programs for parallel processing," *IEEE Transactions on Computers*, pp. 746–757 (Oct. 1966).

48. M. Berry et al., "The perfect club benchmarks: Effective performance evaluation of supercomputers," *International Journal of Supercomputer Applications,* Vol. 3, No. 5, pp. 40 (1989).

49. D. P. Bertsekas and J. N. Tsitsiklis, *Parallel and Distributed Computation*, Prentice-Hall, Englewood Cliffs, NJ (1989).

50. L. N. Bhuyan and D. P. Agrawal, "Design and performance of generalized interconnection networks," *IEEE Transactions on Computers*, pp. 1081–1090 (Dec. 1983).

51. P. Bitar and A. M. Despain, "Multiprocessor cache synchronization: Issues, innovations, and evolutions," *Proceedings of the 13th Annual International Symposium on Computer Architecture* (1986).

52. P. Bitar, "The weakest memory-access order," *Journal of Parallel and Distributed Computing*, Vol. 15, pp. 305–331 (1992).

53. B. Boothe and A. Ranade, "Improved multithreading techniques for hiding communication latency in multiprocessor," *Proceedings of the 19th Annual International Symposium on Computer Architecture*, Australia (May, 1992).

54. S. Borkar, R. Cohn, G. Fox, T. Gross, H. Hung, M. S. Lam, M. Levine, B. Moore, W. Moore, C. Peterson, J. Susman, J. Sutton, J. Urbanski, and J. A. Webb, "Supporting systolic and memory communication in iWARP," *Proceedings of the 17th Annual International Symposium on Computer Architecture*, pp. 70–81 (May 1990).

55. B. Boothe and A. Ranade, "Improved multithreading techniques for hiding communication latency in multiprocessor," *Proceedings of the 19th Annual International Symposium on Computer Architecture*, Australia (May, 1992).

56. K. C. Bowler, and G. Stuart Pawley, "Molecular dynamics and Montecarlo simulation in solid-state and elementary particle physics," *Proceedings of the IEEE*, Vol. 74, pp. 42–55 (January 1984).

57. W. S. Brainerd, C. H. Golberg, and J. C. Adams, *Programmer's guide to Fortran 90*, McGraw-Hill, New York (1990).

58. I. Y. Bucher, "The computational speed of supercomputers," *Performance Evaluation Review: Proceedings of ACM Sigmetrics Conference on Measurement and Modeling of Computer Systems,* pp. 151–165 (Aug. 1983).

59. W. Buchholz, "The IBM System/370 vector architecture," *IBM Systems Journal*, Vol. 25, pp. 51–62 (1986).

60. H. Burkhardt, *Technical Summary of KSR-1*, Kendall Square Research Coporation, 170 Tracer Lane, Waltham, MA, 02154 (1992).

61. D. Callahan, "Task granularity studies on a many-processor CRAY-XMP," *Parallel Computing*, pp. 109–118 (June 1985).

62. D. Callahan, K. Cooper, R. Hood, K. Kennedy, and L. Torczon, "ParaScope: A parallel programming environment," *International Journal of Supercomputer Applications*, Vol. 2, No. 4 (1988).

63. D. Callahan, K. Kennedy and A. Porterfield, "Analyzing and visualizing performance of memory hierarchies," *Performance Instrumentation and Visualization,* R. Koskela and M. Simmons, eds., pp. 1–26 (1990).

64. D. Callahan, "Recognizing and parallelizing bounded recurrences," *Tera Computer Company,* Internal report (Aug. 1991).

65. E. A. Carmona and M. D. Rice, "Modeling the serial and parallel fractions of a parallel algorithm," *Journal of Parallel and Distributed Computing*, Vol. 2, No. 2, pp. 221–229 (1991).

66. N. Carriero and D. Gelernter, "How to write parallel programs: a guide to the perplexed," *Journal of the ACM*, Vol. 35, No. 3, pp. 323–357 (Sept. 1989).

67. CDC, *Cyber 200/Model 205 Technical Description*, Control Data Corporation (Nov. 1980).

68. CDC, "Introduction to Cyber 2000 Architecture," *Technical Report 60000457*, Control Data Corporation, St. Paul, MN (1990).

69. D. Chaiken, C. Fields, K. Kwihara, and A. Agrawal, "Directory-based cache coherence in large-scale multiprocessors," *IEEE Computer*, Vol. 23, No. 6, pp. 49–59 (June 1990).

70. S. C. Chen, C. C. Hsuing, J. L. Larson, and E. R. Somdahl, "Cray X-MP: A multiprocessor supercomputer," *Vector and Parallel Processors: Architecture, Applications, and Performance Evaluation*, M. Ginsberg, ed., North Holland (1986).

71. H. Cheng, "Vector pipelining, chaining, and speed on IBM 3090 and Cray X/MP," *IEEE Computer*, Vol. 22, No. 9, pp. 31–44 (Sept. 1989).

72. C. Y. Chin and K. Hwang, "Packet switching networks for multiprocessors and dataflow computers," *IEEE Transactions on Computers*, pp. 991–1003 (Nov. 1984).

73. P. F. Corbett and D. G. Feitelson, "The Vesta parallel file system," *ACM Transactions on Computer Systems*, Vol. 14, No. 3, pp. 225–264 (Aug. 1996).

74. M. Cosnard and D. Trystram, *Parallel Algorithms and Architectures*, International Thompson Computer Press, London, UK (1995).

75. P. J. Courtois, F. Heymans, and D. J. Parnas, "Concurrent control with 'readers' and 'writers'," *Communications of the ACM*, Vol. 14, No. 10, pp. 667–668 (Oct. 1971).

76. Cray, *CRAY-1 Computer System Hardware Reference Manual*, Cray Research Inc., Eagan, MN (1977).

77. Cray, *CRAY Y/MP Functional Description Manual*, Cray Research Inc., Eagan, MN (1989).

78. Cray, *CRAY Y/MP C-90 Supercomputer System*, Cray Research Inc., Eagan, MN (1991).

79. Cray, "*Cray T3D: Technical Summary,*" Cray Research, Inc., Eagan, MN (Sept. 1993).

80. D. E. Culler, J. P. Singh, and A. Gupta, *Parallel Computer Architecture*, Morgan Kaufmann Publishers, San Francisco, CA (1999).

81. G. Cybenko and D. J. Kuck, "Revolution or evolution," *IEEE Spectrum*, Vol. 29, No. 9, pp. 39–41 (Sept. 1992).

82. W. J. Dally and C. L. Seitz, "The Torus routing chip," *Journal of Distributed Computing*, Vol. 1, No. 3, pp. 187–196 (1986).

83. W. J. Dally and C. L. Seitz, "Deadlock-free message routing in multiprocessor interconnection networks," *IEEE Transactions on Computers*, Vol. 36, No. 5, pp. 547–553 (May 1987).

84. W. J. Dally, "Performance analysis of k-ary n-Cube interconnection networks," *IEEE Transactions on Computers*, Vol. 36, No. 5, pp. 775–785 (June 1990).

85. W. J. Dally, J. A. S. Fiske, J. S. Keen, R. A. Lethin, M. D. Noakes, P. R. Nuth, R. E. Davison, and G. A. Flyer, "The Message Driven Processor: A multicomputer processing node with efficient mechanisms," *IEEE Micro,* Vol. 12, No. 2, pp. 23–39 (April 1992).

86. F. Darema, D. George, V. Norton, and G. Pfister, "A single-program-multiple-data computational model for EPEX/Fortran," *Parallel Computing*, Vol. 7, pp. 11–24 (1988).

87. A. L. Davis and R. M. Keller, "Data flow program graphs," *Computer*, Vol. 15, pp. 26–41 (Feb. 1982).

88. P. J. Denning, "Working set model for program behavior," *Communications of the ACM*, Vol. 11, No. 6, pp. 323–333 (June 1968).

89. P. J. Denning, "Virtual memory," *ACM Computing Surveys,* Vol. 2 (September, 1970).

90. J. B. Dennis, "Data flow supercomputers," *Computer*, Vol. 13, pp. 48–56 (November, 1980).

91. E. W. Dijkstra, "Solution to a problem in concurrent programming control," *Communications of the ACM*, Vol. 8, No. 9 (Sept. 1965).

92. E. W. Dijkstra, "Cooperating Sequential Processes," in F. Genuys, ed., *Programming Languages*, Academic Press, New York (1968).

93. A. Dinning, "A survey of synchronization methods for parallel computers," *IEEE Computer*, Vol. 22, No. 7 (July 1989).

94. J. J. Dongara, ed., *Experimental Parallel Computing Architectures*, Amsterdam: North Holland (1987).

95. M. Dubois and S. Thakkar, eds., *Cache and Interconnect Architectures in Multiprocessors*, Kluwer Academic Publishers, Boston, MA (1990).

96. M. Dubois and S. Thakkar, eds., *Scalable Shared-Memory Multiprocessors*, Kluwer Academic Publishers, Boston, MA (1992).

97. M. Dubois, J. Skeppstedt, and P. Stenstrom, "Essential misses and data traffic in coherence protocols," *Journal of Parallel and Distributed Computing*, Vol. 29, No. 2, pp. 108–125 (Sept. 1995).

98. R. Duncan, "A survey of parallel computer architectures," *IEEE Computer*, Vol. 23, No. 2, pp. 5–16 (Feb. 1990).

99. S. Eggers and R. Katz, "A characterization of sharing in parallel programs and its application to coherence protocol evaluation," *Proceedings of the 15th Annual International Symposium of Computer Architecture* IEEE Computer Society, pp. 384–392 (1988).

100. S. Eggers, J. Zahorjan, and E. D. Lazowzka, "Speedup versus efficiency in parallel systems," *IEEE Transactions on Computers*, Vol. 38, No. 3, pp. 408–423 (March 1989).

101. T. von Eicken, D. E. Culler, S. Goldstein, and K. E. Schauser, "Active messages: A mechanism for integrated communication and computation," *Proceedings of the 19th International Symposium on Computer Architecture*, ACM Press (May 1992).

102. S. Eisenbach, *Functional Programming- Languages, Tools, and Architectures*, Halstead Press/John Wiley, New York (1987).

103. EMC, *EMC CLARiiON FC4700 System, Specifications*, EMC Corporation, Hopkins, Mass., www.EMC.com (2001).

104. Encore, *Multimax Technical Summary,* Encore Computer Corporation, Marlboro, MA (1986).

105. D. G. Feitelson, P. F. Corbett, S. J. Baylor, and Y. Hsu, "Parallel I/O subsystems in massively parallel supercomputers," *IEEE Parallel and Distributed Technology*, Vol. 3, No. 3, pp. 33–47 (Fall 1995).

106. T. Y. Feng, "A survey of interconnection networks," *IEEE Computer*, Vol. 14, No. 12, pp. 12–27 (Dec. 1981).

107. M. W. Ferrante, "Cyberplus and Map V interprocessor communications for parallel and array processor systems," in Karplus, ed., *Multiprocessors and Array Processors*, Simulation Councils Inc., San Diego, CA (1987).

108. J. A. Fisher, "Very long instruction word architectures and the ELI-512," *Proceedings of the 10th Symposium on Computer Architecture*, pp. 140–150, ACM Press, New York (1983).

109. Flexible Computer, *Multicomputing Multitasking Operating System (MMOS) Reference Manual,* Flexible Computer Corporation, Dallas, TX (1986).

110. M. J. Flynn, "Some computer organizations and their effectiveness," *IEEE Transactions on Computers*, Vol. 21, No. 9, pp. 948–960 (Sept. 1972).

111. M. J. Flynn, *Computer Architecture*, Jones and Bartlett, Sudbury, MA (1995).

112. D. E. Foulser and R. Schreiber, "The Saxpy Matrix-1: A general-purpose systolic computer," *IEEE Computer*, Vol. 20, No. 7, pp. 35–43 (July 1987).

113. P. Frederickson, R. Jones, and B. Smith, "Synchronization and control of parallel algorithms," *Parallel Computing,* Vol. 2, No. 3, pp. 265–254 (1986).

114. M. Furtney, R. Kuhn, B. Leasure and E. Plachy, "PCF Fortran: Language definition," *Parallel Computing Forum*, Kuck & Associates, 1906 Fox Drive, Champaign, IL 61820, Version 1 (Aug. 16, 1988).

115. D. Gannon, W. Jalby, and K. Gallivan, "Strategies for global and local memory management by global transformation," *Journal of Parallel and Distributed Computing,* Vol. 5, pp. 587–616 (1988).

116. D. D. Gajski, D. A. Padua, D. J. Kuck, and R. H. Kuhn, "A secondary opinion on dataflow machines and languages," *Computer*, Vol. 15, pp. 58–69 (Feb. 1982).

117. J. L. Gaudiot and L. Bic, *Advanced Topics in Dataflow Computing,* Prentice-Hall, Englewood Cliffs, NJ (1991).

118. D. Gelernter, A. Nicolau, and D. Padua, *Languages and Compilers for Parallel Computing*, MIT Press, Cambridge, MA (1990).

119. K. Gharachorloo, D. Lenoski, J. Laudon, P. Gibbons, and J. Hennessy, "Memory consistency and event ordering in scalable shared-memory multiprocessors," *Proceedings of the 17th Annual International Symposium on Computer Architecture* (June 1990).

120. K. Gharachorloo and K. R. Traub, "Multithreading: A revisionist view of dataflow architecture," *Proceedings of the 18th Annual International Symposium on Computer Architecture* (May 1991).

121. K. Gharachorloo, A. Adve, A. Gupta, J. Hennessy, and M. Hill, "Programming for different memory consistency models," *Journal of Parallel and Distributed Computing* (Aug. 1992).

122. G. Goff, K. Kennedy, and C-W. Tseng, "Practical dependence testing," *Proceedings of the ACM SIGPLAN '91 Conference on Programming Language Design and Implementation*, pp. 15–29 (June 1991).

123. A. Gottlieb, R. Grishman, C. P. Kruskal, K. P. McAuliffe, L. Rudolph, and M. Snir, "The NYU Ultracomputer—Designing an MIMD shared memory parallel computer," *IEEE Transactions on Computers*, Vol. C-32, No. 2, pp. 175–189 (Feb. 1983).

124. G. Graunke and S. Thakkar, "Synchronization algorithms for shared-memory multiprocessors," *IEEE Computer*, Vol. 23, No. 6, pp. 60–69 (June 1990).

125. R. I. Greenberg and C. E. Leisereson, "Randomized routing on Fat Trees," *Advances in Computing Research*, Vol. 7, pp. 345–374 (1989).

126. W. Gropp, S. Huss-Lederman, A. Lumsdaine, E. Lusk, B. Nitzberg, W. Saphir, and M. Snir, *MPI: The Complete Reference (Vol. 2)*, MIT Press, Cambridge, MA (Sept. 1998).

127. A. Gupta, W. D. Weber, and T. Mowry, "Reducing memory and traffic requirements for scalable directory-based cache coherence schemes," *Proceedings of International Conference on Parallel Processing*, pp. 312–321 (1990).

128. A. Gupta, J. Hennesy, K. Gharachorloo, T. Mowry, and W. Weber, "Comparative evaluation of latency reducing and tolerating techniques," *Proceedings of 18th Annual International Symposium on Computer Architecture* pp. 254–263 Toronto (May 1991).

129. J. R. Gurd, J. Watson, "Data driven systems for high speed parallel computing: Part 1: Structuring software for parallel execution: Part 2: Hardware design," *Computer Design*, pp. 91–100, pp. 97–106 (June & July 1980).

130. J. R. Gurd, C. Kirkham, and J. Watson, "The Manchester prototype dataflow computer," *Communications of the ACM*, Vol. 28, No. 1, pp. 36–45 (Jan. 1985).

131. J. L. Gustafson, "Reevaluating Amdahl's law," *Communications of the ACM*, Vol. 31, No. 5, pp. 532–533 (May 1988).

132. J. L. Gustavson, G. R. Montry, and R.E. Benner, "Development of parallel methods for a 1024-processor hypercube," *SIAM Journal of Scientific and Statistical Computing,* Vol. 9, No. 4, pp. 609–638 (July 1988).

133. E. Hagersten, A. Landin, and S. Haridi, "DDM—A cache-only memory architecture," *IEEE Computer,* Vol. 25, No. 9 (Sept. 1992).

134. W. Händler, "The impact of classification schemes on computer architecture," *Proceedings of International Conference on Parallel Processing* (Aug. 1977).

135. J. P. Hayes, T. N. Mudge, Q. F. Stout, S. Colley, and J. Palmer, "Architecture of Hypercube supercomputer," *Proceedings of International Conference on Parallel Processing*, pp. 653–660 (1986).

136. M. T. Heath, ed., *Hypercube Multiprocessors*, SIAM, Philadelphia (1987).

137. J. L. Hennessy and D. A Patterson, *Computer Architecture: A Quantitative Approach*, Morgan Kaufmann, San Mateo, CA (1990).

138. J. L. Hennessy and N. P. Jouppi, "Computer Technology and Architecture: An Evolving Interaction," *IEEE Computer*, Vol. 24, No. 9, pp. 18–29 (Sept. 1991).

139. W. D. Hillis, *The Connection Machine*, MIT Press, Cambridge, Mass (1987).

140. R. G. Hintz and D. P. Tate, "Control Data STAR-100 processor design," *Proceedings COMPCON*, IEEE No. 72CH0659-3C, pp. 1–4 (1972).

141. K. Hiraki, K. Nishida, S. Sekiguchi, T. Shimada, and T. Yiba, "The SIGMA-1 dataflow supercomputer: A challenge for new generation supercomputing systems," *Journal of Information Processing*, Vol. 10, No. 4, pp. 219–226 (1987).

142. C. A. R. Hoare, "An axiomatic basis for computer programming," *Communications of the ACM*, Vol. 12, No. 10, pp. 576–580 (Oct. 1969).

143. C. A. R. Hoare, "Monitors: An operating system structuring concept," *Communications of the ACM*, Vol. 17, No. 10, pp. 549–557 (Oct. 1974).

144. R. W. Hockney and C. R. Jesshope, *Parallel Computers 2*, Adam Hilger Ltd. (1988).

145. J. Hoffman, "HIPPI-6400 technology dissemination," in *Proceedings of the SPIE—The International Society for Optical Engineering: Broadband Access Systems*, Vol. 2917, pp. 422–430 (Nov. 1996).

146. S. J. Hong, and R. Nair, "Wire-routing machines—New tools for VLSI physical design," *Proceedings of the IEEE*, Vol. 73, pp. 57–65 (Jan. 1983).

147. R. M. Hord, *The Illiac IV: The First Supercomputer*, Computer Science Press (1982).

148. J. V. Huber, Jr., C. L. Elford, D. A. Reed, A. A. Chien, and D. S. Blumenthal, "PPFS: A high performance portable parallel file system," *Proceedings of 1995 Int'nl Conf. on Supercomputing*, pp. 385–394 (July 1995).

149. K. Hwang and F. A. Briggs, *Computer Architecture and Parallel Processing*, McGraw-Hill, New York (1984).

150. K. Hwang, *Advanced Computer Architecture, Parallelism, Scalability, Programmability*, McGraw-Hill, New York (1993).

151. IBM Corp., IBM 3838 Array Processor Functional Characteristics, No. 6A24-3639-0, File No. S-370-08, IBM Corp. Endicott, NY (Oct. 1976).

152. IBM Corp., "IBM System/360 principles of operation," *Technical Report GA22-6821-4* (1970).

153. IBM Corp., "IBM System/360 system summary," *Technical Report GA22-6810-8* (1970).

154. Intel, *Paragon XP/S Product Overview*, Intel Corporation, Supercomputer System Division, Beaverton, OR (Nov. 1991).

155. R. Jain, *FDDI Handbook: High Speed Networking Using Fiber and Other Media*, Addison-Wesley, Reading, MA (1994).

156. R. Jain, J. Werth, and J. C. Browne, eds., *Input/Output in Parallel and Distributed Computer Systems*, Kluwer Academic Publishers, Norwell, MA (1996).

157. J. Jájá, *An Introduction to Parallel Algorithms*, Addison-Wesley, Reading, MA (1992).

158. S. L. Johnsson, and C. T. Ho, "Optimum broadcasting and personalized communication in hypercubes," *IEEE Transactions on Computers*, Vol. C-38, No. 9, pp. 1249–1268 (Sept. 1989).

159. H. Jordan, "A special purpose architecture for finite element analysis," *Proceedings of the 1978 International Conference on Parallel Processing*, IEEE Computer Society Press, pp. 263–266 (1978).

160. H. F. Jordan, "Performance and program structure in a large shared memory multiprocessor," in *New Computing Environments: Parallel, Vector and Systolic*, Arthur Wouk, ed., pp. 201–217, SIAM, Philadelphia, PA (1986).

161. H. F. Jordan, "Performance: The need for an in-depth view," Chap. 13 in *Performance Instrumentation and Visualization*, M. Simmons and R. Koskela, eds., ACM Press, New York (1990).

162. H. F. Jordan, "Interpreting parallel processor performance measurements," *SIAM Journal on Scientific and Statistical Computing*, Vol. 8, No. 2, pp. s220–s226 (March 1987).

163. H. F. Jordan, "The Force," in *The Characteristics of Parallel Algorithms*, L. Jamieson, D. Gannon and R. Douglass, eds., Chapter 16, MIT Press, Cambridge, MA (1987).

164. H. F. Jordan, "Shared versus distributed memory multiprocessors," *Proceedings of the Workshop on the Use of Parallel Processors in Metheorology*, European Centre for Medium Range Weather Forecasts, Reading, UK (Nov. 1990).

165. H. F. Jordan, "Scalability of data transport," *Proceedings of Scalable High Performance Computing Conference SHPCC-92*, pp. 1–8, IEEE Computer Society Press, Williamsburg, Virginia (April 1992).

166. H. F. Jordan, "Structuring parallel algorithms in a shared memory MIMD environment," *Parallel Computing*, Vol. 3, pp. 93–110 (1986).

167. H. F. Jordan and B. Rodriguez, "Performance prediction from data transport," *Software for Parallel Computation, Proceedings of 1992 NATO Workshop,* J. S. Kowalik, ed., Springer Verlag, New York (1993).

168. Y-J. Ju and H. G. Dietz, "Reduction of cache coherence overhead by compiler data layout and loop transformation," *Proceedings of 4th Workshop on Programming Languages and Compilers for Parallel Computing,* pp. Q1–Q15, Santa Clara, California (Aug. 1991).

169. M. A. Kandamir, A. Choudhary, J. Ramanujam, and R. Bordewekar, "Compilation techniques for out-of-core parallel computations," *Parallel Computing,* Vol. 24, Nos. 3–4, pp. 597–628 (May 1998).

170. R. M. Karp, R. E. Miller, and S. Winograd, "The organization of computations for uniform recurrence equations," *Journal of ACM,* Vol. 14, No. 3, pp. 563–590 (July 1967).

171. Kendall Square Research Corporation, *KSR-1 Principles of Operation,* Waltham, MA (1991).

172. P. Kermani and L. Kleinrock, "Virtual cut-through: A new communication switching technique," *Computer Networks,* Vol. 3, No. 4, pp. 267–286 Newyork (1979).

173. L. Kleinrock, *Queueing Systems,* Wiley, Newyork (1975). Two volumes.

174. D. E. Knuth, *The Art of Computer Programming: Volume 1/Fundamental Algorithms,* Addison-Wesley, Reading, MA (1968).

175. D. E. Knuth, "Big omicron, big omega and big theta," *SIGACT News (ACM),* Vol. 8, No. 2, pp. 18–24 (1976).

176. C. H. Koelbel, D. B. Loveman, R. S. Schreiber, G. L. Steele, Jr., and M. E. Zosel, *The High Performance Fortran Handbook,* MIT Press, Cambridge, MA (1994).

177. C. Koelbel, P. Mehrotra, and J. Van Rosendale, "Semi-automatic process partitioning for parallel computation," *International Journal of Parallel Programming,* Vol. 16, No. 5, pp. 365–382 (1987).

178. P. M. Kogge, *The Architecture of Pipelined Computers,* McGraw-Hill, New York (1981).

179. J. S. Kowalik, ed., *Parallel MIMD Computation: HEP Supercomputer and Applications,* MIT Press, Cambridge, MA (1985).

180. F. Kröger, *Temporal Logic of Programs,* New York, Springer-Verlag (1987).

181. C. P. Kruskal and M. Snir, "The performance of multistage interconnection networks for multiprocessors," *IEEE Transactions on Computers,* Vol. C-32, No. 12 (Dec. 1983).

182. D. J. Kuck, "ILLIAC IV software and application programming," *IEEE Transactions on Computers,* Vol. 17, No. 8, pp. 758–770 (Aug. 1968).

183. D. J. Kuck, "Dependence graph and compiler optimizations," *8th Annual ACM Symposium on Principles of Programming Languages,* pp. 207–218 (Jan. 1981).

184. D. J. Kuck, R. H. Kuhn, B. Leasure, and M. Wolfe, "The structure of an advanced retargetable vectorizer," in K. Hwang, ed., *Supercomputers: Design and Applications,* pp. 163–178, IEEE Computer Society Press, Los Alamitos, CA (1984).

185. D. J. Kuck, E. S. Davidson, D. H. Lawrie, and A. H. Sameh, "Parallel supercomputing today—The Cedar approach," *Science,* Vol. 213, No. 2 (Feb. 1986).

186. J. T., Kuehn and B. Smith, "The Horizon supercomputer system: Architecture and software," *Proceedings of Supercomputing 1991,* Orlando, FL (Nov. 1991).

187. V. Kumar, A. Grama, A. Gupta, and G. Karypis, *Introduction to Parallel Computing: Design and Analysis of Parallel Algorithms,* Benjamin/Cummings, Redwood City, CA (1994).

188. H. T. Kung and C. E. Leiserson, "Systolic arrays (for VLSI)," Duff and Stewart, eds., *Sparse Matrix Proceedings,* Knoxville, TN, SIAM, Philadelphia (1978).

189. H. T. Kung, *VLSI Array Processors,* Prentice-Hall, Englewood Cliffs, NJ (1988).

190. R. E. Ladner and M. J. Fischer, "Parallel prefix computation," *Journal of ACM,* Vol. 27, No. 4, pp. 831–838 (Oct. 1980).

191. S. Lakshmivarahan and S. K. Dhall, *Analysis and Design of Parallel Algorithms,* McGraw-Hill (1990).

192. L. Lamport, "The mutual exclusion problem," *Journal of ACM,* Vol. 33, No. 2, pp. 313–348 (April 1986).

193. D. H. Lawrie, "Access and alignment of data in a array processor," *IEEE Transactions on Computers* (Dec. 1975).

194. D. H. Lawrie and C. R. Vora, "The prime memory system for array access," *IEEE Transactions on Computers*, Vol. 31, No. 5 (May 1982).

195. F. T. Leighton, *"Introduction to Parallel Algorithms and Architectures: Arrays, Trees and Hypercubes,"* Morgan Kaufman Publishers, San Mateo, CA (1992).

196. C. E. Leiserson, "Fat-Trees: Universal networks for hardware-efficient supercomputing," *IEEE Transactions on Computers*, Vol. 34, pp. 892–901 (1984).

197. C. E. Leiserson, Z. S. Abuhamdeh, D. C. Douglas, C. R. Feynman, M. N. Ganmukhi, J. V. Hill, W. D. Hillis, B. C. Kuszmul, M. A. ST. Pierre, D. S. Wells, M. C. Wong-Chan, S-W. Yang, and R. Zak, "The network architecture of the Connection Machine CM-5," *Journal of Parallel and Distributed Computing*, Vol. 33, No. 2, pp. 145–158 (March 1996).

198. D. E. Lenoski, J. Laundon, K. Gharachorloo, A. Gupta, and J. Hennessy, "The directory based cache coherence protocol for the DASH multiprocessor," in *Proceedings of The 17th Annual International Symposium on Computer Architecture* IEEE Computer Society, pp. 148–159 (May 1990).

199. D. E. Lenoski and W-D. Weber, *Scalable Shared-Memory Multiprocessing*, Morgan-Kaufman Publishers, San Fransisco, CA (1995).

200. R. D. Levine, "Supercomputers," *Scientific American*, Vol. 246, No. 1, pp. 118–135 (Jan. 1982).

201. K. C. Li and H. Schwetman, "Vectorizing C: A vector processing language," *Journal of Parallel and Distributed Computing*, Vol. 2, No. 2, pp. 132–169 (May 1985).

202. K. C. Li and P. Hudak, "Memory coherence in shared-memory systems," *ACM Transactions on Computer Systems*, pp. 321–359 (Nov. 1989).

203. K. Li, J. F. Naughton, and J. F. Plank, "Low-latency, concurrent checkpointing for parallel programs," *IEEE Transactions on Parallel and Distributed Systems*, Vol. 5, No. 8, pp. 874–879 (Aug. 1994).

204. X. Lin and P. K. McKinley, and L. M. Ni, "Performance evaluation of multicast wormhole routing in 2D-mesh multicomputers," *Proceedings of International Conference of Parallel Processing*, Vol. I, pp. 435–442 (1991).

205. X. Lin and L. M. Ni, "Deadlock-free multicast wormhole routing in multicomputer networks," *Proceedings of the 18th Annual International Symposium on Computer Architecture*, pp. 116–125 (1991).

206. D. H. Linder and J. C. Harden, "An adaptive and fault tolerant wormhole routing strategy for k-ary n-Cubes," *IEEE Transactions on Computers*, Vol. 40, No. 1, pp. 2–12 (Jan. 1991).

207. O. Lubeck and J. Moore, "A benchmark comparison of three supercomputers: Fujitsu VP-200, Hitachi S810.20, and Cray X-MP/2," Computer, pp. 10–24 (Dec. 1985).

208. E. Lusk and R. Overbeek, "Use of monitors in Fortran: A tutorial on the barrier, self-scheduling Do loop and Ask-for monitors," *Argonne National Laboratory Report No. ANL-84-51,* Argonne, IL (1985).

209. E. Lusk, R. Overbeek, J. Boyle, R. Butler, T. Disz, B. Glickfeld, J. Patterson, and R. Stevens, *Portable Programs for Parallel Processors*, Holt, Rinehart, and Winston, Orlando, FL (1987).

210. J. R. McGraw, "The VAL language: Description and analysis," *ACM Transactions on Programming Languages and Systems,* Vol. 4, No. 1, pp. 44–82 (Jan. 1982).

211. T. E. Markovich, V. Popescu, and H. Sullivan, "CHoPP principles of operation," *Proceedings of the 2nd International Supercomputer Conference*, pp. 2–10 (May 1987).

212. J. M. May, *Parallel I/O for High Performance Computing*, Morgan Kaufmann Publishers, San Francisco, CA (2001).

213. C. D. Mee and E. D. Daniel, eds., *Magnetic Storage Handbook*, 2nd edition, McGraw-Hill New York (1996).

214. E. L. Miller and R. H. Katz, "Input/output behavior of supercomputer applications," *Proceedings of Supercomputing '91*, pp. 567–576 (Nov. 1991).

215. E. L. Miller and R. H. Katz, "RAMA: An easy-to-use, high-performance parallel file system," *Parallel Computing*, Vol. 23, Nos. 4–5, pp. 419–446 (June 1997).

216. W. L. Miranker and A. Winkler, "Space-time representations of computational structures," *Computing,* Vol. 32, pp. 93–114 (1984).

217. D. I. Moldovan, *Parallel Processing from Applications to Systems,* Morgan Kaufmann Publishers, San Mateo, CA (1993).

218. T. Mowry and A. Gupta, "Tolerating latency through software-controlled prefetching in shared-memory multiprocessors," *Journal of Parallel and Distributed Computing*, Vol. 12, pp. 87–106 (June 1991).

219. T. Mowry, M. Lam, and A. Gupta, "Design and evaluation of a compiler algorithm for prefetching", *ASPLOS V* (1992).

220. *MPI: A Message-Passing Interface Standard*, Message Passing Interface Forum, available from the World Wide Web at http://www.mpi-forum.org.

221. NCR Corporation, *SCSI: Understanding the Small Computer Systems Interface*, Prentice-Hall, Englewood Cliffs, NJ (1990).

222. N. Nieuwejaar and D. Katz, "The Galley parallel file system," *Parallel Computing*, Vol. 23, Nos. 4–5, pp. 447–476 (June 1997).

223. L. M. Ni and K. Hwang, "Optimal load balancing in a multiple processor system with many job classes," *IEEE Transactions on Software Engineering*, pp. 491–496 (May 1985).

224. D. M. Nicol and F. H. Willard, "Problem size, parallel architecture, and optimal speedup," *Journal of Parallel and Distributed Computing*, Vol. 5, pp. 404–420 (1988).

225. A. Nicolau and J. A. Fisher, "Measuring the parallelism available for very long instruction word architectures," *IEEE Transactions on Computers*, Vol. 33, No. 11, pp. 968–976 (Nov. 1984).

226. R. S. Nikhil, "Tutorial notes on multithreaded architectures," *Proceedings of 19th Annual Symposium on Computer Architecture* (1992).

227. R. S. Nikhil and Arvind, "Can dataflow subsume von Neumann computing?," *Proceedings of the 16th Annual International Symposium on Computer Architecture*, pp. 262–272 (1989).

228. M. D. Noakes, D. A. Wallach, and W. J. Dally, "The J-Machine multicomputer: An architectural evaluation," *Proceedings of the 20th Annual International Symposium on Computer Architecture*, pp. 224–235 (May 1993).

229. OpenMP Fortran Applications Program Interface is available from http:// www.openmp.org/ via the world wide web.

230. A. Osterhaug, *Guide to Parallel Programming on Sequent Computer Systems,* Sequent Computer Systems, Inc., Beaverton, OR (1985).

231. D. A. Padua, and M. J. Wolfe, "Advanced compiler optimizations for supercomputers," *Communications of the ACM*, Vol. 29, No. 12, pp. 1184–1201 (Dec. 1986).

232. G.M. Papadopoulos and D.E. Culler, "Monsoon: An explicit token store architecture," *Proceedings of the 17th Annual Intlernational Symposium on Computer Architecture,* Seattle, WA (May 1990).

233. Parallel Computing Forum, "PCF parallel Fortran extensions," Fortran Forum, Vol. 10, pp. 1–57 (1991).

234. G. Paul and W. W. Wilson, "The VECTRAN Language: An experimental language for vector/array matrix processing," *IBM Palo Alto Scientific Center Report 6320–3334* (Aug. 1975).

235. D. A. Patterson, G. A. Gibson, and R. H. Katz, "A case for redundant arrays of inexpensive disks (RAID)," *Proceedings of the 1988 ACM SIGMOD Conference on Management of Data*, pp. 109–116 (June 1988).

236. J. Peterson and A. Silberschatz, *Operating System Concepts*, Addison-Wesley, Reading, MA (1985).

237. G. F. Pfister, W. C. Brantley, D. A. George, S. L. Harvey, W. J. Kleinfelder, K. P. McAuliffe, E. A. Melton, V. A. Norton, and J. Weiss, "The IBM research parallel processor prototype," *Proceedings of the 1985 International Conference on Parallel Processing,* pp. 764–771 (Aug. 1985).

238. G. F. Pfister, V. A. Norton, "Hot spot' contention and combining in multistage interconnection networks," *IEEE Transactions on Computers*, Vol. 34, No. 10, pp. 943–948 (Oct. 1985).

239. C. D. Polychronopoulos, *Parallel Programming and Compilers*, Kluwer Academic Publishers, Norwell, MA (1988).

240. F. Preparata and J. Vuillemin, "The Cube-Connected Cycles: A versatile network for parallel computation," *Communications of the ACM*, Vol. 24, No. 7, pp. 300–310 (July 1981).

241. W. Pugh, "A practical algorithm for exact array dependence analysis," *Communications of the ACM*, Vol. 35, No. 8, pp. 102–114, (Aug. 1992).

242. Quantum, *Quantum DLT1 Specifications*, Quantum Corp., Milpitas, Calif. www.quantum.com (2001).

243. C. V. Ramamoorthy and H. F. Li, "Pipeline architecture," *ACM Computing Surveys*, Vol. 9, No. 1, pp. 61–102 (March 1977).

244. R. Rettberg and R. Thomas, "Contention is no obstacle to shared-memory multiprocessing," *Communications of the ACM,* Vol. 29, No. 12, pp. 1202–1212 (Dec. 1986).

245. K. A. Robbins and S. Robbins, *The Cray X-MP/model 24: a case study in pipelined architecture and vector processing*, Springer-Verlag, New York (1989).

246. B. Rodriguez, *Temporal Characterizations of Parallel Program Demands for Data Movement,* Ph.D. Thesis, Department of Electrical and Computer Engineering, University of Colorado, Boulder, CO (Dec. 1995).

247. B. Rodriguez, H. F. Jordan, and G. Alaghband, "A metric for temporal characterization of parallel programs," *Journal of Parallel and Distributed Computing,* No. 46, pp. 113–124 (1997).

248. E. Rosti, E. Smirni, T. Wagner, A. Apon, and L. Dowdy, "The KSR1: Experimentation and modeling of poststore," *Oak Ridge National Laboratory, Technical Report ORNL/TM-12472* (Nov. 1993).

249. Ja. Rothnie, "Overview of the KSR1 computer system," *Kendal Square Research Report TR 9202001* (March 1992).

250. R. Saavedra-Barrera, D. Culler, and T. von Eicken, "Analysis of multithreaded architectures for parallel computing," *Proceedings of 2nd Annual ACM Symposium on Parallel Algorithms and Architectures,* Greece (July 1990).

251. R. Saavedra, W. Mao, and K. Hwang, "Performance and optimization of data prefetching strategies in scalable multiprocessors," *IEEE Transactions on Parallel and Distributed Systems,* Vol. 22, pp. 427–448 (1994).

252. S. Sakaj, and Y. Yamaguchi, "Prototype implementation of a highly parallel dataflow machine EM-4," *Proceedings of the International Parallel Processing Symposium* (1991).

253. M. Satyanarayanan, *Multiprocessors: A Comparative Study,* Prentice-Hall, Englewood Cliffs, NJ (1980).

254. Sequent, *Balance 8000 System Technical Summary,* Sequent Computer Systems, Beaverton, OR (1985).

255. J. T. Schwartz, "Ultracomputer," *ACM Transactions on Programming Languages and Systems,* Vol. 2, No. 4, pp. 484–521 (Oct. 1980).

256. C. L. Seitz, "The Cosmic Cube," *Communications of the ACM*, Vol. 28, No. 1 (Jan. 1985).

257. J. A. Sharp, *Data Flow Computing*, Ellis Harwood Series on Computers and Their Applications, John Wiley & Sons, New York (1985).

258. H. J. Siegel, *Interconnection Networks for Large-Scale Parallel Processing: Theory and Case Studies*, 2nd edition, McGraw-Hill, New York (1989).

259. H. Simitci and D. A. Reed, "A comparison of logical and physical parallel I/O patterns," *International Journal of High Performance Computing Applications*, special issue (I/O in Parallel Applications), Vol. 12, No. 3, pp. 364–380 (1988).

260. M. L. Simmons, H. J. Wasserman, O. M. Lubeck, C. Eoyang, R. Mendaz, H. Harada, and M. Ishiguro, "A performance comparison of four supercomputers," *Communications of the ACM*, Vol. 35, No. 8, pp. 116–124 (Aug. 1992).

261. V. P. Sirini, "An architecture comparison of dataflow systems," *IEEE Computer*, Vol. 19, No. 3, pp. 68–88 (March 1986).

262. D. B. Skillcorn, "A taxonomy for computer architectures," *IEEE Computer*, Vol. 21, No. 11, pp. 47–57 (Nov. 1985).

263. E. Smirni and D. A. Reed, "Lessons from characterizing the input/output behavior of parallel scientific applications," *Performance Evaluation*, Vol. 33, pp. 27–44 (1988).

264. B. J. Smith, "A pipelined shared resource MIMD computer," in *Proceedings of International Conference on Parallel Processing* IEEE Computer Society, New York (1978).

265. M. Snir, S. W. Otto, S. Huss-Lederman, D. W. Walker, and J. Dongarra, *MPI: The Complete Reference*, The MIT Press, Cambridge, Mass. (1996).

266. P. Stenstrom, "A survey of cache coherence schemes for multiprocessors," *IEEE Computer*, Vol. 23, No. 6, pp. 12–25 (June 1990).

267. P. Stenstrom, T. Joe, and A. Gupta, "Comparative performance evaluation of cache-coherent NUMA and COMA architectures," *Proceedings of the 19th Annual International Symposium on Computer Architecture* (1992).

268. H. S. Stone, "Parallel processing with perfect shuffle," *IEEE Transactions on Computers*, Vol. 20, pp. 153–161 (1971).

269. V. P. Srini, "An architectural comparison in dataflow systems," *Computer*, Vol. 19, pp. 68–88 (March 1986).

270. D. Tabak, *Multiprocessors*, Prentice-Hall, Englewood Cliffs, NJ (1990).

271. V. S. Sundaram, "PVM: A framework for parallel distributed computing," Concurrency: Practice and Experience, Vol. 2, No. 4, pp. 315–339 (Dec. 1990).

272. TMC, *The CM-2 Technical Summary*, Thinking Machines Corporation, Cambridge, MA (1990).

273. TMC, *The CM-5 Technical Summary*, Thinking Machines Corporation, Cambridge, MA (1991).

274. J. E. Thornton, *Design of a Computer: The CDC 6600*, Scott and Foresman, Glenview, IL (1970).

275. D. Tolmie and D. Flanagan, "HIPPI: It's not just for supercomputers anymore," *Data Communications* (May 8, 1995).

276. R. M. Tomasulo, "An efficient algorithm for exploiting multiple arithmetic units," *IBM Journal of Research and Development*, Vol. 11, No. 1, pp. 25–33 (Jan. 1967).

277. P. C. Treleaven, "Control-driven, data-driven, and demand-driven computer architecture," *Parallel Computing*, Vol. 2 (1985).

278. A. Trew and G. Wilson, eds., *Past, Present, Parallel: A Survey of Available Parallel Computing Systems*, Springer-Verlag, Berlin, Heidelberg (1991).

279. L. W. Tucker and G. G. Robertson, "Architecture and applications of the Connection Machine," *IEEE Computer*, Vol. 21, No. 8, pp. 26–38 (Aug. 1988).

280. A. H. Veen, "Dataflow machine architecture," *ACM Computing Surveys*, Vol. 18, No. 4, pp. 365–396 (Dec. 1986).

281. T. Wagner, E. Smirni, A. Apon, M. Madhukar, and L. Dowry, "Measuring the effects of thread placement on the Kendall Square KSR1," Oak Ridge National Laboratory, *Technical Report ORNL/TM-12462* (Aug. 1993).

282. D. W. Wall, "Limits of instruction-level parallelism," *Proceedings of the Forth International Conference on Architectural Support for Programming Languages and Operating Systems*, pp. 176–188 (1991).

283. T. Watanabi, "Architecture and performance of NEC supercomputer SX system," *Parallel Computing*, Vol. 5, pp. 247–255 (1987).

284. W. J. Watson, "The TI-ASC—A highly modular and flexible supercomputer architecture," *AFIPS Proceedings FJCC*, pp. 221–228 (1972).

285. W. Weber and A. Gupta, "Exploring the benefits of multiple hardware contexts in a multiprocessor architecture: Preliminary results," *Proceedings of International Symposium on Computer Architecture*, IEEE Computer Society Press Washington, DC (1989).

286. S. A. Williams, *Programming Models for Parallel Systems*, John Wiley & Sons, New York (1990).

287. M. E. Wolfe and M. S. Lam, "A data locality optimizing algorithm," *Proceedings of the ACM SIGPLAN'91 Conference on Programming Language Design and Implementation,* pp. 30–44 (June 1991).

288. M. Wolfe, *High Performance Compilers for Parallel Computing*, Addison-Wesley, Redwood City, CA (1995).

289. K. F. Wong and M. Franklin, "Checkpointing on distributed computing systems," *Journal of Parallel and Distributed Computing*, Vol. 35, No. 1, pp. 67–75 (May 1996).

290. W. A. Wulf and C. G. Bell, "C.mmp—A multi-miniprocessor," *Proceedings of Fall Joint Computer Conference*, pp. 765–777 (1972).

291. C. L. Wu and T. Y. Feng, "On a class of multistage interconnection networks," *IEEE Transactions on Computers*, Vol. 29, No. 8, pp. 694–702 (Aug. 1980).

292. C. L. Wu and T. Y. Feng, *Tutorial: Interconnection Networks for Parallel and Distributed Processing,* IEEE Computer Society Press, Silver Spring, MD (1984).

293. P. C. Yew, N. F. Tseng, and D. H. Lawrie, "Distributing hot-spot addressing in large-scale multiprocessors," *IEEE Transactions on Computers*, pp. 388–395 (April 1987).

294. H. Zima and B. Chapman, "Supercompilers for parallel and vector computers," ACM Press, New York (1991).

Index